Praise for *Making Shift F*

This book gives us a gift we have needed for a long time—an engagingly written, scientifically grounded treatment of what *specific* steps we each can take to combat the specter of climate change and its toxic effects. Count me impressed.

—Robert B. Cialdini, author, *Influence* and *Pre-Suasion*

Making Shift Happen brilliantly reveals that the only way to make meaningful progress on complex environmental issues is to understand that they must be addressed as *human* issues, requiring far more than traditional, facile solutions. I sincerely hope the remarkable wisdom and practical guidance offered here will be embraced by practitioners and funders. It would be transformational.

—Steve McCormick, managing director, Draper Richard Kaplan Foundation, former president, Gordon and Betty Moore Foundation, former president and CEO, The Nature Conservancy

Making Shift Happen democratizes the research and best practices behind what influences people to make lasting positive change for nature and people. The brass ring is durable, systems-level change and this book is meant for practitioners looking for just this kind of impact.

—Meg Caldwell, deputy director, Oceans, The David and Lucile Packard Foundation

Making Shift Happen brings behavioral science alive, weaving research findings with practical examples. The book provides foundations and principles that can be used to advance a sustainable future. It's timely, grounded in behavioral science, and practical.

—Wesley Schultz, Professor of Psychological Science, California State University

A fascinating workshop-in-a-book that takes practitioners through the entire intervention design and implementation process of creating the conditions under which change happens, grows, and endures. Importantly, the self-care of practitioners and their audience is dealt with in some detail, providing evidence-based explanations of the process involved in and the means of securing resilient, long-term engagement in environmental stewardship. After all, burned out people can't heal the planet.

—Raymond De Young, professor, Environmental Psychology and Planning, University of Michigan, co-author, *The Localization Reader*

Completely fascinating—we've learned a lot about the ways minds work in the last decades and that may help us figure out how to appeal to our better angels more effectively than in the past. Rest assured that people who want to sell us junk are paying attention to these insights—the rest of us better do so too!

—Bill McKibben, author, *The End of Nature*

Provides some much needed, research-based, practical advice on how change agents can actually bring about desirable reductions in human pressures on the environment.

—Paul C. Stern, PhD, president, Social and Environmental Research Institute

As environmental advocates and policymakers work to create lasting cultural changes, they need tools to complement their existing methods. *Making Shift Happen* is an excellent guide to utilizing select tools from a spectrum of disciplines that have explored how to change the behavior of individuals or communities. It will be an invaluable tool for all practitioners in the environmental space.

—Rainer Romero-Canyas, lead senior social and behavioral scientist, Environmental Defense Fund

An invaluable resource for program managers in non-profit groups, government agencies, and companies. Blending a sophisticated understanding of social science with an obvious concern for the environment, this book will become a standard guide for designing behavior change programs.

—Michael P. Vandenbergh, professor, David Daniels Allen Distinguished Chair of Law, director, Climate Change Research Network, Vanderbilt University Law School

Behavior design is the next frontier in environmental policy. We know what we need to do to build a just and sustainable world, but humans are creatures of habit and inertia, and changing course is hard. That's where *Making Shift Happen* comes in. This is the tool kit to get people and institutions moving in the right direction to usher in a much greener and healthier era.

—Jason Scorse, director, Center for the Blue Economy, Monterey Institute of International Studies

A much-needed overview of research-based best practices for encouraging pro-environmental behavior. The authors have sorted through a wide range of cutting-edge and often confusing and complex behavioral science from multiple disciplines and broken these down into a manageable set of behavioral building blocks. The result is a great cheat sheet of guidelines for anyone trying to shift people's behavior on climate change, environmental conservation, or other environmental topics.

—Kaitlin T. Raimi, PhD, associate professor,
Gerald R. Ford School of Public Policy, University of Michigan

Developing and designing effective communication approaches to help frame pro-environmental behaviors in ways that are compatible with people's personal and social motivators is crucial to behavior change initiatives. *Making Shift Happen* includes research-based recommendations on how to do just that, and it does so in a manner that is very user-friendly and easy to digest.

—Katie Abrams, PhD, associate professor,
Center for Science Communication, Colorado State University

If humans came with a manual, this would be it. You won't find a more comprehensive resource for designing effective behavioral interventions.

—Kim Wolske, PhD, research associate professor,
Harris School of Public Policy, University of Chicago

Addressing our most pressing environmental challenges often requires behavioral change from community to global scales. *Making Shift Happen* provides critical understanding, tools and approaches needed to design and implement effective change strategies. It is both practical and thought-provoking.

—Eric Schwaab, senior vice president, Environmental Defense Fund, former acting
assistant secretary, Conservation and Management for the US Department of Commerce,
National Oceanic and Atmospheric Administration (NOAA)

Too often those trying to move society toward sustainability are unaware of the research on decision making and social change. *Making Shift Happen* does an impressive job of introducing science-based strategies for change. It is useful in and of itself and a good starting point for further exploration.

—Thomas Dietz, University Distinguished Professor,
Michigan State University

Making Shift Happen

DESIGNING FOR SUCCESSFUL ENVIRONMENTAL BEHAVIOR CHANGE

Nya Van Leuvan • Lauren Highleyman
Rod Fujita • Ashleigh Kellerman

new society
PUBLISHERS

Cover design by Diane McIntosh.

Cover image: ©iStock

Unless otherwise credited, all tables are copyright the authors.

Printed in Canada. First printing December, 2021.

Inquiries regarding requests to reprint all or part of *Making Shift Happen* should be addressed to New Society Publishers at the address below. To order directly from the publishers, please call (250) 247-9737, or order online at www.newsociety.com

Any other inquiries can be directed by mail to:
New Society Publishers
P.O. Box 189, Gabriola Island, BC V0R 1X0, Canada
(250) 247-9737

LIBRARY AND ARCHIVES CANADA CATALOGUING IN PUBLICATION

Title: Making shift happen : designing for successful environmental behavior change / Nya Van Leuvan, Lauren Highleyman, Rod Fujita, Ashleigh Kellerman.

Names: Van Leuvan, Nya, author. | Highleyman, Lauren, author. | Fujita, Rodney M., author. | Kellerman, Ashleigh, author.

Description: Includes bibliographical references and index.

Identifiers: Canadiana (print) 2021032953X | Canadiana (ebook) 20210329610 | ISBN 9780865719484 (softcover) | ISBN 9781550927412 (PDF) | ISBN 9781771423373 (EPUB)

Subjects: LCSH: Environmental protection—Decision making.

Classification: LCC TD171.8 .V26 2022 | DDC 333.72—dc23

Canadä

New Society Publishers' mission is to publish books that contribute in fundamental ways to building an ecologically sustainable and just society, and to do so with the least possible impact on the environment, in a manner that models this vision.

We dedicate this book to the loving memory of
John "Jack" Culbertson Jr. and Mark Epstein,
and to all the current and future environmental champions.

Contents

Chapter coauthors

Jess Beebe
> Building Block Chapter 10: Longevity

Nicole Hilaire
> Process Chapter 3: Uncover, Process Chapter 6: Methods
> Building Block Chapter 3: Habits

Nicholas Janusch
> Building Block Chapter 8: Rewards

Karina Mudd
> Process Chapter 1: Foundations, Process Chapter 2: Initiate
> Building Block Chapter 7: Optimism

Susan Schneider
> Building Block Chapter 3: Habits, Building Block Chapter 8: Rewards

Introduction

NOBODY WAKES UP IN THE MORNING hoping for bad news about our planet. "Ah yes, I'll take my coffee black, with just a pinch of plastic pollution and some wildfires on the side. Maybe a hurricane or polar vortex, just to round out this hearty breakfast of environmental disasters." We jest, but to make a point—for the most part, humans are not setting out to destroy the environment. Yet, despite this, we consistently act in ways that are detrimental to the environment and ourselves. Even when we have the desire to fix things, we may not know how, or environmental problems may seem so big and intractable that we think only scientists, policymakers, and industry leaders can solve them.

But at their root, all environmental problems are caused by humans acting in specific ways—they are *behavioral problems,* which means the solutions must also revolve around behavior. The fact that environmental problems are behavior problems is good news, because we can all take part in changing behavior. We've written this book to show you how.

• • •

For those who were teenagers in the 1980s and 90s in the United States, you may recall public service announcements that highlighted the negative health consequences of drug use, including infamously dramatized warnings that drugs would fry your brain like an egg in a frying pan, or health education programs at your school that featured cautionary tales about smoking and drug use. One such example is the Drug Abuse Resistance Education (D.A.R.E.) program, which worked to reduce teen drug use by boosting self-esteem and encouraging teens to resist peer pressure. This program was administered by 75% of U.S. schools.[2] Championed by parents and touted by Congress, D.A.R.E. was seen as the silver bullet solution. Until it became clear that it wasn't.

In reality, these campaigns—along with many other anti-drug and anti-smoking initiatives—failed. Many studies have shown that these programs were not only ineffective at reducing drug use among adolescents, but even led to *increased* drug use in some cases.[9] Why? The programs were designed without an in-depth understanding of the audience they were meant to influence.

As it turns out, these anti-drug initiatives piqued teens' curiosity about drugs and presented a great opportunity for rebellion. These initiatives also led kids to believe that smoking and doing drugs was more common than it actually was—and the "cool" and "normal" thing to do. Many kids already understood the health risks associated with smoking, so a lack of knowledge was not the problem. Kids dismissed and ignored the factual arguments presented by the program because these social and emotional factors were more motivating.[8] Ultimately, the designers of D.A.R.E. and similar programs failed to recognize that teens were driven by the influence of social norms and a need for autonomy—a costly mistake, to the tune of hundreds of millions of taxpayer dollars.

In the early 2000s, practitioners launched new anti-drug and anti-smoking campaigns that incorporated these lessons learned about teen behavior. Instead of showing and telling teens what *not* to do, the "Above the Influence" campaign helped teens explore other ways to express their identity and take control of their lives through the pursuit of alternative positive activities they enjoy.[5] Similarly, the "truth" campaign appealed directly to the rebellious side of youth, convincing kids to exercise autonomy by resisting the deceitful solicitations of big tobacco companies.[4] Because these campaigns were tailored to the major motivators of teens, they were more successful at decreasing smoking and drug use.

So why are many environmental initiatives unsuccessful at making positive shifts happen, and how can we improve them? Like the failed anti-drug campaigns, many environmental campaigns are built around the *information deficit model*, which assumes that a lack of knowledge is the main reason people don't act on or support an issue.[12] This can lead to a focus on "educating people about the issue" and "raising awareness." But our behaviors are not just the product of receiving information and acting based on a "rational" assessment of costs and benefits. Behavior is far more complex; it is shaped by our beliefs, temperaments, upbringings, surrounding environments, the media we consume, and many other factors, including biases that often cause us to act "irrationally." The environmental movement has had many crucial successes—but we've also been held back by not always designing our initiatives with this complexity in mind. The next step in the evolution of the movement is for today's environmental changemakers to cultivate a deep understanding of what drives human behavior and to master the tools we have available to shift behavior for the betterment of the planet and for our own well-being.

Fortunately, thanks to a growing body of real-world experience and scientific insights, environmentalists are beginning to integrate innovative behavior change techniques into their ever-expanding toolkit. Organizations and institutions world-wide are creating significant positive environmental impact through simple and targeted initiatives that employ behavior change tools. Energy suppliers, for example, have increased the number of customers in their renewable energy programs tenfold by using behavioral insights to modify enrollment forms.[3] Hotels and universities have reduced food waste by more than 25% just by removing trays from buffet lines.[1,10] Cities have seen an 85% increase in household recycling when they provide free recycling bins and collect both the trash and recycling on the same day of the week.[7] When Rutgers University made double-sided printing the default option, they saved more than 55 million sheets of paper in the first three years—a 44% reduction that saved the equivalent of 4,650 trees.[13]

Using insights from behavioral science to design environmental initiatives doesn't just deliver environmental wins—it often results in an economic return on investment as well. For example, the airline Virgin Atlantic employed different behavioral strategies on different pilots over eight months: feedback on their fuel use performance, providing pilots with personalized monthly fuel efficiency targets, and prosocial incentives (a donation to the pilot's charity of choice). By implementing relatively simple behavior change tools that cost less than $3,000, the airline dramatically reduced their emissions of greenhouse gases and pollutants, and saved over $5 million on fuel in just a matter of months.[6, 11, 14] For Virgin Atlantic, even low-cost interventions produced significant change with far-reaching benefits.

If Virgin Atlantic can make such an impact with just a few behavior change tools, imagine what we could accomplish on a global scale if all initiatives employed the many behavior-based solutions we provide in this book. These behavior change techniques can be used to improve the effectiveness of existing approaches like incentives or regulations, such as by adjusting policy to better account for the most powerful drivers of behavior. Or, they can take the place of these approaches, especially in cases when behaviors, such as those we do in the privacy of our homes, are hard to regulate.

However, given the complexity of behavior, it's easy to see why busy environmental practitioners haven't widely adopted a behavioral approach. For all of the aforementioned efforts to be successful, the program designers had to take the time to understand the factors that influence behavior. This type of understanding can be hard to come by, and implementing a behavior change campaign may not always be easy or straightforward. But it is possible—and this book is here to help. We developed the *Making Shift Happen* process to make it easier for anyone to shift environmental behaviors in the right direction.

This book is for advocates working with organizations and budgets of all sizes; you don't need ample resources and sophisticated marketing to *make shift happen*. Whether you are a community leader, nonprofit manager, environmental advocate, policymaker, philanthropist, or a citizen wanting to spark change, you can use the tools in this book to work toward a more sustainable planet, even if it begins in your own backyard.

•••

Making Shift Happen synthesizes insights from hundreds of academic studies, lessons from our own work at the not-for-profit Root Solutions, and other real world initiatives. We've turned them into a process and a set of tools that will help you understand what drives your audience's behavior and how to use this knowledge to design better policies, campaigns, initiatives, and strategies to motivate actions that will protect and regenerate the environment. In Section 1, we provide a roadmap for how to go from an environmental challenge that you want to address all the way to implementing and scaling a behavior change initiative in the real world.

FOUNDATIONS: We discuss important considerations like ethics, scarcity, and equity that practitioners should always keep in mind when designing an initiative. We also explore some of the processes of the human brain that influence our behavior, such as cognitive biases and emotions.

INITIATE: You'll learn about processes and tools to help you identify, evaluate, and select the environmental challenges, audiences, and specific behaviors on which to focus your initiative.

UNCOVER: You'll learn about the major drivers of behavior, which can roughly be mapped into three categories: Means (can I do it?), Motivation (do I want to do it?), and Memory (can I remember to do it?). Then we show you how to conduct a Behavioral Drivers Analysis, an analytic tool for uncovering evidence-based drivers in your own audience.

DESIGN: You'll learn how to combine the results from your audience research with the intervention design guidance we provide in our Behavioral Building Blocks™. You'll then use these insights to choose and design the evidence-based behavior change solutions that you will use to shift the behavior of your audience. You will also learn how to rapidly prototype your interventions to optimize their success.

IMPLEMENT: We introduce piloting, including how to use pilots as experiments to test the effectiveness of your initiative or variations of your initiative. We also discuss rolling out your full-fledged initiative into the real world, refining your initiative, and considerations for scaling your initiative to even broader audiences.

METHODS: This chapter serves as a resource to you throughout the *Making Shift Happen* process. It provides an introduction to designing and conducting research that helps you uncover meaningful insights to inform your behavior change initiative, including how-to information about methods like interviews, surveys, and experiments. We also discuss how these methods can be utilized at different phases in the process.

Section 2 is focused on how to design behavior change interventions, like the feedback Virgin Atlantic delivered to their pilots or signs in hotel bathrooms that say how much water you'll save by reusing your towels. In this book, we refer to these interventions, or behavior-based solutions, as ***shifters***, which are the tools that *make shift happen*. There are innumerable shifters that a practitioner can employ that have been shown to be effective at changing environmental behaviors. We've categorized the most important or impactful of these into our 10 BEHAVIORAL Building Blocks™, with each letter of the word "BEHAVIORAL" corresponding to a chapter that explores a collection of related behavior change principles: B(elonging), E(asy), H(abits), A(ttachment), V(ivid), I(dentity), O(ptimism) R(ewards), A(ssociations), and L(ongevity).

BELONGING: The need to belong is a powerful driver of our behavior. You'll learn how to use social norms to reinforce and spread environmental behaviors.

EASY: Even the smallest inconveniences can stop behavior change in its tracks. You'll learn how to make environmental actions easy to reduce the intention-action gap.

HABITS: Facilitating habits requires great effort by practitioners, but can reap long-lasting benefits for the environment. Learn how to design initiatives that break bad habits and build positive ones.

ATTACHMENT: You'll learn methods to catalyze your audience's motivation to take action by aligning your initiative with what they care most about.

VIVID: In this age of information overload, competition for people's attention is steep. You'll learn how to design initiatives that are vivid so that your audience notices, pays attention to, and remembers your messages long enough to take the desired action.

IDENTITY: Tapping into our desire to behave in alignment with our identities is a powerful driver of behavior change and for galvanizing environmental champions. You'll learn various methods for doing this, including how to design commitment campaigns.

OPTIMISM: Optimism is crucial for maintaining motivation in the face of daunting environmental challenges. You'll learn how to activate hope and inspire action by strengthening your audience's sense of efficacy.

REWARDS: We are motivated to engage in behaviors when we feel that the benefits outweigh the costs. Learn how to choose incentives wisely to attract people to positive environmental behaviors and deter them from negative ones.

ASSOCIATIONS: Framing information in a way that activates meaningful mental associations is essential for encouraging a shift in mindsets toward environmental engagement. You'll learn about frames that have already been tested, how to avoid detrimental frames, and how to test your own metaphors and frames.

LONGEVITY: You'll learn about the role that exposure to nature, other-focused emotions, and mindfulness play in fostering a change in our underlying relationship to the environment and its inhabitants and achieving permanent, society-wide environmental stewardship.

The concepts presented in each Building Block are rich with information and nuance: each Behavioral Building Block could be its own book, with chapters dedicated to exploring each shifter. But our goal is for *Making Shift Happen* to be a usable guide that highlights the most important elements in each Building Block. If you find yourself particularly intrigued by a chapter, we assure you that there's more to learn on those topics, and we encourage you to dig into the references that we've cited in the back of the book.

•••

Throughout this book, you will see graphic icons like these below that denote major principles, shifters, and case studies to help you navigate the material. Here's what to look for and what to expect:

List of Icons

  In Section 1, you will see these icons signaling a new **step or key consideration** in the *Making Shift Happen* process.

 Principle icons denote core concepts in the BEHAVIORAL Building Block chapters.

 Shifter icons point the way to proven interventions to shift behavior. These icons are found in the BEHAVIORAL Building Block chapters.

 The helpful **Attention** icons signal something to remember or watch out for.

 Your Turn icons accompany checklists and opportunities to put guidance into practice.

 Practitioners must answer many questions throughout this process. **Ask Yourself** icons let you know when to pause to answer a question to help you brainstorm or evaluate.

 You might see any of these **Activity** icons to signal, you guessed it, an activity!

The **telescope** icon tells you when it's time to zoom in on a topic in greater detail.

Section 1

The *Making Shift Happen* Process

Foundations

T O ORIENT YOUR JOURNEY through the *Making Shift Happen* process, we begin with a chapter designed to lay the foundational groundwork on which we build throughout this book. This chapter will introduce you to some of the basic principles that underlie how people think and operate, as well as to the fundamental concepts that underlie our entire *Making Shift Happen* process. Understanding these foundational principles will help to enhance your understanding of our Building Blocks, enabling you to use them strategically as you design a strong, cohesive behavior change initiative.

We begin with an overview of some important cognitive processes to understand how they influence our behaviors. Next, we explore the origins of the *Making Shift Happen* process, which draws from various academic and scientific fields of study as well as problem-solving approaches from a range of professional sectors. Finally, we provide some important ethical guidelines to follow and caveats to keep in mind as you design your behavior change initiative so as to avoid unintended consequences, protect and empower your audience, and maximize your positive impact on the environment.

A Look Ahead: FOUNDATIONS

Foundations of Behavior

Two cognitive systems
Cognitive biases
Emotions
We think and live our lives in narratives

The *Making Shift Happen* Process

Psychological and behavioral sciences
Behavioral economics and choice architecture
Social marketing
Systems thinking
Design thinking

Guiding Principles of the *Making Shift Happen* Process

Take an intersectional approach to environmentalism

Consider culture and context

Follow ethical guidelines

Think carefully about *when* and *whom* you ask: navigating scarcity and worry

Think carefully about *what* you ask: the implications of spillover

Think carefully about *how* you ask: evoking emotions with care

Test, test, test

 Foundations of Behavior

There are many factors that shape human behavior, including beliefs, values, social norms, our perception of ourselves, as well as our built and natural environments. Some of the most significant behavioral influences are the hardest to see, such as cognitive biases. So before we go any further, let's begin with an exploration of why people do the things they do.

Two cognitive systems[13]

Psychologists often describe two different cognitive systems that underlie the way we think and how we navigate the world: automatic and reflective.

The ***automatic system*** is fast, effortless, associative, involuntary, and subconscious. It is often called "fast thinking" or "System 1 thinking" to reflect its earlier evolutionary origin and instinctual nature.

Our automatic system allows us to evaluate situations instantly and without conscious thought, like when we need to swerve to avoid something in the road, when we get a gut feeling about someone's mood during a conversation, or when we're scanning a page and certain things jump out at us as "important." The automatic system evolved for survival so that we could respond instantly to potential threats: when we hear a rustle in the grass, it's better to assume there is a lion than to deliberate and find out the hard way. Automatic thinking also comes into play when we are overwhelmed with information, afraid, overstimulated, or are having a hard time paying attention—which for most of us is pretty often.

The ***reflective system*** is slow, self-aware, voluntary, and conscious. It is often called "slow thinking" or "System 2 thinking." The reflective system is critical for complex problem-solving as well as the continuous self-assessment and monitoring of our own behavior. It's the discipline that keeps us focused on our work when we're tempted to procrastinate and the self-restraint that maintains our composure when we're upset. Reflective thinking is important for tasks that require more concentration such as researching which retirement plan to choose or reading the news, and it's impeded when attention is disrupted or depleted.

Automatic and reflective thinking are not mutually exclusive; they interact with each other to guide our behaviors. Automatic thinking runs, well, automatically, and it continuously feeds reflective thinking its impressions and feelings. Reflective thinking generally accepts those suggestions from automatic thinking, but kicks into gear when it detects we are about to make an error or to solve problems that cannot be processed by automatic thinking. This dynamic is quite efficient, but the general reliance on automatic thinking can also lead to systematic errors in judgment and decision-making, such as cognitive biases.

Cognitive biases

We often use *heuristics* (e.g., mental shortcuts) to facilitate rapid judgment and decision-making, especially when we're navigating with our automatic system.[13] These shortcuts usually save us time and energy, but they can also cause a host of systematic errors in our decision-making, known as *cognitive biases*. As we process information and interpret our surroundings, many different cognitive biases can emerge, each with varying effects on our behavior.

We may not take action to address societal challenges because we believe desirable outcomes are more likely than undesirable outcomes (*optimism bias*). We interpret information differently depending on how emotionally motivated we are to reach a certain conclusion (*motivated reasoning*), and we have the tendency to defend our choices even if the option we've chosen has changed profoundly (*choice blindness*). We make different decisions depending on our current positive or negative emotional state (*affect heuristic*). The more often we hear about something, the more likely we are to believe it, and the stronger our preference for it will be (*mere exposure effect*). We specifically seek evidence that verifies our beliefs while passing up evidence that contradicts them (*confirmation bias*), and we avoid exposing ourselves to information that may cause psychological discomfort even if we know that avoidance could make the situation worse (*ostrich effect*).

Decades of research has revealed hundreds of these biases. Table 1.1.1 is a mini glossary of twenty or so biases that you are likely to encounter in this book; they should give you insight into the ways in which biases influence behavior. We have also included biases in the ***shifters*** (evidence-based behavior change solutions) we introduce in The BEHAVIORAL Building Blocks™ (Section 2); many shifters seek to overcome, reduce, or harness these biases in a constructive manner to help our audiences take actions to protect the environment.

Everybody has cognitive biases—there are no exceptions—but we can consciously engage in processes to identify and overcome some of them within ourselves. Other biases can be leveraged to bring about desired behaviors. For many biases, however, we can do neither, but it's still useful to know when they function as a barrier to behavior change.

Emotions

Distinguished from practical reasoning, ***emotions*** are information processing systems that help us react quickly to situations or events with little to no reflective thought.[11] Emotions are fundamental to our System 1, or automatic thinking. They signal what is important and help us make choices between options that are difficult to compare. They shape our motivation to act, mobilize us for action, and coordinate systems including attention, memory, and decision-making.[11,5]

Some experiences are stored in our memory, "marked" with an associated emotion.[4] Without emotions, these experiences would be only a set of facts; emotions give them meaning. We might "mark" eating sweet foods with the emotion of pleasure and rotten foods with the emotion of disgust. We might also "mark" an activity as dangerous: say you love swimming in the ocean, but after being stung by a jellyfish, you now associate the ocean with the pain from that experience. The next time you swim in the ocean, your emotions prompt you to be more cautious—a clear behavioral shift. Emotions also help prepare the body to take immediate action if necessary; sometimes, taking time for reflective thought can cost us our life. When we experience something that may require a rapid response, our emotions activate the physiological changes (e.g., elevated heart rate and adrenaline) that help our bodies take the appropriate action ("A snake! Run!").

Because emotions shape our behavior at a fundamental level, as practitioners we must understand the role that emotions play in behavior change so that we can evoke appropriate emotions and harness them to instigate behavioral shifts that benefit the environment.

Table 1.1.1: Select Cognitive Biases Pertinent to Environmental Behavior Change

Bias	Definition
Anchoring	When making decisions, we often rely too heavily on the first piece of information presented to us (the "anchor"). We then make subsequent decisions by adjusting from that anchor's value, which results in decisions that are biased toward the anchor. See ASSOCIATIONS (Building Block Chapter 9) for more information. Term coined by Sherif, Taub, and Hovland.[a]
Availability Bias	We overestimate the significance of information that appears to be especially immediate, vivid, and/or mentally "available." We tend to think that an event is more likely to occur when we can readily recall examples of a similar event happening in the past. The availability heuristic also makes it easier for us to remember facts and events that are new, different, or strike us on a personal level, while more commonplace events may be forgotten. See VIVID (Building Block Chapter 5) for more information. Term coined by Gilovich, Griffin, and Kahneman.[b]
Bandwagon Effect	The bandwagon effect is driven by the desire to conform: the rate of uptake of beliefs, ideas, trends, and behaviors increases as others adopt them. In other words, we tend to increase our support of something as it gains popularity.
Choice Overload / Information Overload	We experience choice overload when we are presented with too many options. Information overload occurs when we are faced with too much information, and we can't process it all. Being overloaded by too many choices or too much information can lead to frustration, confusion, poor decision-making, or avoiding decisions altogether. See EASY (Building Block Chapter 2) for more information. Choice overload was popularized by Alvin Toffler in *Future Shock* as was the related term related term "overchoice."[c] Information overload was coined by Bertram Gross in *The Managing of Organizations*.[d]
Cognitive Dissonance	We experience mental stress or discomfort when we're presented with new information that contradicts our beliefs, or when we find ourselves acting in a way that contradicts our beliefs. In response, we are motivated to reduce this stress. Unfortunately, we often resolve our cognitive dissonance by adjusting our thinking so it aligns with our actions, as opposed to changing our actions to align with our thinking. See IDENTITY (Building Block Chapter 6) for more information. Term coined by Festinger.[e]

Table 1.1.1: *Cont.*

Bias	Definition
Confirmation Bias / Backfire Effect	Confirmation bias refers to our tendency to notice, favor, and seek out verification for information that confirms our preconceptions. We tend to interpret ambiguous information as evidence for our position and to ignore information that contradicts our beliefs. This is sometimes called "myside bias" because we primarily do this for beliefs or values that we feel strongly about. The backfire effect refers to a related tendency: when in the face of contradictory evidence, our established beliefs tend to actually get stronger. We are prone to argue when our beliefs are challenged, and the process of creating these arguments solidifies our beliefs. See ATTACHMENT and LONGEVITY (Building Block Chapters 4 and 10) for more information. Confirmation bias coined by Wason.[f] Backfire effect coined by Nyhan and Reifler.[g]
Effort Justification / IKEA Effect	We tend to place higher value on things that we have created or labored over, such as a piece of furniture that we assemble ourselves. The more time or effort we put into something, the more we value it. The original paper that named this effect was looking specifically at IKEA products, but it also manifests with intangible concepts like ideas and beliefs. See IDENTITY (Building Block Chapter 6) for more information. IKEA effect coined by Norton, Mochon, & Ariely.[i] It stems from Festinger's theory of cognitive dissonance.[e]
Empathy Gap	We struggle to detach ourselves from our current physical, mental, or emotional states. If we are well-fed, we can struggle to imagine being hungry. If we are calm, we can have a hard time empathizing with someone who is angry. If we are rested, we have trouble remembering how it feels to be tired. Because of this, it can be difficult for us to connect with issues that do not directly impact our lives or to empathize with people who are in different states from our own. Term coined by Loewenstein.[j]
Fresh Start Effect	We are more likely to tackle our goals immediately following noteworthy temporal landmarks (a new year/month, holiday, special event). These events provide an opportunity to decouple a previous lifestyle from the life that lies ahead, initiating a psychological reset or new period of clarity. See HABITS (Building Block Chapter 3) for more information. Term coined by Dai, Milkman, and Riis.[k]

Table 1.1.1: *Cont.*

Bias	Definition
Hyperbolic Discounting / Present Bias	We tend to value the present more highly than the future, and therefore make choices that increase our happiness in the short term at the expense of future gain. This phenomenon is also known as present bias; in a tradeoff situation, we tend to overvalue immediate rewards, without realizing that delayed rewards can benefit us more significantly in the long term. The related concept of hyperbolic discounting refers to our tendency to discount risks of negative future consequences more than risks in the present. Hyperbolic discounting coined by Ainslie and Haendel.[l] Present bias coined Phelps and Pollak.[m]
Identifiable Victim Effect	We are more inclined to help a specific individual (an identifiable "victim") than a large, nebulous group facing the same problems. We are also more likely to want to punish an individual than a group. See ATTACHMENT (Building Block Chapter 4) for more information. Term coined by Schelling.[n]
Loss Aversion	We hate to lose more than we like to gain. When making decisions, we are therefore more motivated to avoid a loss than we are to achieve an equivalent gain. See ASSOCIATIONS and REWARDS (Building Block Chapters 9 and 8) for more information. Term coined by Kahneman and Tversky.[o]
Mere Exposure Effect	When we are frequently exposed to something, we tend to view it more favorably. See VIVID (Building Block Chapter 5) for more information. Term coined by Fechner[p] but first quantitatively investigated by Zajonc.[q]
Moral Licensing	Moral licensing is a bias that allows us to behave immorally without challenging our moral standing. After we do something considered "good," we feel justified in subsequent "bad" or "immoral" behavior. See LONGEVITY (Building Block Chapter 10) for more information. Term coined by Monin and Miller.[r]
Negativity Bias	We tend to pay more attention, react more quickly, and be more strongly impacted by negative things (e.g., alarming events and unpleasant emotions) than neutral or positive things. See OPTIMISM (Building Block Chapter 7) for more information. Term coined by Rozin and Roysman.[s]

Table 1.1.1: *Cont.*

Bias	Definition
Omission Bias / Decision Regret	We tend to judge harmful action more harshly than harmful inaction. For example, people judged a hypothetical tennis player more harshly when he recommended food that he knew his rival was allergic to, as opposed to when he said nothing and allowed his rival to eat that same food. Similarly, we tend to feel more regret if we experience a bad outcome because of an action we've taken than we do when we experience that same outcome as a result of our own inaction. Omission bias coined by Spranca, Minsk, and Baron.[t] Decision regret was simultaneously developed by Loomes and Sugden, and Bell, and Fishburn.[h]
Risk Aversion	When making decisions in uncertain conditions, we are often less willing to choose an option with a very high payoff if it also has a very high level of risk; we favor options with lower uncertainty, but a lower payoff. Individuals have different thresholds for the amount of risk they are willing to take. Term coined by Sterns on Bernoulli, expanded by von Neumann and Morgenstern.[u]
Scope Insensitivity	Our valuation of a problem, or our willingness to pay to mitigate a problem, doesn't always scale in proportion to the size of that problem. For example, we tend to be willing to pay a similar amount to save 2,000 birds as we would to save 200,000 birds, despite the large increase in number. See ATTACHMENT (Building Block Chapter 4) for more information. Term coined by Desvousges, Johnson, Dunford, Boyle, Hudson, and Wilson.[v]
Single Action Bias	In high-pressure and/or high-risk scenarios, we seek to respond in the form of a simple, single action. Even though it might not be very effective, the single action can reduce our feelings of stress, worry, and vulnerability, so we might not pursue further actions. Term coined by Elke U. Weber.[w]
Status Quo Bias	When faced with difficult choices, we prefer to choose the status quo, or the option that requires no action at all (the default), even if this choice isn't the best one. We tend to prefer our present situation to any other, as the path of least resistance. See EASY (Building Block Chapter 2) for more information. Term coined by Kahneman, Knetsch, and Thaler.[x]

Emotions shape our perceptions of the world and subsequent motivation to act

Emotions shape our attitudes, beliefs, and perceptions of the world around us.[11] For example, if two people are standing on a ledge looking down at the ground below, the person who has a fear of heights will perceive the ground to be farther away than the person who is not afraid. Similarly, we will perceive a hill to be steeper when we are tired or weighed down by a heavy backpack, which can make us feel discouraged.[26] These perceptions and beliefs in turn influence our motivation to act[11] (our psychological willingness to put effort into achieving desired goals such as making it up the hill).[7] This is why one of the most essential things we can do as behavior change practitioners is to remove barriers; it's much easier to take away the backpack (which makes the hill seem less steep and instills confidence) than it is to motivate people to climb a hill that looks insurmountable with their backpack on. We discuss other key motivating factors and how to remove barriers in UNCOVER: Process Chapter 3 and DESIGN: Process Chapter 4.

Emotions help us achieve our instinctual and conscious goals[7]

We all need to do certain basic things to keep ourselves alive; we need to stay fed, clothed, and sheltered. We are often unaware of these instinctual goals, but our emotions help us respond appropriately. For example, the emotion of disgust that arises when we smell rotten food keeps us from mindlessly taking a bite and subsequently getting sick.[11]

Emotions are also involved in the pursuit of goals we may be more aware of, such as the goal of living a life with a certain purpose (e.g., continuous learning), or socio-personal goals (e.g., succeeding at work or being accepted by our peers). Emotions help us prioritize some goals over others, including smaller decisions like whether to go to a surf camp or a language immersion program during holiday, as well as bigger decisions like whether we want a career working with children or working with the elderly. Emotions also help us monitor our progress towards the goals we choose to pursue, such as feeling good when we put money aside for our upcoming holiday and feeling uneasy when we splurge on an expensive a night out.[18]

Emotions help us make decisions between choices that are difficult to compare[25]

How do you logically decide what color is your favorite or which sports to follow? How do you compare apples and oranges? In a world that can sometimes overwhelm us with information, emotions can signal what's most important. As the research of neuroscientist Antonio Damasio demonstrated, contrary to the notion that good decisions come from formal logic devoid of emotion, emotions are actually required for even routine decisions.[4]

Emotions shape our perception and motivation to act, and they play a critical role in decision-making and achieving our goals. Therefore, as practitioners, we must be cognizant of how our initiatives can intentionally or unintentionally trigger emotions, and we must endeavor to evoke appropriate emotions to instigate behavioral shifts that benefit the environment.

We think and live our lives in narratives

Nothing exists for us without narratives. These narratives can be experienced as the mental chatter that accompanies us wherever we go and helps us navigate our surroundings, or they can come in other forms, like the life story we tell about ourselves to others. Without narrative, there is no culture, law, religion, politics, social norms, ideologies, and even our own identities. (How do you "show someone" or physically point to an ideology?) It is through narratives, or stories, that we build our understanding of these things or even think about these things.

For durable change, it's critical for environmentalists to understand that because humans "think in narratives," we are powerfully swayed by them. Environmentalists tend to try to frame their issues as "objectively" as possible (e.g., in terms of how many degrees hotter the planet will become), without appealing to deeply held narratives and engaging with this default way that humans communicate. Instead, we must utilize narratives in our messaging and endeavor to deconstruct environmentally harmful narratives.

When we say that narratives are pervasive, we mean it—even for us, the practitioners. That's why it's important to deconstruct our own narratives before looking at the narratives that drive others. Becoming more aware of our own beliefs, assumptions, and biases will make us more conscientious and effective environmental practitioners. We can learn to detach ourselves from our mental chatter through mindfulness practices (discussed in LONGEVITY: Building Block Chapter 10), but it's impossible to separate our narratives entirely from our decisions and behaviors.

Fast and slow thinking, cognitive biases, emotions, narratives—it's a lot to take in. But don't worry: while it helps to be aware of these concepts, you don't have to become an expert on any or all of them. We've distilled insights from these themes into our *Making Shift Happen* process and its BEHAVIORAL Building Blocks™ to help you design and implement your own behavior change shifters.

 ## The *Making Shift Happen* Process

In addition to our emotions and cognitive processes, many other aspects of our lives influence our behavior, such as cultural and political systems, the built environment surrounding us, and our ideas about how the world works. To shift human behavior for the long-term benefit of the environment, we must take these factors into account. This is why the *Making Shift Happen* process draws on research from many academic fields of study and practical experience from a wide range of sectors. Our process is also informed by systems thinking to help account for system-level factors that will either facilitate or inhibit change. Additionally, the steps of the *Making Shift Happen* process itself originate from design thinking, which aims to ensure that your behavior change initiative is designed with the needs of your specific audience in mind from the start. Following this process will help make your initiatives more efficient, cost-effective, and successful at shifting environmental behaviors. Here we provide a brief overview of the disciplines integrated into our process, and acknowledge the importance of their contributions to our work as behavior change practitioners.

Psychological and behavioral sciences

The *Making Shift Happen* process draws on neuroscience and other behavioral sciences to help us understand the inner workings of the human mind and our subsequent behavioral patterns. Cross-disciplinary areas of study like conservation psychology are especially relevant to environmental behavior change efforts.

Neuroscience and cognitive neuroscience

Neuroscience studies the structure and processes of the human brain and the nervous system. Cognitive neuroscience is a subfield that studies how the chemical and physical processes in the brain affect human cognition. Cognitive neuroscience can therefore help us understand the brain's role in connecting our cognitive processes with our behaviors.

Cognitive psychology

Cognitive psychology is the scientific study of mental processes that shape our behaviors, including (but not limited to) perception, attention, memory, and problem-solving.

Social psychology

Social psychology studies how our behaviors, beliefs, and intentions shape (and are shaped by) other individuals or groups.

Environmental and conservation psychology

Environmental psychology looks at the relationship between humans and their physical surroundings to understand how we affect our environment and how our environment influences our behavior. Similarly, conservation psychology studies the reciprocal relationship between humans and nature, but with the specific goal of increasing protections for the natural world.

Sociology

Sociology examines the causes and consequences of human behavior in social and cultural contexts. It studies social relationships within and between groups, organizations, cultures, communities, and societies, often seeking to explore issues related to race, gender, age, or socioeconomic class, among many other aspects of these groups.

Behavioral economics and choice architecture

We also use insights from behavioral economics to provide deeper insights into our decision-making processes. Choice architecture and nudging are particularly useful concepts in our work as behavior change practitioners.

Behavioral economics

Under classic economic theory, humans are expected to make "rational" decisions by carefully considering all the information available to them and acting in their own best interests. However, in the 1970s, psychologists Amos Tversky and Daniel Kahneman pioneered research that began to paint a very different picture of human decision-making processes. They revealed that our decisions are influenced by things like how information is presented to us and the mental shortcuts that we use to process information. It became clear that insights from psychology could inform economic analyses for a more realistic understanding of human behavior—and thus the intellectual hybrid of *behavioral economics* was formed.

It has since become a robust, interdisciplinary field of study grounded in the concept of **bounded rationality,** which asserts that humans face limitations that prevent us from acting in fully "rational" ways. These limitations can be external (such as a lack of time) or cognitive (such as lacking the mental capacity to process large amounts of information and make logical calculations). Ultimately, we know that our decisions are not made in a vacuum, so we need to consider all of the potential influences when trying to change behavior.

Choice architecture and nudging

Choice architecture refers to the idea that our decisions are influenced by the context or environment in which the decision is made, including the way information is presented and described.[35] For example, consumer habits are influenced by the order of food in a buffet line or the physical layout of a store. A store is a choice environment, and so is a website or even a paper sign-up form. Their design can influence behavior in various ways; for example, we tend toward the most convenient options provided, so we are more likely to fill our plate with food presented early in a buffet line, and select the first option listed on a sign-up form. Therefore, the designer of these environments, the choice architect, has the power to encourage specific behaviors.

One of the fundamental tools used in choice architecture is **nudging**.[33] Cass R. Sunstein, a legal scholar and prominent researcher in the field of behavioral economics, defines nudges in the following way:

> Nudges are interventions that steer people in particular directions but that also allow them to go their own way. A reminder is a nudge; so is a warning. A GPS nudges; a default rule nudges. To qualify as a nudge, an intervention must not impose significant material incentives (including disincentives).

Some nudges are designed to educate people, while some are designed to make specific choices easier, more accessible, or even automatic. Perhaps the most important requirement of all nudges is that the audience fully maintains their freedom of choice (we discuss this further in the section on ethical considerations). Ideally, we can even help our audiences act as their own choice architects,[27] providing people with the tools to shape their own personal environments through self-nudges (like hanging reusable bags on their door knob as a reminder to bring them to the grocery store). When used thoughtfully and appropriately, nudges are one of the most effective tools for influencing behavior.

Social marketing

Originally used in public health initiatives, *social marketing* uses traditional marketing principles not to sell commercial products or services, but to promote specific human behaviors, ideas, or attitudes for the benefit of the greater social good. According to social marketer Dr. Bill Smith, emeritus editor of *Social Marketing Quarterly*, the aim of social marketing is to "offer people something they already value in exchange for a behavior which we believe will benefit not only them as individuals, but society as a whole."[31]

Systems thinking

Every year, we produce 300 million tonnes of plastic waste, (which is nearly equivalent to the combined weight of the entire human population) and yet barely 10% of all plastic ever created has been recycled.[24] Is this entirely the fault of the average consumer? Absolutely not. It's the result of systems and policies that have made it cheaper for oil companies to produce virgin plastic than to recycle plastic products into new ones.[32]

However, it's also true that the larger systems cannot be changed without individual and collective action. Every sixty seconds, one million plastic water bottles are purchased around the world. So decreasing consumer demand for plastic is one way to influence companies to adjust their practices. Changes in individual behavior also accumulate into changes in social norms and expectations, which can influence policymakers to pass new legislation to appease their constituents. By reducing our personal use of plastic as well as pushing for policy changes, we apply pressure from both the bottom and the top of the system.

Individual behavior and systemic factors are inextricably linked. Although much of this book is focused on behavior change at the individual level, it's important for us to consider how individuals and groups are influenced by the natural and social systems and structures surrounding them. *Systems thinking* can help us understand factors interdependent with behavior, such as social norms, social networks, the natural and built environment, institutions, policies, and power structures.[1] We can use a systems thinking lens to help us identify the root causes of the problem we are trying to address—a critical first step in the design of effective programs and behavior change campaigns.

To identify, simplify, and visualize relationships among the different elements of complex socioecological systems, we can use the visual metaphor of an iceberg.[19] Starting from the deepest level, *mental models* form the basic principles that shape the *system structures*. These structures, which include both formal and informal factors (e.g., explicit policies and implicit social norms), shape individual and collective *patterns of behavior*, both directly and indirectly, as well as consciously and unconsciously. These behavioral patterns then result in the outcomes, or *events*, that we observe in the system. Within this general causal sequence, complex interconnections exist between and across levels of the system. Deeper elements of the system such as mental models provide more leverage for change because they are fundamental to the function of the system overall.

Integrating systems thinking with insights from behavioral science provides perhaps the most powerful combination of tools for practitioners; systems thinking allows practitioners to identify the points in the system that will yield the most change, and a behavioral approach can be used to enact the changes themselves.[15] Behavior change strategies can and should be applied throughout all levels of the system—to shift mental models, write policies, or change consumer behavior, among many other possibilities.

Initiatives are particularly effective when they target multiple levels of the system at the same time. For example, let's look at how a multi-pronged effort led to a considerable decline in smoking behavior in the United States. Starting in the 1970s, state and local governments began implementing bans on smoking in public spaces. At the same time, there was an increase in lawsuits against tobacco companies and public health campaigns aimed at reducing the social acceptability of smoking. These efforts simultaneously created shifts in the system at a behavioral level (e.g., reduced smoking in public places), structural level (e.g., indoor smoking bans and high profile lawsuits), and mental model level (e.g., smoking beliefs and attitudes), causing tobacco consumption to be reduced by more than 50% by the end of the century.[8] This behavioral shift reinforced new anti-smoking norms and legitimized the stricter policies, which are still in place today.

When implementing behavioral strategies from this book, we encourage you to take note of any contextual factors that either enable or constrain your desired behavior. In many cases, strengthening enabling factors while weakening constraints can create new conditions that make the desired behavior more likely to occur. Systems thinking will help you identify which contextual factors to target through your initiative. For more detail on tools you can use to incorporate systems thinking into the design of your initiatives, see INITIATE: Process Chapter 2.

Events

Events are observable outcomes of the system that are produced directly by patterns of behavior and indirectly by all of the other components of the system. Events can be thought of as symptoms of a problem, not the cause, so changing them requires shifts at deeper levels of the system.

Patterns of Behavior

Individual and collective patterns of behavior are shaped by system structures and mental models. Most of the shifters in this book are designed to influence this level of the system, and can be applied to behavioral patterns occurring among individuals, households, communities, businesses, and governments.

System Structures

System structures are shaped by mental models, and include formal rules, policies, institutions, and legal systems, as well as informal factors like societal norms. It's important to determine whether behaviors are undermined or supported by system structures; sometimes you may need to redirect your strategy to include changes to the system structures themselves.

Mental Models

Mental models consist of the ideologies, assumptions, and beliefs that shape the foundations of the structures in a system. Although change at this level of a system may take the longest, it can be the most impactful; a shift in mental models can lead to sustained changes in many behaviors at once. More information about shifting mental models can be found in ASSOCIATIONS and LONGEVITY: Building Block Chapters 9 and 10.

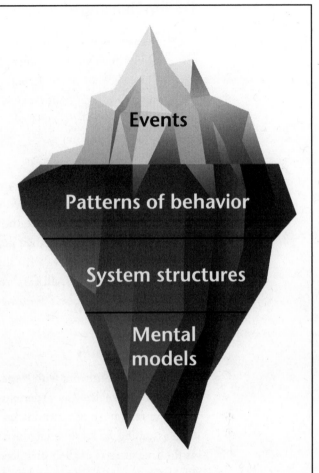

Figure 1.1.1:
The Iceberg Metaphor for
Systems Thinking
CREDIT: GOODMAN, M. *THE ICEBERG MODEL.* (2002). HOPKINTON, MA: INNOVATION ASSOCIATES ORGANIZATIONAL LEARNING. COPYRIGHT 2002 BY M. GOODMAN.

Design thinking

Humans aren't as good as we should be in our capacity to empathize with feelings and thoughts of others, be they humans or other animals on earth. So maybe part of our formal education should be training in empathy. Imagine how different the world would be if, in fact, that were "reading, writing, arithmetic, empathy."

— Neil deGrasse Tyson, astrophysicist, author, science communicator

Because environmental problems are caused by and can only be solved by humans, our process draws on **Human Centered Design** (HCD). HCD uses the perspectives of our intended audience to inform the design of solutions, services, and products that are tailored to their needs. In our case, in lieu of a product or service, we are designing initiatives with the specific goal of encouraging environmental behavior change. As you will see throughout the book, we have incorporated HCD principles into our process. Below are a few of the most important aspects of the HCD process.

Start with empathy

We must begin our work with **empathy**. Empathy refers to our capacity to understand and internalize the experiences of others. Working empathetically means trying to relinquish our own biases, actively listening to our audience and, rather than assuming we know what's best for our audience members, recognizing them as the true experts of their own lived experiences.[14] See LONGEVITY: Building Block Chapter 10 for more on how to build empathy.

Always research, don't guess

It is critical to engage in open-minded, empathetic research at every phase in the design process to learn as much from our audience as possible and discover new insights and ideas as we go. Empathetic research involves interviewing, observing, and conducting surveys with our audience to help us understand their relationship to the issue we are trying to address. These activities can reveal our audience's emotions, beliefs, values, needs, and interactions with their surroundings and help us to identify the barriers and motivators of their behaviors, which inform the design of our initiatives. See UNCOVER: Process Chapter 3 and METHODS: Process Chapter 6 for more information about how to conduct research.

Prototype and iterate

Once we have done sufficient research, we use **prototyping** to test out our initiative's design with our audience. Prototyping helps us save substantial resources in the long run by allowing us to make numerous adjustments to our shifters based on our audience's responses before we implement them on a large scale, preventing us from going too far down the wrong path. This form of iterative feedback provides a valuable guide that may lead us to reevaluate our targeted behavior, or backtrack to a previous step in our design process where we may need to change direction. We discuss prototyping and how to navigate this iterative process in greater detail in DESIGN: Process Chapter 4.

•••

It may be tempting to skip the audience research and go straight to solutions, for fear that this design thinking process could be time-consuming or costly. But remember what happened with D.A.R.E. and teen anti-smoking campaigns? We risk wasting time and resources by rolling out initiatives that don't work. Additionally, there is a risk that our efforts could backfire or even do harm to our audience if we don't thoroughly understand the people and context with which we are working.

Using the *Making Shift Happen* process does not have to be extremely time-consuming or expensive. Even on a shoestring budget, you can incorporate these practices, which can go a long way in maximizing the budget that you do have. You also don't have to use every step and tool in each of the phases we recommend, but we encourage you to use the framework we've laid out as a guide that will help you to design the most effective and efficient initiatives possible.

Table 1.1.2: Words to Describe the *Making Shift Happen* Process

What it is	What it is not
Conscientious	A silver bullet
Creative	Assumption-based
Investigative; Diagnostic	Definitive
Empathetic	Imposing; Authoritative
Equitable	Judgmental
Evidence-based	Linear
Evolving	Manipulative
Inquisitive; Exploratory	Narrow in scope
Iterative; Flexible; Adaptive	One size fits all; Cookie cutter
Problem Solving	Prescribed
Strategic	Rigid
Systems-oriented	
Tailored; Customized	

Guiding Principles of the *Making Shift Happen* Process

In addition to being rooted in many disciplines, the *Making Shift Happen* process is guided by a number of fundamental principles, driven by our belief in an inclusive form of environmentalism that strives for equitable protections of all beings and natural resources on this planet. In this section we call attention to important ethical considerations, including issues of scarcity, our finite pools of worry, behavioral spillover, and some caveats about activating specific emotions. Refer to these guiding principles as you design your behavior change initiatives; they will help to prevent unintended consequences and increase your positive environmental impact.

Take an intersectional approach to environmentalism

> *[Intersectional environmentalism] is an inclusive version of environmentalism that advocates for both the protection of people and the planet. It identifies the ways in which injustices happening to marginalized communities and the earth are interconnected.*
>
> —Leah Thomas, environmental activist

Environmental challenges disproportionately affect marginalized communities and Black, Indigenous, and People of Color (BIPOC): this has been a neglected aspect of environmental activism. Disasters like Hurricane Katrina in the United States, bushfires ravaging Aboriginal communities in Australia, and the threat of pipeline installations on First Nation lands in Canada are blatant reminders of this. But we must look beyond these events that make headlines; marginalized communities endure hardships every day through experiences like the degradation of coastal lands and fisheries, increasingly bad air pollution in urban cities, and the placement of toxic waste dumps.

We will use the terms "environmentalism" and "environmental issues" throughout this book, which are sometimes understood to pertain strictly to natural ecosystems. However, we mean more by them: we believe in an inclusive environmentalism that prioritizes the protection of not only our planet, but all of humanity too—including people of all races, genders, ages, and cultures.

Consider culture and context

Culture has a significant influence on human behavior, so we need to understand the cultural context in which we are designing behavior change initiatives. For example, the concepts of *individualism* and *collectivism* are often used to broadly categorize cultural differences. Western countries such as the United States and the United Kingdom have individualistic cultures that tend to value independence and individual accomplishments. In contrast, many Latin American and Asian countries tend to have collectivist cultures that value interdependence and group accomplishments. These differences have important implications for social interactions and decision-making processes, among many other behavioral patterns.[37] That said, we must note that culture cannot be summed up just by these broad terms. Culture is deeply complex and constantly evolving; even within countries, culture can vary by region, town, and even household. Nonetheless, as long as we remain cognizant of these nuances, we can still identify useful cultural patterns to guide us in the design process.

Beyond culture, there are additional influential aspects of society—including race, wealth, education, and political environments—that shape our behaviors. This is particularly important to note because racial diversity is often lacking among academics, within environmental groups, and in study participants in the social sciences.[21] We must keep this in mind as we design our environmental initiatives, and be sure to test our ideas with our specific audience, as we discuss in more detail at the end of this chapter.

Follow ethical guidelines

When we design programs and initiatives that aim to influence people's behavior—even for the intended benefit of both our audience and the planet—we must be careful to consider some fundamental ethical questions about our work.

There is a continuum of opinions about the ethics of behavior change. For example, some behavioral scientists claim that techniques like nudging can be manipulative in nature, infringing on the autonomy and welfare of the audience.[10] On the other end of the spectrum, there are behavioral scientists who argue that since we are already constantly being influenced by choice architecture (often through marketing that persuades us to buy things that we don't really need), "nudging for good" should in fact be a moral imperative, as long as it's implemented judiciously.[33] For example, pollution is partly caused by unhelpful choice architecture in the form of regulatory defaults designed by those that benefit. This is the case when homeowners are automatically opted into energy programs that don't draw on sustainable sources of energy. Instead, shouldn't we try to change the defaults so that homeowners are opted into more sustainable energy programs?

These divergent opinions—and the many in between—are too complex and nuanced for us to fully explore here (for those interested in reading more on this topic, we recommend the work of Richard Thaler, Cass Sunstein, Leonhard Lades, Liam Delaney, and Pelle Guldborg Hansen). We recommend assessing and employing choice architecture on a case-by-case basis using an empathetic approach that is informed by design thinking and certain ethical considerations. We highlight some of the most important ethical issues for you to consider as you design your behavior change initiatives below. These guidelines should help to ensure that your initiatives come from a place of integrity and serve the best interests of your audience. In general, behavior change efforts should be:

Well-intentioned

Goals should be well-intentioned and not tied to ulterior or self-serving motives.[16] Maintaining honesty and integrity is imperative throughout behavior change initiatives.[34] But even with the best intentions to protect the environment and subsequently improve people's livelihoods, we still need to keep a number of other ethical considerations in mind.

Participatory

It is our responsibility as practitioners to design initiatives that are consistent with the values, interests, and preferences of the community in which we aim to work. But we should be careful to recognize that people in different contexts may have varying ideas of well-being, so we shouldn't jump to conclusions about how we can improve the well-being of others who have a different life experience than our own.[28] We should also be sure to engage with a diverse range of stakeholders and audience segments so that all voices are heard, especially if there are power imbalances among participant groups. A participatory approach provides the most authentic and direct way to learn about the needs, values, and motivations of our audiences and to ensure that they accept and approve of our efforts. Inviting the audience's participation from an early stage also cultivates meaningful relationships instead of transactional ones, which can increase people's long-term investment in the cause, leading to more sustainable and empowering outcomes for the community.[2]

Equitable

Our initiatives should aim to avoid regressive, redistributive effects that take something from a group of people with lesser means and give it to another.[16] We should always be cognizant of how certain behavior changes may have different ramifications for various groups of people due to race, class, gender, and socioeconomic status, among other factors.

Respectful

We must make it a priority to protect the rights of our audience by respecting people's autonomy, dignity, and privacy.[16,34] It is of the utmost importance for us to preserve our audience's freedom of choice. This helps to ensure that our behavior change efforts are not coercive and in no way undermine people's personal agency.

• • •

As you consider these ethical issues, keep in mind that every context you work in will be unique, so you will need to adjust your initiatives accordingly to ensure that they are ethical as well as effective. We will expand on these broad guidelines and discuss a few specific issues in more detail below, which have notable ethical implications.

Think carefully about *when* and *whom* you ask: navigating scarcity and worry

We encourage you to be aware and respectful of the financial and cognitive capacity your audience has to engage with your behavior change initiatives. It's especially critical to understand if your audience's actions are constrained by their socioeconomic status or experiences contributing to their pools of worry.

Scarcity[20]

> Scarcity is not just a physical constraint. It is also a mindset. When scarcity captures our attention, it changes how we think—whether it is at the level of milliseconds, hours, or days and weeks. By staying top of mind, it affects what we notice, how we weigh our choices, how we deliberate, and ultimately what we decide and how we behave. When we function under scarcity, we represent, manage, and deal with problems differently.
>
> —Sendhil Mullainathan and Eldar Shafir,
> authors of *Scarcity: Why Having Too Little Means So Much*

Scarcity is most simply defined as not having enough of something. The basic economic principle of scarcity refers to a limited supply of material goods and services, but there is also the psychology of scarcity, in which cognitive functioning is compromised due to a lack of material or cognitive resources. When our basic needs are unmet (e.g., food, safety, social connection), our mental bandwidth is taxed. This can manifest as *tunneling*, in which we fixate on the resource that we lack, reducing our capacity to focus on other things. In a scarcity mindset, it's more difficult to retain information, reason, make decisions, and adopt new behaviors.

People who live on a tight budget frequently have to make decisions about how to best allocate their limited financial resources to obtain essential things like food and shelter in the short term, rather than invest in things like insulating their home, even though it would save money in the long term. Keep in mind that the scarcity mindset is not limited to the poor; people also struggle with decisions when they are overwhelmed, do not have enough time, or are disconnected from social interaction. A single working parent, for example, might not have much bandwidth for developing new practices in their life that will reduce their carbon footprint. We should therefore be sensitive to the daily pressures that influence the priorities of people dealing with scarcity, whatever form it may take.

Throughout this book, we discuss strategies for reducing barriers to behavior change, but when the mental bandwidth of an audience is diminished due to a lack of material or cognitive resources, simplifying an action or making it more accessible can only do so much. We should therefore design environmental initiatives accordingly: for example, by including elements that reduce our audience's scarcity, and by reducing financial and cognitive burdens associated with the initiative.

Depending on the context and type of initiative, it may simply be inappropriate to choose people facing scarcity as an audience for your behavior change initiative. That said, some conservation initiatives inherently provide additional resources or financial benefits for communities: reforming fishery management, for example, often improves both conservation and positive economic outcomes for fishers. It's also possible to integrate empowering environmental initiatives within programs specifically designed to alleviate poverty.

The topic of scarcity is complex yet important. Within the scope of this book and the *Making Shift Happen* process, we want to emphasize that it deserves the attention of all environmental practitioners, no matter where you plan to work.

Finite pool of worry

Even when we aren't experiencing scarcity, we all have mental and emotional limits to the number of things we can concern ourselves with. This limited capacity to care is sometimes referred to as our ***finite pool of worry***.[17,29] When our concern about one thing increases, our concern for other things may decrease because we can only confront so many challenges at once.

The specific concerns that are in our pool of worry at any given time depend on many factors. Concerns about recessions and job security, for example, tend to override many other worries.[23] In fact, the performance of the United States' economy turns out to be a very good predictor of the public's level of concern for the environment. Researchers found that the degree to which Americans worry about these two issues has an inverse relationship: when concern about the economy increases (such as during economic recessions), concern for the environment decreases.[12] This has significant implications for climate science communications and public engagement with environmental issues.

Other salient events such as terrorist attacks, mass shootings, or the COVID-19 pandemic also consume much of our capacity to worry, especially if we are concerned about where our next paycheck will come from or the health of our loved ones.

• • •

We should be sensitive to the timing and context in which we engage with our audiences and be careful not to contribute anything more to their pool of worry. In some cases, there may be a need to remove scarcity or reduce the number of things occupying the pool of worry before working on behavior change, so we should always work to identify those situations before proceeding.

Think carefully about *what* you ask: the implications of spillover

If someone starts recycling for environmental reasons, are they more or less likely to start carpooling to work? ***Behavioral spillover*** refers to when the adoption of one behavior influences the likelihood of engaging in another behavior.[22] Over the last 20 years, there have been considerable developments in the research on spillover, but our understanding of the phenomenon is still emerging.[6]

In the realm of environmental behavior change initiatives, both positive and negative behavioral spillover can occur: an initiative targeting one behavior may increase or decrease the likelihood of additional environmental behaviors.[36,39] For example, in a study involving an initiative to promote composting, households that started composting also started engaging in other household measures to reduce energy and save water (positive spillover).[30] Conversely, another study found that an initiative designed to reduce household water consumption was successful in doing so, but also led to an increase in household electricity consumption (negative behavioral spillover).[38]

Several phenomena that can cause negative spillover include:

Single action bias	A person or organization might adopt one mitigation strategy or environmental behavior and then—due to a sense of relief at having addressed the problem in some way—stop there, failing to adopt additional measures.[40]
Moral licensing	This related rationalization process can occur if a person considers one environmentally responsible behavior sufficient to justify wasteful or excessive consumption in another aspect of their lives. In other words, our previous good deed makes us feel like we "have done our part" and are now "off the hook."[38]
Rebound effect	Finally, negative spillover can be driven by a ***rebound effect,*** whereby an increase in technological efficiency causes a decrease in operational cost, contributes to an increase in consumption. For example, we might buy a more fuel-efficient vehicle, but because we are saving money on gas, we end up driving more.[9]

The behavioral mechanisms responsible for the kind of spillover we want to see—positive spillover—are currently not as well understood.[22] However, research to date generally suggests that positive spillover stems from a desire for consistency. Decisions made based on identity (e.g., as someone who acts in environmentally responsible ways as a rule, or sees themselves as an "environmentalist"), may be more likely to result in positive spillover than decisions based on social pressure or incentives.[39]

But not everyone sees themselves as "environmentalists." And even among those who do, negative spillover can occur. With every behavioral ask we make, we run the risk of potential negative spillover. And the stakes are high: negative spillover might prevent your next ask, or even another practitioner's ask, from being adopted. This unfortunate reality means that we must put extra care into deciding which behaviors we ask our audiences to adopt. We must also work in tandem with our fellow practitioners to determine which actions are likely to be the most impactful. In INITIATE: Process Chapter 2, we'll dive into considerations like these for identifying and selecting which behaviors to focus on in your initiatives.

Think carefully about *how* you ask: evoking emotions with care

To convey the urgency of environmental issues, communicators often use messaging that triggers negative emotions like fear to motivate action against the threats we face. We understand the temptation of this strategy because we feel the urgency, too! Despite the importance of conveying the reality of environmental threats, however, we recommend erring on the side of caution with respect to evoking negative emotional responses.

As we discuss in detail in OPTIMISM: Building Block Chapter 7, negative emotions can backfire in various ways, especially if they are not paired with messages that promote feelings of efficacy. They may inspire short-term behaviors, but there is little evidence that these behaviors are sustained over the long term—clearly a critical component to environmental issues like climate change. So we should be wary of eliciting negative emotions through our appeals; they may produce the immediate behavior changes we were hoping for, but at the expense of continued engagement with the broader environmental movement. Generally, we prefer eliciting positive emotions when we can, as a more productive and positive way to influence change that can help to uplift each other as we work together to solve challenging problems.

When we aim to change behavior on a large scale, it's inevitable that we will engage with people's emotions. This is one of the reasons why it's so important to test our initiatives, which we discuss further below. Testing helps to ensure that we engage with people's emotions in a respectful way and that we don't inadvertently activate counterproductive emotional responses that could harm our audiences. This is also critical for the sake of protecting the environmental behavior change movement at large.

Test, test, test

Given the range of contextual nuances that affect our work, results from one or a few studies will not necessarily be found again if the same research is conducted in a different setting. This refers to the concept of ***external validity***—the degree to which a study's findings can be generalized.[3]

When reviewing results from a study, we should take note of the context in which the research was conducted and ask ourselves if the participants are similar to our audience. If not, are the findings likely applicable to people from different cultural or socioeconomic backgrounds, geographical locations, or political systems? Asking ourselves these questions can help identify what we don't know about our audience. Testing our ideas and initiatives helps to fill in those gaps, and allows us to tailor our initiatives to better suit our audience's needs. Testing can be as simple as creating basic prototypes or pilot programs, which you will learn more about in DESIGN: Process Chapter 4 and IMPLEMENT: Process Chapter 5. This due diligence is critical, especially before rolling out an initiative that will touch large audiences.

As with all other aspects of our design process, we must be respectful of our audience when testing our initiatives. Use the type of empathetic research promoted by design thinking and the ethical principles described earlier in this chapter to guide your testing processes. We encourage you to keep an open mind and use your deep listening skills, which will help prevent any unintended and unforeseen consequences. Ultimately, it's imperative to test your strategies with your specific audience, in the appropriate context in which you aim to work. We encourage you to keep this in mind as you learn about various behavior change techniques throughout this book.

• • •

We are all trying to make positive changes through our initiatives. However, even the best-intentioned initiatives can overlook things that can end up negatively impacting our audience and our efforts. Our guiding principles are meant to provide a compass you can use to keep your work tracking in a positive direction. Remember to take an intersectional approach to environmentalism that is inclusive and takes both culture and context into consideration. Always take note if some type of scarcity is affecting your audience, and try to remain cognizant of people's finite pools of worry. Be aware of potential behavioral spillover, and be careful when evoking emotions in order to call attention to an environmental issue. At any point in your design process, you can always refer back to our ethical guidelines, which should help ensure your initiative is carried out with integrity.

Conclusion

The issues and considerations presented in this chapter are foundational to any behavior change initiative. This work is far from simple, and we make no guarantees that it will always be easy. But we promise that it's very much worth doing, and we are here to walk you through it. Using our process will not only save you time, effort, and resources in the long run, but it will also help you create a more respectful, equitable, and effective behavior change initiative in whichever context or community you plan to work.

Initiate

T HERE ARE MANY GLOBAL environmental issue areas that need to be addressed—greenhouse gas emissions, plastic pollution, deforestation, and biodiversity loss, to name just a few. Within each issue area, there are myriad ways to effect change—we can try to reduce plastic pollution by focusing on, for example, shifting consumers to use less single-use plastics, working with restaurants and companies to use reusable packaging, working with lawmakers to pass legislation that limits the ability of manufacturers to produce virgin plastic, or by asking manufacturers to use materials other than plastic for their single-use products. How do we choose what to focus our behavior change efforts on?

The INITIATE phase is designed to set practitioners up for success by helping them strategically make this decision. In a nutshell, this phase will help you get from something broad like "reducing ocean pollution" to a specific behavior on which to focus with a specific audience, such as "Tour boat operators in the Great Barrier Reef provide reef-safe sunscreens on all their boats" or "Commercial squid fishermen in the upper Gulf of California, Mexico, will dispose of all damaged fishing gear in designated collection bins."

From there, the INITIATE phase will help you to define one or more goals for your initiative, such as "50% of Great Barrier Reef tour boat operators will provide reef-safe sunscreen on 100% of their boats by December 2025" or "We will double the weight of properly disposed fishing gear in designated port collection bins in the upper Gulf of California, Mexico, this year." In this phase you will also choose the metrics you will use to determine whether you're meeting your goals.

The guidance provided in this chapter will help you complete these steps from scratch, or it can augment your organization's existing strategic planning processes and systems.

The INITIATE phase is rooted in research

To complete the INITIATE phase, we will utilize research of various kinds to select a focus, audience, behavior, and goals for our initiative. Research can take the form of primary research, ranging from interviews to large surveys, or secondary research, such as drawing from academic articles or reports by other practitioners who have worked on the same issue.

To give you a preview, here are some examples of how you might utilize research to inform your decisions in INITIATE:

- When determining and exploring your focus you might review academic literature or conduct interviews with experts and/or potential audience members to gather information on areas of highest need.
- When selecting your audience-behavior pairing you might survey members of several audiences to better understand which behaviors they currently practice and which they are most interested in adopting. You can then use this information along with other data to determine which audience-behavior pairing would have the highest impact on your focus area.
- When defining your goals and selecting metrics you might review academic literature or seek advice from other practitioners to find out what metrics they have used to define success for similar initiatives.

Research throughout the *Making Shift Happen* process

Just as we will use various research methods in the INITIATE phase, we will employ various research methods throughout the entire *Making Shift Happen* process. We recommend that you conduct secondary research, such as looking at case studies or academic papers, throughout the process, but also that you learn information directly from your audience. Your initiative will be more effective at changing the behavior of your audience the more you can interface with, learn about, and include them in the design of your initiative. We present specific techniques you can use throughout the process to get the information you need (including suggestions for ways to adjust the techniques based on your available time and resources). We will describe each of these in detail in their respective chapters, but in sum, we start with a Landscape Exploration and other secondary research, followed by primary research such as interviews, observations, or surveys in INITIATE. Then in UNCOVER, we walk you through conducting a Behavioral Drivers Analysis to uncover barriers to and motivators of behavior. Finally, we recommend a final round of research to test and refine shifters—evidence-based behavior change solutions—in DESIGN. Additionally, we provide tips and overarching considerations in METHODS, which is designed to guide you through how to conduct various types of research.

At the end of this chapter, we go into more detail about how you can utilize various research methods to get the information you need.

The INITIATE phase will take a different shape for every initiative

The exact path each practitioner takes will vary depending on their starting point, expertise, resources, constraints, competing priorities, and goals. Because of this, the INITIATE phase will develop in different ways for every initiative.

The components of the INITIATE phase are interconnected

Although we present these elements in separate sections of this chapter, the focus, audience, and behavior components of an initiative are interconnected. The entire *Making Shift Happen* process is iterative—meaning that you may revisit and revise your approach as you go—but you should plan to iterate especially during the INITIATE phase. Although you select your focus first, you might uncover new information when researching potential audiences and behaviors, causing you to rethink and adjust your focus. Because of this phase's iterative nature, you may find it's more appropriate to proceed through this phase in a different order than presented, or do several of the steps detailed below simultaneously.

Ultimately, what matters is that you move forward to UNCOVER with a clear audience and behavior on which to focus your initiative. When you discover something through your research during the INITIATE phase that causes you to revisit a selection you already made, think of this as something to celebrate, because it means you have adjusted your initiative to make it more effective.

The INITIATE phase is designed for practitioners at different stages

Even though we present these steps and provide guidance as if you are starting from a relatively blank slate (i.e., with only a vague idea of what your initiative could focus on), we understand that you may be starting your initiative with some variables already determined. For example, your geographic location or organizational mission may dictate what focus area you will work on, or your role might mean that you are limited to only working with certain audiences (such as university staff or students). Table 1.2.1 gives examples of initiatives that are starting with certain aspects already determined.

Table 1.2.1: Examples of Being Locked into an Audience, Behavior, or Location

Environmental Issue: Ocean Health	Audience	Behavior	Location
Focus: Improving fishing practices **Audience:** Your NGO works with fishing **cooperatives on the Pacific Coast of Mexico.**	You already know your general **Audience.**	From your longitudinal research, you know illegal fishing is rampant and significantly impacting fish populations, so you choose to focus on fishers staying within catch limits.	You choose to work with the cooperative that fishes the grounds where monitoring behaviors would be the least obtrusive and enforcing them would be the most feasible.
Focus: Protecting sea life **Behavior:** Your NGO works on marine mammal protection and has funding to prevent ship strikes (a leading cause of death for whales) by **lowering the speed at which boats travel through shipping lanes and bays.**	Through audience research, you determine to work with shipping captains.	You already know the *general* **Behavior.**	After researching, you choose to start with bays with the highest concentration of ship strikes.
Focus: Reducing debris entering the marine environment **Location:** You have a grant specifically to work on single use plastic marine debris prevention in **San Francisco.**	Through audience research, you narrow the audiences to just a few, such as teens, tourists, and fishers.	Through primary and secondary research, you determine that proper disposal of cigarette butts (one of the most littered items) is a high impact potential behavior.	You already know your **Location.**

If you have preexisting ideas for some of these components, we still encourage you to read each step of the INITIATE phase with an open mind. You may find that the research and thought exercises provided in this chapter help you identify faulty assumptions, clarify your theory of change, or shift your focus, audience, or behavior to one that is more realistic, impactful, or otherwise desirable. And if you don't have specific ideas in mind for these elements of your initiative, that's no problem! Following the steps in this process will help you get there.

A Look Ahead: INITIATE

Choose and Explore Your Focus

Choose your focus
Explore your focus

Choose Your Priority Audience and Behavior

Identify potential priority audiences
Identify potential priority behaviors
Evaluate possible audience-behavior pairings
Define your audience-behavior pairing statement

Set Your Behavior Change Goals and Choose Metrics

Make your goals SMART
Set or refine your overarching goal
Set specific behavior change goals
Choose metrics to measure progress toward your goals

Use Different Research Methods to Get the Information You Need

Secondary research
Primary research

To kick off the INITIATE phase, let's strategically identify a problem area on which to focus our efforts. If you are starting from a broad environmental issue like "reduce ocean pollution" use this process to narrow to a more specific issue on which to focus, based on criteria like impact, need, and organizational fit. In this section, we'll also conduct research and mapping exercises to better understand our focus, so that we're fully prepared to move on to selecting audiences and behaviors.

Choose your focus

So what exactly is a "focus"? This list shows examples of broad environmental issues each with two examples of a *focus*—a specific component of that issue that your behavior change initiative will aim to solve, improve, prevent, reverse, or mitigate:

- **Climate Change**
  - "My initiative will increase carbon sequestration through farming practices that restore soil health."
  - "My initiative will reduce methane emissions from cattle ranching in Mato Grosso, Brazil."

- **Threats to Wildlife**
  - "My initiative will reduce the poaching of sea turtle eggs from nesting grounds on the Nicoya Peninsula, Costa Rica."
  - "My initiative will reduce the destruction of bird habitats during nesting season."

- **Ocean Pollution**
  - "My initiative will reduce the amount of gear abandoned from fishing vessels."
  - "My initiative will reduce the amount of toxic sunscreen entering the water."

Next we outline some criteria to consider as you work to choose your focus. Many practitioners will have a strategic planning process to think through their mission, theory of change, intended outcomes, and the tactics they will use to reach them.

The criteria below can complement existing processes or provide a starting point if you're starting from the ground up.

Impact:
- How much impact does, or would, this focus area have on the environmental problem?

Need:
- Which focus areas are not already being effectively addressed by other organizations?
- Which focus areas address multiple needs (e.g., overfishing impacts both ocean health and food security)?

Fit:
- How does this focus match with your organization's mission and expertise? If you do not have an in-house expert on the topic, do you have access to advisors or thought partners in the field? How does this focus fit current and upcoming priorities?
- Does your team have the necessary bandwidth?

Feasibility:
- What level of funding will be required if you choose this focus?
- What are the potential sources of support available for this focus area?
- Are there other institutions who will partner with you on this initiative?
- Do you have, or can you form, the stakeholder relationships necessary to succeed?
- Do you have buy-in from your board or senior leadership team?
- Will you need government support and/or public approval of your initiative?
- What external threats are there to your success?
- What enabling conditions exist to support your success?

Systemic challenges or opportunities:
As we discussed in the last chapter, systems thinking can help us identify how system structures might support or undermine our behavior change strategies. We take a closer look at how to use systems thinking to strengthen initiatives later in this section of INITIATE. If we will be pushing up against large systemic barriers, we likely need to focus our initiative on changing policies or breaking down

institutional or structural obstacles in addition to individual behavior change. If it isn't possible to lower these systemic barriers, we may need a different focus.

- What are the political, legal, economic, natural, and cultural forces that may influence this focus area, such as legislation, cultural movements, or economic or demographic trends?

If you already have a focus in mind, the above criteria can help you evaluate it. For example, as you work through these considerations, you may decide to adjust your focus to address an unseen area of need or in response to a realistic assessment of your organization's bandwidth and priorities. If you end up adjusting your focus from thinking through these considerations, that's great! That means you are now even more informed about your issue, and you are ready to progress to the next step with more knowledge and clarity. Conversely, if you find yourself needing more information before deciding on a focus, you can also do some of the research and mapping described below to help you get there.

Let's illustrate the first step of the INITIATE process by presenting an example that we will carry forward periodically throughout this chapter to illustrate some of the steps and considerations we detail. We will use this icon to draw attention to this example.

 Imagine the environmental issue of concern is climate change. We'll need to drill down quite a bit to carve out a behavior change project. We start by determining if our initiative will seek to reduce greenhouse gas emissions, increase carbon sequestration, increase resilience to climate change, or something else. Using the above criteria, we decide based on organizational fit and expertise within our team, to focus on carbon sequestration to increase the amount of carbon stored in natural landscapes such as soils, forests, or mangroves. We then consider these criteria again to narrow from carbon sequestration as a general method for combating climate change to a small subset of carbon sequestration methods:

- **Impact:** Forest management, mangrove restoration, and certain farming practices all have the potential to sequester carbon. But, because there is an abundance of farmland that is not sequestering carbon to its full potential, we can maximize our impact by focusing on the agricultural sector. Moreover, many farming practices currently implemented have negative impacts on the environment, so changing those practices on a large scale would increase the sustainability of our food system in addition to the carbon sequestration benefits.

- **Need:** Historically, many governments and organizations have worked on carbon sequestration through forest management but fewer have focused on farming. We know that healthy soils—those that are rich in organic matter— retain more water and sequester more carbon. A number of common farming practices are depleting agricultural soils of moisture and nutrients, such as monocropping (planting the same type of crop every season instead of rotating crops) and tilling (mechanically disturbing topsoil by digging and overturning it in preparation for planting and to control weeds). As a result, many farmers are struggling with less resilient crops, lower yields, and slimmer margins. Taking all of this into consideration, we can identify the need to increase organic matter in soils, both to help farmers and to sequester more carbon.

- **Systemic challenges or opportunities:** The food system is extremely complex and has many political and market-based barriers that create resistance to change, meaning we would likely need to focus on changing policies or breaking down institutional or structural obstacles in addition to individual behavior change.

Based on our evaluation, we choose to focus on farming practices that can rebuild organic matter in soils. We now have our focus: "Our initiative will increase carbon sequestration through farming practices that restore soil health."

Write a focus statement

As we work to clarify our focus area, the next step is to synthesize everything into a statement like the one in our example above. Our focus statement should be approximately as narrow as this. Putting our focus into a clear statement helps us set the parameters for the subsequent research and mapping exercises we'll do to explore our focus area.

Importantly, this focus statement also serves as an overarching goal for our initiative: there is a ***desired outcome***—the change we intend to create as a result of our initiative—embedded in the statement (e.g., "reduce methane emissions" or "increase carbon sequestration" or "reduce the amount of sunscreen entering the water").

While the focus statement provides us with parameters and an overarching goal, note that it does not specify an audience or behavior. Exactly how the desired outcome will be achieved (i.e., which audience we're going to prioritize and what behavior they'll do) will be determined in the "Choose Your Priority Audience and Behavior" section of the INITIATE process. We will revisit our overarching goal at the end of the INITIATE phase, where we'll also set measurable behavior change goals based on the audience-behavior pairing we've chosen.

Explore your focus

The research and mapping exercises described in this step will help you explore the focus area that you chose. This is an opportunity to gather and synthesize information from a variety of sources to inform your initiative and to enrich your understanding of the problem, as well as its surrounding systems. Exploring the landscape of the focus area will help provide the information you need before you move on to the next phases of INITIATE. Alternatively, if you feel like you need to gather more information about your issue before you select a focus, the research and exercises posed in the next step can also help you do that.

> The more time you spend doing your due diligence up front, the less likely you are to repeat work that's already been done, and the more value you can add to collective efforts to solve environmental problems.

Exploring your focus is an essential step that will set you up for success. The more time you spend doing your due diligence up front, the less likely you are to repeat work that's already been done, and the more value you can add to collective efforts to solve environmental problems. For this reason, we recommend that everyone spends time exploring their focus.

Learn about your focus with a Landscape Exploration

In the context of the *Making Shift Happen* process, conducting a **Landscape Exploration** entails engaging in secondary research (i.e., a literature review, collecting and analyzing datasets, resource gathering interviews) to evaluate the current state of the field for your focus.

The level of specificity of your research depends on how defined your focus currently is.

 For our focus statement of "My initiative will increase carbon sequestration through farming practices that restore soil health," our Landscape Exploration might entail (but not be limited to): researching existing government conservation programs designed to encourage sustainable farming practices as well as other goverment programs and laws that affect farming practices (e.g., subsidized crop insurance); scanning United States census data to understand who owns or rents farmland and what type of crops are most prevalent; reviewing previous academic studies focused on the uptake of various farming practices; conducting interviews with knowledge partners who work in the agricultural industry; and informal conversations with stakeholders like farmers and landowners.

If we had determined that we didn't know enough to arrive at a focus as specific as carbon sequestration via farming practices, we may have needed to conduct a broader Landscape Exploration, such as by researching both farming and forest management practices as ways to improve carbon sequestration. Our analysis may have included (but not been limited to) interviewing organizations that work in these sectors and reading through the science on the carbon sequestration storage potential for both forests and farmland.

Why conduct a Landscape Exploration?

A Landscape Exploration will reveal many details about the focus area. It will provide valuable information that will inform choices later in the process. Specifically, you may discover:

- Potential audiences to prioritize
- Potential behaviors to prioritize
- Potential barriers to and motivators of behavior
- Solutions that have succeeded, failed, or are yet to be tested
- System factors that influence our focus area

Importantly, a Landscape Exploration will tell you what has worked and what hasn't worked for other researchers and organizations, which helps you avoid reinventing the wheel. As with the rest of the INITIATE phase, a Landscape Exploration is an iterative process that can be revisited and expanded throughout the *Making Shift Happen* process.

Conduct your Landscape Exploration

To conduct a Landscape Exploration, you will need to mix and match several different kinds of secondary research, such as literature reviews, knowledge gathering interviews, and stakeholder interviews. See METHODS: Process Chapter 6 for more details on conducting secondary research via literature review and resource gathering interviews.

Literature review	A literature review using desktop research—reading news articles, case studies, government reports, results from public opinion surveys, academic literature, and reports from other organizations about past surveys or focus groups with this audience—is low-cost yet invaluable.
Knowledge gathering interviews	Conduct informal interviews with knowledge partners—colleagues, community members, clients, and others who are familiar with the topic and research—to obtain advice, lessons learned, or connections to others.
Stakeholder interviews	After your literature review and knowledge gathering interviews help you identify pertinent stakeholders, it is important to consult these stakeholders; they will almost always have important insights and may know your focus area quite well.

Guide your exploration with questions

We recommend formulating some research questions to help guide your research. Thinking about what you would need to know about your focus ahead of time can be a great way to direct your research toward the most useful and promising sources of information. However, it is also important not to be too restrictive with your Landscape Exploration; you may need to revise or adjust your list of research questions as you discover new information. Remember, your goal at this stage should be to use various research methods to uncover as much relevant information about your issue as possible. You can use the following list as a starting point, but we also encourage you to create your own list:

System influences questions:

- Who are the people and what are the elements within the different layers of the system surrounding your focus? What are the relationships and dynamics among these elements?

- What are the underlying root causes of the problem?
- Where are the positive or negative feedback loops?
- What are the biggest systemic and behavioral enablers? What are the biggest systemic and behavioral barriers? For example, are there rules or regulations that must be followed that are leading to the problem?

Potential audiences questions:
- Who are the stakeholders involved with your focus area?
- From which stakeholders would a change in behavior lead to mitigating or solving the problem?
- Are there any stakeholders that are off-limits to work with, or that aren't likely to be receptive to an initiative?
- Who is particularly influential?
- Do any stakeholders have respected peers that already support your cause?

Potential behaviors questions:
- What behaviors are the biggest contributors to the problem?
- What behaviors do potential audiences currently engage in? When? How frequently?
- What are the barriers to behaviors you want changed? What has motivated people before to adopt these behaviors?
- What perceptions or concerns do audiences have about a particular behavior?

Similar past initiatives questions:
- What approaches have been tried?
- What has worked and what has failed with similar past initiatives, and why?
- What resources are available (surveys, data, reports)?
- Who else might be important for you to speak to?
- Where might there be opportunities for partnership?

A landscape exploration will reveal answers to many, but not all, of these questions. If you can't find sufficient information in the literature or from talking to knowledge partners or stakeholders, you may need to conduct your own primary research—such as through an Audience Analysis (discussed later).

Involve stakeholders in the process

A key goal of the Landscape Exploration is the identification and inclusion of a diverse range of *stakeholders* (individuals or groups that would be impacted in some way by the outcomes of your initiative) early on. For example, the stakeholders for an initiative to improve access to public buses might include bus drivers, people riding the bus, public transit agencies who might experience an increase in ridership, businesses located near bus stops, and the local community, who might benefit from reduced air pollution and increased bus access. In FOUNDATIONS, we explain that the *Making Shift Happen* process should be participatory, meaning that we invite our audience to participate in the design and implementation of our initiatives, and we engage with a diverse range of stakeholders and audiences so that all voices are heard. This participatory approach begins as soon as you start researching your focus area via your Landscape Exploration.

 We would want to be sure we've heard from farmers as part of our research into carbon sequestration through farming practices. Farmers might reveal that they are aware of the benefits of certain farming practices but their adoption of them is influenced heavily by financial constraints imposed by annual bank loans, or that they would fear being judged by the local farming community if they adopted certain practices (e.g., not tilling the soil could appear as if they were neglecting their crops). Farmers might also express concern about how long it would take (multiple years) to benefit from increased yields and profits that result from transitioning to new farming practices. Keep in mind that there is often considerable variation within stakeholder groups; for example, farmers who grow corn in the midwest will not have the same challenges or experiences as farmers who grow fruits and vegetables in California, so be sure to recognize the diversity of stakeholders when considering who to involve in your process.

As you engage with stakeholders, also remain cognizant that anecdotal information gathered from informal conversations should not be overgeneralized as universal truths. Ideally, that information should be corroborated by additional research. When you feel that you have collected sufficient information to answer your research questions, you can begin to organize the information into a map of the systems surrounding your focus area.

Explore the system

In your Landscape Exploration, you gathered information about your area of focus. This information can be used to map the system surrounding that focus area. No matter what issue you choose to focus on, there are systemic factors such as political, regulatory, economic, natural, and cultural forces that influence the problem you are trying to solve.

As we discussed in FOUNDATIONS, systems thinking can help us identify how systemic structures might support or undermine our behavior change strategies.[1] If we will be pushing up against large systemic barriers, we likely need to focus our initiative on changing policies or breaking down institutional or structural obstacles, in addition to individual behavior change. If it isn't possible to lower these systemic barriers, we might need to rethink our focus.

Visualize and assess using the iceberg model

To identify leverage points in the system, it can be helpful to determine where the information we have uncovered about our system falls in the iceberg model presented in FOUNDATIONS. We start by listing out what we know about our system under the four iceberg categories: events, patterns of behavior, system structures, and mental models (see the example in Figure 1.2.2). Importantly, we are not only listing the people involved in the system, but their relationship to other elements in the system, such as the processes and forces that shape relevant power dynamics, like political pressure from a local government or a lack of enabling infrastructure.

 Here, we have started to sort some of the observable patterns of the food system in the United States,[4,5] garnered from our Landscape Exploration, into the four levels of the iceberg model: events, patterns of behavior, system structures, and mental models.

Label elements as enablers or inhibitors

Look at each of the elements you have listed and identify and label those that are **enablers** in the system, which support the positive systemic change we are working toward, as well as those that are **inhibitors,** which perpetuate the negative aspects of the current system.

 From the list of food system elements, "banks give short-term loans that disincentivize farmers from adopting new practices that improve soil health" would certainly be an inhibitor. Meanwhile, some consumers' willingness to "pay a premium for organic or sustainably farmed products" could be an enabler.

Assess your iceberg

Once you have listed all the elements of your system that you have uncovered, take a step back and analyze what you created. Your goal in this phase is to think critically about the elements of your system, looking at the people and elements involved, assessing how they are interrelated, and identifying points of leverage at which you can intervene. What does the structure of the iceberg reveal about causal relationships between elements?

Table 1.2.2: The U.S. Food System, Using the Iceberg Model of Systems Thinking

System Level	Food System Elements[4,5]
Events System events, or observable outcomes, are produced directly by patterns of behavior and indirectly by all of the other levels of the iceberg.	• Empty grocery store shelves when supply chains are disrupted (e.g., during the COVID-19 pandemic) • Farmers struggle to keep up with operating costs • Low crop diversity • Soil erosion and water pollution • Loss of biodiversity • Food waste • Widespread food insecurity despite food surpluses for certain crops
Patterns of Behavior Individual and collective patterns of behavior are shaped by system structures and mental models.	• Consumer demand for year-round availability of all food products • Some consumers are willing to pay a premium for organic or sustainably farmed products • Lobbying by agribusiness corporations • Farmers' reliance on government support and bank loans to cover annual operating costs due to small profit margins • Banks give short-term loans that disincentivize farmers from adopting new practices that improve soil health • Major universities with specialized agriculture schools teach farming methods that prioritize the maximization of yields • Monocropping and tilling • Overuse of pesticides and herbicides to maximize yields
System Structures System structures are shaped by mental models and include formal rules, policies, institutions, and legal systems, as well as informal factors like social norms.	• Industrialization of agriculture • Subsidized government programs that reward high yields over soil health • Barriers to land access and land ownership • Social pressures within farming communities to use certain farming practices (social norms) • Consolidated retailers, distributors, and supply chains that maximize efficiency at the expense of resilience
Mental Models Mental models consist of the ideologies, assumptions, and beliefs that give rise to system structures and human behavior.	• Resources are to be extracted from the land for profit as efficiently as possible • Short-term gains are more important than long-term benefits • The only way to "feed the world" is through large-scale production of basic commodities like wheat, corn, and soy • If we begin to deplete our resources, technology will solve the problem

We can identify that the mental model "the only way to 'feed the world' is through large-scale production of basic commodities like wheat, corn, and soy" has impacted several elements in higher levels of the iceberg, such as what farming techniques are taught in agriculture departments at universities and the resulting behaviors like tilling or monocropping, which both aim to maximize yield.

Map the system[1]

Once we have a better sense of our system's main elements, we can use system mapping to illustrate the system's most important elements and the relationships among them. By the end of this process, you'll have a sketch similar to Figure 1.2.1. In this case, we've decided to focus on the elements most closely related to U.S. agriculture within the food system more broadly.

Begin by physically mapping out all of the elements in the system, drawing connections where we see them. During this process, patterns or themes may surface that seem particularly influential in the system. You will likely find that you need to keep shifting elements around as you go—as you realize certain elements are more connected than others—so have lots of scratch paper handy. Alternatively, it can be helpful to use a stylus pen with a tablet or websites like Kumu.io or MentalModeler.com.

When we have sketched out a map that lays out the elements of the system, we next want to identify the causes and effects of patterns within the system. For example, we might notice that a mental model influences a pattern of behavior (an *upstream cause* of the behavior), and that this pattern of behavior directly influences an event (the *downstream effect* of the behavior). But we also have to look beyond upstream and downstream, as systems are not linear in nature. We should also consider feedback loops that illustrate how system elements interact. There are both *virtuous* and *vicious loops* (either progressing toward or away from your goals), as well as *stabilizing loops* that maintain and reinforce particular systemic patterns.

When we map out our food system (Figure 1.2.1), if we look at the elements starting with the word "farm," we identify a vicious loop that has a significant impact on farming practices. Farmers rely on bank loans to cover their annual operating costs (demonstrated by the arrow from financial lending → farm capital), but those loans are typically based on the previous year's yields (farm yields → farm capital). New practices take time to adopt and may decrease yield in the short term, disincentivizing farmers from experimenting with new practices that would increase soil health and carbon sequestration (farm capital → farming practices).[10]

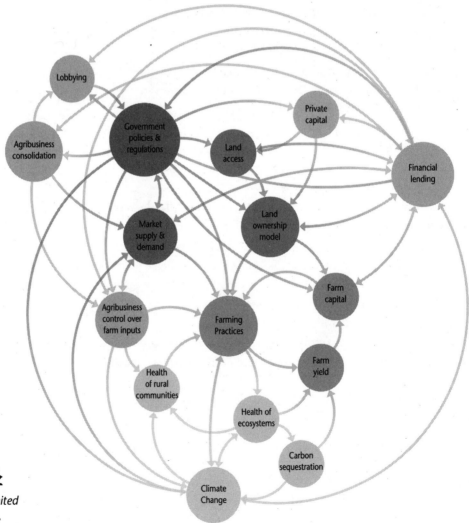

Figure 1.2.1:
Systems Map: United States Agriculture

Our system map, with its virtuous, vicious, and stabilizing loops, helps us to identify potential *leverage points*—points in the system connected to other elements and stakeholders, where we can intervene to produce the most wide-spread effects throughout the system.[9] Identifying the most powerful leverage points will help us focus our efforts within the system we are trying to change. As we become more aware of the ripple effects that a small shift in one element can have on seemingly unrelated actors in a distant part of the system, we also become better equipped to prevent unintended consequences resulting from our initiative. To learn more about systems thinking, we recommend starting with *Thinking in Systems: A Primer*, by Donella H. Meadows.

 We can see in Figure 1.2.1 that government policies and regulations as well as financial lending have a particularly significant influence in the system because they are connected to so many other elements. These two elements of the system could be considered high impact leverage points. As we begin to think about audiences to work with through our initiative, we should consider the stakeholders connected to those system elements—government officials and banks, for example.

Stop and Assess: Are You Missing Stakeholders?

As you learn more about the complexities of the system you are working with, note the roles of the various stakeholders involved; you should begin to see who stands to gain or lose from changes made to the system. Mapping exercises can illuminate critical stakeholders that perhaps you have not yet spoken with. This includes people or groups that may not have much power in the system, but bear the burden of the problem you are seeking to address. Although it is not the responsibility of disempowered groups to create systemic change (nor is that often even a possibility), it's still important and informative to consult them when planning your initiative.

Whether you started INITIATE with a clear idea of the issue you'd like to focus on or you waited until you gathered initial research to select a focus area, by the end of this section, you should have created a clear focus statement and collected a lot of information to aid you as you determine your audience and behavior.

❓ *Ask Yourself: Choose and explore your focus*

Choose your focus

- **Impact:** What is the impact you intend to have with your initiative? If you are deciding between multiple focus areas, which criteria are most important to you?
- **Need:** Would working on this initiative duplicate efforts? If so, can you help others scale their efforts instead? Would working on this solve multiple problems?
- **Fit:** How good of a fit is the initiative for your organization?
- **Feasibility:** What is the likelihood that you would succeed working on this focus?

Explore your focus

- **Research:** What can the research you've collected tell you about your focus area? What additional research might you need to select your focus, audience, or behaviors? We recommend perusing these sections so you are familiar with what you need to know.
- **Audiences and behaviors:** How much do you know about the audiences and behaviors impacting your environmental challenge?
- **Similar initiatives:** What lessons can be learned from similar initiatives?
- **Stakeholders:** Have you identified and included the appropriate stakeholders in your process?
- **System Influences:** What forces are at play at different levels of your system's iceberg? Do you understand the root causes of the problem you're trying to solve? Have you identified the people and elements in the system and the relationships and dynamics among them?
- **Leverage:** Have you identified the critical leverage points at which you could intervene in the system?

Choose Your Priority Audience and Behavior

Now that we've learned more about the focus within our environmental issue and the systems in which it exists, we are ready to start the process of identifying the behavior we want to change and the people from whom we want this change. In this section, we'll walk you through a process for identifying potential audiences and behaviors that can help address the problem you are focusing on. We will also walk you through techniques for narrowing them down to a manageable number of audiences and behaviors to evaluate. Then, we provide guidance for assessing several audiences and behaviors in tandem to select one ***audience-behavior pairing***: the single audience and behavior that will be the focus of your behavior change initiative. Finally, after you've selected your priority audience-behavior pairing, you'll write your ***audience-behavior statement***, which clearly defines your audience and behavior and will be used as a guidepost for your work.

> ## Choose Your Audience and Behavior
>
> - Identify potential priority audiences, considering impact, equity, potential to scale, and likelihood of success
> - Brainstorm behaviors contributing to the problem and identify desired replacement behaviors
> - Identify the sequence of distinct behaviors leading up to the one that directly leads to the outcome
> - Use prioritization criteria to select an audience-behavior pairing(s) on which to focus your behavior change initiative using a priority filter
> - Define your audience-behavior statement

Prioritization criteria

A key mentality to adopt when selecting audiences and behaviors is to try to make your selections as specific and narrow as possible. Different audiences and behaviors have different barriers and motivators, which require different strategies and tools to successfully shift behaviors. Therefore, it's important to be as specific as possible when selecting audiences and behaviors, which we'll discuss more in the audience-behavior section below.

At each step of the way, similar to our process for determining our focus, we will be looking at criteria such as the ones below. These *prioritization criteria* can help us brainstorm, narrow our choices, and finally evaluate our audience-behavior pairings.

Impact:	We want to consider how big of an effect the audience and behavior we are considering will have on our environmental issue and which would most help us achieve our desired outcome. We want to consider both the short and long-term impacts of potential audiences and behaviors. This includes determining where you might have the most *leverage*.
Potential to spread and scale:	*Scaling* is the process of expanding or replicating your initiative in order to increase participation from your existing priority audience or spread your initiative to new audiences. One way to do this is by designing an initiative that targets leverage points in the system (e.g., reforming a policy that affects many aspects of the system), which is a powerful way to achieve widespread behavior change. Other ways to scale your initiative are to make it "sticky" (such as when they are funny, catchy, repeatable, or "meme-able"), or to work with audiences who are extremely receptive to change and influencers who encourage your initiative's adoption. And, finally, utilizing tools we provide in the BEHAVIORAL Building Blocks™, such as invoking norms or tapping into salient identities, will increase the chances that your initiative will scale to other audiences.
	If you intend to scale your initiative, such as from a neighborhood to a county or state, it's important to plan and design your initiative to scale from the start. We go into greater detail on designing initiatives to spread on their own, as well as intentionally replicating your initiative, in the section on scaling in IMPLEMENT: Process Chapter 5.
Likelihood of success:	We want to consider how likely we are to succeed with the parameters we choose. This includes evaluating the success of past behavior change initiatives that have been applied to similar audiences, as well as whether your audience has already adopted related behaviors. It also includes the *probability of adoption*, which is usually predicated on the ease with which the behavior can be adopted, combined with the receptiveness and motivation of your

Continued on page 59

audience. Additionally, it includes considering your **organizational ability**—do you have the expertise, resources, bandwidth, and relationships you would need to work with these audiences or behaviors?

Equity: Especially if your initiative is not providing a service or benefit, consider whether asking particular audiences to change certain behaviors might be placing undue burden on them, even if the audience or behavior may have the largest impact on the issue. No matter how important or relevant your issue might be to them, when people's basic needs are not met, they are less likely to have bandwidth for behavior change. For more on designing equitable initiatives, see the ethical guidelines in FOUNDATIONS: Process Chapter 1.

Identify potential priority audiences

To start honing in on an audience-behavior pairing, we need to identify the people that have direct impact on the problem we are trying to solve (e.g., residents using electricity) and also identify those that have influence over the focus area we've chosen (e.g., utility providers). Examples of broad audience groups would be farmers, bankers, homeowners, policymakers, commuters, fishermen, tourists, or CEOs. But these groups are still too broad for a behavior change initiative.

Initiatives aimed at changing the behavior of many tend to change the behavior of only a few. Often, the group of people impacting an environmental issue is a very large group, such as "all United States residents" or "all adults in Canada." But even if we may wish for "everyone" to replace their appliances with more energy-efficient ones, a behavior change initiative with an audience this broad is unlikely to be very effective because it is more likely to be made up of people with very different behavioral barriers and motivators. For example, renters generally don't have the ability to replace appliances, and not everyone can afford expensive items. When our audience is too broad, we might waste resources on messages that only appeal to a small portion of the group and which may even turn off some portions of the group, or on addressing barriers that only a few people face.

Instead, we want to identify subgroups of those broader audiences that are more homogenous. In other words, these smaller audiences should have characteristics in common that might make them likely to respond to a behavior change initiative in a similar way. The important thing is that the characteristics we use to define our audience are meaningful. In general, if a characteristic (like whether someone is a parent) isn't likely to cause a group of people to respond differently to an initiative, then it's probably not worth narrowing the audience based on that characteristic.

There are no hard and fast rules for how specific or narrow to get with our audiences, but examples of reasonably narrow audiences to identify at this stage would include:

- Waterfowl hunters who hunt at wildlife preserves in Northern California
- Employers at companies in X county with more than 50 employees
- Drivers that pick up children from X school
- Tour boat operators in the Great Barrier Reef that provide tours to more than 100 guests per week
- Brazilian cattle ranchers with over X heads of cattle

The idea is for the audience we select at this stage to be large enough to make a *meaningful* impact on the issue we're focused on while having at least one meaningful characteristic in common. Even though this narrower audience is smaller, by crafting our strategies around a more homogenous audience, we're likely to see higher rates of behavior change per amount of effort and resources put in. Audiences like those listed above are narrow enough to be a manageable size to move forward with.

Similar to the process for deciding your focus, and later your behavior, we recommend that you brainstorm and then prioritize several audiences. But unlike in the "Choose and Explore Your Focus" section, you don't have to pick just one quite yet; we suggest narrowing your list to roughly three potential audiences.

Generate a list of potential audiences

Take a moment to create a list of as many potential audiences that influence your focus area as possible. Who were the stakeholders you identified through your Landscape Exploration, systems mapping, or in your iceberg model? Who were the audiences with the greatest leverage in your system? At this stage, there is no need to worry about whether these audiences are practical or feasible—just list them out freely. If you are struggling to identify and brainstorm potential audiences, you can preview the next section and use the questions we list for each criteria to help you think of ideas.

 If we look back to the lists we brainstormed about the food system using the iceberg model, we can see there are a number of different stakeholders and potential audiences involved, including:

- Consumers
- Farmers
- Food purchasers (retailers)
- Distributors
- Banks
- Policymakers

Include Both Upstream and Downstream Audiences

Try to include both upstream audiences (e.g., policymakers, businesses, employers, etc.) and downstream audiences (e.g., consumers, homeowners, employees, etc.) in your initial list. It can be tempting to only focus on downstream audiences because they may seem easier to reach, understand, and influence. Indeed, many of the studies and real-world initiatives discussed in this book are focused on downstream actors, as most behavioral research has been conducted with individuals downstream (particularly on consumers and college students).

But no matter the level within the system you are seeking to influence, you are still seeking to change the behavior of individuals. Corporations, governments, and other institutions might seem large, impersonal, and impervious to change, but they are made up of humans who have beliefs and cognitive biases just like the rest of us. Furthermore, upstream actors are not only capable of change, they can be especially impactful leverage points in a system. They are often among the largest contributors to environmental problems—for example, just 100 fossil fuel companies were responsible for 71% of global emissions from 1988 to 2017.[3] As many practitioners point out, focusing on getting powerful business leaders and politicians to take more responsibility for these issues is critical; we won't make enough progress addressing environmental challenges if we only ask households to curtail their energy use.

Therefore, we encourage you to seriously consider upstream audiences during this audience identification process. And even if you determine that it is more feasible or appropriate for you to select a downstream audience as your priority, you will likely still want to enlist the support of midstream and upstream audiences to help pave the way for your initiative, as they can have a significant influence on how difficult or easy a certain behavior is for a downstream audience to adopt.

Prioritize audiences

When you feel that you have included all the audiences that you can, you can start narrowing your list, considering the *prioritization criteria* we presented earlier. Early on, try to eliminate audiences that seem unsuitable to avoid spending unnecessary time and resources learning about them.

As you prioritize, try to divide your audience into groups of people who are likely to respond similarly to an initiative. We recommend that you narrow your list down to roughly three audiences before moving on, approximately as specific as "Waterfowl hunters who hunt at wildlife preserves in Northern California" or "Rangers at Volcanoes National Park in Rwanda."

The guidance and questions below will help you to brainstorm, identify, and narrow potential audiences.

Impact and influence in the system

- To what degree does each audience contribute to the problem?
- To what degree would a change in this audience's behavior mitigate or solve this problem?
- Which groups, policies, or influencers are contributing most to the problem? Why?
- Who are the most influential actors?
- Who are the main decision-makers that affect this issue?
- Who has access to levers that can be pulled (e.g. through policies, rules, or regulations), where a small amount of pressure will result in the most possible change throughout the system?

Note that out of all the audiences in our list, only farmers are the ones that can engage in any of the behaviors that will directly achieve our outcome (increased carbon sequestration via farming practices). The other audiences' impact on this outcome would be indirect, but some may have a significant influence on farmer behavior. If we look back to our systems map (Figure 1.2.1), we can see that banks are a broad audience with significant indirect influence, since the current structures of bank loans present a considerable barrier to changes in farming practices. Even if farmers want to shift their practices to increase soil health and sequester more carbon, they may not be able to because they are bound by the annual pressures of bank loans that require them to maximize yield. So if we try to change farmer behavior without addressing lending practices from banks upstream, we may not get very far.

As we consider the potential impact of other audiences on our list, we can eliminate distributors, who function more as a middleman in the food system and don't have much influence on farming practices. Although consumers can influence the food system through the foods and products that they demand, purchasing habits are influenced by many other things like product availability, pricing, and advertising. Since sustainably-produced products are often more expensive, a smaller percentage of consumers can afford to demand those products, so the resulting impact from this audience will likely be reduced. Because of these factors, we eliminate consumers too. Policymakers and food purchasers certainly affect farmer behavior, but there are more barriers to overcome in the short term to instigate change within those audiences, which we explore further below.

Potential to spread and scale

- Will working with this audience pave the way to expand your project to other groups?
- Is this audience likely to spread your message?

 Let's say that we identify certain farmers who may be particularly influential among their peers because they are community leaders or members of farmer associations in a particular region. If we can get these farmers to adopt new practices first, their peers will likely be more receptive to following suit. Therefore, we will aim to interview and work with these farmers early on in our process.

Likelihood of success

Success of past initiatives:

- Has this audience adopted related behaviors in the past?
- Have successful behavior change initiatives been applied to similar audiences?

Organizational ability:

- Are there audiences on your list that you simply can't work with (for example, if you can't work with audiences that operate outside your county)? Which can you eliminate right now?
- Do you have the ability to reach this audience and observe or measure their behaviors?
- Do you have access to the media channels these audiences use most?
- Do you have a good working relationship and trust with this audience?

 Due to the significant financial influence of agribusiness lobbying, policymakers have in the past been resistant to attempts to reform the food system through legislation. Additionally, let's say that our organization doesn't have expertise working with policymakers or many contacts within the United States government. Due to a lack of past successes and organizational limitations, policymakers would be a challenging audience to work with, so we remove them from our list.

Probability of adoption and receptivity:

It's worthwhile to identify which audiences and subgroups of those audiences are likely to be most receptive to your initiative. You can consider this for a specific behavior or behaviors, or in terms of general open-mindedness. Receptivity encompasses things like how interested, willing, and motivated an audience might be to change their behavior. Receptivity is also influenced by the strength of your relationship with the audience. For example, if you already work extensively with certain audiences, your positive relationship with them may increase their receptivity to change a particular behavior even if they aren't yet particularly interested or motivated to do so.

 Food purchasers (e.g., supermarkets) have a huge amount of influence in the food system from the demand side. However, for most farmers to make enough money to support a shift in their farming practices, food purchasers would have to pay above market price for products coming from their farms. This is a difficult lever to pull in the system because most food purchasers are constrained by the need to keep prices low so they can stay competitive. Since they are less likely to be receptive, we may remove food purchasers from our list of broad audiences.

To help us consider how receptive different audiences might be to our initiative, we can draw on two theories of behavior change: the Stages of Change Model, which categorizes people based on how ready they might be to adopt a particular desirable behavior or terminate an undesired behavior,[11] and the Diffusion of Innovation Theory, which categorizes people based on when (and why) they adopt new innovations and behaviors more generally (e.g. innovators vs. laggards).[12]

Drawing on these theories and frameworks, we can consider questions like:

- Which audiences have responded well to previous behavior change initiatives? Which subgroups have been "innovators," "early adopters," or the "early majority" when it comes to trying new behaviors, vs. those that lagged behind other groups or never adopted the behaviors at all?
- Are there any audiences who pride themselves on being the first to adopt new innovations and ideas?
- Which audiences tend to be open to change and willing to take risks?
- Have any audiences already expressed an interest in or motivation to make change in this focus area?

- Do you already know whether certain audiences hold values, attitudes, beliefs, and perceptions that might make them more or less receptive to change related to this focus area or specific behaviors?

While it is still possible to work with audiences who are less receptive (and we provide advice to that effect in several later chapters, such as ATTACHMENT: Building Block Chapter 4), it is often easiest and most cost-effective to identify "low hanging fruit": the audiences who are more likely to respond positively to your initiative, rather than throwing resources at audiences that have no intention or motivation to change. By first prioritizing these more receptive groups, their adoption of the behavior sets a positive example that makes it more likely that the behavior change will spread to the less receptive groups—once these groups see that the behavior is widely accepted, they are more likely to jump on the bandwagon.

 Given that we've eliminated the other broad audiences from our list, we can start getting more specific about the two remaining audiences (farmers and banks). For example, we can start identifying whether some banks are more receptive than others to changing their policies for sustainable purposes. (Are there banks that have made statements about their commitments to climate change or have previously changed their policies for the social good? If you don't know which banks are most eager to collaborate, this is a good time to do some audience research.) However, keep in mind that you can still choose to work with banks who aren't as receptive to reforming their lending practices—and design shifters that increase their receptivity.

Equity

- Is asking this audience to change their behavior placing an undue burden on them?
- Are there audiences that tend to be overlooked but for which your initiative could improve their lives or livelihoods?
- When mapping your system, did you identify any stakeholders who you should consider while planning your initiative, even if they don't ultimately become your priority audience?

 Even though you may primarily focus on farmers with larger farms that have more acreage on which to increase carbon sequestration, you may still want to include small farmers as a priority audience to ensure equal access to the benefits of participating in your initiative.

Demographics

Derived from the Greek words for people (*demos*) and picture (*graphy*), the term **demographics** refers to statistical data about a population and particular groups within it. Examples of demographic information include (but aren't limited to) geographic location, age, gender, race, ethnicity, preferred language, literacy level, religion, income, employment, education level, political affiliation, marital status, family size, health and disability status, and home ownership status.

Demographic factors can be great for narrowing audiences in part because demographic data are relatively easy to find (such as via census data) or collect through primary research. Additionally, demographic factors can be highly relevant to how an audience might respond to an initiative. For example, it's often effective and practical to limit our audience to people living in a certain location. However, we should ensure that the demographic data we are using is meaningful.

Before narrowing your audience based on a demographic characteristic, think carefully about whether that demographic factor is likely to be relevant to how that audience thinks or behaves in regard to your focus area. For example, if the potential behavior is an expensive one, like purchasing an electric vehicle or an efficient water heater, then considering income during audience selection is important, but it wouldn't be as relevant for a behavior like recycling or turning off the lights. Additionally, even when a demographic factor is *relevant*, that demographic factor alone is *insufficient* for understanding and predicting behavior, as we will discuss more when diving into the drivers of human behavior in the next phase, UNCOVER. Relatedly, it's critical to remember that even if a group shares demographic characteristics like income or ethnicity, they can differ widely in their beliefs and behaviors.

 We could narrow our two potential audiences based on the following:

Banks

- Banks in a certain region
- Banks that specialize in agricultural loans
- Small vs. large banks
- Banks that operate as franchises vs. those that have a centralized corporate structure

Farmers

- Farmers in a certain region
- Farmers that lease vs. own their land
- Farmers who are particularly influential among their peers in a specific region
- What type of crops are grown
- Small-scale vs. large-scale farms
- The age of the farmer or amount of farming experience

By the end of this section, you should have audiences that have been narrowed by one or more characteristics like location, and are at least as specific as the ones above. You will get more specific later: you will learn a great deal about your audience in the next phase (UNCOVER) and will have another chance to further narrow your audience, based on this information, in DESIGN: Process Chapter 4.

Choosing an Appropriate Audience for Plastic Shotgun Wad Reduction

When a shotgun is fired, the shot is encased in a plastic wad that falls away in midair. These wads, when fired over water, contribute to ocean plastic pollution. In 2019, Root Solutions began an initiative with the Greater Farallones Association to reduce the amount of plastic shotgun wads entering the water in the San Francisco Bay Area, by encouraging hunters to pick up any shotgun wads they saw on the ground or in the water.

We considered two potential priority audiences for our initiative: recreational shooters and waterfowl hunters. While recreational shooters attend gun clubs and shooting ranges and fire at clay pigeons that are launched into the air, hunters go to wildlife preserves and target live waterfowl, like ducks. Meetings with range managers and other key stakeholders revealed that our potential priority audiences were very different.

We initially thought that recreational shooters could be an easier priority audience to work with because they fire from a single location mostly over land, making wad retrieval easier than it is for hunters, who, in this region, primarily fire over the water (making wad retrieval nearly impossible). To gather more information on both potential audiences, we visited gun clubs and wildlife preserves and spoke with staff at both. Managers at the gun club in our region informed us that shooters are already required to use biodegradable wads and that club employees already clear the site of shells and wads. However, these same requirements and policies did not exist for waterfowl hunters. In the end, we chose hunters as our priority audience because it would have a larger impact on reducing shotgun wads entering the marine environment.

Identify potential priority behaviors

As the title of this book suggests, our goal is to make shift happen—namely, shifts from current problematic behaviors to positive environmental ones. But for each focus area that we can choose, there are many behaviors that would help us achieve our desired environmental outcome. How do we decide which one to focus our initiative on? In this section, we define behavior and provide guidance on generating numerous potential behaviors on which to focus (and we explain below why it is important not to assume you have already selected the best one). Then, in true INITIATE fashion, we walk you through how to narrow your broad list of possible behaviors to create a "shortlist" of a few key/priority behaviors.

What exactly does "behavior" mean?

Before you begin generating behavior ideas, it's important to understand what we mean, and don't mean, when we say "behavior."

Behavior change comes in many forms

Behavior change can take different forms: maintaining or increasing an existing desirable behavior, modifying an existing desirable behavior, beginning a new desirable behavior, or stopping a current undesirable behavior. In some cases, you may even ask your audience to not change at all, but to simply refuse to adopt a new, undesirable behavior.

Knowledge and awareness are not behaviors

As you begin brainstorming behaviors, remember that even when making the audience aware of a problem is a prerequisite for them to do the priority behavior, awareness or knowledge are not behaviors themselves and are almost never sufficient to result in behavior change. So "the audience is aware that composting food is beneficial to the environment" is not a behavior.

 Just because farmers know that certain farming practices can store more carbon in the soil, increase soil health, and even increase crop yield over time doesn't necessarily mean they will adopt those practices on their farms.

Vague asks and outcomes are not behaviors

Outcomes, like the one you defined earlier as part of your focus statement (increased carbon sequestration, the reduction in the amount of food waste entering landfills, etc.) are the environmental changes you wish to see as a result of your initiative. *Behaviors* are the actions people need to take to make that outcome a reality, and there are usually *numerous behaviors that can help achieve an outcome.*

Even initiatives with the best intentions can fail by being too vague in what they are asking of their audience. Asks like "stop climate change" or "save the ocean" (which are *outcomes*) might draw attention to an issue, but they don't present the audience with specific actions they can take to make a difference.

Instead, our priority behaviors should be as **distinct** as possible, meaning that the behavior takes the form of a single action that cannot be broken down further into smaller behaviors.[8] Even asking families to "decrease food waste," (as a way to mitigate climate change) is too vague. Instead, ask for distinct behaviors such as "place food scraps in your compost bin instead of the trash" or "immediately store extra food in the freezer instead of the refrigerator" that can move the needle toward our desired outcome.

Identify behaviors

Now it's time to identify potential behaviors for each of the priority audiences you are considering. We want you to start broad by brainstorming behaviors with an open mind. This should be a fun activity that generates some great ideas! After you brainstorm, you will go through a prioritization process to narrow your potential behaviors for each audience down to roughly three, based on several of the same prioritization criteria we have used already, such as impact or equity.

Research Options to Guide Behavior Selection

You can use the information you collected through your Landscape Exploration and systems mapping to help brainstorm problematic behaviors that are contributing to your environmental issue and the positive behaviors that will help. You may also decide to conduct additional research on potential behaviors. In the "Use Different Research Methods to Get the Information You Need" section below, we discuss the ways that you can explore potential behaviors via informal primary research (e.g., direct observation and intercept surveys), as well as a more formal *Audience Analysis*.

Brainstorm desirable behaviors

Start with brainstorming a large quantity of potential behaviors for each potential priority audience. You do not yet need to assess and evaluate the behaviors—let ideas flow freely. In a perfect world with no constraints, what could audiences at all levels of the system do to address your environmental issue?

Brainstorming

The purpose of this brainstorming session is to produce a large quantity of potential behaviors from which we can prioritize. A successful, creative brainstorm session first requires certain mindsets: being open-minded, encouraging wild ideas, thinking without constraints, and building off of one another's ideas.

In a brainstorming session, you should feel empowered to contribute ideas that go outside the box. You will use these ideas both to craft creative solutions, and as inspiration for even more ideas. One should aim to let ideas flow freely and quickly. Try to keep the following in mind:

Aim for a large number of ideas:
Set a goal for the number of ideas you will generate.

Defer judgment:
There are no bad or good ideas at this point. Later you can evaluate your ideas. For now, just let your ideas flow.

Let one person talk at a time:
Avoiding side conversations allows everyone to follow the flow of ideas and build upon them.

Build on ideas:
Build on one another's ideas by adopting a "yes and" mindset. When one person proposes an idea, the next person can say "yes and" and contribute an idea that builds on the previous one.

Try "rolestorming":
Encourage group members to take on others' (team or audience members) identities during the process to expand perspectives.

Consider brainstorming separately first:
Consider asking team members to brainstorm on their own. Later, add everyone's lists together. This allows everyone to contribute on an individual level before being influenced by anyone else, and it can help include those that do not like to brainstorm in groups.

We could focus on a number of different behaviors for both farmers and banks that would help achieve our desired outcome. To sequester more carbon, farmers could (among other things) plant new or different types of crops that sequester more carbon, switch to low till farming, or plant cover crops on their existing fields (which helps to retain more organic material in the soil). Meanwhile, banks could remove clauses requiring that farmers do not engage in new practices to be eligible for loans, offer loans with interest rates based on a running five-year average of farmers' yields instead of their performance from the previous year, or even reward farmers for investing in new practices that will improve soil health (which can increase yield, as well as climate resilience, over time, ultimately making the farmer a lower-risk borrower for the bank).[10]

Look for "Bright Spots": Which Behaviors Are Working?

We can also try to find out if some people in the audience are already engaging in positive behaviors. These behaviors may be good candidates to spread to a larger audience. For example, when investigating childhood malnutrition in Vietnam, Jerry Sternin, founder of the Positive Deviance Institute, discovered that one key to promoting child health had already been found—it simply hadn't spread to the majority of the population. Sternin and his colleagues observed that even though many impoverished children in certain villages were malnourished, there were some equally impoverished children who were not. They found that the parents of the healthy children incorporated proteins such as tiny shrimp, crabs, and snails into their children's meals. They also tended to provide more frequent, smaller meals throughout the day. Once the solution had been identified, Sternin helped these successful families provide hands-on foraging and cooking classes to other parents in the community. One year after the program began, 80% of the children enrolled in the program were adequately nourished.[7] By learning from the "bright spots"—those parents who were already practicing effective behaviors—Sternin was able to focus his initiative on behaviors that were proven to work in that specific context.

Identify problematic behaviors

We started with positive behaviors so we could brainstorm without being influenced by all the problematic behaviors contributing to the problem. Here, we use our Landscape Exploration and systems thinking to identify and list out the problematic behaviors.

Let's brainstorm the problematic behaviors of both our broad potential audiences: farmers and banks. We can identify several farming practices that deplete the soil of nutrients, preventing it from storing more carbon. Some of the most detrimental ones include:

- monocropping
- tilling the soil frequently
- overuse of pesticides and chemical fertilizers

We can also identify practices of banks that pose a barrier to farmers adjusting their behaviors, such as:[10]

- short-term loans, which disincentivize farmers from experimenting with new practices that can take a few years to increase yields and produce a profit
- loan interest rates based on annual yields, which incentivizes behaviors that maximize yield in the short term such as monocropping, frequent tilling, pesticide usage, among other behaviors
- loans do not reflect the reduced risk that comes with practices like diversifying crops, low tillage, and planting cover crops, which all increase a farm's long-term resilience to things like extreme weather

In the process of identifying problematic behaviors, you might end up thinking of a new audience. That's great—you certainly aren't locked in to any audiences at this point, even if you've already gone through the process of brainstorming and narrowing your audiences. And remember, at any point in this process, you can always move back to a previous section and evaluate a new audience or behavior using the same criteria.

Make negatives behaviors into positive

Identify replacement or alternative behaviors for all the problematic behaviors you listed in the last step. Asking for the behavior you want instead of the behavior you don't want makes it easier for your audience to see a clear path forward. For example, instead of only asking your audience to avoid driving single occupancy vehicles, suggest that they carpool or telecommute instead. Not every undesirable behavior can be replaced by a desirable behavior. Sometimes audiences should simply avoid doing something, like feeding wildlife in national parks. Table 1.2.3 has a list of problematic and positive replacement behaviors related to single-use plastics.

Table 1.2.3: Problematic and Positive Replacement Behaviors Related to Single-use Plastics

Audience	Problematic Behaviors	Positive Replacement Behaviors
Individuals	• Take/use plastic straws. • Take/use plastic utensils when ordering takeout. • Purchase produce wrapped in plastic. • Take/use plastic bags when shopping.	• Ask for no straw. • Bring your own straw. • Ask for no utensils. • Bring your own containers when eating out. • Purchase produce in bulk. • Bring your own shopping bag. • Vote for a plastic bag ban in your town.
Restaurant Owners	• Hand out plastic straws without being asked. • Use plastic containers for takeout. • Provide plastic utensils without being asked.	• Offer paper straws. • Only give plastic straws when asked. • Purchase and use compostable takeout containers. • Become a certified sustainable business that doesn't use disposable plastic.
Distributors or Retailers	• Offer plastic bags to your customers. • Wrap produce in plastic. • Only provide plastic bags for bulk goods (e.g. grains, beans, and granola). • Use plastic containers for prepared foods. • Inadequately train staff on store policies regarding customers' ability to use their own containers.	• Encourage your customers to bring their own bags. • Charge for plastic bags and provide reusable alternatives. • Purchase and use compostable packaging or no packaging for produce. • Allow and encourage customers to bring their own containers for prepared and bulk foods. • Train and educate staff on bring-your-own container policies and monitor staff adherence to new policies.

Convert your list of brainstormed problematic behaviors into desirable behaviors. Ask yourself, what do I want my audience to do instead? If you are still considering several audiences at this stage, brainstorm behaviors for each potential audience.

Our list of behaviors that could lead to increased carbon sequestration include:

Banks

- Remove clauses requiring that farmers do not engage in new practices to receive loans
- Provide long-term loans (e.g. 5–10 years instead of annual loans)
- Offer loans with interest rates based on a running five-year average of farmers' yields instead of their performance from the previous year
- Lower interest rates on operating loans to farmers who plant cover crops

Farmers

- Plant different crops that sequester more carbon
- Switch to low till farming
- Plant cover crops

Note: while these behaviors are already fairly prescribed to our audiences of farmers and banks, many behaviors, like carpooling or biking, can still at this point be done by multiple audiences, like commuters and parents taking their kids to school.

Identify behavioral sequences

When you look at your brainstormed list and break down broader behaviors into distinct ones, you might notice that they are often connected in a sequence, or chain, leading to your desired outcome. For example, the distinct behavior of "place food scraps in the compost bin instead of the trash" is preceded by several other distinct behaviors, including "buy a compost bin" or "research which types of food are allowed in the compost" (each of which can usually be broken down into more distinct behaviors themselves). Try to identify the full sequence of behaviors needed to perform this behavior.

After you've identified the sequence, ask yourself: "Have I identified the final behavior in the sequence?" and "Which behavior will most directly lead to my intended outcome?" Most of the time, we are going to want to focus our initiative on the final behavior in the sequence, because this is usually the behavior that actually produces the outcome we seek (e.g., lower emissions and therefore a healthier climate)—the *outcome-producing behavior*. If we only identify earlier behaviors in the sequence, then our audience may complete the earlier behaviors but never the behavior that actually achieves results. Outlining the full sequence helps us ensure we're not accidentally picking a behavior that's really early in the sequence, such as "research what you can compost."

In UNCOVER: Process Chapter 3, we'll revisit this sequence and will use it to help brainstorm potential barriers and motivators and to write targeted survey questions for our Behavioral Drivers Analysis survey. After beginning your research into your audience's barriers, you may ultimately decide to choose a different behavior in the sequence.

Prioritize behaviors

Now it's time to assess our list and narrow it down. Here we revisit the *prioritization criteria* to help you determine which behaviors to focus on.

Impact and influence in the system

Environmental impact of the behavior:

- Which desirable behaviors would have the most positive impact on the focus area?
- Which problematic behaviors have the most negative impact on your focus area?

 We identify two particularly impactful behaviors: banks offering loans with interest rates based on a running five-year average of farmers' yields; and banks rewarding farmers for planting cover crops by offering lower interest rates on operating loans for investing in new practices that specifically improve soil health.

Frequency and magnitude of the behavior among the audience:

If you have an audience or several audiences in mind, think about how each engages in the behavior.

- **Frequency**
  - How often does this group engage in negative behavior(s) associated with the problem you are trying to address?

- **Magnitude**
  - To what magnitude or intensity does this group engage in the negative behavior(s) associated with the problem you are trying to address? For example, some groups may engage in a behavior relatively infrequently (e.g., showering only every few days), but when they do, it may be with greater intensity than others (e.g., extremely long showers).

Behaviors with potential for positive spillover:

This is also an important moment to recall the discussion of positive and negative behavioral spillover from FOUNDATIONS: Process Chapter 1. We need to be cognizant that a change in behavior can influence the adoption of future behaviors. We should of course do everything in our power to anticipate and avoid causing negative spillover—the reduced likelihood that our audiences will adopt future environmental behaviors that we, or other practitioners, ask of them. Because of the possibility that the behavior we choose could cause future behaviors not to be adopted, we should select the highest impact behaviors for our initiatives. Additionally, we should consider which behaviors might have the highest potential for positive spillover—the increased likelihood that our audience will adopt additional environmental behaviors.

Potential to spread and scale

Behaviors acting on leverage points in the system:

- Where can a small change in behavior result in subsequent changes across other areas of the system?
- Are there any structural barriers preventing people from doing this behavior, like laws or institutional practices?

Behaviors likely to spread:

- Does this behavior have any inherent spreadability? For example, is it fun, or does it provide more rewards than costs?

Likelihood of success

Success of past behavior change efforts:

- Have other initiatives succeeded at changing this behavior?"
- Have other initiatives with your priority audience succeeded at changing a behavior similar to this?

Organizational ability:

- Does your organization have the expertise and partnerships to focus on changing this behavior?

Level of difficulty:

- How easy or difficult is this behavior?
- Does your audience know how to do this behavior?

Switching to low till farming or planting a new and different set of crops requires farmers to invest in different equipment, knowledge, and skills. This may not be feasible for many farmers, so let's strike these from our list.

Equity

- Would asking this behavior of your priority audience raise any equity concerns?

• • •

By the end of this section, you should have a list of one or more potential audiences and one or more potential behaviors. Next you will be evaluating these and selecting a single audience-behavior pairing on which to focus your initiative.

❓ Ask Yourself: Priority behaviors

- Have you brainstormed numerous positive and negative behaviors relevant to your focus area?
- Have you done a quick pass to remove truly nonviable options?
- Have you identified replacement behaviors, or positive behaviors you want your audience to do instead of their negative behaviors?
- Have you confirmed that your list only contains actual behaviors, and not other outcomes like knowledge, awareness, beliefs, or skills?
- Have you identified the distinct behaviors in the behavioral sequence that lead to your outcome-producing behavior?

Evaluate possible audience-behavior pairings

Whether you brainstormed audiences or behaviors first, by now you should have a list of several potential audiences and a short list of high priority behaviors for each one. Now it's time to begin strategically evaluating them as pairs to narrow down your options until you select the pairing that you will focus on. We will be visiting our prioritization criteria a final time!

 Pairing together our lists of audiences and behaviors from the previous sections, we create a list of three audience-behavior pairings. Note that in reality we would likely want our potential audiences to be more specific at this point, like banks in a certain region or farmers in a certain county who own their land, but for the purposes of creating a simple example, we'll keep our audiences broad:

Banks:

- Banks in my county offer loans with interest rates based on a running five-year average of farmers' yields instead of their performance from the previous year.
- Banks in my county reward farmers for planting cover crops by offering lower interest rates on operating loans.

Farmers:

- Farmers in my county plant cover crops.

Use prioritization criteria to evaluate your audience-behavior pairings. Similar to the process of choosing and refining audiences and behaviors individually, the process of selecting an audience-behavior pairing should take many different criteria into account. You can consider potential audiences using these criteria based on information and knowledge you already have. However, if you have the time and resources, we recommend gathering additional information about your potential audience(s) for each of the following criteria.

There are many things to consider when evaluating different audience-behavior pairings. Below we provide some criteria (similar to the criteria used in "Choose and Explore Your Focus"), that will help guide you, including: impact now and in the future, likelihood of success, equity, and the ability to evaluate outcomes. Use these to test assumptions and help narrow down your potential audience-behavior pairings.

Impact and influence on the system

If this audience changes this behavior, what level of impact will it have? Consider these questions:

Environmental impact of the behavior:

- Which behavior would have the most positive impact on the focus area (e.g., reduce the greatest amount of food waste, reverse habitat loss the fastest, save the most energy)?

Leverage on the system:

- Would this behavior from this audience lead to a larger audience adopting a desired behavior (e.g., if the owner of a big box retail store mandated that all suppliers must meet certain sustainability requirements)?
- Is it necessary for an upstream audience to perform a certain behavior to achieve the primary behavior change you desire?

 Implementing new farming practices (e.g., planting cover crops) can be costly initially, and therefore risky to pursue without adequate financial support. It may therefore be necessary to prioritize the pairings that are targeted toward banks to pave the way for farmers shifting this behavior.

Size of the audience:

- How large is each potential audience? The more people doing the behavior, the more likely they are to have a greater impact.

Saturation of the behavior among the audience:

- How many people in the audience already perform this behavior? For example, if most of an audience already has low-flow showerheads, focusing your initiative on installing low-flow showerheads will not have as high an impact.
- Is it a priority to get the remaining audience members to perform the behavior, or is it a higher priority to move on to another behavior with lower saturation?

Future impact and influence

Potential for negative and positive spillover:

We want to choose audience-behavior pairings with high potential for *positive spill-over* and avoid choosing ones with a higher likelihood of causing *negative spillover*. Spillover is difficult to predict, but research to date suggests that positive spillover stems from a preference for behavioral consistency, so it's more likely to occur between similar behaviors, such as those that share a common goal or require similar skills or knowledge to adopt. Thus, selecting target behaviors that are similar to actions the audience is already taking could lead to greater adoption.[13,14] See FOUNDATIONS: Process Chapter 1 for more about spillover.

- What is the likelihood that the audience adopting this behavior would lead to them adopting future positive environmental behaviors?
- What is the likelihood the audience would adopt this behavior but then adopt environmentally unfriendly behaviors or fail to adopt other future positive behaviors?

If banks change their lending practices to allow, or even incentivize, farmers to shift practices to those that improve soil health, then we would be more likely to see farmers experiment with new practices such as planting cover crops. The resulting decrease in costs spent on fertilizer might encourage farmers to explore other practices as well, such as switching to low till farming or rotating their crops. In contrast, working with farmers on a single behavior (like planting cover crops) may have less potential for positive spillover.

Potential to serve as proof of concept:

- Would focusing on this audience-behavior pairing demonstrate the feasibility of expanding this or similar initiatives to other audiences or addressing other behavioral issues? Will this lead to greater buy-in from stakeholders to replicate your initiative or adopt other behavior change efforts?

Potential to spread through systems change:

We considered leverage on the system when evaluating immediate impact above, but certain audience-behavior pairings can help an initiative spread and scale through time as well. We recommend that you read the section on scaling in IMPLEMENT: Process Chapter 5 to learn more.

- Would this change in behavior in this audience result in subsequent pro-environmental changes widely across the system?
- Would this audience adopting this behavior likely lead to additional audiences adopting this behavior?

Likelihood of success

Probability of adoption:

How likely is it that the priority population will adopt this behavior? This depends on how easy the behavior is and how motivated the audience is. When motivation is low, we will have the most success changing easier behaviors. As motivation increases, we can succeed in changing more challenging behaviors. For example, an audience that cares a lot about fitness might be quite willing to bike a long distance to work each day. Consider these questions for your initiative:

- **Motivation**
  - To what degree is the priority population already motivated to address this issue?

- **Ease/difficulty of the behavior:**
  - How many steps are involved in performing this behavior? Taking a single bus to work is easier than planning a commute involving a train, a bike, and a bus.
  - How easy or difficult is this behavior? Biking 30 miles roundtrip for work each day is likely more difficult than driving.

Organizational ability:

- Does your organization have the resources (e.g., time, staff, expertise, money) to adequately support an initiative that focuses on this audience-behavior pairing? Be realistic about your organization's strengths, weaknesses, and limitations.

Potential for controversy:

- Would stakeholders agree that it is appropriate to focus on this audience-behavior pairing?
- Could controversies surrounding this issue derail your initiative? For example, if people are upset to learn that agriculture is using most of a county's water supply in a drought, they may not be receptive to taking shorter showers.

Potential for unintended consequences:

- Could the initiative lead to perverse outcomes? For example, taxing people for the weight of their trash to promote recycling can backfire and instead motivate people to dispose of their trash elsewhere.

Equity

- Would working on this audience-behavior pairing create or provide equity for all groups affected?

  Note that in some cases, equity considerations and other considerations like impact or receptivity may not be in alignment. For more detailed ethical guidelines for behavior change initiatives, refer back to FOUNDATIONS: Process Chapter 1.

Ability to evaluate success

- **Ability to directly observe behavior:**
  - Are you able to directly observe the effectiveness of an initiative for this audience-behavior pairing, or will you need to rely on indirect measures?

Some behaviors, such as many of those done in the home, cannot be directly observed. Thus, evaluation typically relies on self-reporting from the priority audience or other indirect measures.

- **Ability to collect data:**
  - ○ Are you able to collect data pre- and post-initiative to demonstrate whether there was a change in behavior?

Other criteria that are important to you or your organization

- Do you have other organizational priorities that align with this choice? For example, do you want a long term relationship with this audience, or with others working with this group or on this behavior?

Use a scoring system to finalize your audience-behavior pairing

To help you weigh the strengths and weaknesses of your potential audience-behavior pairings, we recommend using a scoring system like the one depicted in Table 1.2.4.

This tool rates each category from 1–4, with higher numbers representing better outcomes. Once you've rated all of the relevant categories for your initiative, you will add up the scores to help you identify the best candidate for your priority audience-behavior pairing. Note that three of these criteria (Saturation of behavior, Potential for controversy, and Potential unintended consequences) are scored in the opposite direction than the others because you want to have less of these things instead of more. Here are a few other things to consider about the way you evaluate:

Range of Criteria:

You don't need to use all of the criteria above (e.g., you may choose to focus on only one aspect of "Future Impact" if it is the only aspect that is relevant or feasible for you to evaluate).

Weight of Criteria:

You can create a multiplier to *weigh* certain criteria as more important than others. For example, if "Potential for unintended consequences" is more important to your goals than other criteria, like "Potential to serve as proof of concept," you could multiply the former by 2.

Table 1.2.4: Scorecard for Potential Audience-Behavior Pairings

Potential audience-behavior pairings ➤		1	2	3	4
Impact and Influence	Positive environmental impact of the behavior (greatest positive impact=4, least=1)				
	Leverage on the system (greatest leverage=4, least=1)				
	Size of the audience (greatest size=4, smallest size=1)				
	Saturation of behavior (least saturation=4, greatest=1)				
Future Impact and Influence	Potential for spillover (greatest positive spillover=4, worst negative spillover=1)				
	Potential to serve as proof of concept (greatest potential=4, least=1)				
	Potential to spread through systems change (greatest potential=4, least=1)				
Likelihood of Success	Probability of adoption (greatest probability=4, least=1)				
	Organizational ability (greatest ability=4, least=1)				
	Potential for controversy (least controversial=4, greatest=1)				
	Potential unintended consequences (least potential=4, greatest=1)				
Equity	Potential equity effects (greatest equity=4, least=1)				
	Ability to evaluate success (greatest ability=4, least=1)				
Score:					

When Is It OK to Pick More Than One Audience or Behavior?

At this point, you should have narrowed down your options and selected an audience-behavior pairing. But while you should always narrow your ask down to one behavior per audience, there are some cases when it would be beneficial to address two different audiences as part of the same overarching initiative. Here are some scenarios:

Multiple audiences:

If you do have the ability to work with more than one audience, remember what we discussed in FOUNDATIONS: Process Chapter 1. Initiatives are especially effective when they target behaviors at multiple levels of a system simultaneously and apply pressure from both the bottom and the top, all directed toward a common goal. You may decide to work with both upstream and downstream audiences at the same time, especially if the upstream audience only indirectly influences the end behavior. This could entail developing two different programs or campaigns—one focused on an upstream audience and one focused on a downstream audience—under the umbrella of an overarching initiative. Both prongs of this initiative could take place at the same time, or you may decide to tackle them in two different phases.

 Since farmers are the only broad audience that can directly enact farming practices that increase carbon sequestration, our initiative should make sure that farmers actually change their behavior. However, simultaneously working to encourage banks to change their lending practices would in tandem remove an important barrier that would enable farmers to adopt the desired farming practices. Working to create a virtuous loop in the system (instead of the vicious loop we originally identified) by targeting multiple audience-behavior pairings at different levels of the system can be a particularly effective approach.

Even if you don't have the organizational capacity to work with multiple audience-behavior pairings, consider partnering with other organizations that might already be working with another priority audience. This type of integrated approach has the potential to produce powerful shifts within a system.

Multiple behaviors:

We don't recommend asking the same audience to adopt multiple behaviors. We see this type of ask a lot with lists of "100 Ways to Save the Planet." While these lists include some good advice about all the behaviors we can change, for most people, even just thinking about changing 10 behaviors can be exhausting, so these lists tend to miss the mark on effecting behavior change.

Why is it important to be specific and avoid asking people to change too many behaviors? First, we live in a society where demands on our attention are often overwhelming, but we have limited attention capacity (see more on this

(Continued on page 86.)

in VIVID: Building Block Chapter 5). If we give people too much new information to absorb, they're likely to tune out even if they care about the issue. Second, when asked to do or choose between too many things, we often experience *choice overload* and end up doing nothing at all (see EASY: Building Block Chapter 2 for information on overcoming choice overload). By asking too much, we set our audience up for failure and face the risk of audience disengagement rather than the intended long-term behavior change.

Define your audience-behavior pairing statement

Once you've selected an audience-behavior pairing, you'll want to write an audience-behavior statement such as the ones below. The "behavior" portion of the statement—denoted with [ ]— will be used in most of the questions you will ask during deep audience research in UNCOVER: Process Chapter 3 and will ensure you stay focused and obtain data on exactly the behavior you are trying to shift. Additionally, you can use this portion of the statement to set goals, which we will talk about in the next section. Your audience-behavior statement should clearly identify the priority audience and the ideal behavior.

Examples of Audience-Behavior Statements

- Employees at X company will [donate the maximum amount their employer will match to X charity].
- Parents and other caretakers picking up children at X school [always turn off their car while waiting in school pick-up and drop-off lines].
- Companies X, Y, and Z [institute a "guaranteed ride home" policy].
- Tour boat operators in the Great Barrier Reef [provide reef-safe sunscreens on all their boats].

Say we narrowed our audience-behavior pairings down to two (one for farmers and one for banks), and we decided to launch an initiative that would target both pairings simultaneously, to influence both upstream and downstream audiences. Our two audience-behavior statements would look like:

- Farmers in my county who grow more than X acres of X crop will [plant cover crops on X% of their fields].
- Banks in my county will [reward farmers for planting cover crops by offering lower interest rates on operating loans].

• • •

At this point, you have already done most of the work of the INITIATE phase. Congratulations! You may have already revised your priority audience and behavior several times. You may have even adjusted your focus. In the last stage of this phase, you will build on everything you've already selected and will set goals for your initiative, as well as identify the metrics you will use to measure success.

🔲 Ask Yourself: Audience-behavior pairing selection

- Have you assessed the strengths and weaknesses of potential audience-behavior pairings?
- Have you selected one priority behavior for each audience?
- Have you defined your audience-behavior pairing statement for each audience?

 Set your Behavior Change Goals and Choose Metrics

At this stage in the INITIATE phase, we have defined our focus, selected a priority audience and behavior, and defined our audience-behavior statement. When writing our focus statement, we also defined our overarching goal, or the desired outcome we hope our initiative will create, such as reducing greenhouse gas emissions, reducing abandoned fishing gear, or reducing the number of wildlife hit by cars. In this section, we'll revisit that overarching goal, as well as set specific behavior change goals. We'll also discuss considerations for how we'll measure whether we've achieved our goals.

Why is it important to set goals this early in our project? Setting well-defined goals helps provide us direction and milestones to work toward, and choosing metrics early lays the groundwork for evaluating our progress in relation to those goals. And of course, you also may be required to set goals for grant proposals or other funding opportunities. While we recommend setting specific, measurable goals at this stage (based on what you already know about your audience, behavior, and what you want to accomplish), it doesn't mean that your goal has to be set in stone for the remainder of your project. Because the *Making Shift Happen* process is iterative, it's quite possible that steps in another phase will reveal information that warrants adjusting your goal. For example, after learning more about your audience in the UNCOVER phase, you might discover that the level of behavior change you were hoping for is simply not realistic given the barriers your audience faces.

Make your goals SMART

All the work you've already done to strategically select your focus, audience, and behavior comes into play to help you define a SMART—specific, measurable, achievable (yet ambitious), relevant, and time-bound—goal for your initiative.[2,6] If you have completed all the steps in the INITIATE phase, that should mean that you've already got the *specific* and *relevant* components covered.

Ideally, goals are also:

Measurable:
We should strive to set goals that are possible to measure, and should think through *how* we'll measure whether we've achieved each goal. We'll discuss choosing metrics in more detail below.

Achievable (yet Ambitious):
Try to find the sweet spot between a goal that is realistically attainable and one that is aspirational enough to inspire your team to meet its full potential. For example, it's probably not realistic for a new anti-idling program to aim for 100% of drivers to turn off their cars while waiting to pick up kids from school, but 20% may be. Use any available relevant data to inform your goal, such as the current saturation of the behavior in your audience, or the success rates of past similar programs. For example, if we're starting a brand new carpooling program and we've learned that a majority of employees already carpool, then a 20% increase on top of that may not be realistic, but if only 10% of our employees currently carpool, then increasing that number by 20% might be a realistic goal to set.

Time-bound:

Finally, set a time frame for meeting your goals, to help you plan and keep on track (i.e., by May 2025). For simplicity, we won't include a time frame for all of the example goals we share in this section.

Set or refine your overarching goal

Now that you know more about your focus area and what's realistic given the audience-behavior pairing you chose, add a time component and measurable outcome to the overarching goal embedded in your focus statement (if you haven't already).

Here are examples of overarching, outcome-based goals:

- Decrease the number of cigarette butts littered on the street in San Francisco by 25% by 2025.
- Decrease the number of pages printed at X university by 20% compared to the previous year.
- Decrease the number of shotgun wads found on the ground at hunting reserves by 25% within two years.
- Increase halibut populations in the North Pacific by 30% over the next ten years.
- Vessel strikes on marine mammals in our bay will not exceed 10 per year.

It can be difficult or even impossible to measure some environmental outcomes (e.g., for a reduction in GHG emissions or an increase in carbon sequestration). If we are unable to measure these outcomes, we can still set directional goals and simply say "increase/decrease/reduce" (e.g., "increase carbon sequestration") to make our vision and intentions clear.

Set specific behavior change goals

In addition to setting an overarching, outcome-based goal, we also recommend setting behavior change goals, especially when the actual environmental outcomes are difficult to measure. The specific behavior change goals you set for your initiative (e.g., collect at least X pounds of abandoned fishing gear, increase pounds of food composted by X percent) will draw heavily from the audience-behavior statement you defined earlier. While the audience-behavior statement specifically defines the audience you're focused on and the behavior you want them to do, your goals will define the results that you'd like to see.

For example, specific goals for an initiative with an audience-behavior statement of "Drivers will turn off their cars while waiting to pick up or drop off their kids" could be: "The number of drivers who turn off their car while waiting to pick up/drop off their kids will increase by 30%," or "By the end of this school year, 5 out of 10 drivers will turn off their cars while waiting to pick up/drop off their kids. By the end of next year, this will be up to 8 out of 10."

Other examples include:

- The percentage of hunters that pick up their plastic shotgun wads while hunting will increase from 10% to 30% within two years.
- The number of commuters that ride the express bus will increase by 20% within five years.
- The number of smokers littering their butts will decrease by 10%.

 Let's focus on just one of the audience-behavior statements we chose earlier: "Banks in my county will reward farmers for planting cover crops by offering lower interest rates on operating loans." We can set specific behavior change goals for this audience-behavior pairing: "Within three years, 50% of bankers in my county will lower interest rates on operating loans to farmers who plant cover crops."

Choose metrics to measure progress toward your goals

Now that you know where you've set your goal, how will you know when you've reached it? Earlier when setting goals, you were encouraged to set goals that you could realistically measure progress toward. That's where metrics come into play. *Metrics* are what we use to quantify progress toward our desired environmental and behavior change goals, such as reductions in the amount of fertilizer entering a river, the pounds of trash a college campus diverted from landfills, or the number of people who switched their primary mode of transportation to cycling. More specifically, metrics that measure environmental and behavior change outcomes are called *outcome metrics* (in IMPLEMENT: Process Chapter 5, we'll also introduce another type of metric, *process metrics*). Metrics not only tell us whether our initiative was successful in the end, but they also help us track progress toward goals or milestones during the implementation of the initiative, so that we can make midcourse corrections if we have any hiccups along the way.

To evaluate whether your initiative has been successful, you will want to measure environmental and behavior changes as directly and accurately as you can. For example, it's more direct and accurate to measure actual changes in paper use (e.g., number of pages printed) than the amount of paper purchased or the number of people that have pledged to save paper. In other words, if our goal is to reduce paper use, the number of pages printed is a direct metric, while the amount of paper purchased is a more indirect metric. Even if you can collect data on **direct metrics**, you may also want to use **indirect metrics** to provide a more detailed picture of the outcomes your initiative achieved, such as increased levels of awareness, knowledge, acceptance or support, willingness, and intention to change behavior.

When choosing your metrics, it's helpful to do a bit of time traveling—think ahead to the future version of your team that will be collecting these metrics. Will you actually be able to reliably collect the data you need? Your aim should be to judiciously choose metrics that are direct, accurate, and reliable indicators of progress toward your goal, while still being realistic and feasible to measure; if you select something that is too difficult to observe or track, you won't be able to measure your progress.

It's helpful to consider and choose metrics early in your design process, because in many cases, you will be seeking to measure how your initiative resulted in a *change* in environmental outcomes, behaviors, or other factors like knowledge and attitudes. In order to measure change, you'll need to collect data on your metrics before the initiative ever takes place (**baseline data** or **pretest data**), and then collect data on those metrics again after the initiative (**posttest data**). For example, if one of our goals is to increase the percentage of our audience that cycles as their primary mode, we would collect data for the percentage of the audience who cycled as their primary mode of transportation before the initiative, and compare that with the percentage who used cycling as their primary mode after the initiative.

There are many options for collecting data on your metrics, including via surveys and observations, and you may also decide to evaluate the effect of your initiative by designing it as an experiment. In IMPLEMENT: Process Chapter 5, we discuss evaluation options in more detail, and in METHODS: Process Chapter 6, you can find more information on *how* to collect the data you need to measure the impact of your initiative.

❓ Ask Yourself: Goal-setting and metrics

- Have you set an overarching goal, as well as any specific behavior change goals?
- Have you referenced available data to inform the design of your goals?
- Are your goals realistically attainable?

- Do the goals inspire you? If not, can you make them a bit more ambitious or provide more detail to help bring the statement to life?
- Have you set a time frame within which to achieve each goal?
- How will you measure whether you have achieved each goal? Have you selected metrics that you can realistically collect data on while still measuring progress as directly as possible?

 ## Use Different Research Methods to Get the Information You Need

Throughout the chapter, we've mentioned how various kinds of research are useful for choosing and narrowing your focus, audience, and behavior. Toward the end of the chapter, we also touch on using research methods to collect the data you need to measure progress toward your goals. Research in this phase can also prepare you for your Behavioral Drivers Analysis survey, which you will conduct in the UNCOVER phase (see "Using Research to Inform Questions for Your Behavioral Drivers Analysis Survey" below for more).

The types and depth of research you'll use will be determined by many different factors, including the scale and goals of your project, your resources and expertise, and how much access you have to participants. Research for the above purposes can take the form of:

- **Secondary research:** Any secondary research you did as part of your Landscape Exploration (e.g., knowledge partner interviews, literature reviews), as well as any additional secondary research you did to learn about your audience and behavior or to set goals and choose metrics.
- **Primary research:** Observations, interviews and focus groups, and short or longer surveys (Audience Analysis).

Below, we describe how we can use these research methods to meet different needs during the INITIATE Phase. In METHODS: Process Chapter 6, you can find more information about each of these research methods, including how-to tips and their overall advantages and disadvantages.

Table 1.2.5: Summary of Research Purposes and Methods during INITIATE

	Choose focus	Choose audience and behavior	Collect baseline data	Inform Behavioral Drivers Analysis survey
Secondary research	x	x	x	x
Observation		x	x	x
Interviews and focus groups	x	x		x
Short surveys		x	x	x
Audience analysis survey		x	x	x

Using Research to Inform Questions for Your Behavioral Drivers Analysis Survey

In the UNCOVER phase, we will conduct what is called a Behavioral Drivers Analysis (BDA) Survey, which will ask questions designed to reveal our priority audience's barriers to and motivators of the specific behavior we've chosen. Observation, interviews, focus groups, and open-ended questions within short or in-depth surveys can inform which questions we ask in the BDA, as well as how we ask them, and we can use the most common responses from this initial research as the response options for closed-ended questions. If you plan to use primary research during INITIATE to inform your BDA survey, we recommend reading UNCOVER: Process Chapter 3 before finalizing your questions.

Secondary research

If the information gathered during your initial Landscape Exploration is insufficient for choosing your focus or selecting your audiences and behaviors, you can take time at any point to conduct additional secondary research (such as revisiting the literature for new sources and reaching back out to knowledge partners with more focused questions). Sometimes secondary research reveals existing sources of robust baseline data, but in many cases you'll need to collect your own baseline data via primary research for the metrics you've chosen. You can also use secondary sources to inform the questions and closed-ended responses you write for your BDA survey during the UNCOVER phase. We discuss secondary research throughout this chapter, as well as in more detail in METHODS: Process Chapter 6.

Primary research

Often, secondary research won't be sufficient to get the information we need or want during the INITIATE phase. We have several primary research methods at our disposal. Below, we describe how they can help us meet our needs in this phase. As a reminder, we describe how to conduct this research (observation, interviews and focus groups, and surveys) in METHODS: Process Chapter 6.

Observation

Observing people in the setting in which we plan to work allows us to gain insights about potential audiences and their behaviors. For example, for a campus paper reduction project, we could observe the department's print center to see which paper materials students discard or leave unclaimed on the printer, which audience is primarily leaving their print jobs (e.g., students or faculty), as well as how the print center is set up to encourage scrap paper use. After choosing an audience and behavior, we can also use observations to collect baseline data, such as by counting the number and proportion of people that we see do the desired behavior in a given day (compost properly, ride a bike to the bus, etc.). Observing an environment or observing people engaging in a behavior helps us observe patterns and barriers firsthand. This not only helps us draft a much better BDA survey, but also provides information to supplement our findings; people are unaware of a lot of things that they do, which means these things would therefore not be reported to us in a survey.

Interviews and focus groups

Like observations, interviews and focus groups can give us an opportunity to ask questions that could help us choose audiences and behaviors and inform our BDA survey. Depending on who we have recruited for our interviews and focus groups, they could also help inform our focus. Interviews and focus groups are generally not well-suited for collecting baseline data, because you will usually not be interviewing enough people to get an accurate sense of the baseline levels of behaviors or other measurements of interest.

Surveys

Both short and in-depth surveys can inform audience and behavior selection, serve as baseline data, and can inform your BDA survey. They are not suitable for helping you choose a focus because they are conducted after one has already been selected.

Short surveys

Even the briefest of surveys can provide valuable information about one audience; or, if you survey more than one audience, you can see how answers vary across audiences. Among other things, short surveys can be used to gather basic demographic and logistical information and to help you choose certain audiences (if you ask them about their behaviors, willingness, ability, etc.).

Examples of questions you could ask in a short survey in the INITIATE phase include:

- How often do you engage in [X behavior]?
- Which of the following behaviors do you do most often?
- Which of the following behaviors would you be most likely/willing to try?
- What makes it difficult to do [X behavior]? What are the benefits of doing [X behavior]?

Short in-person surveys (intercept surveys)

Intercept surveys (also known as "intercept interviews") are short surveys where you briefly "intercept" someone to ask them one or a few questions (such as from the list above). Often, you'll collect responses in the settings in which you plan to work, but you don't have to. When you can, start by observing the audience, then ask your survey questions. Consider, in addition to the above, a question like "Can you describe your experience doing [X behavior]?"

Short online surveys

There are numerous online platforms to host short surveys. There are also platforms for A/B testing, where you can quickly gauge an audience's perception of multiple options. For example, if you want to ask locals to regularly help with one aspect of maintenance at your nearby coastal state park (e.g., beach cleanup, trail cleanup, critical park habitat restoration, tree planting, or mapping invasive species), but are unsure of which behavior they'd be most willing to do, you can present the audience with pairs of behaviors to "vote" between until they have seen each behavior paired against every other behavior. The results can help you choose which behavior to focus on.

Audience Analysis survey

We call the type of in-depth survey we do in the INITIATE phase an Audience Analysis (AA) because of its focus on helping you choose an audience, a behavior to seek from the audience, or both. An AA can also help you collect baseline data for your initiative. While the methods described above can accomplish the same purposes, an AA survey is a more robust method for doing so. Because you can survey more people than you would through an interview or intercept survey (e.g., for a survey in advance of changing a federal law that will impact behavior nationwide you might want tens of thousands of responses), you can obtain data on numerous parameters to help you define and prepare for your initiative in a way you can't through less rigorous methods.

Who should conduct an Audience Analysis survey?

Conducting an Audience Analysis survey before conducting the BDA during UNCOVER isn't necessary for all projects. You wouldn't need to conduct an AA if you were able to gather all the information needed to choose a specific audience-behavior pairing through less intensive methods. For instance, you may already have gathered ample information about your potential audience-behavior pairings from literature reviews or interviews.

In our work on reducing plastic shotgun wad marine debris on the Northern California Coast, we were able to arrive at a sufficiently narrow audience-behavior pairing without needing to do an Audience Analysis survey. To begin with, the potential audiences for our chosen focus were fairly limited. As discussed above, we were able to determine through knowledge partner and stakeholder interviews that we should prioritize waterfowl hunters over sport shooters or manufacturers. We determined our priority behavior after desktop research and interviews with range managers and hunters revealed that, in California, picking up shotgun wads was a more viable option than purchasing ammunition with biodegradable wads. Once we had our audience-behavior pairing, we moved straight on to a BDA.

However, for projects that would benefit from doing an AA, we recommend it when your circumstances allow it. We always recommend an Audience Analysis for projects that are starting with a larger scope, have a longer time frame, or have a larger budget. Taking this additional step during the INITIATE phase will set your project up for success.

Here is an example of a project for which we would recommend an AA survey. Let's say a county-wide transportation authority wants to shift travel to more sustainable, active modes. They are embarking on projects that will take place over the next five to ten years and will determine how millions of dollars will be spent. In this case, they'd be starting with a very broad audience (all county residents) and almost limitless transportation behaviors that they need to narrow down. If they don't already have robust data on county residents' transportation behaviors, then it's a wise use of resources to conduct primary research that helps them make evidence-based decisions on which audiences and transportation behaviors to prioritize before investing significant resources.

In this example, we would conduct an Audience Analysis survey of county residents. Our survey can include questions that help us consider the criteria interspersed within every step of the INITIATE phase, including questions we have drafted throughout, to help us determine (among other things):

- Information about current behaviors, including how often people are driving vs. using shared or active modes of transportation (Purpose: determining how prevalent the behavior is, and how often people are doing it, helps us to assess the impact of the audience or behavior and can serve as baseline data)

- Information about audiences' ability, receptivity to, and interest in using various shared or active modes of transportation (Purpose: assess which audiences are receptive to which behaviors, and what can be asked of whom)

- Relevant demographic information, such as location, age, mobility and physical impairments, etc. (Purpose: helps choose audiences and behaviors by assessing feasibility or equity, for example)

- Other questions to gather any information they might not have been able to collect through secondary research

Based on the responses to this survey, the transportation authority can use this information to prioritize audience-behavior pairings. For example, which alternative modes of transportation are frequent drivers most willing to adopt? Based on this, they might choose "residents of X city between the ages of 25–34" as an audience and to promote the behavior of "telecommuting twice per week." Since this is a large project, they'd also likely conduct behavior change initiatives for several audience-behavior pairings under the umbrella of one overarching initiative.

You can also conduct an AA once you have narrowed to one or a few potential behaviors. This allows you to ask specific questions to help you write questions for your BDA, and, importantly, identify the closed-ended responses for them. If you have ever coded open-ended survey responses, you will know how much time this can save you later.

What if you want to do an Audience Analysis survey, but can't?

You might want to do an Audience Analysis to help choose your audience, but might not have the time, resources, or even the ability to survey your audience more than once. In these cases, you'll still need to choose a priority behavior using whatever information you have available, but you can move on to the UNCOVER phase to conduct a BDA with a slightly broader audience (e.g., all county residents rather than a subgroup of county residents). If you're not doing an AA, then in addition to behavioral drivers questions, your BDA will include questions that you would have asked in your AA, getting at receptivity, impact, and other information that would help you narrow your audience further.

Conclusion

Here again we want to emphasize the iterative nature of the INITIATE phase. We encourage you to celebrate any adjustments you made throughout—your initiative is likely to be far more effective because you went through this process. And remember, the whole *Making Shift Happen* process is iterative, not just the INITIATE phase; in the next phase, UNCOVER, you will conduct primary research on your chosen audience to understand their barriers and motivators for doing the behavior you want them to adopt. At this time, you may discover information about your audience that requires you to revise your goals to make them more realistic or appropriate. That's not a bad thing—in fact, it's a sign that you are doing your due diligence, and you will save time, energy, and resources down the line. In DESIGN, we'll also have the opportunity to interface with our audience one more time to choose the most effective interventions to deploy during the final phase, IMPLEMENT.

Uncover

I N INITIATE, you refined your focus, selected a priority audience and specific behavior for your initiative, conducted preliminary research on your audience, and identified your goals. Now it's time to build on what you already know about your audience members to uncover the factors that are truly driving their behavior. What's stopping your audience from taking action, and how can you help them overcome it? It can be tempting to skip straight to solutions, but taking the time to listen to and deeply understand your audience is at the heart of the *Making Shift Happen* process—ignoring or making assumptions about why people are or are not adopting a behavior can waste resources or even backfire.

In the UNCOVER phase, we'll introduce you to the major drivers of behavior and walk you through how to survey your audiences to uncover which of these drivers are motivating or deterring their behavior. Specifically, we will introduce you to our recommended method of using a **Behavioral Drivers Analysis** (BDA). The BDA is a systematic, evidence-based method for uncovering which factors are driving your audience's behavior, which will help you choose the appropriate evidence-based behavior change solutions—or **shifters**—in the next phase, DESIGN.

A Look Ahead: UNCOVER

Introduction to the Drivers of Human Behavior

Understand the Key Behavioral Drivers: Means, Motivation, and Memory

Means—can you do it?
Motivation—do you want to do it?
Memory—can you remember to do it?
Other notable drivers

Uncover the Drivers: Prepare and Conduct a Behavioral Drivers Analysis

Prepare to start your Behavioral Drivers Analysis
Write questions to screen for eligibility
Write questions to distinguish between Doers and Non-Doers

Write questions to uncover behavioral drivers
Write questions to identify relevant demographic information
Write questions to gather additional information
Put it all together to conduct your BDA

Analyze and Interpret Your Behavioral Drivers Analysis Results

Get to know your participants and your data
Understand which results represent significant drivers
Understand why to deprioritize all other results
Analyze your data to identify the highest priority results
Finalize your list of high priority results

 ## Introduction to the Drivers of Human Behavior

In this book, we refer collectively to the many factors that influence human behavior as **drivers**. Behavioral drivers can refer to both the things that motivate and facilitate action, as well as the barriers that can deter action.

It is by amplifying the motivators and lessening or removing the barriers that we can achieve the greatest changes in behavior. Since we can't amplify every motivator or address every barrier, we have to be strategic about which to prioritize, but to do so, we must have a deep understanding of the many drivers and how they interact. Here we introduce to you how to think about drivers, and in the next section we provide an overview of some of the most important drivers of human behavior.

Multiple drivers usually influence each behavior:

For any given behavior, there are usually multiple barriers and motivators at play. For example, someone could be motivated to bike to work by certain benefits—wanting to be environmentally friendly, wanting exercise, wanting to avoid traffic, knowing that it's socially acceptable to bike to work—and at the same time, they could be discouraged by certain barriers—if it's rainy or cold outside, lack of safe bike lanes, lack of a place to shower at work, distance, etc.

What drives us can be external or internal:

Whether they function as a barrier or motivator for your audience, drivers can be more external (e.g., financial status, physical environment, laws and policies), or more internal (e.g., our knowledge, values, attitudes). Of the internal drivers, some are temporary (state-like) and are relatively easy to change (e.g., emotions, attitudes), while others are more lasting (trait-like) and are relatively stable (e.g., values, ideology). The lines between external and internal drivers can be blurry. For example, there are external social norms and expectations in every community, but the way we think and feel about them is an internal process.

Both reality and perception drive behavior:

As discussed in FOUNDATIONS: Process Chapter 1, reality does not always drive behavior—our perception of reality does. This is why it's so critical to do research to uncover and understand your audience's perceptions. For example, your audience might already have the access they need to do a behavior, would experience positive consequences as a result of doing the behavior, and have many peers that perform the behavior. But if they *perceive* that they don't have access, that they would experience negative consequences, or that their peers don't approve, they are unlikely to adopt the behavior. It's the audience's perception that matters.

The audience may be unaware of their drivers:

We may not be aware of some of the factors influencing our behavior, such as the layout of a store or the opinions of our peers. Because of this, it's important to gather driver information in ways other than surveying; when the audience isn't aware of how something is influencing them, they can't report it in a survey. When possible, a Behavioral Drivers Analysis should be complemented by other methods, such as stakeholder and resource gathering interviews and observations of the environment. See METHODS: Process Chapter 6 for more on each of these tools.

The same driver can be a barrier or a motivator:

Most drivers can be motivators or barriers depending on the context. Let's use social norms as an example. If 80% of your friends talk about climate change (i.e, they engage in the desirable behavior), then the norm in this context is a *motivator:* wanting to fit in may motivate you to start talking about climate change. But if only 20% of your peers talk about it, then most people aren't doing the desirable behavior, and in this context the norm is a *barrier:* you might be reluctant to bring up climate change around your friends. Similarly, if someone believes a problem is important, then perceived importance is a *motivator,* but if they believe the problem is unimportant, then perceived importance is a *barrier.*

Wow, that's a lot to think about! But don't worry—while thinking about drivers in terms of different categories or groups can help you understand them, at the end of the day, what's important is not that each driver fits neatly into a category, but that you do the work to understand how they are influencing your audience. This chapter provides a framework for helping you understand and apply these drivers.

Theories and Models of Human Behavior

Many different factors drive human behavior. Over the years, researchers across many fields have created theories and tested models to explain and predict human behavior. Some of the most widely-used and well-studied models include the Theory of Planned Behavior, the Theory of Reasoned Action, and the Health Belief Model, which provide the foundation for our Behavioral Drivers Analysis. We also draw on and incorporate factors from many other models, such as the Transtheoretical (or "Stages of Change") Model, Social Cognitive Theory, Gifford's categorization of the "Dragons of Inaction," and the work of other established researchers, such as Kahneman, Tversky, Bandura, and Stern. Researchers and practitioners have applied these models and theories to develop actionable frameworks (e.g., the Fogg Behavior Model and the COM-B Model) to explain and influence environmental behavior.

 ## Understand the Key Behavioral Drivers: Means, Motivation, and Memory

For the *Making Shift Happen* process, we've found that the most useful and intuitive way to think about the many drivers of behavior is to think about your audience's Means (*Can* they do it?), Motivation (Do they *want* to do it?), and Memory (Can they *remember* to do it?). We call these the "Three Ms." Within these three broad categories, there are many drivers. We have summarized these in Table 1.3.1, and we discuss each one in further detail after the table.

Below, we provide descriptions of major behavioral drivers, along with questions that can be asked to reveal whether that driver is influencing your audience's behavior. We do not intend for you to ask every single question we present. Instead, think of these as possible questions to choose from for each driver. A full-length BDA survey (described in depth in a later section) will often include one or two questions for each behavioral driver, while a shorter version may ask only one question per driver, or only ask questions for some drivers.

You'll want to use both open-ended and closed-ended questions in your BDA, and you will see both types referenced throughout the chapter, identified in parentheses after each driver sample question.

- **Open-ended:** With open-ended questions (e.g. "What makes it difficult for you to bike to work?"), respondents are not given predetermined response options and can answer however they would like. Their answers might end up being a single sentence or even an entire paragraph. You can use the most frequent answers as inspiration when writing a closed-ended version of this question in future surveys.

- **Closed-ended questions:** Closed-ended questions are ones in which the audience must select from a predetermined list of answers. There are numerous types of closed-ended responses, such as yes/no, lists of items to choose from, and rating and ranking scales. For example, when you see "(rating scale—agreement)" listed after an example question, this signifies that we recommend a rating scale closed-ended question type. You will also see that we present some sets of closed-ended survey questions that have a name like "Environmental Self-Identity" and the "Environmental Portrait Values Questionnaire." These sets of questions have been tested to confirm their efficacy at measuring a particular concept. You can find more information about these scales in their corresponding references.

While the questions we present with each driver are designed for a formal survey, keep in mind that incorporating these kinds of questions into more limited or informal audience research can be invaluable. For example, if you don't have the capacity or permission to do a formal survey, you can still ask your audience about their drivers through a handful of open-ended questions in informal conversations or short interviews.

You can find more support for the development of both formal and informal interviews and surveys in METHODS: Process Chapter 6, including more about question types (e.g., more information about Likert scales), sampling (i.e., who to survey), study procedures, and more.

Table 1.3.1

Behavioral Drivers: Means—Motivation—Memory		
Means (Can I?)	**Motivation** (Do I want to?)	**Memory** (Can I remember to?)

Policies and practices
 	
Physical environment
 	
Access to resources
  Tools and services
  Financial
  Time
  Security
  Information
  Social support
Ability and self-efficacy
  Ability
    Knowledge
    Skills
  Self-Efficacy
	Perceived positive consequences
	
	Perceived negative consequences
	
	Perceived social acceptability
	
	Perceived action efficacy
	
	Perceived importance
	
	Perceived severity
	
	Perceived susceptibility
	
	Perceived responsibility
	
	Identity
	
	Value systems
		Attentional capacity
		
		Presence of cues
		
		Existing behaviors and habits

Other notable drivers: Personality Traits Emotions and Cognitive Biases		

Means—can you do it?

Now let's dive into our first grouping of drivers: Means. People cannot engage in a behavior if they do not have the means to do so. The Means group of drivers includes both internal factors (e.g., whether we believe we have the ability to do the behavior) and external factors that can influence our ability to take action. External factors that may prevent or facilitate behavior include the complex systems we live in (e.g., laws, regulations, common practices), the resources that may or may not be available to us (e.g., time, money, social support), and our physical environment. On the other hand, some of these factors may be in perception only. For example, we might think there is a law in place that is not actually there or believe that a behavior will take more time than it will. So even if we "technically" have the means to do the desired behavior, we might believe we do not—and the *belief or perception* that we lack the means can prevent us from trying.

Policies and practices

Every behavior your audience does or does not adopt takes place within multiple systems (e.g., cultural customs, formal and informal institutional practices, laws and policies), each with an impact on the behavior. These systems can necessitate specific behaviors, or, at the opposite extreme, can prohibit them. Even if a policy or practice doesn't require or prohibit a behavior outright, policies and practices can make behaviors easy or difficult for your audience. It can be challenging, if not impossible, to change behavior without first addressing these systemic factors in some way. You can learn more about Systems Thinking in FOUNDATIONS: Process Chapter 1 and INITIATE: Process Chapter 2.

Examples of policies and practices that can influence environmental behavior include:

- Renters cannot make energy efficiency upgrades to their home because of the terms of their lease.

- Farmers cannot adopt conservation practices because their farming techniques are largely determined by market demand and dependency on short-term bank loans.

- Health and safety regulations prevent restaurants from allowing customers to use reusable containers.

- During the COVID-19 pandemic, many grocery stores prohibited customers from using reusable bags.

> **Sample Questions: Policies and Practices**
>
> - To what extent do any policies or systems make it difficult for you to [behavior]? (open-ended)
> - If [x policy/system] was changed, would this make it easier for you to [behavior]? (yes/no)
> - What policies/systems would need to change or be created to make it possible/easier for you to [behavior]? (open-ended or list of options)

Understanding the Context for Plastic Shotgun Wad Marine Debris

In 2019, Root Solutions worked with the Greater Farallones Association, the nonprofit partner of the federal Greater Farallones National Marine Sanctuary, to reduce plastic shotgun wads, a form of marine debris, on north-central California coastal beaches. Waterfowl hunters, the main source of these wads, can reduce the harm wads cause to sea life and the marine ecosystem by picking up the wads they see or by switching to biodegradable shotgun wads. To understand why hunters might or might not be willing to engage in these behaviors, we first had to understand more about the context hunters find themselves in.

When researching past initiatives involving our priority audience, as well as initiatives aiming to solve the problem of plastic shotgun wad debris, we discovered that two of the barriers for switching to biodegradable wads were a lack of awareness about the existence of biodegradable wads and a lack of access to affordable options. Currently, traditional ammo is less expensive to produce and purchase than ammunition containing biodegradable wads, yet the cost of the latter will not decline until hunter demand increases. Until then, companies are reluctant to invest the capital needed for less expensive large-scale production. Because demand for ammo with biodegradable wads is low, most stores don't stock it. Because stores don't stock it, most hunters aren't aware that biodegradable wads exist. Furthermore, even if these hunters seek to purchase ammunition with biodegradable wads online, they can't, because California passed legislation outlawing online ammunition sales. These feedback loops and policies mean that affordable wads are not currently available to our priority audience.

Due to these means-based barriers, asking hunters to switch to biodegradable wads in the short term was unreasonable. This is one of the reasons why, in the INITIATE phase, we chose to focus our initiative on encouraging waterfowl hunters to pick up and dispose of any wads they spotted while hunting. (In this case, we were able to discover these means-based barriers early, so we were able to adjust our priority behavior early in the process, but we likely would have needed to adjust our priority behavior in a later phase if we had discovered these barriers later). We recommend that future efforts seek to increase the demand for biodegradable wads while simultaneously making them affordable and available in stores.

Physical environment

Whether we live with cold winters in Chicago or hilly topography in San Francisco, our physical environment has a tendency to heavily influence what we do and what we think we can do. Specific characteristics of our homes, workplaces, neighborhoods, and cities can all constrain or facilitate our ability to enact a behavior. For instance, our ability to take public transportation can be determined by the distance between our home and workplace, infrastructure (e.g., roads, sidewalks, bicycle lanes), and transit services along the way.

In many cases, asking your audience about their physical environment may not be as useful as directly observing the audience in that environment, because people are often unaware of how physical surroundings are influencing their behavior. We share tips for observation in METHODS: Process Chapter 6. Additionally, you may find it useful to consult digital resources like images, Google Maps, GIS (Geographical Information Systems) data, and other tools or reports that help you better understand your audience's physical environment. For instance, Google Maps can tell you if there are viable bike routes near your location of interest.

> **Sample Questions: Physical Environment**
>
> - Do any characteristics of your [home, workplace, neighborhood, etc.] make it challenging for you to [do the behavior]? How so? (open-ended)
> - If [aspect of the physical environment] were to [describe change/improvement], would that make it easier for you to [behavior]? (yes/no)
> - Which of the following changes to the physical environment would make it easiest for you to [behavior]? (list of options)

Access to resources

Even when your audience is motivated and cares about your issue, behavior change can be impeded if they lack information, necessary tools, services, or social support. Importantly, the audience's perception of their access to these resources matters most. You may have reason to believe the audience has the resources needed to complete a behavior, but if the audience doesn't think they do, they are unlikely to perform it. Some examples of resources that people may need access to include:

Tools and services:
Some behaviors require specific materials or goods to complete. For example, composting requires access to a compost bin.

Financial:

Some behaviors hinge on having enough money to purchase an item or service. For example, not being able to afford energy-saving appliances or insulate one's home makes it harder to make a home energy-efficient.

Time:

Your audience may not have time to do the behavior or to seek out resources needed to do the behavior. For example, people may not have time to bike to work after dropping their kids off at school.

Security:

Is everyone able to do the behavior safely? For example, if compost and recycling bins are stored on a dark street or alley, some people may not feel that they have access to them.

Information:

It's hard for your audience to do the behavior if they can't access information about how to do it. For example, a farmer might not know where to find information about how to use less fertilizer. (See Ability and Self-Efficacy below.)

Social support:

Social support is also considered a resource. Having a strong support network is imperative to many types of behavior change, including those that are good for the environment.[20,21] Such is the case for all sorts of environmentally friendly

---

Sample Questions: Access to Resources

- What resources would you need to [behavior]? (open-ended or list of options)
- How difficult is it for you to get the resources you need to [behavior]? (rating scale—difficulty)
- Do you have access to the following? (list of options)
- Do you have the support you need from others [or list specific groups] to successfully [behavior]? (yes/no)
- Whose support would make [behavior] possible/easier for you to do? (open-ended or list of options—such as colleagues, employer, spouse, children, parents, neighbors, other family members, etc.)

behaviors—changing travel behavior hinges on the support of significant others,[18] reducing meat consumption requires buy-in from our families who eat dinner with us, and lowering the thermostat requires agreement with roommates.

Ability and self-efficacy

Willingness to engage in a new behavior or to continue a behavior once we have begun is highly influenced by whether we have the ability to do the behavior and whether we *believe* we have the ability (also known as self-efficacy).

Ability

If someone has the ***ability*** to perform a behavior, this generally means they know the steps that are necessary to complete the behavior, how to perform the steps, and they have the skills to do so.

How-to knowledge:

How-to knowledge includes both knowing the steps involved in performing the behavior and knowing how to complete each step. Does the homeowner know the steps involved in securing affordable solar (e.g., researching both solar installers and rebates) and how to complete each step (e.g., how to properly fill out the rebate forms)?

Skills:

Do people have the skills to do the behavior? When we talk about skills, we mean skills like problem solving, creative thinking, and communication, as well as the skills specific to the task. For example, installing an insulating blanket on a hot water heater requires someone to have the skills to measure, cut, and fasten the blanket onto the heater.

Ability is different from access to resources. Someone can have the ability to play a sport (e.g., knowing the rules and having the technical skills to play) but still not be able to access the resources (e.g., having equipment and a field to play on) to do it. Knowing the rules of the game and having the technical skills to play a sport is *ability,* having equipment and a field to play on is *access to resources.*

Sample Questions: Ability and Self-Efficacy

Ability questions

One way to determine our audience's ability level is by asking them questions that test their knowledge or skills. For example, we can ask: "Choose all the items you can compost in your city" and provide a list of options that include items that are and are not compostable. Their answers will indicate to you the level of knowledge present in your priority audience.

- What is the ideal temperature at which to set your water heater? (open-ended or list of options)
- Where is the perimeter of where you are allowed to fish? (open-ended or list of options)
- How far away should you stay from seals and other marine life? (open-ended or list of options)
- How do you [behavior]? (open-ended or list of options)

We can also ask questions that measure ability less directly:

- What (if anything) makes it challenging/difficult for you to [behavior]? (open-ended or list of options)
- What would make it easier for you to [behavior]? (open-ended or list of options)
- How easy/difficult is it to [behavior]? (rating scale—easiness/difficulty)

Self-efficacy questions

- What makes you confident/not confident in your ability to [behavior]? (open-ended)
- How confident are you that you have the knowledge and skills needed to [behavior]? (rating scale—confidence)
- How confident are you in your ability to [behavior]? (rating scale—confidence)
- Of the following, which do you feel confident in? (list of options)
- I believe I can succeed at [behavior]. (yes/no)
- To what extent do you agree with the following statements: (rating scale—agreement)[14]
  - "There's so much information out there that I am confused about how to make this change."
  - "I don't understand enough of the details about how to make this change."
  - "I'd like to change but I'm not sure where to begin."

Self-efficacy

Closely related to ability is self-efficacy. *Self-efficacy* turns out to be one of the most important drivers of behavior.[1] Even if your audience is capable of carrying out a behavior, if they are not confident in their ability—if they think that performing the behavior requires more knowledge and skills than they have—their self-efficacy will be low. When self-efficacy is high, we are more likely to be motivated to do the behavior and more likely to make progress.[2] Note here that self-efficacy also influences motivation, and thus overlaps with the drivers discussed below in "Motivation—do you want to do it?". Many factors influence self-efficacy, including:

- **Ability:** When one has low ability (how-to knowledge and skills), their self-efficacy is likely to be lower.
- **Feedback/Lack of Past Success:** People may know how to perform the behavior but still not feel effective at implementing it if they haven't received feedback that they are doing it well.
- **Resources:** If someone doesn't have—or perceives they don't have—access to tools or information, their self-efficacy may be low. See the driver "Access to resources."

It's important to understand which of many possible factors are causing our audience to feel low self-efficacy so we can design shifters that address the root cause. See EASY, HABITS, and OPTIMISM (Building Block Chapters 2, 3 and 7) for more about how to overcome this barrier.

Motivation—do you want to do it?

Motivation is the psychological willingness to put in effort to achieve desired goals.[7] We need little motivation to perform behaviors that are easy, but as the required effort increases, the amount of motivation we need increases. Motivation is driven by internal factors, such as perceptions of the positive or negative consequences of the behavior, perceptions of the social acceptability of the behavior, and the degree to which personal identities and value systems align with the behavior.

Many of the drivers in this category are issue- and behavior-specific. In other words, they refer to the audience's beliefs about the specific problem and behavior at hand. But others, like identities and value systems, are not specific to a particular issue or behavior. These drivers fundamentally underlie the way we see the world and decide what's important to us, and thus what motivates us. If a behavior doesn't align with our values or identities, our motivation to take action is low, and we might even be motivated to actively oppose the behavior.

Perceived positive consequences

Perceived positive consequences are the benefits the audience believes will result from performing the desired behavior or abandoning the undesired behavior. When someone believes they will experience positive consequences as a result of the behavior, they are more likely to be motivated to engage in it. In fact, this is one of the most important drivers of behavior.

We almost always recommend asking about perceived positive consequences as an open-ended question because perceived positive consequences are often unforeseen by those not in the priority audience. When you ask this question in an open-ended format, your audience—both those who do the behavior and those who don't—may share benefits they have experienced that you may not have been aware of previously. These benefits can be amplified through the shifters you design.

What does your audience believe are the benefits and advantages of performing the behavior? Here are examples of common perceived positive consequences:

- **Environmental benefits:** It's not just practitioners who recognize positive environmental consequences—your audience may be excited about helping the environment, too.

- **Health:** Some environmental behaviors, like biking to work or using a shared office printer rather than an individual desktop printer, provide people with the opportunity to get moving. Other behaviors may impact water and air quality or other things that affect our health.

- **Financial:** In many cases, environmental behaviors can save money. Does your audience believe there are financial benefits?

- **Convenience:** Does your audience believe that the desired behavior can save time or effort? For example, some people may not want to deal with the hassles of driving in traffic to work every morning, so they take the train,

---

Sample Questions:
Perceived Positive Consequences

We recommend always asking these as open-ended questions, like those below, but you can also follow them with closed-ended questions in which you ask the audience to choose from a list of specific benefits (such as the last question on this list).

- What do you see as personally beneficial about [behavior]? (open-ended)

- In your opinion, what are (or might be) the advantages/positive consequences of [behavior]? (open-ended)

- Which of the following are the most important benefits of [behavior]? (list of options)

---

which means that they have a faster commute, and also that they don't have to pay close attention to the road and potential hazards.

- **Social benefits:** If the desired behavior is in line with a social norm, your audience may already be aware that their peers will approve of them if they are seen doing it.

- **Intrinsic benefits:** Does your audience see doing the behavior (e.g., biking or walking) as fun or enjoyable? Does your audience perceive the behavior as an opportunity for growth, autonomy, or creativity (e.g., learning about and designing a native plant garden in one's yard)? See REWARDS: Building Block Chapter 8 for more on the intrinsic benefits of behaviors.

Perceived negative consequences

Perceived negative consequences are the negative things a person thinks will result from performing the desired behavior or abandoning an undesired behavior. In other words, these are the perceived costs, downsides, or disadvantages of the behavior. Keep in mind the emphasis on perception; if an audience thinks it's safer to drive than to ride a train, they will be less likely to ride a train even if they are actually safer than cars. You'll likely find that many of the negative consequences perceived by your audience overlap with topics from the means category, such as cost and safety.

As with perceived positive consequences, perceived negative consequences can be wide-ranging and surprising to practitioners, so it's important to ask open-ended questions about them. Some common examples of perceived negative consequences include:

- **Inconvenience:** Are the sustainable behaviors perceived as less convenient or more time-consuming?

- **Financial cost:** Is the behavior seen as more financially costly than the status quo?

- **Lack of safety and security:** Are there real or perceived safety concerns about the behavior? For example, you might know that shared multifunction printers have security features like key codes or ID card requirements, and are easier for IT staff to keep secure from hacking. However, audience members might believe that shared multifunction printers are less secure than desktop printers and feel reluctant to use them.

- **Social costs:** Does the audience perceive social costs (e.g., being scorned or made fun of) for doing the behavior? See "Perceived social acceptability."

- **Less freedom of choice:** Does the audience perceive the behavior as limiting their freedom of choice?

- **Uncertainty:** Does the audience believe that changing their behavior would lead to an uncertain future? Uncertainty about the future can prevent change for some people. See risk aversion, loss aversion, and status quo bias in FOUNDATIONS: Process Chapter 1.

- **Conflicting goals and priorities:** Does the behavior conflict with other goals the audience has? For example, they may want to reduce emissions by busing to work, but if the bus experiences frequent unpredictable delays, they may drive in order to consistently arrive on time to work.

- **Lower quality:** If the desired behavior is to use a more environmentally friendly product or method, it could be perceived as being lower quality than the alternative, less sustainable version. For example, people may perceive that a cleaning product using "nontoxic" or "sustainably-sourced" ingredients won't be as effective as a more traditional product.

Sample Questions: Perceived Negative Consequences

We recommend always asking about perceived negative consequences with an open-ended question (like the first few questions below) to avoid bias and reveal consequences not readily predicted by those outside the audience. However, you can follow the open-ended question with closed-ended questions in which you ask the audience to choose from a list of specific negative consequences (such as the last two questions on this list).

- What (if any) are the negative consequences of [behavior]? (open-ended)

- What, if anything, do you see as the disadvantages of [behavior]? (open-ended)

- If you used to [behavior] but don't anymore, why did you stop? (open-ended)

- Which of the following would deter you from [behavior]? (list of options)

- To what extent do you agree with the following statements? (rating scale—agreement)[14]

  - Making this change would interfere too much with my other goals in life.

  - I'm concerned that this change will take up too much of my time.

  - I can't change because I'm invested in my current lifestyle.

  - These issues are important to me, but it's too hard to change my habits.

  - I haven't changed because I'm afraid this wouldn't work.

Perceived social acceptability

Every group or community has some behaviors that are considered normal or acceptable and others that incur sanctions and negative consequences. These **social norms** are one of the most powerful motivators of human behavior; our desire to belong motivates us to behave in ways that make us fit in.

Perceived social acceptability is about norms. It refers to a person's belief that a behavior is a norm, meaning that it is accepted, approved of, or even performed by one's community (also called one's **social reference network**—e.g., colleagues, community, family, or others who are important to us). The effects of norms vary with context and observability; for example, many of us are more likely to deviate from social norms when we're not being observed by others. Most of the time, perceived social acceptability affects *motivation* to do a behavior. For example, if someone perceives that their neighbors will disapprove of them for buying solar panels (which some see as an eyesore), they'll be less willing to do so. However, there are cases where perceived social consequences are so severe that they impact a person's *means* to do the behavior. For example, when someone could lose their job or be cut off by their family, they could still technically do the behavior, but for all intents and purposes, they really don't have the ability.

To uncover the influence of perceived social norms, determine whose approval is important to your audience, what behaviors your audience's peers approve of, and how important social acceptability is for the behavior (e.g., is it performed in public?). It's also key to determine whether the majority of the audience is already doing the desired behavior.

In many cases, what people think is socially acceptable aligns with what the majority of the group is actually doing. But sometimes, people don't have accurate perceptions of what their peers are actually doing (called a **mistaken norm**).

If people have a misperception that the norm is worse than it actually is, you have a great opportunity to correct this mistaken norm. For example, if most people believe that everyone else is littering cigarette butts, but only 20% actually do so, an initiative that corrects this misperception can positively influence behavior. (But if people perceive the norm is actually better than it really is, you don't want to correct the mistaken norm.) In the sample questions below, we show you how to determine if there is a mistaken norm.

Refer to BELONGING: Building Block Chapter 1 for more about how social norms drive behavior and how to leverage and change norms.

Sample Questions: Perceived Social Acceptability

Question to determine if there is a mistaken norm

To determine if there is a mistaken norm, we need to compare the perceived norm to the actual norm. To identify the actual norm (i.e., what percentage of the audience does the behavior), use your Doer/Non-Doer screening questions (which you will learn about soon) or observe the behavior directly. Then, use this question to measure perceptions of the norm. Use the answers to these questions to compare the perceptions of the norm to the actual norm.

- What percentage of people in your [community/institution] do you think [do the behavior]? (open-ended or list of options—such as 0 to 20, 21 to 40, 41 to 60, 61 to 80, and 81 to 100)

Other social acceptability questions

- Who are the people that are most/least in favor of you practicing the behavior? (open-ended or list of options)
- Of the individuals or groups mentioned above, whose approval is most important to you? (open-ended)
- To what extent do you agree with the following statements: (rating scale—agreement)[14]
  - Making this change would be criticized by those around me.
  - I would be letting certain people down if I made this change.
  - I'm worried that my friends would disapprove if I made this change.
  - If I made this change, I would probably be embarrassed when others noticed what I was doing.

Perceived action efficacy

Perceived action efficacy refers to the belief that doing the behavior will help solve or mitigate the problem. Many people struggle to conceptualize how their actions can have a global impact given the scale and lack of proximity of most environmental problems. It's our job to keep people motivated by helping them see how their actions will make a difference. We address this concept in depth in OPTIMISM: Building Block Chapter 7.

Perceived importance

Perceived importance refers to the degree to which the person believes that the environmental problem is a priority. As discussed in FOUNDATIONS: Process Chapter 1, we all have mental and emotional limits to the number of things we can concern ourselves with. Our limited capacity to care is sometimes referred to as our **finite pool of worry**. Even if your audience thinks that the environmental issue is important, they may have competing challenges that they believe they should pay attention to, be concerned about, or take action on. As practitioners, we want to figure out where our environmental issue ranks within our audience's pool of worry (if it is in their pool of worry at all).

Sample Questions: Perceived Action Efficacy

- How effective do you think [behavior] is at addressing/helping solve [problem]? (rating scale—effectiveness)
- How likely is it that [behavior] will mitigate or solve [problem]? (rating scale—likelihood)
- Do you think [behavior] would influence [policy-maker, decision-maker, influencer] to take action? (yes/no)
- To what extent do you agree with the following statements? (rating scale—agreement)[9,14]
    - I can make a positive impact on the environment and society by [behavior].
    - If enough of us do [behavior], we can make a difference together.
    - As long as other people do not [behavior], my efforts to [behavior] are useless.
    - Humans are powerless when it comes to saving the earth, so there is no need to [behavior].

Sample Questions: Perceived Importance

- What are the most important issues facing your [campus, community, etc.]? (open-ended or list of options)
- How important is [problem] compared to other environmental problems? (rating scale—importance)
- Please rank these issues in order from the most important to the least important. (ranking scale with a list of options)

Perceived severity

Perceived severity refers to the degree to which the person believes that the environmental problem is or will be serious, harsh, impactful, and widespread. If someone doesn't believe that a problem is severe or will have a large impact, they are less likely to do anything about it. For example, people who think "I like warmer weather, so global warming sounds like a good deal to me" might have a sense that increased carbon emissions is not a very severe issue. A lack of perceived severity is exacerbated when we don't feel the environmental effects of a problem immediately, even if long-term consequences are quite severe. See ATTACHMENT: Building Block Chapter 4 for more.

Perceived susceptibility

Perceived susceptibility refers to the extent to which people believe the problem will impact their lives. This is important because people are more likely to take action when they believe an issue will impact them or those they care about.

There are many reasons people may not perceive themselves as susceptible to environmental challenges. Some environmental issues may arise so incrementally they go unnoticed even if they are happening in our own backyard. Some people have not made the connection between their personal experience and larger environmental issues. And finally, we often do not feel susceptible to something (e.g., climate change) that is seemingly happening far away, to other people, or in the future.

Additionally, although it may seem like people who have experienced or are experiencing environmental issues will generally have higher awareness of their susceptibility, this is not always the case. So instead of making assumptions, we recommend asking about perceived susceptibility directly. See ATTACHMENT: Building Block Chapter 4 for more on connecting to your audience's personal experience.

It's important to note that even if we don't feel susceptible to an issue, we may still take action (as environmental practitioners, many of us may work on issues that we don't feel particularly susceptible to). This is true for beliefs about other potential drivers we talk about in this chapter as well, like action efficacy (e.g., many of us recycle even if we don't believe it is all that effective), severity, and even social norms.

Perceived responsibility

Perceived responsibility refers to whether a person believes it is their duty to address a problem. Factors influencing perceived responsibility include perceptions of who is the source of the problem (e.g., "farms use 80% of the water in my area, so even if I took shorter showers, it wouldn't make a difference"), values such as fairness (e.g., "other people aren't doing their part, so why should I?"), ideology (e.g., "it's the government's job to fix it"), and morals (e.g., "humans have a moral imperative to protect the Earth"). Read more about values, ideology, and morals in ATTACHMENT: Building Block Chapter 4.

The cognitive bias called **moral licensing** can also reduce perceived responsibility. When we are partaking in moral licensing, we feel justified engaging in a "bad"

Sample Questions: Perceived Susceptibility

- How does [problem] impact [you/your organization, etc.]? (open-ended or list of options)
- Does [problem] impact you and people you care about? (yes/no) If so, how? (open-ended)
- Which of the following impacts may affect you or those you care about? (list of options)
- How likely is it that [impact/problem] will happen if we don't [behavior]? (rating scale—likelihood)

Sample Questions: Perceived Responsibility

- In your opinion, whose responsibility is it to address [problem]/do [behavior]? (open-ended or list of options)
- To what extent do you agree with the following statements? (rating scale—agreement)
  - Humans caused/have contributed to [the environmental issue], and therefore it's our responsibility to solve it.
  - I didn't cause [problem], so it is not my responsibility to [behavior].
  - I already engage in other environmentally friendly behaviors, so I don't need to also [behavior].
  - It's not fair for me to have to [behavior], since [industry/government/corporations] is/are to blame for the majority of the problem.
  - Technological advancements will make a much bigger impact than me [doing behavior], so I don't see much point.

behavior because we did something else we consider "good" (e.g., "I didn't eat meat today, so why can't I drive to work?"). For more on this topic, see the discussion of **negative behavioral spillover** in FOUNDATIONS: Process Chapter 1.

Finally, beliefs fueled by misinformation can also affect perceived responsibility. For example, if someone believes that humans are not the cause of climate change, they are unlikely to think it is the responsibility of humans to address it. For more, see ASSOCIATIONS: Building Block Chapter 9.

Identity

Identity is an individual's sense of self. We each carry multiple identities, such as that of a student, sibling, professional, or parent. Each identity is shaped by our individual expectations for ourselves as well as our affiliations and the expectations placed on us by others. The significant impact of identity on human behavior is highlighted in numerous theories which share the idea that we are motivated to keep or bring our behaviors and identities into alignment, so as to not let down ourselves or others.[5,6]

Environmental self-identity is the extent to which someone perceives themself as the type of person who acts in environmentally friendly ways. This identity in particular is an important driver of environmental behaviors.[4] When we know that our audience has an identity that corresponds with environmentally positive behaviors, we can highlight and tap into it to motivate behavior change. For more about identity and how to leverage it for behavior change, see IDENTITY: Building Block Chapter 6.

Sample Questions: Identity

- Which of the following do you identify with most strongly? (list of options—such as environmentalist, parent, student, or vegetarian—with an option to fill in identities not listed)
- "I would call myself an environmentalist." (yes/no)
- To what extent do you agree with the following statements? (rating scale—agreement)(options below come from the Environmental Self-Identity survey instrument[22])
  - I am the type of person who acts environmentally friendly.
  - Acting environmentally friendly is an important part of who I am.
  - I see myself as an environmentally friendly person.

Project Cane Changer:
The Importance of Audience Research for Uncovering Drivers

Runoff from pesticides, herbicides, and fertilizers from nearby sugarcane farms is a critical threat to the Great Barrier Reef in Australia. Based on knowledge of behavioral science, the Project Cane Changer research team hypothesized that an initiative to help cane farmers take up and become accredited in recommended best management practices would likely need to focus on reducing financial barriers and amplifying environmental benefits.[16]

However, as they got to know their audience of farmers, the research team learned that the main behavioral drivers were not the financial or environmental ones they anticipated. Rather, they were drivers related to identity, and a lack of established record-keeping habits (which itself is a behavior that has its own drivers, including identity-related drivers). The farmers saw themselves as stewards of the environment with a history of adapting their practices to be more sustainable. Being asked to change their behavior felt like vilification, and changing their behavior was seen as an admission of fault and a threat to their identity as stewards.

Based on this audience research, the project team designed shifters to address the appropriate barriers. One example is the "Setting the Record Straight" slogan that represents and reinforces farmers' identities as protectors of the reefs and their commitment to both keeping written records and to become accredited in the best management practices program moving forward.

The results have been dramatic. Since the project commenced in 2016, accreditation in best management practices has increased by over 500% in the Project Cane Changer region—significantly greater than in regions where Project Cane Changer interventions are not yet in place.[17] This example shows how critical it is to avoid making assumptions about an audience—even a project team educated in behavioral science had not accurately predicted the most significant barriers. Directly researching our audience is an irreplaceable step that can mean the difference between an initiative's success and failure.

Value systems

It's important to understand your audience's value systems. In particular, it's key to understand your audience's perception of whether the behavior aligns with their values (how we decide whether something is important[10]), morals (how we evaluate what is acceptable and what is not[12]), and ideologies (shared philosophies of how the world does and should work[11]). Environmental issues are often deeply intertwined with value systems, and it's important to keep in mind that people will not engage in, and will often actively oppose, behaviors that aren't aligned with our value systems.

Value systems can directly drive behavior, but they also often indirectly influence some of the other drivers we discuss in this chapter. For example, if someone's ideology espouses the belief that environmental issues such as climate change are not caused by humans, this might impact perceived severity (e.g., "how can anything that is natural be bad?") and perceived responsibility (e.g., "humans aren't causing it; therefore we don't have to fix it").

Although it's difficult to change our audience's value systems, it is crucial to understand them so that we can design shifters to work with these systems. We also need to know if our audience holds values, morals, or ideologies that might cause them to oppose a certain environmental behavior. For example, someone's religious ideology might drive the perception that doing the behavior would be against *divine will* (their god's wishes), their religious doctrine, or the practices of their church, mosque, or synagogue. If your audience thinks that doing a behavior goes against their religious ideology and you still want to move forward with prioritizing this audience, you'll likely need to design your initiative to work with their religious leadership to bring them on board first. In some cases, our audience's value systems may be so strongly opposed to our cause that we decide that it's not worth spending limited resources to influence their behavior, when we could achieve behavior change with a more amenable audience.

On the other hand, if we discover that our audience holds values that could lead to environmental behavior (e.g., riding a bike to work for health reasons), our messages can tap into those values to motivate behavior change. Thus, being aware of value systems that encourage or impede environmental behavior can help us design our shifters to work with and not against these systems.

See ATTACHMENT: Building Block Chapter 4 for more on value systems.

Sample Questions: Value Systems

People can feel uncomfortable answering questions about their values, so we recommend testing your survey questions ahead of time in small focus groups or in conversations with the audience. Finding the questions that are the most acceptable and least polarizing can help obtain higher response rates in your audience surveys. See METHODS: Process Chapter 6 for more on survey question design.

Environmental Portrait Values Questionnaire

If you have the space in your survey, we recommend using the E-PVQ (Environmental Portrait Values Questionnaire), which is based on the widely used Schwartz Values Survey.[4] It is designed to measure four human values considered to underlie individuals' environmental beliefs and behaviors. The survey respondents rate how much they think the hypothetical person in each description is like them.

Here is a sample list of questions, used to measure biospheric values (one of the four values measured by the questionnaire):

- It is important to them to prevent environmental pollution.
- It is important to them to protect the environment.
- It is important to them to respect nature.
- It is important to them to be in unity with nature.

You can see the full list of items and learn more about this methodology for measuring values here: https://www.epgroningen.nl/epvq/.

American Environmental Values Survey

Alternatively, you could ask one or several questions from EcoAmerica's American Environmental Values Survey.[19] Respondents are instructed to rate their level of agreement with each statement. Below is just a sampling of the questions from the survey.

American Environmental Values Survey— Values questions (rating scale—agreement):

- I am concerned about environmental issues.
- I worry about the effects of environmental pollution on my family's health.
- I am worried about climate change.

American Environmental Values Survey— Ideology questions (rating scale— agreement):

- We can achieve environmental protection and economic growth at the same time.
- Environmental progress slows innovation.

Morals questions

- To what extent do you agree with the following statements? (rating scale—agreement)
  - It's important to [behavior] to be a good person.
  - Even when no one is watching, I do [behavior].

Additionally, be on the lookout for insights about value systems that show through in questions about other drivers. For example, while we only occasionally ask about drivers related to religious ideology and divine will directly, these drivers can come up in the answers to some of the other questions (such as perceived social acceptability or perceived consequences).

Memory—can you remember to do it?

Who can relate to planning to ask for no utensils when ordering takeout, but then forgetting? Even when we have the means to do a behavior, and the motivation to do it, we must also remember to do the behavior. Thus, the final group of drivers revolve around memory—factors that make our audience more or less likely to remember to engage in the behavior. While most drivers present themselves as both barriers and motivators, (the lack of) attentional capacity and memory are likely to always fall under the barrier category.

Attentional capacity

We can safely assume that attentional capacity is almost always going to be a barrier for our audience, either because of information overload, scarcity, or both. *Attentional capacity* refers to the ability to focus sufficiently on something to be able to understand it or take action. It's common for people to have reduced attentional capacity, or *attention fatigue*, which is exacerbated by things like *information overload* and *choice overload* (when we're presented with so much information or so many choices that we can't process it all). This influences our ability to pay attention to issues, and can also lead to poor decision-making and inaction. Attentional capacity, and how to address it, is covered in depth in VIVID and LONGEVITY: Building Block Chapters 5 and 10.

This also connects to the means category of drivers because attentional capacity can be especially depleted for people who are experiencing scarcity. In the case of scarcity—when our basic needs such as food, shelter, social connection, or safety are unmet—we can lack the cognitive bandwidth to devote mental capacity to anything else. Therefore, it's important to keep scarcity in mind as you consider potential attentional barriers for your audience. See FOUNDATIONS: Process Chapter 1 for more on scarcity.[15]

Limits on attentional capacity can mean that our audience can overlook a behavior—they might not even notice it at all. Or the audience might be aware of a behavior but have difficulty remembering 1) to do the behavior or 2) the steps involved in doing the behavior. Just because our audience knows they should do a behavior and knows how to do it, it doesn't mean they will remember to do it; we all know how to grab our reusable shopping bags, but actually remembering to do so is another story.

Presence of cues

Cues are a driver of behavior, because for behavior to happen, there must be an effective cue that reminds us to perform an action, even if motivation and means are both high. (This also makes cues a highly valuable shifter, as HABITS and VIVID: Building Block Chapters 3 and 5 discuss.) Even eating meals or snacks each day is prompted by some kind of cue, such as the physical feeling of hunger, smelling cookies in the oven, seeing snacks on the counter, or hearing the clock strike noon.

Our physical environment is a major source of cues. That is, what we encounter can trigger or remind us to do something. For example, the route that we take to and from work can lead us to stop at a farmer's market or a favorite cafe as we pass signs and familiar landmarks. Hanging our reusable bags next to our car keys reminds us to bring the bags to the grocery store. There are also a number of other types of cues that we're exposed to in our day to day; the time of day, our emotions, and other people can trigger us to behave in a certain way. Over time, cues counteract deficits like attentional capacity because they signal behavior automatically.

Sample Questions: Attentional Capacity

- How easy/difficult is it (or would it be) to remember to [behavior]? (rating scale—easiness or difficulty)
- How easy/difficult is it (or would it be) to remember the steps involved in [behavior]? (rating scale—easiness or difficulty)
- What percentage of the time do you remember to [behavior]? (open-ended, or list of options—such as 0–25%, 26–50%, and so on)

Sample Questions: Presence of Cues

- When are you most likely to remember to [behavior]? (open-ended or list of options)
- When are you most likely to forget to [behavior]? (open-ended or list of options)
- What might help you remember to [behavior]? (open-ended or list of options)
- Is there anything in your [home, office, etc.] that helps you or might help you remember to [behavior]? (open-ended)

Existing behaviors and habits

Our past behavior is one of the best predictors of future behavior. Our current behaviors and habits are affected by all the other drivers covered in this chapter, but they're also a driver in and of themselves for future behaviors.

Habits are actions that have been repeated so many times that they require little conscious effort. Most of the time, this is advantageous—habits free up our attention so we can focus on other, more important things. However, when a series of cues, actions, and rewards become a bad habit, it can be very difficult to change. Thus, we want to know as much as we can about existing habits that might facilitate or conflict with the priority behavior. We also want to consider the strength of the habit and how the habit may impact our ability to change people's behavior.

On the other hand, we can use the presence of strong good habits to foster a new habit, effectively piggybacking on it. For instance, knowing that our audience uses reusable grocery bags provides a foundation for the introduction of a new habit, like package-free shopping. Grabbing one's shopping bags can cue one to also grab any reusable containers they may need to store items from bulk sections in stores. Similarly, one can use an enjoyable habit, like reading, to incentivize oneself to commute on public transit instead of driving.

See HABITS: Building Block Chapter 3 for more about how to build and break habits.

Sample Questions:
Existing Behaviors and Habits

- What habits do you have that might get in the way of [behavior]? (open-ended)
- What habits do you have that might help you [behavior]? (open-ended)
- What are your favorite daily rituals and activities? (open-ended or list of options)
- What do you wish you had more time for? (open-ended)

Additionally, be on the lookout for insights about environmental habits that come through in other questions. For example, Doer/Non-Doer questions like "How often do you [behavior]?" can help us get at how habitual or strong the desired behavior is.

Other notable drivers

Above, we outline the drivers that tend to most directly influence whether someone does a specific behavior. Yet, we know that there are other, broader forces that shape our thoughts and behaviors. These broad drivers tend to have widespread impact on our behaviors in many aspects of life (e.g., health, environment, finance), influencing our behavior "through" many of the drivers listed above. That is, these drivers can influence narrower, context-specific drivers, that in turn influence our behavior. For example, a strong ***present bias*** (where we give more weight to rewards and costs that are incurred in the present than those that are incurred in the future) may cause someone to believe the immediate *perceived negative consequences* of a behavior far outweigh the *perceived positive consequences* that would happen in the future. So if you ask your audience about their perceptions of the positive and negative consequences of flying two less times per year, their present bias is likely to come through in their response.

Personality traits

There is no doubt that personality traits like those detailed in the OCEAN model (i.e., the "Big Five"—openness to new experiences, conscientiousness, extroversion, agreeableness, and neuroticism) influence our behavior. Personality traits tend to be better for understanding and predicting broad patterns of behavior (e.g., sustainable practices), rather than specific behaviors (e.g., electric vehicle purchasing behavior or reusable bag use).[3] That's because personality traits are somewhat removed from these narrow, outcome-producing behaviors. For example, those with more conscientious or altruistic personality traits may be more likely to engage in environmental behaviors in general, but it may be difficult to predict which specific behaviors they will be drawn to or will successfully adopt.

Emotions and cognitive biases

Emotions and cognitive biases are both drivers that influence the way we interpret information and can prevent us from engaging in environmentally friendly behaviors.

Emotions

Emotions are complex internal reactions to situations or events and are linked with a variety of cognitive processes, including perception, attention, learning, and memory. We discuss them in more detail in FOUNDATIONS: Process Chapter 1, OPTIMISM, and LONGEVITY: Building Block Chapters 7 and 10.

Cognitive biases

Cognitive biases are systematic errors and biases in our decision-making that arise from the mental shortcuts we use to facilitate rapid judgment and decision-making. You can learn more cognitive biases in FOUNDATIONS: Process Chapter 1 and in every Building Block chapter.

• • •

While they are important behavioral drivers, emotions and cognitive biases are difficult to measure directly in a survey. And even if you don't measure them directly, know that many of the shifters within the Behavioral Building Blocks™ work to overcome often unseen biases and to elicit fruitful emotions.

Despite their overarching importance, we generally don't recommend including specific questions for these drivers because it's difficult to succinctly ask about them in a survey, and people tend to have a hard time answering them. With little room to spare in our BDA survey, it's important to reserve space for the most actionable questions. Remember, these other drivers will "come through" in response to the questions we ask about other drivers. For example, the personality trait of "conscientiousness" might come through in someone's responses to questions about perceived responsibility. Emotions may be revealed when asked about the consequences of a behavior. And someone with a tendency to be high in loss aversion might reveal their fears when asked about perceived severity.

 ## Uncover the Drivers: Prepare and Conduct a Behavioral Drivers Analysis

Now that we've described the most common and important drivers of behavior, it's time to turn to our audience to uncover which drivers are influencing whether they adopt our priority behavior. There are several important reasons for taking this step before starting to design shifters:

- To learn, not guess, your audience's true barriers and motivators
- To uncover unexpected barriers and motivators
- To ensure that your resources are spent on the most influential drivers of the desired behavior—addressing the most important barriers and amplifying or leveraging the most relevant benefits and motivators.

Our preferred method for understanding and measuring an audience's behavioral drivers is called a **Behavioral Drivers Analysis (BDA)**—a systematic, relatively rapid tool that uses in-depth surveys or interviews to uncover an audience's significant barriers and motivators. With a BDA, you are not only uncovering your audience's barriers and motivators, but you are also revealing the statistically significant differences between people who do the behavior (Doers) and people who don't (Non-Doers). In other words, a BDA survey is designed to answer: "Who is doing the desired behavior, and why? Who is not doing the behavior, and why?" (We discuss statistical significance later in the "Analyze and Interpret Your Behavioral Drivers Analysis Results" section.) The BDA we present here is adapted from the Barriers Analysis developed by Tom Davis and updated by Bonnie Kittle and colleagues, which was designed for public health and development contexts and is used by many organizations worldwide.[13]

By asking all respondents the same questions about their behaviors and perceptions and then statistically evaluating how the Doers and Non-Doers' answers differ, we can see which factors are critically influencing behavior. For example, let's say that you're working with restaurant decision-makers (people who make decisions or recommendations about serviceware purchases in their restaurant) to uncover their key drivers for providing only reusable serviceware (e.g., plates, utensils, trays, etc.) to dine-in customers. You find that both Doers and Non-Doers report that they don't see plastic pollution as a responsibility of restaurants to solve. This means that perceived responsibility probably *isn't a* key driver, because Doers are providing reusable serviceware despite this perception. Let's say you also find that Non-Doers are more likely than Doers to feel that washing and reusing serviceware on site would be too expensive. This suggests that the perceived negative consequence of additional expenses is a *key barrier* to actually doing the behavior, and that in the DESIGN phase, you should focus on correcting this misperception instead of trying to convince your audience that they bear responsibility for addressing plastic pollution.

This half of UNCOVER will help you understand the ins and outs of conducting a Behavioral Drivers Analysis to promote environmental behavior change.

> The 20 drivers we shared with you in the first half of UNCOVER can be thought of as *potential* drivers of behavior. With the Behavioural Drivers Analysis, we are uncovering which of those potential drivers are *actually* driving whether our audience does the behavior or not.

Prepare to start your Behavioral Drivers Analysis

Before you start your BDA, make sure you have what you need to start writing it. This includes information you got from primary or secondary research in the INITIATE phase, as well as a specific audience-behavior statement. We also encourage you to start thinking of your priority behavior as part of a sequence, which we define below.

Confirm that you've completed the steps from INITIATE

The work we did in INITIATE: Process Chapter 2 sets us up for success in the rest of the *Making Shift Happen* process, starting with the BDA in UNCOVER. Before continuing with a BDA, we recommend that you have gone through the entire process of INITIATE, but that you especially have the following:

Preliminary research about your focus, audience, and behavior

Because a BDA involves the development of a questionnaire, it is often preceded by observations, focus groups, and exploratory surveys and interviews. As discussed in INITIATE: Process Chapter 2, the more research you can do with your audience before conducting a BDA, the more specific you can get in your BDA. Secondary and primary research (such as observations, interviews, or an Audience Analysis) can help you ascertain your audience's current behaviors or receptivity to change. This research can even include things like where your audience goes for information on your issue or whose advice they listen to. Importantly, these also help narrow potential questions and identify potential relevant responses to use in closed-ended questions for our BDA. Additionally, these analyses can also be used to gather baseline data. Performing research beforehand also allows you to focus your BDA almost entirely on the drivers of behavior.

A clearly defined audience-behavior statement

You'll want to make sure that you clearly defined your audience-behavior statement at the end of the INITIATE phase before continuing with a BDA. Having a clear and specific audience-behavior statement is critical for writing meaningful and useful survey questions and for uncovering barriers and motivators that are unique to a specific behavior.

If you haven't yet identified a specific audience-behavior statement, return to INITIATE: Process Chapter 2. There, we provide you with decision-making criteria and guide you through the types of primary and secondary research that you can use to select an audience-behavior pairing and then define an audience-behavior statement.

As a refresher, here are examples of audience-behavior statements:

- Restaurants in my county will serve dine-in customers using only reusable serviceware.
- Employees at X company carpool to and from work at least 2x per week.
- Boaters in Guerrero Negro stay at least a football/soccer field's length away from whales.
- Tour boat operators in the Great Barrier Reef provide reef-safe sunscreens on all their boats.
- Members of the House of Representatives vote in favor of a bill to raise emission standards on new automobiles to standards set by California.

Consider the behavioral sequence

Before you move on to drafting your questions, it's helpful to revisit the behavioral sequence that you may have already mapped out in the INITIATE phase. As a refresher, below is what the behavioral sequence would look like for an initiative aimed at encouraging people to bike to work three days per week.

- Purchasing a bike, if needed (this alone involves many steps!)
- Obtaining accessories like a helmet and a backpack that holds a change of clothes and other workday essentials
- Researching safe bike routes and whether a bike can be accommodated on public transportation
- Figuring out if there are lockers at work and where to store the bike both there and at home
- Planning new evening and morning routines, such as setting an earlier alarm and packing work clothes
- Following through with the new evening and morning routines (e.g., getting up when the new alarm goes off)
- Biking to work!

In the INITIATE phase, you most likely considered this sequence and chose to focus your initiative on the last behavior of the sequence, the *outcome-producing behavior* (in this case, biking to work). Note, however, that to ultimately complete the behavior of biking to work, people must also engage in these earlier behaviors. Therefore, you should also consider the full behavioral sequence when designing your BDA survey questions.

In the UNCOVER phase, most of your questions in the BDA (especially your open-ended questions) will ask about this behavior (e.g., "What makes it difficult to ride your bike to work?" and not "What makes it difficult to go to bed early enough to bike to work in the morning?" or "What makes it difficult to research safe bike routes?"). But there is also value in asking some questions specifically about earlier steps in the sequence, or to incorporate earlier steps in the sequence into your closed-ended questions. For example, you could ask your audience, "What makes it difficult to ride your bike to work?" and have them select all that apply from options that include: "lock up my bike," "research safe routes," "I don't have a bike," etc.

Even if you don't ask specifically about earlier behaviors in the sequence, by asking your audience open-ended questions about the outcome-producing behavior, they are likely to share with you rich information about their barriers and motivators related to earlier steps in the sequence (e.g., someone might share that planning their route is what makes it difficult to bike to work).

An activity called *journey mapping* can help you refine the behavioral sequence that you originally identified in INITIATE and identify which points in the sequence might be particularly important to include questions about.

 ### Activity: Use Journey Mapping to Identify the Sequence of Behaviors

One way to help you begin to identify potential barriers and motivators along the behavioral sequence is to create a journey map where you visualize the steps of the process your audience goes through in order to complete an outcome-producing behavior.[8] You can expand on your existing behavioral sequence outline by adding detail to each of the steps in the sequence, informed by observations, conversations and interviews with your audience, or activities where you ask them to lay out the sequence of events and narrate their experiences to you. The goal is to identify any steps in the sequences that you might have missed, as well as to better understand which ones might be the most challenging, inconvenient, confusing, or daunting.

Journey mapping will be most useful when you can interact directly with your audience. Can you watch someone complete the steps in person, in a video, or over screen share? Can you ask potential audience members to walk you through the steps and describe what they are feeling and thinking at each point along the way? This can reveal information about which steps or behaviors are most difficult for them and which ones tend to prevent them from proceeding further along the sequence. See METHODS: Process Chapter 6 for interview and observation best practices.

If you are unable to connect with your audience directly to do journey mapping, you can still glean useful insights by imagining your audience going through an experience. For example, put yourself in the shoes of a commuter and imagine what it is like to navigate through the process of biking to work, from start to finish.

Finally, always keep in mind that journey mapping is intended to be a starting point for identifying your audience's potential barriers and motivators. Although some potential behavioral barriers and motivators may be revealed in the process (such as what makes it difficult for someone to safely secure their bike at work), journey mapping should not be a replacement for the in-depth research of our Behavioral Drivers Analysis. Rather, journey mapping is a tool to help you design an even stronger and more useful BDA.

•••

When you're sure that you have what you need to be able to write specific questions for your BDA, the next step is to write your survey.

Write questions to screen for eligibility

For the rest of this section, you will be drafting survey questions. One of the first things we must do when designing a BDA is write questions that screen potential participants for eligibility. Members of the priority audience you selected during INITIATE are the only individuals who should participate in the BDA. Usually, a handful of questions can help us determine someone's eligibility.

Let's continue with the reusable serviceware example we included in our list of audience-behavior statements above: "Restaurants in my county will serve dine-in customers using only reusable serviceware." In this case, by "reusable," we mean durable dishware and utensils, which could be plates, baskets, utensils, cups, etc., that can be washed many times and be reused. This is in contrast to single-use items, whether plastic, "compostable," or otherwise, that are discarded after a customer uses them once. As you will see, we will also need to be explicit about what we mean by "reusable" in the introduction to our survey, even if we don't include the full definition each time we ask a question.

We will need to create screening questions that cover every aspect of the definition of our priority audience.

For example, let's say that we decided in the INITIATE phase that we would prioritize restaurants in our county that serve customers in-house (for dine-in service) and have at least one dishwashing machine. We therefore need to be sure that we are only surveying decision-makers at restaurants that serve dine-in customers, and which own dishwashers. (In the future, we might work with decision-makers at restaurants that don't currently have a dishwasher, but for now we chose to focus on those that already have a dishwasher.)

Additionally, we need to be sure that the person answering the survey is able to make decisions about what kind of serviceware to use. In the audience-behavior statement, we use "restaurant" for simplicity, but the specific people we will be focused on are the decision-makers at the restaurant (those who make decisions or recommendations about serviceware purchases at the restaurant).

We can ask the following screening questions to verify that the people taking the survey are part of our priority audience:

- Do you make decisions or recommendations about serviceware purchases at one or more restaurant(s) located in X county? (yes/no)
- How many dishwashing machines does your restaurant have? (0–8+)
- Your restaurant serves customers for: a) dine-in b) take out (Check all that apply)

If a respondent doesn't make decisions about serviceware purchases at a restaurant in X county, doesn't have a dishwasher at their restaurant, or doesn't serve dine-in customers at their restaurant, they wouldn't be eligible to take the survey.

Write questions to distinguish between Doers and Non-Doers

We just wrote questions to ensure that our respondents are actually part of our priority audience (that the right people are taking our survey). But we also need to determine who among these respondents are Doers and who are Non-Doers. To conduct a scientifically sound BDA, you will need to survey a sufficient and relatively equal number of Doers and Non-Doers. Ideally, your sample should include at least 90 participants, 45 of whom are Doers and 45 of whom are Non-Doers.[13] A larger sample size makes it easier to determine how Doers and Non-Doers differ, helping us to pinpoint which behavioral drivers are most influential. When we have less than 45 participants in either group, it can be difficult to determine if there are statistically significant differences between Doers and Non-Doers.

Below, we walk you through how to clearly define the criteria that make someone a Doer, and how to write the survey questions that determine whether the respondent meets those criteria.

Define what it means to be a Doer or Non-Doer

Generally speaking, a **Doer** is someone who already engages in the behavior as described in the audience-behavior statement defined during INITIATE: Process Chapter 2. In the case of our reusables example, Doers must "serve dine-in customers using only reusable serviceware."

To sort people into Doers and Non-Doers, we need to ask questions that determine whether a respondent "does" the behavior or not. Sometimes, this is as simple as asking "Do you [behavior]?" But usually, asking this question alone is insufficient. For example, if we only asked, "Do you compost?" then someone who has only composted once or twice in their life could answer "yes" and be counted as a Doer. This person might be very different from someone who composts regularly and has been composting for years. So, to get more specific about who "fits the bill" of a Doer vs. a Non-Doer, we usually need to ask questions that determine how well or to what extent someone does the behavior.

This usually requires refining or expanding on your audience-behavior statement to consider details about the behavior that are critical to determining whether the initiative achieves its goals. This might include the following details:

- **How?**
  - To be a Doer, does someone have to do the behavior in a specific way, like using certain tools, products, or methods?
- **When (at specific times)?**
  - To be a Doer, does someone have to do the behavior at particular times (e.g., a particular time of day, like watering the lawn in the morning or nighttime) or before or after specific events (e.g., always shutting off automatic sprinklers prior to a forecasted storm or turning off all lights and unplugging appliances before leaving for vacation)?

- **To what extent?**
  - **How often? (Frequency):** How often should someone engage in this behavior to be considered a Doer? For example, does someone have to carpool to work always (5x a week) or only some of the time (2x a week)?
  - **How much? (Magnitude):** To what extent does someone have to do the behavior to be considered a Doer? For example, does someone have to shower for less than 10 minutes? 5 minutes? Does a farmer have to adopt no-till practices on all of their fields or only some of them?
  - **How well? (With how much accuracy or skill):** To be a Doer, does the person have to do the behavior with 100% accuracy? For example, if we are studying composting behavior, do we need Doers to know how to properly compost or to only attempt to compost?
- **Where? (In what context)**
  - To be a Doer, does the audience have to do the behavior everywhere or only in some places? For example, if we are trying to promote home recycling, we might decide to only require that Doers recycle in their home—not at work.

Note that you don't need to include all these criteria in your definition of who is a Doer. For example, it may be important to specify that employees bike to work at least two days per week, but if it is not important what route they take, how long it takes them, etc., then those specifics shouldn't be in our Doer definition.

Make sure that our definition of a Doer is neither too strict nor too relaxed

We must balance defining Doers as those that do our desired behavior exactly as we wish they would with our need to sample enough Doers. We want to make sure that our Doers are the people who are doing the behavior well, most of the time, or both, and that the Non-Doers are the people who aren't doing the behavior sufficiently.

If our Doer definition is too relaxed or too strict, then our survey data becomes less meaningful. The more we relax the definition of a Doer away from the level of the behavior we seek, the less the results of an analysis between groups will illuminate what is driving the differences in behavior. The two groups mean less—you might have people classified as Doers who are really more like Non-Doers, and thus the barriers and motivators of the people we defined as Doers won't align with the barriers and motivators of those who fit the essence of a "Doer" in the "real world." Conversely, if we make the Doer definition too strict, we'll classify people as Non-Doers who are really more like Doers. Because the goal of our survey is to measure the differences between Doers and Non-Doers, incorrectly grouping respondents in our survey means that the differences, and therefore the results of our survey, are less meaningful and useful.

In addition to having a less meaningful survey, if your definition of a Doer is too strict, you may find it challenging to get at least 45 Doer responses in your survey. But if it's too relaxed, you may not be able to find enough Non-Doers. You may find that you need to adjust your definition depending on how likely it is that you will get at least 45 Doers and 45 Non-Doers to respond. If it's a common or relatively easy behavior like discarding one's trash in a trash bin (i.e., not littering), you may be able to be more strict with your definition of who is considered a Doer, such as by requiring that Doers are people who *never* litter. However, if the behavior is rare, or even the most basic version of the behavior is inherently difficult, you may need to relax your definition of what it means to be a Doer, just for the purposes of the survey. For example, if the behavior for your initiative is that people bike to work twice per week, you might have to relax the definition of a Doer to anyone that bikes once per week, or even once every two weeks.

To craft a realistic and useful Doer definition, we should draw on our existing primary and secondary research as much as possible. For example, if we conduct primary and secondary research before drafting our BDA, we can get a sense of how difficult the behavior is and how common it is among our audience, which will help us avoid making our definition too strict or unattainable. There's not a science to creating these definitions, but the more we know about our audience ahead of the BDA, the more we can avoid having to make adjustments to our definition later on. However, it is OK to need to make adjustments if needed: for example, if you're having trouble finding Doers as you begin conducting your survey, you can relax your Doer definition then.

When defining Doers and Non-Doers for our reusables example, the most important criteria is magnitude: how much of the serviceware items restaurants provide to dine-in customers must be reusable? While in an ideal world, each restaurant would use 100% reusable serviceware for dine-in customers, that might not be realistic. For example, some restaurants may provide reusable utensils, plates, and bowls, but still give out plastic cups if requested by a customer. These restaurants are still doing the desired behavior almost all of the time, so they likely share many of the barriers and motivators of Doers, rather than of Non-Doers. Therefore, we may define Doers as "restaurant decision-makers who use reusables for at least 75% of the serviceware provided to dine-in customers."

Our Doer definition doesn't necessarily change our audience-behavior statement or the goals of our initiative

The Doer definition we create does not necessarily change our audience-behavior statement or the goals of our initiative. That is, if for our survey we relax our definition of Doers from "restaurants that provide 100% reusable serviceware to dine-in customers" to those who "provide 75% or more," our audience-behavior statement for our initiative can still be "Restaurants in my county will serve dine-in customers using *only* reusable serviceware"—we wouldn't need to relax that, too. We create our relaxed definition of Doers only for the purposes of classifying people as Doers and Non-Doers for our survey. In most cases, our BDA would still ask people about the behavior we defined in our audience-behavior statement, and we would still intend for our initiative to achieve the goals we set in INITIATE. We would only modify our audience-behavior statement or the goals of our initiative if, through this process, we determine that the behavior we used in our audience-behavior statement is entirely unrealistic, at which point we could relax the behavior we want our initiative to promote, or even select a new behavior entirely.

Introducing a new behavior: when there aren't any true Doers in the audience

Sometimes, we want to introduce a completely new behavior to our audience (a behavior that no one in the audience has even had the opportunity to perform yet), such as using autonomous shuttles in a city that is about to introduce autonomous shuttles for the first time. In this case, a Behavioral Drivers Analysis can't be performed because there would be no true Doers to compare to the Non-Doers. That's because any responses we get from our groups would reflect their *perceptions* of what it would be like to do the behavior, rather than barriers and motivators gained from experience, so we wouldn't be able to identify any true drivers.

While we can't technically do a BDA, we can still do meaningful audience research to get a sense of what our audience's perceptions are regarding the new behavior. For example, we might identify that some people have misperceptions about the safety of the shuttles. We can use this information to try to correct these misperceptions before the shuttle program is implemented. We can also compare the responses of different groups within our audience: Are some people more willing and interested in trying out the behavior than others? Are these the people that have more accurate perceptions of the barriers and benefits of the behavior? What might be influencing any differences in beliefs and perceptions about the behavior (e.g. demographic factors, experience with similar behaviors)?

Examples of questions you might ask in a survey for a brand new behavior include:

- What might make it difficult to [behavior]?
- What (if any) are your concerns with [behavior]?
- What might make it easier for you to [behavior]?
- How likely are you to [behavior] when it becomes available?
- How interested are you in trying [behavior] when it becomes available?
- What are the potential benefits of [behavior]?

And of course, secondary research is very useful in cases like these: Has this behavior been introduced to similar audiences as yours? What lessons can be learned from their experience? Within your own audience, what are the barriers and motivators for similar behaviors that have been introduced to this audience (e.g., introduction of e-scooters or other kinds of shuttles)?

Draft your Doer or Non-Doer survey questions

Once you have defined what it means for someone in your audience to be a Doer, you can start drafting the survey questions that you will use to separate Doers from Non-Doers in your survey audience. We almost always need to ask a minimum of two questions to ascertain whether someone is a Doer, meaning they meet all aspects of the behavior portion of the audience-behavior statement.

See the box to the right for examples of questions you can use to determine whether someone is a Doer or a Non-Doer.

Before deploying your survey, make sure you know exactly which responses (and which combinations of responses) will lead to someone being counted as a Doer, a Non-Doer, or neither. We recommend creating a table or matrix like the one in Table 1.3.2 to help you organize how the responses will determine Doer or Non-Doer status. In our example, we ended up being able to determine whether restaurant

---

Sample Questions: Doers and Non-Doers

- How often do you [behavior]?
- Within the past [time period], how many times have you [behavior]?
- In an average [time period] how many times do you [behavior]?
- Approximately what percentage of the time do you do [behavior]?
- Which of the following [tools/methods/products] do you use to [behavior]?
- At which of the following [times/places] do you do [behavior]?

Table 1.3.2: Example Doer / Non-Doer Classification

Audience-Behavior Statement: Restaurants in my county will serve dine-in customers using only reusable serviceware.

Survey question asked	Possible answers	Doer answers	Non-Doer answers	Neither (exclude from Doer/ Non-Doer analysis)
Think about all of the serviceware items you provide to dine-in customers (e.g., cups, plates, baskets/trays, utensils). Approximately how many of those items are reusable?	A 100% (All) B 76–99% C 51–75% D 26–50% E 1–25% F None G I'm not sure	A 100% or B 76–99% or C 51–75%	D 26–50% or E 1–25% or F None	G (I'm not sure)

decision-makers meet the Doer criteria with a single carefully worded question. If your Doer/Non-Doer determination is more complicated (e.g., if they have to meet multiple criteria to be considered a Doer), your matrix should also note how combinations of responses will work together (e.g., if someone does not answer "yes" to every question, are they a Non-Doer, or can they answer "no" to one question and still be considered a Doer?).

Each response option should mean something and be worded clearly. Often, we use yes/no questions and scales (e.g., a 5 or 6-point scale) for Doer/Non-Doer questions. Scales that have fewer options (e.g., "always, sometimes, never") don't give the respondent much to choose from, and they also don't provide us with as much information about the respondent, which can make it more challenging to decide which group to place them in. It's especially important to have a more detailed list of response options when we are only asking one question to determine who is a Doer. For example, because we only used one question to determine Doer or Non-Doer status for our reusable example, we provided six clearly differentiated options ("None, 1–25%, 26–50%, 51–75%, 76–99%, and all," rather than providing fewer, less specific options like "none, few, most, all"). No matter how many response options you provide, make sure you're clear on which responses make someone a Doer vs. a Non-Doer.

Finally, make sure you offer people the option to answer "I'm not sure" and determine which responses would classify someone as a "neither":

Offer people the option to answer "I'm not sure":
You'll notice that we have offered the option to respond "I'm not sure" to our Doer/Non-Doer question. This is because we don't want people to pick a response that does not accurately reflect reality. If someone truly doesn't know how to respond, we don't want them to just respond arbitrarily. Usually, anyone that responds "I'm not sure" to any of the Doer or Non-Doer questions will need to be counted as a "neither," because we won't be able to accurately determine whether they fit better into the Doer or Non-Doer category. These "neithers" will *not* be included in the Doer/Non-Doer analysis. However, note that if you are using your BDA to collect baseline data about your priority audience, you can still allow this person to complete the survey; as long as they passed the screening questions, they are still part of your priority audience.

Special cases of "neithers":
Ideally, you won't need to classify anyone as a "neither," because if we have to exclude too many respondents, it might be difficult for us to find enough responses to have at least 45 Doers and 45 Non-Doers. But there may be unique cases where you decide that if someone provides a certain combination of responses, you can't confidently decide whether they should be considered a Doer or a Non-Doer. For example, this might be the case if a respondent answered one question as a Doer—they compost regularly—but then answered another question as a Non-Doer—they haven't composted in the past week.

Write questions to uncover behavioral drivers

Now it's time to write the questions that will help you identify your audience's behavioral drivers. We provided examples of questions for each driver in the first half of this chapter, such as "What would make it easier to [behavior]?," which you can use as a starting point for your survey.

The behavior part of your audience-behavior statement is what would go in place of the [behavior] in the sample questions we provided above, as in "What would make it easier to bike to work?"

Not all questions about drivers will include the [behavior] part in them. Some drivers questions (like those getting at the perceived severity of an environmental problem) are not asking about the behavior specifically, so you would not include the behavior in the question. For example, "Does air pollution affect you or the people you care about?" is about a specific issue that a behavior [bike to work] addresses, not about the behavior itself.

Select which drivers questions to include

As mentioned earlier, ideally you can include at least one question for each of the drivers you learned about above. However, this can make for a fairly long survey, which may not always be feasible or appropriate. So, at a minimum, your survey should include these driver questions:

One perceived positive consequences question (Open-ended)	What, if anything, do you see as personally beneficial about [behavior]?
One perceived negative consequences question (Open-ended)	What, if anything, do you see as the disadvantages of [behavior]?

By asking these first two drivers questions about perceived consequences in an open-ended format, you aren't biasing your audience with a list of positive or negative consequences.

One means question (Open-ended)	What makes it difficult to [behavior]? or What would make it easier to [behavior]?

Asking an open-ended question like this can uncover many of the means-based drivers, such as *ability*, or whether there is an inhibiting policy in place.

One or two motivation question(s) (Open- or closed-ended)	*Social Norms:* Social norms are one of the most powerful drivers of our behavior, so in almost all cases, you should ask about them. Because social influences often operate outside of our awareness, they can be easy to overlook and don't often show up as answers to open-ended questions about consequences. In the extremely rare cases where there is no social component to the desired behavior, you would skip this. (However, keep in mind that we as researchers could be overlooking relevant social influences.) *Importance:* You might prioritize a question for this driver when you have reason to believe that the audience has competing priorities that would need to be addressed. *Values or Identities:* If you don't already have this information about your audience and you anticipate that your initiative will need to target some of the audience's underlying drivers like value systems, identities, etc., then we would recommend asking questions about these in your BDA.
Zero or one memory question (Open- or closed-ended)	It can be helpful to ask "what would help you remember to [behavior]?" when you have reason to believe memory is a key driver (e.g., remembering to take reusable bags with you to the grocery store) or you want to design memory solutions (e.g., a reusable bag that can fold up so small it can fit on your keychain). However, we often do not ask a memory question—in lieu of asking an extra means or motivation question—and instead design our shifters with memory in mind. It is safe to assume we could all use help with our memory!

Which drivers you choose to ask about will depend on what you already know about your audience. If your prior primary and secondary research has already revealed to you a lot about certain overarching characteristics of your audience (e.g., values and identities), then your BDA can be more focused on drivers specific to the behavior (e.g., self-efficacy) or to the issue (e.g., perceived importance). But if you don't have general audience information yet, you may choose to ask about things like values or identity.

Word questions differently for Doers and Non-Doers

When you conduct this survey in person, or when you use advanced survey tools like Qualtrics™, you may be able to ask Doers and Non-Doers questions with slightly different wording. For example, you would ask Doers, "what are the benefits of [behavior]?" and ask Non-Doers, "what might be the benefits of [behavior]?" If you can't include different versions of the questions for Doers and Non-Doers (such as through an online survey), you can include both versions of the wording in the same question—for example, "What are (or might be) the benefits of [behavior]?"

Write questions to identify relevant demographic information

In the INITIATE phase, you may have collected demographic information about your audience such as their age, gender, ethnicity, preferred language, literacy level, religion, income, employment, education level, political affiliation, marital status, family size, health and disability status, and home ownership status, among other things. You likely used at least one demographic factor to select your priority audience.

In UNCOVER, there are several reasons we may want to include demographic questions in our BDA survey:

- **To screen for BDA eligibility:** If you limited your priority audience to people of a certain demographic (such as people of a certain age and income level) during INITIATE, then you'll only want people with those characteristics to take your BDA survey. You will need to include questions about these demographics to screen survey participants, unless you can ensure that you are only surveying people that meet this criteria (such as if you are only surveying in a particular city).

- **To assess how representative your sample is:** Collecting demographic data in your BDA will help you assess whether the sample population that took your survey "represents" the actual audience population in terms of factors like gender, age, race and ethnicity, language spoken, and income. Refer to METHODS: Process Chapter 6 for more on representative samples.

- **To further narrow your audience or identify subgroups of your audience in the DESIGN phase:** You may have already used at least one demographic factor to choose your priority audience (such as location or language spoken). But you may want to ask about additional demographic factors in your BDA, especially if you think that a demographic factor might cause your audience to react differently to your initiative. This will allow you to further narrow your audience or tailor your initiative to different audience segments in the DESIGN phase.

- **To discover how demographic factors are influencing behavioral drivers:** Demographic factors can influence behavior directly and indirectly. For example, someone's income can affect their ability (*means*) to do a behavior, but it can also affect their *motivation*, such as by influencing their perception of an issue's relative importance.

While demographic factors *can* influence behavior, it's important that we don't assume that a demographic factor is driving behavior. Demographic information is insufficient for understanding and predicting behavior: on their own, demographics don't get at the "why" or the motivation behind behavior, so they should never be used as a replacement for research that uncovers an audience's beliefs and perceptions. If we rely on demographics alone or don't think about them critically, we might make incorrect assumptions about why an audience is or isn't taking action. For example, just because someone is a parent who needs to drop off their children at school in the morning doesn't mean they will automatically be unwilling or unable to bike to work. Rather than assuming they are unwilling or unable because they are a parent, we should ask them about their drivers for biking to work. We may find that some are, or could be (through our behavior initiative), motivated to bike with their kids to school on the way to work as a form of bonding or instilling an exercise routine in their children.

Write questions to gather additional information

A BDA is a great opportunity to collect data from your audience that you didn't get a chance to collect in INITIATE. While the main purpose of a BDA is to uncover drivers, you can also use it to collect baseline data if you don't have that already, or to ask other questions (that don't fit into one of the categories above) that help you further narrow your audience.

Questions that provide baseline data

Your Behavioral Drivers Analysis can be a great opportunity to collect baseline data if you haven't already collected it through secondary or primary research. As discussed in INITIATE: Process Chapter 2, we want to collect baseline data so that we can measure whether our initiative resulted in changes to environmental outcomes as well as behaviors. For example, if we are deploying a new employee carpooling program, we'll want to know what percentage of employees already carpool, and how often, so that we can later see whether our initiative resulted in changes in this behavior. If we don't already have this data, the BDA is one opportunity to collect self-reported information on these metrics. We can also use the BDA to collect baseline data on other outcomes of interest, such as changes in beliefs, knowledge, and skills.

Keep in mind that a BDA is not suitable for collecting baseline data if we aren't surveying a sample that is relatively representative of our entire priority audience. If you're going to use your BDA to collect baseline data, then you should seek to recruit a large and representative sample from your audience.

Other questions to help you better understand or narrow your audience

The Doer/Non-Doer and drivers questions you ask are going to tell you a lot about your audience and their behavior. However, you might want to ask additional questions to help you better understand or narrow your audience. For example, you might want to find out who in the audience would be willing to sign a pledge to do the behavior, or ask any additional questions about criteria from INITIATE, like impact or receptivity, that might not have been captured in the other categories. Below, we profile one such example: receptivity.

Receptivity questions

Even if you asked about or considered receptivity in the INITIATE phase, there are reasons why you might decide to ask your audience questions about their receptivity (e.g., willingness, interest) to adopting the behavior again in your BDA. First, asking about receptivity can help you identify the most receptive subgroups within the audience you've selected. By determining whether and how many Non-Doers would be willing to start doing the behavior, you can identify "low-hanging fruit"—the Non-Doers who are most likely to adopt the behavior. Second, you can check to make sure that creating an initiative around this behavior still makes sense—are there enough Non-Doers who are willing to change that your initiative can still be impactful? Additionally, a willingness question is also a good way to get data for social norms messaging (see BELONGING: Building Block Chapter 1). If the majority of people are *willing* to start doing a behavior, you can emphasize their willingness as a norm even when most people aren't actually doing it yet. Finally, as discussed above, if your behavior is brand new, asking about willingness can help you define potential Doers to use as substitutes for actual Doers.

Example questions to measure receptivity include:

- How willing are you to [behavior]?
- How interested are you in [behavior]?

Put it all together to conduct your BDA

Once you have your questions drafted, you'll need to assemble them into a full survey before you administer it to your audience. It's important to consider all aspects of your survey, including how the introduction will sound and how the questions are ordered to ensure that all the pieces fit together into a cohesive, unbiased, and easy-to-navigate experience for your audience. More guidance on surveys can be found in METHODS: Process Chapter 6.

Structure your Behavioral Drivers Analysis

In the box on page 148 is an outline of our recommended survey structure. If you're able, ask at least one question for every driver that we outlined in the first half of this chapter. We recommend that you use the structure outlined on page 148 even when you administer a shorter survey.

It's essential to ask open-ended questions about perceived consequences (positive and negative) before asking about any of the other drivers to avoid leading the respondents and biasing their answers. For example, if you asked a question asking whether doing a behavior is difficult to remember, and then asked the open-ended question, "what makes it difficult to do [behavior]," respondents might be predisposed by the previous question to say they can't remember. We also recommend asking your open-ended questions about a particular driver first, followed by any closed-ended questions you are including about the same driver. For example, ask an open-ended question about perceived social acceptability of doing the behavior before asking a closed-ended question that lists groups that might approve or disapprove, because otherwise respondents might be predisposed to list the same groups in their open-ended response.

Recommended BDA Survey Structure

1. Eligibility/Screening question(s)

2. Doer/Non-Doer question(s)

3. Motivation: Perceived positive consequences question (open-ended)
   - e.g., "What do you see as personally beneficial about [behavior]?"

4. Motivation: Perceived negative consequences question (open-ended)
   - e.g., "What, if anything, do you see as the disadvantages of [behavior]?"

5. Means: Perceived ability question (open-ended)
   - e.g., "What makes it difficult to [behavior]?" or "What would make it easier to [behavior]?

6. Other means drivers question(s)

7. Other motivation drivers question(s)

8. Memory drivers question(s)

9. (Relevant) Demographics (closed-ended questions)

10. Other questions you need for baseline data, to narrow your audience, etc. (These can be interspersed above; they do not necessarily need to be at the end of the survey)

11. Is there anything else you would like to share? (open-ended)

Conduct your survey

Once you have created a BDA survey that asks the necessary questions in an unbiased, easy to follow way, you can begin administering it to your audience. We encourage you to read METHODS: Process Chapter 6 for more tips about the ins and outs of conducting survey research, such as how to recruit participants and how to reduce bias.

Keep in mind that because you may need to remove some people from your BDA, you will likely need to survey more than 90 people to obtain at least 45 Doers and 45 Non-Doers in your sample.

Analyze and Interpret Your Behavioral Drivers Analysis Results

Now it's time to analyze the data you collected through your survey. This step may seem daunting if you've never done this before, but it's the big reveal! Between UNCOVER and METHODS: Process Chapter 6, we'll present basic instructions on conducting the analyses that are most relevant to your BDA, but other analyses can be conducted to dive deeper into the data. All of this can be accomplished in Excel®, Google Sheets, or a more advanced statistical software package (e.g., SPSS®, R, STATA®, Python). If you've never worked with data before, you might consider getting outside help. But even if you can't do advanced analysis, simply tallying up responses can give you helpful information. By running the statistics, we're using a scientific approach to identify drivers with greater certainty.

Get to know your participants and your data

Here are some of the first steps to take to analyze the results of your BDA.

Prepare your data

Data preparation is a vital step in analyzing data collected for your BDA or any other study. If you aren't familiar with how to do this, check out METHODS: Process Chapter 6, where we briefly discuss and provide additional resources for preparing qualitative and quantitative data.

Get the big picture of your data

Especially if you are using this survey to collect baseline data, you want to get a sense of the overall results of your survey (the "big picture") of your sample and their data before removing the "neithers" from the data. For example, what percentage of all respondents currently carpool? How often?

Assess whether you have a representative sample

One of the first "big picture" things to assess is the degree to which you've recruited a representative sample. Regardless of whether you have the ability to survey more people to make your sample more representative, knowing the discrepancy helps with interpretation of your results. In METHODS: Process Chapter 6, we discuss why representative samples are important and how to do your best to obtain one.

Remove "neithers"

Remember how we mentioned that sometimes people don't fit neatly into Doer or Non-Doer groups? At this stage, it's time to exclude these people from our analysis. While some survey platforms can be set up to exclude people who provide certain responses, sometimes we will need to manually determine Doer and Non-Doer status and remove participants based on their responses after everyone has taken the survey. We can remove participants using a filter in our statistical software package or by deleting their row of data. But be careful! You should always keep a backup copy with all of your responses.

Understand which results represent significant drivers

When analyzing the results of our BDA, the most important thing we are looking for is whether there are differences between Doer and Non-Doer responses. Specifically, the most important results are those where:

- a barrier is reported at significantly greater levels by Non-Doers than by Doers
- a benefit or motivator is reported at significantly greater levels by Doers than by Non-Doers

Results that meet these criteria reveal what we call *significant drivers.* These results reveal the barriers and motivators that are driving behavior, and they shed light on

---

What Does It Mean to Find a "Significant Difference Between Doers and Non-Doers"?

Without checking for significance, we don't know whether the differences we find are the result of error (or chance) or a real, meaningful difference between our Doers and Non-Doers. Ideally, we can conduct a *statistical test of significance*, which tells us the probability that we found a difference when there isn't actually a difference at the population level (i.e., that we found a difference due to error or chance). If you cannot conduct a statistical test of significance, such as a t-test or chi-square, a good rule of thumb is that a difference of at least 15% between Doers and Non-Doers is likely to be significant. For now, just keep this explanation of significance in mind. Later, you'll calculate whether any of your BDA results are significant.

---

potential leverage points—the places where shifters will be the most effective in encouraging the desired behavior. Below, we explain why these results are most important and why other results should be deprioritized (including significant results that don't fit this pattern).

Result: The barrier is significantly more common among Non-Doers

When a barrier, like not having the time to do something or not perceiving a problem as important, is highly common, or prevalent, among Non-Doers but significantly less common among Doers, it's likely that this barrier is driving behavior. We can infer that this barrier is stopping Non-Doers from doing the behavior, and that Doers either overcame this barrier at one point or didn't face it in the first place. Therefore, it's likely that this barrier is (at least in part) driving whether people are Doers and Non-Doers, and that by addressing or removing this barrier, we can help Non-Doers adopt the behavior.

For example, let's say that we want to know why some people are not taking advantage of a program offering free LED lightbulbs to homeowners and renters. In our BDA, we find that Non-Doers are significantly more likely to have trouble navigating the online order form than Doers. By helping Non-Doers navigate the order forms (such as by simplifying the website or providing paper forms as alternatives), we can make it more likely that they will order an LED lightbulb kit.

Sometimes, Non-Doers will share perceptions of negative consequences of a behavior that do not align with reality. For example, in Root Solutions' work to replace desktop printers with shared multifunction printers on college campuses, Non-Doers often incorrectly believed (at greater rates than Doers) that shared multifunction printers are less secure than desktop printers. (In fact, these shared multifunction printers have stronger security features like "secure print," which require ID cards or codes to release print jobs.) Even though these perceptions about barriers aren't accurate, they're still drivers that we should seek to address by correcting the misperception.

While the above example was about perceived negative consequences, it's also common to uncover misperceptions related to perceived social acceptability. Non-Doers often perceive that the desired behavior is not the norm, or is not socially acceptable, while Doers are more likely to think that the desired behavior is the norm. In these cases, in the DESIGN phase, we would select and design shifters from BELONGING: Building Block Chapter 1 (all about social norms) to correct Non-Doer misperceptions.

Result: The motivator is significantly more common among Doers

The other time a significant driver arises is when Doers report a benefit at a greater rate than Non-Doers. This may indicate that this benefit is motivating Doers, while Non-Doers simply aren't aware of it. For example, Doers' positive perceptions of the behavior sometimes form only after they engage in the behavior, so Non-Doers would naturally be unaware of those benefits. When this is the case, we can make these benefits more visible to Non-Doers to encourage behavior change.

However, we can't always assume that because Non-Doers don't report a benefit, they simply aren't aware of it. In some cases, Non-Doers just don't see something as personally beneficial (i.e., it's not motivating to them). For example, many Doers might note that taking the bus to and from work allows them to relax and "clear their heads" as they transition from home to work or vice versa. If you message or amplify this benefit and it's something Non-Doers haven't considered, they may be delighted by the prospect of gaining this downtime. But there's also a possibility that your Non-Doers are aware that the bus provides this opportunity, but they don't personally see it as a benefit (maybe they don't feel that they can relax on a public bus, or they just don't really care about the ability to relax on the bus). Note that in this case, messaging about the benefit is unlikely to motivate them.

Understand why to deprioritize all other results

We should deprioritize any result that does not fit the above criteria. Here we'll discuss the other types of results you'll come across (significant results that don't fit the required pattern, and nonsignificant results) and why they should be deprioritized. As you'll see, these results can provide insights that help us understand our audience, but do not reveal what is driving behavior.

Deprioritize results that fit the opposite pattern of drivers

It may at first seem counterintuitive to deprioritize significant results, but we want to deprioritize statistically significant results that fit the opposite pattern of the two types of results that classify drivers. Below, we explain why these results are not considered drivers of behavior, and why they should be deprioritized. (Note that in addition to being unimportant, these findings tend to be relatively uncommon.)

Result: The barrier is significantly more common for Doers

Sometimes, Doers will bring up a concern or barrier that Non-Doers don't express. Since Doers regularly engage in the behavior, they may be well-attuned to the inconveniences or difficulties of doing the behavior (even though these things aren't stopping them from engaging in the behavior). For example, regular bike riders might note specific barriers related to riding in the rain, infrastructure, or road conditions that Non-Doers might not even be aware of as possible barriers. Since these perceived negative consequences aren't stopping current Doers, but may just be small inconveniences, they're not drivers of behavior and should therefore not be a focus of your initiative. While we could address these barriers, there are likely to be other reasons that Non-Doers aren't doing the behavior, which should be addressed first. We can act to address these perceptions at a later date, to help Doers continue to do or improve upon the behavior, but the priority is to get Non-Doers on board first.

Result: The motivator is significantly more common for Non-Doers

Sometimes, a significantly greater number of Non-Doers will report a benefit of the behavior than Doers. This result does not reveal a driver of behavior: Non-Doers aren't doing the behavior despite being aware of this benefit, and Doers must be doing the behavior for other reasons. For example, Non-Doers might report the environmental benefits of biking to work at much greater rates than Doers. This shows that environmental motivations are likely not why Doers are biking to work, and these motivations are also not causing Non-Doers to bike to work (despite being aware that it's better for the environment to do so).

Note that this result tends to be uncommon, because Doers are usually more likely to identify any benefits or advantages of a behavior than Non-Doers are. When this result does occur, keep in mind that it might be because Non-Doers mistakenly believe that the behavior will deliver this benefit. It goes without saying that if the benefit being identified by the Non-Doers is inaccurate (it's not actually a benefit that this behavior provides), you should not seek to promote this benefit.

If this benefit identified by Non-Doers is a real benefit of doing the behavior, you could include this benefit in your messaging, but it is unlikely to have much of an impact; Non-Doers already note this as a benefit, and they still aren't doing the behavior. Thus, this is not a high-priority result.

Deprioritize nonsignificant results that are common for both Doers and Non-Doers

In general, we should deprioritize any nonsignificant results, even if there is a response that is highly common for everyone. Your BDA might reveal a factor that is highly prevalent among both our Doers and Non-Doers, but for which there is not a significant difference between the two groups. For example, let's say that 56% of Doers and 58% of Non-Doers reported that there was a long wait time for the bus. It might be tempting to start brainstorming shifters to address long wait times.

But let's take a moment to think about what this means. A *barrier* that is reported at similarly high rates for Doers and Non-Doers is *not* a driver of behavior: our Doers are engaging in the behavior despite this barrier. And a *benefit* that is reported at similarly high rates for Doers and Non-Doers is also *not* a driver of behavior: our Non-Doers know about this benefit and are still not engaging in this behavior. Thus, no matter how counterintuitive it may seem, we should not prioritize acting on these highly prevalent factors. (At least not yet!) Let's consider these examples:

- **Barriers:** Let's say that the majority of both groups reported that a barrier to using their programmable thermostat is that it's difficult to program, but there was no significant difference between Doers and Non-Doers. If we made programming the thermostat easier for everyone, we would not be addressing a driver of using a properly programmed thermostat; we know it's not a driver because Doers are still using it even though they also said that programming it was difficult. Note that it doesn't hurt to try to address a barrier that is commonly cited by both Doers and Non-Doers, but it is not a top priority. If a majority of both groups found programming the thermostat to be difficult, this is something that we could improve (especially if it's relatively easy to fix), but it shouldn't take priority over addressing any of our significant drivers. Addressing this may also be more useful to promote behavioral maintenance later on, for example, to help Doers more quickly reprogram their thermostat when the seasons change.

- **Benefits:** Perhaps the majority of Doers and Non-Doers identify "the ability to work during the commute" as an important benefit of taking the bus. Because our Non-Doers are already aware of this benefit, and yet they are still not taking the bus, messaging this benefit wouldn't be all that useful for shifting Non-Doers to adopt this behavior. Messaging the benefit of being able to work from the bus doesn't hurt, but it most likely will not positively influence Doers or Non-Doers to a meaningful degree, so it shouldn't be prioritized above other significant results.

Analyze your data to identify the highest priority results

We've introduced you to which types of results are most important and which should be deprioritized. Here, we outline the calculation and analysis steps necessary to classify these results.

Determine how common the result is among Doers and Non-Doers

The first step in determining what is influencing behavior is to determine the prevalence of each response among Doers and Non-Doers. The **prevalence** of a response refers to the proportion of the group that gave that response (e.g., the number of group members who said "yes" divided by the total number of group members).

Let's say that we surveyed 100 restaurant decision-makers about providing only reusable serviceware for their dine-in customers. Of these decision-makers, 53 happened to be Doers, and 47 were Non-Doers. To measure the driver of self-efficacy, we asked them, "Are you confident in your team's ability to serve dine-in customers using only reusable serviceware?" with the option to answer either "yes" (representing higher self-efficacy) or "no" (representing lower self-efficacy). To calculate the prevalence of self-efficacy among Doers, start by counting the number of Doers who said "yes" and divide this by the total number of Doers in the sample. Repeat this process to calculate the prevalence of the response for Non-Doers. For example, our survey results might indicate that 85% (45 of 53) of Doers responded that they felt confident in their ability to provide reusable serviceware, whereas only 28% (13 of 47) of Non-Doers said they felt confident, indicating that self-efficacy is more prevalent among Doers relative to Non-Doers.

Determine the size of the difference between Doers and Non-Doers

To make use of our data, it's not enough to just consider whether there *are* differences between Doers and Non-Doers. We also want to look at the *size* of the differences between the two groups. The bigger the gap between Doers and Non-Doers, the more likely it is that this factor is driving whether people are doing the behavior or not.

To calculate the size of the difference between Doers and Non-Doers, subtract the smaller percentage from the larger percentage. This gives us the **prevalence difference** between the two groups.

Following our example, 85% of Doers minus 28% of Non-Doers equals a difference in prevalence of 57% between groups for self-efficacy. That's huge! Let's say that another question on our survey revealed that 72% of Doers and 60% of Non-Doers believed that it was important to reduce the use of single-use plastic (*perceived importance*). Here, the gap between Doers and Non-Doers is not as large (only 12%). These results suggest that perceived importance may not be driving behavior as much as self-efficacy.

Looking at our results graphically makes the size of prevalence differences between Doers and Non-Doers more obvious and helps us compare multiple results side by side, as you can see in the graph comparing the results of these two questions (see Figure 1.3.1).

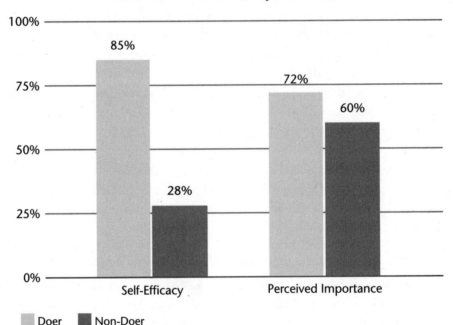

Behavioral Drivers Analysis Results

Fig: 1.3.1:
% of Doers and Non-Doers who answered "yes" and "very important" to each item.

Questions:
Are you confident in your ability to serve dine-in customers using only reusable serviceware? (Yes/No)
In your opinion, how important is it to reduce the use of single-use plastics? (Not at all important/Very important)

Once you've calculated the prevalence for your results, you can start to classify them based on what pattern they fit (a motivator that is more prevalent for Doers, a motivator that is more prevalent for Non-Doers, etc.) If you identify any results that should be deprioritized (i.e., results that don't match the pattern of drivers as described earlier), you don't have to take them any further into the process (you don't need to bother with calculating their significance). However, you can return to these deprioritized results if you find that you don't have any significant drivers—we talk more about this below.

Determine whether the differences between Doers and Non-Doers are significant

We determined the size of the differences between Doers and Non-Doers, but now we need to measure the *significance* of those differences. Continuing with our restaurant example: since we found differences between Doers and Non-Doers for both self-efficacy and perceived importance, we might be tempted to conclude that *both* factors are driving behavior. But there is still a key question to answer: Are the differences we found between our Doers and Non-Doers due to chance or error, or are the differences *significant*—real and meaningful?

Generally speaking, a difference between Doers and Non-Doers of 15% or more is likely to be significant (as long as we have the recommended sample size of at least 90 people).[13] So we can be pretty confident that the 57% difference we saw between Doers and Non-Doers on self-efficacy is significant. On the other hand, we can't be as confident about the much smaller 12% difference between Doers and Non-Doers on their perceptions of importance.

However, there's a way to be even more confident about both results: while the 15% rule of thumb is helpful if we have limited resources or statistical capabilities, the best way to ensure that our findings are not simply due to chance (especially for smaller differences) is to conduct a statistical test of significance. Without doing a significance test, it's difficult to know whether the differences we see are the result of error (or chance) or a real, meaningful difference between our Doers and Non-Doers. A statistically significant difference between groups (a p-value smaller than .05) tells us that there's less than a 5% chance (i.e., a low probability) of obtaining the difference that we found when there isn't actually a difference within our priority audience. Therefore, we can be more confident in results with p-values of .05 or smaller than those with larger p-values.

With our restaurant decision-makers, we find that the difference between Doers and Non-Doers for self-efficacy is significant (with a p-value smaller than .001), but that the difference for perceived importance is not significant (with a p-value of .20). This confirms what we hypothesized above—that self-efficacy is driving behavior more than perceived importance.

In the METHODS: Process Chapter 6, we provide additional resources to help you with statistical analysis. If you aren't familiar with how to do significance testing, there are many books and websites that could help, or you could partner with graduate students or professors with statistical expertise. But if you don't have the resources to do significance testing on your results, don't fret. Even using the methods we described above (calculating the prevalence difference and looking at the results graphically) can tell you a lot about your audience and their drivers.

Interpreting and Communicating Significant Differences With Prevalence Ratios

Another way to characterize the size of the difference in prevalence between our Doers and Non-Doers is to calculate the *prevalence ratio*. This tells us that a response is "X times more prevalent among one group than it is for the other group." Thinking about it this way can make the interpretation and communication of significant differences more accessible.

The prevalence ratio is calculated by dividing the larger prevalence by the smaller prevalence. A ratio of 1 indicates that the prevalence is the same among our two groups. The larger the number, the greater the magnitude of the difference between the Doers and Non-Doers, and the more likely it is to be an important driver. Following our example of self-efficacy among restaurant decision-makers, 85% of Doers divided by 28% of Non-Doers (85 divided by 28) gives us a prevalence ratio of 3.04. This means that Doers said they were confident in their ability to provide reusable serviceware three times more often than Non-Doers. Or, in other words, Doers are 3 times more likely than Non-Doers to say that they are confident.

Finalize your list of high priority results

Now that you have analyzed and interpreted the results of your BDA, you'll want to loosely prioritize your findings before moving on to DESIGN. You will use the criteria above to prioritize and then consider which category—Means, Motivation, or Memory—the driver falls under. You will design shifters around your highest priority results in DESIGN: Process Chapter 4.

Sort results into significant drivers and all other results

First and foremost, your highest priority results are the statistically significant results that fit the criteria for significant drivers (i.e., the more prevalent barriers for Non-Doers and the more prevalent benefits or motivators for Doers). If you found many significant drivers (with a p-value smaller than .05 or, if you aren't calculating significance, a difference greater than 15%), then your highest priority among them are those with the largest gaps.

If you didn't find any significant drivers, however, the next most important results are those that match the same patterns as our significant drivers, but are not statistically significant (i.e., those with the greatest prevalence gap).

You should carefully consider whether to act on all other results: among the remaining types of results (other nonsignificant results and any results in the opposite direction of significant drivers), we recommend prioritizing results where many Non-Doers have noted a barrier. Just keep in mind that because this is likely not a significant driver, addressing this barrier may have little to no effect.

Loosely prioritize the results in terms of Means, Motivation, and Memory

For the high priority results you identified in the previous step, we also recommend considering which category of drivers each result falls under—Means, Motivation, or Memory. To begin, label each high priority result with which "M" category it belongs to. Refer back to our general discussion of drivers (and Table 1.3.1) in the beginning of this chapter to find which "M" category your driver belongs to.

Thinking about our results in terms of Means, Motivation, and Memory can help us to prioritize them. Specifically, MMM can help us think through which "ingredients" are missing and which drivers might be most and least difficult to address. Considering your results in terms of broad MMM categories can help you think about what is missing that might help your audience adopt the behavior. Do your Non-Doers have the ability to do the behavior, but aren't motivated? Are they motivated but can't remember to do the behavior? Can they remember to do it but they don't have the ability to follow through?

Thinking about your drivers in terms of MMM can also help you consider which drivers might be easiest or most difficult to address. While we aren't yet in the DESIGN phase (that comes next), it can be helpful to begin thinking on a broad level about how you might address a driver. Are there any drivers that might be more difficult to address (e.g., it would require more resources)? Conversely, are there any that would be relatively easy to address? Note that you will also have another opportunity to consider feasibility after you've brainstormed a robust list of potential shifters in DESIGN.

You may find that in some cases, the considerations above may contradict one another. Regardless of whether you prioritize drivers in this step, you may still find it helpful to think about how your results relate to one another and to begin the process of brainstorming how you might address these drivers in the DESIGN phase—are your shifters going to focus on means, motivation, or memory, or a combination thereof?

Memory-related drivers

If your audience has high ability and/or motivation, all they may need is a well-timed reminder. For example, if you uncovered that your audience has no significant barriers related to means or motivation, but you did discover that an inability to remember to do the behavior was a driver, you could focus your brainstorming on shifters that cue the behavior. Even when motivation is low, if the behavior is easy enough, cues can be sufficient to trigger a desired behavior. Cues like reminders and prompts are "low-hanging fruit," as they are generally easier to create and implement than shifters that address means or motivation. Just remember that memory alone is not sufficient: if means and motivation are both low, increasing memory alone likely won't do much.

Means-related drivers

When behaviors are difficult, it requires greater motivation to take action, but when behaviors are easy, they require little to no motivation to complete. Therefore, if you have uncovered means-based barriers *and* low motivation, we recommend starting by trying to make the behavior easier before trying to increase your audience's motivation. Focusing on increasing someone's means to do the behavior (by improving their ability or making the behavior itself easier) is usually more cost-effective and less complicated than trying to increase someone's motivation to overcome obstacles on their own (increasing motivation is tough!). Sometimes, if you can make the behavior easy or automatic enough, no motivation is required at all!

Motivation-related drivers

Increasing motivation can be the most difficult driver to address, so generally speaking, we recommend working to increase motivation after any means and memory barriers have already been addressed. However, if a behavior is very difficult and you are unable to make the behavior easier to complete, you may have no choice but to try to increase the audience's motivation—if a behavior is difficult, the audience's motivation must be high for them to take action.

• • •

Ultimately, means, motivation, and memory all matter, and it's not always easy to prioritize based on these considerations. You might need to address all three of them, or you might only need to address one of them. You'll return to your list of high priority results in the next phase, DESIGN.

Conclusion

By this point in the *Making Shift Happen* process, you've done most of the necessary preliminary work for setting up a well-informed, well-planned initiative that centers on a specific behavior and audience. In the UNCOVER phase, you've learned a lot about your audience by conducting your own Behavioral Drivers Analysis to uncover insights about what drives their behavior. Now that you're equipped with a list of the drivers that are most important, impactful, and meaningful, you're ready to design your initiative!

Design

NOW THAT YOU ARE EQUIPPED with the extensive preparation and research you did in INITIATE and UNCOVER, you're ready to begin designing solutions to shift your audience's behavior. In this phase (DESIGN), you will use what you've learned about your issue area, audience, and behavior to design a complete suite of behavioral *shifters*, evidence-based behavior change solutions, to achieve your goal.

The basic idea underlying the design of your initiative is to address the barriers and amplify the motivators that you uncovered during your BDA. Your solution can take the form of a new product, service, communication strategy, policy, choice architecture, or a combination of these. These shifters must address the specific barriers the audience faces and should use the most effective behavior change techniques to motivate and inspire them. You'll use science-backed shifters from the BEHAVIORAL Building Blocks™ to accomplish this.

A Look Ahead: DESIGN

Determine Your Audience Segmentation Approach

Segment based on meaningful and practical characteristics
Decide if you will use an undifferentiated, concentrated, or differentiated approach

Generate Shifter Ideas Using Your Drivers-to-Shifters Roadmap

Brainstorm shifters to address drivers related to Memory, Means, and Motivation
Look to initiatives that have already been attempted

Evaluate and Prioritize Potential Shifters

Consider impact
Consider feasibility
Select the shifters with the highest potential

Make Your Shifter Ideas More Concrete

Determine the content of your shifters
Determine the delivery mode
Choose the best messenger

Carefully consider placement
Determine the ideal timing to launch shifters

Assemble Shifters as a Suite

Prototype Your Shifters
What is prototyping?
What shifters will you prototype?
What kind of feedback do you want?
Create your prototype
Test and evaluate the prototypes

Before you begin: do you need to refine or revise your priority behavior?

Before you begin designing shifters, pause to ensure that you are adapting as much as possible to the information you discovered during the UNCOVER phase. Does the priority behavior you selected in INITIATE still make sense given your new insights about the audience? For example, did you realize that the original behavior you chose was unrealistic? If your priority behavior was biking to work three days a week, but you found in your Behavioral Drivers Analysis that much of your audience lives too far to make even biking once per week feasible, you likely need to select a different behavior, such as carpooling.

Questions to help you refine your priority behavior include:

- Did you discover that a different priority behavior is better suited to address the problem?
- Did you originally define the behavior too ambitiously (e.g., asking your audience to walk to work too far or too often)?
- Can your audience reasonably do the priority behavior? Are there too many barriers that are prohibitively difficult to change or outside of your control?
- Is the behavior opposed to the audience's values, identities, or ideologies?

Determine Your Audience Segmentation Approach

In INITIATE, you began the process of *audience segmentation:* using the demographic, geographic, psychological, and behavioral characteristics of the audience to identify subgroups with the aim of determining who to prioritize with your initiative and how to tailor your shifters to one or more of those subgroups. Now, in DESIGN, you have the opportunity to use what you uncovered in your BDA to further narrow your priority audience. Even just dividing your audience into two groups based on one characteristic is a basic form of audience segmentation. Or, if you can't or don't want to further narrow your audience, you may decide to design different sets of shifters for different subgroups within your audience. Even if you ultimately decide to do neither, going through this process of considering how different segments of your audience might respond differently to your shifters will help you to design your initiative more strategically.

Here is an example of how someone in the DESIGN phase might choose to segment their audience based on insights from their BDA. Let's say you decided on an initiative to encourage smokers in San Francisco to properly dispose of their cigarette butts. You began narrowing down your audience in INITIATE and have so far gone from "everyone in San Francisco that smokes" to "young adult smokers":

- Everyone in San Francisco that smokes
  → Young adult smokers in San Francisco (aged 18–25)

Then, in your BDA, you identified that many young adult San Francisco smokers litter their cigarette butts because they perceive that it's the norm to litter cigarette butts. You can now further segment your audience based on this information:

- Young adult smokers in San Francisco (aged 18–25)
  → Young adult smokers in San Francisco (aged 18–25) who perceive that the norm is to litter cigarette butts

You can also choose to subdivide this further and further based on other characteristics like language spoken, more precise locations, values and identities, etc. As you can see, you could keep segmenting until you have a relatively homogenous group. But even just segmenting a bit can go a long way. For example, if you are seeking to reduce cigarette butt littering in San Francisco, even just segmenting by citizens and tourists can enable you to design tailored shifters, which are likely to make your initiative more effective.

Whether or not (and how) you segment your audience will depend on many factors, including the characteristics of your audience, the resources available to you, and how much you eventually want your initiative to scale to other populations (see IMPLEMENT: Process Chapter 5 for more about scaling). When you have an audience composed of diverse subgroups, the more you segment and subsequently tailor your shifters, the more likely they are to be effective. However, this also requires more effort and resources up front, both to identify these segments and to design many different versions of your shifters. On the other hand, trying to design a single shifter to influence multiple diverse subgroups can also be challenging. You have to make tradeoffs about how narrow you want to get with your segments. Here we will discuss various considerations for effective audience segmentation.

Segment based on meaningful and practical characteristics

Just as in INITIATE, you will be deciding whether and how to divide your audience into subgroups (segments) based on their shared characteristics: factors like age, location, income, and language. But this time, you will also be using what you learned about your audience's barriers and motivators from the BDA that you completed in the UNCOVER phase.

While you *can* segment your audience by almost any characteristic, you want to segment based on the most *meaningful* characteristics: those that are most likely to influence how people might respond to various shifters. In addition to creating *meaningful* audience segments, practitioners should also consider whether those segments are *practical*: Are you actually able to deliver the shifters differently based on this characteristic? If not, there is no reason to segment based on the characteristic. For example, if everyone in an office is going to pass by the same sign, this sign can't be tailored for different values, so segmenting by values is not possible.

Many Audience Characteristics, Many Segmentation Methods

There are many characteristics and ways of grouping those characteristics that you can use to segment your audience. Some require asking your audience a set of very specific questions. If you have the ability to ask your audience many questions or survey them several times, you might consider using one of the segmentation methods below. Even if you do not use the specific survey questions suggested by each method, you can still use the main ideas when considering the types of characteristics you will use to segment your audience.

Values Modes:

It's possible to segment your audience via characteristics related to people's core needs, what they value most, and what they want to get out of life.[8] One method of audience segmentation refers to these characteristics as *values modes.* An audience's values modes affect how receptive they are to certain shifters. For example, while some people may want to become involved in cause movements (if you're reading this book, you likely fall into this category), not everyone wants to. In fact, those particularly interested in the esteem of their peers may actively avoid engaging in—or even bringing up—cause movements so as not to risk alienating their peers. When focusing on this audience segment for an environmental initiative, you may find that it's effective not to make it about the environment at all.

Diffusion of Innovation:

We first introduce this theory in INITIATE: Process Chapter 2 as a means of narrowing your audience. Can you segment your audience based on whether they are likely to be early adopters or laggards? If you can identify early adopters, you may want to start your initiative with them as the "low hanging fruit." Then, social proof provided by the innovators can influence the rest of the population to follow suit.[1,9]

Stages of Change:

Consider the Stages of Change model from INITIATE: Process Chapter 2. Your research may indicate that certain segments of your audience are more prepared to act than others. For example, if your audience can be segmented into a group of people in precontemplation and contemplation and another group in the preparation stage, it may make sense to concentrate your efforts on those already preparing to make the change, as they are the "low-hanging fruit."[7]

Decide if you will use an undifferentiated, concentrated, or differentiated approach

The degree to which you can or should segment depends on many factors. In some cases, segmenting your audience will not be in your best interest or even possible. For example, if there is not a clear distinction of subgroups within your audience (e.g., they are all the same age, have similar experiences and values, and share common barriers and motivators), you may neither want nor be able to segment at all. Or, you might be short on resources or have reason to believe that most of the audience will respond similarly to a single set of shifters. In either case, an **undifferentiated approach** can be a good choice. This means that you are applying the same shifters to all segments of the audience (e.g., billboards advertising the benefits of biking where every driver in your priority audience would see it). In this case, you would be designing your shifters based on commonalities across the entire audience to appeal to all of them at once.

When you can or should segment your audience, there are two segmentation approaches to consider, which we detail below. Each approach has its own advantages and disadvantages.

Concentrated approach (narrow audience, tailored shifters)

A **concentrated approach** is a continuation of the process of narrowing your audience based on their characteristics, which you began doing in INITIATE. Here, you will further narrow down your audience to a single segment and deliver an initiative to only that audience segment. For example, rather than attempting to get all people in a city to bike instead of drive to work, you might focus only on those who live close to work and are interested in exercising more, as they will likely be particularly receptive and ready to adopt the desired behavior.

To ensure that you concentrate your initiative on the most promising audience segment, be sure to revisit INITIATE: Process Chapter 2 and consider who will be the most influential, impactful, receptive, etc., to your initiative.

Differentiated approach (multiple audience segments, tailored shifters for each segment)

A **differentiated approach** entails creating a multi-pronged initiative that delivers shifters tailored to each distinct audience segment. For example, you could send emails to parents about how healthy it is for their children to bike to school, but send emails to young professionals with social norms messaging about their peers who are biking to work. Differentiated approaches work well when it is clear what kind of shifter, or version of a shifter, each audience segment would respond to best.

In Table 1.4.1, we highlight several pros and cons for undifferentiated, concentrated, and differentiated approaches.

Table 1.4.1: Audience Segmentation Approaches — Pros and Cons

	Pros	Cons
Undifferentiated (Not Segmented)	Requires only a one-pronged initiative, which may be cheaper and easier to implement	Lower likelihood of success because it is less targeted than the other approaches
Concentrated (Narrow Audience, Tailored Shifters)	Higher likelihood of success than an undifferentiated approach because shifters are designed for a specific segment Less resource-intensive than a differentiated approach: you only have to design a one-pronged initiative and fund its roll out to a smaller audience	Limited scope: The level of impact on the problem is limited because a smaller audience is changing their behavior
Differentiated (Multiple Audience Segments, Tailored Shifters for Each Segment)	Higher likelihood of success than an undifferentiated approach because shifters are tailored to each segment Potential to have the largest impact, because you are tailoring to multiple audience segments	More resource-intensive: You will need to design multiple prongs of the initiative and fund their roll out to multiple audience segments

Once you have determined which segmentation approach your initiative will take, you can begin designing your initiative's shifters.

 Generate Shifter Ideas Using Your Drivers-to-Shifters Roadmap

Now that you've uncovered and prioritized your audience's key barriers and motivators and decided on your audience segmentation approach, you're ready to develop a list of shifter ideas. The shifters you brainstorm should address barriers and amplify motivators by supplying the means, motivation, and memory to incite behavior change. The goal in this step is to brainstorm shifters that directly address the drivers you uncovered while being as open-minded and creative as you can. Later, you'll evaluate your shifter ideas based on those criteria at this stage.

Note that when we talk about designing shifters to influence our audience's behavior, we're primarily referring to designing shifters for the people in our audience who aren't doing the behavior yet, or aren't doing it as well as we wish they were. In other words, our primary audience for our shifters is the Non-Doers (people that aren't doing the behavior at all, or aren't doing it at sufficient levels). Even though we surveyed Doers (generally, people that are already doing the behavior) in the UNCOVER phase for the purposes of identifying significant drivers, we aren't really concerned with changing the behavior of people who are already doing the behavior. We of course would like if Doers continue the behavior, to start doing it with greater consistency, or to form a habit, but this is not usually the main purpose of our shifters. Unless otherwise specified, we are designing our shifters to change the behavior of the people who are not yet doing the behavior or are doing it infrequently. This doesn't mean that only the Non-Doers are going to see or interact with our shifters, but it does mean that these are the people for whom we are designing the shifters.

Put another way, "smokers aged 18–25" might be the more general priority audience you selected in INITIATE, but when you're talking about who you are designing shifters for, you're referring to "smokers who litter their butts" or "smokers who aren't properly disposing of their butts as often as we'd like."

Brainstorm shifters to address drivers related to Memory, Means, and Motivation

As discussed in UNCOVER, drivers can be grouped into three main categories: means, motivation, and memory. Depending on the drivers you identified in your Behavioral Drivers Analysis, your shifters will need to address low means, increase motivation, help the audience remember to do the action, or a combination of these.[4,6] In the sections below, we'll walk you through how to use the information from your Behavioral Drivers Analysis to inform your selection of shifters.

A key step of brainstorming relevant shifters is to make sure that they're addressing key behavioral drivers. So, before you start brainstorming, make sure you have a list of the highest priority drivers you discovered through your Behavioral Drivers Analysis in the UNCOVER phase. We recommend creating a table with the priority drivers you identified in the left-hand column. Create a right-hand column that you will later use to write down your shifter ideas for addressing the drivers from the left column.

Using Table 1.4.2 as a guide, group your list of drivers into Means, Motivation, and Memory if you haven't already. Be careful not to lose any of the prioritization you did in the UNCOVER phase.

```
B - Highlight norms to leverage BELONGING
E - Make it EASY
H - Cultivate powerful HABITS
A - Activate ATTACHMENT
V - Design it to be VIVID
I - Leverage our need for consistent
    IDENTITY
O - Inspire through active OPTIMISM
R - Judiciously use REWARDS
A - Frame for the appropriate ASSOCIATIONS
L - Expanding the self to ensure nature's
    LONGEVITY
```

After you've grouped your drivers, you're ready to start brainstorming shifters for them. You will find these shifters in Section 2 of this book, where we distill insights from scientific literature and practical experience into the BEHAVIORAL Building Blocks™: tools that you can use to shift behavior. Our Building Block chapters explain how each shifter works to address barriers or amplify motivation and provide ideas and advice for how to use them in your initiatives.

Use Table 1.4.2 and the following sections to guide you to the appropriate Building Block chapters as you brainstorm shifters for each of your drivers in the steps below.

Table 1.4.2: Behavioral Drivers and Building Blocks Mapped to Means-Motivation-Memory

	DRIVERS → → →	SOLUTIONS: BEHAVIORAL Building Blocks™
Means (Can I?)	Policies and practices Physical environment Access to resources Ability and self-efficacy	Make it EASY Cultivate powerful HABITS Judiciously use REWARDS
Motivation (Do I want to?)	Perceived positive consequences Perceived negative consequences Perceived social acceptability Perceived action efficacy Perceived severity Perceived susceptibility Perceived responsibility Identity Value systems	Highlight norms to leverage BELONGING Cultivate powerful HABITS Activate ATTACHMENT Design it to be VIVID Leverage our need for consistent IDENTITY Inspire through active OPTIMISM Judiciously use REWARDS Frame for the appropriate ASSOCIATIONS Expanding the self to ensure nature's LONGEVITY
Memory (Can I remember to?)	Attentional capacity Presence of cues Existing behaviors and habits	Design it to be VIVID Expanding the self to ensure nature's LONGEVITY Cultivate powerful HABITS

Brainstorm shifters for drivers related to Means

If you've uncovered drivers related to barriers like policies and practices that inhibit the behavior, barriers in the physical environment, low knowledge or skills, or inadequate resources (e.g., tools, finances, or time), brainstorm shifters that can address these. The shifters that you brainstorm will depend on the specific drivers you uncovered, but they can include making the behavior easier by reducing hassle factors and increasing the audience's ability (see EASY: Building Block Chapter 2), or offering subsidies or rewards (especially for financial means—see REWARDS: Building Block Chapter 8).

Brainstorm shifters for drivers related to Motivation

If you uncovered drivers that indicate that your audience has low motivation, such as low perceived severity, susceptibility, responsibility, or social acceptability, or the perception that doing the behavior will result in negative consequences, you can brainstorm shifters that increase motivation by addressing these barriers. For example, if your audience doesn't think that the problem is very severe, you could brainstorm shifters that relate the problem to what the audience cares about.

Additionally, if you found that the Doers you surveyed identified certain benefits or shared certain motivations significantly more than Non-Doers, you could also brainstorm shifters that amplify those. However, keep in mind the caveats we laid out in UNCOVER—just because a Doer is motivated by something, it doesn't guarantee that your Non-Doers will also find it motivating.

Most of our Building Blocks have shifters that help to increase motivation. It's important to remember that motivation is closely linked to emotions, as FOUNDATIONS: Process Chapter 1, OPTIMISM: Building Block Chapter 7, and LONGEVITY: Building Block Chapter 10 discuss in detail. Other Building Blocks seek to increase motivation by tying your initiative to identity (see IDENTITY: Building Block Chapter 6), highlighting the norms of your audience's community (BELONGING: Building Block Chapter 1), providing incentives (REWARDS: Building Block Chapter 8), making impacts more salient and concrete (VIVID: Building Block Chapter 5), tapping into what your audience cares about (ATTACHMENT: Building Block Chapter 4), and framing issues in a way that resonates with your audience (ASSOCIATIONS: Building Block Chapter 9). Finally, building habits can reduce the need for deliberate, conscious motivation by setting inertia in favor of the desired behavior (HABITS: Building Block Chapter 3).

Keep in mind that motivation to engage in certain behaviors is not constant; it can vary from moment to moment and can fade over time. For example, even if someone is really motivated when they first start doing a behavior, it doesn't mean they will sustain that same level of motivation forever. In HABITS: Building Block Chapter 3 and VIVID: Building Block Chapter 5, we also discuss how to time your shifters to leverage moments when motivation is already high.

Brainstorm shifters for drivers related to Memory

If you uncovered drivers that are related to memory, start by brainstorming shifters that will address those. For example, if your audience shared that they frequently forget to do the behavior, you could brainstorm shifters that create noticeable cues and prompts. Pay special attention to VIVID: Building Block Chapter 5 to ensure your reminders and prompts get noticed, and visit HABITS: Building Block Chapter 3 to learn more about the role of cues in forming habits.

Look to initiatives that have already been attempted

Don't forget to look to past initiatives to help design your own. If you haven't already researched other initiatives that addressed your issue, a closely related issue, or that worked with an audience similar to yours (in a similar context and facing the same behavioral drivers), now is an excellent time to do so. By exploring why the initiatives did or did not work, you can learn from the solutions that have failed or succeeded, and think of specific ways that you can apply these insights to your own initiative. This step can save you time, effort, and resources.

When researching past initiatives, keep an open mind. Even examples that appear dissimilar on the surface may provide invaluable insight. Academic literature, popular media, and nonprofit and corporate white papers are full of examples of both successful and unsuccessful environmental behavioral shifters, initiatives, and design ideas that you can use as sources of inspiration. See INITIATE: Process Chapter 2 for a summary of the secondary research we recommend and METHODS: Process Chapter 6 for more on how to conduct a literature review and resource gathering interviews.

Lessons from our collection of case studies (the *Making Shift Happen* examples and other examples found throughout this book) are also good places to start.

❓ *Ask Yourself: Shifters that have already been attempted*

Answers to these questions should help you thoroughly understand past shifters:

- Has your priority audience (or a similar audience) been exposed to initiatives for this behavior or a similar behavior before?
- If the audience was exposed to a previous initiative, how did they respond to it? How long ago was it? If you were to implement your initiative now, would they be fatigued by it?
- Were any of the attempts you've looked at successful, unsuccessful, or mixed? Why? What could have been done differently to improve the outcome of past initiatives?
- Are you able to consult with people who have run past attempts (either with your audience or elsewhere)?

• • •

At the end of your brainstorming, you will likely have several shifter ideas for each driver you identified. Each shifter or combination of shifters should:

- Directly address one or more of your audience's key barriers (such as low means or memory) or amplify one of their motivators .
- Be supported by behavioral design principles (e.g., the Building Blocks) or evidence from past initiatives.

Going back to our earlier cigarette butt example, your shifter brainstorming might look like the table on page 174. (The example is not intended to be comprehensive of all shifters that could address the identified drivers.)

Next, you will refine this list of shifters, so that you can focus on the most promising ones when you eventually prototype them.

Table 1.4.3

Prioritized Significant Drivers (from your high priority list generated in UNCOVER)	Shifter Ideas
DRIVERS: Norms and perceived social acceptability Many smokers litter their cigarette butts (there is a high percentage of Non-Doers). When the audience observes many other smokers littering their cigarette butts, it signals that it is the norm to litter one's butts rather than dispose of them properly.	**BELONGING** - When the current norm reinforces the undesired behavior (a lot of people are littering), emphasize a more environmentally friendly one (such as the norm that most people think that littering isn't the right thing to do), and spread this norm through social networks. **VIVID** - Include these normative messages in vivid displays, on signage such as prompts, and on pocket ashtrays.
DRIVER: Perceived negative consequences Non-Doers identified that properly disposing of cigarette butts is difficult.	**EASY** - Eliminate hassle factors by placing more cigarette receptacles around popular smoking areas. Choose receptacles that allow for quick and easy disposal of butts. Supply pocket ashtrays to smokers to enable proper disposal on the go. **ASSOCIATIONS** - Avoid repeating and reinforcing the negative consequences (that it takes longer to properly dispose of a cigarette butt than to litter), while articulating your own framing about the positive consequences of the behavior.
DRIVER: Attentional Capacity Non-Doers struggle to find cigarette butt receptacles and to remember to dispose of butts properly.	**VIVID** - Create cigarette butt receptacles that are noticeable and novel. Place prompts at popular smoking areas reminding smokers to dispose of their butts properly.
DRIVER: Perceived Susceptibility Perceived susceptibility is low. Non-Doers don't believe that cigarette butt litter impacts them or the people, places, and animals they care about. Non-Doers are not aware that cigarette butts are plastic and that storm drains lead to the ocean.	**ATTACHMENT** - Reduce psychological distance by telling a story that brings to life the negative impacts of cigarette butts on water quality, marine life, and seafood safety. **LONGEVITY** - Help smokers feel empathy for marine life impacted by plastic waste.

Evaluate and Prioritize Potential Shifters

Now we need to evaluate and prioritize the shifter ideas that we brainstormed in the previous step. It's tempting to pick shifters that seem the most fun or look cool, but it's most important to choose the shifters that will be effective. By brainstorming shifters to address your audience's high priority drivers, you're already on the right track to choosing effective shifters. In this step, you'll narrow down your list by considering each shifter's potential impacts and feasibility (similar to the process of narrowing down audiences and behaviors that you did in the INITIATE phase).

When evaluating a potential shifter, try to imagine it as concretely as possible and consider all the details you would need to fully implement it—the more details you consider, the easier it will be to determine whether it has potential. Revisiting and utilizing what you learned about your audience and your issue in INITIATE and UNCOVER will also help with this process.

A successful shifter has many dimensions, and just because a shifter is strong in one criterion doesn't mean it will be the best option. For example, a shifter that is likely to have a huge impact may end up being too expensive or otherwise unfeasible for your organization. The criteria below are designed to help you think through some of these dimensions and choose the shifters that are the most promising all around.[2,3,10] This can be done subjectively by your team, or you can include knowledge partners or other outside experts if you think they can help you make more accurate judgments. Since different individuals will have different perspectives on shifter benefits and feasibility, gather your team and do this exercise collectively.

Consider impact

Consider which of your shifters are likely to have a positive effect on your environmental issue: How likely are the shifter ideas you've generated to achieve the desired outcome? What could help, or hinder, their success? This includes the shifter's immediate impact, as well as its potential to scale to other audiences and contexts. Additionally, this holistic view of "impact" includes thinking about the equity impacts of the shifter. There are several factors that contribute to impact:

- **Effectiveness:** Do behavioral design principles (e.g., the Building Blocks) and evidence from past initiatives suggest that this shifter will be effective at addressing one of your audience's key barriers, and/or amplifying one of their key motivators? How have similar shifters fared in past research or real-world implementation?

- **Receptivity:** How likely is the audience to respond positively to the shifter vs. have concerns about it or react against it? How much of a commitment does it require of the priority audiences? Will it create a large or small change in the lifestyle of the priority audience?

- **Potential for positive spillover:** Is the shifter more likely to encourage negative or positive behavioral spillover? See FOUNDATIONS and INITIATE: Process Chapters 1 and 2 for more about behavioral spillover.

- **Attentional demand:** Does the shifter require a lot of directed attention to work? Conversely, does the shifter restore directed attention? See LONGEVITY: Building Block Chapter 10 for more on directed attention and attention restoration.

- **Speed of change:** How quickly do you expect behavior to change after the shifter is implemented? Keep in mind that the more complex the behavior change is, the longer it will take for the shifter to have an effect.

- **Durability:** How long do you expect the impact of the shifter to last? Does continued success require continued application of or exposure to the shifter? How likely is the shifter to create durable behavior change?

- **Roadblocks:** Are there any insights you have about your audience or issue suggesting that your shifter may not work? Are there systemic or structural impediments to achieving the goal even if all the desired behavioral changes are achieved?

- **Unintended consequences:** Might the shifter have any negative unintended consequences?

- **Equity and ethics:** Might the shifter reduce quality of life for your audience? Could it negatively impact the well-being of some audience segments more than others? See FOUNDATIONS: Process Chapter 1 for more about equity and ethical considerations.

- **Adaptability and scalability:** If scaling is a priority for you, how easy might it be to adapt your shifter to work in other contexts, or to reach broader audiences or a larger number of people? See FOUNDATIONS and IMPLEMENT: Process Chapters 1 and 5 for scaling guidance.

Consider feasibility

How feasible is it for your organization to implement this shifter? If a shifter isn't feasible, its potential positive impact becomes irrelevant. Consider the following:

- **Resources:** Does your organization have the resources (e.g., staff, skills, budget, influence) to effectively implement this idea, including making adjustments when prototyping and piloting? Even if you have enough resources to implement, will you have enough resources left over to adapt and make needed adjustments over time? If scaling is a priority, will you have enough resources to scale this shifter?

- **Practicality:** How practical is it to design your shifter idea? Once designed, how realistic is it to implement?

- **Permission to implement:** Can your organization obtain any needed permissions to implement this shifter?

- **Timeline:** Does the amount of time needed for the shifter to change behavior match the time you have allotted for your initiative?

Select the shifters with the highest potential

Use the activity below to rate each shifter idea based on its overall impact vs. its feasibility. For example, a shifter with many positive attributes like high receptivity, effectiveness, and speed of change (i.e., that is likely to have a lot of positive impact) and that is also quite feasible has a lot of potential. This exercise, which can be done on your own or in a group, can help you to zero in on which shifters you want to carry forward to the prototyping phase. Don't hesitate to combine existing ideas, update your ideas with the latest information, or make any other necessary modifications.

Activity: Prioritizing shifter ideas

- On a whiteboard, paper, wall, or tabletop, draw a box with quadrants like the one in Figure 1.4.1. You can also use digital collaboration tools like Miro, MURAL, or a shared online document.

- Read out a shifter idea and give team members some quiet time to reflect on its potential impact and feasibility.

- Have each member come up to the wall or table, and place a sticky note (with the name of the shifter idea) at some level of impact and feasibility, and explain briefly the reasoning behind placing the sticky there.

- Once each team member has given their explanations, allow the group to decide whether to adjust the position of any of the notes.
- Shifters clustered in the high impact and high feasibility (upper-right) corner are your highest priority shifters.
- For shifters that have high impact but low feasibility, it may be worthwhile to consider how you could increase their feasibility (e.g., lower costs, work with a different audience, etc.) before discarding them.

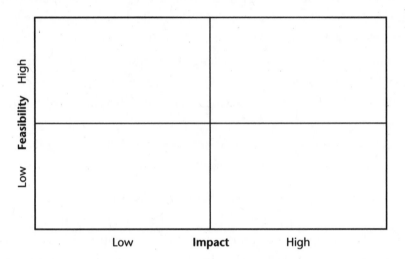

Figure 1.4.1:

Prioritizing Shifters

CREDIT: ROOT SOLUTIONS

 Make Your Shifter Ideas More Concrete

Now that you've chosen the most impactful and feasible shifters, it's time to zero in on the details of the shifters' design, such as the specific wording or images used, how or by whom the shifter is delivered, where it is placed, and how it is timed. You don't have to finalize these details now, though—in fact, we encourage you to come up with several variations of these details that you can later test during prototyping.

Determine the content of your shifters

Whatever the form your shifter or suite of shifters takes, its content should address one or more of the three Ms (e.g., captures attention or provides a reminder, increases motivation, or helps to increase means, such as by providing how-to information). Let's say that one of your shifter ideas is to put up signage.

Should the content, size, shape, images, or colors used in the signs be tweaked to ensure they are VIVID (see Building Block Chapter 5)? Do the words that you are using on the sign resonate with your audience (see ATTACHMENT and ASSOCIATIONS: Building Block Chapters 4 and 9) and draw on the appropriate emotions (OPTIMISM and LONGEVITY: Building Block Chapters 7 and 10)? Does the message invoke social norms (BELONGING: Building Block Chapter 1) or identities (IDENTITY: Building Block Chapter 6) that are aligned with the call to action? Does it supply information that makes the behavior easier for the audience to complete (EASY: Building Block Chapter 2)?

Determine the delivery mode

How are you going to deliver your shifter? Different audiences prefer different modes and channels of communication, and they interact with information in different ways, so it's wise to scope this out before you decide how to deliver your content. For example, is your audience more likely to read your message, hear it, or watch it? Which magazines does your priority audience read, what television shows do they watch, and what podcasts do they listen to? Even if you have a great, well-crafted shifter, using the wrong delivery mode can render it ineffective.

Choose the best messenger

The messenger matters. Who is delivering a message can be just as important as what the message says. Think about which individual or group would be the best to deliver your messages to your audience. Who does your audience perceive as credible and trustworthy? Who is well-known and respected among your audience? Who has the most charisma or is the most likeable? Is there someone in a position of authority? Sometimes audiences will only listen to these people.[11] For more on the importance of messengers, see BELONGING and ATTACHMENT: Building Block Chapters 1 and 4.

Carefully consider placement

Where exactly you put shifters, like signs, can greatly influence whether they grab attention and motivate action. Placing a shifter at the point of decision-making is much more effective than putting the shifter somewhere else, because this reduces the amount of time that the audience needs to keep the message in their memory. See EASY, HABITS, and VIVID (Building Block Chapters 2, 3, and 5) for more.

Determine the ideal timing to launch shifters

Audiences sometimes vary in their receptivity to shifters, depending on the time of year, the occurrence of a widely-reported event, and even whether or not they've had lunch yet, along with many other factors. Use what you've learned about your audience in the INITIATE and UNCOVER phases, as well as the guidance about timing that we provide in various Building Block chapters, to determine the ideal time to launch shifters. The frequency with which a shifter is applied can also have dramatic effects.

 Assemble Shifters as a Suite

You now have a refined list of detailed shifter ideas. Now it's time to decide whether to use a single shifter or combine them into a complementary, well-rounded suite of shifters. A single shifter can sometimes result in significant and lasting behavior change. For example, changing the default option to a green alternative can dramatically increase the percentage of people that choose that option. However, most environmental behavior change initiatives make use of more than one shifter in order to address means, motivation, memory, or all three. Often, getting over the threshold means employing multiple shifters.

It is also common to combine Building Blocks and shifters within one tool to make it as effective as possible. For example, if you are creating a sign to prompt your audience to use less water, you can use messaging that invokes a social norm (BELONGING: Building Block Chapter 1), images to capture attention (VIVID: Building Block Chapter 5), and messaging that activates identity (IDENTITY: Building Block Chapter 6) and core values (ATTACHMENT: Building Block Chapter 4). A single sign might have an attention-grabbing image, how-to information, and state, "80% of Californians do their part and save water during the drought. Each time you shower, stay in only for as long as your favorite song."

Additionally, if you have decided to take a differentiated approach for multiple audience segments, you can choose different shifters to address the different segments. One segment might need shifters focused on increasing motivation, while another segment might need help increasing ability.

With all this in mind, take a moment to decide whether you want to go with just one shifter or use a combination of shifters to achieve your goal. For all the reasons we discussed above, using a combination of multiple shifters all at once

Combining Multiple Shifters in a Paper-Saving Campaign at UC Berkeley

Root Solutions began working on a staff and student campaign to reduce student paper use at the University of California, Berkeley, Haas School of Business in 2018. Through interviews and surveys, we uncovered behavioral drivers facilitating and preventing student paper reduction. We designed the subsequent initiative, The Haas Paper-Saving Challenge, to address identified behavior levers through a suite of shifters that included how-to knowledge, prompts and reminders, feedback, pledges, social norms, and incentives. Designed as a competition, students were entered into a raffle to win various prizes for participating in the challenge, and the top two paper-saving students won $100 each. The initiative successfully achieved its goals of reducing student paper use, shifting existing norms on paper use, and increasing awareness of the environmental consequences of paper waste. Some of the shifters we used in this initiative included:

Messages that were framed to match the audience's goals, values, and identities

Survey results and conversations with students revealed that, not surprisingly, undergraduate business students enjoyed competition and highly valued being leaders and innovators. The students' love of competition is why we made the initiative into a challenge. Additionally, we used messages that tapped into these values and identities whenever possible. Students were also passionate about making Haas the first zero waste building on campus and achieving carbon neutrality, so paper-saving messages were also tied to these goals (drawing on the ATTACHMENT, IDENTITY, REWARDS and ASSOCIATIONS: Building Block Chapters 4, 6, 8, and 9).

Multiple forms of incentives and feedback that encouraged student participation

The competition utilized social recognition and tangible rewards to incentivize group and individual participation (drawing on HABITS and REWARDS: Building Block Chapters 3 and 8). Students won a variety of prizes for low-effort behavior (such as taking a photo of themselves engaging in a paper-saving behavior, or referring friends to sign up for the competition) as well as for higher-effort participation (such as printing zero pieces of paper during the competition).

Social incentives

Mid-campaign updates provided ongoing feedback about which teams were leading the way, and the winning team ultimately won bragging rights.

Participating students submitted pictures of themselves taking paper-saving actions and posted them in the competition's social media accounts.

Tangible incentives

These were offered for recruiting friends, following the Challenge on social media, and signing up for the pledge. Each participation point entered students into a raffle to win a variety of smaller prizes such as gift cards. The two individuals with the lowest paper usage received $100 prizes (courtesy of a print management company).

Continued on page 182

Fifty-dollar raffle prizes were also offered to incentivize participation in a follow-up survey.

Information presented at new student orientation

Because starting a new school year is a great time to develop new habits (see HABITS: Building Block Chapter 3), we shared information to encourage paper reduction in the new student orientation presentation (the first time that information about saving paper had been shared during orientation). The information included multiple behavioral best practices, and used identity statements like "Paper Saver" (drawing on IDENTITY: Building Block Chapter 6). In addition to incoming students, we sent all matriculated students the slides from the presentation. We created various other signage and materials to highlight a positive social norm of paper consciousness for new Haas students (drawing on BELONGING: Building Block Chapter 1).

Prompts for students to save paper at the appropriate time and place

We also created prompts for the Haas computer labs, including tabletop tent cards to be placed next to print lab computer monitors (the ideal location for reminders). Per best practices, prompts also included the same normative and identity messaging discussed above (drawing on BELONGING, EASY, HABITS, VIVID, and IDENTITY: Building Block Chapters 1, 2, 3, 5 and 6).

Various signs and messages that highlighted positive social norms about paper use

As mentioned above, messaging about the Paper-Saving Challenge frequently highlighted positive social norms (drawing on BELONGING: Building Block Chapter 1). For example, several signs mentioned that "71% of Haas students don't print lecture slides often," and that "89% of Haas students support or strongly support paper-saving efforts."

Paper-savers who socially modeled desirable behavior

We encouraged students to share instances of their paper-saving behaviors. They were given extra points in the Challenge for sharing photos on social media of themselves committing to the Paper-Saving Challenge or taking paper-saving actions, such as using scrap paper to take notes. We further circulated the images when we shared them on the Paper-Saving Challenge Instagram account (drawing on BELONGING: Building Block Chapter 1).

Outcomes of the initiative

- Paper use decreased by 32.5%.
- Students reduced printing of non-mandatory lecture slides.
- Student print credits allocated by the university each semester were reduced from $200 to $150 and then again to $100.
- Student awareness of the negative impacts of paper consumption increased.
- Student knowledge of how to use less paper increased.
- Student support for paper-saving policies and behaviors increased.
- A majority of students completed two or more paper-saving actions during the challenge.

can amplify their effects and increase the likelihood of behavior change. Just keep in mind that if you don't test each shifter individually, it makes it difficult to know which shifters worked best or drove the change. For example, if you used multiple shifters and you see an increase in bike ridership, was the increase due to incentives or because you made it sound easy? Finding out exactly which shifter has the most effect can be invaluable for future efforts. Both approaches have their benefits, but we encourage you to test individual shifters whenever possible. See prototyping below for more on quickly evaluating variations of shifters, METHODS: Process Chapter 6 for an introduction to experimental design, and IMPLEMENT: Process Chapter 5 for an overview of using your pilot to test shifters.

 Prototype Your Shifters

Once you have decided on your shifter or suite of shifters, it is time to start testing them via prototyping. From now until you implement your solutions, you will be taking your designed shifters through iterative rounds of testing—starting with iterative prototyping all the way through to piloting in the IMPLEMENT phase.

What is prototyping?

Prototyping is the final step before the IMPLEMENT phase. Here, you create prototypes to test your potential shifters in a rapid, low-cost manner on members of your priority audience. The goal of prototyping is to generate valuable, tangible feedback while assessing how your audience will react to your shifters. Even the most well-researched shifters might not go as planned, and could engender unexpected consequences when people are exposed to them in a real-world setting. Prototyping allows you to keep your users' needs at the forefront of your plans, identify problems, and make necessary changes to your designs quickly and affordably before you use substantial resources to roll out shifters. There are many possible approaches to prototype design and testing. Depending on the nature of your idea, the ideal prototyping method may range from roleplaying within your team, to testing the design of a product, poster, or communications strategy with a focus group, to some combination of these and other strategies.

The prototyping process can and should be repeated multiple times before the design is finalized, allowing you to innovate and adapt in order to zero in on your best designs.[5] Depending on the feedback you get from each phase of prototyping, you can add to, change, or even abandon your shifters.

Prototyping should include the following steps:

1. Determine what shifters you will prototype.
2. Determine what kind of feedback you want.
3. Create your prototypes.
4. Test and evaluate the prototypes.

At the end of prototyping, you should have a refined shifter or suite of shifters ready to pilot in the IMPLEMENT phase.

What shifters will you prototype?

Before you prototype, we suggest that you prioritize your refined list of shifters one more time. You may need to narrow your list based on budget, resources, and time constraints, but keep in mind the importance of investing a small amount now to reduce costs for your final implementation. You can use the following guidelines to help you prioritize what you will prototype.

Prototype whenever possible and especially when:

- The shifter is easy or inexpensive to test.
- Past attempts at using this shifter have had mixed results, or (to your knowledge) the shifter has never been attempted before with your audience or a similar audience.
- There is something from your audience research that suggests the shifter or suite of shifters has the potential to backfire.
- The shifter includes messaging for values, frames, or emotions. See ATTACHMENT: Building Block Chapter 4 and ASSOCIATIONS: Building Block Chapter 9 for more on the importance of testing this messaging.

What kind of feedback do you want?

Be clear on what you want to learn and which parts of your prototype will help you learn it. Remember that the objective of prototyping is to learn more about your audience and how they will interact with your shifters, not to get it right the first time.

Testing should address the following things:

- **Effectiveness:** Does the shifter prompt the desired behavior?
- **Audience experience:** How did the audience feel about the experience?
- **Comprehensibility:** Is the shifter, and how to interact with it, understandable to the audience?
- **Expected results:** Are there any unexpected outcomes?

Create your prototype

In this step you will consider the different aspects of your shifter that you would like to test. You will then need to determine which prototyping method is best for each shifter you will be testing, as well as the fidelity (quality and realism) of the prototype. Prototyping will help you develop and refine those details.

Test the details of the shifter

There are a lot of important details that can influence the effectiveness of a shifter or suite of shifters. (Recall the list of shifter details mentioned earlier: content, messenger, placement, delivery mode, and timing.) For example, if you are prototyping the pledge card for a commitment campaign, you could test how many and which commitment options to give your audience, the wording used on the card, or the look, feel, and shape of the card. Try prototyping a message in both written and spoken form to see which your audience responds best to. Can you test out different messengers in the prototyping process? Or try different placements and timing as part of the prototyping process? You may choose not to prototype all of these details, but you will still need to determine these details by the end of the DESIGN phase.

Determine the prototyping method you will use

There are a variety of ways that you can prototype, ranging from simple sketches or storyboards to live role-playing.

Poster or Sketch

Sketches can be as simple as doodles in a notebook. They help make your ideas clear so that you can better explain your shifter to test audiences and get realistic feedback. Sketches should not take long to draft—they're meant to be a rough outline of your idea.

Storyboard

A storyboard is a series of sketches, similar to a comic strip, that should help you imagine every way that people will interact with your shifter. For example, if your shifter is a sign that encourages people to compost in a restaurant, you might create sketches depicting how a person from each segment of your audience might approach, read, and behave after seeing the sign. The storyboard can also help you test out different elements of the shifter—does it make a difference where in the restaurant the sign is placed? A storyboard helps you think through and understand the flow of people's interaction with your shifters.

Storyboards of physical interactions usually take the form of comic strips, drafting all of the ways a person may interact with your shifter. Storyboards of conversations usually take the form of a flowchart that maps out potential directions the conversation may go. Both will help you and your testers holistically think through the discrete behaviors that lead to the outcome-producing behavior.

Capture every interaction an audience member has with your shifter. For example, if you plan to follow up with audience members a few weeks after they make a pledge, your storyboard should capture both interactions. Creating timelines can help you see a clear picture of how quickly you are expecting change to take place.

Presentations

Deliver presentations about your shifter to a test audience to elicit feedback. Ask them if they find the idea clear and motivating, or what could be done to improve it.

Role-play

Create an interactive skit or scenario in which your user can participate. This could imitate how a user would interact with a service, how an initiative would occur, or other possible interactions. Role-play scenarios can either be presented to a user or have a loose script that involves the user in the interaction. Utilizing props and costumes can make these interactions more realistic.

When you're first creating your prototypes, you can role-play as your priority audience to determine how you feel about your prototype. Jot down your impressions as you interact with it. Do you think you would change your behavior as a result of the shifter? Did you enjoy interacting with your prototype? Do you feel like something might be missing? Note that although this method can help you create a prototype that is developed enough to put in front of a tester, your feedback should not be substituted for that of others.

Interactive models

Models in the prototyping phase can be made out of anything—cardboard, ribbon, plates, paper, boxes, etc. These do not need to be as fully functional as your final product will be, especially if it will involve technology or engineering. For example, if you are designing an interactive waste disposal system, have a team member act as the machine part that would respond to the user.

• • •

In the list below, we provide prototype examples for two shifters for a campaign to encourage food composting.

Shifter: Create signs that prompt the audience at a food court to compost

Possible prototypes include:

- Create a few sketches or images of signs, varied by size, font, color, or images used.
- Create a few different variations on the wording of the sign, such as "Please remember to compost" versus "90% of diners at this food court compost their food."
- Role-play among the team at the food court to determine where composting signs and bins would be most visible.
- Create a storyboard of the steps diners usually go through when eating at the food court, and add composting signs and bins in different frames in the storyboard to see which work best.

Shifter: Rearrange the layout of the food court to make composting easier and more visible

Possible prototypes include:

- Create a computer, paper, or clay model of the food court to help visualize different iterations of the layout.
- Role-play among your team where the office is turned into a mock food court, and the team tests different layouts as they pretend to eat and dispose of their food.
- Conduct a focus group with target audience members testing out different layouts.

We encourage you to mix and match prototyping methods, and go through as many iterations of prototypes as is necessary to increase the likelihood of your shifters' success.

Keep costs in mind

Keep early prototypes simple and inexpensive. Of course, a sophisticated prototype would yield more realistic information on how your audience may react to your shifter, but there is a tradeoff between the expense and effort required and the additional information you might gain.

Low-fidelity prototype

A *low-fidelity prototype* is one that is inexpensive, rough, and easily modified as feedback starts coming in—for example, a poster, a sign, or a set of social media posts. These are best when your funds are limited or when a higher-fidelity prototype is not necessary.

High-fidelity prototype

A *high-fidelity prototype* is one that you spend more time and resources on, closer in quality to what the final shifter will be. Some examples include detailed 3D models, digital app mock-ups, glossy printed posters, and other detailed models with higher quality materials. The increased investment in these more realistic prototypes should allow you to better see the way the user would interact with the design.

• • •

We recommend that you start with a low-fidelity prototype and then move to a higher-fidelity prototype. Limit the amount of time you spend making your first draft—maybe even just a few minutes. Do not strive to create a perfect prototype, especially for initial testing. Since initial prototypes gauge the audience's initial reactions, they do not need to be expensive and refined. You can then move to higher-fidelity prototypes as you refine your solution. These are best for second or third drafts, when you only have one chance to get feedback from your audience, or when it is extremely important to get your shifters right before rolling them out.

Keep in mind that prototypes should be inexpensive; only spend as much time and money as is necessary to test the concept. Before beginning, consider setting a budget for your prototyping (e.g., ten minutes on a primary sketch, $15 on a product model).

Test and evaluate the prototypes

Once you have created your prototype, test them with strategically selected users who can give helpful feedback.

Who to test with

Prototyping can be conducted by formally or informally interviewing individual members of audiences, or it can be conducted through focus groups. Although you can start by testing early-stage prototypes on your teammates or colleagues, it's important that prototyping is done with members of your priority audience. Test your prototype on members of your actual audience as early as possible, and test often throughout the process. You want to know if you're on the right track early on, rather than finding out that the audience doesn't respond to your shifter after you've fully developed it.

Consider testing your shifters with the users that have the most extreme needs within your audience, like the young or elderly, those who are disabled, those with high or low levels of comfort with technology, etc. These extreme users can provide feedback specific to their needs. For example, a practitioner seeking to increase food composting in restaurants by using prompts might want to test potential new signage with those representing the youngest and oldest people in their audience, in order to design a shifter (or multiple shifters) that will be effective with both audiences.

Fig: 1.4.2: *Prototyping resulted in this final version of a "vote with your shotgun wad" bin to capture waterfowl hunters' attention and encourage them to pick up and dispose of plastic shotgun wads.* CREDIT: ROOT SOLUTIONS

How to test

When testing a prototype, give testers as little background information on the initiative, the goal of the shifter, and the prototype as possible. This allows you to avoid influencing them with your hopes and expectations about how the shifter will work. Provide the tester with only as much guidance as they would receive if they were encountering the prototypical situation in real life. For example, while prototyping a sign showing how much paper is being saved (e.g., a progress thermometer of paper savings), you can specify how the shifter would be presented in the real world: where you would post the sign, how often the thermometer would be updated, etc. However, you would not specify the goal of the thermometer or the actions you want to evoke. You can also ask a colleague to administer and collect the feedback to avoid biasing the testers with your gestures, voice tone, and other actions; you would still be able to be present in the room as an observer recording or taking notes.

It can also be helpful to break your prototype down into smaller components to allow the audience to provide more specific feedback. For instance, if you are testing the prototype of a poster and receiving a mixed response, consider testing the wording and graphic design of your poster separately. They may be eliciting different responses that are muddled in the joint feedback.

Additionally, consider offering your user multiple versions of a prototype to compare. Sometimes, people don't know how to articulate their feedback, so having comparisons to talk about may reveal some valuable insights.

You will want to elicit detailed feedback at every stage of testing, either while the test is being done or after-the-fact. Eliciting feedback could entail:

- Asking the audience questions directly
- Conducting focus groups
- Observing the audience (in person or on video, with permission)
- Distributing questionnaires and surveys
- Tracking usage statistics

Questions you might ask when soliciting feedback include:

Effectiveness

❑ Do you think you would change your behavior as a result of this?

❑ Do you think people would take any of these steps after seeing this?

User experience

❑ What were your impressions as you interacted with the prototype? Did you enjoy interacting with it?

❑ Is there an aspect of this that stands out to you in some way?

❑ How could you improve the prototype to address the issues that arose?

Comprehensibility

❑ Please tell me in your own words what this is trying to say.

❑ Do you see any words that you think some people might have a hard time understanding?

- ❏ [Aspect of prototype X] means different things to different people—what does it mean to you?
- ❏ Does this help you know what to do? After reading this [sign, document, etc.], do you feel prepared to/for [behavior]?
- ❏ Do you feel like something might be missing?
- ❏ Who do you think this [document, poster, etc.] is for?

Conduct a tiny experiment or A/B test with your prototypes

If you have the resources and access to a large enough test audience, you can conduct a tiny experiment with your prototypes to see if a single shifter is effective, or you can compare different versions of a shifter.

A/B tests are tests that evaluate which of two options is more effective. These are great for online audiences. If you send out a newsletter to your membership asking for a commitment, you can test two different subject lines or the content of the commitment message on a subset of your audience. In this type of experiment, your feedback is coming in the form of results as opposed to verbal feedback (e.g. does your audience click on the link? Donate?) The more feedback you can collect, the more it can help you to adjust and improve your design. Refer to METHODS: Process Chapter 6 for more on experiments.

• • •

As you go through the prototyping process, remember that it is iterative. We encourage you to remain in this stage for as long as you need, and to celebrate when you learn something new about what works and what doesn't with your shifters!

Conclusion

At the end of the DESIGN phase, you will have used the BEHAVIORAL Building Blocks™ to design shifters based on both your understanding of the issue and your knowledge of your priority audience's barriers and motivators to action. You will then have undergone prototyping and used feedback from your priority audience to modify the prototypes until you were satisfied that the shifters you designed are likely to be successful. It's time to move on to IMPLEMENT: Process Chapter 5, where you will plan, pilot, implement, iterate, and scale your initiative.

Implement

P REPARATION, RESEARCH, DESIGN, AND TESTING are all necessary for coming up with a solution to an environmental problem. But the problem will not go away unless the solution is rolled out effectively to and taken up by key audiences. IMPLEMENT, the final phase of the *Making Shift Happen* process, involves planning a full-fledged initiative, testing it on a small portion of the audience, making refinements, fully implementing the initiative, and then scaling it. We'll also discuss how to adapt to unforeseen changes and how to evaluate your initiative using the metrics you selected in INITIATE.

A Look Ahead: IMPLEMENT

Plan for Scaling Your Initiative

Piggyback on things that are already widespread

Shift attitudes and beliefs to favor your initiative

Spread your initiative through norms and existing social networks

Distribute your messages through media

Empower others with necessary skills

Secure resources for scaling

Plan Out Your Full-Fledged Initiative

Determine How You Will Evaluate Your Initiative

Design your initiative as an experiment or quasi-experiment

Finalize your outcome metrics and collect baseline data

Determine your process metrics

Pilot Your Initiative

Design your pilot initiative

Implement, evaluate, and refine your pilot

Share results and lessons learned

Implement Your Full-Fledged Initiative

Plan for Scaling Your Initiative

Before diving into implementation, we need to talk about *scaling*—the process of expanding or replicating your initiative in order to increase participation from your existing priority audience or spread your initiative to new audiences. You may have noticed that we've referenced scaling in previous chapters. This is because even though scaling happens after an initiative is first implemented, scaling principles should be considered as soon as you start designing your initiative and creating your implementation strategy.[1]

In rare cases, a single behavior change initiative may be enough to solve a problem. For example, this is the case when the scale of the environmental problem is small (e.g., litter in a local park), or when the priority audience is very influential but relatively concentrated (e.g., a few chemical companies that together could stop the production of most ozone-layer-destroying chemicals). But, most of the time, you will likely want your desired behavior to catch on beyond the relatively narrow priority audience you selected in INITIATE.

Scaling can occur in many ways, but the main ones seem to be through systems change, "spreadability," and intentional replication:

Systems change:
Intervening at a high leverage point in the system (e.g., by reforming a policy that affects many aspects of the system) is a powerful way to achieve widespread behavior change.

"Spreadability":
Many of the behavior change tools we present in the BEHAVIORAL Building Blocks™ (Section 2) are considered best practices for scaling any type of initiative. For example, when a message is funny, catchy, repeatable, or "memable," or when you invoke salient norms or identities, you can increase the chance that the initiative will spread to other audiences.

Intentional Replication:
If you are planning to replicate your initiative with other audiences, you'll need to start planning for this during the INITIATE phase. Your intention to replicate your initiative will influence which audience you choose, what behavior you focus on, what audience research you conduct, and many more elements of your initiative.

If you intend for others to adapt and implement future iterations of the initiative, you'll need to make sure these individuals are included in the design and implementation of your original initiative in order to give them time to master needed skills.

Sometimes it seems like initiatives have scaled "overnight" or "automatically," with little effort or intentionality. However, in most cases, scaling requires strategic planning, effort, and resources. The literature suggests that most conservation initiatives do not scale automatically; rather, those that do scale share certain attributes.[1] We have distilled these attributes into the scaling principles below, which you can use to design your initiative with scaling in mind.

Piggyback on things that are already widespread

Developing sufficient infrastructure (e.g., tools, services, physical resources, social networks) for scaling often requires a major investment of resources. Instead of building new infrastructure, piggyback on tools (e.g., mobile phones), services (e.g., public distribution systems), and media channels or platforms (e.g., social media) that have already successfully scaled. For example, if *feature phones* (inexpensive mobile phones with some functionality but not as much as a smartphone) are already used by fishers, develop solutions that allow fishers to use those to solicit catch data, track fishing behavior, or increase enforcement in order to solve fishery challenges, rather than trying to get everyone to use an app that can only be used on a smartphone. You can piggyback on *soft infrastructure* like social networks and influential people, as well as *hard infrastructure* like feature phones. In addition to piggybacking on infrastructure by yourself, form strategic partnerships with people who can help you expand your program, enter new geographies, work with new audiences, and co-create locally tailored solutions. Engage these partners in scaling activities like peer-exchanges and learning networks to facilitate the spread of your messages and shifters.

Shift attitudes and beliefs to favor your initiative

You can shift attitudes and beliefs to favor your initiative with current audiences as well as with new audiences to pave the way for a future initiative. While shifting attitudes and beliefs can be difficult and time-consuming, it's more than worthwhile because pro-environmental attitudes and beliefs can make people more likely to protect the environment for generations to come. To start making these shifts, use frames, metaphors, and stories that promote environmental behaviors and mindsets, and repeat them often. See ASSOCIATIONS: Building Block Chapter 9 for design advice and more on the power of shifting frames and mental models for durable, scaled change, and see ATTACHMENT and LONGEVITY (Building Block Chapters 4 and 10) for more ways to change long-term values, ideologies, mindsets, and attitudes.

Spread your initiative through norms and existing social networks

When designing an initiative, utilize the power of norms to increase the likelihood that the behavior will be picked up. For example, if you have 20 solar panel systems to give away, install them close together to set a norm in that neighborhood, as those without panels will see that numerous neighbors have them.

One way to spread norms and new behaviors is through social networks. It can be particularly effective to focus your efforts first on opinion leaders and influencers—individuals who can spread new norms and thus new behaviors to the members of their social networks—because many other people look to them for advice and as role models.[2] For more information on norms and social networks, see BELONGING: Building Block Chapter 1.

Distribute your messages through media

Obviously, various media (e.g., television, radio, print media, or social media) can be great for increasing awareness—especially for initiatives that generate a sense of injustice or outrage, which can spread awareness particularly quickly. However, awareness alone seldom results in behavior change. Fortunately, media can also be great for spreading behavior change—it can spread new norms, frames, and mental models, and even change culture in some cases, and carry our messages, stories, and other shifters.[3,5] Read more about the power of media in shaping norms in BELONGING: Building Block Chapter 1, and the value of stories in ATTACHMENT: Building Block Chapter 4.

Empower others with necessary skills

Running an environmental behavior change initiative requires specific skills. Therefore, if you are planning to scale your initiative to a new audience but aren't going to run that initiative yourself, you may need to teach stakeholders or practitioners from other organizations how to adapt this initiative to new audiences and how to run it without you. Make sure these individuals are included in the design and implementation of your original initiative to give them time to master needed skills. For example, one of the authors of this book was engaged in an initiative that trained several local leaders from disparate fishing villages in the Philippines in how to regulate their fisheries in sustainable ways. With some coaching, these leaders were able to create more sustainable fisheries in their own villages.

Secure resources for scaling

Having adequate resources to scale and adapt your initiative to another location or audience is essential. If you intend to replicate your initiative, be sure to budget for that and secure additional funding.

❓ Ask Yourself: Scaling your initiative

- Which tools, services, media, or other infrastructure that have already scaled will you use to piggyback aspects of your initiative on?
- How can you shift frames and mental models to increase support for your initiative over time?
- How might you spread your initiative through social networks?
- How might you use media such as television, radio, print media, or social media to spread your initiative?
- Which practitioners or audience members will need to learn the necessary skills to spread the initiative?
- How will you secure the necessary resources for scaling?

 Plan Out Your Full-Fledged Initiative

By the end of DESIGN, you selected, designed, and refined a suite of shifters to address your audiences' barriers and motivators. You thought about when and where you would apply shifters, and to which audiences you would deliver them. And by now, you've also considered how you might scale your initiative. Now, it's time to design the full-fledged initiative, and determine how you will implement and evaluate it. While it's beyond the scope of this book to address all of the intricacies of designing and implementing an initiative, the following are important considerations for planning yours:

Logistics:

In DESIGN, you planned the steps you will need to take in order to implement your shifters: where and how frequently will you engage your audience with each shifter; how many times will you apply shifters and when; and which shifters will go in which places. Now, it's time to plan for your whole initiative: What infrastructure do you need? What permits and permissions do you need? You will also want to consider who on your team will deploy, observe, and monitor shifters and plan estimated dates for important tasks and milestones. Remember to include scaling considerations in your planning.

Timing:

Consider when to begin and end your initiative. Certain audiences have set schedules like school years, hunting seasons, or harvest times that need to be considered. In fact, many shifters rely on timing, like efforts to introduce new habits during times of transition (such as the beginning of a school year). See HABITS: Building Block Chapter 3 for more about leveraging periods of transition and disruption.

Duration:

Your initiative should run at least long enough to see the whole trajectory of the behavior that you are trying to change. For example, if you are trying to reduce paper use on campus, you would likely want to pilot or implement your initiative for an entire semester to capture all the periods of high paper use (e.g., the beginning of semesters when reading materials are being printed as well as middle and end of semester when reports are being turned in). You may even want to run it for the entire year to ensure you capture end-of-year capstone and thesis printing.

Location:

In the DESIGN phase, you thought about where you will implement your shifters (e.g., right above the compost bin or in the computer lab): do these locations still make sense in light of all the shifters together and the initiative as a whole? And if you are recruiting participants to take part in the initiative, are the locations you are using to recruit your audience appropriate for reaching them?

Budget:

Plan your budget for implementing, sustaining, and evaluating your initiative. If you plan to scale the initiative, remember to budget for that as well.

Stay in touch with your stakeholders:
Continue to engage your stakeholders along the way, such as the knowledge partners you consulted for your Landscape Exploration in INITIATE or the members of your priority audience who were involved in the design of your initiative. Anyone from the community or priority audience who will take over implementation and/or scaling should shadow your team as much as possible so they are prepared to take the reins.

❓ Ask Yourself: Plan your initiative

- Is there anything that could impact the optimal timing of your initiative? Have you considered how certain routine events (e.g., school years, seasons) might affect your initiative? Have you taken these into account while planning for baseline data collection?
- Are the locations you are using to recruit providing a representative sample of participants? Are they enabling you to reach the intended audience?
- Is the duration of your initiative long enough for you to see the entire trajectory of the behavior?
- Have you ensured that your plan is feasible given the resources you have?
- Are you involving all necessary stakeholders in the design and implementation of the pilot?

 Determine How You Will Evaluate Your Initiative

In addition to planning how you will implement the initiative, you will also want to plan how you will measure its success, both in terms of keeping it on track with your plan and in terms of the desired environmental and behavioral outcomes that you identified in INITIATE.

Design your initiative as an experiment or quasi-experiment

Designing your initiative as an experiment is the most robust way to measure its effectiveness. We can use experiments to test the impact of our initiative overall, but also to compare the effectiveness of different shifters or different variations of a single shifter (e.g., to compare incentives to how-to information, or to compare two different types of incentives).

There are several types of experiments and quasi-experiments that we can use to measure cause and effect. Each type of experiment has its advantages and disadvantages, and you may be limited to using one type or another. "True experiments" include all three elements of experimental control: a treatment, a treatment group and a control group, and random assignment into groups. By controlling for factors like differences between groups, and by examining the behavior of a control group in addition to your treatment group, experiments enable you to more confidently attribute changes in behavior to your initiative. The most robust type of true experiment, a "classic controlled experiment," involves all three elements of control as well as pretest (baseline) data. A "posttest-only control group experiment" includes all elements of control, but does not require baseline data. If you're conducting a quasi-experiment (an experiment that lacks one or more of the experimental elements of control), we strongly recommend collecting baseline data.

Let's say you want to change the way people get to work in order to reduce greenhouse gas emissions, and you have access to two offices in the same building, but one is a marketing firm (Office A) and one is an accounting firm (Office B). You make Office A your treatment—everyone in Office A receives the entire initiative (e.g., assistance with route-planning and an incentive). You make Office B your control—no one in Office B is exposed to any shifters of your initiative.

You collect baseline data for the current transportation behavior of both groups—this helps us see if the groups began the experiment with any differences. These two groups of people are likely to begin with meaningful differences between them, since you are not using random assignment. After the pilot period, you look at how transportation behavior changed from baseline (pretest) to posttest for each of the two offices. You might see some natural change among your groups (perhaps the weather got warmer during the course of your initiative) captured by a subtle change in the control group (Office B), but should see much greater change in the treatment group (Office A) if the shifters were effective. You could also add additional treatment groups (offices) to your experiment if you wanted to compare shifters to one another.

The above is just one example of how you can utilize experimental design to test the effectiveness of your initiative. In METHODS: Process Chapter 6, you can find more information about what constitutes an experiment, descriptions of different types of experiments, and considerations for how you can integrate experimental design into your work.

Finalize your outcome metrics and collect baseline data

In the INITIATE phase, you set an overarching goal for the desired environmental outcome you seek, as well as goals for specific behavior change outcomes. You also tentatively selected *outcome metrics* to measure whether you've achieved your goals (e.g., the number of people riding the bus, the pounds of food composted in the school cafeteria, or the percentage of farmers that have converted to no-till farming). As a reminder, you should seek to measure your desired outcomes as directly and accurately as possible, while still being able to feasibly collect data on those metrics.

Now is also the last chance to collect *baseline data* (data on your metrics prior to implementing your initiative), if you did not already do so in either the INITIATE or UNCOVER phases. If you have not already obtained baseline data, you have several options:

- **Pause to collect baseline data now**
- **Design your initiative or pilot as a posttest-only control group experiment (without baseline data):** If you choose to design your pilot or your full-scale initiative as a posttest-only control group experiment, you can adequately measure the effectiveness of your initiative without collecting baseline data, because the way you are measuring effectiveness is by comparing the two groups (your treatment vs. your control group) to one another only after the shifters have been applied. An added bonus is that if you run a pilot as a posttest-only control group experiment, you can use the posttest data from the pilot's control group as baseline data for your full-scale initiative.
- **Use less direct metrics:** If you haven't collected baseline data because you found that the metrics you originally identified to measure environmental or behavior change are too difficult or impossible to collect data on, you likely need to use indirect metrics. For example, if you want to measure the pounds of food composted in the school cafeteria but find it difficult or impossible to obtain this data, you can instead measure how many students walk up to the compost bin and dispose of their food, or ask students about what percentage of their food scraps they compost. Just remember when interpreting your results that less direct metrics may not be as reliable as direct metrics. For example, if you ask students about the food they compost, they may overstate the amount they actually compost to avoid disappointing you.

Determine your process metrics

Now is also the time to consider and define your process metrics, if you haven't already. *Process metrics* measure whether or not you are doing things according to plan. An example of how to use a process metric is to keep track of the number of brochures that were actually sent out and compare this to what was planned. Process metrics don't necessarily tell you whether you've achieved your behavior change or outcome goals (sending out brochures doesn't guarantee that people have received them, read them, or acted on the information in them), but they are essential for tracking your initiative's progress, identifying any problems with implementation, and figuring out how to adjust the initiative or how to do things differently in future iterations.

Additional examples of process metrics include:

- **Outreach:**
  - Number of brochures distributed, calls made, events held
  - Number of social media posts
  - Number of conversations with audience members
- **Milestones:**
  - Approvals (e.g., permission has been granted to install waste receptacles at the beach)
  - Decisions made
  - Tasks completed
  - Shifters launched
  - Deliverables submitted
- **Performance:**
  - Efficiency of staff time (e.g., how many audience members did each team member talk to in one hour?)
  - Return on investment and other resources devoted to this initiative

Any data on process metrics that we collect during a pilot (see the following section on piloting) can help us to identify unusual patterns and where we might aim to do better during full implementation. For instance, a dip in participation in a paper use reduction initiative on a college campus one week might be linked to a line in our recruitment log denoting that the campus was closed that week, leading to fewer people than normal. Further, these process data can help us to understand which parts of our procedures were particularly valuable and what parts were less essential to the success of our campaign.

Outcome metrics

- Have you chosen metrics that will allow you to evaluate whether the initiative results in desired behavior change and environmental outcomes?
- Have you collected all necessary baseline data?
- What changes to external factors might influence the outcome data (e.g., season and weather, political events)?

Process metrics

- Have you chosen metrics that will allow you to evaluate whether the initiative is being implemented as designed and is meeting its outreach, milestones, and performance goals?
- Have you planned out all the needed tasks and milestones for implementing the initiative, from start to finish?
- Have you decided how often you plan to evaluate how your initiative is going?

 Pilot Your Initiative

We strongly recommend piloting your initiative prior to full implementation. In a *pilot*, the polished versions of your designed shifters are deployed on a small fraction of your audience, or a small fraction of an audience very similar to your priority audience, to see whether they work, the reasons why they may not work, and how you might change them so that they work better.

Even though you will be referring to the notes from prototyping when piloting, piloting is quite different from prototyping (see DESIGN: Process Chapter 4). Instead of testing one shifter at a time, in a pilot you get to see them all together in action. Prototyping is like trying different versions of costumes, sets, or even actors before putting on a play, whereas piloting is like a dress rehearsal of the play. Through piloting, you'll see whether you need to make adjustments to your implementation plan before investing significant resources in full-scale implementation. You'll also be able to evaluate your shifter design to determine whether each shifter worked as intended, and whether adding them all together resulted in any unexpected outcomes, such as multiple shifters either complementing or working against each other.

Making Shift Happen: Using Pilot Farming Programs to Improve Crop Yields and Soil Conservation

The Master Farmer program, run by Peace Corps Senegal and the United States Agency for International Development, included an initiative to encourage farmers to pilot sustainable farming practices on their own land, such as by planting trees to prevent erosion and implementing practices to improve the nutrients in the soil.[6] Farmers carried out pilots to ensure that these methods worked before risking their livelihoods with full implementation. Additionally, they helped spread the methods to other farmers. For example, Dembo Tigana, a lifelong farmer who had been part of the program since 2010, was able to produce four times his usual amount of corn after he tested multiple ways to plant corn on side-by-side plots. Tigana became committed to passing on his knowledge to other farmers. In 2012, he trained nearly 200 farmers in new techniques. This is a good example of how pilots can accomplish even more than testing the effectiveness of an initiative—the pilots themselves can be used to spread confidence and new behaviors throughout a community.

Through piloting, you can test part or all of your initiative before rolling it out to a wider audience. Piloting allows you to:

- **Evaluate and adjust your implementation process**
  - Discover any unexpected implementation challenges.
  - Ensure your chosen metrics measure behavior as directly and feasibly as possible.
  - Assess whether you need to make adjustments to your implementation plan.
  - Adjust to challenges before investing significant resources in full-scale implementation.

- **Evaluate and adjust the design of your initiative**
  - See all your shifters in action together.
  - Test shifter variations on a subset of your audience.
  - See how your initiative works in its intended context, including timing, duration, location, and audience.
  - Gauge your audience's reaction to your shifters.
  - Assess the potential for success in a real-world setting.
  - Gain insights on how to scale your initiative.
  - Discover and take advantage of any unexpected successes to amplify the impact of full-scale implementation.
  - Refine your shifters and overall initiative before full-scale implementation.

Design your pilot initiative

To glean useful information about how successful your full-fledged initiative might be and how you can improve upon it, it's important to conduct your pilot in a way that reflects the context, conditions, and audience of your full initiative as much as possible. This requires planning, which begins with considering the logistics of your pilot, such as how you will use it to collect data, who the audience will be, how big it will be, and how long it will last.[4,7]

Design your pilots as an experiment

A pilot is a great opportunity to conduct an experiment so that you can test the effectiveness of your initiative (or individual shifters) before rolling them out to a larger percentage of your audience. Even if you won't be designing your full initiative as an experiment, we strongly recommend designing your pilot as an experiment, especially before rolling out a large, long-term, or expensive initiative. Recall that we discuss using experiments for evaluation above; we also discuss them in greater detail in METHODS: Process Chapter 6.

Choose the pilot audience with full-scale implementation in mind

A dress rehearsal aims to be as close to the real thing as possible. If you design an initiative with a certain audience in mind, your pilot should include a subset of that audience. If that's not possible, pilot with an audience that is as similar as possible to your priority audience.

Determine the pilot audience size

Remember that your pilot is only a test run before full implementation—your audience size should be much smaller than the number of total priority audience members, yet still large enough to test your initiative's feasibility and effectiveness. The size of the pilot may also depend on how the priority audience is structured. For example, if full implementation will be city-wide and the city has many neighborhoods that could have different responses to your shifters, you may need to pilot in more than one neighborhood, or pilot with a small percentage of people from each neighborhood, to ensure your sample is as similar as possible to the whole city. You'll also need a larger pilot audience if you plan to create a control and treatment group—something we strongly recommend. And if you are creating multiple treatment groups, you'll need to pilot with an even larger audience.

Determine if you will run the pilot with a representative, or specific, subset of the audience

The more representative your pilot sample is, the more accurately you can predict what will happen during your full initiative and make any needed changes. On the other hand, choosing a more targeted subset of your priority audience (such as early adopters, influential people, environmental champions, and anyone who is already interested in the topic or is especially willing to work with you), your pilot will be more likely to succeed. These audience members may promote your cause and encourage people to join your initiative when you fully implement it.

There are tradeoffs between these two approaches, and each has its own advantages and disadvantages. Most often, we recommend using a representative sample rather than a targeted sample as your priority audience for the pilot. But, it can be difficult, and sometimes impossible, to pilot an initiative with a truly representative sample of your audience. For example, if your initiative involves using signs to influence visitor behavior at national park information centers, you may choose to run a pilot at one or two parks rather than at all of them. In this case, only the type of visitors to visit those specific parks will be exposed to your pilot.

Determine if you will pilot with a subset of the priority audience or one very similar

Running a pilot with a portion of your actual audience (people who are among the population that will later receive the full-fledged initiative) can provide you with more accurate feedback, and if your pilot shifters are well-received, the participants can help spread the initiative to the rest of your audience.

On the other hand, running a pilot with a similar but separate audience (e.g., your audience is really the hunters at reserves A, B, and C, but you piloted at reserve D) may produce results that can't be generalized as well to your priority audience, but can help prevent problems during full implementation in case any aspect of the pilot didn't sit well with the audience. Additionally, some initiatives rely on surprise; if it is important that the priority audience doesn't hear about the initiative, then you will want to conduct the pilot with a similar but separate audience, not a subset of the priority audience.

Determine the pilot location

You'll also need to plan where your pilot will be conducted. Location can strongly affect what you learn from the pilot because audience characteristics and factors that influence the effectiveness of your shifters can vary dramatically from place to place.

One such consideration is when to pilot in just one neighborhood and when not to. Let's say that you're planning a city-wide initiative to reduce energy use. Neighborhood A is dominated by people who share values aligned with lower energy use, whereas in some other neighborhoods, the opposite is true. A pilot only targeting Neighborhood A may be successful, but this doesn't mean your shifters will successfully scale to the other neighborhoods. By only piloting with Neighborhood A, our pilot becomes less useful for determining what works and doesn't with our full priority audience.

But there are other times when we might want to pilot in a single neighborhood. Take the example of leveraging norms to spread the use of solar panels as a way to lower energy use: if you keep your initiative concentrated in one area like a single neighborhood (e.g., when installing solar panels), you may be able to spread the behavior more quickly due to social norms, as people will be more likely to see and be influenced by their neighbors' behavior. In this case, you will still want to choose a pilot neighborhood that best "represents" the majority of neighborhoods you plan to scale the initiative to. See BELONGING: Building Block Chapter 1 for more on spreading behaviors through social networks.

Determine how you will recruit the audience for your pilot

Most likely, you have chosen to pilot with a representative sample of your priority audience. If your pilot relies on recruiting people to volunteer to become members of your pilot (like asking volunteers to sign up for a new online energy program before it is rolled out to all customers in full implementation), you should pay special attention to your methods of recruitment to ensure that this self-selecting group is as representative of the priority audience as possible. For example, simply asking for volunteers for the new online program would likely encourage a lot of early adopters who are excited about the new innovation. While it will not be possible to prevent this type of *self-selection bias* entirely, intentionally seeking out people that represent the audience and prototyping your recruitment materials to reduce the chances that they are appealing only to one type of person can help mitigate this. Include as many people as possible in the pilot to account for a diversity of participants and also monitor the proportion of responses from each demographic so that you can put more effort into recruiting underrepresented demographics as needed. See METHODS: Process Chapter 6 for considerations for choosing and recruiting participants.

Decide on timing and duration of your pilot

In addition to determining the size of your pilot and choosing participants, you will also need to decide when your pilot will be administered and how long it will last.

Timing:
Generally, you should aim to administer your pilot at the same time of year, or at the same time within a cycle that you are planning to implement your full initiative (e.g., when tourists arrive for a cruise) to ensure that changes in timing and schedules don't affect the success of your initiative.

Duration:
Ideally, your pilot has the same duration as your initiative. However, sometimes this isn't possible—particularly if your full-fledged initiative will take place over years or will permanently apply shifters. In these cases, run your pilot for as long as is feasible and realistic so that you have enough time to see its full effects. Think of it this way: if you will be running your initiative permanently, you want to know as much as possible to get it right. The shorter the pilot, the less information you can use to iterate and refine elements of your initiative before implementing it in its entirety.

Determine when you will collect baseline data and outcome data

If your evaluation plan requires collecting baseline data (as most do), make sure you've collected baseline data on the pilot group (including treatment and control groups, if applicable) for your outcome metrics before launching your pilot program.

While you can start collecting process metrics as soon as you begin implementing the pilot, you should wait to collect outcome metrics until enough time has passed such that there is a reasonable expectation that behavior or environmental quality could have changed in response to your initiative. For example, if the initiative is designed to use signage to increase bus ridership, process indicators like the number of signs put up can be collected right away, but it may take months to observe an actual increase in bus ridership.

When possible, we recommend collecting outcome data more than once after your pilot ends. For example, if your initiative is intended to encourage people to unplug their unused electronics, measuring energy use shortly after the shifters are applied might show only a very small drop in energy use because people need time to develop the habit. And measuring again six months after the initiative might—if a habit has formed—show an even greater drop in energy use. Conversely, if you measure again a year later, you might see an uptick in energy use, indicating that people have lost motivation to continue unplugging their unused appliances and that you may need to reintroduce the shifters or try new shifters to remotivate them. Measuring later is essential for understanding the durability of the behavior change initiative.

❓ *Ask Yourself: Designing your pilot*

Pilots as experiments

- If you'll be using experimental design, what type of experiment will you conduct?

Choose your pilot audience and location

- Will your pilot audience be a subset of your priority audience, or will you sample your pilot audience from elsewhere?
- Will you choose a pilot audience that represents your full implementation audience as closely as possible, or will you have a different method of selecting your pilot audience that means it will be a little less representative?
- Is the location of the pilot representative of where you will conduct full implementation?
- Is the pilot audience large enough to be representative of the full audience for the initiative?

Determine the timing and duration of your pilot

- How closely can you match the duration and timing of your pilot to that of your full implementation?

Implement, evaluate, and refine your pilot

Now that you have designed your pilot, it's time to implement it, evaluate it, and refine it.

Implement your pilot

Roll out your pilot initiative to your pilot audience. Periodically monitor your shifters; are they still in operation? Collect process metrics and data throughout the pilot. Then it's time to move on to evaluation.

Evaluate your pilot

The point of conducting a pilot test is to learn what works, what doesn't work, and why, so that your shifters will work optimally when fully implemented. The evaluation of pilots and initiatives is a whole field unto itself. You will have to decide yourself whether you need a more rigorous evaluation by experts, which can take months and be expensive (but also can be very informative), or whether you would be satisfied with a more basic evaluation you can do yourself. If possible, ask members of the pilot audience for their perceptions and feedback on what did and did not work. Ultimately, you're seeking to answer the question: did my initiative achieve the goals I set in the INITIATE phase?

The goals of evaluating your pilot are to:

- Determine whether the initiative resulted in environmental change, behavior change, and other outcomes of interest
- Obtain insight into what worked, what didn't work, and what lessons can be used to improve future initiatives
- Share results and lessons learned, if applicable

Collect process data

During your pilot, you should collect data for the process metrics you identified as described above; periodically collect these data to evaluate progress against milestones and assess whether the program is progressing as intended. Doing so will provide valuable insight into whether you need to adjust your tactics or strategy if progress seems slow or blocked altogether. You might have to measure some metrics more frequently than others if they change more rapidly.

Check in with your team regularly to see how things are coming along. Take notes about how you and your team think the pilot is going. Is everything going to plan? Checking in is not only satisfying; as you check off tasks and celebrate progress, it's also crucial for adapting to unforeseen changes, mishaps, and strategic or tactical errors, as well as for taking advantage of unforseen successes.

Collect and evaluate outcome data

One of the most exciting parts of an initiative is discovering the effect it had on people's behavior. Now is the time to collect and analyze data on your outcome metrics to evaluate the effect of your pilot.

Did everything go according to plan, but behavior didn't shift? One possible explanation is you waited too long or not long enough to measure outcomes. Did behavior shift for some people but not others? Is there a pattern to these results (e.g., employees who live within 30 minutes of the office shifted to taking public transportation, but those that live farther did not)? Troubleshoot your initiative and consider why your pilot might not have been effective and if there is anything you can do to address that, but remember that a potential implication is that your pilot demonstrated that it is not worth the resources to fully implement your initiative.

Refine your initiative based on your pilot

Once you have run your pilot, you can apply what you learned. Is there anything that you need to adjust about your initiative? This could be tweaking things that didn't quite work or adding new components to amplify what worked really well.

Consider information from many sources—look at your outcome data, your process data, notes on how smoothly the pilot went, your evaluation of how well the shifters worked together, and audience and stakeholder feedback. Use this feedback to evaluate and refine your initiative before you launch the full-fledged version. (See prototyping in DESIGN: Process Chapter 4 for how to gather audience feedback.) Use the following categories to guide your refinement.

Audience selection and recruitment

Did anything about the pilot reveal something unexpected about your chosen audience that might cause you to reevaluate your selection or segmentation? Did you face any recruitment challenges, such as with obtaining a representative sample? If so, how might you overcome them for full implementation?

Location, timing, duration, and budget

Did you implement your suite of shifters in the best location? Were there any unforeseen issues with the timing of your pilot (e.g., a recurring event that conflicts with your initiative timing)? Might you be more successful if you implemented it for a longer period of time? Did your pilot incur unforeseen costs that make implementing it at full-scale unattainable?

Data collection procedures

Are there process or outcome data that you did not collect that you wish you had? Sometimes it can be difficult to anticipate all of the data, especially process data, that might be useful until you implement your pilot. For example, you may wish that in addition to collecting data on the number of people you asked to sign a pledge, you had also collected data on where you were doing the asking so that you knew which locations resulted in the most pledge sign ups. Formalize the collection of this data moving forward, so that you can use it to guide recruitment efforts during full implementation.

Share results and lessons learned

Even if you aren't planning on implementing your initiative at full scale, it's still good practice to debrief and consider lessons learned. Consider sharing your results publicly if possible (both what worked and what didn't) to help other practitioners.

• • •

To increase the likelihood that your full initiative will be successful, we strongly recommend that you first pilot your initiative, evaluate the pilot, and then adapt the initiative once you learn more about what is working, what's not working, and why. Piloting an initiative provides an opportunity to tweak the initiative, based on your evaluation of it, before it's rolled out. Piloting can also be a way to increase buy-in before full implementation, as participants in the pilot model the new behavior to their peers.

❓ *Ask Yourself: Implement, evaluate, and refine your pilot*
General
- How well do you think your pilot went?
- Did anything unexpected arise during your pilot?
- Overall, how did the audience react to your initiative? Were you able to gather audience feedback?
- Based on results and feedback from your pilot audience, what worked with your initiative, what didn't work, and why?
- How well did your shifters work when applied together?
- How can you use the insights gained during the pilot to modify the initiative and shifters?

Process and outcome metrics

- How closely did your pilot remain "on plan" (e.g., timing, cost, duration, audience selection)?
- Are you evaluating outcome metrics after sufficient time has passed to see a change in behavior?
- Are you evaluating outcome metrics after sufficient time has passed to see if the behavior returned to pre-initiative levels?

- What did the outcome and process metrics indicate about the effectiveness of the initiative?
- Was your pilot effective enough that you plan to fully implement your initiative?
- How will you share results and lessons learned?

 ## Implement Your Full-Fledged Initiative

Now that you've piloted your initiative, you're ready to roll it out to your full audience. This is mostly the same process that we outlined for piloting, but at a larger scale. You may have already planned your full implementation (considering details such as how big your audience will be, how long your initiative will last, when it will occur, and where it will take place), but you should take the time to reflect on your pilot and make necessary changes to ensure success. There are some key considerations for implementing:

- If your pilot did not go well, will you refine your pilot and run another pilot, fully implement your refined initiative immediately, or wait for months or longer before full implementation? Will you rebrand your initiative?
- Your audience may already be familiar with your initiative. How can you leverage any positive attention you garnered from the pilot?
- If you plan to scale your initiative, it is critical that anyone from the community or priority audience who will take over implementation and scaling should shadow your team as much as possible.

Conclusion

Congratulations—you've reached the end of the *Making Shift Happen* process! Successfully implementing your initiative requires careful planning, testing, and iteration, but it's well worth it. We hope that in this phase, you were able to see your hard work pay off in the form of slowing, stopping, or reversing environmental degradation. By carefully designing and implementing your initiative, and by deploying innovative and evidence-based behavior-based solutions, you have enhanced the prospects that more audiences will take up the desired behavior change, producing results that are commensurate with the large scale of many environmental problems. Consider sharing your results and lessons learned with others, so that they too can *make shift happen*.

Methods

Y OU CAN'T MAKE SHIFT HAPPEN without doing your homework. Researching and understanding important aspects of your priority audience is at the core of *Making Shift Happen*. This chapter will help you kick start your behavioral research. In the following sections, we will introduce common methods for doing research and provide advice on how to design your research effort. By choosing the right research methods, you can uncover meaningful insights to inform your behavior change initiative. Once you have a sense of your research direction, we urge you to consult more comprehensive resources such as those we have compiled at the end of this chapter.

A Look Ahead: METHODS

Research Methods for Different Stages of the *Making Shift Happen* Process

Secondary Research Methods

Review relevant literature

Resource gathering interviews

Primary Research Methods

Observations

Surveys

Interviews

Focus groups

Experiments and quasi-experiments

Designing Primary Research

Collecting data on and measuring key variables

Sampling from your priority audience

Analyzing Primary Research

Analyzing qualitative data

Analyzing quantitative data

Additional Resources

Research Methods for Different Stages of the *Making Shift Happen* Process

You have a variety of research methods in your toolbox that you can employ at various points in the *Making Shift Happen* process. Which tools you use and which types of data you collect will depend on where the gaps are in your understanding of the environmental problem, your priority audience, and your audience's behavior.

Different research methods are best used at different stages of the *Making Shift Happen* process. For example, literature reviews and resource gathering interviews are a great starting point to help us uncover what is already known about our environmental issue, our audience, and their behaviors. Observations tend to be particularly useful during INITIATE: Process Chapter 2 and in the early stages of UNCOVER: Process Chapter 3, when we are trying to wrap our minds around the issue and our audience. Experiments, on the other hand, may be premature during the early stages of the process, but help us test our ideas and, ultimately, the efficacy of our *shifters*—evidence-based behavior change solutions—during DESIGN: Process Chapter 4 and IMPLEMENT: Process Chapter 5.

Biases in Research: What Biases Do You Bring to the Table?

When designing and conducting research, remind yourself about common cognitive biases that can impact your research design decisions (e.g., confirmation bias, the availability bias, and the planning fallacy; see FOUNDATIONS: Process Chapter 1 for an introduction to common cognitive biases). For example, your opinions on an issue may influence the sources you seek out and choose to accept when doing research. This could cause you to miss valid and valuable information from sources that reflect other perspectives. While it's impossible to avoid or overcome our cognitive biases entirely, you can limit them by including outsider perspectives and using techniques such as those described in LONGEVITY: Building Block Chapter 10.

Below is a table outlining how different research methods can help us at different stages of the research *Making Shift Happen* process. Keep this table about the different stages of the process in mind as you learn about each method in more detail below.

Table 1.6.1: Research Methods at Each Stage of the *Making Shift Happen* Process

Stage	Purpose / Goals	Research Methods
Initiate	• Identify and learn about potential priority audiences • Identify and learn about potential priority behaviors • Set behavior change goals • Identify appropriate metrics	• Literature reviews • Resource gathering interviews • Observations • Surveys (in particular, an Audience Analysis survey)
Uncover	• Identify barriers to behavior change • Identify motivators of behavior	• Literature reviews • Resource gathering interviews • Observations • Focus groups • Interviews • Surveys (in particular, a Behavioral Drivers Analysis survey)
Design	• Determine how you should segment your audience • Get more information about things like audience preferences and tendencies to better design your shifters • A/B test different versions of a shifter • Solicit feedback on prototypes	• Literature reviews • Resource gathering interviews • Observations • Focus groups • Interviews • Surveys • Experiments
Implement	• Pilot your initiative • Implement and evaluate your initiative	• Observations • Interviews • Surveys • Experiments

Secondary Research Methods

At its broadest level, research is classified as primary or secondary. The research methods you will use to inform your initiative draw on both primary and secondary methods. The rest of this chapter organizes research methods by primary and secondary, and discusses in more detail what each type of research is.

Secondary research involves reviewing and analyzing information created or collected at another time, in another location, or for another purpose. Existing data, reports, publications, and articles serve as information sources for secondary research. This can take the form of internal data (e.g., your own organization's records and documents or results from past surveys or focus groups), or it can take the form of external data (e.g., published case studies, reports, or academic journal articles). Secondary research gets us started, and mostly happens early in the process, but it is helpful later as well, as we seek inspiration for designing shifters and fine-tune our ideas.

Secondary research may even give you access to more and better information than you could gather yourself. For example, social scientists may have already surveyed thousands of people in your priority audience and critically evaluated the results. Take advantage of these existing pools of information, but remember that no two research objectives are alike. We may still have a number of unanswered questions about our audience or their behavior.

Although there are other forms of secondary research out there, here we discuss two that are most relevant to the *Making Shift Happen* process: literature reviews and resource gathering interviews. We recommend that all practitioners start their initiatives with this type of research. Each is described in detail later in the chapter.

- **Review relevant literature:** an examination of existing information sources, most commonly journal articles, government reports, or datasets
- **Resource gathering interviews:** a semistructured conversation with knowledge partners to gather information about the issue or audience

Review relevant literature

Searching for literature is an iterative process that takes some patience and skill. Although it can take a bit of work to gain access to and review existing sources, diligent research will ultimately help your initiative be more successful. It can be quite interesting and rewarding to learn more about environmental issues, your audience, and how people have used shifters in the past. When reviewing the sources you find, pay close attention to any relationships, themes, and major gaps that emerge.

Be a Critical Consumer of Research

Most of our behavior change recommendations are based at least in part on academic research, so we want to take a moment to recognize a few of its potential limitations. Studies conducted in a lab can only attempt to replicate real-life scenarios, and are usually limited by smaller sample sizes. Academic studies also often use college students as study participants, which can be a problem for generalizing the results to different audiences. Below we provide a brief overview of some of the most common limitations built into many academic studies.

Culture and context

In both academia and applied contexts, there is a tendency to conduct studies using participants from Western, Educated, Industrialized, Rich, and Democratic countries (sometimes referred to as "WEIRD" countries). Yet, WEIRD countries represent a relatively small percentage of the world's population.[3] The lived experience of people from WEIRD countries can be markedly different from those living elsewhere in the world, which has considerable psychological and behavioral ramifications. So we need to be careful about over-generalizing conclusions from studies conducted in WEIRD countries among largely white populations.

Relatedly, the social sciences have been criticized for their lack of replicability (known as the "replication crisis"), particularly for experiments that study cognition and behavior.[18] Unlike natural or physical sciences that (in theory) should be able to replicate results many times over, the study of the human mind is extremely complex, and results are shaped by various contextual factors that can cause a shifter to work in one scenario but not in another. Data collection in the social sciences can also be challenging, as it often relies on observational data or self-reporting from participants (which can be skewed by biases).[9]

Correlation vs. causation

It's also more difficult for social science research to demonstrate *causality*, which means that we can show that the shifter we applied directly influenced behavior.[6] Without the right conditions to show causality (discussed in greater detail in our section on experiments and quasi-experiments below), we are looking at *correlation* instead, which shows a pattern or relationship between factors, but not that one thing caused another. Correlational data is more common and it still provides very useful insights, which we draw from often in our behavior change work. It's simply important to be aware of the difference between correlation and causation when you are conducting research or interpreting results.

Preparing for a literature search

To prepare for your search, start by clarifying what you need from your research. Conversations with your client, relevant decision-makers, and other technical experts will help you to hone in on what is known about the issue and give you insights into the language used to discuss the topic. These conversations can help you identify, among other things, the following information that can be used to improve your literature search process:

- **Identify useful keywords:** Whether you use Google Scholar or an academic search engine, you'll need to generate relevant keywords to guide your search. Finding the right search terms to fit your needs can be a process of trial and error, but you can focus on those that come up repeatedly in your materials and client conversations. For example, to find articles about past behavior change initiatives, you should search using words like "initiative," "campaign," "intervention," or "nudge."
- **Identify the experts:** Find the people and organizations who are investigating similar issues. Identifying and communicating with experts on a given topic often reveals a wealth of information. Similarly, you will find that some organizations are centered around a given topic of research. Those that regularly conduct or fund research on the issue may catalog relevant press releases and reports in research repositories on their websites.

Conducting a literature search

When conducting your search, it's useful to consult a variety of resources to learn from unique perspectives. Seek out academic articles, books, white papers or reports, presentations, datasets, and website content from researchers in academia, private companies, nonprofits, and government agencies. Further, reputable news outlets can provide high quality articles and press releases. It can also be helpful to search social media for posts and discussions about your issue. Just remember, when reviewing sources of any kind, it's better to seek out and read the original source than to get your information secondhand.

Tips for using a search engine

Consult industry and academic sources by using Google, Google Scholar, or an institution's academic literature search engine (we recommend using an aggregated search tool that searches multiple databases, rather than one database at a time) to search for your keywords. Regardless of which search engines you use, there are a number of things you can do to optimize your literature search.[8] Here are a few basic tips:

- **Try advanced search options:** You can filter your results by the type of publication and year it was published.

- **Use search notation:** Putting search terms in quotes (i.e., "environmental behavior") tells a search engine that any results must have exactly that word or phrase. This is particularly helpful when searching terms that can return thousands of unrelated results. We can also use the term AND (to search multiple keywords), OR (to search one keyword or an alternative one), or NOT (to find one keyword but exclude another) in a search. For example, we might search for: "active transportation" + "behavior change" + (bike OR cycling OR bicycle) + (barriers OR motivators) + (campaign OR initiative OR intervention).

- **Follow the paper trail:** It's useful to see who your source cites, as well as who cites them! You can do so by looking at information about the article on the search engine (e.g., "Cited by…" and "Citations"). Citation count can also convey valuable information about the quality of a source—papers that are classics in their field tend to have counts that can be anywhere from several hundred to several thousand!

Tips for gaining access to resources

Academic articles can be tricky to access: they may be unavailable without a journal subscription. However, there are several strategies you could use to access these articles. You can oftentimes find links to the PDFs posted on researchers' academic websites by searching for the article title on a search engine. In many cases, you can directly email the author (many article previews display the lead author's primary email address). ResearchGate, a free social media platform for researchers, is another useful resource for accessing published resources.

Resource gathering interviews

When conducting secondary research, you can scour the internet for published material, but don't forget to reach out directly to peers and colleagues for their insights! Whenever possible, contact other practitioners and researchers directly to ask if they have any articles, data, or materials (e.g., questionnaires) they could share. Many will be happy to share the latest information they have with you.

Because it can take months or even years to publish a paper, their information is almost always more up-to-date than the published literature.

In some cases, you may wish to conduct a ***resource gathering interview***, an informal conversation with knowledge partners to discuss the environmental problem you're looking to address. Researchers may have lots of insights and practical information to share from their experiences with similar past and current initiatives. These conversations can shed light on possible drivers and shifters. Importantly, knowing what hasn't worked is just as valuable as knowing what has! Note that resource gathering interviews are good for the bigger picture, but shouldn't replace direct contact with your audience.

Although less formal, the quality of your resource gathering interviews would benefit from many of the same tips used to design interviews with your audience. Consider the best practices shared in the later section about interviews. We also discuss more on the value of conducting resource gathering interviews with knowledge partners and provide guidance on what to ask in INITIATE: Process Chapter 2.

• • •

While secondary research is invaluable, primary research is often necessary in order to gain a deeper understanding of your audience. For the rest of this chapter, we discuss primary research: how to pick primary research methods, how to design your primary research, and how to analyze primary research results.

Primary Research Methods

Looking at the work and efforts of others is invaluable for the design of your initiative. But if existing research hasn't sufficiently answered all of your questions (and it rarely will), it's time to start thinking about conducting original, or primary, research. Understanding how your audience thinks and behaves is at the heart of the *Making Shift Happen* process, and the most thorough way to do this is by conducting primary research to gain insights directly from your specific audience.

Primary research refers to firsthand data collection: directly observing, surveying, or interviewing your audience. This kind of research might sound difficult and time-consuming, and it certainly can be, but it's generally worth the effort. When choosing primary research methods, don't let perfect be the enemy of good; you don't have to be an expert to do it! Even if you lack the time and resources to use some of these methods, you can still gain valuable insights by asking a few targeted questions. For the rest of this chapter, we discuss how to choose primary research methods, how to design your primary research, and how to analyze the data you collect through your primary research. We start by exploring five common primary research methods for gathering audience insights below:

- **Observation:** Non-intrusive monitoring of the audience in a natural setting
- **Survey:** A fixed series of questions posed by you to participants
- **Interview:** A structured conversation between you and the participant
- **Focus group:** A facilitated discussion with a small group of participants
- **Experiment or quasi-experiment:** Implementing and examining a change for the purpose of determining cause and effect

Observations

Direct observation—the non-intrusive monitoring of your audience in a real-world setting—is one of the oldest data collection methods used to understand human behavior.[7,10] It may involve, for example, sitting in a restaurant and watching how people dispose of leftover food. People aren't always accurate in reporting their own behavior, so observation is usually a more accurate way to measure behavior than surveys, interviews, and focus groups. Observation can help us to learn more about our audience's behavior, as well as to measure behavior before, during, and after our initiative. When paired with self-reported data, direct observations can also illuminate contrasts between people's reported intentions and their actual behavior, which can be invaluable for designing shifters.

Before you begin your observations, you'll need to be clear on what exactly you want to observe. For example, if you're interested in composting behavior in a restaurant, you may have to decide whether you want to look for correct composting behavior or simply observe whether people are attempting to compost at all. You may also note the location of composting bins, or look for signage instructing people how to compost their food. You might observe the weather or types of homes found in the neighborhood to help inform your observations on energy use. Environmental factors can include anything that prompts behavior, like signs or other subtle cues, as well as external barriers to behaviors. What you already know may influence what you choose to prioritize in your observations.

Besides what to observe, there are many other factors to consider when preparing for your observation. How will you collect your data (i.e., by observing in real-time vs. video-taped lab sessions)? How long will you need to observe to understand the behavior adequately? How and when can you best observe the specific audience? There are no right or wrong answers to any of these questions. What's most important is how these decisions fit your initiative's goals and constraints.

A key thing to remember when making observations is to stay unnoticed: be as unobtrusive as possible, as people often alter their behavior if they know someone is observing them. When you're in the field, make sure to station yourself out of the way so that you don't interfere with your subjects' activities, while respecting any rules and signage in the area. Try to match the dress code of the area: don't show up at a fancy restaurant in flip flops or a hunting area in a lab coat. In some instances, you'll need (or want) to secure permission to make your direct observations, such as in a private business.

Finally, while it's important to maintain field notes and diaries, don't let note-taking distract you from the observation itself. Photographs and video recordings, when appropriate, can come in handy when you have lots of information to capture. Having help can also make it easier to spot as much relevant information as possible in a busy scene. Additionally, by increasing objectivity, visual records like these and additional observers help fight *observer bias*, the tendency for researchers to see what they want to see in the environment.

Surveys

While observations help us see behavior in action, surveys, interviews, and focus groups help us gather information about things we can't easily observe, like our audience's thoughts, attitudes, and past experiences. Surveys can be long or short, and they can be administered online, on paper, or in-person (i.e., intercept surveys). Surveys are useful to collect data from larger and more diverse groups of people than is possible with interviews or focus groups. Additionally, collecting survey data tends to be relatively inexpensive and fast. Though surveys are an effective method of gathering quantitative data, including open-ended questions can enhance the survey by allowing for qualitative insights.

Below we give advice for designing your survey: keeping your survey focused and actionable, writing strong survey questions, reducing survey bias, and testing your survey.

Keep your survey focused and questions actionable

A survey should take no longer than 20 minutes to complete, so you'll have to focus and prioritize your questions. As we know, we have limited opportunities to capture our audience's attention, even when we're presenting fun and engaging content! Participating in research isn't something most people want to spend their time doing, so we have to make the experience as painless as possible, otherwise our data quality may suffer. Your questions should be highly tailored to your priority audience and their situation, as you can quickly lose your audience's attention when your questions begin to sound irrelevant. For instance, a series of questions about one's workplace can quickly frustrate a full-time student. To remedy this, consider adding instructions in your interview script about skipping questions that do not apply, or design your online survey to automatically skip questions or sections that are not relevant to certain audiences.

There are an endless number and type of questions you can ask your audience. You can probably think of almost a dozen in the span of a couple of minutes! Listing your survey's specific goals is a necessary step to focus and limit the number and type of questions you ask.[14] There are many things that would be "nice to know" or interesting about our audience, but that we can't do anything about. For a question to make it into the study, being interesting is not enough.

We need to choose questions that are most likely to deliver useful, actionable insights about our audience. For example, when studying bus ridership, you might be tempted to ask questions like "What features would make taking the bus more attractive?" However, if we cannot implement these types of upgrades, this question is not only inactionable, it may be highly disappointing when suggestions go unmet. Therefore, you should always think to yourself: "What will I do with the answer to this question?" or "How will this information help me answer my research questions?"

Carefully design your survey questions

It's important to carefully word our survey questions to make sure we produce data that are helpful, accurate, and easy to interpret. How you ask your questions depends on what you need to get out of the answers.[11]

If your aim is to understand and collect information on all possible types of answers, an *unaided* or *open-ended* question is preferable. With open-ended questions, participants write in or verbalize their own responses. Their responses could end up being a few words, or even a few paragraphs. Collecting these types of responses can be invaluable, particularly if you don't yet know a lot about your audience, as it allows you to hear perspectives that you wouldn't have thought to put in as possible answer choices. However, note that open-ended questions can be a bit challenging for participants, who are responsible for generating their own responses. Additionally, interpreting and coding open-ended answers can be time-consuming for the researcher, especially when working with large sample sizes.

If you are looking to restrict answers and just compare a few options against one another, an *aided* or *closed-ended* question, like a yes/no, multiple choice, or ranking question, is preferred. Closed-ended questions are ideal for large sample sizes, as responses are easily quantifiable and take much less time to analyze than open-ended responses. However, since the researcher is responsible for providing the response options, closed-ended questions require a clear understanding of the range of possible responses. For this reason, we almost always recommend including an "other" option for respondents to fill in in case you missed an important close-ended response. If you have time, we recommend conducting a few interviews or deploying a brief survey to ask important questions in open-ended form to generate a robust list of potential responses for closed-ended survey questions.

Open-Ended Questions	Closed-Ended Questions
What modes of transportation do you use?	Which of the following modes of transportation do you use?
_____	*Select all that apply.*
_____	❑ city bus
_____	❑ private shuttle
_____	❑ personal vehicle
_____	❑ bicycle/scooter
_____	❑ Uber/Lyft/taxi
_____	❑ Other, please specify:
_____	_____

Below we share more information about some of the most commonly used closed-ended question types.

- **Yes/No:** Survey participants must select either yes or no.
- **List of Options:** Survey participants choose the best option(s) from a list you provide. For example, you might ask participants to select what makes it difficult for them to bike to work (e.g., weather, topography, distance, road conditions, infrastructure). You can ask respondents to select one option, several, or all that apply.
- **Ranking Scale:** A ranking scale question asks respondents to compare items to one another. For example, you might ask participants to rank which factors make it the most difficult for them to bike to work.
- **Rating Scale:** There are many established rating scales to choose from. Rating scales are often formatted as Likert scales (more information on these below).

Likert scales are a popular closed-ended question type that allow participants to rate their response using a range of values. These scales are useful for measuring agreement ("strongly disagree" to "strongly agree"), frequency ("never" to "always"), importance ("not at all" to "extremely"), and likelihood ("not likely" to "extremely likely"). We can also use a Likert scale when we want our audience to rate difficulty, interest, willingness, or virtually anything that can be rated (e.g., we could even rate how cute people find kittens). Here's just one idea for how you might use a Likert scale in a closed-ended question for a behavior change initiative about composting:

I am willing to pay to have compost collected at my home.

Strongly Disagree	Disagree	Agree	Strongly Agree
◯	◯	◯	◯

   Likert scales usually offer four to seven options that range from one extreme (not at all likely, not at all important, not at all difficult, etc.) to the other (very likely, very important, very difficult, etc.). For example, when we use an *agreement scale*, respondents rate how much they agree with a statement on a scale from "strongly agree" to "strongly disagree." Likert scales should be symmetrical (e.g., with equal numbers of agreement and disagreement), and they should measure just one idea. For example, rather than asking a question on a scale ranging from "extremely brave" to "extremely shy," you should instead use a scale ranging from "extremely brave" to "not at all brave." Why? Bravery is not necessarily the opposite of shyness. *Unipolar scales* like these are easier for people to wrap their heads around. Unipolar scales also leave us, the researchers, more sure about the validity and soundness of our measure.

Reduce survey bias

Because surveys are administered with minimal interaction from you, they require a great deal of care to elicit accurate responses. Part of this means avoiding different kinds of bias from your participants. *Response bias* refers to the myriad ways in which participants respond inaccurately (whether intentionally or unintentionally). Participants may not answer accurately because they want to tell you what you want to hear, they may get tired, or the order of the questions may prime them for certain answers. There are many ways to reduce response bias, including making the survey anonymous, randomizing question order, using clear and accessible language, and making sure your questions really capture what you intend to measure. It's especially important to use neutral language when writing your survey questions. For example, word your questions in ways that don't reveal your personal stance or beliefs (i.e., favoring one answer over another):

- Is taking the bus less stressful than driving?
  - → Which mode of transportation is less stressful to you:
    a) taking the bus or b) driving?
- Is a vegetarian diet less expensive than one which includes meat?
  - → Is it less expensive to eat:
    a) a vegetarian diet or b) one that includes meat?

Researchers can also introduce bias when they reveal the exact purpose of their research. For example, avoid starting with "We are trying to stop the use of disposable utensils, a leading source of trash that kills wildlife" because introductions like these can lead respondents to answer how they think the survey designer or administrator wants them to (in this case, respondents might underreport the amount of disposable utensils that they use to avoid the administrator's disapproval). Instead, you could use a more neutral introduction like "Our goal is to learn more about how serviceware is used by restaurants in the county." Sharing the exact purpose of the survey can also influence whether or not people decide to partake in the research in the first place. Frequent users of disposable utensils might choose not to take the survey at all if the introduction makes them feel attacked or ashamed. Thus, we also find it helpful to have language in the introduction that makes it clear we are seeking to understand equally both those who do the behavior and those who don't. As you continue to learn more about research, keep an eye out for other ways to reduce response bias.

Test your survey

Always pretest your survey with a group similar to your priority audience before you administer it to make sure that it is understandable and not too long in length. Testing, or "piloting," your survey will also give you a sense of timing and the opportunity to work out any potential issues with wording.

A Special Type of Survey: Intercept Surveys

Intercept surveys are typically short encounters with the audience in the setting where they perform the behavior. For example, we can intercept a customer as they're shopping for lightbulbs with a quick question or two about their experience.

There are several advantages of intercept surveys:

- Intercept surveys are useful when you can observe the behavior or you can find your audience by visual cues or by going to a specific location, or if finding your priority audience online might be difficult.
- Intercept surveys are useful for getting people's quick, spur-of-the-moment responses to questions.
- Intercept surveys are great to conduct prior to larger, more formal surveys. The data you gather can help you draft your longer questionnaires.

Some limitations of intercept surveys include:

- You can only interview or survey one person at a time. This means you may also get a smaller sample size than online surveys.
- At certain locations, intercept surveys may be more objectionable than observation. Many locations, like hardware stores, have rules against soliciting customers on their property. You may have to obtain permission from the site before conducting your survey.
- You may only be able to intercept a non-representative portion of your audience. The practitioner interviewing customers who are buying lightbulbs, for example, will not have the opportunity to survey those who are not yet shopping for new lightbulbs.

Interviews

Interviews are documented conversations held between a researcher and a participant. You might choose your interview participants for their ability to represent a priority audience, for their diversity of perspectives, or because they are well-connected within their group. Your goal is to select participants who represent the range of opinions held by your priority audience, and keep interviewing until you no longer hear new perspectives.

It's helpful to create an interview guide, a series of prepared questions before beginning to interview participants. Like with surveys, your interview questions should use neutral language to avoid biasing responses. Interview questions should also be open-ended to elicit detailed responses. Your interview guide can also include examples of follow-up or prompting questions that you might ask after a respondent gives their initial answer. For example, after asking a participant about their opinions on a particular transportation mode, you can also ask participants to recall past experiences with that mode to get more detailed information.[4]

Your interview guide can stick to a predetermined list of questions (called a structured interview), or it can consist of questions and topic areas to facilitate a less formal conversation that could include new questions or topics (a semistructured interview). A structured interview format promotes consistency across interviews with different individuals, while a semistructured interview promotes a more comfortable, conversational tone, and the interviewer has the ability to follow up on interesting responses.

In addition to planning your questions via an interview guide, it's also helpful to conduct a practice interview with a colleague or friend to help you work out potential issues (e.g., confusing wording, questions that need altering, and the approximate duration of the interview). When practicing your interview, also be cognizant of time. As a rule of thumb, interviews should last no longer than an hour; it's important to be considerate of the time and energy of interview participants.

Once you are prepared, you can conduct your interviews in several ways. While phone or video calls are increasingly popular and may be more convenient when dealing with geographic, physical, or other constraints, they may lose some of the depth and nuance of in-person interviews.

Focus groups

Focus groups are documented conversations among five to ten people led by a facilitator.[12] The role of participants is to educate the facilitator about their thoughts and experiences as representatives of the priority audience (or a specific subgroup of the priority audience). While focus groups share many similarities with interviews, a key difference is that with a focus group, you are viewing the responses you collect as reflective of the entire group, rather than tracking individual responses. This is because individuals respond differently if they are being interviewed in a room with their peers as opposed to in a one-on-one setting. Focus groups allow you to get a variety of perspectives in a potentially shorter time frame than interviews. They also help you observe how social dynamics or social norms might be influencing audience members' opinions or the uptake of a behavior. While providing a lot of detail about focus group facilitation is beyond the scope of this book, we want you to be aware of focus groups as an option and some of the advantages and limitations of this method.

Many aspects of planning a focus group, such as identifying participants, writing your interview questions ahead of time, and practicing beforehand to work out potential issues, involve the same steps that you would take for planning an interview. Just like an interview study, you know that you've gathered enough data when you stop encountering new ideas or perspectives. However, one additional consideration for focus groups is which participants will be assigned to each focus group. Try to group individuals who share similar characteristics like profession, geographic region, or pay grade to increase their comfort with sharing to the group.

Once you've planned out all aspects of your focus groups, you're ready to conduct them. There are a few considerations for conducting successful focus groups. First, it can be helpful to plan ahead of time how you will introduce yourself to the participants. To ensure that all participants share an understanding of why you are meeting and what to expect, this introduction should establish 1) overall initiative goals, 2) goals for this focus group, and 3) respective roles. Next, it's important to establish ground rules with your participants, which can prevent potential communication issues. Some example ground rules include "don't interrupt others," "agree to disagree with respect," and "what we discuss in this room will not leave this room." Consider drafting a few of your own before the meeting, then encouraging the group to add to your prepared list.

Once the focus group is underway, your role transitions to that of a facilitator, where you're primarily ensuring that everyone stays on task and on time, and that everyone has the opportunity to be heard. During the focus group, you may find that some participants are hesitant to speak. Lean into the silence and allow participants to contemplate a response. If you don't fill the silence, then your participants will, which will help you hear more from them. Try to only interrupt if a discussion is veering off-topic. In this case, politely redirect the conversation back to the topic at hand. You may also want to take this opportunity to remind participants of the agenda, ground rules, and the limited time that is set to accomplish the focus group goals, ensuring that your time spent together is valuable.

Experiments and quasi-experiments

When you're ready to test the impact or efficacy of your overall initiative or of specific shifters, we recommend designing your efforts as an experiment. *Experiments* enable us to make inferences about cause and effect to determine whether our shifters affected behavior. In other words, they can answer: "did our shifter change behavior, and how well?" Although experiments and quasi-experiments are a primary research method on their own, they rely on other data collection methods, such as observations or surveys, to evaluate outcomes.

By holding constant as many variables as possible that could impact our audience's behavior, experiments enable us to isolate a shifter's (or whole initiative's) impact on an outcome. For example, let's say we want to encourage towel reuse in hotel rooms. We can design an experiment in which we randomly assign guests to rooms that either have signage wishing them a nice stay and mentioning that the majority of guests reuse their towels (invoking social norms), or that simply have signage wishing them a nice stay. We flip a coin to determine which rooms get which condition: the sign invoking social norms or only the "nice stay" sign. If we set up an experiment this way, if there is a change in behavior among those who received messaging about social norms, we can more confidently conclude that it alone nudged them to reuse their towels.

Complete control in an experiment is impossible, but that doesn't mean we shouldn't strive for it. The three main elements of control in an experiment are:[17]

Manipulation:

The *experimental manipulation,* or *treatment,* is a new thing, like a shifter, that is designed and introduced by the researcher. It's this treatment that's expected to change participants' thoughts or behavior. In our context, the "treatment" might be an individual shifter or the initiative as a whole (i.e., a suite of shifters). In the hypothetical hotel experiment above, the experimental manipulation was the extra line on the sign invoking social norms.

Comparison:

Another key element of experimentation is comparison: dividing your participants into at least two groups—a treatment group and a control group. The *experimental* (or *treatment*) *group* is exposed to the manipulation (i.e., the new shifter or initiative), and the second group (the *control group*) is not exposed to the manipulation (i.e., the status quo or current way of doing things). In the hotel experiment, we have two groups: guests who were wished a nice stay (the control group) and those who received additional messaging about social norms (the treatment group). We could also add another treatment group to compare more than one variation of our shifter in a single study. We could create a third group of hotel guests to whom we would offer a small gift, like a chocolate, along with our message invoking social norms to see if this is even more effective than simply words invoking social norms. Including this third group is a great way to test out multiple shifters before designing our full-fledged initiative.

Randomization:

Another essential element of experimentation is randomization. Ideally, the only thing that differs between the treatment and control groups is exposure to our shifter. We can prevent systematic differences between groups by using ***random sampling*** to select participants from our priority audience (discussed in greater detail later in the chapter, in the section about sampling) and then using ***random assignment*** to put them into the groups described above. In the hotel example, we randomly assigned guests to either the control group (no signage) or the experimental group (signage) by flipping a coin prior to their arrival. By contrast, assigning hotel floors 1–5 to the control group and floors 6–10 to the treatment group would be non-random assignment; in this case, we wouldn't be able to tell as confidently that changes in behavior between the two groups were due to our shifter alone. What if the rooms on floors 6–10 are more expensive? The guests on those floors may behave differently than those on other floors, regardless of our shifter.

Although not a required feature of an experiment, another factor that increases control and our ability to detect an effect is ***repeated measurement***: testing (collecting data on) the same participants both before and after the treatment. By including a ***pretest*** or ***baseline*** measure, we complement the required elements of experiments—further removing "noise." Collecting pretest data enables us to examine whether there were any preexisting differences between our groups (despite random assignment), and account for it by subtracting it from the posttest data. It also helps us determine the amount of change that can be attributed to the treatment. That is, it shows us just how great an effect the manipulation had on our treatment group's behavior (i.e., the magnitude or size of the impact).

There may be times when you can't run a true experiment: a study featuring all three elements of an experiment (manipulation, comparison, and randomization). In these cases, you can run a ***quasi-experiment,*** which is similar to an experiment, but is missing one or more of those elements. In our experience, it's most common to a) have a control group but lack random assignment into groups, or b) lack a control group all together. It's less likely that we'll design a study which lacks experimental manipulation, though sometimes researchers are limited to examining the effects of ***natural manipulations,*** treatments that are not introduced by the researchers, such as natural disasters or policy changes.

On page 234, we'll discuss common experimental designs (e.g., classic controlled experiment, between-groups experiment) and quasi-experimental designs (e.g., one-group designs, nonequivalent groups designs) used in behavioral research. Table 1.6.2 summarizes the elements included in each type.

Table 1.6.2: Common Experimental and Quasi-Experimental Designs

	Design	Treatment	Control group	Random assignment	Pretest	Posttest
True Experiments	Pretest-posttest control group design (i.e., classic controlled experiment)	X	X	X	X	X
	Posttest-only control group design (i.e., between-groups experiment)	X	X	X		X
Quasi-Experiments	Pretest-posttest nonequivalent groups design	X	X		X	X
	Posttest-only nonequivalent groups design	X	X			X
	Pretest-posttest one-group design	X			X	X
	Posttest-only one-group design	X				X

Designing a true experiment

The following experimental designs contain each of the three elements of control required to be a "true experiment." They only vary in their use of pretest data.

Using a pretest-posttest control group design

The **pretest-posttest control group design**, also known as the **classic controlled experiment**, involves all of the classic elements of an experiment—designing a treatment, randomly assigning participants to a control or treatment group, along with added control from also collecting pretest and posttest data on both groups. Though not always feasible, this type of experiment is the gold standard.

Let's say that we want to encourage employees at a large, national company to cycle to work. To do so, we can use the company contact list to randomly assign people to receive a personalized travel plan via email or not, and examine the number of days members of each group ride to work in the month before receiving their travel plan, as well as during the months after receiving it. Then, we can subtract the pretest scores from posttest scores for both groups and compare the amount of change in the treatment group to the amount of change in the control group. The advantage of collecting pretest data here is identifying the magnitude of the effect, the disadvantages are that it can be expensive and time-consuming.

Using a posttest-only control group design

You won't always have the ability to collect baseline data (pretest data). The next best thing to demonstrate the impact of your shifters is a ***posttest-only control group design*** (also called a ***between-groups experiment*** or ***randomized controlled trial***). Like the previous experimental design, the between groups experiment compares two randomly assigned groups (the treatment and control groups). Unlike the previous design, however, data from these groups are only collected after the treatment. An advantage to this approach is that it can be a shorter study because you only need to collect data from your groups one time. However, a disadvantage of this approach is that since you will not have pretest data (which strengthens your study), you generally need more participants to identify effects.

Designing a quasi-experiment with two groups (non-random assignment)

Sometimes, it's difficult or impossible to randomly assign participants to groups. Continuing with our bike-riding example where we're testing a reward for a large company with multiple offices, we may not be able to randomly assign office participants if we have to offer (or not offer) the reward to each of the company's offices as a whole. (This could be for various reasons: perhaps because office policies would prohibit you from assigning some employees within an office to the treatment group and others to the control, or because it would be impossible for some employees within an office to not find out about the program). In this case, participants would be grouped into treatment and control groups by the office they work at.

We can't consider this design to have random assignment because there may be systematic differences between the members of each office that affect our participants' behavior (e.g., one office might be located in a much hillier area than another office, making for a much more strenuous bike ride). However, this doesn't mean that we can't use this design. It just means that we need to be aware that non-random assignment limits how much we can attribute changes in behavior to our reward program (e.g., did Office A perform better than Office B because of the incentive, or because Office A has an easier bike commute than Office B?). To reduce this limitation, strive to create groups that are as similar as possible to each other (e.g., try to choose offices with similar topography).

There are two variations of the quasi-experiment without random assignment, which we discuss below.

Using a pretest-posttest nonequivalent groups design

Although there are various types of quasi-experiments, one of the most relevant to our work is the *pretest-posttest nonequivalent groups design*. Here, you would have two groups of participants (Office A and Office B) and expose only one office to the shifter (bike-riding reward program). In this case, you measure both groups before introducing the shifter, and then measure both groups again after introducing the shifter to the treatment group. Then, you compare how Office A changed from pretest to posttest against how Office B changed. Through the pretest/posttest comparison, you are also accounting for unintended systematic differences between groups, because you know where each group's behavior started out.

Using a posttest-only nonequivalent groups design

The *posttest-only nonequivalent groups design* is like the previous design (groups are not assigned at random), but in this case, we are only collecting posttest data; we don't know where each group started from. In our biking example, this would mean introducing the reward program in only one office (office A, the treatment group), then measuring the rates of bike-riding at office A and comparing this to rates of bike-riding at a different office (office B, the control group), where the reward program was not introduced. This quasi-experimental design is not ideal because it does not account for preexisting differences between our groups. Therefore, we recommend using a pretest-posttest design whenever possible if you aren't able to randomly assign your groups.

Designing a quasi-experiment with only one group

For one reason or another, we're not always able to include a control group (and therefore cannot engage in random assignment), but we still want to evaluate the impact of our treatment. It's important to reiterate that our ability to interpret one-group data is limited. Without a control group, it's difficult to say whether it was our shifters or other events that had an effect on our audience's behavior. Though less rigorous than previously described designs, we describe two designs that allow us to do so.

Using a pretest-posttest one-group design

A common quasi-experiment is the *pretest-posttest one-group design*, which involves evaluating a single group of participants before and after exposure to a treatment. In our bike-riding example, this would mean offering the incentive to everyone in a single office (or everyone in the entire company) and measuring how often employees ride their bike to work before and after initiating the reward program. In such cases, you're studying the effect of your initiative on only one group. This study design is common due to practical constraints (it can be challenging or impossible to have a control group), but remember that without a control group to compare the treatment group to, we don't know whether any behavioral changes we see are due to factors out of our control that affect participants' scores between the pretest and posttest (such as the natural shift in ridership that occurs as the season changes from winter to spring) and not our shifter.

Using a posttest-only one-group design

The least robust quasi-experimental design is implementing a treatment and measuring outcomes for a single group, without collecting baseline data. This is called a *posttest-only one-group design*. Researchers use this design when baseline data are hard to come by and measuring outcomes for more than one group isn't possible. For example, let's say that we are working to stop ship strikes of whales. The goal of our initiative is to have fewer than 10 ship strikes per year, and we record 5 whale deaths by ship strikes in the year during which our initiative took place. We technically met this goal, but if we don't know how many whale deaths from ship strikes occurred in the year prior (we don't have any baseline data), then we don't actually know if deaths by ship strikes increased or decreased compared to the previous year. This type of study has limited utility, because it doesn't tell us whether our shifter made a difference.

● ● ●

You'll need to consider feasibility when choosing and designing the primary research that you'll conduct. Your research choices will depend on your research needs, your capabilities, and the stage you are at in the *Making Shift Happen* process. You'll also need to be realistic about the time and money at your disposal. For example, a qualitative analysis of interviews can lead to rich insights, but can be very time-consuming. Therefore, interviewing many people would not be appropriate for an initiative with a quick turnaround. Ultimately, each research method has its advantages and disadvantages; be judicious about the methods you choose, so you can get the most accurate insights about your audience that you can.

Table 1.6.3: Advantages and Disadvantages of Each Research Method[15]

Method	Advantages	Disadvantages
Observations	• Occur in a natural setting • Can reveal discrepancies between actual and self-reported behavior • Provide understanding of context • Don't require much training	• Time intensive • Don't get at the "why" or reasoning and motivation behind behavior • Produce findings that are highly time- and location-dependent • Can be difficult to observe busy locations or larger groups • Subject to observer bias
Surveys	• Adaptable for high numbers of participants • Identify broad patterns • Standard across participants • Can obtain more candid responses than interviews/focus groups • Cost-effective	• Prone to sampling bias • Less objective data than observation • Highly rigid format • Potential low response rates
Interviews	• Measure things you can't directly observe • Build rapport and credibility • Highly flexible and adaptable • Can record body language • Able to explore topics in-depth	• Costly and time intensive • Less anonymity than observations • Require high level of skill • Particularly subject to researcher bias • Result in small sample • May not be representative of the population • Results are not generalizable • Produce a large volume of qualitative data that can be difficult to organize and evaluate
Focus Groups	• Capture social dynamics • Potentially more time efficient than individual interviews • Inexpensive • Can provide a diversity of perspectives	• Require greater skill • Discussion may be challenging to control • Social dynamics may bias results if participation isn't equal across the group • May not be representative of the population • Produce a large volume of data
Experiments	• Allow for greater control • Can be used to infer causal effects	• Can require extra resources • Creating controlled conditions may be challenging • Can be difficult to generalize if they become too controlled • May require large sample sizes

CREDIT: CONTENT ADAPTED FROM ALMEIDA ET AL. (2017)

Designing Primary Research

In this section, we review some of the basics on how to design your primary research, including measuring and collecting data on key variables, choosing sampling methods, and other considerations for designing research, like ethics.

Collecting data on and measuring key variables

We may need to collect our own data about key variables like behaviors (and the environmental outcomes associated with those behaviors), psychological factors (i.e., how people think and feel), contextual factors (i.e., aspects of the environment with bearing on thoughts and behavior), and demographics. The purpose of collecting this data might simply be to understand an audience and their behavior better, or it might be to measure it for the purpose of evaluating our initiative. As you'll see, these goals can be accomplished by collecting quantitative or qualitative data. Here we will provide key considerations for choosing what type of data to collect and measuring key variables.

Collecting qualitative and quantitative data

Primary research can produce data that are either qualitative or quantitative.[1] Both types of data are useful and serve different purposes.

Qualitative data include descriptive narratives of beliefs, attitudes, perceptions, behaviors, or experiences. These data reveal rich details about the audience that can help us to both describe and explain behavior; they get at the "why"—the motivational factors underlying the numbers. For example, qualitative data can take the form of narratives like "I don't feel safe while on the train after 8 p.m.," "I love the exercise that I get by biking to work," or "I feel stressed whenever I have to drive in traffic." We can collect qualitative data like these through open-ended, exploratory research via surveys, interviews, or focus groups. Qualitative research tends to be conducted when we do not yet know much about a given topic. We can use this research to inform hypotheses and formulate the purpose of our research, as well as to help us write specific questions to ask a larger audience in future quantitative research. For all of its advantages, qualitative research tends to be time intensive and sample sizes tend to be smaller; because of this, findings are not typically generalizable to large populations.

While qualitative data are descriptive, **quantitative data** enable us to measure or count something. For example, quantitative data can help us find out how prevalent a behavior or belief is, how frequently something occurs, or how severe a problem is. Quantitative data can tell us the percentage of people who drive to work alone, how many gallons of water households use per week, and how often people change their air filters. We can use quantitative data to get a better understanding of large patterns within our issue or priority audience (rather than the specific experiences of a few people) or to evaluate our initiative or our shifters. For the ambitious researcher, a well-designed study with a large sample size and rigorous sampling procedures can also be used to understand cause and effect and the relationships among multiple factors, such as the relationship between a particular attitude and a particular behavior, or which of several barriers best predict action.

You don't always have to choose between qualitative and quantitative data. By mixing methods, or blending elements of quantitative and qualitative research, we can paint a more accurate picture of reality than we would have by relying on any single method.[13] In an ideal world, we would have the opportunity to conduct a series of studies using different research methods. Oftentimes, this means starting with qualitative research to gain a deeper understanding of an issue before moving on to a quantitative survey. There are also times when we might start with a quantitative survey and find ourselves following up with qualitative research. This tends to happen when we're met with unexpected findings that we would like to explore more deeply. Even if we can only conduct a single study, we can incorporate both qualitative and quantitative elements. For example, we might deploy a survey to measure whether people support a particular cause, but also ask them "Why?" to determine what motivates their level of support.

Measuring key variables as directly and accurately as possible

Regardless of what we are collecting data about, we need to make sure we are measuring behaviors and other variables as directly and accurately as possible. In other words, we want to ensure that we're measuring what we think we're measuring.

Measure behavior

Measuring behavior is a critical component of the *Making Shift Happen* process. Ideally, we can directly observe behavior, such as watching how many people properly compost at a restaurant or cafeteria compost bin. But for various reasons, sometimes we won't be able to directly measure behavior, such as if the behavior takes place in a remote or private location, or if there are other reasons that it would be difficult or resource-intensive to observe or track the behavior. In these cases, we'll need to rely on self-reported data: asking the audience to tell us how they behaved. For example, we might ask, "How many times did you take the bus to work this past week?" or "Approximately how many miles do you drive in an average week?"

When asking participants to self-report their behavior, it's especially important to be specific about the context and time span, or our data may lose usefulness. For example, if we're interested in measuring transportation behavior, we must be sure to specify whether we are interested in how people get around "in general" or "when traveling to and from work." The same can be said of time spans: it's important to articulate whether we're interested in behavior that has occured in the last day, month, or even year. For infrequent behaviors or new habits, be sure to ask about a time span that's large enough for the behavior to have occured.

In UNCOVER: Process Chapter 3, we provide many examples of questions you can use to measure behavior. We present these in the context of a Behavioral Drivers Analysis, but you can also use these questions for evaluative purposes.

Measure psychological factors

Understanding psychological factors such as perceptions, beliefs, and attitudes is also critical to designing an effective behavior change initiative. In order to analyze how factors like these are influencing behavior, we need to be able to measure them. Since we can't observe these factors, we must rely on asking our audience questions about them, and use our audience's responses to measure the presence and magnitude of these factors. For example, as a stand-in for our audiences' actual attitudes about the importance of recycling, we can ask, "How important do you think it is to recycle?" and provide them with a scale from "not at all important" to "very important."

Some psychological factors important to environmental behavior change (such as "environmental concern"[5]) have already been operationalized in the form of standardized scales. These scales typically use several questions to measure a single concept. We strongly recommend using existing "validated" scales when possible—you won't have to worry about writing your own questions, and these standardized scales have gone through a rigorous statistical process to demonstrate that they really measure what they say they measure.

We share many examples of questions to measure the most important psychological factors or "drivers" of behavior in UNCOVER: Process Chapter 3, including several standardized scales for factors like environmental values and identity. Remember, you can use these questions not just in the context of a Behavioral Drivers Analysis, but also to measure psychological factors before and after your initiative.

Measure contextual factors and demographics

We talk extensively in the process chapters about the importance of understanding various contextual factors (e.g., policies, social networks, resources, infrastructure) and demographic factors (e.g., income, geographic location, education level) that may be influencing your audience's behavior.

We may be able to obtain these data from secondary sources like Census data, or we can directly observe these factors, such as by mapping where our audience lives in relation to the closest bus stop or taking note of local regulations affecting their city. As with behavior and psychological factors, we can also ask our audience about these factors; we provide examples of questions in UNCOVER: Process Chapter 3.

When asking about demographics, we strongly recommend using questions designed by expert researchers who have spent years perfecting their wording. A lot of hard work goes into framing questions about demographics in ways that make participants feel comfortable providing (sometimes) sensitive, identifiable information. The United States Census Bureau and Pew Research Center have extensive survey databases and resources on their websites to guide question-asking on a wide variety of demographic factors.

Sampling from your priority audience

Sampling is the process of selecting a group of participants that represents the target population whom you will include in our research, whether it be interviews, focus groups, surveys, or experiments. Your *target population* is the priority audience you chose in the INITIATE phase—this is the group that you will draw participants from whenever you need to collect primary research on your audience.

When sampling, we want to avoid (intentionally or unintentionally) recruiting in a way that systematically selects a group of participants that is not representative of your target population. Inviting a highly homogenous group, like a single office or school, to participate in research is appropriate if that location alone is your target population, but not if your target population is broader, such as all parents in the county or all employees of an international company.

Here we'll tell you more about how to collect data from a meaningful sample, including how to recruit your target population and how to determine how many people should participate.

Recruit a representative sample

Based on the audience you've identified during the *Making Shift Happen* process, think about who should be included and who should be excluded from your study. Ideally, we want to collect data from a ***representative sample***—that is, a subset of the priority audience that closely resembles them on key demographics like gender, age, race and ethnicity, language spoken, and income. For example, if our priority audience is approximately 65% women, we would want our sample to have roughly the same percentage of women.

To recruit a sample that matches your target population as closely as possible, you will need to uncover demographic information on your target population through secondary research. In some cases, you can find demographic characteristics of your target population through sources like Census data, employee data from Human Resources, or enrollment data from a university. We may not always have access to robust demographic data on our audience, but when we do, we can use it to guide sampling. Use this information to select recruitment procedures (e.g., methods of contact, locations, etc.) that give you the best access to individuals with these characteristics.

Representativeness is important for generalizing study findings to the broader target population and, therefore, designing successful initiatives. Failing to represent the target population can have significant implications for the decisions we make for our initiative, such as the audience or behaviors we choose, the barriers and motivators we identify, and, ultimately, the shifters we select and design. Insights from a nonrepresentative group could mean drawing conclusions about and catering efforts to a group that ultimately isn't very similar to our priority audience as a whole. (However, note that sometimes, there are benefits to subjectively curating participants representing diverse sectors of your audience, or who are particularly capable of representing the perspectives of their group. It's OK to introduce some subjectivity in your participant selection for strategic reasons or resource limitations, as long as you acknowledge it when interpreting results.)

Here we will provide guidance on how to recruit a representative sample from your priority audience.

One of the best ways to select your sample is by recruiting through *simple random sampling*, in which you randomly select people from your priority audience to participate in your survey. Simple random sampling ensures that each participant is chosen purely by chance and that the people you are surveying aren't systematically different from your target population. True random sampling requires great access to the target population because you have to be able to identify and reach everyone from your target population to give each member a chance at being selected. For example, researchers might contact a randomly selected portion of residents from a county's mailing list or employees from the business directory.

The surest way to obtain a representative sample is by recruiting through *stratified random sampling*, in which you divide the target population into meaningful subgroups, and then randomly sample from within these subgroups. This sampling method ensures adequate representation of specific groups, like students or communities of concern, who may be underrepresented using simple random sampling. This method is more rigorous than simple random sampling: not only does it require the ability to identify audience members, but it also requires the ability to segment them into meaningful groups.

Random sampling can be difficult to achieve—we rarely have the ability to identify and access every member of our target population. Thus, in most cases random sampling won't be possible. *Convenience sampling* is the term for recruiting participants who are very easily accessible to the researcher. For example, if you aren't able to send emails out to every single member of your potential target audience, you might instead send emails out to all of those who have signed up for your mailing list. This method is usually considered biased because those who are easily accessible may be inherently different than those who are not. For instance, those who sign up for a mailing list may be more receptive to your organization than those who didn't sign up. Convenience sampling is acceptable as long as the researchers acknowledge and account for the bias.

Somewhere between random and convenience sampling, you can aim for a sample that is as representative as possible within the practical constraints of your study. When you can't access your entire priority audience, you can strive to sample from as large of a portion of your audience as you can manage. For example, you can supplement your recruitment email by mailing survey recruitment postcards to your priority audience. Further, you can make your selection as random as possible: you can select homes at random across all neighborhoods rather than settling for all homes in a single neighborhood.

Bias in Sampling

When conducting primary research on your priority audience, there are several sources of bias you should be aware of. Bias is never 100% avoidable; you will always have a little of it, but it helps to be aware of it and do what you can to counter it. Awareness of these limitations will help you make arrangements to counteract unintentional biases in your sampling procedures. In this section, we introduce two sources of bias: bias due to the researcher and bias due to the participant. Both types of bias can lead to samples that are not representative of your target population.

What's most in our control is the bias we introduce when designing our sampling and recruitment procedures. We introduce bias when we intentionally or unintentionally give some participants a higher or lower chance of being selected to participate in our research. This can occur when participants are not invited to participate when they should be (e.g., our contact list is missing whole neighborhoods or new employees). Another common way this occurs is when participants have unequal access to a survey or interview; those who are able to participate are often systematically different from those who aren't. For example, surveys administered online can suffer from this bias, because online surveys can unintentionally exclude low-income earners without internet access and older adults who are less technologically savvy. As another example, those who have a hearing impairment may struggle to complete a phone interview or participate in a focus group. To address this bias as much as possible, try to consider all the different ways you can access the full range of the target population (e.g., flyers versus emails versus public announcements) so as not to systematically exclude certain groups.

Participants also introduce bias into the sampling process. There are some members of your audience who will be unwilling to participate in your survey, and those members may be fundamentally different from those who choose to participate. For example, some people may choose not to participate in a survey about climate change because they believe that climate change is a hoax. The same can be said of those who are highly willing to participate: those who have strong opinions on the research topic may be particularly eager to share them with you. Most research suffers from this bias, since participants almost always have the choice to participate in a study (unless they are unaware that they are taking part in an experiment, for example). To reduce this bias as much as possible, make sure your recruitment materials include a compelling yet neutral introduction, which can set the tone and influence whether or not a respondent completes the survey or signs up to participate. For any study type, behavioral science tools—such as normative messaging and incentives—can be used to guarantee reasonable participation rates.

As you progress through data collection, you can monitor your sample and target underrepresented groups to course-correct along the way. To do so, periodically review demographic data from your ongoing study and compare it to the demographic information for your priority audience. Whether you have the ability to survey more people to make your sample more representative or not, knowing the discrepancy helps with the interpretation of your results.

Determine how many participants to recruit

The size of the sample we will collect data from (our *sample size*) depends on the goals of our research, the size of the target population, the resources that we have, and on which research methods we are using.

If we're conducting observations, interviews, focus groups, and intercept surveys, sample sizes tend to be smaller. While there is no magic number, we should aim for at least 12 individual interviews or 3–6 focus groups per sub population.[2] In some cases, we can glean insights from as few as 10 participants. The deciding factor here is whether we feel we've stopped observing new perspectives or reached saturation. Does every new interview start to sound like one you've heard before? If so, it may be time to stop. If not, reach out to a couple more participants.

Determining our sample size for surveys and experiments can be a bit trickier. To conduct quantitative analyses, sample size calculations tend to be more precise. In general, our goal is to collect enough data to detect an effect or be reasonably sure our results are not due to chance. The larger the sample size, the more representative our results are of the broader population. While it's best to calculate an appropriate sample size using a sample size calculator, novices can apply a general rule of thumb. In general, we should aim to collect data from at least 50 participants when examining relationships among variables (via correlation or regression) or at least 30 participants per group (but ideally more) when detecting differences between two or more groups (using statistical tests like the t-test or ANOVA).[16]

• • •

Finally, when designing and conducting your primary research, always treat your participants with the utmost respect. In FOUNDATIONS: Process Chapter 1, we discussed some considerations for designing ethical initiatives that apply to all of the primary research methods. Research conducted outside of universities doesn't necessarily need to go through the same approval process, but ethics are still imperative when planning and carrying out your initiative. Most of all, you should be sure to ask for informed consent from participants for interviews, surveys, and some types of experiments. Tell them enough information about the study—your goals, what you will ask of them, and how you will use their information—for them to make an informed decision about participating. Other ethical concerns may vary based on the project. For a review of research ethics, refer to ethics resources on the American Psychological Association's website, and discuss your plans with your HR department whenever you are able.

 Analyzing Primary Research

After collecting your data, it's time to analyze it. Your methods for analyzing results depend on your research question and the type of data that you collected. While data analysis can seem daunting, there are plenty of people and resources out there to help get you through it! We share an introduction to data analysis below.

Analyzing qualitative data

Whether collected via interview or open-ended survey questions, qualitative data are considered descriptive—collecting qualitative data (such as through open-ended survey questions), arms you with rich information that can provide more detail and insights than quantitative data alone (such as if you only asked closed-ended questions). Once you have this rich data, your goal is to evaluate the content of participants' responses to better understand how your audience thinks, feels, and acts. For example, when evaluating bus system descriptions, you may ask yourself the following questions to get a robust picture of the data: What were participants' descriptions like? What specific words did people use? Did they describe buses as clean, safe, and efficient, or as dirty, dangerous, and inconvenient? Did anything surprise you? What kinds of themes emerged?

At this stage of analysis, it's standard practice to code transcripts of interviews or field notes of observations. In qualitative analysis, *coding* means assigning a thematic label to short segments of text. You can code by hand with a pencil, highlighter, or sticky notes, or you can code in a spreadsheet or using qualitative analysis software, such as NVivo or Atlas.ti. The purpose of coding is to condense and organize data so that you can make sense of the information yourself, as well as to be able to better communicate about it with others. For example, if a participant said

"I had nowhere to sit; the seats were covered in trash," you may label, or code, that sentence with two labels: "dirty" and "lack of seating." If you had another response that said "the bus is too full and I always have to stand," you would also label this as "lack of seating." Codes can be grouped into themes, and themes can be grouped into broader categories to understand how the issues relate to one another. You may find at the end of your coding that you have a bunch of small groups of codes. Do any of those codes "hang together"? For example, you may decide to group reliability and speed into one larger category about service quality.

There is no right or wrong method when it comes to coding; it's part art, part science. The way you segment the data (e.g., by sentence, sentence fragment, or even paragraph) and the codes you assign to segments is up to your discretion. But a word of caution: it's easy to get carried away with the number of codes and ways that you can categorize responses! Too many different categories can make analysis more difficult, so it's important to keep this in mind as you go. Once coded, you can go a step further to quantitatively analyze your qualitative data.

Analyzing quantitative data

The ultimate goal of quantitative data analysis is to describe, compare, or predict patterns in the data. Whether you have extracted data directly from a survey platform or quantified your qualitative data, analyzing and interpreting quantitative data involves many steps. Quantitative analyses are often conducted using a statistical software package (e.g., SPSS, R, SAS), but many simple analyses can be accomplished in Excel®.

Preparing quantitative data

First, you'll need to get your data into an electronic format (if they aren't already). Electronically administered surveys are already ready to go, but if you administered your survey on paper or are using other data, you will ideally want to copy the data into Excel® or something similar. Then, once your data are entered, there is always some level of data cleaning and preparation involved. **Data cleaning,** just like it sounds, involves looking for errors and outliers in your dataset. For example, you might remove participants who did not fit the criteria of your priority audience, who did not make it to the end of the survey, or who took the survey very quickly and selected the same response for every single question (i.e., "straightlining").

Conducting quantitative analyses

There are several different ways that you can analyze quantitative data. We offer a brief list of some of the most common methods below. Depending on your comfort levels with data analysis, you can conduct your analysis at varying levels of complexity. If you are new to research, you may begin by simply running some basic descriptive analyses and creating graphs to visualize your data. If you're more comfortable with basic statistics, you may add some more elements, like tests of differences or association, to your analysis. Since whole books have been written about how to describe, visualize, and analyze data (some of which we list at the end of this chapter), we only provide a brief summary here.

Describing your sample and your data

Begin analyzing your data with descriptive analyses that summarize the basic features of the sample and your participants' responses.[16] For example, if you're considering a bike-to-work initiative, you may want to get a sense of how many of your respondents live within five miles of their workplace, what the average age and mobility level of the participants is, or even how many of them are parents. A few common descriptive analysis measurements that can help you get this "big picture" summary are:

Averages

- **Mean:** A value that takes into account all data points to represent the middle of the data. Add up the values for each case and divide by the total number of cases. For example, to get the mean number of people who live within five miles of their workplace, add up all the people who do, and divide by the total number of respondents.

- **Median:** The value at the center of an ordered dataset. If we have a set of 5 respondents who live 0.5, 0.5, 1, 5, and 10 miles from their workplace, the median for that dataset is 1.

- **Mode:** The value that occurs most often in the data. In the above dataset, the mode is 0.5, because it occurs twice.

Frequency

- **Prevalence:** The prevalence of a response refers to the proportion of a group that gave a particular response. For example, to calculate the prevalence of those who said "yes" among a group, start by counting the number of people in the group who said "yes" and divide this by the total number of people in the group.

Distribution and deviation

Measurements of distribution and deviation, such as range, standard deviation, and confidence intervals, help us to understand the extent that behavior and other factors (e.g., attitudes, beliefs) vary among our audience.

- **Range:** The spread, or the distance, between the lowest and highest values of a variable. In the above dataset of people who live different distances from their workplace, the minimum and maximum are 0.5 and 10, respectively, and the range is 9.5.
- **Standard Deviation:** The average distance that scores are above or below the mean. The smaller the value, the closer the individual scores cluster around the mean.
- **Confidence Intervals:** A range of values likely to contain the "true" value within the population. This helps us understand how much error has affected our estimate. For example, if our confidence intervals are 33% to 37% we can be 95% confident that the true answer is within that range, though we can't say exactly because of error.

Depending on your research question, you may stop here. To further expand the analysis, a researcher can apply other analytical methods such as testing the relationship between two or more variables, variable changes over time, or differences between two or more groups. The following quantitative methods are useful to examine the relationship between variables.

Testing for relationships and differences

There are many cases throughout the *Making Shift Happen* process where more sophisticated statistics are useful. Often, we'll want to identify which variables are related to or influence another variable (e.g., whether self-efficacy positively relates to bus ridership), to test whether a measurement changed significantly over time (e.g., variation in ridership from pretest to posttest), or to test whether two groups are significantly different from one another (e.g., if Doers vs. Non-Doers or a control vs. treatment group differ on a barrier or motivator). If you're interested in comparing groups, or tracking changes in individuals across time, you might be interested in using chi-square, t-test, or ANOVA.

While these more advanced tests can be extremely useful, you can still do important and impactful research without them. And remember, there are many practitioners and researchers out there that you can hire or who may be willing to partner with you on this kind of analysis.

Conclusion

In this chapter, we aimed to give you a brief introduction to some of the main research methods that can help you design the most effective behavioral initiative. Rather than overload you with scientific details, we hope to empower you to carry out your own study! Remember, even the simplest application of any of these research methods can make your work significantly more effective—maximizing your impact and saving you time and resources in the long run.

Use this chapter as a jumping off point as you explore the wealth of other resources on behavioral research. As you go, remember some of this chapter's main takeaways:

- Behavioral research is an important way to make our initiatives as effective as possible.
- There are a range of diverse methods you can use to explore a given topic.
- Research can (and should!) be adapted for your goals and limitations.
- Research doesn't have to be complicated, expensive, or time-consuming to be effective.

Additional Resources

Overview of research methods

O'Leary, Z. (2017). *The essential guide to doing your research project* (3rd ed.). Sage.
Privitera, G. J. (2019). *Research methods for the behavioral sciences* (3rd ed.). Sage.
Patton, M. Q. (2014). *Qualitative research and evaluation methods* (4th ed.). Sage.
Westat, J. F. (2002). An overview of quantitative and qualitative data collection methods. In Joy Frechtling Westat (Ed.), *The 2002 user-friendly handbook for project evaluation* (pp 43–62). The National Science Foundation Directorate for Education & Human Resources Division of Research, Evaluation, and Communication.

Secondary research methods

Centre AlphaPlus Centre (2004). *Tips for conducting a literature search*. Centre AlphaPlus Centre.
Flisser, B. (2014, June 9). *How to Find Anything Online With Advanced Search Techniques*. Envato. https://bit.ly/2fytWVS.
Ridley, D. (2012). *The literature review: A step-by-step guide for students*. Sage.

Primary research methods

Observations

Girard, J. M., & Cohn, J. F. (2016). A primer on observational measurement. *Assessment, 23*(4), 404–413.

Surveys

Krosnick, J. A. & Presser, S. (2010). Question and questionnaire design. In P. V. Marsden & J. D. Wright (Eds.) *Handbook of survey research* (2nd ed., pp. 263–324). Emerald.

OECD (2012). Good practices in survey design step-by-step. In OECD. *Measuring regulatory performance: A practitioner's guide to perception surveys* (pp. 29–43). OECD.

Interviews

Kvale, S. (2007) *Doing interviews.* Sage.

Rubin, H. J., & Rubin, I. S. (2011). *Qualitative interviewing: The art of hearing data* (3rd ed.). Sage.

Focus groups

Bloor, M., Frankland, J., Thomas, M., & Robson, K. (2001). *Focus groups in social research.* Sage.

Liamputtong, P. (2011). *Focus group methodology: Principles and practices.* Sage.

Experiments and quasi-experiments

Loda, J. (2015). *LISA Short Course: Designing Experiments.* Vimeo.

Seltman, H. J. (2018). *Experimental design and analysis.* Carnegie Mellon.

Data analysis

Creswell, J. W., & Poth, C. N. (2016). *Qualitative inquiry and research design: Choosing among five approaches* (4th ed.). Sage.

Field, A. (2013). *Discovering statistics using IBM SPSS statistics* (4th ed.). Sage.

Gravetter, F. J., Wallnau, L. B., Forzano, L. A. B., & Witnauer, J. E. (2020). *Essentials of statistics for the behavioral sciences* (10th ed.). Wadsworth.

Silverman, D. (Ed.). (2016). *Qualitative research* (4th ed.). Sage.

Section 2

The BEHAVIORAL Building Blocks™

IN THE FIRST THREE PROCESS CHAPTERS IN SECTION 1 (FOUNDATIONS, INITIATE, and UNCOVER), you identified which behaviors you wanted to shift and uncovered what drives your priority audience's current behaviors. But understanding your audience, while an essential step, is just the first phase of the process. *Making Shift Happen* also involves strategically developing and implementing solutions that are rooted in behavioral science. We call these evidence-based behavior change solutions ***shifters.***

We have distilled the key insights from behavioral science—from both experimental research and real-world application—into ten BEHAVIORAL Building Blocks™. Section 2 consists of one chapter for each of these Building Blocks, and within each chapter we introduce you to a dozen or more shifters. While Process Chapters 4 and 5 (DESIGN and IMPLEMENT) focus on the process of developing and delivering these shifters, the Building Block Chapters in Section 2 introduce you to what these shifters are, how they work, and provide ideas and advice for how to use them in your initiatives.

We recommend that you read through and familiarize yourself with all of the shifters within the BEHAVIORAL Building Blocks™ before you begin designing—having a strong understanding of the myriad behavioral shifters will help you select the best possible ones for your initiative. We also find it helpful to read or skim these again before designing each new initiative; there are so many behavioral shifters, each with their own nuances, and we find that we are reminded of something important every time we revisit them. (As we mentioned in the introduction, each Building Block could be its own book, with chapters dedicated to exploring each shifter within them!)

Remember, there is not a one-size-fits-all approach to behavior change. The better you understand your audience, the better you can mix and match shifters to design your behavior change initiative. We also encourage you to be adaptive, creative, and open to new ideas in your approach—after all, this is an emerging and dynamic field. If you design something new, consider publishing your work!

BELONGING

Learn how to leverage people's fundamental need for belonging by highlighting a desired behavior that is commonly performed, spreading desired behaviors through social networks, and choosing influential messengers trusted by the audience.

EASY

Learn how to make desired behaviors easier and more likely to be adopted by removing barriers like access issues, simplifying the choice through defaults, reducing the number of choices and steps, making actionable information easier to find and understand, and adding friction to undesired behaviors.

HABITS

Learn how to create and leverage disruptions to break old habits, introduce cues and create implementation intentions to support new habits, and use tools like feedback and rewards to reinforce habits.

ATTACHMENT

Learn how to align your initiative with your audience's experiences, their values, morals, and ideologies, as well as what is close to them personally, geographically, and temporally.

VIVID

Learn how to attract attention with vivid imagery and displays, make abstract concepts more concrete, connect action to impact, and nudge at the right time and place through positioning, reminders, and prompts.

IDENTITY

Learn how to highlight the appropriate identities, reinforce identities that align with environmental action, draw on the power of commitments, and build an environmental identity.

OPTIMISM

Learn how to inspire active optimism by pairing a realistic portrayal of environmental threats with messages that build your audience's efficacy and tap into productive emotions. You will also learn to empower your audience by building confidence and fostering a sense of collective action.

REWARDS

Learn how and when to administer a reward that is appropriate for the audience, well-timed, deployed in a way that reduces the risks of undesirable outcomes, and makes the best use of limited resources.

ASSOCIATIONS

Learn how to present—or frame—information to trigger the right mental associations for the audience.

LONGEVITY

Learn how to build intrinsic motivation in people so that taking actions to protect the environment springs naturally from empathy and compassion for nature and for other people.

Highlight norms to leverage BELONGING

> **Key Takeaway:** *The need to belong is a powerful driver of our behavior. Highlight and build social norms to ensure that environmental behaviors spread and are durable.*

Belonging is a fundamental behavioral driver

WHY DO YOU SAVE ENERGY? Is it to protect the environment? Benefit society? Save money? Because others are doing it? If you're like most people, you don't believe that knowing what your peers are doing has much, if any, effect on your behavior. Indeed, in one study, California homeowners rated messages about how their neighbors were saving energy as less motivating than homeowners who received messages about the environmental, societal, or financial benefits of doing so. However, the normative messages were actually the most effective: the homeowners who received them conserved the most energy.[19]

Although people tend to underestimate the degree to which others influence their own behavior, *social norms* are among the most powerful motivators of behavior change. This may be rooted in our instinctive need to belong, which likely evolved early in our history as a species, when fitting in to share food, labor, and defenses against predators was key to survival.[2] Even today, we frequently look to the behaviors and beliefs of family, friends, coworkers, and neighbors for guidance, especially when we are unsure of what to do. When we conform to social norms, we gain a sense of belonging and security through cooperation and communal acceptance. We also look to norms to conserve our limited mental energy; if we just do what most others are doing, we don't have to spend more of our own energy figuring out what the right behavior is.

Highlight norms to leverage belonging

Environmental practitioners can leverage the need to belong by highlighting what is known as *social proof.* Showing, telling, or implying that most of an audience is engaging in a behavior can significantly increase the chances that others will begin doing it, too.[5,13] Social proof is provided when people (or the surrounding context) model the behavior, but it can also be depicted in visuals or described in written communications. Because people want to fit in with—or perform better than—their peers, practitioners can also highlight certain norms to leverage *social comparison.*[10,13] People will compare themselves to those in their *social networks* (such as family members, friends, neighbors, or coworkers) or to people of high status such as celebrities.

This Behavioral Building Block focuses on tapping into existing norms, although we briefly examine changing an undesirable norm.

Principles and Shifters for the BELONGING Building Block

Highlight Positive Social Proof

Avoid negative social proof

Stop the spiral of silence

Draw attention to the desired norm

Highlight a relevant reference network

Emphasize a Better Social Norm

Use injunctive norms

Provide dynamic norms

Emphasize intentions

Model the norm through fiction

Signal social proof using policies

Spread the Norm Through Social Networks

Choose the right messenger

Collaborate with community pioneers

Foster connection through group activity

Change the Norm

Give people a reason to change

Coordinate the change

Establish new norms at moments of transition

As practitioners, we can prove to the audience that an environmentally friendly behavior is in line with a norm by highlighting when people are engaging in that behavior and by not drawing attention to undesired behaviors.

Avoid negative social proof

Even the most well-intentioned environmental initiatives can backfire when they draw attention to people doing the undesired behaviors. This is why the anti-drug campaigns mentioned in the introduction backfired. Another illustrative example is an environmental ad that aired in the 1970s and 80s. It showed a Native American man shedding a tear after people threw trash out of a car. The intention of the advertisement was to admonish people to properly dispose of their trash. However, later research suggested that highlighting people who were littering may have unintentionally suggested that littering was the norm.[4]

> Even the most well-intentioned environmental initiatives can backfire when they draw attention to people doing the undesired behaviors.

Stop the spiral of silence

Like money, religion, and politics, environmental issues often are contentious, stressful topics that many would rather avoid or do not feel comfortable discussing with friends or family. We may avoid these topics because we believe that we are alone in our environmental concern or that we might be drawn into a hostile debate about our beliefs. However, at least in regard to climate change, that's not necessarily true anymore. As of November 2019, the majority of Americans were classified by the Yale Program on Climate Communication as "alarmed" or "concerned" about global warming, and, for the first time, more people were alarmed than concerned.[30] If most people are worried about climate change, why can it still be so tough to talk about?

Norms can become locked in a *spiral of silence*[18] in which everyone secretly disagrees with a norm but follows it anyway because they observe other people following it. This silence can spiral: as fewer people voice their opinions, more become convinced that those opinions are unpopular. This can lead to a situation where a norm, behavior, or belief is entrenched in a society even though most people might not actually agree with it.

There is a strong spiral of silence in the United States around climate change, as evidenced by one experiment in which participants consistently underestimated how many people believed in human-caused climate change. While one survey on climate change attitudes indicated that 76% of the United States population agreed with the statement "global warming is caused by human activity," participants in the study consistently guessed that only 46–56% of people agreed.[17]

The spiral of silence can have substantial effects on policy, as policymakers themselves are also subject to it. When the same researchers surveyed congressional staffers in the United States, they found evidence of population underestimation: while 60% of the U.S. population believed (according to the survey) that carbon dioxide should be regulated as a pollutant, staffers thought that only 40–55% of the population supported this idea.

How can you stop the spiral of silence? Drawing attention to these kinds of discrepancies can help you move your audience toward action.[17] Break through the spiral of silence by providing your audience with social proof of the environmental concerns present among their peers, making them less afraid to voice their own concerns. Group discussions led by a moderator in a safe, neutral setting are a powerful way to break the spiral, as they can empower people to talk about their true beliefs among their peers. A key element of this process is thoroughly understanding your audience so that you can identify which prevailing norms, beliefs, and concerns to highlight. See INITIATE: Process Chapter 2 and UNCOVER: Process Chapter 3 for more on the research you can do to understand your audience.

Draw attention to the desired norm

We are always looking for proof of what other people are doing (whether we are aware of it or not), and we use diverse cues to determine what the best behaviors are in a given situation. Below we detail some of the ways that you can make the desired norm more visible.

Tell your audience about common behaviors

Descriptive norms refer to behaviors that the majority of people in a given group actually do (regardless of what is considered "the right thing to do").[4] Descriptive norms can prompt social comparison: seeing what our peers are doing shows us how our behavior compares to that of others. Sometimes you can provide social proof just by telling your audience about a descriptive norm. Statements like "80%

of the people in this community recycle" or "join the hundreds of people pledging to bike to work" can reinforce an existing norm.

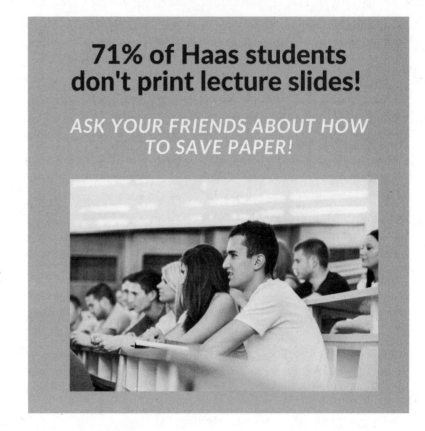

71% of Haas students don't print lecture slides!

ASK YOUR FRIENDS ABOUT HOW TO SAVE PAPER!

Fig. 2.1.1: *University of California, Berkeley, Haas School of Business used survey data to provide positive social proof that the majority of students don't print their lecture slides.*
CREDIT: ROOT SOLUTIONS FOR UNIVERSITY OF CALIFORNIA, BERKELEY, HAAS SCHOOL OF BUSINESS

Making Shift Happen: Using Descriptive Norms to Encourage Towel Reuse

At a hotel chain in the southwestern United States, researchers compared the effectiveness of two messages in guest bathrooms encouraging towel reuse. One sign urged guests to help save the environment by reusing towels, while the other invoked descriptive norms by stating that 75% of previous guests who had stayed in the same room reused their towels. The researchers found that guests who viewed the descriptive norm were significantly more likely to reuse their towels than those who viewed the "save the environment" sign. By simply telling people what their peers were doing (leveraging the descriptive norm), the researchers were able to increase the number of people performing the desired behavior.[13]

Model the behavior

Someone *modeling* a behavior can signal that the behavior is the norm, especially when we are unsure or inexperienced and need instructions on what to do. Modeling can also provide us with useful information—such as what cafeteria items can and can't be composted—that makes it easier for us to follow the desired behavior. Modeling is especially important when we are introducing new and complex behaviors. See EASY: Building Block Chapter 2 for more on making actions cognitively easier.

By enlisting people to model norms, you can highlight your desired behavior. For example, in a study conducted at three fast-food establishments, researchers found that diners were more likely to correctly compost their leftovers when they witnessed others correctly composting. This was more effective than when people only viewed instructional posters.[26] The more we see others engaging in a behavior, the more likely we are to follow them to fulfill our need for belonging.

Contextually reinforce the norm

When no one is around and we are unsure of how to act, we will likely take our cues from the surrounding context. For example, if the light is switched off when we enter a bathroom, it might signal that we are expected to turn it off when we leave. On the other hand, if the light is on, we might think that we should keep it on.[9] In one study, researchers found that when people entered a parking garage free of litter, they were more likely to properly throw away flyers that were placed on their cars. Conversely, an environment full of trash seemed to encourage people to litter their own flyers because it demonstrated that many other people were littering.[4,8] Our aim in contextual modeling is thus to create an inferred social norm that best prompts the desired behavior.

⚙ Highlight a relevant reference network

How we respond to normative information is affected by many factors, including which norms are salient to us and which of our *reference groups* we are looking to for cues about how to behave. Our reference group may be the people who stand out to us, who are valued by us, or who are perceived to be similar to us in our current context.[7,21] Because it can be difficult to predict which of a person's reference networks will impact the salience of norms and behaviors, it is important to test your messages to ensure that they are highlighting a reference group that is salient to the audience.

Making Shift Happen: Selecting the Right Reference Group for Towel Reuse

In a follow-up of the hotel towel reuse study mentioned above, the researchers tested a number of reference networks in their messages, such as gender ("76% of the women and 74% of the men participated in our new resource savings program by using their towels more than once") and reference groups shaped by context ("75% of the guests who stayed in this room (#xxx) participated in our new resource savings program by using their towels more than once").[13] On one hand, people generally see their gender identities as highly important, and would therefore be expected to place a lot of value on what others of their own gender (their reference group) are doing. (For more on how identity affects environmental behavior, see IDENTITY: Building Block Chapter 6.) However, contextual reference groups such as other guests in the same room might also have an effect. Norms can be dependent on context, so people may want to emulate the behavior of those whom they perceive as similar to them in their current situation.

So, which reference group had the largest effect on towel reuse? The study found that, in this case, the *contextual* reference group had the largest effect: guests had higher towel reuse rates in the "same room" condition, despite participants rating the gender condition as more important to them.

This is not to say that reference groups tied to important identities, like gender, will always have less influence on behavior than contextual reference groups. Instead, this study demonstrates the importance of testing normative messages to find the right reference group.

 Emphasize a Better Social Norm

What if you don't yet have a well-established positive norm? What if the current norm is undesirable? First, you don't want to provide social proof of negative behaviors. (For example, you don't want your messages to portray that most smokers litter their cigarette butts.) Fortunately, there are many approaches to emphasizing and strengthening a positive norm you want to build when the current norm is not the behavior you want to promote.

⚙ Use injunctive norms

Injunctive norms refer to perceptions of what other people consider to be right or wrong (what society thinks we "ought" to do in a situation), regardless of whether or not people actually follow these standards of conduct.[8] You may have seen injunctive norms represented on signs that say "prohibited," with symbols and emojis (e.g., signs using a red circle and bar, the use of sad faces and smiley faces), or similar messaging that conveys whether your behavior is desirable or problematic. Injunctive norms are strongly embedded into our culture. We all know that society looks down upon littering, leaving shopping carts in a nearby empty parking spot, and failing to hold the door open for the next person. Therefore, to feel like we are good members of society—that we belong—we try to follow injunctive norms and may feel discomfort when we do not.

Since many environmental behaviors are reinforced by injunctive norms—we know that we are expected to recycle, conserve energy, and not waste water—practitioners can leverage these norms to encourage environmental behaviors. Statements like "we recycle here," "it's not cool to leave the lights on," and "be a team player; turn off the tap" can be ways to remind your audience of injunctive norms.

Sometimes, descriptive and injunctive norms may conflict. For example, during a drought, we know that we are expected to conserve water (injunctive norm). But seeing that everyone in our neighborhood has perfectly green lawns suggests that it is OK to water our lawn because everyone else is doing it (descriptive norm). While combinations of injunctive and descriptive norms work well whenever they are aligned, it is best to draw attention to injunctive (rather than the descriptive) norms in cases where these norms are not aligned. For example, when working with smokers in San Francisco to encourage them to properly dispose of their cigarette butts, we found that the majority (80%) thought it was unacceptable to litter their butts. Rather than focusing on the large percentage of smokers that litter, we recommended injunctive messages like "80% of San Francisco smokers don't think it's cool to litter our butts."

Even when injunctive and descriptive norms don't conflict, injunctive norms can be used to augment descriptive messages. For example, one downside of using descriptive norms is that people who are performing better than their peers (i.e., saving more energy than their neighbors) tend to drift back to the average when they see what the norm actually is. Emphasizing injunctive norms can help prevent this backward drift.[23]

Making Shift Happen: Using Injunctive Norms to Prevent a Boomerang Effect in Energy Bills

In a southern California neighborhood, researchers provided residents with information on how their energy usage compared to that of their neighbors (descriptive norm). They anticipated that households would alter their energy consumption to match the descriptive norm: while households consuming more energy than average might reduce their energy use, those consuming less than average might increase their energy consumption. In an attempt to prevent the backward drift for better-than-average energy savers, the researchers added an injunctive norm to their messages for some of these households by including smiley faces for households who saved more energy. These messages proved to be effective, resulting in lower energy consumption for all households.[23] Use injunctive norms to help your audience keep up the good work and not slip into less desired behaviors.

🌣 Provide dynamic norms

If you notice that people are moving toward a desired behavior, consider drawing attention to the *dynamic norm.* Dynamic norms indicate how people's behavior is changing (in this case, that people are increasingly adopting the desired environmental behavior).[24] Dynamic norms can be effective for establishing a new norm or strengthening an existing one. For example, if there are people in your audience who have just begun recycling, try enlisting them to talk to others in their community about why they made the switch. This would emphasize that there are many people who are changing their behavior and starting to recycle.

Making Shift Happen: Using Dynamic Norms to Reduce Meat Consumption

Dynamic norms can be powerful when descriptive norms don't signal a majority. Over a two-week period, researchers at Stanford University surveyed people waiting in line at a campus cafe, asking about consumer preferences.[24] Embedded in the survey were either descriptive norms ("30% of Americans made efforts to eat less meat in the last 5 years"), dynamic norms ("30% of Americans have started to make efforts to eat less meat in the last 5 years"), or a control that presented a dynamic norm unrelated to food consumption. After two weeks, 34% of people presented with the dynamic norm ordered a meatless lunch compared to 17% in the descriptive norm group and 21% in the control. This study shows how dynamic norms can be used to stimulate action. Use dynamic norms with your audience to give them a sense that others are starting to take action, so they should, too.

Table 2.1.1: Examples of Normative Message Types

Descriptive norm	✓	90% of San Francisco smokers properly dispose of their butts.
	✓	The majority of students don't print their lecture slides.
	✓	98% of scientists agree that climate change is happening now.
Descriptive norm (DON'Ts)	✗	90% of San Francisco smokers litter their butts.
	✗	Many park visitors litter their trash on the ground.
Injunctive norm	✓	80% of San Francisco smokers don't think it's OK to litter butts.
	✓	San Francisco smokers don't think it's cool to litter butts.
	✓	89% of students support efforts to reduce paper use on campus.
Dynamic norm	✓	A growing number of San Francisco smokers are using pocket ashtrays.
	✓	The number of people following a plant-based diet has increased by 30% over the last five years.

⚙ Emphasize intentions

Additionally, if the descriptive norm does not support your desired behavior, try focusing on an intention to act that people hold regardless of their actual behavior. Sometimes, just exposing your audience to others' intentions to perform a behavior is enough to provide social proof. When a person makes a public commitment to do (or not do) a behavior, they risk damaging their reputation if they go back on their word. When enough people (or the right people) commit to making a change, it promises others that the change will actually happen.[3] For example, if the data suggest that most people don't recycle even though they know they should, we might say (if accurate), "90% of the people we surveyed expressed the desire to recycle more often." See IDENTITY: Building Block Chapter 6 for more on leveraging commitments.

⚙ Model the norm through fiction

Role models don't have to be real to be effective. Fictional characters in theater, movies, and soap operas can be powerful influencers of social norms. When these characters are relatable, they can help show a community that not everyone follows a certain norm.[3]

For example, in Brazil, a series of novelas that featured female protagonists with few or no children were estimated to have played a role in the country's 4% decline in fertility rates between 1980 and 2000, even during a time when the advertising of contraception methods was illegal.[15] Declines in birth rates are associated with lower populations and lower consumption of resources, causing environmental benefits.

When using fictional characters as examples of alternative norms, it is most important to ensure that the characters are representative of your audience. In Brazil, the effect of the novelas on fertility rates was strongest for women who were in the same age range as the women in the novelas. If the characters are not relatable, the audience will not see them as role models and likely won't change their behavior.

It is also important to show characters successfully deviating from a norm or adopting a new one. Unsuccessful characters would only discourage the audience from following suit, since viewers will imagine the same consequences for themselves as those that befell the characters.[3]

Keep in mind that a single fictional character who does not follow the established norm or who behaves according to a new norm may not be enough to spark societal change. Additionally, people have to believe that their peers are changing, so they have to know that others in their community are watching the same characters and receiving the same messages.[3]

⚙ Signal social proof using policies

Policies and laws can be powerful signals of social proof. Indeed, some laws, such as banning or charging five-cent fees for plastic bags, seem to exist mostly to change behavior by signaling what the social norm is (though a five-cent penalty might not be a strong enough deterrent on its own).[25]

New laws can signal to people that their peers will change their behavior. If using plastic bags was suddenly subject to a legal penalty, it's reasonable to expect that most people would stop using them.[25]

While laws can reinforce norms, they can also backfire or have unintended consequences.[25] For example, imposed penalties can be more severe than intended; while banning plastic bags can signal that it is frowned upon to use them, charging a harsh penalty for using them could unfairly punish the poor or trigger backlash. In addition, laws with monetary penalties can crowd out intrinsic motivations for engaging in a behavior. For example, mandating recycling and imposing a financial penalty on those who do not recycle could turn what was a moral issue into a financial one, giving those who can afford to pay the penalty license to do so.[25] See ATTACHMENT: Building Block Chapter 4 and REWARDS: Building Block Chapter 8 for more on intrinsic and extrinsic motivations.

Because laws can be complicated, changing a norm by working with a community is preferable to top-down legislative changes.[25] However, here are a few tips to help make legislative interventions more effective:[3]

- The law must come from a recognized authority that is seen by the community as fair and trusted.
- If the community does not respect the body that issued the law, they will be less likely to follow it. In addition, if the process that created the law is not seen as fair and appropriate, the law will not be respected.
- Laws must be fairly enforced for people to respect them. Everyone in the community who disobeys the law must be subject to the same penalties and have an equal chance of getting caught. Those who enforce the law must be seen by the community as fair and honest.
- The law must align with the community's views. The further the new law is from the community's existing values and norms, the less likely it is to be followed. The law should encourage new behavior, but not expect change that is too extreme.

When we see members of our social network such as friends, family members, colleagues, or neighbors performing a behavior, our desire to belong drives us to want to adopt that behavior. As practitioners, we can use *social diffusion*—the spreading of an innovation or concept through a social network[22]—to propagate a desired behavior. For example, a Swedish study found that peer discussions increased adoption rates of solar technology.[20] When information comes from somebody we know and trust, we perceive that information as being more accurate.[1]

> When we see members of our social network such as friends, family members, colleagues, or neighbors performing a behavior, our desire to belong drives us to want to adopt that behavior.

Because people look to their social network for cues on how to behave, you can engender widespread uptake of a desired behavior or idea by encouraging your audience to post about it on social media, providing tokens (e.g., "I voted" stickers), showcasing the names of environmentally friendly actors, and asking your audience to talk to their friends and family. See IDENTITY: Building Block Chapter 6 for more on the power of public commitments.

Choose the right messenger

Who delivers a message is crucial to its effectiveness. We are generally more willing to follow the lead of, or seek out and accept information from, those we trust, such as those in our social networks or who share similar beliefs and values, as opposed to outside experts.[28,29] For example, one study showed how building concern for climate change into a middle school curriculum could spread outward to the wider community. Students were such effective messengers that even the most conservative parents expressed concern over climate change.[16]

Whenever possible, recruit members of the audience's relevant social networks to be messengers, or show the behavior of other audience members as social proof. For example, Portland Community College (PCC) recruited two important campus figures, the president and a school dean, to model giving up personal desktop printers. The images were advertised in the campus' weekly news along with a story about PCC's paper reduction initiatives.[27] The more a norm or any message is seen as coming directly from the audience's peers, the more potent its influence will be.

Deliver messages in person

Audiences who receive a message face-to-face may follow a social norm more readily than those who receive information another way. In one field study, face-to-face canvassing increased voter turnout by 12.8 percentage points (from 44.5% to 57.3%) while telephone calls led to no increase and direct mailing resulted in only a 2.5% increase.[11] One specific approach is to use **block leaders** or **peer educators**; these are trained volunteers who act as opinion leaders and help spread a message through their social networks. Block leaders have been found to have large, positive effects on behavior.[1]

Foster a connection between messenger and audience

To make your messenger as effective as possible, try the following:[5]

- **Find a charismatic messenger** who is well-liked and respected by the audience. Good messengers often come from within the audience's social network.

- **Highlight similarities,** such as shared experiences, hobbies, or favorite sports teams, between the messenger and the audience.

- **Have the messenger praise the audience** for things that matter to them (e.g., "I know you are all hardworking parents, so thank you for taking the time to listen today").

- **Highlight that the messenger and the audience are on the same team;** they are all working toward the same goal.

- Try to **keep the message positive and hopeful.** Messengers who are associated with bad news are more likely to be disliked.

- **Have the messenger bring** refreshments to meetings and ensure that people are comfortable so the audience associates the messenger with positive experiences.

⚙ Collaborate with community pioneers

As mentioned in INITIATE: Process Chapter 2, if you start by focusing your initiative on the members of your audience who are the most receptive to change, you can provide even more social proof to the rest of your audience. As a behavior becomes more popular, it is adopted faster and more readily. Our desire to belong drives us to adopt popular behaviors (to "hop on the bandwagon") with less scrutiny than we do for less popular behaviors. Therefore, by working with trendsetters, you will more effectively build behavior change momentum for the rest of your audience.

Trendsetters are those who have broken from the old norm or adopted a new one; they can be anyone in the community who is willing to break from tradition for a variety of reasons. If you can identify potential trendsetters, you should prioritize them with your interventions as they are the most likely to change their behavior. Additionally, others in your audience will be more likely to follow suit because they now have role models they can look to.[3] People with one or more of the following characteristics might be more likely to be trendsetters:[3]

- **The current norm does not align with their beliefs:** If a current norm does not align with a person's values and/or beliefs, and they are only following it because they want to fit in or avoid social stigma, they are a good candidate to be a trendsetter.
- **High degree of autonomy:** Individuals who are not as sensitive to the need to fit in are more likely to be trendsetters. If those individuals are highly esteemed and respected in their communities, they will be even more effective role models.
- **High sense of self-efficacy:** People who believe they have a lot of control over their own actions tend to be more likely to deviate from a norm.
- **Low risk-sensitivity:** Individuals who aren't as worried about the risks of deviating from a norm will be more likely to do so. This could be because they perceive the risk of deviation as small, or because they are not as afraid to take risks.

Spotting trendsetters can be challenging. A person's likelihood to be a trendsetter can vary in different contexts and from moment to moment. Additionally, a person's status as a trendsetter for one norm may not predict their likelihood to be a trendsetter for a different norm.

⚙ Foster connection through group activity

Creating a group or team to tackle an issue is a great way to connect people to new or existing members of their social networks (e.g., neighborhoods, schools, places of worship). This can significantly increase their uptake of behaviors or values demonstrated and held by other members of that community.[12] In addition, by turning your environmental initiative into a team exercise, you can create or strengthen social connections that reinforce your desired behavior(s). For example, involving your audience in a "green team" can help create a sense of cohesion and belonging as members all work toward a common goal. Group cooperation can help foster dramatic and lasting environmental change.

Change the Norm

Norms can be hard to change, as they are often deeply entrenched in a community's value system. Norm change is achieved through an understanding of why the norm exists within the community. Then, change requires a sustained application of multiple norm change techniques. Social norm change is rarely linear—it may be gradual, sudden, or fluctuating—and often, continued application of multiple change strategies is necessary before the old norm is fully abandoned by the community.[3,14] That being said, there are many tools and strategies that a practitioner can employ to induce social norm change within a community.

Norm change can entail the creation of a new norm, like making it commonplace for people to compost their food. It can also call for the abandonment of an undesired norm, like convincing poachers that it's not socially acceptable to illegally hunt for sport. However, it may require a combination of both, like normalizing biking to work rather than driving. Norm change requires two steps: first, we must give a community a reason to change their behavior; then, we must provide social proof of the new norm.

Give people a reason to change

When attempting to convince others to abandon an existing norm or adopt a new norm (or both), you must give them a reason for doing so. Norms exist for a variety of reasons; to create change, it is essential to understand why a norm has sway over a community.

If the problem is a spiral of silence, you could highlight the actual beliefs of the community.[3] For example, emphasizing that a majority of people in the United States support regulating carbon as a pollutant could convince lawmakers to take more action on climate change.[17] But for norms that have widespread support, simply presenting corrective evidence often isn't enough. Instead, you can enlist allied community members to provide testimonials about the negative impacts of the norm or create vivid demonstrations of the negative impacts of the norm. For example, with open defecation, a serious public health and environmental problem, practitioners created a village display of human waste next to some food.[3] Soon, flies started to gather, traveling freely between the waste and the food, to the horror and disgust of the villagers. This disgust served as an impactful motivator to change the village's norm of defecating freely.

We generally want to avoid directly challenging or dismissing a norm that is rooted in a community's culture, values, ideologies, or identities, such as men eating meat because their community believes it is manly. In these cases, providing a reason to change may be more difficult. Instead, it is best if we can find a different value, ideology, identity, or cultural custom that the community also holds, which is in conflict with the current behavior. For example, if people are getting too close to wildlife to get good pictures for social media, and their social media presence is an important part of their identity, avoid trying to convince them that social media isn't important (e.g., avoid messages like "Don't take pictures too close to wildlife—social media likes aren't worth it"). Instead, try emphasizing a value or identity that's equally important to them. If you find that most of your audience is visiting the preserve due to a deep passion for animals, you can demonstrate that taking pictures from too close is actually damaging the wildlife they love. Now, you can leverage this equally important value of theirs to enforce a different norm without having to challenge their deeply held beliefs (e.g., "Thank you for valuing our wildlife; please show this appreciation by keeping your distance").

The process of giving people a reason to change must be done at the same time that you provide social proof that the community is changing (discussed later), or it risks highlighting the ubiquity of the undesired norm. See VIVID: Building Block Chapter 5 for more on making a message stand out, and ATTACHMENT: Building Block Chapter 4 for more on working with those whose values are in conflict with your message.

⚙ Coordinate the change

Even if an individual is convinced that they need to change a behavior, they may still not do it. They must also have social proof that their peers are changing, too.3 If someone believes that the production of single-use plastics will only stop when purchases stop, that person may continue to buy plastic products until they are convinced that a large group of people has also stopped. All of the previously discussed techniques for creating and highlighting social proof can be used to coordinate norm change. Additionally, bringing your audience together to discuss a norm can both convince them that they need to change and assure them that others are changing, too.

⚙ Establish new norms at moments of transition

It's easier to establish a new norm when people are in new groups, new environments, or in moments of transition. (See HABITS: Building Block Chapter 3 for more.) Look for situations where you are able to create new groups or reach a group of people when it is first coming together, like orientations of new cohorts. Creating "green teams" or intervening right when new people are being added to a group can allow the desired norm to take root as the group grows its bonds. For example, we timed our paper reduction campaign at the University of California, Berkeley's Haas School of Business to coincide with the orientation of a new class. Read more about this initiative in DESIGN: Process Chapter 4.

Moments of transition, such as the rapid changes induced by the COVID-19 outbreak, can be particularly good times to establish new norms or sustain norms. For example, in areas with shelter in place mandates, workers went paperless while their offices were closed for the pandemic; this new norm may well continue even when employees return to the office. Start messaging the new norms when changes happen, and, if possible, enlist large groups of people to continue with the new norm and spread messages endorsing it.

Conclusion

As we have seen, our need to belong drives our need to conform to social norms, which can have a powerful impact on environmental behavior. By providing your audience with social proof, you can change behaviors, beliefs, and even norms themselves. Social proof is most powerful when it can be reinforced by multiple kinds of norms at the same time (e.g., descriptive plus injunctive). Yet it is also possible to reinforce your desired behavior even when most people are not engaging in it by using injunctive and dynamic norms. Finally, norms can spread to large audiences via social networks, so building or enhancing group connections and choosing relatable messengers can accelerate the uptake of a desired behavior.

Stopping Petrified Wood Thieves in Their Tracks [6]

It is all too easy for visitors to take small pieces of petrified wood from Arizona's Petrified Forest National Park. Although the wood supply may look plentiful to individuals, rampant theft over many years led the park to be placed on a list of America's 10 most endangered national parks in the early 2000s.

To curb the thievery, the park put out signs pleading with visitors to stop taking wood. The signs read, "Your heritage is being vandalised every day by theft losses of petrified wood of 14 tons a year, mostly a small piece at a time." However, a group of researchers, including behavioral psychology heavyweight Robert Cialdini, had some doubts about the sign's effectiveness. What was going wrong?

The researchers hypothesized that the current signage being used by the park was actually subtly encouraging thievery by conveying the descriptive norm that everybody was doing it. They decided to test different messages to see if any of them would be more effective.

Over a five-week period, the experimenters rotated signs with different messages through three popular locations in the park, and they counted the amount of petrified wood stolen while each sign was up.

The researchers were right. Nearly 8% of wood pieces were stolen under the watch of a sign with a descriptive norm ("Many past visitors have removed the petrified wood from the park, changing the state of the Petrified Forest," accompanied by pictures of three visitors taking wood). However, less than 2% of the wood pieces were stolen while the sign displayed an injunctive norm ("Please don't remove the petrified wood from the park," accompanied by an image of people stealing wood from the park with a red circle and bar symbol over it.)

This example shows that when most people are engaging in an undesired behavior, drawing attention to it, even to admonish it, can encourage more people to do it. It also shows that emphasizing an injunctive norm can be an effective way to convey norms and change behavior even when the actual norm is undesirable.

📋 Your Turn

What are some ways that you can highlight or change norms to reinforce the desired behavior? Use the questions below to brainstorm.

Highlight positive social proof

❑ Are people engaging in any undesirable behaviors that you should avoid highlighting?

❑ Is there a spiral of silence around your issue? How can you help your audience break out of that spiral?

❑ How can you (or a community representative) model a norm for others to follow?

❑ Is the majority of your audience engaging in the desired behavior, and, if so, can you highlight it?

❑ What are some context cues that could signal your desired behavior, or, conversely, any that might be encouraging the undesired behavior?

Emphasize a better social norm

❑ Do most people think they are expected to engage in the desired behavior, and, if so, can you highlight that belief?

❑ Has your desired behavior become more popular recently? Can you highlight that dynamic norm?

❑ Are there any popular works of fiction, such as TV shows or movies, that can be used to reinforce your norm? Do you have the resources to create something that does?

❑ Are there any policies or laws that reinforce your desired behavior? Can you emphasize them? Are there any existing policies that enable the undesired behavior? Do you have an opportunity to help pass new laws or policies?

Spread the norm through social networks

❑ Can you use social media, signs, logos, or public group activities to encourage your audience to spread the desired behavior to their social networks (e.g., friends, families, neighbors)?

❏ Can you identify potential recruits to talk about your desired behavior with their social networks? Can those people teach others about the behavior, such as by leading a workshop?

❏ Can you create group coherence through a team setting, such as a "green team" within your audience?

Change the norm

❏ What are some of the reasons an undesirable norm is present for your audience? Do they already see reasons to change?

❏ Can you provide reasons to change by hosting a vivid demonstration or by emphasizing a value held by your audience that conflicts with the undesirable norm?

❏ What are some ways that you can provide social proof to convince the entire community to change their behavior?

❏ Are there any periods when new people will be initiated to groups within your audience? Can you message a new norm during this time?

Building Block Chapter 2

Make it EASY

> **Key Takeaway:** *Even the smallest inconvenience can stop behavior change in its tracks. By making environmental actions easy, we reduce the intention-action gap.*

Small inconveniences can prevent action

HOW MANY OF US HAVE WAITED until the last minute to file our taxes? How many times have you stopped filling out a form when it took too long? Sometimes, we even put off actions that result in huge personal benefits. For example, millions of eligible students in the United States do not receive federal financial aid because the application is notoriously long and complicated.[5]

In today's busy and ever-changing world, we are asked to take many different actions every single day and even every hour. To optimize our limited time, attention, and energy, we often take the path of least resistance. Even minor inconveniences, or **hassle factors**, can cause us to move on to easier or more pressing matters.

Of course, we can all think of people—ourselves included—who have accomplished some incredibly difficult tasks. When we are motivated, we can pursue difficult tasks; however, if the task is easy enough, very little motivation is needed.

Unfortunately, even if someone is highly motivated, there can still be a gap between intentions and actions—this is known as the **intention-action gap**.[30,59] Because even the smallest inconvenience or friction can result in intentions not translating into actions, it's always in our best interest to reduce hassle factors. Reducing the hassle factors involved in each step increases the capacity for more actions to be completed, which is important if we want people to take many environmental actions or become environmental champions.

A key point to remember about hassle factors is that they are all about perception! An inconvenience that seems minor to you might be perceived as a major inconvenience by your audience. That's why it's important to observe and talk with your audience to find out what makes them tick (and what might make them quit)!

Make it easy to reduce the intention-action gap

Make it EASY is about making environmental behaviors obvious, convenient, enjoyable, affordable, and accessible, so that less motivation is required.

So what can we do to help close this intention-action gap? This chapter isn't about increasing motivation—you'll find solutions for that in other Building Blocks (e.g., tapping into identities or values, highlighting social norms, or offering rewards). Rather, here we discuss tips for making the desired behaviors as simple, seamless, and convenient as possible. We'll also explore adding *friction* to make undesirable behaviors difficult to complete.

Principles and Shifters for the EASY Building Block

Lay the Foundation for Easy Action

Improve access to necessary infrastructure
Make the desired behavior safer and more affordable
Create policies and processes that facilitate change

Simplify the Choice

Make it the default
Consider active choice or enhanced active choice
Reduce the number of choices
Reduce the number of steps

Ensure Information Is Easy to Understand, Access, and Remember

Make the ask clear
Emphasize "how-to" information
Use visuals to aid understanding
Make useful information easy to find
Use easy-to-understand language
Use chunking and nesting to aid information processing
Make it easier to remember with mnemonics

Add Friction to Undesirable Behaviors

Make it less convenient
Make it more costly

Lay the Foundation for Easy Action

We should first consider if the context supports or discourages a behavior. Financial constraints, physical infrastructure, and laws or policies can all make environmental behaviors easier—or harder—to complete. Practitioners may need to remove, work around, or—at the very least—be aware of contextual factors before asking an audience to change a behavior.

- We want people to bike to work, but there is no place to store their bikes.
- We ask hunters to use biodegradable ammunition, but it is either too costly or unavailable in local stores.
- We want employees to use less paper, but policies require hard copies of certain documents.

Supportive resources and conditions are essential for achieving environmental behavior change. For example, a Swedish study found that written information did not improve the sorting of food waste in households, whereas, providing sorting equipment did, in both the short and long term.[8] Ensure that your audience has access to necessary infrastructure, that the behavior is safe and affordable, and that rules and policies support it.

Improve access to necessary infrastructure

It's critical to ensure that the infrastructure and environment make the desired behavior accessible. For example, 41% of smokers report that they don't have access to proper disposal bins for their cigarette butts at work. Fortunately, Keep America Beautiful found that for every additional ash receptacle, the rate of littering decreases by 9%.[27] Similarly, studies find that when recycling stations are placed in highly convenient locations—such as hallways outside of student dorm rooms—recycling increases by as much as 147%.[13] Simple access improvements like these can have significant impacts.

Making Shift Happen: Using Convenient Gear Disposal Locations to Address Ocean Pollution

Each year, fishers discard thousands of tons of gear into the ocean, such as fishing lines, nets, and traps. Gear may be thrown overboard if space is tight or if the gear is illegal and demands quick disposal, and unattended gear may wash away during severe weather.[33] Derelict fishing gear remains in the ocean where it can trap and kill marine wildlife, in a phenomenon known as ghost fishing.

To combat this pervasive problem, the National Oceanic and Atmospheric Administration (NOAA) and the National Fish and Wildlife Foundation (NFWF) created the Fishing for Energy project in 2008.[38] They installed collection bins at ports to make it convenient (and free) for commercial fishermen to properly dispose of old and unwanted gear. As of 2018, more than 2,000 tons of run-down fishing gear has been collected from 58 ports in 13 U.S. states. Metals from the gear are recycled, and non-recyclable materials are converted into energy. In fact, one ton of nets can create enough electricity to power a home for 25 days! This success story illustrates how practitioners can support desired behavior simply by providing convenient physical infrastructure.

⚙ Make the desired behavior safer and more affordable

Be aware of safety and affordability issues when planning behavior change initiatives; otherwise, you may exclude some people from being able to participate, or worse, you may add risk or burden to their lives.

Make it safe

It's important not to encourage behaviors that could put your audience at risk and to understand their perceptions and concerns about safety. For example, a discussion about this topic at one of our training sessions revealed that many women in St. Louis felt unsafe entering alleys to access recycling and composting bins after dark. Similarly, many people cite safety concerns about dimly lit park and ride lots as a barrier to taking public transit.

Make it affordable

Understand your audience's socioeconomic status before designing shifters and ensure the desired behavior does not involve additional expenses that make the action unaffordable. For example, we may want students to reduce their car trips to reduce greenhouse gas emissions, but asking students to move closer to campus may be too expensive for them. Instead, the University of Colorado launched a one-year pilot program that enabled students to use their student ID cards as unlimited bus passes for an annual fee of only ten dollars. By the end of the year, the number of student bus rides increased from 300,000 to over 1 million.[25]

Incentives or subsidies can be effective when the cost of an environmental behavior is a primary barrier, but they should be implemented judiciously. For more information about applying shifters like incentives, see REWARDS: Building Block Chapter 8.

⚙ Create policies and processes that facilitate change

Have you ever wanted to use your reusable container for takeout orders to reduce your packaging waste only to be told that it wasn't allowed? Do you know someone who wants to raise chickens in their backyard, but their city doesn't allow it? These examples reflect that it can be commonplace for policies to complicate or even prohibit environmentally friendly actions.

Conversely, policies that make your priority behaviors easier to adopt may not exist.

However, relatively simple changes to policies and processes can result in meaningful change. For example, Bank of America saw 56% cost savings when it created software that enabled employees to print letterhead on an as-needed basis. This reversed an inconvenient and wasteful policy of ordering letterhead in bulk for every title or address change.[44]

Making Shift Happen: Using Policy to Increase the Convenience of Curbside Recycling

The Edinburgh City Council combined several shifters to make it easier to recycle.[17,39] First, the Council provided residents with free recycling bins that were significantly larger than their trash bins. This made it easier to recycle many items and signaled an expectation for more recycling than garbage. Additionally, the Council changed its policies so that trash and recycling were picked up on the same day of the week so that residents only had to remember to set out their discards once per week. These changes resulted in a recycling rate that was 85% higher for participating households than the city average—exceeding Scotland's country-wide recycling goal.

Simplify the Choice

We tend to think having more choices is always a good thing, but in many cases, too many choices can be overwhelming, cause confusion, and make it difficult for us to choose. Thus, to encourage your audience to change their behavior, simplify the choice. You can do this by making the environmentally friendly behavior the default, reducing the number of choices, or reducing the number of steps.

⚙ Make it the default

Sometimes, doing nothing is the easiest action of all. By making an environmental action the default, we can effortlessly increase the uptake of environmentally friendly choices. Whether or not individuals are automatically enrolled into sustainable options has significant consequences for the environment. For example, most households in the United States are automatically enrolled in energy plans that use fossil fuels to power their homes. Customers, therefore, need to exert additional effort to opt in to an alternative if they want to use a clean energy plan (assuming that it's even an option offered by their utility). Imagine if the majority of us were automatically enrolled in renewable energy plans by our utility providers! Well, this is exactly what was tested in a randomized controlled trial in Germany. When households had to exert extra effort by opting in to green energy, only 7.2% of participants enrolled. However, when green energy was set as the default (still allowing people to opt out if they didn't want the green plan), 69.1% stuck with the green option—an impressive tenfold increase.[15]

This is an example of the power of defaults in action—a *default* is the option you automatically receive when you don't actively make a choice. Defaults differ from two other common situations we frequently encounter: mandates and active choice. With *mandates* we are given no choice at all, whereas, with *active choice*, several choices are presented to us, and we are forced to make an explicit choice among the alternatives before we can proceed.

> Sometimes, doing nothing is the easiest action of all. By making an environmental action the default, we can effortlessly increase the uptake of environmentally friendly choices.

With defaults, although one option is pre-selected for us, we still maintain the freedom to choose a different option if we wish.

- **Mandate:** A restaurant does not provide straws.
- **Active choice:** When ordering a drink, you must actively choose between plastic, paper, or no straw.
- **Default:** A restaurant provides paper straws unless you request plastic or no straw.

The power of defaults has been demonstrated across issues

Defaults can even determine whether someone becomes an organ donor and how much one saves for retirement. The participation rate in one company-sponsored retirement plan more than doubled to 86% after automatic enrollment was put into place.[34] Another example is when printers are set to automatically print double-sided unless you choose a different setting. Many universities and businesses have adopted double-sided printing defaults. When Rutgers University made double-sided the default, they decreased paper usage by 44% over four years, saving the equivalent of 4,650 trees![52]

How can something so simple have such a powerful effect?

In short, defaults work because of the *status quo bias*—our tendency to prefer the current state of affairs.[23] A great deal of research explores the status quo bias and the effect of defaults on decision-making. Scholars and defaults experts Cass Sunstein and Lucia Reisch summarize the following underlying reasons for status quo bias and why defaults tend to stick: inertia and procrastination, risk and loss aversion, and social norms and endorsement.[54]

Inertia and Procrastination	To reject the default, people have to make the cognitive and physical effort to consider the tradeoffs and then take action. To avoid this effort, we often procrastinate (defer) or ignore the decision altogether. We choose the path of least resistance by continuing with the status quo and sticking with the default. Studies of brain activity confirm that this tendency to stick with the default is amplified when decisions become more difficult.
Risk and Loss Aversion	Defaults establish reference points for decisions. Once a default is used as a reference point, any deviation from the status quo may be perceived as risky and costly. Even the cognitive costs of merely *thinking* about making the switch can be perceived as a loss. Especially when the audience doesn't have strong preferences on the issue, these perceived immediate costs outweigh the immediate and future benefits. To avoid such losses, we stick with the default.
Social Norms and Endorsement	To save cognitive energy and avoid losses, especially in the presence of uncertainty or when we lack expertise, we look to the behavior of others to help us make decisions about our own behavior.[55] Thus, we are more likely to stick with defaults because we tend to perceive them as the socially accepted and popular choice. We might also believe that the default is a recommendation chosen by experts for a good reason. For more information about the power of social norms, see BELONGING: Building Block Chapter 1.

Unfortunately, environmentally friendly options are often not set as the default. Practitioners can flip the script by advocating for environmentally friendly options as the default, requiring people to make the extra effort to opt out if they want to choose a less environmentally friendly option. Similarly, if someone wishes to do the unsustainable behavior, we can require them to make an extra effort to opt in (or request to do so). Remember that with both types of defaults, the person's freedom of choice is still maintained—they have the ability to reverse the default if they so wish.

Table 2.2.1: Using Defaults to Promote Environmentally Friendly Choices

People have to make an effort if they want to *opt out* of the environmentally friendly default.	People have to make an effort to *opt in* to a less sustainable choice.
Conferences automatically add a carbon offset fee for air travel unless you opt out.	Hotel guests must make a special request if they want fresh towels.
Customers are enrolled in a renewable energy plan by their utility unless they opt out.	Restaurant customers must request a straw to receive one.
You receive a public transit pass from your employer unless you opt out.	Customers must make a special request if they want to receive billing statements by mail.

Now that we've covered what defaults are and why they work, let's talk about how to design them. Although research shows that there is a high degree of receptivity to environmental and public health defaults, they work best when practitioners are well-informed about their audience's preferences and underlying interests. Knowledge of the impact that different options will have on the audience's well-being and the environment will also help design defaults tailored to our audience.[53,54]

Weigh the benefits to the audience and environment

First and foremost, consider to what degree the chosen default will benefit or harm the audience as well as the environment. When both the environment and the audience clearly benefit, such as when renewable energy plans are cheaper than dirty energy, defaults are an easy choice. However, if a renewable energy plan is significantly more expensive, defaulting consumers into this plan raises equity concerns. Such a default may especially affect customers who may be less able to afford it, and who, due to being in scarcity, have less capacity to take the actions necessary to opt out.[7,47,54] See FOUNDATIONS: Process Chapter 1 to learn more about the importance of considering scarcity when designing behavior change initiatives.

Understand your audience's preferences

Defaults work best when they are well-aligned with audience preferences; they are likely to fail if your audience has a strong opposing preference. If you don't know your audience's preferences well, choose defaults that are not too extreme. Consider this example from a study conducted at the Organization for Economic

Cooperation and Development (OECD): a one degree difference in temperature was acceptable to the audience, whereas a two degree change was not. When the new default room temperature was set 1°C cooler than the usual temperature, the default stuck.[10] However, in the group where the default was set to 2°C degrees cooler than the baseline setting, many employees noticed and raised the temperature, reversing the benefits of the default. This example demonstrates how defaults can backfire when audience preferences are not well understood. If the audience is diverse in their preferences, practitioners can personalize or tailor defaults for different audience segments.

Consider the complexity of the decision and audience's relevant expertise

We are more willing to let an expert choose for us when we don't have relevant expertise or when the decision is complex. When the audience has expertise in the topic, they are less likely to stick with the default. For example, in advance of a European conference, environmental economists were presented with one of two default types to offset their flight's carbon emissions. The experiment required some economists to actively opt in to pay the carbon offset fee, whereas some needed to opt out if they did not want to pay. However, because the economists were a group of experts quite familiar with carbon offsets, setting a default option did not significantly affect whether they paid the carbon offset or not.[32]

Consider the level of trust

We are especially likely to stick with a default when we trust the designer and believe the default has been designed with our best interests in mind. But the opposite also holds. We are less likely to stick with the default—and may even react against it—when we doubt the motives of the persons setting the default.[54]

Make it clear that there is still a choice

Some audiences are particularly sensitive to encroachment on their freedom of choice and may react negatively to a default even if they agree with its intent. Present the default in a way that still makes it clear that there is a choice. For example, at a restaurant, this might be as simple as putting a placard on the table that says, "Because of the drought, we do not automatically serve water. Please ask for water if you would like some."

Making Shift Happen: Setting Defaults to Reduce Single-Use Plastics

People in the United States consume about 175 million straws per day, making them one of the top items collected at environmental cleanup events.[57] Rather than choosing solutions that may be unpopular, such as bans or fees, use defaults, like making straws available only when requested (customers must opt in to the undesired behavior of using single-use plastic straws). The city of San Luis Obispo, CA, successfully used this method: three months after food establishments were required to offer straws by request only, plastic straw use decreased by an average of 32% per business. Initial feedback about poor customer service was addressed by adding "Want a straw? Feel free to ask" to the messaging. This example demonstrates how you can set simple defaults that positively affect behavior while still enabling your audience to choose.

• • •

Ideally, practitioners will use defaults whenever possible, but we should always be aware of the above considerations and pay particular attention to equity issues. If we are not well-informed about our audience's preferences or if a default would reduce the well-being of a segment of our audience, then defaults are not recommended. Additionally, if it's important that our audience learns about the issue or if we want them to seek out information before choosing, we can use active choice or enhanced active choice, which are discussed below.

Considery active choice or enhanced active choice

If you've determined that, based on the considerations above, setting a default is not preferable, feasible, or ethical, an alternative is to offer what some call active choice and enhanced active choice.[28] *Active choice* is when we are presented with a menu of choices and we must affirmatively choose one of them before we can proceed.

Active choice is preferred for controversial decisions, when audiences are especially diverse in their preferences, or if you are not well-informed about your audience's preferences. It is also well-suited to situations where it's important to you that your audience gain a deeper understanding of the issue. In order to make an affirmative decision, they will need to spend time learning about (or at the very least, thinking more critically about) the choice you are asking them to make.

Active choice can lead to better outcomes than passive choice. For example, when a firm required employees to explicitly choose between enrolling or not enrolling in a 401(k) retirement plan, it resulted in a 28% increase in enrollment compared to when employees had to actively opt in to a plan.[11]

The same concept can be applied to various environmental behaviors:

- Airlines could require customers to select whether to purchase carbon offsets or not before they can book their flight.
- Conference organizers could require customers to choose between vegetarian or non-vegetarian meals before their conference registration is finalized.
- Restaurants could require customers to decide if they want plastic utensils or no utensils before purchasing their to-go order.

Practitioners can take active choice a step further with **enhanced active choice,** in which you intentionally enhance the preferred option by dispelling concerns about and highlighting the advantages of the environmentally friendly choice while highlighting the disadvantages of the less sustainable alternative.

Consider the choice involved in buying a car. Consumers must actively choose from a large possible set of cars with a range of energy efficiencies because there is neither a reduced choice set nor a default. In this case, practitioners could enhance the greener option by using a number of behaviorally informed strategies, such as those discussed in BELONGING, VIVID, and ASSOCIATIONS (Building Block Chapters 1, 5, and 9), to make electric or hybrid vehicles more appealing. For example, we could call attention to the cost-efficiency of electric vehicles and the abundance of charging stations, while simultaneously highlighting the disadvantages of gasoline-powered vehicles.

Reduce the number of choices

Before you consider other potentially more time- or resource-intensive intensive strategies to promote the behavior, simply ask yourself: Can I just remove a few choices? In Western cultures in particular, freedom of choice is highly valued, and we are often attracted to situations where we have more choices because we believe that more choices will enable us to make the most optimal decision. Yet, in reality, more choices tend to result in suboptimal decision-making. Choice expert Sheena Iyengar tested this by offering shoppers 24 kinds of jam in one location and six types in another. While a jam stand offering 24 types generated more interest from shoppers, customers were far less likely to actually purchase any jam when faced with so many options, with only 3% making a purchase. On the other hand, when the choice was simplified and only six types of jams were offered, jam purchases went up tenfold—jumping to 30%![21]

> Before you consider other potentially more time- or resource-intensive strategies to promote the behavior, simply ask yourself: Can I just remove a few choices?

Although there are other factors at play here like the complexity and difficulty of the choice at hand, large choice sets do tend to result in less optimal decisions, decreased motivation to choose, a delay or deferral of choice, lower satisfaction or decision regret, or no decision at all.[45]

This phenomenon of **choice overload** affects decision-making across topics, from the selection of food items to 401(k) retirement plans.[21] Unsurprisingly, environmental behaviors are no different. For example, a study found that people were 10% less likely to say they would switch from a poorly performing electricity service provider when they were given a longer list (17 providers) vs. a shorter list of two alternative providers.[22]

To prevent choice overload, reduce the number of options you present. You might be promoting dozens of different environmental behaviors (e.g., transit agencies need people to bike, take the bus, carpool, rideshare, and more; energy efficiency organizations want people to seal cracks, improve their insulation, and replace energy-guzzling appliances), but reducing the number of options is one of the least resource-intensive ways to make environmental actions easier to adopt.

> To prevent choice overload, reduce the number of options you present.

Reducing does not mean "severely restricting" choices. Rather, by removing some options, you can make it easier for your audience to take action by providing more limited, but more impactful and realistic, options. Below are some tips and considerations for reducing the number of choices.

Present only the most impactful and timely choices

Among a list of 100 actions individuals can take to reduce their carbon footprint, which five are the most impactful? If your community is facing a drought, what is the #1 most important habit for your audience to build? If action is urgently needed, don't give your audience too many options to sift through. What are the options most relevant to the current time period? To feature more options over time, feature a different action each month to draw attention to one specific behavior change at a time.

Present only the most realistic choices

What are the actions your specific audience can realistically take? For example, if your audience rents their homes, avoid sharing information about more expensive energy-efficiency upgrades like new insulation and new water heaters.

Point out which behaviors work for your audience's peers or for "most people"

Within a reduced set of choices, show your audience the options that work for "most people" in their community to increase their motivation. See more on the power of social norms in BELONGING: Building Block Chapter 1.

Carefully Consider Cultural Differences

Always consider how cultural differences shape views of choice. In *The Art of Choosing,* Sheena Iyengar discusses the broad distinctions between individualist and collectivist cultures when it comes to choice.[20] Generally speaking, for people raised in collectivist cultures like Japan, China, or India, fulfilling one's duties to family and society is prioritized over one's individual preferences. People raised in these cultures tend to prefer fewer choices, especially when those options are supported or recommended by people they respect. In contrast, people from individualistic cultures like the United States and other Western societies tend to highly value personal choice and view it as an expression of one's identity.

These patterns should, therefore, inform the way you present choices to audiences from different cultures. For audiences from individualistic cultures, it may be helpful to emphasize the freedom to choose and the ability to express individuality and identity through choice, while being cautious about presenting no choice at all. For audiences from collectivist cultures, consider presenting a limited number of options and emphasizing those that are most supported by the audience's community, including elders, neighbors, and others whose opinion they value.

While it is important to be aware of these general patterns, this information should not replace learning about the preferences of your specific audience and tailoring your messaging and choice presentation accordingly.

⚙ Reduce the number of steps

Make desired behaviors easier by always asking yourself: "Can I eliminate any steps in this process?" Decreasing the number of hoops your audience must jump through makes it more likely they will follow through and complete the desired behavior. If we are motivated enough, we will persevere, but when our motivation is low, too many steps will lead to us abandoning the task.

Practitioners can take cues from companies like PaperKarma that have reduced the number of steps needed to take positive environmental action. According to the United States EPA, Americans receive more than 100 billion pieces mailed to homes each year![58] When we try to unsubscribe from junk mail, the process can take many steps—where do we even start, which is the right form? In contrast, with the PaperKarma app, you simply snap a picture of your unwanted mail and press "Unsubscribe" to remove yourself from a company's marketing list.[41] To date, PaperKarma has processed more than eight million unsubscribe requests. That's a lot of paper saved!

Ensure Information Is Easy to Find, Understand, and Remember

Once our audience has the access to perform the desired behavior, we need to look at other factors that may prevent follow-through. The way we present information, for example, can have a significant impact on behavior. While providing information is insufficient to motivate behavior, not providing information about what behaviors to undertake and how to execute them can be a barrier to change—even for people who are already motivated.[1,19,30,46,50] Practitioners should provide useful and actionable information in a way that does not overwhelm our audiences. Below we share strategies that make useful information easy to find, understand, and remember.

Make the ask clear

Don't leave your audience guessing: make your call to action crystal clear! "Stop Climate Change" or "Save Water" are familiar requests, but they don't make the desired action clear. We discussed this in INITIATE: Process Chapter 2, but it's important enough to mention again.

Instead of vague requests like, "Don't bother the wildlife," make your ask specific: The United States National Park Service asked visitors to stay "two bus-lengths" away from most wildlife and "about four bus-lengths" away from black bears.[2] For tips on how to turn a broader goal into a specific, distinct behavior, see INITIATE: Process Chapter 2.

Once you've identified and developed a specific call to action, you can focus on making that behavior easier for your audience!

⚙ Emphasize how-to information

Providing how-to information is an effective tool for encouraging behavior change.[16,46] In order to increase *self-efficacy*—or confidence in one's ability to succeed at a behavior—practitioners may need to provide information that explains what to do and how to do it properly.[6] This can take a more traditional form, like an instructional diagram or video, or it can take the form of hands-on skill building.

Provide how-to information

Provide detailed instructions, diagrams, personalized information, or other forms of how-to information to your audience.

Here are a couple examples:

- The Monterey Bay Aquarium's Seafood Watch app provides easily accessible guidelines for consumers and businesses to choose sustainably fished seafood. It also helps users easily locate nearby restaurants serving sustainable options.[37]
- The "Way to Go Durham" program aims to reduce single occupancy vehicle trips. Its staff emails participants personalized route maps with options for walking, biking, busing, or ridesharing to work that also compared travel time, cost, and weight loss potential for each option.[12]

Provide hands-on instruction and support

If a behavior is particularly new or difficult, you may need to provide hands-on guidance and support to help your audience build skills and confidence. Some of the strategies to promote self-efficacy for environmental behavior change include:

- Opportunities for observational learning (allowing the audience to watch you or someone else performing the behavior)
- One-on-one coaching or support
- Opportunities for the audience to practice under your guidance

To learn more about the importance of self-efficacy and how to promote it, see UNCOVER: Process Chapter 3, and OPTIMISM: Building Block Chapter 7, respectively.

Making Shift Happen: Using Hands-On Composting Training to Reduce Waste

Composting is one of the most effective ways to divert organic waste from landfills and reduce emissions of methane, a potent greenhouse gas; yet, consumers frequently avoid composting because they don't understand how to do it.[56] In Canada,

Vancouver's Compost Coaching initiative offers free bin delivery and educational services, such as one-on-one training sessions, assistance with compost bin set-up, and follow-up troubleshooting resources.[26] Surveys and waste audits revealed that, as a result of these efforts, residents felt more confident in their composting skills, produced higher quality compost, and increased the amount of materials composted up to 450 kg/year among households with no history of composting and up to 25% among households already composting. These results show how you can use effective how-to information and hands-on support to make sustainable practices more understandable and accessible.

⚙ Use visuals to aid understanding

Visuals are powerful aids for making information easier to understand, remember, and act upon. Many studies have found that when images are successfully integrated within texts, learning significantly improves and people are better able to follow instructions.[18,31] Visuals, like infographics and illustrations, also help people understand and remember information over longer periods of time.

Visuals can sometimes replace words, especially when language barriers might be an issue. This is one reason we see visuals commonly used in situations where understanding information is particularly critical, such as in airports or airplanes.

Making Shift Happen: Using Visual Aids to Improve Recycling

In one study on recycling, researchers tested the impact of different recycling and trash bin lids: a trash bin with a traditional flap lid, a paper recycling bin with only a two-inch wide slit in the lid, and a glass/aluminum/plastic recycling bin lid with a small, circular hole for disposing of bottles.[14] The lids visually signaled what items belonged in each while also creating barriers to placing items into the wrong bin. These specialized lids not only increased recycling rates by 34%, but they also reduced contaminants entering the recycling bins by a whopping 95%. As the study authors cleverly conclude, something as simple as lid design "matters a HOLE lot." Use visual aids to make it easier for your audience to identify and successfully complete the desired behavior.

In another example, researchers placed green signs above recycling bins with images depicting recyclable paper products and red signs above trash bins with images of non-recyclable items. These visual aids increased recycling up to 84%.[4] Examples like these show how providing audiences with easy-to-understand visual instructions can increase positive environmental behaviors.

⚙ Make useful information easy to find

Even if you've created or curated great resources to facilitate behavior change among your audience, it won't translate to impact if your audience can't easily find it. If your audience perceives the information as difficult to access, they may give up. The Seafood Watch app, mentioned above,[37] is a great example of making actionable information easy to find, because it's all organized in one place.

Fortunately, even the smallest tweaks, such as directly linking to pertinent information in an email, can increase actual and perceived access to information.[61] For example, the United Kingdom's Behavioral Insights Team launched the "midata" program to help consumers easily access their energy bill information online. Energy companies are required to include a Quick Response (QR) code on energy bills. By simply scanning the code, the customer is directed to an app that shows them their past energy usage and helps them easily compare options and switch to the most suitable energy plan.[48]

⚙ Use easy-to-understand language

> *If you care about being thought credible and intelligent, do not use complex language where simpler language will do.*
> —Daniel Kahneman, *Thinking, Fast and Slow*

Have you ever noticed that popular or memorable quotes are rarely complicated? That's because the most effective messages are simple. Technical terminology or jargon may be appropriate for conveying nuanced information to specialists, but we don't want our audiences to become frustrated as they use up their mental energy and patience just trying to comprehend our message. If you want your message to hit home, make it easy to understand and translate complicated information into commonly understood terms. For example, instead of referring to "anthropogenic climate change," say, "human-induced" or "man-made." When trying to explain a complex topic, we can also utilize metaphors (see ASSOCIATIONS: Building Block Chapter 9) and storytelling (see VIVID: Building Block Chapter 5) to help our audience understand and engage.

⚙ Use chunking and nesting to aid information processing

When too much information is presented alongside key points, it becomes harder to process the most important elements. Try not to overwhelm your audience with too much information, but if your audience wants or needs more, use *chunking* and *nesting*.

Use chunking

Have you ever visited a web page or picked up a pamphlet only to lose interest when faced with never-ending blocks of text? Avoid the same fate with your messaging by breaking text into shorter chunks, which are less cognitively taxing. Use these tips to help your audience make associations between pieces of information and improve comprehension and recall:[36]

- Organize information into short sections with labels or headings.
- Keep related information together.
- Stick to one main point per chunk.

Use information nesting

If you need to convey additional details, consider a nested structure. Give your audience the basics first, then offer the option for them to learn more if they wish. This approach works well if your audience includes people with a range of exposure to and expertise in your issue; those that want the basics can stop at the first level, while those that want to dig deeper can do so.

Chunking and nesting can be used together. Imagine you're designing a website to share a list of environmentally friendly lifestyle changes your audience can take. You can group these behaviors into categories based on the level of impact, the time needed, or what environmental issue they address, and use a drop-down menu to direct users to additional resources.

Make it easier to remember with mnemonics

Making things easier to remember closely links to VIVID: Building Block Chapter 5, which introduces concepts that help to not only capture our attention, but also to recall information later because it has been made vivid in our memories. For example, placing a brightly colored magnet on the fridge can make it easier to remember to take the recycling out on collection day.

Another simple and fun way we can make behaviors easier to remember is through **mnemonics**. A mnemonic (or **mnemonic device**) is anything that aids us in storing and recalling specific information. Mnemonics have been found to increase recall tenfold,[40] so it's no wonder that mnemonics can be found all around us! Many of us still use the mnemonic PEMDAS to help us remember the correct order of operations for math problems (Parentheses, Exponents, Multiplication, Division, Addition, Subtraction). This is an example of an expression or word mnemonic that uses the first letter of each item in a list to form a phrase or word.[35] This is by far the most common type of mnemonic. Our BEHAVIORAL Building Blocks™ use this (you are reading the E block right now).

Mnemonic devices can take many forms, both verbal and visual, including a play on words, a rhyme, an image, or other unique patterns that make it easier for us to remember information.

Examples of mnemonics used to promote environmental behavior include the well-known "Reduce, Reuse, Recycle." Some other, lesser-known, examples include:

- **"Think before you ink!":** Yale's Office of Sustainability uses this mnemonic to help people avoid unnecessary printing.[60]
- **Mnemonics for plant identification:** A study in the United Kingdom showed that using mnemonics could help people remember plant names and characteristics better than other methods, such as identification keys.[49] For example, the mnemonic for Lungwort was: "Leaf like a pair of lungs upside down, with white blotches like warts."

Incorporate mnemonics into your messages to make it easier for your audience to remember not only to take an action, but also *how* to take that action.

 Add Friction to Undesirable Behaviors

The issues we've discussed so far in this chapter can essentially function in reverse; in order to discourage detrimental environmental behaviors, we can make them less convenient or more costly. A critically important thing to note about this technique is that nothing is being taken away from an audience. The same options remain in place—it's just that some options may be made less convenient.

We must be careful that this added inconvenience does not create any consequential burden for an audience—for example, initiatives often unintentionally create "effort burdens" that fall disproportionately on people with lower incomes and on other vulnerable populations.

⚙ Make it less convenient

Make the behavior less convenient by requiring more time and effort, making it harder to find and access, or requiring additional steps.

Require more effort or time

For example, in one German town, not only must residents opt out of the town's default renewable energy option, but they must also identify an alternative energy provider themselves if they do opt out.[42] The additional effort required has deterred nearly 100% of residents from opting out.

Move it farther away

When Google moved the snack table farther from the coffee machine, where employees spent time every day waiting for their coffee to brew, snacking was reduced by up to 23%.[9] Similarly, an office focused on reducing paper consumption might consider moving its office printer to a less convenient location. This additional effort required may encourage people to think twice before printing nonessential items.

Make it harder to find

An office that's trying to reduce paper consumption might store new paper reams in a cupboard while visibly displaying scrap paper in a convenient location near the printer. This requires employees to actively seek out the new reams for special print jobs.

Require additional steps

Some organizations have an extra approval process that is required when people want to engage in less sustainable behaviors, such as printing extra copies or renting fuel-guzzling vehicles. For example, at one company, the fleet manager removed the majority of large SUVs from the primary car selection list and placed them on a separate list. By adding extra steps along with cost disincentives for choosing an SUV, the company's fleet emissions have been reduced by more than 20%.[29,51]

Making Shift Happen: Designing to Reduce Buffet Food Waste

Food waste is a ubiquitous issue in "all you can eat" college cafeterias in the United States. An experiment, conducted by food service company Aramark, removed carrying trays from 25 colleges and universities on select days, making it harder for students to grab more food than they could actually eat. The days without trays resulted in 25–30% food waste reduction per person.[3]

Providing smaller plates is another way to reduce food waste. One study conducted by a hotel chain demonstrated that providing smaller plates in buffet lines reduced food waste by nearly 20%.[24] Even the size or shape of serving utensils can influence the amount of food people pile on their plates.[43]

These examples illustrate how you can use small changes to make undesirable behaviors more difficult, resulting in behavior shifts that benefit both the audience and the environment.

⚙ Make it more costly

In some cases you may consider making discouraged behaviors more expensive. To learn more about disincentivizing undesirable behaviors, including equity considerations, see REWARDS: Building Block Chapter 8.

Conclusion

When even the smallest inconvenience can prevent action, we can't underestimate the importance of making sustainable behaviors physically and cognitively easier to adopt. The more barriers we can address—both big and small—the more successful we'll be in engaging our audience in our initiatives.

📋 Your Turn

What are some ways that you can make your desired behavior change easier? Use the questions below to brainstorm.

Lay the foundation for easy action

- ❑ How accessible (in terms of availability, distance, and convenience) is the infrastructure required to complete the desired behavior?
- ❑ Might your audience have any safety concerns about the action(s) you are proposing?
- ❑ Can you reduce the cognitive, time, and financial costs associated with the desired behavior?
- ❑ Are there changes you could make to the policies or procedures that would allow for easier adoption of the behavior? What policies should be removed, or, conversely, added?

Simplify the choice

❏ What are the cultural values and preferences of your audience around making choices?

❏ Can you design a default so that the desired behavior happens automatically?

❏ How can you reduce the number of choices your audience must make? Can you remove the irrelevant or least impactful choices?

❏ How can you reduce the number of steps required to complete your desired behavior?

Ensure information is easy to find, understand, and remember

❏ Have you made a specific ask, rather than a vague appeal? How can you be clearer about the action(s) you want your audience to take?

❏ What how-to information would make it easier for your audience to successfully complete the behavior?

❏ Are there ways to work alongside your audience and provide personalized, hands-on support as they learn the skills necessary to perform the behavior?

❏ What kind of visual aids can help your audience more easily understand the information you are presenting?

❏ Have you made useful information about the behavior easy to find?

❏ Can you simplify the language used in your initiative?

❏ Can you remove nonessential details and use chunking or nesting to feature the most important information?

❏ Can you make your information easier to remember, such as by using mnemonics?

Add friction to undesirable behaviors

❏ How can you add friction to an undesirable behavior so it requires additional effort to complete?

❏ Can you make undesirable behaviors less convenient by adding distance, time, or extra steps?

❏ Can you make aspects of an undesirable behavior more difficult to see or access?

❏ Can you make an undesirable behavior cost more than environmentally friendly alternatives?

Cultivate powerful HABITS

> **Key Takeaway:** *Designing initiatives that break bad habits and build positive habits requires great effort by practitioners, but can reap long-lasting benefits for the environment.*

Habits free up our attention

HAVE YOU EVER DRIVEN HALFWAY TO WORK without even realizing it? While learning a new behavior, like driving a car, requires focused concentration, with frequent repetition the brain creates neurological pathways that reinforce a pattern to the point where the behavior becomes so automatic we don't have to pay attention at all. To save time and energy, our brain turns these repeated behaviors into subconscious habits.[57] We especially rely on established habits to move about the world when our attention is fatigued. Nearly 40% of our daily activities are shaped by habits formed throughout our lifetime.[56]

Bad habits are born from convenience

Because our brains are constantly trying to save time and energy, the "path of least resistance" subconsciously guides much of our daily behavior. Unfortunately, many of our bad habits are born from convenience. It requires less mental effort to throw all of our waste in one bin than to remember to put plastics in one bin, papers in another, and compost in yet another. Likewise, it takes more effort to carry our own water bottles when we leave the house or to turn the car on and off instead of idling the engine. Immediate benefits (e.g., saved time, effort, and attention by buying individually-wrapped snacks) often outweigh the delayed costs (e.g., increased production of plastic packaging). Good habits, on the other hand, tend to work in the opposite way—the up front costs (e.g., time and effort to pack snacks in reusable containers) seem to outweigh delayed benefits (e.g., reduced production of plastic packaging).

Because they're automatic, habits are hard to break.[31] Even when our goals and values change, our habits don't automatically follow.[8] Luckily, this inertia works both ways: once we establish a *good* habit, it too can be powerful and hard to break.

How can we cultivate environmentally friendly habits?

While any action for the environment is beneficial, we can maximize the effectiveness of our initiatives by turning individual actions into automatically repeated behaviors, or habits. This chapter provides a variety of tools to support our target audiences in building durable positive habits by shaping the first actions toward change, introducing new contextual cues to trigger desired actions, and reinforcing these actions with practice, feedback, and incentives. This chapter also provides a variety of tools to support breaking habits by disrupting old cue and response links. By designing these shifters into our initiatives, we can help our audiences transform negative habits and create positive ones that are in tune with environmental goals.

Because they're automatic, habits are hard to break. Luckily, this inertia works both ways: once we establish a *good* habit, it too can be powerful and hard to break.

HABITS

Principles and Shifters for the HABITS Building Block

Lay the Foundation for Habit Change

Understand the habit loop
Start with small shifts in behavior
Influence the first choice
Foster meaning through goal-setting

Disrupt Old Cues and Responses to Break Habits

Remove cues from the surroundings
Capitalize on periods of change
Change the reward
Target the response

Design Cues to Support New Habits

Add new cues to the surroundings
Link desired behaviors to existing habits (and their cues)
Encourage implementation intentions

Reinforce New Habits with Practice, Feedback, and Rewards

Encourage repetition through practice
Cue and reward with feedback
Solidify habits with temporary incentives

Although many habits are formed outside of our conscious awareness, intentionally creating new habits or altering existing ones often requires concerted effort. Forming new habits takes anywhere from 18 to 254 days, with an average of 66 days.[30] Regardless of the exact number of days, building a new environmental habit is a challenge that requires time, energy, and a supportive environment to develop and reinforce the new practice. This can be daunting! This first set of shifters addresses the importance of understanding the habit loop, starting small, influencing the first choice, and inspiring actionable goals.

Understand the habit loop

An American Psychological Association task force on psychology and climate change pinpointed habits as "one of the most important obstacles to the mitigation of climate change impacts."[50]

> An American Psychological Association task force on psychology and climate change pinpointed habits as "one of the most important obstacles to the mitigation of climate change impacts."

To change habits, we must understand that there is more to a habit than the behavior we observe. To better understand how to break a bad habit or instate a new one, we can evaluate some of the less visible aspects of the habit loop.

The *habit loop* has three (though some say four) primary phases.[34] First, something in our internal or external environment (a *cue*) reminds us of a past behavior or reward, consciously (*motivation*) or unconsciously propelling us to engage in the behavior (a *response*). After starting or completing the behavior, we receive the *reward*, which strengthens the association between the cue and the response. We discuss each of the phases in more detail below:

Cue	At any given time, we are surrounded by hundreds of things with the potential to be cues. When visual elements, other people, events, or emotional states trigger us (consciously or unconsciously) to act in anticipation of a reward, they become cues for a response.[37] For example, someone who bikes to work every morning may be cued by their phone to check the weather forecast and cued by their bicycle to put on their helmet.
Motivation (Craving)	Sometimes cues trigger conscious desire, or *motivation*, to get an anticipated reward. For our most ingrained habits, however, conscious motivation to get a reward is bypassed. That is, cues in the environment directly trigger a response. For example, seeing your bike triggers you to put on your helmet without thinking about how safe it will make you feel.
Response (Behavior)	The response is the visible part of the habit loop—this is the behavior that we can observe people engaging in. Whether or not a response occurs depends, in part, on how motivated the person is and how easy they think the behavior is.
Reward (Consequence)	Rewards complete the habit loop by reinforcing the response. When someone receives an unexpected or expected reward—or multiple rewards—after engaging in the behavior, they are more likely to perform the behavior again the next time they are cued. A reward provides benefits, relieves any internal cravings, and signals to us which cues are worth noticing, thereby restarting the habit loop.[46] For example, someone may recall the joy their morning bike commute brought them the next time they see a sunny forecast.

When designing initiatives, our choice of shifters depends on a) whether we're promoting new habits or discouraging old ones and b) the sticky point in the habit loop (where the problem is occurring).[7] Figure 2.3.1 (based on Clear's Four Laws of Behavior Change) lists the approaches that best address each step of the loop when creating or breaking habits.

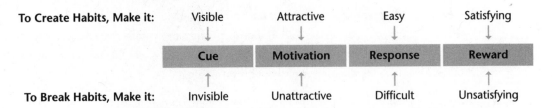

To Create Habits, Make it:	Visible	Attractive	Easy	Satisfying
	↓	↓	↓	↓
	Cue	**Motivation**	**Response**	**Reward**
	↑	↑	↑	↑
To Break Habits, Make it:	Invisible	Unattractive	Difficult	Unsatisfying

Fig. 2.3.1: *Whether creating or breaking habits, each stage of the habit loop requires a different type of behavioral shifter. What is used to create a habit (e.g., making cues visible/salient), must be used in the opposite way when breaking a habit (e.g., making cues invisible).*

⚙ Start with small shifts in behavior

Breaking old habits and establishing new ones can be difficult. Thus, it's no surprise that a number of habit experts suggest starting small. This can be done, of course, by asking for small, gradual behavior changes in your audience, but it can also be done by strategically choosing which behaviors you will influence to start a chain reaction that leads to greater change.

Size your behavioral ask appropriately

In the beginning of an initiative, it is important that we "meet people where they are at." As we'll emphasize throughout the chapter, it's often easiest to build on the cues, behaviors, and rewards that already exist for our audience. B.J. Fogg, a researcher at Stanford, suggests starting habits with the ***minimum viable effort***. "To create a new habit," he says, "you must first simplify the behavior. Make it tiny, even ridiculous. A good tiny behavior is easy to do—and fast."[15] Pick up three pieces of trash, reduce your shower time by two minutes, or walk to the store just once. Encourage any step in the right direction and build from there.

⚙ Influence the first choice

By influencing our audience's very first choice (e.g., by providing a free reusable bag at a grocery store opening), we can set them on the path to developing more environmentally friendly habits. We prefer to stick with the first choice we made the next time it is given as an option, and this preference can even intensify with time so that we come to view our original choice more positively while also potentially becoming more dismissive of the alternatives.[6] Seeing our past choices in this positive light fuels future repetition of the behavior.

⚙ Foster meaning through goal-setting

People may be concerned about particular environmental issues, but lack the drive to get started. Formulating goals helps motivate us to take the first steps toward change.

Encourage detailed goals

When encouraging people to set goals, follow these simple practices:

- **Make it specific:** Goals that lack specific details will not be as actionable. "I will ride my bike every Saturday" gives more guidance than "I will ride my bike more this year." Given our tendency to underestimate what is needed to meet our goals (i.e., the **planning fallacy**),[24] it's important to be as specific as possible about the anticipated time, effort, and other resources required. For example, in one study on energy saving, those who had no specific goal saved only 1.5% on their household energy compared to 11%—the average of those with specific, realistic goals.[22]

- **Make it measurable:** Encourage people to set their sights on goals they can easily track. For example, the number of trips made via active modes vs. by car is more easily tracked than the amount of time spent in the car per week.

- **Make it time-bound:** Finally, goals should be focused around outcomes that are bound by time. For example, rather than "I will ride my bike more this year," coach your audience to give themselves a deadline such as, "I will ride my bike at least once before May 15th."

Call it a fresh start

Leverage the **fresh start effect**, which refers to people's tendency to tackle goals following **temporal landmarks**, or important milestones that signal new beginnings.[9] People are particularly motivated to commit to goals around special occasions (e.g., an anniversary, a birthday, a graduation) or calendar events (e.g., a new season, a holiday, a new month or year), which mark the passage of time. These temporal landmarks are effective because they separate experiences into those belonging to a past self and those belonging to an ideal future self.

Design initiatives with this in mind by capitalizing on the turn of a new year or new semester, or by connecting their causes to a special birthday, season, or holiday to increase engagement.[48] For instance, we may encourage the onset of a new transportation habit by giving people a one-week rail pass on their birthday, or a coupon for a local cycling shop to use on the first day of spring.

 Disrupt Old Cues and Responses to Break Habits

Returning to our discussion of the habit loop, we must understand the cue, motivation, response, and reward before trying to break a habit.[7,11] Through mindfulness we can notice a cue and choose to not respond with our habitual behavior, and through introspection we can determine how to intervene in the loop to enact behavior change. (See LONGEVITY: Building Block Chapter 10 for more on fostering mindfulness.) We can take similar steps to understand our audiences' habits:

- **Identify the response:** What response or behavior do you want to change? Reflecting on the series of actions that you find problematic is the first step in the process.

- **Identify the motivation and reward:** Why is your audience engaging in the response or behavior? When breaking habits, it's important to understand the underlying cause that drives the current habit. Is the behavior driven by motivations discussed throughout the book, such as the desire for consistency, connection, or comfort?

- **Identify the cue:** What context cues trigger the response? An awareness of the cues that trigger the action and subsequent reward helps us break the cycle. Thus, we'll want to determine whether the habit surfaces at a particular time or location, in response to another event, or when people are in a particular emotional state.

Answering these questions gives us insight into the possible points of intervention for creating lasting change. We'll discuss each in greater detail below.

✿ Remove cues from the surroundings

If your environment doesn't change, you probably won't either.

—James Clear, *Atomic Habits*[7]

Two major ways to alter context cues are to completely change the environment or to capitalize on change that's already taking place. Known as ***environmental reengineering***, this process involves both cue disruption and the introduction of new or altered environmental features to foster positive environmental behavior.[55]

Altering the environment in which an undesirable habit typically occurs can eliminate context cues—the key triggers for the unwanted behavior. By eliminating such cues, we create space for new habits to form that are more in tune with our current goals. Importantly, habits are often triggered by the whole context, not just individual cues.[46] So when possible, alter more than just a few individual cues in the environment. For instance, rearrange the whole office in a way that disrupts cues to use paper. You can provide suggestions to encourage your audience to reengineer their own environments as well.

Replacing bad habits with new ones may also involve adding cues to the environment. We speak more to this later in the principle "Design Cues to Support New Habits."

✿ Capitalize on periods of change

Interruptions to one's daily routines, like a vacation or the birth of a child, disrupt established habits and behavioral patterns. During these periods, we are already undergoing behavioral transitions to adapt to new circumstances and are, therefore, more receptive to further change.[51] The ***habit discontinuity hypothesis*** posits that old habits die more quickly and are more painlessly replaced with healthy, new habits during big changes in our lives.[52] Identify moments of change, both big and small, to better time your shifter.

Look for major life transitions

Big changes tend to disrupt our habit loops, creating space for new habits to form: as an example, the COVID-19 pandemic disrupted the habit of driving to work for many people. With their driving habit having now been disrupted, an effort to promote a new habit (like an initiative to promote active modes of transportation) is more likely to be effective. Similarly, studies on combating addiction have shown that people are often more successful at kicking a habit when they change their surroundings by moving (even a short distance), or starting a new job. Such transitional events maximize the effects of cue disruptions.

Engage with audiences who can be identified as going through major transitions (e.g., new students, employees, homeowners, or parents). We can seek them out in existing relevant contexts (e.g., schools, hospitals, offices) or by targeting completely new places (e.g., new housing developments, parks, train stations, stores, or offices). By targeting these times and places of transition, we can count on broken routines and the energy brought about by newness to increase the likelihood that the new habits stick after the dust settles.

Making Shift Happen: Using Life Transitions to Promote Sustainable Behavior

In Cambridgeshire, England, a campaign promoted sustainable behaviors like recycling, reducing food waste, and becoming more energy efficient to 800 adults.[53] While 400 had moved within the past six months, the other half had not. Movers and non-movers were further separated into test and control groups. Test participants were given sustainability information and items such as reusable shopping bags, eco-friendly dish soap, vegetable oil, a bus timetable, and a shower timer. All reported how often they performed 35 environment-related behaviors at the beginning of the study and again eight weeks later. The results? The intervention was more effective among participants who had recently moved. In particular, individuals who had moved within three months prior to the study were most likely to adopt new sustainability habits. This example demonstrates how we are more likely to form new habits after a larger change. Leverage this knowledge to design initiatives specifically targeted at audiences that have just moved or experienced other major life events.

Capitalize on temporary disruptions

While larger, more permanent changes like becoming a parent are conducive to developing new habits, even temporary changes can provide opportunities for behavior change that outlast the disruption. Such was the case in 2002, when the winter Olympics caused traffic and parking shortages in Salt Lake City, Utah.[3] This major driving inconvenience caused over half of study participants to use public transportation at least once during the Olympics. Encouragingly, researchers found that many people who began using the light rail during that time continued to use it even after the Olympics were over.

When possible, capitalize on the temporary disruptions people encounter in everyday life to kickstart a habit. Whether planned or unexpected, the following events could be leveraged to change environmental behavior: major construction or road closures, special events coming to town (e.g., sporting events, conferences, festivals or fairs), power or water outages, building renovations, vacations, short-term visitors, illness, and auto accidents or car repairs. Shifters that capitalize on temporary cue disruptions are particularly effective when the behavior of interest is closely linked to the event, such as the case above (encouraging alternative transit modes while parking was disrupted during the Olympics).

Making Shift Happen: Taking Advantage of Temporary Infrastructure Change to Help Travelers Shift Modes

From 2004 to 2015, King County, Washington, helped around 23,000 Seattle-Metro-Area travellers shift from drive-alone trips to walking, ridesharing, use of public transit, or biking.[27] The county's In Motion program identifies areas where major construction projects will be happening and connects with community members who will be affected by this change in transit. In addition to capitalizing on road repair disruptions, the campaign implemented tools such as motivational interviewing, commitments, rewards, norms appeals, and weekly feedback. After a 12-week program, participants reduced their drive-alone trips by 10.7 trips, drove 151 fewer miles, and saved 7.5 gallons of gas on average. At 18 months, participants still took 6.4 fewer trips over 12 weeks, reduced miles driven by 90.6, and saved 4.5 gallons of gas. This example of capitalizing on temporary disruptions is also a great example of how practitioners can work with local governments to implement behavior change initiatives to have large and lasting impacts.

Change the reward

Can you change the behavior by targeting the reward? Yes—by adding a new reward (or highlighting an existing one) and by making it more desirable or more frequent than the reward for the old behavior. For instance, if someone is eating a lot of meat-heavy dinners because they enjoy the taste, using plant-based alternatives in the same recipes can preserve the taste (the existing reward) with the added benefit of a more heart-healthy diet (a new reward). Keep in mind that rewards can take many forms—for example, social recognition and acceptance commonly serve as rewards. Social norms are especially powerful at reinforcing habits: what others are doing can serve as a cue and feelings of fitting in can serve as a reward. See REWARDS: Building Block Chapter 8 for more about different types of rewards.

⚙ Target the response

It's not always possible to remove cues or wait for external forces to disrupt unhelpful cues, nor can we always weaken motivation for a particularly desirable reward. Sometimes we need to challenge the behavioral response itself. Challenging existing responses may require ***vigilant monitoring***[41]—the audience must notice they have been cued and then consciously align their actions with their intentions. See LONGEVITY: Building Block Chapter 10 for more on fostering mindfulness to raise awareness.

Deter the unwanted behavior with friction or penalties

When addressing the behavior head on, adding friction or penalties can effectively deter an unwanted habit.

Discourage the behavior with friction

While removing salient cues is one way to reengineer the environment, you can also add *friction* to the unwanted behavior: additional steps or barriers that make it more difficult to engage in the unwanted habit. For example, to counter food waste in the dining hall, researchers made it difficult for patrons to take excess food by removing access to trays.[42] In effect, they are adding friction to the undesirable behavior, making it exceedingly effortful to take too much food at once. For more on adding friction to deter both ongoing and one-time behaviors, see EASY: Building Block Chapter 2.

Discourage the behavior with penalties

In some cases, penalties may also be used to deter behavior. For example, a plastic bag tax at the checkout counter punishes an unwanted behavior: using plastic bags. While penalties won't build a habit around bringing reusable bags to the grocery store, they can help disrupt preexisting bad habits. A more extreme example of this is a ***commitment device***—a service or program that locks people into giving up bad habits with the threat of an unwanted penalty—commonly used by people who want to change their habits. For more on carefully designing penalties and for an overview of commitment devices, see REWARDS: Building Block Chapter 8.

Find a replacement response

We can replace the problematic response (or behavior) with a more environmentally friendly response. For example, in *The Power of Habit*, Duhigg gives a salient example of overriding his mid-afternoon cookie addiction.[11] After identifying the underlying reward (socialization with colleagues), Duhigg makes a plan to change the response: when triggered each day by the time (3:30pm), instead of seeking a cookie that situates him in a social context (the cafeteria), he stops by a friend's desk for 10–15 minutes. By replacing his current response with a different response that provides the same reward, Duhigg was able to reduce the unhealthy consequences of his original habit. You can help your audience do the same.

Importantly, practitioners will need to help replace the response with a positive environmental behavior that gives people a reward of equal or greater value. Returning to our earlier example about meat consumption, we see this in the work some companies are doing to create plant-based alternatives to meat that provide the same taste (i.e., reward). Which replacement behaviors can be triggered by the same cues and also provide the same, or similar, reward as the problematic behavior? If this is difficult to answer, it may be an indicator that more research is necessary to understand your audience's drivers.

 ## Design Cues to Support New Habits

As discussed earlier, actions are triggered by prominent cues in the surrounding environment and, over time, can turn into powerful triggers for automatic behavior.[19] Practitioners can take advantage of this by introducing new cues to the environment (in addition to removing cues from the environment), piggybacking on existing habits and cues, and encouraging implementation intentions.

Add new cues to the surroundings

Redesign environments so that they help automatic processes kick into gear. You can utilize cues, such as well-placed recycling bins, that directly trigger the behavior, or you can use cues that do this while also increasing motivation, by reminding people of the benefits of engaging in the behavior.[38,54]

If a behavior is easy enough or if someone is motivated to do the behavior, introducing a cue that simply serves as a reminder to do the behavior is sufficient. For example, for some audiences, simply introducing a helmet as a cue can result in the new habit of riding one's bike to the grocery store. But we will often want to provide explicit reminders of the benefits of the behavior (the reward) along with the cue in order to tap into existing motivation or increase motivation to do the

Create a Stable Context

If a person's environment is not stable, cues may not be reliably present, making repetition of the behavior difficult; to form habits, people must have access to a stable, supportive environment that provides a consistent physical setting, ample opportunity to repeat the behavior, and social support.[39] Before introducing cues, it's worth ensuring that the surrounding environment is stable so that new behaviors stand a fighting chance to become established habits. To support the formation of a habit like using cloth napkins at home, for instance, meals should be eaten in a consistent location (physical setting), cloth napkins should be clean, abundant, and easily accessible (enabling conditions), and their use should be integrated into current routines like setting the table.

behavior. For example, we can post a picture of a beautiful forest on a sign that encourages people to reduce their printing or encourage people to put a sticky note that says "enjoy the fresh air!" next to their bike helmet.

No matter what type of cue you use, make sure your cue is highly visible. For example, cues can prominently display environmentally friendly options near the cash register. Ultimately, we want to display or encourage visual reminders that work in people's everyday lives. Determine, through prototyping and testing, which cues and placements will lead to the most success. You can also encourage your audience to alter their own environments (e.g., suggesting they hang their reusable shopping bag with their keys). For more on designing salient cues, see VIVID: Building Block Chapter 5.

Link desired behaviors to existing habits (and their cues)

It's often easier to make use of existing cues than to create entirely new ones. Try linking a new behavior with an existing habit through a process called **piggybacking** or **habit stacking**.[11] This works best when there is a natural connection between two behaviors: for instance, someone might be cued to pack a change of clothes (new habit) after they make their lunch in the evening (existing habit), ensuring that they're prepared to bike to work in the morning. In a similar vein, if someone wants to exercise more, they could add extra mileage to their daily bike commute rather than trying to carve out separate time for exercise. It's more likely to happen when piggybacking on other tasks.

New desired behaviors don't have to piggyback on existing *environmental* habits. Through a process called **temptation bundling** (also known as the Premack Principle), they can also be linked to or reinforced by enjoyable actions that are unrelated to the environment.[12,35] In other words, you only get to do the pleasurable (tempting) behavior if you do the positive environmental habit you are trying to build. For example, ask your audience to reserve listening to an interesting new podcast (pleasurable behavior) for when they are picking up trash at the beach (new habit) or to only read their favorite book series (pleasurable behavior) while they ride the bus (new habit).

⚙ Encourage implementation intentions

It can be difficult to carry out behaviors that are foreign to us. To help our audience break through the *intention-action gap*, we can encourage them to create specific plans of action called *implementation intentions*. Implementation intentions use "if/then" statements to help people determine the details of how they will implement a desired behavior—such as what they will do at a certain time of day, after a given event, or when a particular thought arises. For instance, if your goal is to assist an audience with their desire to reduce consumption of single-use plastics, you can ask them to make a concrete plan: If I go to the grocery store, then I will use reusable cloth bags for my produce.

We can also encourage people to create a backup plan as part of their implementation intention: Overly rigid routines or goals can be detrimental to habit formation—since life inevitably gets in the way.[1] Help your audience by brainstorming potential barriers that could derail their intention to act. Then create a plan for overcoming those barriers, so that the anxiety associated with a new task is reduced and goals are more likely to become action.[21] Following the example above, that might be: If I forget my bags, then I will purchase the food unbagged and wash my produce extra well when I get home.

Going through the steps of designing a specific plan to carry out goals and commitments (especially brainstorming ways to overcome possible barriers) makes the behavior no longer feel so unfamiliar and daunting. By prompting people to recall their goals and act accordingly, these relatively simple and cheap plans have been found to help people to follow through with their intentions.[20,43,47]

Making Shift Happen: Using Implementation Intentions to Create Alternative Transportation Habits

As you know by now, information alone is seldom sufficient to change behavior. In one Japanese study of car use, all participants received lessons on the environmental impacts of driving cars and reported their car and public transit use.[18] A subset of this group created implementation intention plans for how they would reduce car use. Post-intervention data showed that the families who created implementation intentions reduced their car trip duration by 27.7% and their car-use days by 11.6%, while the group that only received information did not significantly reduce their car use. Help your audience create a plan of action—if they know what to do and how to do it, they'll be more likely to follow through.

Reinforce New Habits with Practice, Feedback, and Rewards

As we all know, engaging in a behavior once or even a few times doesn't guarantee that it will become a habit. As practitioners, we can reinforce our audience's newly established behaviors by facilitating practice, providing feedback that serves as both a cue and reward, and using temporary incentives to reinforce repetition.

⚙ Encourage repetition through practice

Habits are automatic responses formed through repeated action. When practiced over time, associations between context cues, responses, and rewards are strengthened, thereby cementing habit representations in memory—a process called *associative learning.*[23] Think about what it was like tying your shoe for the first time as opposed to now. It took real concentration the first time, didn't it?

Interestingly, practicing a new skill or behavior leads to neural connections that do not form when merely observing others.[40] Instead of telling, or even showing, people what to do, create opportunities for hands-on learning and time for the audience to practice the desired behavior. Trial and error is an excellent teacher. Over time, unconscious habits can be formed with enough motivation, simple repetition, and other support.[46,57]

⚙ Cue and reward with feedback

> *Feedback is the breakfast of champions.*
> —Ken Blanchard, PhD, *The One Minute Manager*

One way to keep your audience motivated to repeat a new behavior is to provide them with *feedback:* information about their performance on a given task or the effect of actions toward a specific outcome. Feedback functions as both a cue and reward—when we see that we have made progress, or that our actions have made a difference, our enhanced sense of achievement can continue to cue the desired behavior and boost motivation.[2,5]

Behavioral feedback is commonly provided in the energy sector, likely because of the ease with which providers can give feedback about energy use and track its impact. Over 30 years of research has shown that feedback can result in between 5% and 20% energy reduction depending on variability in the frequency, duration, and specificity of the feedback.[16] The important behavior change mechanism underlying feedback's effectiveness is the *feedback-standard gap* (i.e., enabling comparison of one's performance to a standard or reference). To turn behaviors into habits, feedback must be specific enough to easily act upon or relevant enough to our audiences' values and concerns to spark behavior change.[45]

Find the most motivating type of feedback

In general, feedback is an effective strategy for motivating a variety of positive environmental behaviors, especially when comparing current behavior to one's historic behavior, referencing social norms, and reminding people of pre-set commitments or goals.[28] The effectiveness of such feedback can be maximized by making it specific and vivid, making it span longer periods of time, and combining it with other shifters,[25] as will be discussed in greater detail below.

Giving historical (self-comparison) feedback

Information, such as our past and current energy usage or the number of days we have gone without a vice we are trying to forgo, serves as reinforcement and gives us the ability to monitor our behavior. Historical feedback that is highly specific makes it easier for us to identify and resolve problem areas while also allowing us to see where our initiatives will have the most payoff. For example, receiving feedback about the energy use of each household appliance allows us to target our behavior to the appliances with the highest consumption, which would not be possible if we are only provided with household-level energy consumption.[14]

Showing progress toward a goal

One way to make feedback specific and meaningful is to show the audience the progress they've made toward their goal. The hard road to the finish line feels more achievable when we know we are already part of the way there. Without a clear view of our progress, we're more likely to feel that our efforts are futile.[32] Progress feedback helps us to stay persistent by showing us that our goals are attainable and can be accomplished, the problem is not beyond repair, and our effort is building momentum.

As a general rule, when encouraging the audience through progress, draw attention to the smallest distances.[29] In the beginning of an initiative, we should show the audience how far they've come, rather than the work they have yet to accomplish. However, when close to the end of a goal, it's most motivating to focus on the remaining distance between the audience and their goalpost.[33]

Providing social comparison feedback

Social comparison feedback shows us how our behavior compares to that of others or to a social standard. Social feedback often builds upon an existing base of historical feedback. For example, energy bills sometimes compare an individual household's average consumption against the average for the neighborhood. Ensure your social feedback is based on a reference group that is relevant to your audience. See BELONGING: Building Block Chapter 1 for more on highlighting relevant reference groups, and how to invoke the power of social norms to influence behavior.

Consider the Tone of Your Feedback

It's important to keep in mind that the feedback we give can be positive or negative—it can serve as a confidence boost that sustains engagement, or it can tell us we need to step it up. Positive feedback is usually preferred, whereas negative or judgmental feedback is more hit-or-miss.[10] Negative feedback can lead to *information avoidance,* where people react by ignoring or denying that there is a problem, or abandoning the desired behavior altogether.[26] If framed constructively (e.g., by acknowledging room for growth), people will likely respond well to reminders that they have not yet reached their best potential, especially with regard to something they have committed to.[13]

Consider the timing of feedback

Well-timed feedback can promote lasting behavior change. Feedback can be provided periodically, such as information in a monthly energy bill—or continually, such as a home display panel that relays constant, real-time energy usage information. Although there are several dimensions of feedback timing to consider (e.g., frequency, duration, immediacy, granularity), we focus primarily on immediacy below.

Using immediate feedback

Immediate or *real-time feedback* is especially powerful because it allows us to see the consequences of our ongoing actions as the decisions are being made and while we are still in a position to change them. Immediately seeing the direct connection between our actions and their consequences increases the chances that we'll change our behavior.

However, note that real-time feedback, like feedback communicated via in-home displays, can be costly and difficult to implement, thus limiting scalability.[4] Furthermore, engagement varies over longer periods of time; significant reductions in participation rates have been observed for several energy savings initiatives. Evidence suggests that engagement wanes as batteries die, the novelty wears off, and devices are put away.

Making Shift Happen: Using Real-Time Feedback to Reduce Fuel Consumption

Can timely feedback lead to increased conservation behavior? Perhaps one of the most successful feedback examples can be found in the automotive sector. Makers of the Toyota Prius developed an information display that provides drivers with real-time feedback on how actions, like how fast they accelerate, influence their gasoline consumption.[44] This immediate feedback on mileage effectively teaches people to drive in ways that help them save money and positively impacts the environment. Calling themselves "Hypermilers," some Prius owners have even gamified this effort. In the most recent Hybridfest competition, the winner achieved a stunning 180 mpg. Taking a cue from the Prius playbook, give your audience real-time information so they too can adjust their behaviors in the moment.

Giving delayed feedback

Delayed feedback (or periodic feedback), such as billing statements comparing our energy usage now with usage a year ago, occurs after-the-fact, providing information about our decisions days or weeks after the relevant behavior has occurred. This type of feedback can illuminate behavioral patterns that are hard to see with immediate feedback, is relatively easy to implement, and is scalable to a larger segment of the population unlike more costly immediate feedback. Delayed feedback helps to keep good habits going strong. Seeing our progress over time offers both information plus motivation to restart established environmental habits that have lapsed. An occasional lapse is less likely to cause a discouraging slowdown in effort when the overall trend is still moving in the right direction.

Provide your audience with periodic prompts and feedback to encourage their ongoing behavior. Because feedback is provided some time after consumption, the information it contains can be highly customized, for example, to provide neighborhood comparisons. We all differ in the type of information we like to receive and how we receive it, so allowing for customization can also help individuals make specific behavioral adjustments more easily while also enhancing the user's sense of control. Thus, delayed feedback can sometimes be a more appropriate approach given our specific goals.

⚙ Solidify habits with temporary incentives

To strengthen certain behaviors, practitioners can offer *reinforcers* in the form of incentives.[36] Incentives and reinforcement can help reinforce habit loops, especially in initial stages when the connection between cue and reward may not be well established. Whether an incentive is a reinforcer depends on whether or not it successfully influences the intended behavior. The type and timing (or schedule) of reinforcement can affect whether behaviors become habits: behaviors that are immediately rewarded are more likely to be repeated.

Use incentives to kickstart learning

Incentives can also be a great way to overcome barriers to forming new habits. While incentives should be used sparingly, temporary ones can overcome inertia and kickstart learning. For example, providing new bus riders with a free one-month pass can provide the needed incentive to overcome their resistance to researching bus schedules and stops. Temporary incentives work as initial positive reinforcements that strengthen and cement behaviors, as well as enhance neural pathways that are associated with the reward.

Making Shift Happen: Employing Temporary Financial Incentives to Create Transit Habits

How can we use financial incentives to motivate more people to use public transportation? At Kyoto University in Japan, some of the participants in an experiment were given a bus ticket that allowed them to travel on all bus routes in Kyoto for one month for free.[17] This group ended up using public transit more often than the control group even one month after the bus ticket became invalid, and their frequency of bus use was 20% higher than their initial frequency before the intervention. This example demonstrates how temporary financial incentives can lead to sustained behavioral change if used appropriately.

Use incentives to ramp up efforts

You can also use incentives to gradually guide your audience to adopt more challenging habits. Although we may encourage people to start small, we shouldn't leave them only performing tiny behaviors. Use *shaping* to reward the audience for each step taken as they gradually ramp up to the more challenging behavior or habit.[49] For instance, if someone is not sorting recycling from trash, reward them for starting to recycle their aluminum cans and as they begin to do so consistently, increase your ask to include paper waste, then PET plastics, and so on.

• • •

See REWARDS: Building Block Chapter 8 for more on deciding whether to use incentives, the different types of incentives that can be offered, and best practices for implementing incentives on a schedule of reinforcement.

Conclusion

Guiding our audience to create new habits not only helps us achieve our goals as practitioners, but it helps our audience ditch harmful behaviors and adopt positive environmental habits that are more in line with their goals and values. Ultimately, adopting durable habits promotes more than short-term change—it can lead to a lifetime of positive environmental stewardship. LONGEVITY: Building Block Chapter 10 is another Building Block that focuses on creating durable behavior change with useful content for those working on making and breaking habits.

> Adopting durable habits promotes more than short-term change—it can lead to a lifetime of positive environmental stewardship.

☱ Your Turn

What are some ways that you can nurture positive habits through your initiative? Use the questions below to help you:

Lay the foundation for habit change

- ❏ Are you trying to get people to merely break habits or would you like them to replace old habits with new ones? Where are they in the habit loop?
- ❏ How can the desired behavior be broken down into smaller actions?
- ❏ Which of your audience's goals can be leveraged to inspire habit change?

Disrupt old cues and responses to break habits

- ❏ What are the cues, motivations, and rewards associated with the habit you want to break? Are there cues that you (or your audience) can remove from their environment?
- ❏ What recent life transitions or temporary disruptions have members of your audience experienced, or will soon experience? How might you capitalize on this period to help your audience start a new desired habit?
- ❏ Is it possible to disrupt the habit loop? If not, how can your audience replace their behavior with a more desired one?

Design cues to support new habits

- ❏ How can your audience's context be altered in order to inspire new habits?
- ❏ Can you introduce new cues to remind the audience to do the behavior and/or remind them of the benefits of the behavior?
- ❏ Does your audience have preexisting habits you could link to a new behavior?
- ❏ How can you help your audience develop their own personal implementation intentions (if/then statements) and backup plans?

Reinforce new habits with practice, feedback, and rewards

- ❏ How can you incorporate opportunities for practicing the new behavior?
- ❏ Which types of feedback will your audience respond best to—self-comparisons or social comparisons? Immediate or delayed?
- ❏ Can you make your feedback specific enough to allow your audience to see how different behaviors contribute to the desired environmental outcome?
- ❏ How can you structure your rewards to help your audience maintain the habit over time?

Activate ATTACHMENT

> *Key Takeaway:* By aligning our initiative with what our audience cares most about, we can activate their motivation to take action.

We prioritize what we are attached to

WE ALL HAVE THINGS THAT WE ARE ATTACHED TO, such as the people, animals, or places we love the most, our favorite activities, and our culture. When we deeply care about something, we experience powerful emotions that motivate us to protect or preserve it, and we prioritize the things that are in line with the morals and ideals that guide our judgments. Emotions play an integral role in this process, as they serve as guides that help us evaluate our world. For example, when we observe cruelty, we may feel disgust and anger, which may lead us to judge the behavior as wrong.[24]

We sometimes lose sight of how integral our environment is to all the things we are attached to. But we all have reasons to prioritize environmental action: the things we care most about, our favorite places and activities, and even our culture and way of life can be threatened by environmental issues. Even if we aren't being directly impacted, engaging in anti-environmental behaviors may run counter to the values, morals, and ideologies that guide our sense of how we want to live our lives. So how can we, as practitioners, inspire our audiences to prioritize environmental issues?

Connect with the heart

As practitioners, we can help our audience see the connection between the environmental issues we work on and the things that they are most attached to. We can do this by reducing their sense of psychological distance from the issue: by reminding them of their past experiences of environmental issues, focusing on local environmental impacts, and helping them to feel more connected to distant people and places that are experiencing environmental degradation. We can show our audience how the issue relates to their most pressing worries without adding on new worries. We can also help our audience see how their deeply held values, morals, or ideologies may be opposed to anti-environmental behaviors or make it imperative that they take action to protect the environment. One powerful vehicle for decreasing psychological distance is storytelling. Being able to tell a good story is an extremely effective way to help your audience see how environmental issues can affect what they are attached to.

An important note for this Building Block is that when we tap into what our audience most deeply values, we are playing with fire: what our audience cares about can be nuanced, and the strong emotions at play mean that getting it wrong can be especially detrimental to our cause. With this in mind, it is imperative to test your messages before using them.

Principles and Shifters for the ATTACHMENT Building Block

Align Your Message With Your Audience's Value System

Appeal to core values
Appeal to morality
Work with, not against, ideology
Avoid competing values in a message

Reduce Psychological Distance

Relate it to what people care about
Reduce our sense of emotional distance from others
Reduce temporal distance
Reduce geographic distance
Reduce experiential distance

Tell a Story

Set your story framework
Focus on individuals to encourage empathy
Enlist the right storyteller
Capture attention
Be authentic
Ensure your audience can relate to the story

Make the story optimistic

Connect through positive emotions

Don't ditch all the facts

Leave the audience with something to hold onto

Know your audience and test your stories

Align Your Message With Your Audience's Value System

Environmentalism is intertwined with core values, morals, and ideologies.[9,36] These are interrelated concepts, and this principle covers not just what they are but how they are related, starting with values.

We love to talk about *values*. Companies and organizations have "core values"; we are encouraged to "be true to our values"; we search for partners who "share our values." But what exactly are values? Most literature defines values along the lines of "how we decide something is important."[9,23] So we might determine the importance of an idea, policy, initiative, statement, or behavior by how fair we perceive it to be, or by how much happiness it brings us, and so on. Everyone prioritizes different sets of values—criteria by which they evaluate the world.[55] These values are relatively stable over our lifetimes.[13]

Messages based on policies or issues alone (e.g., "we need to cut carbon emissions") are often ineffective for many audiences because they fail to engage our value systems (e.g., "we need to cut carbon emissions to ensure that our children have a healthy planet"), which often means the messages do not resonate or inspire action.

Appeal to core values

Researchers have classified values in many different ways.[9,55,61] However, a main theme shared by many of the categorizations is the idea that values associated with materialism, consumerism, social power, wealth, ambition, success, hedonism, or other forms of self-enhancement are typically linked to less environmental concern and engagement, while those centered on transcending the self, justice, honesty, fairness, responsibility, protecting the welfare of others, or equality have been shown to be more strongly associated with greater environmental concern and engagement.[9,13]

> Not every audience will hold the following values equally. Value appeals will only be successful if you choose values that are prioritized by your audience.

Values that tend to be associated with environmentally friendly behavior

Below we discuss a number of different value types that, through testing, have been associated with environmentally friendly behavior.

Universalism[55] — Universalism involves an appreciation for people, the world, and the natural environment. Those who esteem universalism tend to value open-mindedness, a world of beauty, a world at peace, wisdom, equality, harmony, protecting the environment, and social justice. Emphasizing these values by using phrases such as "I know that you share our vision of a future in which people and nature thrive alongside one another" tend to elicit environmentally friendly behavior.[9] In several studies, universalism was one of the most influential values that resulted in environmentally friendly behavior.[27,44]

Biospheric values,[61] which place a high value on the ecosystem, are similarly strong drivers.[15]

Self-Direction[55] — Self-direction revolves around each person's freedom to think, act, and explore for themselves. It relates closely with freedom, curiosity, creativity, independence, self-respect, privacy, and the ability to choose your own goals. Self-directed messaging may use words such as "choosing," "creating," "learning," "exploring," and "discovering."[9] In one study, researchers found that self-direction was the second most important value, after universalism, for influencing pro-environmental behavior.[27]

Benevolence[55] — Benevolence refers to prioritizing and protecting the welfare of other people, especially those whom we care about most and see most frequently. Love, helpfulness, friendship, responsibility, honesty, forgiveness, and spirituality are generally connected with benevolence values. For example, someone who values benevolence might feel a responsibility to engage with their community to ensure that everyone has access to parks and other green spaces. Similar to benevolence is *altruism,*[60] which involves care for the well-being of others in the community and in future generations. For example, someone who values altruism may personally engage in climate action in order to safeguard the health of others, both now and in the future. As with biospheric values, environmental behaviors may be especially likely to last in the long term when the audience values altruism.[15]

Fairness between places[56]

People who esteem fairness between places are concerned with equal access to opportunities and resources, such as clean air and water, no matter where you live. It encourages people to think about how they, as individuals, fit into a larger community. Messages targeting people who hold this value may be particularly effective when environmental issues are related to important social justice issues, such as racial equality, environmental public health, immigration rights, and rural or urban policies. It can also have strong impacts when tied to government and policy interventions.

Achievement[55]

Achievement refers to personal success that meets social standards. Someone who values achievement might esteem characteristics such as intelligence, capability, ambition, and influence. While this value is not associated with overt concern for the environment, it has been associated with environmental behavior, particularly for behaviors that give people a sense of competence. Achievement messaging should encourage active participation and opportunities for people to make sustainable decisions, at both the individual and group levels. Research that tested which values most encourage people to use energy-efficient behaviors in the home concluded that achievement was highly influential.[44]

Preparation for the future[56]

Preparation for the future refers to the desire to engage in behaviors now in order to prevent problems in the future. For example, an individual concerned with preparation for the future may be more inclined to engage in environmental activism in order to reduce the long-term effects of climate change. Messaging should highlight the proactive steps people can take in order to ensure sustainability.

Values that tend to be associated with anti-environmental behavior

The values below have generally been associated with anti-environmental behavior. However, some have suggested ways to tap into these values to promote pro-environmental behaviors, which we include in the list.

Egoism[61]

Egoism is about self-interest. While egoistic values (such as focusing on economic savings when reducing electricity use or the personal health benefits of clean air and water) can lead to pro-environmental behavior, researchers have suggested that emphasizing these values may not result in durable behavioral change, and is therefore best suited for short-term rather than long-term environmental behavior change.[15]

Materialism[5]

Those who esteem materialism are concerned with wealth, material goods, and personal possessions. This value has been associated with less engagement in pro-environmental behaviors (such as turning off unused lights, cycling, buying secondhand, or recycling).[9] These values are also associated with viewing humans as consumers of, rather than part of, nature. They can be triggered negatively by interventions that make things more expensive (e.g., a carbon tax). However, some have suggested that they can be used in a positive way by advertisements marketing cool green products (e.g., a luxury Tesla).

Hedonism[55]

Hedonism centers around self-gratification and self-indulgence. These values may be associated with lower levels of environmental engagement because they prompt people to maximize their rewards in the short-term rather than considering long-term goals.[62] Someone might value the convenience and freedom of driving a car over taking public transit and not even think about car emissions. However, some have suggested that messages such as "Feel good knowing you're helping save a species" and "Enjoy a candlelit sustainable dinner" can be used to elicit hedonistic values for positive environmental behavior.[9]

Values that have been associated with both pro- and anti-environmental behavior

The values below have been associated with both pro- and anti-environmental behavior. The effect they have may vary depending on audience characteristics, the environmental issue, or how they are elicited.

Security[55]	Security is related to safety and stability, such as cleanliness and social order, at both the personal and societal levels. While the value of security can sometimes be pro-environmental (e.g., viewing climate change as a threat to national security, or to personal security due to the increased severity of natural disasters), it can also be anti-environmental (e.g., not buying sustainable products in the interest of financial security). Phrases such as "extreme threat," "dwindling supplies," or "food security" can evoke this value.[9]
Tradition[55]	Tradition centers around respect for cultural and/or religious customs. If someone grows up in a community where it's traditional to hang clothes to dry rather than use a drying machine, they may be likely to continue this tradition in the future. If meat is an important part of a cultural diet, people may be less likely to switch to a plant-based diet. The phrases "helping to preserve their way of life" and "respecting the cultures and needs of local people" are examples of messages that draw upon this value.[9]
Power[28]	Those who value power are concerned with status and authority over other people and/or resources, especially in relation to social power, public image, wealth, and recognition. Environmentalism can be in conflict with the pursuit of power, but messages like "Help our community become a leader in the environmental movement!" can tap into this value to support pro-environmental behavior. However, when linked to issues of individual dominance over others or choosing between the environment and the economy, this value may have anti-environmental impacts (e.g., an entrepreneur who values power may choose more economical options over environmentally friendly options).

Continued on page 328

ATTACHMENT

Protection[56]   Those who esteem protection are concerned with the government's role in keeping its citizens safe from threats. In general, people who hold this value support government-based interventions but can be reluctant to engage in individual lifestyle changes. Encouraging people to lobby politicians for clean water and climate change action is a way to positively appeal to this value.

Frame your messages to align with the values that increase support for your environmental issue. Metaphors and stories can be particularly powerful ways to make your message trigger deeply held values[34] and establish connections between those values and the desired environmental behavior. You can read more about stories later in this chapter, and learn more about metaphors in ASSOCIATIONS: Building Block Chapter 9.

After determining your audience's values, connect environmental issues to them. Some researchers have proposed that people are not only at risk from the physical impacts of environmental issues (which can threaten health and safety), but that their social and cultural values are also at risk. For example, not only does food security affect health and well-being, but food can also play a powerful cultural role, and many cultural values and customs could be at risk if certain dishes or routines became unavailable due to climate change.[49] Other researchers have suggested that a multitude of values related to health, belonging, safety, esteem, and self-actualization are potentially threatened by environmental issues such as sea level rise.[23] This is because such changes force people to alter their customs and behavior in order to adapt. The way we live—which may include financial and job security, water and sewer infrastructure, a sense of community and identity, and even freedom—might be forced to fundamentally change in a society affected by environmental problems. Emphasizing how environmental issues threaten the values that are embedded in our way of life could make the problems more significant and salient to your audience. Make sure to offer appropriately-scaled solutions whenever you are emphasizing particular threats. For more on this, see OPTIMISM: Building Block Chapter 7.

One final note: evidence suggests that as we encounter certain values more frequently over time, those values become more important to us. Some researchers argue that messages should appeal only to values that are most likely to prompt long-term concern for the environment, such as intrinsic values that emphasize concern for others, while avoiding messages that appeal to extrinsic values, such as "you will save money by investing in solar panels."[9] When possible, frame your initiatives around the intrinsic values that your audience already holds, such as those related to connection with nature, a passion for outdoor activities, a love of animals, or concern for their community.

There will be cases where the only values you can appeal to are extrinsic. The key is understanding your audience: because value systems vary widely between and within audiences, and because messages that clash with the audience's value system can be catastrophic to campaign efforts, researching and testing messages that appeal to core values is crucial.

> Because messages that clash with the audience's value system can be catastrophic to campaign efforts, researching and testing messages that appeal to core values is crucial.

The Values That People Hold Can Vary Dramatically[55]

Everyone prioritizes different values. Often, these value priorities are due to individual differences. However, they can also arise from cultural or ideological differences. For example, collective values relating to interdependence and group accomplishments tend to be more common in Eastern cultures, while individualistic values, relating to independence and individual accomplishments, tend to be prevalent in the West.[63]

Additionally, some of the most deeply held ideals in the United States, such as freedom, equality, and fairness, may not mean the same thing to every person and may trigger different reactions depending on who you're talking to. For example, the concept of freedom is often understood differently depending on political ideology. Cognitive scientist George Lakoff argues that, for progressives, environmental freedom represents the freedom to enjoy nature. Taxation and government intervention is a necessary step to preserving these kinds of freedoms. However, conservatives have their own version of freedom, which sees taxation and government intervention as oppressive and restrictive of freedom.[35] This is all to say that using words that trigger a freedom ideal might elicit very different understandings of and reactions to your message. This example underscores the importance of testing your messages.

ATTACHMENT

Activate ATTACHMENT • 329

⚙️ Appeal to morality

Morals—how we evaluate what is acceptable and what is not[25]—are core components of our value system. On one level, morals are shaped by one's culture and experiences and can vary widely even within relatively homogenous groups. A study asking college students whether climate change was a moral issue elicited varied responses: 42% said "yes," 36% were "unsure," and 23% answered "no."[41] However, research by psychologists, most notably Jonathan Haidt, suggests that all people share six higher-level "moral foundations" regardless of culture (though to different degrees, as we discuss in more detail below).

People share moral "taste buds"

According to Haidt, moral foundations are hardwired in our brains and act like taste buds; they serve as powerful determinants of what humans, regardless of culture, will find palatable and distasteful.[24] For example, seeing a photo of someone suffering can activate the "care/harm" receptor in our brain, and we would experience discomfort, pity, and an urge to protect or alleviate the suffering of the person in the picture. Haidt's six moral receptors ("taste buds") are:

1. **Care/harm:** People universally react with disgust to cruelty and want to help those suffering or in need.

2. **Fairness/cheating:** Centers on ensuring that people who work together benefit equally and fairly from their work.

3. **Loyalty/betrayal:** Urges us to punish traitors and reward those who cooperate and work together.

4. **Authority/subversion:** Makes us notice things like status and rank and spurs us to preserve hierarchical relationships.

5. **Sanctity/degradation:** Revolves around cleanliness and purity, and may be at play in many religious ideals.

6. **Liberty/oppression:** Helps us to ensure that hierarchical relationships don't become too strong, with the people in power exploiting everyone else.

While these moral receptors or values seem to be universal, individuals place different degrees of emphasis on each one. One way to address moral differences may be to make your message appeal to different moral "taste buds." For example, researchers found that a message emphasizing a need to purify and clean our environment that has become polluted and contaminated (appealing to the "sanctity/

degradation" receptor) had a different effect across audiences than a message emphasizing the harm and destruction humans are causing to the environment (appealing to the "harm/care" receptor).[19] Both messages were equally effective at eliciting pro-environmental attitudes among liberal participants. Conservative participants, however, showed similar pro-environmental attitudes to liberal participants when they read the purity and sanctity message but showed significantly lower pro-environmental attitudes than liberals when they read the harm and destruction message. This demonstrates that appealing to different "moral taste buds" can affect how supportive your audience is of your initiative.

Work with, not against, ideology

Moral values, when shared by a lot of people, give rise to *ideologies* such as political or religious views on the world. For example, people who value empathy may feel that it is morally right for a government to support the elderly, disabled, and homeless, giving rise to a progressive ideology.[34] Alternatively, those who value discipline may believe that taxing the wealthy is morally wrong because it in effect "punishes those who are prosperous," giving rise to a conservative ideology.

Ideology comes in many forms. Here we talk about two pertinent dimensions of ideology: political and religious.

It is important to work with, and never against, ideology. Directly contradicting deeply held ideologies will backfire.

Work with political ideology

Political ideology has been associated with levels of environmental support; for example, people who identify as conservative tend to be more skeptical of environmental issues such as climate change. However, environmental issues are not inherently polarizing. Everyone, no matter their ideology, can become engaged in protecting and preserving the place they call home, other species, or the planet. There are many who identify as conservative that support environmental protection, especially when that protection takes the form of individual behavior, and not government intervention. Often, opposition to environmental policies on the part of those who identify as conservative stems from opposition to the types of solutions that are proposed—for example, taxation or regulation. People who identify as conservative are more likely to believe in well-managed markets as the primary driver of environmental progress.[10] In fact, pushback on environmental regulation started, in part, with scientists living through the Cold War conflict between authoritarian regimes and democratic countries who feared that environmental issues would provide governments with too much power to infringe on the rights of the people.[51]

Messaging that directly contradicts our audience's ideologies is rarely effective. For better or worse, we are not built to constantly change our beliefs. We often suffer from **confirmation bias** (also sometimes called myside bias[43])—a bias that arises when we actively avoid information that contradicts what we already believe, and pay more attention to and even seek out information that supports our beliefs. This may be in part because we experience **cognitive dissonance** (mental or even physical discomfort) when our values, beliefs, and norms are contradictory to new information we've received.[21] We are also prone to argue when our beliefs are challenged, and the process of creating these arguments solidifies our beliefs. This is known as the **backfire effect.**[48] It is therefore best to avoid directly challenging our audience's values and ideologies as much as possible.

Instead, look for inconsistencies between the audience's behavior and values that the audience already holds.[7] For example, if an audience opposes pollution regulation because they believe it is an overstep by the government, avoid directly contradicting that belief. Instead, if the audience also values their legacy, emphasize the negative impacts of pollution on the community that would be harmful to their legacy, and offer solutions that are rooted in the community, rather than those that come from the government. This approach should extend to both the design and communication of the policies. If, for instance, one community chooses to provide economic incentives to promote the desired action and another chooses regulation to constrain undesired behavior, and there is reason to believe the environmental outcome will be the same in both cases, there are no strictly environmental grounds to favor one community's choice over the other.

It can be important to understand what works for groups that don't traditionally support environmental causes.

When communicating with those who hold conservative values, avoid partisan cues that can easily shift a dialogue from open learning to defensive debate. You could choose, for example, to say "elected official" or "civic leader" instead of "politician," and "our state" or "our community" instead of "our government."[20] The same logic applies to issues like carbon taxes. During a study by the Columbia University Earth Institute, 52% of people said they would support a program to raise the cost of emission-intensive products when it was framed as a carbon "offset," while only 39% supported it when framed as a carbon "tax." And it was politically conservative people who strongly preferred the offset label to the tax label.[29] (To learn more about the importance of considering how we present, or frame, information, see ASSOCIATIONS: Building Block Chapter 9.) An important point to remember is that this approach should never be misleading. It is a genuine effort to help people of all values, morals, and ideologies become allies in protecting our shared environment because doing so actually aligns with the things they value the most—or, as we said at the start of this chapter, aligns with the things to which they are most attached.

Work with religious ideology

Several key religious values (e.g., compassion, fairness, purity, responsibility) are strong influences on people's willingness to take pro-environmental action.[18] For example, Islamic texts, which were developed during a time of water scarcity, present guidelines for water conservation. Religious figures such as the Dalai Lama have urged the public to take action against climate change to align with Buddhist values.[26,53] Christian leaders have also advocated for climate action: Reverend Richard Cizik of the National Association of Evangelicals, for example, helped to organize a collective of scientists and Christians to reframe climate change as a religious issue.

Through the Interfaith Power & Light program, thousands of congregations have already pledged to reduce carbon emissions. Reverend Sally Bingham of Interfaith Power & Light has recognized the ties between faith and climate, recommending that religious leaders focus less on guilt and more on morals: being good stewards of God's Creation; offering solutions to fix environmental problems that we helped create; and ensuring that we show love for our neighbors by recognizing the impacts of the environment on the health and well-being of others (especially vulnerable communities).[8]

Appealing to religious values and moral frameworks can help people see environmental issues from a new perspective and encourage them to take a stand.

Avoid competing values in a message

It's tempting to appeal to numerous values in a single message to try to reach disparate audience segments at the same time. However, certain opposing values, like opposing ideologies or intrinsic and extrinsic values, can inhibit each other: the more a person focuses on one frame or set of values, the more inhibited the other set becomes.[34,9] It has even been suggested that commonly used messages such as "save money *and* the environment" have the potential to backfire: appeals to extrinsic values of money and profit may be in direct conflict with the intrinsic values engaged by "save the environment."[9] Therefore, according to some scholars, optimizing a single message for disparate audiences is tricky. It can work, as discussed in the "Appeal to morality" shifter earlier in this chapter, but if you try to appeal to opposing values, morals, or ideologies at the same time in the same message, you may not be successful.

Reduce Psychological Distance

Generally, it's more difficult to care about something when it seems **psychologically distant.** This happens when people who aren't like us are being affected by an issue, when impacts are in the future or far away, or we haven't experienced something ourselves.[64] For example, researchers in the United Kingdom found that people were more concerned about climate change when they believed it would affect their local region, affect those similar to them, and occur soon.[59]

As practitioners, we can frame our issue to reduce psychological distance, helping our audience move from detachment to attachment.

⚙ Relate to what people care about

You can increase the likelihood that your message will be heard by connecting environmental issues to things that your audience already prioritizes. Priorities refer to things that motivate us, like obtaining what we need for survival, or our children's well-being, or causes that are dear to us. Our **finite pool of worry**[38] refers to our limited capacity to care about multiple things simultaneously, so if a new issue of importance comes along that fills our metaphorical "worry bin," others might become less important.[68] You can increase receptivity by tailoring your messages to remain pertinent to the priorities, concerns, and identities of your audience (see IDENTITY: Building Block Chapter 6).

> You can increase receptivity by tailoring your messages to remain pertinent to the priorities, concerns, and identities of your audience.

Environmental behavior can be motivated by myriad reasons. For example, a 2009 British study showed that the majority of people who engage in the environmentally preferable behaviors of using public transportation, turning off lights, or buying organic food were largely driven by convenience, saving money, and health reasons, respectively.[70] So before appealing to an audience, it's important to understand what they care about most.

Self-Interest Is Not Necessarily a Predictor of Behavior

For example, many people will vote for a political candidate because he or she appeals to their values, even though that candidate's policies work directly against their self-interest.[34]

⚙ Reduce our sense of emotional distance from others

When we do not relate to the people being harmed by environmental issues, we can be less likely to care. Reduce the social component of psychological distance by encouraging empathy and perspective taking, using relatable messengers, and fostering a human connection through stories of affected individuals.

Encourage perspective taking

Perspective taking is important for reducing our emotional distance from others because it allows us to see things as they might see them. See LONGEVITY: Building Block Chapter 10 for more on perspective taking.

Create a direct connection

You can foster a connection between your audience and the people or animals being affected by the issue by communicating in a way that is relatable. We react more strongly to information that describes the impact of environmental issues on people, rather than technical or complicated statistics.[47] Use images of familiar people and common items that your audience interacts with in their daily lives rather than intricate graphs and abstract photographs (see VIVID: Building Block Chapter 5 for more on how to use images to increase salience and capture

---

When Deploying Emotional Appeals, Consider the Impact Your Message Can Have on Your Audience's Quality of Life

Adding to your audience's pool of worry can distress them. While it's important that your audience is not complacent about an issue, it's worth being mindful about the amount of stress you may be adding to their lives.

ATTACHMENT

attention).[30] As with stories (discussed in the "Tell a Story" principle to come), focusing your communications on one individual can increase the likelihood of making a connection.

⚙️ Reduce temporal distance

Psychological distance is increased when environmental consequences occur in the distant future and when there is uncertainty over what those consequences will be. Reduce this distance by focusing on what is happening right now or on what has already happened, and by presenting consequences in as certain (yet honest) terms as possible.

Show the issue is here now, not in the distant future

Emphasize impacts that are happening right now. In general, we prioritize immediate threats over those on the distant horizon, especially if the consequences are uncertain.[40] By discussing immediate consequences, we can counteract the human tendency to discount faraway events, and we can make our issues stand out.[57] However, it is important to remember that emphasizing immediate impacts can engender negative emotional reactions, such as fear. See OPTIMISM: Building Block Chapter 7 for information on how to cultivate efficacy in the face of environmental threats.

Finally, focus on the concrete consequences of a particular event, rather than the likelihood that it will occur within a particular period of time. When we focus on a time period (e.g., a tsunami in 6–12 months) rather than the issue itself (e.g., the impacts of tsunamis), we may be seen as "crying wolf" if the event does not occur when predicted.[40]

Decrease uncertainty

When things seem less likely to happen, we tend to perceive them as more distant from ourselves.[64] Uncertainty is inherent in many environmental issues. As practitioners, we do not want to gloss over or ignore uncertainty, but we can present uncertainty in ways that still motivate action. See ASSOCIATIONS: Building Block Chapter 9 for how to do this.

⚙️ Reduce geographic distance

Often, environmental issues take place on a massive scale and yet require local and regional cooperation to solve. Focusing on global impacts increases psychological distance. Instead, focus on local consequences that bring the issue home for decision-makers.

Don't focus on global impacts

Focusing on global impacts can prompt individuals to care less because they seem more psychologically distant.[12] Emphasizing general global effects also magnifies the sense of uncertainty around the issue,[67] which can lead to fear or paralysis, or even give us permission to ignore the issue. If the impacts are distant and uncertain, motivation to spend time and energy mitigating them might not be high.

Focus on local impacts

By shifting the focus toward local impacts,[54,69] such as the property damage caused by sea level rise or the regional effects of air pollution, you can reduce psychological distance for your audience and motivate behavior change. This can also help you appeal to a broader range of values, since people are very attached to their homes, communities, and environments.[23]

In British Columbia, Canada, researchers found that people who read a message emphasizing the potential impacts of climate change in their local area (such as pine beetle deforestation) scored higher on measures of climate change engagement than those who read about the potential global impacts of climate change.[54]

Some researchers suggest that emphasizing local environmental consequences can sometimes override ideological beliefs. One study found that conservative support for fracking was lower when fracking was taking place close to where respondents lived, but that support for fracking became more polarized when it was occurring far away.[12]

⚙ Reduce experiential distance

We remember things more vividly that we have experienced firsthand. Often, memories are tied to powerful emotions, such as fear or nostalgia. These memories help shape how we respond to new experiences; knowing how it feels to be stung by a bee might encourage us to avoid all beehives in the future.[3] As environmental practitioners, we can reduce psychological distance and promote behavior change by identifying experiences our audiences relate to and tying our cause to these personal experiences, by simulating a relevant experience, and by helping our audience create new positive experiences in nature.

Relate it to personal experience

Highlighting the connection between your audience's personal experience and the environmental issue at hand can promote positive behavior change.

Some studies have demonstrated that people who have experienced the effects of environmental degradation show enhanced support for environmental causes. For example, residents in Florida who were surveyed before and after the arrival of Hurricane Irma were more likely to attribute the cause of Irma to global warming and reported an increased willingness to pay higher taxes to protect the environment after the hurricane struck.[6]

However, environmental problems can often develop so incrementally that many people do not notice them, even if they are happening in their backyard. It can be particularly difficult for individuals to detect that they have personally experienced the effects of climate change, as they must be able to pick out changes that occur relatively slowly, distinguish differences in climate from everyday variations in weather,[68] and recognize climate change's wide-reaching impacts.

As practitioners, we can highlight our audience's personal experience with an environmental issue, such as water pollution, air pollution, or climate change, which can in turn increase their support for our cause and the likelihood that they will respond to our call to action. For example, you can make the connection for your audience that the plastic marine debris they encounter on their local beach is a result of both individual actions and systemic issues (like a lack of policies that require producers to be responsible for the environmental impacts of their products). Then, be sure to give your audience clear ways that they can take action against this problem that they have personally experienced. For ideas on how to make vivid connections between action and impact, or to capitalize on the saliency of recent events, see VIVID: Building Block Chapter 5.

As with many shifters in this book, the effectiveness of this shifter depends on the existing beliefs of your audiences. Audiences that are already concerned about an environmental issue may be more likely to change their behavior in response to messaging that highlights their personal experience. Conversely, those who are in denial about an issue may be reluctant to acknowledge that their personal experience was caused by the issue and are not likely to take related environmental actions.[46] For example, a farmer who does not believe in climate change may be reluctant to support climate mitigation and adaptation measures, even after experiencing several catastrophic extreme weather events. Thus, highlighting their personal experience may have little effect on their behavior.

Simulate personal experience

You can simulate personal experience through interactive displays or vivid stories (discussed in the "Tell a Story" principle below). Interactive and virtual experiences such as video games and virtual reality can be particularly effective at reducing psychological distance. For example, people who participated in a virtual experience of cutting down a tree (in which they heard and felt a chainsaw start and were instructed to move a joystick back and forth to cut the tree down) later used 20% fewer napkins compared to those who simply read a description about deforestation.[2]

Build new positive personal experiences

Help your audience reduce psychological distance and strengthen their connection with nature by helping them create new positive experiences in nature. See LONGEVITY: Building Block Chapter 10 for more.

 Tell a Story

Successful campaigns reduce psychological distance and align messages with an audience's value system. But how to do that in practice? Hands down, the best vehicle for this is *storytelling*.

The human brain is wired for stories. We communicate with each other by telling stories, we become immersed in stories of people who are not even real and events that never even happened, and we even dream in stories. Stories are the default ways that we think, helping us to process information and store it in long-term memory.[14]

Stories help us navigate everything from social dilemmas to moral decision-making. They also help us empathize with others by allowing us to see the world through others' eyes.[11] (For more on building empathy and compassion, see LONGEVITY: Building Block Chapter 10.) Through stories, we can imagine real-life scenarios or daydream about possible ones.

Stories are easier to process than facts and statistics,[14,56] and they are engaging, interesting, and accessible for audiences.[14,16] This may be why good stories are riveting—we don't have to force ourselves to pay attention to a good novel or a friend's enthralling story the same way we sometimes have to force ourselves to pay attention to a lecture. When hearing or watching a story, our brain isn't a spectator; it's a participant in the action. When tested, narratives consistently outperform facts in terms of persuasiveness.[16]

Stories can even diminish polarizing issues, including environmental ones,[45] as people tend to be less resistant to a convincing narrative—even if they know it is fictional—than to facts.[14] Through stories, practitioners have a unique ability to share how-to knowledge and convey ideas, attitudes, and visions that can spread contagiously. Stories come in many forms, such as testimonials from those affected by environmental issues, speeches, short stories, newspaper or magazine op-eds, and plays, films, or TV shows.[11]

But for stories to work, we must be transported. How do we, as practitioners, do this for our audience? There are copious resources devoted to this. Below we present some of the elements of a good story.

⚙ Set your story framework

Many stories have five ingredients:

1. **Context:** start with the big picture, then zoom into the story
2. **Characters:** a hero, villain, love interest, or mentor
3. **Conflict:** failure, disappointment, fear to overcome, or another internal struggle
4. **Plot:** once the context is established, connect characters through a plot containing the main conflict and the outcome or resolution
5. **Outcome:** something learned, a moral proved, or an environmental win

A powerful yet simple way to craft a story is to use a framework like the one in Table 2.4.1.

Table 2.4.1: Framework for Crafting a Story

	Plot / Sequence	Example
Characters and Context	• Once upon a time, there was a... • ... **and** • ... every day	I am from Missouri, **AND** every evening I heard the sound of frogs in the marsh nearby. This was the sound of my childhood.
Conflict	• ... **but** • ... because of that	**BUT** over time, the frog sounds disappeared as the marsh was drained for development. I realized I couldn't remember the last time I had heard them.
Outcome	• ... therefore • ... **so** • ... finally • ... ever since then • ... to this day • ... in response	**SO**, I, along with a group of other locals, reached out to the development company and came up with a plan to restore some of the land. Last night, I closed my eyes and smiled as I heard the familiar sound of a frog in the distance.

CREDIT: ADAPTED FROM KENN ADAMS "STORY SPINE" AND THE ABT (AND; BUT; THEREFORE) FRAMEWORK[1],[50]

Focus on individuals to encourage empathy

Focusing your story on just one individual can help your audience connect. Our valuation of a problem, or our willingness to pay to mitigate a problem, doesn't always scale in proportion to the problem or the number of people or beings affected; this is known as *scope insensitivity*. For example, in Canada, Toronto residents were willing to pay higher taxes to preserve fish populations in a small area of Ontario lakes, but were only slightly more willing to pay to preserve populations in the entire region.[31] Similarly, people expressed similar levels of willingness to pay to protect migratory birds—regardless of whether the conservation program was described as protecting 2,000, 20,000, or 200,000 birds.[17]

When stories focus on the individuals being harmed, we become more engaged.[58] This seems to work for a number of reasons, including the fact that the plights of single individuals are more emotionally available to us than those of abstract groups, and because it may be more compelling to know we can help a single individual in need, rather than being faced with all those we won't be able to help.[37] Images of single individuals who are affected by environmental problems can inspire people to help more than when they are given statistics or even told stories about groups of affected people.[37]

Make sure the individual is valued by the audience. For example, the image of a single polar bear stranded on melting ice was meant to catalyze a more powerful emotional response than providing cold, impersonal statistics about climate change's impacts.[39] But as we know, images of polar bears have not spurred widespread behavior change. It has been suggested that only wildlife lovers find images like these compelling.[39] Images of polar bears have also been criticized for overdoing the emotional appeals and unintentionally resulting in psychological distance—something we discuss briefly below and at length in OPTIMISM: Building Block Chapter 7.

Enlist the right storyteller

By featuring storytellers and messengers who are relatable and diverse, you can increase your credibility.[22,42] Recruit people from your audience's social networks, or use unexpected yet trustworthy messengers who are involved in the issue.[22] For example, enlist military officers to talk to an audience about the national security implications of climate change, or local business owners to discuss the impacts of environmental damages such as oil spills. By enlisting the appropriate storytellers, you can help your audience to understand that your issue relates to them, does not have to be polarizing, and that many disparate people can band together to address it.

The storyteller doesn't always have to be real. For instance, soap operas have been used successfully to motivate behaviors and attitudes related to standing up against violence in Rwanda[52] and promoting sustainable fishing in Belize,[66] among other issues. For more on choosing the right messenger and using fiction to model behaviors, see BELONGING: Building Block Chapter 1.

Capture attention

Create engaging stories that capture and keep your audience's attention. We give a few tips below, but see VIVID: Building Block Chapter 5 for more on how to capture and hold your audience's attention and make abstract issues more concrete through vivid language.

- **Show, don't tell:** For example, instead of just telling people that beaches need to be protected, you can embed your call to action in a story of a family enjoying the beach, utilizing vivid descriptions to paint a mental picture of the waves hitting the shore, sand that is pleasantly warm to their bare feet, and the salty smell in the air. This can help audiences connect to their own beach experiences, increasing their motivation to respond to your ask.[22]

- **Pique curiosity by holding something back:** Keep your audience guessing by holding something back, adding an element of mystery. The audience will want to keep listening or reading to find out what will happen next, and by guessing or trying to figure it out, they will also process the information at a deeper level.[32]

- **Finally, surprise the audience** with an unexpected plot twist or outcome.

Be authentic

People can tell when a story isn't authentic: we can pick out staged stock images from photos of real people in real situations, and we are put off by stories and photos that appear forced or contrived.[4] Additionally, because we tend to accept convincing stories with less scrutiny than we do facts and statistics,[14] it is ethically imperative to present stories truthfully.

Ensure your audience can relate to the story

Audiences will form a deeper connection to your content when they can relate to the characters in the story, or can imagine themselves in the characters. By featuring relatable characters enjoying the environment and actively participating in solutions, you can help your audience imagine themselves doing the same.[4,22] Additionally, when the elements in the story highlight values, morals, ideologies, identities, and emotions that the audience is attached to, they can see how the environmental issue is connected to what they value.[22] Your stories are likely to be ignored by your audience if they do not connect to their value systems,[32] as we discussed previously in the "Align Your Message With Your Audience's Value System" principle.

Make the story optimistic

While elements of fear, concern, or danger may be important for creating a dramatic narrative, make sure to focus on the solutions to environmental problems, and emphasize how the audience can enact that solution.[22,42,65] See OPTIMISM: Building Block Chapter 7 for more on fostering optimism.

⚙ Connect through positive emotions

Certain elements, like emotional language and heartwarming storylines, can activate positive emotions and foster emotional connection. For example, "she stared out at the vast ocean in wonder" can spark positive feelings of awe in an audience. Heartwarming themes include the long-suffering finally getting rewarded, being reunited with a long-lost loved one, or close relationships like friendships and family. Even aspects of nature can serve as a long-lost loved one: "One day, I no longer heard the sound of frogs in the balmy summer air, something that was ever present in my childhood. But then we came together and restored the marshland. Just last night I heard the frogs once again."

⚙ Don't ditch all the facts

While stories can be more persuasive than facts alone, this doesn't mean we should remove all facts. Embedding facts in a story can be an excellent way to communicate the importance of those facts by providing needed context and allowing the audience to process the information on both an emotional and a logical level. Additionally, facts can help put smaller stories about individuals into the context of a larger system.[33,65]

⚙ Leave the audience with something to hold on to

A compelling ending leaves the audience with a gift—new wisdom, how-to information, a new way of seeing the world, and/or potential solutions to environmental problems. Be sure to give your audience a clear takeaway.

⚙ Know your audience and test your stories

It is important to test your stories on your audience. Stories are subject to all of the risks of backfire discussed throughout the chapter, and should not be used indiscriminately. Stories that are not tested can also be unintentionally misleading.[32] Additionally, stories that focus on individuals have the potential to obscure the systemic causes of problems.[33] Testing your stories with your audience can enhance your ability to reach them while helping to prevent backfiring.

• • •

Storytelling is an incredibly powerful tool to help you connect with your audience. Stories that meet the above criteria are more likely to be memorable and engaging, create attachment in our audiences, and to inspire action. We recommend that you use the above features to not only create new stories, but also to evaluate how much merit a particular story has. Good stories might take time to find, so consider starting to collect and curate stories now. Pay attention to stories that pop up in the news, and try enlisting the members of your audience to share their stories.

Conclusion

The things to which we are most strongly attached (e.g., the people, places, and things that we love; the values, morals, and ideologies that we espouse; and our stories about them) help us to make sense of the world around us and determine what's right and what's wrong, guide us in deciding what's important in life, and shape how we think the world should work. When our attachments are activated, we often experience powerful emotions that guide our decisions and behavior. By aligning your message with the things to which your audience is attached, you can tap into what they care about the most, prompting positive environmental and behavioral engagement.

📋 Your Turn

How can you align your message with what the audience is attached to the most to promote behavior change? Use the questions below to brainstorm.

Align your message with your audience's value system

❑ What are some things that your audience values the most? Which of those values align with environmentally friendly behavior?

❑ Does your audience have a moral connection to the environment? Can you connect your issue to their moral beliefs?

❑ How can you craft your message to align with your audience's ideologies? Is there anything you should emphasize or avoid (such as emphasizing local solutions over governmental ones for conservative ideologies)?

❑ What are some ways that you can incorporate intrinsic values into your messaging? Can you avoid extrinsic or self-serving values and still prompt engagement?

Reduce psychological distance

❑ What are the consequences of your environmental issue? Has your audience experienced any of them? How can you highlight those experiences?

❑ Can you create a simulated or virtual experience of these consequences?

- How might your issue affect your audience's local community? How might you highlight this?
- What are the specific solutions and consequences of your environmental issue that you can emphasize?
- What does your audience already have on its plate? How might your message affect what they're already worried about? Can you alleviate this worry without decreasing motivation?
- Who are some messengers that you can enlist as allies in engaging with the rest of your audience?
- Who are all the potential stakeholders in your issue? Are there any that are surprising (e.g., military officers, business owners)?
- Are there any individuals who have been harmed impacted by your issue? Can you showcase their stories?

Tell a story

- How many of the best practices do your stories include?
- While researching your issue, did you come across any compelling stories of people harmed by the issue, or of related challenges or successes?
- Can you ask your audience to share their stories with you?
- Have you integrated feedback from testing and presenting your stories?

Design it to be VIVID

> *Key Takeaway: In this age of information overload, competition for people's attention is steep. By designing our initiatives to be vivid, we can help our audiences notice, pay attention to, and remember our messages for long enough to take the desired action.*

Attention fatigue is ubiquitous

WHY DO WE NOTICE and remember some things, while others "go in one ear and out the other"? In our fast-paced and technology-driven society, we are bombarded by messages competing for our attention every day—from billboards, to pop-ups on our phones, to signs in the grocery store. We've gone from seeing about 500 ads a day back in the 1970s to as many as 5,000 a day today.[25] And that's just advertising—many things, like our work and families, also compete for our attention.

The sheer volume of information—all of which claims to be important—results in ***information overload*** and, ultimately, ***attention fatigue***. We simply can't process and respond to all the messages presented to us—even those about things that are truly important to us. So our brains are always sifting through information, deciding where to place our attention based on whatever is most compelling or salient at that moment, rather than what might actually be more important to us.

Attention fatigue has significant consequences: whatever can manage to successfully capture our attention and stick in our memory is more likely to influence our behavior. This is known as the ***availability heuristic***:[27] the easier we can bring something to mind, the more important we perceive it to be, and thus it bears greater weight on our decision-making than something that is not as immediately available.

347

Unfortunately, environmental messages are often not what come most easily to mind. Many other things compete for our audience's attention. But as passionate environmental practitioners, we often underestimate this challenge. Because we think our issue is so important and think about it all the time, we think: "How can someone NOT pay attention to this? It's so important!"

This is one of the most difficult—if not *the* most difficult—challenge for contemporary changemakers. Your cause is important, and you might even know that your audience already cares, but by some accounts, we have only seconds to capture our audience's attention. So how can we make sure our calls to action are the ones people pay attention to? How can we break through the noise? We must design our initiatives to be vivid. While **vividness** can have different meanings across disciplines, a commonly accepted definition from social psychology is that vivid communication is "likely to attract and hold our attention and to excite the imagination to the extent that it is emotionally interesting, concrete, and image provoking."[36]

Capture attention with vividness

> *It is a notorious fact that what interests us most vividly at the time is, other things equal, what we remember best.*
>
> —William James, American philosopher and psychologist

Given the critical importance of what information is most noticeable and memorable, environmental practitioners face a critical challenge and opportunity. To be successful, we must design initiatives that not only take attention fatigue into account, but also overcome it.

And while attracting attention does not guarantee behavior change, it is a critical first step: a message can't influence an audience if they never see it. When a message captures our attention, we are more likely to act on it; when an item catches our attention, we are more likely to choose it.[18] For example, eye-tracking research found that for every additional second of visual attention, the likelihood of purchasing shade-grown certified coffee increased by 22 percentage points.[48]

Fortunately, there are many ways to make something stand out to our audience and to stick more vividly in their memory. For example, we can make it novel or unexpected, concrete and easy to process, or well-timed. By the end of this chapter, you will better understand how to design vivid initiatives that help your audience notice, pay attention to, and remember your message long enough to take the desired action.

VIVID

Principles and Shifters for the VIVID Building Block

Get Noticed

Make it novel

Create contrast

Craft curiosity-generating questions

Put it in verse

Repeat, repeat, repeat

Say their name, say their name

Make the Abstract Concrete

Engage the senses

Make invisible impacts more visible

Connect actions to impact

Use illustrative and attention-grabbing images

Paint a mental picture with vivid descriptions

Tell an engaging story

Nudge at the Right Time and Place

Arrange choices strategically

Time calls to action to current events

Give reminders at the right time

Use prompts in the deciding moment

Whether it's crafting a catchy slogan or designing a flashy recycling bin, there are many ways to make something stand out. In Copenhagen, surveys found that while the public overwhelmingly considered littering unacceptable, there was a gap between this reported belief and a high littering rate. To reduce this **intention-action gap**, researchers placed eye-catching green footprints on the sidewalk leading to trash cans. This simple vivid shifter made the locations of trash cans more noticeable and nudged people to use them, resulting in an impressive 46% reduction in litter. The footprints were also cheaper and more effective than trying to enforce anti-littering laws.[22] Keep Britain Tidy and Zero Waste Scotland have also used the same technique with promising results.[9,42]

Here we discuss how you can use novelty, contrast, intriguing questions, rhyming, repetition, and personalization to make your messaging and desired behavior stand out from the noise.

Make it novel

Novelty and surprise attract attention. New and unexpected information draws interest and makes an idea sticky (e.g., more likely to be remembered). Novelty is also vital in fighting **attention habituation,** or our tendency to lose interest in things over time; what was once new and exciting can soon become predictable and boring.[3]

Students from the National Taiwan University of Arts used novelty to create an unexpected yet powerful twist on a classic treat: popsicles. The students created popsicles using water from polluted sources around Taiwan. While we usually think of popsicles as refreshing, these contained plastic trash, cigarette butts, and waste oil. By presenting a surprising twist, this project drew attention to water contamination issues and connected those issues to daily consumption and problematic behaviors.[21,24]

Making Shift Happen: "Vote with your butt" Bins Use Novelty and Fun to Capture Attention

Using novelty doesn't have to be as serious as it was with the popsicle example. It can also be fun and lighthearted. "Vote with your butt" bins or "ballot" bins are a novel way to capture smokers' attention and have been shown to reduce cigarette butt litter by up to 46%.[19] The clever containers are a novel twist on otherwise boring, easy-to-miss cigarette butt bins. This new style of bin invites people to "vote" on fun questions, from favorite soccer players to dream superpowers, by placing their cigarette butt in different slots in the receptacle. The bins also went viral on social media and attracted inquiries to use them worldwide.[20] The bins exemplify how incorporating a little humor and novelty into your initiatives can go a long way. We used this same concept to have hunters "vote" for their favorite duck species using plastic shotgun wads they picked up—see DESIGN: Process Chapter 4.

Create contrast

When we scan visual information, we unconsciously search for what stands out and thus notice things that contrast with their surroundings. We can harness the power of contrast in various ways, such as by using contrasting colors, sizing, and backdrops to make our most important point or call to action stand out.

For example, one study found that only 52% of university students recycled when both the trash can and recycling bins were grey.[34] But when researchers placed a vividly colored (green), contrasting recycling bin next to a gray trash can, the recycling rate increased significantly to 88%. This same study also found that green was the most memorable color for a recycling bin, followed by blue, red, and then grey.

You can apply this concept to make a message contrast with surrounding information or to make a desired choice contrast with other options. For example, we could use a green box to highlight the most environmentally friendly carbon offset plan or energy plan on a website while the other options are grey.

Craft curiosity-generating questions

What is it about a good question that hooks us and leaves us wanting to know more? Questions capture our attention by generating curiosity, especially when they highlight a gap in knowledge. We are then motivated to resolve the posed question, so we keep reading or listening. Examples of the types of questions that you can use to pique your audience's curiosity and capture their attention include: Why is it that…?, How is it that…?, or What happened when…?

⚙ Put it in verse

In addition to making your message simple, try to make it memorable. Put your ideas in verse if you can; they will be more likely to be taken as truth.

—Daniel Kahneman, psychologist and
winner of the Nobel Prize in Economics

Make your messages simple and easy to understand (see EASY: Building Block Chapter 2), but also make them catchy (e.g., likable and memorable). Of course, there is no magic formula for making something catchy, but using rhyme helps. People rate rhymes as more likable, more original, and easier to remember.[13] For this reason, they are often used as mnemonic devices. For example, the humorous rhyming mnemonic "If it's yellow, let it mellow" can help serious water savers remember not to flush unnecessarily. For more on mnemonics, see EASY: Building Block Chapter 2.

Rhymes have another advantage, known as the ***rhyme-as-reason effect***: people perceive rhymes as more accurate, truthful, and persuasive than phrases that do not rhyme.[13] For example, students given a list of rhyming aphorisms like "woes unite foes" rated them as more accurate than non-rhyming versions like "woes unite enemies."

In sum: if you take the time to create a rhyme, your behavior change campaign will be sublime!

⚙ Repeat, repeat, repeat

If your audience isn't taking action, consider how often you shared your message or call to action. Maybe your audience only saw your message once, so they figured it wasn't that important, or they simply forgot about it. Studies show that repetition makes a message more prominent in our minds, helping us process and recall that message.[23] Hearing a message multiple times can even subconsciously lead people to have a more positive regard for it, in a phenomenon known as the ***mere exposure effect.***

However, researchers have also found that this phenomenon has a declining rate of return. Extreme overexposure can cause our audience to be bored or even irritated by our message.[7] It's essential to strike a balance between making the message salient and not overloading the audience. One way to counteract overload can be to repeat the core message, but with new imagery or colors designed to capture attention. It's also essential to present your message at the appropriate time and place (as covered throughout this chapter) for it to remain useful and relevant to your audience.

⚙️ Say their name, say their name

Have you noticed that you immediately pay attention when someone calls out your name, no matter how preoccupied you are or how noisy the environment is? Enter the *cocktail party effect*: research consistently shows that personalized appeals, such as those using a name, are more effective than more generic messages. Messages using our name not only capture our attention, but we also tend to believe that they hold greater relevance.[2]

Putting this effect to the test, the UK Behavioral Insights Team found that while only 5% of Deutsche Bank employees who received a generic "Dear Colleague" email from the CEO donated a day's salary to charity, donations went up to 12% when the email addressed the employee by name.[5] While these percentages may seem small, this simple and inexpensive messaging tweak can have a significant positive impact, especially if implemented at scale.

 ## Make the Abstract More Concrete

Environmental issues like climate change, deforestation, and ocean pollution can seem abstract and far removed from our daily experiences, which can result in a lack of concern or a lack of understanding of how our actions contribute. Environmental issues are even harder for people to conceptualize when, instead of making our messages vivid, practitioners rely on technical language and complicated statistics to communicate.

Vivid communication that engages the senses and makes something feel closer in time or space can enhance a message's persuasiveness, increase people's ability and motivation to review the information carefully, and ultimately, initiate behavior.[2,36] Below we discuss several ways to use vividness to make abstract concepts more concrete, especially to make the connection between environmental actions and their impacts more clear.

⚙ Engage the senses

> *The more you can engage people's senses and transport them to a place, the more success you will have getting them to see why taking a certain action to protect that place is so important—and what is at risk if they fail to act.*
>
> Heartwired to Love the Ocean: A Messaging Guide for Advocates

Vivid messages that engage the senses may enable the brain to assimilate and process information more effectively than messages that don't.[2] Yet, environmental communications often fail to take advantage of this opportunity. In a survey about the ocean, 84% of respondents agreed that they "love feeling the sand between my toes, the sound of the waves, the smell of the salt air, and the sights and tastes of being at the ocean," yet many messages about ocean conservation do not include these sensory elements.[38] By incorporating more concrete, multi-sensory language like this, we can transport people to the place they love and motivate them to protect it.

While many of the shifters in this chapter engage our sense of sight, we can also incorporate our other senses like hearing, smell, taste, and touch into our initiatives.

Making Shift Happen: Creating Tactile Activities to Make Carbon Footprints More Concrete

The California Academy of Sciences has used clever cubes to make the carbon footprint of our food choices more concrete. Adapted from cubes created by chef Anthony Myint and local art students,[43] each cube is wrapped with images of one type of food (produce, poultry, grains, etc.) and weighted according to that food's relative carbon footprint (including emissions from growing, processing, transporting, and producing the food). As participants interact with heavier cubes such as beef and lighter cubes such as beans and greens, they can begin to better understand and remember the relative carbon impacts of different food choices, inspiring and empowering them to adjust their diets accordingly. Practitioners can use tactile tools like this to engage several senses at once while making impacts and solutions more concrete to audiences of all ages.

⚙ Make invisible impacts more visible

The adage "seeing is believing" still rings true—it's easier to grasp new ideas when we can see them with our own eyes. Yet environmental practitioners and organizations often communicate with facts and figures, rather than making problems and solutions more visible to our audiences.

For example, people tend to overestimate how much energy is saved by visible practices (like turning off the lights) and underestimate less visible uses (like heating water).[17] Instead of just providing facts, we can use tools like in-home energy displays to make real-time energy use visible, helping households identify which appliances are using the most energy.

Visualizations can also help us better understand future impacts that we can't yet see. For example, seeing images of a familiar landscape altered due to climate change can promote a more in-depth consideration of adaptation and mitigation measures.[17] Some practitioners are even painting blue lines on buildings and infrastructure like telephone poles and mailboxes, making the height of future sea levels vivid. Seeing these blue lines helps paint a concrete image of how sea level rise will affect communities.

But remember: it's essential not just to make *problems* vivid and visible, but their *solutions,* as well. See OPTIMISM: Building Block Chapter 7 for more about the importance of sharing solutions to increase hope and motivation.

> It's essential not just to make *problems* vivid and visible, but their *solutions,* as well.

Making Shift Happen: Using Thermal Imaging to Make Heat Loss Visible

A series of studies in the United Kingdom tested the effects of vivid thermal images and found that "making heat visible" influences energy conservation behaviors.[17] Thermal images show a sharp contrast in the coloration between different temperatures, making it clear where heat is escaping or cold air is entering a home. Households that received a thermal image took significantly more energy-saving actions and were nearly five times more likely to take draught-proofing action (like installing insulation) than households that only received an energy audit. In a second study, households that received a thermal image reduced their energy use by more than 14% at a one-year follow-up, while homes in the control group and those that received a carbon footprint audit demonstrated no change. Why were thermal images so effective? They drew attention, were personally relevant, and provided a vivid visual to help households identify how to save energy in their home.

Connect actions to impact

Often, people don't believe that their individual actions make a difference—in both positive and negative directions. We can make the connection between an individual or group's actions and their environmental impact more concrete by vividly demonstrating the consequences of behavior. Numerous studies show that once people believe that their actions do matter, they are more likely to perform environmentally friendly behaviors.[31] See UNCOVER: Process Chapter 3 and OPTIMISM: Building Block Chapter 7 for more about *action efficacy*—the perception that a recommended action will be effective.

In one example of visually connecting action to impact, advertising agency Saatchi & Saatchi designed paper towel dispensers for the World Wildlife Fund with a see-through outline of South America.[31] Every time you pull a towel from the dispenser, you receive real-time visual feedback that demonstrates how each piece of paper used contributes to deforestation in the Amazon, making the impact of everyday actions and solutions more concrete.

Similarly, but with greater emphasis on the positive effects of our actions, researchers tested the effect of a series of images showing the positive impact of recycling old clothing. The recycling bins in the images contain a translucent person-shaped cutout that makes the positive impact of recycling clothes more visible and concrete. Compared to images that did not include the cutout (but were

Fig. 2.5.1: *Paper towel dispenser and clothing recycling bins vividly connect action to impact.*
Credits: Top: Saatchi & Saatchi Copenhagen, Bottom: Dr. Marijn Meijers

identical otherwise), the cutout images increased the belief that recycling clothing makes a difference and resulted in stronger intentions to recycle.[31]

Demonstrating cumulative impacts via physical displays can be particularly engaging and effective at helping the audience connect the dots between frequent, small actions and their cumulative significance, which can be otherwise easy to overlook. For example, at Portland Community College, sustainability coordinator Elaine Cole collected empty paper ream boxes and stacked them in a high-traffic area to help people visualize what just a fraction of the school's annual paper use looks like (see Figure 2.5.2). Importantly, the display also included actionable information about how to use less paper. For more about the importance of pairing vivid information about negative impacts with solutions, see OPTIMISM: Building Block Chapter 7.

Making Shift Happen: Creating Vivid Visual Displays to Demonstrate How Food Waste Adds Up

"Weigh the Waste" campaigns, popular on hundreds of college campuses, have students discard their food scraps into see-through bins, so students can better visualize the scale of campus food waste.[14] At the end of each day, the containers are weighed, demonstrating the cumulative impact of each person's discarded food. At Chapman University, this initiative resulted in a 30% decrease in food waste.[10] Practitioners can implement activities and displays like this to make cumulative impacts more vivid.

Fig. 2.5.2:
Portland Community College created a vivid paper ream display to help students visualize paper use.
CREDIT: ELAINE COLE / PORTLAND COMMUNITY COLLEGE

⚙ Use illustrative and attention-grabbing images

We all know the phrase "a picture is worth a thousand words." The *picture superiority effect* means that we process, retain, and recall information from images better than text.[53] Images also elicit stronger emotional responses than text-based information. Images can be powerful communication tools on their own, but they can also supplement written messages, helping to enhance the audience's understanding of environmental issues and solutions.

But what kinds of images should environmental practitioners use? The considerations presented below are supported by existing research, but imagery is not as well-researched as other environmental communication topics.[11] Images are an area where we especially recommend testing to see what is most effective for your specific audience, context, and goals.

Portray real people

Contrary to what many nature-loving environmentalists might think, images of beautiful landscapes and wide-angle vistas are less memorable than pictures of people.[8] Human figures are particularly effective at grabbing our attention, even in online environments full of distractions. Yet, imagery of humans is underutilized in environmental communications. For example, a recent review of the marketing materials and websites of ten well-known ocean conservation organizations found that most were missing any humans in their images and messages—only about one in ten included a human.[38]

Showing humans in images also serves to remind us that issues like climate change affect people (not just "the environment"), and that human action is both the cause of and solution to those problems. If we only use images of nature and abstract landscapes, we may miss opportunities to make these connections and engage people's emotions. See ATTACHMENT: Building Block Chapter 4 for more about how to engage values and emotions in your messaging.

Show human faces and emotions

People tend to remember and be most responsive to photos with only one or a few individuals, as opposed to large groups of people.[11] We also recognize human faces faster than other elements in an image, especially faces that convey recognizable human emotions. Additionally, evidence suggests that being able to make "eye contact" with the subjects in photos is a powerful way to elicit a moving emotional response. Images need not only show negative emotions. For example, showing people experiencing the powerful emotion of awe in the ocean's presence can be particularly effective.[38]

Show real people in relatable, realistic situations

Use images that show people interacting with the issue at hand. For example, to depict the dire consequences of wildfires, it's more effective to show people's experience (e.g., a family surveying a lost home or wearing masks in heavy smoke), than to show a burning landscape.[11]

However, remember to use authentic imagery that portrays real, everyday people your audience can relate to. While depicting celebrities is common in advertising, there is evidence that this is not always beneficial for environmental causes. Some studies have shown that politicians or celebrities' images can appear inauthentic, which can produce negative responses like reduced feelings of efficacy.[11,39]

Consider both salience and efficacy

Research suggests that imagery tends to either heighten people's perceived importance of environmental issues (*salience*) or their perception of their ability to effect change (*efficacy*), but rarely both at the same time.[39]

Images showing people engaged in solutions, like making their home more energy-efficient, can increase perceived efficacy but don't do much to increase the salience of the issue. Catastrophic or fear-inducing imagery, such as aerial views of flooding or images of climate refugees, attract attention and increase perceived importance by vividly communicating a high level of risk or threat.[8] However, these alarming visuals can also evoke anxiety, hopelessness, guilt, or shame, which can backfire by undermining our audience's sense of efficacy. If you use images demonstrating environmental problems and threats, be sure to pair them with empowering information, like the steps your audience can take to address the issue portrayed in the image.

Ultimately, visuals can be powerful aids in our environmental initiatives, but we need to carefully consider our specific audience and goals when choosing imagery and corresponding text. See OPTIMISM: Building Block Chapter 7 for more on how to balance capturing attention with ensuring your audience still feels empowered to take action and is hopeful for the future.

VIVID

Depict intriguing animals

Photos showing animals can also be particularly useful for capturing attention and eliciting emotion, both of which are associated with increased action.[35] It's no wonder that many conservation organizations use animals on their logos (e.g., the World Wildlife Fund's iconic panda), websites, and social media.

While research on animal imagery for environmental behavior change is limited, here we share a few essential considerations.

Which species to show?

There are tradeoffs to consider when deciding what species to depict. Do you show *charismatic megafauna*—widely popular, easily identifiable, large, and usually aesthetically pleasing species such as the Bengal tiger, polar bear, or elephant? Do you go with *flagship species,* creatures that serve as symbols or ambassadors for a particular habitat or environmental cause? Or should you show local species or lesser-known species that your audience might perceive as less interesting or valuable?

Some research has shown that flagship species can increase donation amounts relative to non-flagship species.[49] While using flagship species can increase support for environmental initiatives, it may also devalue species that aren't used as icons.

Another major downside of depicting iconic species is the potential distancing effect. Although images like the polar bear on a melting ice cap can capture attention, they can also create a distancing effect—making the problem seem far away—which can make us feel less able to do anything about it. For more about how to counteract this distancing effect, see ATTACHMENT: Building Block Chapter 4.

Happy and free? Or sad and suffering?

Shocking photos of animals suffering from various environmental issues have gone viral, from turtles entangled in plastic to pigs and chickens in factory farms. And, of course, images of suffering polar bears fall into this category as well. Just as images of catastrophic events or human suffering can backfire, despair-inducing images of animals can also result in disengagement. For more on considerations related to fear appeals and threat appeals, see OPTIMISM: Building Block Chapter 7.

⚙ Paint a mental picture with vivid descriptions

Showing is usually better than telling, but sometimes we have to rely on words. Vivid descriptions can evoke images in the listener's mind, making abstract concepts concrete, understandable, and easier to remember. Below are some of our favorite vivid descriptions:

- **Conveying the scale of California's waste problem:** Rather than stating that Californians produce upwards of 40 million tons of waste per year, try depicting this massive amount in vivid geographic terms: "enough to fill a two-lane highway, ten feet deep from Oregon to the Mexican border."[6]

- **Illuminating energy inefficiencies:** Trained energy efficiency auditors described excessive cracks around and under doors to homeowners in terms of their cumulative impact. They compared cracks to the equivalent of "a hole the size of a football in your living room wall" rather than in less vivid terms like "cracks around the door" or kWh of electricity wasted. The energy auditors also used other techniques, such as personalized recommendations and commitments (see IDENTITY: Building Block Chapter 6), resulting in significantly more customers applying for retrofit finance programs.[16]

- **Meaningful carbon footprint descriptions:** Online footprint calculators, like the EPA's "Household Carbon Footprint Calculator,"[50] calculate the tons of annual CO_2 pollution they create, helping people connect their actions to their impacts. However, some carbon footprint calculators make this information more vivid by also sharing the number of Earths that would be required to support the world's population if everyone adopted that lifestyle.[45]

⚙ Tell an engaging story

Stories are another powerful way to capture attention for various reasons. We're wired to like stories because they help us make sense of the world. That's why movies, TV shows, and radio soap operas are so popular. Stories can also make messages more memorable compared to information not presented in a story-like format. People are more likely to trust vivid descriptions in stories about other people's experiences than statistics. For advice on how to craft attention-grabbing, relatable, and memorable stories, see ATTACHMENT: Building Block Chapter 4.

Nudge at the Right Time and Place

Even the most well-crafted message will be ineffective if presented at the wrong time or place. But when presented when and where our audience is most receptive and able to act, our messages can successfully promote desired behaviors.

⚙ Arrange choices strategically

Intentionally arranging options or information to influence people's decisions can affect behavior in meaningful ways. Because we rely on mental shortcuts to make quick decisions in our busy lives, even the smallest change in the way a choice is presented can influence our behavior. Changing the order and placement of choices may have modest impacts, but it's generally found to be effective, easy, and inexpensive to implement.[4]

> Even the most well-crafted message will be ineffective if presented at the wrong time or place. But when presented when and where our audience is most receptive and able to act, our messages can successfully promote desired behaviors.

Don't underestimate order effects

The order in which choices are presented (***presentation order effect***) influences which options stand out. In particular, people tend to place a disproportionate emphasis on the first piece of information they see, also known as the ***primacy effect***. Take, for example, how ballot order influences voting. A study found that the arrangement of choice options on voting ballots significantly influences choice, both within and between parties. Due to this ***ballot order effect***, for example, candidates listed first on ballots across 118 Ohio races received, on average, 2.5% more of the vote than those listed last.[33] This effect has led U.S. states like Ohio to rotate the order of the candidates on ballots.

In other cases, such as on menus, both the first and last positions are preferable to the middle. People are more likely to remember and select the items at the top and bottom positions of lists.[12] We can apply these findings in any instance where our audience is selecting from a list of options. Essentially: put the choices you most want your audience to choose either first or last, but not in the middle. For example, food providers can list meat-free options first and last on menus and put plant-rich options first in buffets.

Purposefully pick your placement

Why are candy bars and tabloids always positioned by the grocery checkout? Supermarkets know that these items are impulse buys. What better place to tempt us than when we are in line, ripe for something to distract us from the wait? Supermarkets also know that people tend to choose items that are by the checkout, at the end of aisles, and at eye-height.

Fortunately, you can also use these techniques to promote healthy and sustainable choices. Various studies show that placing healthier food options closer to the checkout makes people more likely to choose them. For example, at train station snack shops in the Netherlands, people chose fruit and other healthy snack options more often when they were next to the cash register.[29] Schools and universities are increasingly using choice architecture in cafeterias to promote healthy and more environmentally sustainable eating, such as by placing plant-rich dishes in a more visible position in self-service displays.[44]

While common in cafeteria and grocery store settings, this technique can also be applied to promote environmental behaviors in other store settings. For example, place native, drought-resistant plants next to the checkout and on the corner of aisles at garden and hardware stores.

You can also apply this concept outside of a store setting as well, by always considering how to put the preferred choice or item in the most prominent or noticeable position.

⚙ Time calls to action to current events

The familiar saying "timing is everything" is particularly pertinent to changing behavior. By syncing our efforts to significant events that are top-of-mind, we can increase the likelihood that our messages will capture our audience's attention. In the immediate aftermath of extreme environmental events, conservation and climate issues may be more mentally prioritized; the salience of the environmental problem spikes dramatically following unplanned disturbances such as a hurricane or an increase in gas prices.[30]

Tailoring our message to reflect our audience's current situation and concerns can make them more receptive to our message. This applies even if the audience is hearing about these events on the news or from other people, but especially if our audience has been personally affected by them. For example, several studies find that people are more likely to purchase flood and earthquake insurance after experiencing one of these events.[37,40] However, when connecting our message to events like these, we must also be careful to be sensitive to recent losses, tragedies, or traumatic experiences.

When possible, you should also wait for events that cut against your message to pass before delivering your message. For example, people are less likely to support environmental legislation in an economic downturn,[26] and if you're in the middle of a storm, the audience may struggle with the idea of conserving water to mitigate drought. Similarly, people are less likely to respond to wildfire prep messages in the winter than during the height of wildfire season. We should either wait for a more appropriate moment to engage our audience or craft our message in a way that acknowledges and responds to the issues that are most important to them in that moment. For more about relating your environmental issue to your audience's personal experiences and concerns, see ATTACHMENT: Building Block Chapter 4.

⚙ Give reminders at the right time

Reminders are external cues that help us remember to do a behavior we have previously committed to, such as walking the neighbor's dog or showing up to an appointment. As such, they are another tool that helps us close the intention-action gap.

Thanks to new technologies, reminders are becoming easier and more relevant, and have successfully changed behaviors from physical activity and healthy eating to taking malaria medication.[46] Mail, texts, and email are some different ways we can remind people to take action, and studies find that the most effective reminders are short and to the point.[41] But we need to use them at the right time—giving reminders too far in advance won't stick, and therefore, won't lead to the desired outcome.

While digital messaging may seem easiest, postal mail can still be effective when timed correctly. The United States government saw a 1.68% increase in landowner participation in a conservation program when they sent reminder letters during the program's sign-up period rather than before sign-ups opened. This seems like a small percentage, but by simply optimizing the timing of reminders, the government conserved hundreds of thousands of additional acres per year and lowered the costs of outreach to landowners. This resulted in an estimated benefit-cost ratio of more than 20:1, all without the need for costlier financial incentives.[52]

⚙️ Use prompts in the deciding moment

Prompts are similar to reminders, but they trigger us to take a specific action right at the point of decision-making. For example, a sticker next to the faucet reminding us to turn off the tap while brushing our teeth, or the message "These Come from Trees" on paper towel dispensers may cause us to think twice about how much we use at the exact moment we perform that action. In a potent example of how effective prompts can be, a study found that in bathrooms that had signs asking occupants to turn off the light as they left, lights were eight times more likely to be turned off.[47]

Besides signs, prompts are prevalent in online pop-ups and phone notifications. For example, some airfare sites prompt travelers to help the environment by purchasing carbon offsets right as they finalize their booking. Auditory prompts, such as a buzzer, can signal us to end our shower early to reduce water usage. We can even be prompted by seeing others act, such as seeing someone turn off the water while shampooing in a communal washroom.[1] See BELONGING: Building Block Chapter 1 for more about modeling norms.

Critical characteristics of prompts are that they:

- Happen at the point of decision-making (in time and space)
- Call out a specific behavior
- Call out a behavior the audience already knows how to do, or one that requires little instruction

Remember: Reminders and prompts are most effective when our audience is already motivated to do the desired action and when there aren't significant barriers to taking action. All the reminders in the world won't help if your audience doesn't have the financial resources or materials they need to take action. Here we'll share specific best practices for making prompts as effective as possible.

Prompt behavior as close as possible to the point of decision-making

Present the prompt when and where the intended audience is most likely to be receptive and able to take appropriate action. A prompt to print double-sided will be more effective if placed near the computer or as an on-screen pop-up rather than at the printer, when it may be too late to change the print settings. Another example is "no idling" signage prompting people to turn off their engines at locations like school drop-offs so that parents receive the nudge in the moment rather than

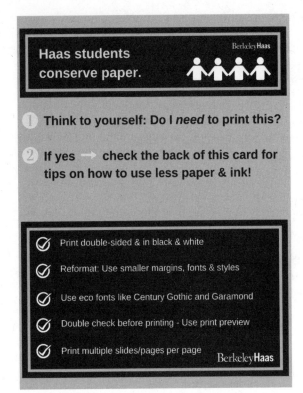

 appears above; the figure content:

Haas students conserve paper. — BerkeleyHaas

1. Think to yourself: Do I *need* to print this?

2. If yes → check the back of this card for tips on how to use less paper & ink!

- ✓ Print double-sided & in black & white
- ✓ Reformat: Use smaller margins, fonts & styles
- ✓ Use eco fonts like Century Gothic and Garamond
- ✓ Double check before printing - Use print preview
- ✓ Print multiple slides/pages per page

BerkeleyHaas

Fig. 2.5.3: *Table tent prompt (showing both the front and back side) to promote paper-saving in the University of California, Berkeley, Haas School of Business computer lab.* CREDIT: ROOT SOLUTIONS FOR UNIVERSITY OF CALIFORNIA, BERKELEY, HAAS SCHOOL OF BUSINESS

before or after the fact, such as in school newsletters or at parent meetings.

Be simple and specific

General statements asking individuals to "Conserve Electricity" or to "Keep California Beautiful" are less effective than ones that target specific behaviors, such as "Please unplug appliances when not in use" or "Please throw all food items in the compost bin." Precise language is especially helpful when people aren't as familiar with the behavior.[32] For example, composting is an example of a newer behavior, where using specific language is valuable, such as "please compost all food scraps." We recommend pairing this with photos of what can and can't be composted.

However, while some simple and specific how-to information can be included in a prompt, prompts are not the place to try to teach a complex behavior to your audience. Rather, prompts are intended to activate an already familiar behavior—or a relatively simple new behavior—at the right time and place. To be effective, prompts should not include long, detailed instructions, but they can include relatively self-explanatory and easy-to-follow how-to information, such as a rule of thumb for what you can compost, or a tip on how to use less water when showering. If your desired behavior is more complex, see our advice in EASY: Building Block Chapter 2.

Make it noticeable

Your audience is presented with many reminders and prompts throughout the day, so it's critical that they notice yours. Design prompts to stand out, using techniques discussed above in the "Get Noticed" principle, e.g., adding bright colors or pictures to otherwise neutral or text-heavy signage.

Incorporate normative information

Show your audience that the desired behavior is the social norm and that people like them are already doing it. Describing others' actions can make prompts more effective, such as "80% of beachgoers keep our shores clean and 'stoop to scoop' their dog's poop." Adding the face of an influential person or peer can also heighten interest and reinforce that the action is normal and sensible. For more on messaging social norms, see BELONGING: Building Block Chapter 1.

Keep it polite, uplifting, and non-demanding

Positive prompts can create positive associations with the desired behavior. They can also help avoid adverse reactions to requests that some audiences may perceive as curtailing their freedom. Using non-demanding and polite language, such as the word "please" can reduce the possibility of negative reactions such as resentment or the perception of infringement of freedom of choice.

Keep prompts fresh

We can quickly grow acclimated to the same message, no matter how exciting, and eventually, fail to notice it at all. This is less of a concern in places like airports where the prompt is new to people, but in situations where the same people will see the same prompt daily, finding new ways to express our message can help ensure that it stays noticeable. Other shifters discussed in this chapter, like "Make it novel," can help you keep your prompts fresh.

Combine prompts with other behavioral shifters

It's also important to consider combining prompts with other shifters from various Building Blocks, such as making the behavior easier (see EASY: Building Block Chapter 2) or introducing habit-building techniques so that the behavior lasts long after the prompt is gone (see HABITS: Building Block Chapter 3).

Making Shift Happen: Placing Prompts to Promote Cold Water Washing at Oberlin College

To reduce energy consumption, Oberlin College used a combination of prompts and other shifters to motivate students to do their laundry with cold water.[15] Focus groups showed that 50% of students had no water temperature preference and that most students either used the default setting or the same setting they had learned at home. The college put up posters in the laundry rooms that spelled out the benefits of cold water washing on clothes and the environment and addressed misconceptions about hot water washing. Additionally, prompt stickers that read "Cool is clean, use cold water, please choose bright colors setting" were placed on laundry machines near the settings to prompt students right before they chose an option.[51] The stickers provided important yet simple how-to information to students who may not have known that the "bright colors" setting is the cold water setting. And for those that knew, but might have forgotten to override the default, it served as a reminder. Combined, these changes led to an impressive increase in the number of machines set to cold water, from virtually 0% to 45%. Practitioners can use simple, informative prompts like these at the point of decision-making to spur behavior change.

Fig. 2.5.4: *This sticker, placed on Oberlin College laundry machines, prompts students to wash their laundry with cold water.*
Credit: Oberlin College

Conclusion

Capturing your audience's attention is both a critical challenge and an opportunity. Although the competition for your audience's attention is steep, the good news is that you have many tools you can use to break through the noise. With these shifters in your toolkit, you can make your calls to action more vivid, increasing the chances that your initiatives are the ones your audience notices, remembers, and—most importantly—takes action on.

🗒 Your Turn

How can you employ vividness to make your initiatives more attention-grabbing, memorable, and motivating? Use the questions below to brainstorm.

Get noticed

❑ Is the information presented in a novel or surprising way?

❑ Are there opportunities to create a contrast that makes your message stand out?

- What questions can you ask to generate curiosity?
- Can you make your message catchier and memorable, such as by using rhymes?
- Can you utilize repetition to make a message more salient without bombarding the audience?
- Are the messages you send to your audience personalized, referring to the people by their names?

Make the abstract more concrete

- How can you engage multiple senses to draw attention to your message?
- Are there ways you can make environmental impacts more visible or tangible?
- How can you emphasize the connection between individual action and environmental outcomes?
- Can you present individual environmental impacts in a way that helps the audience understand the cumulative impacts?
- Can you use imagery depicting people or animals rather than abstract vistas?
- How familiar are people with the metrics you're using? Can you translate those metrics into real-life terms that are more concrete, easier to understand, and meaningful?
- Can you tell a story to make your message more memorable?

Nudge at the right time and place

- Have you considered how the arrangement of options can affect people's decisions and ordered them strategically?
- How can you place information or choices to influence people's behaviors positively?
- Have you considered the timing of your message in relation to events significant to your audience?
- Where can you incorporate appropriately-timed reminders?
- How can you use clear, noticeable prompts to nudge your audience to take a specific action at the point of decision-making? Have you consulted the prompts best practices?

Leverage Our Need for Consistent IDENTITY

> **Key Takeaway:** *Tapping into our desire to behave in alignment with our identities is a powerful driver of behavior change and for galvanizing environmental champions.*

Identity drives our behavior

IDENTITY IS SHAPED BY OUR VALUES, BELIEFS, AND BEHAVIORS. We each carry multiple identities, such as that of a student, sibling, professional, or parent. Each identity is shaped by our individual expectations for ourselves and by the expectations placed on us by others. If we fail to fulfill the expectations associated with our identity, we risk appearing inconsistent and disappointing ourselves and others.[8] Our drive to be consistent with our most strongly held values and societal roles shapes every aspect of our lives, including how we interact with others, how we respond to messages in our environment, and how we behave on a daily basis.

> Our drive to be consistent with our most strongly held values and societal roles shapes every aspect of our lives, including how we interact with others, how we respond to messages in our environment, and how we behave on a daily basis.

How can we tap into our need for consistency?

This chapter provides tools to leverage your audience's drive to be consistent with their identities so as to encourage environmental behaviors. These tools include: highlighting identities that align with environmental behavior while avoiding those that may be polarizing or alienating for the audience, catalyzing a connection between identities and environmental behaviors, obtaining commitments, alleviating cognitive dissonance, and building an environmental identity by utilizing a ladder of increasingly involved environmental behaviors.

Practitioners should seek to promote positive **behavioral spillover**, discussed in FOUNDATIONS: Process Chapter 1, in which adopting one environmental behavior encourages our audience to adopt more. When positive spillover occurs, research and theory suggest that it stems from a preference for consistency.[23] This means that when we evoke and cultivate environmental identities in our audience, they may be more likely to engage in additional environmental behaviors, particularly if those behaviors are similar to each other (e.g., they have a similar goal or require similar skills and knowledge).[20,32,33] Thus, when our audience members have environmental identities, it is important to connect our initiatives to those identities, because not doing so may distract our audience and can be a lost opportunity to promote positive, identity-driven spillover. For similar discussions, such as why appeals to self-interest should be used sparingly or why incentives should only be administered when they are needed, see ATTACHMENT: Building Block Chapter 4 and REWARDS: Building Block Chapter 8, respectively.

Principles and Shifters for the IDENTITY Building Block

Highlight Appropriate Identities

Accentuate and reinforce identities that align with environmental behavior
Beware of polarizing identities
Choose whether to emphasize specific or broad identities

Connect the Identity with the Behavior

Use identity-activating words
Remind people of their past environmental actions
Harness community pride

Tap into Our Desire for Consistency

Draw on the power of commitments
Give your audience solutions that alleviate cognitive dissonance
Foster an environmental identity through a ladder of engagement

Once you know through your preliminary research which identities your audience values the most (INITIATE: Process Chapter 2 and UNCOVER: Process Chapter 3), you can highlight those that are connected to environmental behavior while avoiding those that may be alienating.

⚙ Accentuate and reinforce identities that align with environmental behavior

Choose and highlight your audience's identities that align with environmental behavior.

Select the identities that align with environmental behavior

Most of us relate to a number of different identities, such as "doctor," "wife," "parent," "American," "student," or "outdoor enthusiast." Each of our identities carries with it a different set of behavioral expectations,[29] and many identities may have direct or indirect connections to positive environmental behavior. For example, parents might consider protecting the environment for the sake of their children's futures to be part of their identity as parents.

Highlight and reinforce these identities

Emphasizing the appropriate identities can inspire stronger environmental engagement.

Our myriad identities are salient to us at different times, and different identities are activated in differing situations. For example, you may generally consider yourself to be a safe driver. However, if you're running late for work, your identity as a "punctual person" may lead you to drive faster and more carelessly than you would if your "safe driver" identity was activated.

The most obvious identities to evoke are those that are overtly associated with environmental behaviors. So does that mean we should highlight and reinforce the most obvious environmental identities—such as "water warrior" or "environmental steward"? Well, it depends. People who consider it important to be identified as someone who engages in environmental behaviors are more likely to recycle, save water and energy, and shop and eat sustainably,[39] and therefore highlighting this aspect of their identity can encourage environmental behavior. However, not everyone considers "environmentalist" to be a positive label (see the "Beware of polarizing identities" shifter below), so your approach will depend on your target audience.

Even if it wouldn't work to evoke environmental identities (e.g., "environmentalist") directly in some audiences, we can still evoke positive environmental attitudes and intentions. We can do so by using language that activates identities with indirect connections to environmental protection (e.g, "hunters"). For example, in a resource management game, researchers found that people who were told they were completing a "Consumer Reaction Task" reported feeling less personally responsible for environmental problems. They conserved less water and exhibited higher levels of selfish behavior than those who were told they were completing a "Citizen Reaction Task," even though it was the same exercise.[3] We need to understand which of our audience's most valued identities are connected with environmental behavior and leverage those identities to encourage desired behaviors.

Our goal as environmental practitioners is to identify, highlight, and reinforce the identities that are both important to our target audience and most in line with environmental behavior.

> Our goal as environmental practitioners is to identify, highlight, and reinforce the identities that are both important to our target audience and most in line with environmental behavior.

⚙ Beware of polarizing identities

Because identity is closely tied with values, ideologies, and emotions, triggering an identity can be powerful—but it can also backfire. Be sure to avoid triggering identities that your audience will see as polarizing, or identities that will work against your cause.

Avoid identities your audience doesn't hold

Even if it seems like some identities align with environmental behavior, be aware that for certain audiences, some identities are inherently polarizing—i.e., they aren't identities that are held by your audience. For example, many people see activists, including environmentalists, as radical, militant, or eccentric outsiders to be avoided.[2] Some audiences may engage in the same behaviors as environmentalists but would not identify themselves as such.[7] In these cases, avoid drawing attention to these identities as much as possible.

If your research reveals that your audience is sensitive to activist and environmentalist labels, consider emphasizing an identity that encompasses the desired

IDENTITY

Fig. 2.6.1: *Signage designed to tap into hunters' identities, prompting them to pick up their shotgun wads.* CREDIT: ROOT SOLUTIONS FOR GREATER FARALLONES ASSOCIATION

We know you already pick up your shells.

If you spot a wad, please pick those up too!

HUNTERS LEAVE NO TRACE

environmental behavior but avoids any associations with the labels to which they are sensitive. For example, the vast majority of hunters in the United States (81%) consider themselves to be conservationists, regardless of political party affiliation.[31] However, not all hunters identify with the label "environmentalist," which can carry negative connotations and bring to mind points where they disagree with environmental groups.[15] For this reason, when working with waterfowl hunters on a project to reduce marine debris caused by plastic shotgun wads, we used language aligned with hunters' conservationist legacies and identities, such as "resource conservation" and "hunters leave no trace."

Be aware of polarizing identities your audience does hold

Additionally, your audience might hold some identities, which, when activated, can be directly opposed to environmental behavior. For example, research shows that wording that evokes certain political identities, such as "Republican," can adversely affect acceptance of environmental issues like climate change.[13] If you want to de-emphasize a particular identity, do so by highlighting a more desirable identity held by your audience. For example, reminding your audience that they are avid hikers may make them more willing to engage in environmental behavior than reminding them that they are Republicans.

••••

It is crucial to test your language so that you are aware of the identities held by your audience; if you use language that opposes or contradicts any of your audience's identities, they may interpret you as a threat to the core of who they are. As a result, they may no longer be receptive to you or your message. Be sure to affirm—not oppose—identities. See ATTACHMENT: Building Block Chapter 4 for more on how to avoid opposing your audience's values.

Making Shift Happen: The Polarizing Effects of Highlighting Right-Leaning Identities on Climate Change Beliefs

Reminding people of their right-leaning identities can negatively shift their environmental attitudes. Australian researchers found this to be true when polling right- and left-leaning students about climate change.[34] When the researchers asked left-leaning students what proportion of climate change they attribute to human causes, they found that on average, the left-leaning students attributed about 60% to human causes, regardless of whether researchers reminded them of their political affiliation beforehand. But when they asked right-leaning students the same question, there was a major difference: those who were reminded of their political affiliation reported that only 40.5% of climate change is human-caused, compared to 64.4% for those who weren't reminded. This study suggests that bringing polarizing aspects of identity to the forefront of a person's mind can adversely affect their reported belief in environmental issues.

To learn more about how to reach those with right-leaning ideologies, see ATTACHMENT: Building Block Chapter 4. To learn more about the strategies that some think tanks use to delegitimize the environmental movement, see ASSOCIATIONS: Building Block Chapter 9.

⚙️ Choose whether to emphasize specific or broad identities

Research suggests that it's better to emphasize a specific identity, such as "paper saver," when promoting a specific behavior. However, emphasizing broader identities, such as "environmental steward," may be more effective when you're trying to encourage a broad range of behaviors, such as recycling, saving energy, and sustainable transportation all at once.[39]

Table 2.6.1: Examples of Identities and Their Relationships to Environmental Behavior

Words/ Identities	Behavior Evoked	Environmental Behavior
Frugal[11]	Pro-environmental	Frugal identities are associated with environmental behaviors and energy conservation. A frugal consumer identity is associated with a low carbon lifestyle and waste reduction including money, waste, gas, and electricity reduction.
Moral[11]	Pro-environmental	A moral consumer identity is strongly associated with behaviors such as buying green, buying fair produce, and plastic bag avoidance. See ATTACHMENT: Building Block Chapter 4 for more on morals and the environment.
Wasteful[11]	Anti-environmental	A wasteful consumer identity maps onto self-enhancement values such as egoism, hedonism, and materialism that have been associated with less environmentally friendly behaviors. This identity is associated with disposable plastic bag usage and a higher consumption of resources than needed.
Liberal / Progressive / Democrat	Pro-environmental	Reminding people of their identity as Democrats has been shown to increase certainty about the issue of climate change.[6] Note: Since values and identities are often intertwined, see ATTACHMENT: Building Block Chapter 4 for more on the different values, morals, and ideologies that are linked with positive environmental behaviors.
Vegetarian[36]	Both Pro- and Anti-environmental	Labeling certain dishes as "vegetarian" may appeal to those who identify as vegetarians. However, it may also signal to non-vegetarians that the dishes are exclusive to those identifying as vegetarians. In addition, the word vegetarian can be alienating for some, such as men who connect eating meat with masculinity.

Connect the Identity with the Behavior

By using words that trigger certain identities in your communications and by reminding people of their past environmental actions, you can activate the connection between a valued identity of your audience and the desired behavior.

Use identity-activating words

Using statements that activate desirable identities can evoke the behavior we'd like to see. When trying to activate an identity, use *identity-activating phrases*, such as "steward" (a person can be a steward), as opposed to *identity-neutral phrases*, such as "stewarding" (a person can engage in stewarding). For example, in a study conducted in New Jersey, researchers asked a group of registered voters: "How important is it for you to vote in the next election?" They asked another group: "How important is it for you to be a voter in the next election?"[4] The latter question was designed to evoke a sense of voter self-identification. Results showed that 89.9% of those who were asked the identity-activating version voted in the election, compared to 79% of those who were asked the identity-neutral version. Results like this show that we can have a powerful impact on behavior with simple changes in wording that tie actions more directly to positive identities. You can turn almost any environmental behavior into an identity statement; for example, in our work at UC Berkeley, instead of asking students to "save paper," we incorporated identity language into messaging that claimed "Cal Bears are paper savers!"

When an identity is very broad (such as "environmentalist"), you may need to establish a connection between it and the desired behavior (for example, bringing reusable bags to the grocery store instead of using the provided disposable bags). Use phrasing that further reinforces the connection, such as "continue to be a [identity-activating word] by pledging to...[behavior]," or even "environmentalists bring reusable bags."

Remind people of their past environmental actions

Identity can trigger action, and actions can trigger identity. People who see themselves as environmentally friendly are generally driven to perform a range of environmental tasks.[35] Research has found that when people are reminded of a range of past environmental behaviors, such as recycling, composting, and taking sustainable transportation, they are more likely to identify as environmentalists, or as the type of people who engage in behaviors that are good for the planet. These reminders can activate an environment-related identity and make people more likely to adopt the new behavior you are asking of them.[35]

⚙ Harness community pride

Pride evokes positive feelings associated with taking responsibility for favorable outcomes.[38] Our identities can be tied to a sense of community pride; we experience feelings of dignity when we're part of a social group, especially when we contribute to collective efforts on a local or even national scale.[19] It's helpful to use locally relevant language and images to activate a sense of community pride and identity. For example, the nonprofit Rare designs its signature Pride campaigns to increase communities' pride in their natural surroundings to strengthen conservation efforts.[27] They employ several strategies to boost local pride, such as promoting mascots that represent local wildlife and granting "local hero" badges to individuals engaging with sustainable behaviors.

Increasing this sense of local responsibility can bring previously distant issues toward the forefront of people's minds through a heightened sense of personal significance and urgency. See ATTACHMENT: Building Block Chapter 4 for more on reducing psychological distance by focusing on local impacts.

Making Shift Happen: Using a Local Slogan to Decrease Litter

In the 1980s, Texas had a problem with littering: the Texas Department of Transportation was spending $20 million per year on cleanup, yet littering was only getting worse.[22,24] In 1985 they launched an anti-littering ad campaign to stem the problem; they called it "Don't Mess With Texas." The slogan was created by Texan Tim McClure, who was inspired by the deep pride that Texans have for their state—their identity is shaped starting at a very young age by chants and slogans such as "Remember the Alamo" and songs like "Deep in the Heart of Texas." The campaign officially launched in 1986 with an ad featuring celebrity Stevie Ray Vaughan in front of a Texas flag. As part of the initiative, bumper stickers were distributed all over the state. To make it feel more owned by Texans, they did not highlight that the campaign was from the transportation department. It was an instant success: littering went down by 29% in just a year, and, by 1990, was down by 72% from 1986. The slogan tapped into state pride, and Texans adopted the slogan as their own and began using it in contexts outside of littering—for example,

President George Bush himself used the slogan in a speech. The slogan is still in use today, printed on trash cans and available on merchandise. This incredibly successful campaign illustrates how practitioners can leverage local culture to make positive change, especially for communities that take great pride in where they live.

Although pride is generally associated with positive individual and community action, we want to avoid *hubristic pride*, which entails an unconditionally positive view of oneself, or the idea that we are "better" than others.[40] Hubristic pride can lead to negative social behaviors such as discrimination and exclusion, which can also manifest at the group level. We should never promote pride in one group at the expense of another; this leads to *in-group bias*, in which we favor people similar to us (members of our "in-group") over those who we perceive to be unlike us ("outsiders").[30] Be sure to prevent this type of unethical favoritism by focusing on the productive types of pride that enhance positive feelings around collective action and *self-efficacy*. (See OPTIMISM: Building Block Chapter 7 for more details.) Consider expanding the level of your group to one that does not reinforce rivalries (e.g., if you have University of California, Berkeley and Stanford students in the same audience, avoid rivalries by focusing on their identities as Californians).

Tap Into Our Desire for Consistency

We are driven by a desire to remain consistent with our identities, past behaviors, and commitments to future behaviors. You can tap into this desire for consistency by asking for commitments, by encouraging environmental behaviors that alleviate cognitive dissonance, and by building an environmental identity through a ladder of engagement.

Draw on the power of commitments

Commitment-based shifters are powerful tools that catalyze people to take up environmental behaviors. Commitments (often taking the form of pledges) to adopt certain behaviors work for two reasons. First, our need for consistency drives us to uphold our commitments: we don't want to see ourselves, or for

> Our need for consistency drives us to uphold our commitments: we don't want to see ourselves, or for others to see us, as the type of person who does not follow through on promises.

Fig. 2.6.2:
Commitment campaign to save paper at University of California, Berkeley, Haas School of Business CREDIT: ROOT SOLUTIONS FOR UNIVERSITY OF CALIFORNIA, BERKELEY, HAAS SCHOOL OF BUSINESS

others to see us, as the type of person who does not follow through on promises.[8] Second, when we promise to perform a behavior, we see ourselves as the type of person who would do that behavior, and this new aspect of our identity drives us to remain consistent with our commitment. The following best practices will help audiences follow through on their commitments to environmental behaviors.

Make commitments voluntary

It's key for a commitment to be voluntary: if external factors—such as coercion through large rewards—are used to secure our commitment, it won't be associated with our internal identities and therefore may be less likely to stick and to spill over into other behaviors.[8,18]

Make commitments public

Make it more difficult to act inconsistently by publicizing a commitment.[8] Dutch farmers who received information on how to make their farms more supportive of biodiversity—and also made a public commitment to do so—were more likely to follow through than those who did not make a public commitment.[17]

In addition to promoting participant follow-through, public commitments can encourage others to follow suit. We can tap into the human desire to fit in with peers by enlisting people who have already publicly committed to a behavior to ask others to make a similar pledge.[8] Ask your audience to spread the word by sharing their pledge with their peers, such as on social media. Other examples of public commitments include honor rolls or pledge boards (or any kind of map or list that shows who has made the same pledge), lawn signs, banners on social media, pins and badges, and bumper stickers. To learn more about the influence of social norms, see BELONGING: Building Block Chapter 1.

Make commitments specific

While participants are likely more willing to sign a pledge that is vague, specific commitments in a pledge tend to engender greater adherence and stronger behavior changes.[1] Design the commitment to be as specific as possible (e.g., "I commit to turning off the lights every time I leave the room"), as opposed to offering a general commitment (e.g., "I commit to saving energy").[12] In addition, reduce mental effort by asking people to do only one thing, or have them choose one or two actions from a handful. Asking people to pledge to do ten different things may overwhelm them.[14] Specific commitments should also include a time frame. For example, you might ask your audience to make an appointment for a home energy audit by the end of the week.

Commitment statements that include an inherent cue (e.g., "every time I leave the room") will be easier to remember and more likely to promote habit formation, even after the commitment time frame has ended. For more information about building habits, see HABITS: Building Block Chapter 3.

Making Shift Happen: Committing to Reuse Hotel Towels

A field experiment at a hotel compared guests who were asked to sign a general commitment to be "environmentally friendly" during their stay with those who were asked to sign a specific commitment to reuse their towels during their stay.[1] Although a greater percentage of guests agreed to the general commitment (98%) compared to the specific commitment (83%), the vague commitment did not effectively encourage the desired behavior. Those who were asked to make a specific commitment hung a greater percentage of used towels (32%) than those who were asked to make a general commitment (24.8%). In fact, those in the vague commitment condition performed similarly to people who had not been asked to make any commitment at all (24.4%). While more people may be willing to make vague or general commitments, specific action-oriented commitments are more effective at eliciting desired behaviors.

IDENTITY

Encourage the audience to write commitments

Requiring someone to actively commit to an idea promotes the internalization of that commitment.[8] Actively writing down, or even just signing, a commitment is often more effective than a verbal commitment because the latter is more easily forgotten or minimized. Additionally, when someone puts more effort into making a commitment, such as when they take the time to write it down, they are more likely to value what they committed to.

Provide tokens of commitment

Offering a token of the commitment when the commitment is made will remind pledgers of their promise and reinforce their identity as the type of person who would engage in that behavior.[1] For information about designing tokens that act as a cue, see VIVID: Building Block Chapter 5.

Tokens of commitment can also serve as a means to make pledges public. They enable people to see which of their peers have committed and help the pledger to represent a socially desirable identity. For example, wearing an "I voted" sticker signals to your peers that you perform your civic duty, and it reinforces the idea that it is normal to vote, encouraging others to do the same. In the previously described study on towel reuse at a hotel, 80% of guests who made a specific commitment and received a small "Friend of the Earth" lapel pin were likely to hang towels for reuse, compared to 64% of those who made a specific commitment but did not receive a pin. These results show how coupling specific commitments with small representative tokens can help motivate desired behaviors.[1]

Follow up on commitments

Sending reminders about the commitments that people made can help your audience remember to follow through. Because of our motivation to appear consistent to others and to uphold social expectations, we're more likely to follow through on commitments when someone checks up on our behavior. Even the possibility that someone might follow up with us can motivate follow-through. For more information about feedback and reminders, see HABITS: Building Block Chapter 3 and VIVID: Building Block Chapter 5.

Use implementation intentions

Enlisting audiences to use implementation intentions can also help with follow-through. ***Implementation intentions*** are if-then statements that allow your audience to formulate a specific, concrete plan to carry out their commitment and brainstorm ways to overcome possible barriers.[12] For more information on implementation intentions, see HABITS: Building Block Chapter 3.

I PLEDGE TO RISE ABOVE PLASTIC POLLUTION

Scientists estimate that by 2050 the weight of PLASTIC in the ocean will be equal to the weight of ALL THE FISH in the sea

But there is something YOU can do about it!

Pick ONE habit to build during the next 30 days:

Break up with the bottle
☐ I want the ocean to be plastic-free, so when I leave home I will carry my reusable bottle with me.

Be plastic bag free
☐ I want the ocean to be plastic-free, so when I leave home I will carry my reusable bag with me.

Ditch disposable to-go-ware (utensils and containers)
☐ I want the ocean to be plastic-free, so when I leave home I will carry my reusable utensils with me.

Ditch disposable cups, lids, & straws
☐ I want the ocean to be plastic-free, so when I leave home I will carry my reusable mug or straw with me.
☐ To make single-use plastic-free living a breeze, I will order my drinks with "no straw please".

Be a smart shopper
☐ I will be fantastic and only buy fruits and veggies that are not wrapped in plastic.

Email Address: _____ Zip Code: _____

------- Write down your chosen habit and cut here -------

I, _____ , pledge to Rise Above Plastic Pollution!
(name)

(copy the chosen habit from above)
_____
_____
_____

Date: _____

Flip for tips & next steps!

* Keep this as a reminder of your pledge *

SURVEY - Tracking our positive impact!

Question 1
Which ONE of the following options best describes why you choose your specific item?

☐ I think this item causes the biggest plastic pollution problem
☐ I think avoiding this item will make the most positive impact
☐ I can remember to avoid it
☐ I already have the reusable items I need to avoid this single-use item
☐ I already wanted to create this new habit
☐ It is the easiest option
☐ It is the most challenging option and I wanted to challenge myself

Question 2

Single-use Item	About how many do you use in a week?	How difficult or easy is it for you to avoid this single-use plastic item?				
		Very difficult	Difficult	Neutral	Easy	Very easy
Plastic bottles						
Plastic bags						
Plastic to-go-ware						
Plastic straws						
Plastic lids						
Produce in plastic						

Email Address: _____

------- Cut here -------

Visit riseaboveplasticpollution.org to:
- Invite a friend to pledge!
- Get tips on how to Rise Above Plastic Pollution
- Get more info on Rise Above Plastic Pollution Month

Share your pledge on social media!
- For images and posts that are share-ready, visit riseaboveplasticpollution.org
- Tag us! #RiseAbovePlasticsOregon @SurfriderOregon

Fig. 2.6.3: *Pledge card for Surfrider Oregon Rise Above Plastic Pollution Month*

CREDIT: SURFRIDER FOUNDATION--OREGON REGION

"I want the ocean to be plastic-free...
so when I leave home I will carry my reusable utensils with me."

"I want the ocean to be plastic-free...
so when I leave home I will carry my reusable mug or straw with me."

"I want the ocean to be plastic-free...
so when I leave home I will carry my reusable bag with me."

To make single-use plastic-free living a breeze...
I will order my drinks with "no straw please!"

Fig. 2.6.4: *Social media icons for the Rise Above Plastic Pollution campaign include a rhyming cue to help the audience remember their specific commitment.*

CREDIT: ROOT SOLUTIONS FOR SURFRIDER FOUNDATION—OREGON REGION

Give your audience solutions that alleviate cognitive dissonance

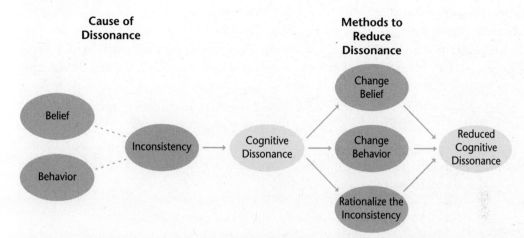

Despite our best efforts, we sometimes fail to avoid inconsistency between our identities and our actions. This can result in *cognitive dissonance*, the mental discomfort and stress we experience when our sense of internal consistency is challenged.[9] To relieve these negative feelings, we seek to resolve cognitive dissonance by eliminating the inconsistency, through changing our behavior, changing our beliefs, or rationalizing the inconsistency.[28]

As an example, consider environmentalists who believe that plastic waste is bad for the environment but continue to use plastic straws. When their inconsistency is pointed out or realized, they experience cognitive dissonance. To relieve the dissonance, they may shift to thinking that plastic pollution is not as big of a deal as it is made out to be (change beliefs) or that their use of straws isn't really a problem because of all the plastic they otherwise avoid (rationalizing the inconsistency). Their behavior would not change, but it would no longer be inconsistent with their beliefs and identity.

This is where environmental practitioners can be of service: we can help our audiences change their behaviors rather than their beliefs by first gently highlighting the disconnect between beliefs and actions. Then, by making the necessary behavior change obvious, specific, easy to remember, and immediately available when dissonance arises, we can help our audience maintain their beliefs while restoring needed consistency.

It is imperative to provide people with a specific action to alleviate their cognitive dissonance and help them behave in a way that aligns with their beliefs.

Fig. 2.6.5:
Cognitive dissonance theory

IDENTITY

Otherwise, we run the risk that people may change their beliefs to match the unfavorable action or rationalize their action instead of changing the behavior itself.

It is vital to consider potential points of cognitive dissonance that your audience may face. By identifying the beliefs and identities they hold, and determining whether any of their behaviors conflict with those beliefs and identities, you can alleviate cognitive dissonance as it comes up.

Practitioners can also create situations of dissonance, then offer a means for their audience to alleviate it by engaging in the desired behavior.

Making Shift Happen: Dissonance and Environmental Donations

Informing people of the discrepancies between their beliefs and behaviors can help spur behavioral change motivated by cognitive dissonance. Researchers in France, posing as staff from an ecological association, had participants complete one of three tasks: to write a speech that promoted ecological behavior, to read a message stating that people should adopt ecological behaviors, or to read a message stating that a majority of people have adopted ecological behaviors.[26] The researchers then induced cognitive dissonance in half of the participants by asking them to report times when they did not engage in environmental behavior. Those who were reminded of their inconsistency were more likely to donate to the organization when asked than those who were not reminded or were in the control group that did not complete an initial task. (Don't worry—donations made during the study were promptly returned to the participants.)

⚙ Foster an environmental identity through a ladder of engagement

Our behaviors can shape our identities; engaging in even a small environmental behavior can cause people to see themselves as the type of person who cares about the environment. We can foster an environmental identity in our audiences by encouraging them to complete small actions at first and then gradually build up a history of environmentally friendly behaviors.

As your audience invests increasingly more effort and energy into your cause, they are more likely to endorse it. This is the concept of *effort justification*, the idea that the more effort we put into something, the more we value it. We don't like to identify ourselves as time-wasters or poor investors, so when we spend time on something, we justify our efforts by increasing our perceived value of the thing or activity in which we've invested.[9]

When you want someone to commit to something that might be too large of an initial request, you can ask them to agree to something much smaller and more attainable, and then work up from there (sometimes known as the *foot-in-the-door technique*).[5,8,10] Asking your audience to perform a similar behavior to the first, and ones that generate *intrinsic motivation* (the enjoyment of the behavior itself), are more likely to lead to positive spillover (see FOUNDATIONS: Process Chapter 1). Your audience members' environmental identities may become more robust as they complete behaviors up this *ladder of engagement* and increasingly see themselves as "the kind of person" who engages in environmental behavior.

Completing each task is a key requirement for moving up the ladder of engagement. You can probably relate to the *IKEA effect*, the idea that we tend to place a higher value on things that we have created or labored over (such as a piece of furniture that we assembled ourselves), and we place even greater value on things we have seen through to completion, as opposed to those we gave up on.[25] Environmental practitioners can use this concept by promoting actions our audience can realistically complete and by providing support like reminders, clear instructions, and the resources necessary to complete the task at hand.

As practitioners, we ideally want our audience members to move up the ladder of engagement until they see themselves as environmental champions.

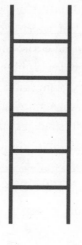

5 Speak at a public event in support of a cause

4 Attend an in-person event to show support

3 Share a video on social media or click a link to show support

2 Answer questions via email or text indicating support for the organization or cause

1 Answer questions via email or text indicating support for the message

Fig. 2.6.6:

Ladder of engagement

IDENTITY

Structure your ladder of engagement to gradually increase the effort required to complete related but increasingly difficult behaviors. An example would be the ladder of engagement developed by practitioners from the Analyst Institute, Climate Advocacy Lab, and San Diego-based organizations Climate Action Campaign (CAC) and Mid-City Community Advocacy Network (CAN). They designed a test to bring CAC and Mid-City CAN supporters up a ladder of engagement to encourage people to become champions of sustainable and equitable transportation. They classified actions on a 1–5 scale of engagement, with level 1 being the easiest, entailing answering questions such as "how important is a better transportation system to you?" via email or text. The ladder progressed, with level 3 entailing behavioral action such as sharing a video on social media or clicking a link to show support, and level 5 involving acts of volunteer leadership like speaking at a public event in support of a sustainable transportation cause.[21]

Making Shift Happen: Encouraging Environmental Champions in a University

A ladder of engagement can transform people from reluctant participants to environmental and social change champions. At McGill University in Canada, sustainability officers designed four programs to progressively move its community of students, faculty, and staff up its ladder of engagement from individual actions to collective change initiatives.[16] Each rung of McGill's ladder of engagement contained an environmental and social sustainability program more involved than the last. Staff formed small teams to tend to a garden where they received training in sustainability practices and learned about other rungs of the ladder. Students and faculty worked together to make events sustainable, moving from four sustainable events in 2017 to 100 in 2019. Departments participated in a Sustainable Workplace Certification Program, which required at least 75% of the people in the office to commit to socially and environmentally responsible behaviors. The program provided them with guidance in the form of checklists and incentives, trainings, and social support (e.g., taking lunch breaks and learning about campus mental health resources). Unit Level Action Plans were also developed so that departments could create a sustainability strategy tied to their own context as well as to the campus-wide Climate & Sustainability Action Plan. Like McGill University, practitioners can strategically develop programs that start with smaller sustainability efforts, but that build on successes to make more impactful and ambitious changes.[37]

Conclusion

The powerful personal and social desire to be consistent with our past behaviors, identities, and commitments can motivate us to perform and stick with positive environmental behaviors. As practitioners, we want to help our audience deepen their connection with their environmental identities and internalize their commitments as parts of those identities. This will help build environmental behavior into the fabric of our society.

▤ Your Turn

What are some ways that you can leverage identity in your initiative? Use the questions below to brainstorm.

Highlight appropriate identities

- ❏ Which identities are most valued by your audience, and what beliefs and behaviors are associated with those identities?
- ❏ Is there any polarizing language about your issue that you should avoid?
- ❏ Are there any identities associated with undesirable behaviors or anti-environmental identities you should avoid triggering?

Connect the identity with the behavior

- ❏ If your desired behavior is not explicitly connected with your audience's valued identities, can you make the connection more obvious?
- ❏ Can you replace identity-neutral language with identity-activating language?
- ❏ Can you reinforce identity by reminding your audience of their past environmental actions?
- ❏ Does your audience have any community identities (e.g., school mascots, state pride) that you can connect with your desired behavior?

Tap into our desire for consistency
Leverage the power of commitments

- ❏ How can you word the commitment to refer to a specific behavior rather than a vague goal?
- ❏ What are ways you can encourage your audience to actively make the commitment (e.g., make it written, have them sign it)?

- How can you or your audience publicize their commitments?
- Can you ask existing supporters to recruit and motivate more people to make the commitment?
- How will you remind your audience of their commitments? Are you able to collect contact information so that you can remind your pledgers using a follow-up call, text, email, or visit?
- Can you provide tokens that serve to remind people of their commitment?

Alleviate cognitive dissonance

- Can you observe whether your audience is acting in accordance with their valued identities and associated beliefs?
- What immediate actions can you suggest to your audience to alleviate cognitive dissonance and bring their beliefs and behaviors into alignment?
- Can you make the desired behavior as easy and convenient as possible so your audience doesn't change their beliefs or trivialize an inconsistency instead?

Foster an environmental identity through a ladder of engagement

- Is there a small task your audience is likely to complete to get them involved initially?
- Can you create a ladder of engagement of increasingly involved tasks to help your audience become supporters?
- What are some ways that you can help your audience along the ladder (e.g., encouragement, confidence building, support)?

Empower through active OPTIMISM

> **Key Takeaway:** *Optimism is crucial for maintaining motivation in the face of daunting environmental challenges. Activate hope and inspire action by strengthening your audience's sense of efficacy.*

"Doom and Gloom" is disheartening

SEA LEVELS ARE RISING. Wildfires are blazing out of control. Species teeter on the brink of extinction as ecosystems are threatened by human activity and a changing climate. When this is all we hear about the environment, it's no wonder we find ourselves feeling overwhelmed or even paralyzed.

The truth is, most of us do care about the health of the planet, but many environmental issues feel daunting, abstract, and outside of our individual control. These feelings are amplified when environmental practitioners highlight the catastrophic nature of a problem, guided by the mistaken assumption that this strategy will not only grab people's attention but also make them more likely to act. Although doomsday messaging may evoke concern momentarily, it is less likely to motivate long-term engagement.[35] Instead, it can make us feel hopeless, causing us to give up, ignore the problem, and even deny its existence entirely.

Lead the way with optimism

> *Let's understand [Optimism] in its broader sense—let's understand it as courage, hope, trust, solidarity.*
>
> —Christiana Figueres, former Executive Secretary of the United Nations Framework Convention on Climate Change

By *active optimism*, we mean the kind of optimism that is rooted in action. Active optimism isn't just about believing that the outcome will be positive, it's also about

391

> Active optimism isn't just about believing that the outcome will be positive, it's also about feeling empowered and capable of taking action to make that outcome a reality.

feeling empowered and capable of taking action to make that outcome a reality. This kind of optimism is a crucial driver of transformational, enduring environmental change. Therefore, much of this chapter focuses on cultivating *efficacy*: the belief that we can indeed bring about the change we seek.[3] As author and researcher Daniel Pink notes, it's not fear that drives motivation, but the human need for autonomy, mastery, and purpose.[38] As practitioners, we need to reinvigorate our audience's sense of efficacy and purpose by demonstrating that individual actions do make a difference. Our audience might feel that their efforts only amount to a drop in a bucket—it's our job to relay the significance of that drop rather than fixating on the bucket's size.[7]

In this chapter, you will learn to empower your audiences through active optimism. We will first discuss the importance of balancing the reality of the threats we face with positive messaging. We'll then demonstrate how to increase your audience's sense of efficacy by providing concrete solutions, setting appropriately-scaled goals, facilitating opportunities to practice, and highlighting role models. Finally, we'll discuss how to convey that no one is in this fight alone, which can inspire the powerful collective action needed to tackle environmental issues.

Principles and Shifters for the OPTIMISM Building Block

Be Intentional with Emotional Messaging

Carefully navigate negative emotions
Motivate through positive emotions

Build Confidence Through Efficacy

Offer concrete solutions and immediate actions
Set appropriately-scaled goals and provide positive feedback
Facilitate opportunities for your audience to practice
Depict success through social modeling

Energize Through Collective Action

Connect individual behaviors to larger environmental movements
Demonstrate the aggregate effect of individual actions

Be Intentional with Emotional Messaging

As we discuss in FOUNDATIONS: Process Chapter 1, our emotions have a powerful influence on our actions. Given the urgent nature of environmental issues, it's tempting to use messaging that evokes strong emotional responses. Although we must convey the reality of our environmental problems, we should be careful to do so in a productive way that maintains our audience's optimism and efficacy. Thus, the tone and content of our messages should be chosen carefully to avoid negatively affecting our audience's motivation to perform environmental behaviors.

Here we present some caveats to activating negative emotions, as well as some guidance on how to leverage humor and engage positive emotions like pride and hope. Generally, positive emotions have a broadening effect on our thinking and behavioral patterns, while negative emotions produce a more limited range of reactions that are linked to evolutionary survival mechanisms (escape! hide!).[17] That said, it's important to recognize that every emotion is unique, even within those broad categories of "positive" and "negative." For example, fear may trigger the desire to escape, while anger may trigger the urge to attack.[13] We should therefore pay careful attention to their differentiating characteristics, several of which we will discuss here.

Also keep in mind that even if you are able to evoke a desired emotion in an audience, it does not guarantee that people will act on that emotional response, or act in the way you intended. Therefore, emotional responses are best viewed not as a vehicle for guaranteed action, but as behavioral tendencies. We can use these emotional response tendencies in the design of our behavior change initiatives as long as we remember that human behavior is complex, context-dependent, and varies from person to person. Even when we do not intend to trigger specific emotions, we should try to anticipate a range of possible emotional responses.

Carefully navigate negative emotions

Due to a phenomenon called **negativity bias**, humans tend to be more attentive and reactive to negative information than positive information.[30] We are also loss averse, which means we're often more responsive to potential losses than we are to equivalent gains.[24] (To learn more about loss aversion, see ASSOCIATIONS: Building Block Chapter 9.) Consequently, environmental communicators often present issues in a threatening way that highlights what we have to lose if we don't act. Indeed, doomsday stories and images can certainly sound the alarm and capture attention, often by evoking fear, guilt, or other negative emotions that may heighten the importance of an issue, at least momentarily. However, these stories rarely inspire the kind of long-term, sustained engagement that we need to tackle our planet's most pressing problems. Therefore, it's critical that we carefully consider which emotions our messages may evoke.

Never shame individuals

Some research suggests that shame may be an effective tool for influencing large-scale changes in institutions, corporations, or governments.[23] For example, many campaigns have successfully shamed a corporation into changing its environmental or human rights practices. However, we never suggest activating shame to influence *individual* behavior change, as it can be hurtful to those individuals. Shame targets the self ("I am bad"), whereas other negative emotions like guilt may target a specific behavior ("I did something bad").[9] Targeting the self in a negative way rarely has productive outcomes, as it projects unwanted identities on people. For example, if someone is pegged as an "anti-environmentalist," it can become a self-fulfilling prophecy through negative self-talk: "I guess I won't bother recycling since I'm not really an environmentalist." Instead of shaming people for not being environmentally conscientious, highlight aspects of their identities that align with positive environmental behaviors. For more on how to leverage identity for environmental behavior change, see IDENTITY: Building Block Chapter 6.

Go easy with guilt appeals

Guilt appeals, commonly used to encourage more sustainable lifestyle choices, evoke negative feelings such as regret.[11] Because guilt appeals target specific behaviors instead of the self, people are more likely to maintain self-empathy, which helps them stay open to making behavioral changes.[9] Subtle guilt appeals that evoke a sense of social responsibility can be effective with people who already believe they have an obligation to mitigate their impact on the environment. These appeals can hold people to their social commitments and personal standards, motivating them to participate in a desired behavior to avoid the anticipated guilt of failing to live by their principles.[11,44] For people who have committed to reducing their carbon footprint, for example, an effective appeal might be: "Your community is counting on you to reduce your carbon footprint. Don't drive when you can bike." See the closely related concept of cognitive dissonance in IDENTITY: Building Block Chapter 6.

More accusatory appeals that create feelings of guilt about people's current or past behaviors can backfire, particularly for audiences who are already environmentally conscious.[11,44] For example, community members who have been involved in efforts to conserve water in their neighborhood are more likely to react negatively to an overt guilt appeal such as "Your long showers are a letdown to your community. Buy a low flow shower head and save water today." Especially when people are highly conscious of an issue, they are more likely to view related guilt appeals as manipulative or threatening; if they feel that their current efforts are being dismissed or undervalued, they may become defensive and subsequently less likely to adopt the desired behavior promoted in the appeal. Regardless of who your audience is, overt guilt appeals aimed at current or past behaviors tend to produce negative, reactive responses and should be avoided, whereas more subtle guilt appeals that elicit anticipatory guilt can be effective when employed judiciously.

Use threat appeals cautiously

Threat appeals are a widespread yet controversial technique in environmental communications that introduce a threat with the goal of motivating the audience to take action to avoid the consequences of that threat. *Fear appeals* are a common type of threat appeal, which specifically aim to persuade people to respond by activating emotions of fear or anxiety.[43] Both threat appeals and fear appeals can motivate environmental action, but if not designed carefully, they can backfire, leaving our audience feeling hopeless, defensive, or disengaged.[47]

When presented with images or messages that convey impending danger, we often experience the urge to fight, take flight, or freeze. Threat and fear appeals often evoke avoidant responses such as denial (flight) or shutting down emotionally (freeze), which we use to control our internal fear.[47,31] When fear triggers these avoidant responses regarding an environmental issue, our audiences may disengage and "bury their heads in the sand" to avoid the negative information (*the ostrich effect*).[18] In extreme cases, people may deny the issue entirely, such as with climate denial.

Of course, we hope people will respond to threat appeals about our planet by fighting (addressing) the threat directly. In many cases, threat appeals do lead to a fight response, but it depends on the audience's perception of how serious the threat is (*perceived severity*) and whether it will harm them directly (*perceived susceptibility*).[21] Critically, how someone responds also depends on their sense of

OPTIMISM

efficacy: when they believe there is a solution to the threat and they feel confident in their ability to enact that solution, they are more likely to take action.

So, how can practitioners effectively communicate about environmental threats? For ethical reasons, we do not recommend using appeals that explicitly aim to evoke fear (who wants to live in a society where we constantly walk around in fear anyway?). However, threat appeals can be an effective tool if used correctly: do not word them so strongly that they evoke paralyzing fear, and always pair them with efficacy messages. We discuss efficacy in more detail throughout the rest of this chapter.

Also keep in mind that because fear tends to narrow our behavioral responses, in cases when threat or fear appeals do lead to a "fight" response, that response may motivate people to adopt short-term or one-time behaviors instead of broader, lasting behavior change.[17, 43] In other words, these appeals can be effective at influencing specific behavioral shifts, but they aren't enough on their own to address the many widespread and ongoing environmental issues we're up against. For a more holistic and sustainable approach, we also need to rely on other shifters that can promote longer-term lifestyle changes, such as those from IDENTITY, ASSOCIATIONS, and LONGEVITY (Building Block Chapters 6, 9, and 10).

Making Shift Happen: Pairing the Threat of a Loss with Actionable Solutions to Increase Recycling Among Hotel Guests

In a study conducted at a hotel in the United Kingdom, researchers analyzed the recycling behaviors of hotel guests after providing double-sided door hangers to 360 rooms.[19] One side of the hanger described either the threat of a potential loss ("By not recycling, we waste over 12.5 million tonnes of paper and cardboard") or a potential gain ("By recycling, we gain over 12.5 million tonnes of paper"). The other side of the hanger either shared abstract reasons for the importance of recycling or specific instructions for how the guests should recycle using the bins provided in their rooms. Overall, the signs that paired the loss message on one side with instructions of how to do the desired recycling behavior on the other were the most successful at increasing guests' recycling rates. In fact, the study showed a 22% increase in recycling compared to the positive message paired with the same concrete instructions. This study highlights the power of pairing a description of an environmental threat with specific guidance for engaging with the solution, thereby building the audience's sense of efficacy. We further explore loss and gain frames in ASSOCIATIONS: Building Block Chapter 9.

•••

If we want to ensure that we motivate our audience to address environmental threats directly, we must be careful when using any kind of negative messaging, as it may activate a range of counterproductive emotional responses. Additionally, as you will see in the rest of this chapter, much of our optimism and motivation stems from a strong sense of efficacy. So, if you (judiciously) decide to use negative messaging, it should always be presented in tandem with solutions-based messages that empower our audience to confront impending challenges.

And remember, there are many other ways to capture your audience's attention and help them grasp the gravity of an issue without using negative appeals. For more on this, see VIVID: Building Block Chapter 5.

⚙ Motivate through positive emotions

Positive emotions are more likely than negative emotions to lead to reinforcing cycles of environmentally friendly behavior.[41] This is because positive emotions tend to broaden our scope of attention, leading to a wider range of thoughts and actions.[17] Some evidence suggests that when our mindset is more open, playful, and exploratory, we are more likely to act on our positive intentions. Evoking positive emotions can not only make environmental behavior change initiatives more effective, but also more enjoyable for all parties involved. In this shifter, we discuss the benefits of tapping into people's pride, as well as guidance on how to use humor and constructive hope to motivate our audience. See more about how to evoke warm, positive emotions like gratitude and awe in LONGEVITY: Building Block Chapter 10.

> Positive emotions are more likely than negative emotions to lead to reinforcing cycles of environmentally friendly behavior.

Tap into pride

Pride is generally a positive feeling of satisfaction associated with one's achievements, but it can also be elicited prior to completing a task.[45] To inspire your audience members to take environmental action, encourage them to imagine the pride they will feel once they've adopted a certain behavior rather than the guilt they'd feel for not doing it.

In Australia, researchers set out to test the influence of pride versus guilt when making environmental decisions. To test the motivational strength of each emotion, they used various prompts to evoke feelings of pride and guilt among participants prior to making a series of choices. For example, participants were asked to choose between a sustainably made sofa in an outdated style and a modern sofa made from non-environmentally friendly chemicals and synthetic fabrics. They found that people were more likely to choose the sustainable options when they anticipated feelings of pride associated with purchasing the environmentally friendly option as opposed to guilt for choosing the non-environmentally friendly option.[41]

We can also experience pride when we engage in a behavior that is practiced and valued by people who are important to us. In another study conducted among university students, researchers assessed how feelings of pride and guilt influence daily participation in environmentally friendly behaviors such as recycling, taking public transportation, and turning off digital devices when not in use. People were more likely to take these actions if they reported feeling proud of their environmental behaviors and also believed that most of their peers participated in such behaviors.[6] This is why it's helpful to highlight others who have adopted environmental behaviors through acknowledgments or awards so people know that others in their circles are taking action.[39] For more on the importance of our peers' behavior, see BELONGING: Building Block Chapter 1, and for more about harnessing the power of community pride, see IDENTITY: Building Block Chapter 6, where you will also see a warning against the promotion of hubristic pride.

Research has also shown that pride can motivate people to persevere through challenging tasks—even ones that have higher initial costs, as is often the case when tackling environmental issues.[45] Evoking feelings of pride tends to boost people's confidence in their abilities, which, as we will discuss later in the chapter, is a critical component to strengthening our audience's sense of efficacy.

Uplift with humor

Humor can provide a cathartic release that builds resilience and energizes people to participate in social movements.[12] Humorous ads, for example, have shown to be more effective at increasing positive attitudes and engagement with an issue than non-humorous ads.[20] Researchers have proposed that through a phenomenon called **humorous threat persuasion**, humor can mitigate defensive emotional responses triggered by purely fear-based appeals and can effectively encourage threat-reducing behaviors. Additionally, humorous appeals tend to be easier to remember and can reach a larger audience, partly because people are more inclined to share and laugh about them with others.[8] Especially for polarized environmental issues, humor can help bridge political divides by reducing message resistance, even among those with opposing views.[33]

Comedy in particular can be a powerful tool for empowering disenfranchised communities to engage with environmental justice efforts. In Norfolk, Virginia, where largely low-income Black communities live in low-lying coastal areas prone to flooding, comedians collaborated with the town's Black community leaders to create "Ain't Your Mama's Heat Wave," a multimedia comedy show with both film and live stand-up.[12] Their participatory approach to its creation increased community awareness and political mobilization aimed at building resilience in the face of future disasters. Comedy provided a platform through which people could safely challenge the status quo, reshape unhelpful or harmful narratives, and humanize people affected by environmental issues.

We should always be thoughtful and judicious in our use of humor: it should never be used in a demeaning or offensive way. Humor can also backfire if it trivializes an issue, so it's important that the problem or threat is still clearly conveyed.[20] But with this in mind, humor can encourage more positive interactions with environmental challenges and can help to unite and uplift our audiences through shared laughter.

Making Shift Happen: Creating Funny Ad Campaigns to Save Water in Denver

In 2006, as the city of Denver was recovering from a serious drought, Denver's Board of Water Commissioners worked with Sukle Advertising to launch the "Use Only What You Need" campaign with ambitious goals of reducing water consumption.[1] They employed hilarious stunts that captured the city's attention: for example, someone dressed in a toilet costume ran across the field of Mile High Stadium in the middle of a football game (and was promptly tackled by a security guard) as the scoreboard projected "Stop running toilets." They also ran a campaign featuring the tagline: "Grass is dumb. Water 2 minutes less. Your lawn won't notice." Over the years, these clever ad campaigns worked in conjunction with policy and pricing changes to prompt a cultural shift in Denver's water use habits: despite a 15% increase in population, water use decreased by more than 20% over a period of 15 years.

OPTIMISM

Fig. 2.7.1: *Denver promotes saving water with a humorous ad campaign.*
CREDIT: COURTESY OF DENVER WATER, SEPTEMBER 15, 2020

Note that the success of Denver's ads was largely due to the combination of humor with a specific ask of their audience. This is important because vague humorous appeals can leave room for misinterpretation of the intended message behind a joke.[33] When we include explicit directives like "Water 2 minutes less" the audience knows exactly what they are being asked to do. For more on identifying and selecting specific behaviors, see INITIATE: Process Chapter 2.

Inspire with constructive hope

We can motivate our audience by presenting our vision of the future we are working toward, rather than harping on the problems we are trying to solve. That said, we should also be careful about depicting environmental challenges through rose-colored glasses. If we oversimplify environmental problems and pretend they will be easy to address, we risk eliciting a form of denial that people can use to justify inaction. Studies have shown that hope based on denial or a false sense of reality decreases people's engagement with solutions because it causes people to downplay the need for human intervention.[34]

To find a balance, we can use *constructive* hope as a motivating force. We build constructive hope by realistically depicting the challenges we face, identifying viable solutions to those challenges, and highlighting our progress toward overcoming them.[28] For example, to help a coastal community prepare for rising sea levels, we might emphasize the

> We build constructive hope by realistically depicting the challenges we face, identifying viable solutions to those challenges, and highlighting our progress toward overcoming them.

urgent need for mobilization, coupled with assurance that there are actions the community members can take, like restoring sand dunes, which offer protection and greater resilience. Constructive hope helps to maintain positivity, increasing the likelihood that people will adopt environmental behaviors, take political action, and support environmental policies or movements.

•••

In sum, evidence suggests that an effective approach to shifting behavior is to clearly convey the importance, severity, and urgency of environmental threats, coupled with the activation of positive emotions like hope and pride, as well as solutions-oriented messaging.[37] Ultimately, we can find utility in both positive and negative messaging as long as we instill a strong sense of efficacy, which is a critical determinant of motivation.[25] The remainder of this Building Block thus focuses on how to increase our audience's sense of efficacy, empowering them to take action.

Fig. 2.7.2:

CREDIT: iStock.com / ArtMarie

Build Confidence Through Efficacy

Whether you think you can or think you can't—you're right.

—Henry Ford

How do we keep our audience hopeful and engaged when confronted with daunting environmental challenges? We have little incentive to act if we doubt our ability to produce a desired outcome,[3] so having a sense of efficacy is key. Widely studied in psychology, efficacy is known to be one of the most important drivers of human agency, and therefore of human behavior. Efficacy promotes active optimism because it helps people to view obstacles as challenges to be overcome instead of threats to be avoided.[4]

Empower through active OPTIMISM • 401

There are two types of efficacy that are important for making behavioral shifts happen. Sustained participation from our audiences will require them to have both *action efficacy* (their belief that a specific action will result in the desired outcome) and *self-efficacy* (their belief in their ability to perform that action).[2,26] In other words, we need to have faith in the recommended solutions to an environmental problem, as well as confidence in our ability to carry out those solutions.[27] The shifters outlined in this principle are designed to strengthen both types of efficacy, which are often closely intertwined.

As practitioners, we can increase efficacy by outlining concrete solutions, aiming for achievable goals, providing encouragement, and highlighting progress already made.[22] It is also important to provide our audience with the information and practice needed to carry out the desired action, as well as to offer examples of positive role models performing the same behaviors.

Offer concrete solutions and immediate actions

When we believe that proposed solutions are adequately designed to address the problem at hand, we are more likely to engage in those solutions.[47] To increase your audience's action efficacy, connect the dots for your audience by explaining how and why the recommended actions will help to reduce the challenge your initiative is addressing. Once your audience believes that the recommended action will address the problem, give them specific examples of steps they can take.[37]

The immediacy with which our audience can take action is another critical consideration. For example, working toward a "fossil-free future" fails to convey an immediate plan for action.[37] Instead, offer your audience tangible behaviors they can do right away, like "take your bike for a test ride tomorrow and make a plan to start biking to work next week." As discussed earlier in this chapter, this is especially important when using emotionally charged messaging to convey the threat.[14,42] We will boost both our audience's action efficacy and self-efficacy if we can instill confidence that there are available solutions immediately within reach for tackling the problem.

⚙ Set appropriately-scaled goals and provide positive feedback

Environmentalists often present recommended actions in terms of their contribution toward the end goal or global-scale problems, like "ending global warming" or "ridding the ocean of plastics." But research suggests that environmental messages focused on high-level goals that are too large or abstract are less likely to lead to the adoption of positive behaviors.[32] Reaching such high-level goals doesn't feel achievable for one person, or even one community, and can exacerbate feelings of helplessness. Instead, we should make sure that our stated goals match the scale of what can be accomplished by the behaviors we are proposing. This helps the audience believe that their actions matter, even if they're small. In particular, we boost action efficacy when we help people see impacts from their efforts in their own homes or communities.

Making Shift Happen: Setting Low-Level Goals to Reduce Computer Energy Use at Universities

Low-level goals, which refer to more familiar actions and outcomes, tend to increase the perceived impact of an individual's contribution. A study conducted in Switzerland showed that students were more likely to turn off their computer screens at the end of a work session when they were presented with a message focused on low-level goals ("I turn off my computer screen in order to save energy at the university") versus high-level goals ("I turn off my computer screen in order to help phase out nuclear power in Switzerland").[32]

In addition to setting low-level goals, we can also strengthen our audience's self-efficacy by commending past achievements and ongoing contributions to a cause. Highlighting how our audience has already made some progress toward a certain goal can be a motivating factor in itself.[29] For more tips on setting goals and providing feedback to increase motivation, see HABITS: Building Block Chapter 3.

⚙ Facilitate opportunities for your audience to practice

Another way to help our audiences build self-efficacy is to create opportunities for them to practice desired behaviors in low-pressure scenarios with a high probability of success.[2] When we have successfully completed a task, we gain confidence in our ability to repeat it and are more likely to take on increasingly difficult actions of a similar nature. Practice is also important because many of us are kinesthetic learners, meaning that we learn by physically doing things. Provide your audience

OPTIMISM

with opportunities to practice through classes, trainings, or workshops that will increase their self-efficacy. For more on providing how-to information, see EASY: Building Block Chapter 2.

Making Shift Happen: Mastering Behaviors to Protect a Threatened Plant Species

For some conservation behaviors, a lack of knowledge or technical skill may stand in the way of action. This was exemplified in Belize, where a native wild palm plant called xaté was threatened by overharvesting.[46] In 2005, the Belize Botanic Garden provided xaté seeds to farmers in four villages and offered a training program on domestic cultivation of xaté as a way to augment household incomes and decrease pressures on the wild plant population. Five years after the training sessions, researchers compared the attitudes and behaviors of the trained farmers to those who did not participate in the program. The training gave the farmers greater confidence in their ability to cultivate xaté and access necessary resources. Technical knowledge and faith in their cultivation skills were the strongest predictors of whether farmers continued to cultivate the palm. This illustrates how skill-building programs can have a significant influence on our audience's self-efficacy and their subsequent adoption of environmental behaviors.

⚙ Depict success through social modeling

Watching someone similar to ourselves succeed at a task we are attempting to learn can boost both action efficacy and self-efficacy.[5] Role modeling demonstrates how to perform a behavior and also showcases the positive outcomes of a task.[22] For example, if we witness our neighbors getting their home insulated and then learn about the money they subsequently saved on their energy bills, we may be inspired to follow suit.

Role modeling doesn't always have to take place in person. When using imagery and narratives, depict people performing tangible actions that your audience can imagine themselves doing with relative confidence so they feel more empowered to act.[36] For example, energy efficiency campaigns should depict energy-saving behaviors such as adjusting a thermostat, replacing a lightbulb, or sealing window cracks—actions that people are familiar with and can apply in their own homes.[40]

By showcasing the environmental achievements of individuals or groups similar to our audience members, we can make them feel more optimistic about their own ability to succeed at related actions. For more on modeling social norms, see BELONGING: Building Block Chapter 1.

Energize Through Collective Action

Because many environmental issues are large-scale, even global, in nature, one individual's actions alone didn't cause them, and one individual can't fix them. Even if our audience feels capable and confident in their abilities to perform certain actions, individuals may get discouraged if they feel that their personal impact is a mere "drop in the bucket."[7] To demonstrate that individuals are not alone in bearing the burden of environmental challenges, illustrate how they are part of a collective effort that can have significant positive impacts.[3]

Connect individual behaviors to larger environmental movements

Our hope—and therefore motivation—is amplified when we perceive that many people are contributing to a shared cause.[3,15] In a national study conducted to assess Americans' feelings about humanity's ability to address climate change, the most common sources of hope came from the belief that collective awareness was increasing and from evidence that others were taking action.[28]

One way we can energize our audience around collective efforts is to help them conceptualize how their actions work in tandem with larger environmental movements.[37] While we should still demonstrate to our audience members how their individual behaviors address lower-level goals (like those within their community), it's also helpful to show people how those goals are connected to progressive initiatives happening at a regional, national, or global scale. By highlighting how their actions are supported by more powerful systems and movements, we can increase our audience's confidence in the power of collective efficacy. When we do this, our audience is more likely to set goals, strengthen their commitments to reaching those goals, and remain resilient in the face of obstacles.[3]

Demonstrate the aggregate effect of individual actions

Demonstrating the aggregate effect of many people working in tandem is common in environmental communications, driven by the idea that "if X people all do Y action, then Z outcome will be achieved."[10] Research shows that this strategy can increase the perceived impact of solutions,[44] which is helpful because sustainable choices sometimes require short-term personal sacrifices for the longer term, collective benefit of the planet. Energy-efficient lightbulbs, for example, are usually more expensive, but people may be more motivated to purchase them if they understand the large-scale energy-saving impacts we could have if consumers nationwide purchased them. For tips on how to make demonstrations of these positive collective impacts salient for your audience, see VIVID: Building Block Chapter 5.

When highlighting collective efforts, you may run the risk of people believing: "Since there are so many others available to work on this issue, surely they will take care of it!" This is the *diffusion of responsibility*, a phenomenon in which individuals feel less responsibility to take action when there are more people available to help.[16] To combat this diffusion of responsibility, be sure to communicate that while a larger group is indeed taking action, every individual's contributions are critical to making the collective effort a success.[26] Additionally, you can counteract the diffusion of responsibility by tapping into our innate desire to belong; by highlighting your audience's peers that are taking action, your audience will be motivated to "join their team." Read more about belonging and social proof in BELONGING: Building Block Chapter 1.

We can strengthen a community's perception of its collective efficacy by highlighting how our audience's individual actions are tied to more systemic environmental movements and multiplied by other individuals working toward the same goals. By doing so, we help motivate our audience to continue working toward a more sustainable future.

Conclusion

Hope—largely driven by perceived efficacy—is crucial for maintaining long-term motivation to tackle the environmental challenges we face. We can think of hope as the "gasoline that keeps the motor running" on the journey toward societal behavior change.[15] That's why this chapter focuses on inspiring active optimism in our audience by building a strong sense of efficacy in the following ways: striking a balance between positive and negative messaging, setting realistic goals that match the scale of the solutions, helping our audience build confidence through practice, and highlighting how individual actions are part of collective efforts. All of these are designed to empower our audiences, instilling hope and confidence in their ability to influence positive environmental outcomes through their behaviors.

📋 Your Turn

How can your environmental initiatives help your audience maintain active optimism? Use the questions below to brainstorm.

Be intentional with emotional messaging

❑ Are you using doomsday messaging? Instead, what are some positive messages that would be less overwhelming and more inspiring?

❑ Are you trying to motivate your audience by tapping into shame, guilt, or fear? Can you inspire them by activating emotions like pride or hope instead?

❑ If you are using threat appeals, how can you incorporate strong efficacy messages that help empower your audience to address the problem?

❑ How can you help your audience feel pride for behaviors they have already done, or imagine the pride they will feel after they do a new environmental behavior?

❑ How might you use humor to capture attention and encourage specific behaviors without trivializing the issue?

❑ Are you sugarcoating the environmental issue you hope to tackle? How can you be realistic about the challenge but still inspire constructive hope?

Build confidence through efficacy

❑ Are you offering concrete solutions and immediate actions your audience can take?

❑ How can you break down the larger goal so that it matches the scale of the proposed solutions?

❑ How can you give your audience positive feedback as they make progress toward (and/or reach) their goals?

❑ What kinds of opportunities can you provide for your audience to practice desired behaviors in low-pressure scenarios?

❑ Are there people similar to your audience who are succeeding at the desired behaviors? How can you highlight them?

Energize through collective action

❑ How can you portray your audience's actions as part of a larger environmental movement?

❑ How can you illustrate the aggregate impact of your audience's actions, multiplied by others who are doing the same?

Judiciously use REWARDS

> *Key Takeaway:* We are more likely to engage in behaviors when we feel that the benefits outweigh the costs. By choosing incentives wisely, we can attract people to positive environmental behaviors and deter them from negative ones.

Rewards act as motivation boosters

IN AN IDEAL WORLD, everyone would be motivated to engage in environmental behaviors all of the time. Everyone would believe that the costs of environmental behaviors (like the extra time it takes to sort our food into compost bins) are outweighed by the benefits (like the reduced emissions from food in landfills), even if those benefits will be realized far into the future. However, in reality, few of us are sufficiently motivated by distant, diffuse, or intangible rewards. Some people may have no motivation to engage in environmental behaviors at all and require external incentives to engage. Moreover, even motivated people may face constraints to adopting environmental behaviors, like being unable to afford solar panels or to spend the time researching which solar panels to buy. Furthermore, since environmental costs and benefits are rarely distributed equally, people aren't always motivated to minimize their environmental impact. For example, if a farmer uses too much groundwater to increase their yields, people elsewhere might run out of water. But since the farmer would increase their profits, they might lack motivation to conserve water, since other people would bear the costs.

For all of these reasons and more, sometimes your audience will require an extra incentive to make the benefits of environmental behavior outweigh the costs and to overcome the psychological and social barriers to behavior change.

Judiciously incentivize behavior change

To encourage an audience to engage in environmental behaviors, consider incentivizing them to do so with rewards or penalties. (Note that in this chapter, we generally use the terms "reward" and "incentive" interchangeably.) **Rewards** can provide the extra incentive needed for audience members to overcome the psychological and social barriers to behavior change. In addition to rewards, practitioners can also employ penalties. **Penalties** can be used to make undesirable behaviors less appealing to the audience by adding costs (e.g., financial, time) to performing them. While we discuss penalties in this chapter, we mainly focus on rewards, as they are generally preferable to penalties.

Rewards are often thought of as tangible items like money or goods. However, rewards are frequently intangible, too; they can include social recognition or feelings of enjoyment and accomplishment. For example, rewards can take the form of the positive emotions you feel when you toss a piece of litter in the trash and someone nods and smiles at you, or the pride an organic farmer feels at the farmer's market when her customers tell her how much they enjoy her vegetables.

> Rewards are often thought of as tangible items like money or goods. However, rewards are frequently intangible, too; they can include social recognition or feelings of enjoyment and accomplishment.

By creating rewards for certain behaviors or by increasing the size or visibility of existing rewards, you can boost your audience's motivation to take action. Rewards and penalties can also even out disparities in the costs and benefits of some behaviors. For instance, rewarding a farmer for keeping more water in the ground can help ensure that there is enough water for all households. Similarly, funds generated from a penalty for overuse of groundwater could be used to connect homes to a municipal water supply or to help households purchase water-saving appliances.

Application of rewards and penalties must be judicious: there are some cases where they aren't the best option. For example, rewards are best for one-time behaviors, or when the audience is not already intrinsically motivated (such as when a task is extremely mundane). When the behavior is intrinsically rewarding, incentives may be unnecessary and sometimes even ill-suited.[31]

In this Building Block, we will focus on how you can use tools like these to design and deliver rewards and penalties to motivate positive environmental behavior.

Principles and Shifters for the REWARDS Building Block

Determine the Incentive

Decide whether a reward or penalty is needed
Decide if you will penalize instead of reward
Design rewards to be meaningful and useful

Watch out for unintended consequences

Determine whether to reward behaviors or outcomes

Reward at the individual or group level

Consider the Timing of Rewards

Utilize the power of immediacy

Reward one-time behaviors

Reward on a schedule for long-term change

Give Your Rewards a Boost

Use lotteries

Make it a game

Tap into loss aversion

Imply that the reward is scarce

 ## Determine the Incentive

First, you must decide whether and what kind of reward to administer. Keep in mind that there are no "silver bullet" incentives for motivating environmental behavior change. To produce the most effective reward, you must know your audience and provide the benefits that are aligned with what the audience finds most attractive.

Decide whether a reward or penalty is needed

Your first step in choosing your reward or penalty is to decide whether or not you even need one. If most of your audience performs the desired behavior with some regularity, adding an incentive is likely unnecessary. Be sure to only proceed with an incentive if your audience needs an extra boost to begin doing the behavior or to do it more frequently.

> Be sure to only proceed with an incentive if your audience needs an extra boost to begin doing the behavior or to do it more frequently.

Providing unnecessary rewards is not only a poor use of resources, it can also hurt your behavior change efforts. In some cases, certain rewards (like financial ones) can impede positive spillover and "crowd out" intrinsic motivation to engage in a behavior. (We discuss intrinsic motivation in more detail to come).

⚙ Decide if you will penalize instead of reward

When you're unable to reward a desired behavior, you can instead penalize an undesired one, either by directly prohibiting it or by making the undesired behavior more difficult. For example, raising the price of parking may discourage people from driving their car to the office. See EASY: Building Block Chapter 2 for more on adding friction to undesired behaviors.

Penalties can range from financial disincentives (e.g., fines, taxes, or surcharges) to the suspension of privileges (e.g., when governments closed parks during the COVID-19 pandemic because too many people weren't taking appropriate precautions). Even not receiving a reward can be seen as a penalty (as we later discuss in the shifter "Tap into loss aversion"). When designing a penalty, keep in mind that it must be substantial enough to outweigh the benefits of the problematic behavior, or it won't work.

We must be especially careful when using penalties because of their risk for creating unintended consequences, including creative misbehavior, negative reactions, and undue burden on particular groups.

When a penalty is in place, people will be motivated to find ways to "game the system" to continue to do the undesired behavior while avoiding penalties. For example, when a fine was implemented in Vancouver, British Columbia, for driving alone in a carpool lane, people built and dressed mannequins to appear as extra passengers.[8] As a more serious example, the United States Endangered Species Act, which penalizes people for harming endangered species, has also led to perverse outcomes; some landowners clear habitats in order to prevent endangered species from being discovered,[1] and there is even a phrase some landowners have for what to do if they find an endangered species on their land: "Shoot, shovel, shut up."

Such undesirable reactions can take place not just because people want to avoid the penalty, but also because they want to rebel against perceived restrictions on their freedom to behave as they desire.[4] For example, in Dade County, Florida, cleaning products containing phosphates were made illegal, and some residents rebelled against this restriction by turning to smuggling and hoarding the products, even traveling to neighboring counties in "soap caravans" to purchase these products. The ban also led to another unintended consequence: some people began to see the banned cleaning products as having higher quality, and therefore as more desirable.[6]

Finally, be sure to pay attention to the magnitude of your penalty. Audiences may react negatively or creatively to penalties that they perceive as especially severe or unfair.[4] Additionally, it's particularly important to make sure the penalty doesn't

REWARDS

result in excessive costs for vulnerable members of your audience. For example, we might wish to raise bridge tolls to increase the cost of driving to work, but too high of an increase can make it prohibitively expensive for those with low incomes to get to work. This means that to support the shift away from driving, we should provide alternative infrastructure or programs, like ensuring easy access to cheap alternative modes of transportation, or offering subsidies or exceptions for those groups.

Making Shift Happen: Combining Incentives and Penalties in Calgary

If you have to use a penalty, consider combining it with an incentive. In response to increasing demand for parking downtown, the City of Calgary, Alberta, created a disincentive to park downtown by raising the price while simultaneously incentivizing a desired substitute behavior by reducing the cost for park and rides.[13] The share of downtown workers taking public transit increased from 37% in 1998 to 50% in 2014. This example shows that combining incentives with penalties may be especially effective in facilitating behavior change.

Before implementing penalties, consider how likely (and how serious) any unintended consequences like these might be. We recommend that before turning to penalties, you try to use rewards and other shifters to positively reinforce desired behaviors. Finally, if you do use penalties, pair them with programs that make the desired behavior easier and more appealing, as described in the City of Calgary park and ride example.

⚙ Design rewards to be meaningful and useful

Rewards come in many forms and can function in different ways to achieve behavior change—they can tap into different types of motivation, they can be designed to address specific barriers, and they can sometimes simply highlight benefits that are already inherent in the behavior itself. When designing incentives, consider the characteristics that will be most meaningful and useful to your audience. See UNCOVER: Process Chapter 3 for more on understanding what impedes and motivates your audience's behavior.

Tap into intrinsic motivation, extrinsic motivation, or both

The purpose of offering rewards is to increase the motivation for your audience to complete or avoid a certain behavior. Motivation can arise intrinsically and extrinsically (note that the two aren't mutually exclusive, as we discuss more below).

Intrinsic motivation arises automatically in your target audience when they perform a behavior and experience things like a sense of meaningfulness, competence, growth, autonomy, exploration, enjoyment, or positive feelings from helping others.[9,34] You can boost motivation by tapping into these intrinsic motivators (e.g., by providing the opportunity to learn new skills). *Extrinsic motivation* arises from a source external to your audience, such as when they receive financial benefits or social recognition for performing or avoiding the behavior.[9,34] Extrinsic benefits come in many forms: financial (e.g., rebates, discounts), tangible (e.g., food, toys, vacations), reputational (e.g., public recognition), or progress-based (e.g., gamification).

Below are some examples of rewards that can motivate your audience.

Table 2.8.1: Examples of Rewards

Reward Type	Description	Tips and Examples
Material (tangible) rewards and penalties: money, goods, and services	Material rewards are tangible things that your audience can use and benefit from. The most obvious example is money, but they could also be food, school supplies, toys, stickers, household appliances … the list is endless! Courses, trips, or other services may also be a strong material incentive because these are things that people would otherwise have to pay for.	• Make sustainable behaviors cheaper: offer a discount for bringing a reusable container, mug or bag. • Make unsustainable behaviors more expensive: charge for printing or plastic bags. • Use celebration as a reward: throw a pizza party for the team that reduces their energy use the most. • Offer small rewards: place snacks next to shared office printers. • Offer relevant tokens that facilitate sustainable behavior: tote bags, reusable straws, etc.
Social rewards: recognition, status, and connection	Humans are a fundamentally social species: we go to incredible lengths, even risking our lives, for recognition (feeling acknowledged for our efforts), status (feeling equal or superior to others), and connection (feeling close to others). What type of social rewards does your audience most respond to, and which	• Use physical or virtual badges, scores, and awards to publicly showcase members' success: NOAA's Turtle Trash Collectors program does this by giving youth badges for collecting trash in their local community.[37] • If possible, continually update public scores, as this combines social rewards and progress tracking. The League of Conservation Voters' National Environmental Scorecard does this for elected officials.[26]

Table 2.8.1: *Cont.*

Reward Type	Description	Tips and Examples
Social rewards: *Cont.*	will be most effective in achieving your goals? See BELONGING: Building Block Chapter 1 for more on social norms.	• Provide opportunities for teamwork and social bonding: require participants to work together in order to achieve group energy-reduction goals. • Don't forget that even smiling and thanking someone can be a reward!
Other non-tangible rewards: purpose, accomplishment, autonomy, competence, novel experiences, and spiritual connection	Don't underestimate the importance of having a sense of purpose! It can be profoundly motivating to do meaningful work that we believe will make a difference. For example, people can be highly motivated to achieve autonomy, competence, novel experiences, and spiritual connection.	• Provide the audience with a sense of purpose or accomplishment by highlighting the positive environmental impact of doing the desired behavior. See VIVID: Building Block Chapter 5 for examples. • Frame benefits in terms of personal goals in addition to environmental ones: emphasize the exercise benefits, like a rush of endorphins, from biking to work. • Emphasize how the sustainable behavior will increase the participant's autonomy: biking instead of taking the bus provides you with more control over when you leave for work and which route you take. • Provide experiences or practical training that increase participants' autonomy and competence while facilitating sustainable behavior: organize a workshop on bike maintenance or teach bike riding in a beautiful outdoor setting.

Extrinsic motivation can "crowd out" intrinsic motivation; that is, it can overshadow the inherent reasons to engage in a behavior. Consider what happened at a group of Israeli day care centers: within weeks of implementing a new policy that fined parents a small amount for picking up their children late, the number of late pickups almost doubled.[16] Apparently, the relatively small penalty was interpreted as a reasonable amount to pay for cheap childcare, crowding out parents' intrinsic motivation to be good citizens and pick up their kids on time. Even when this penalty was reversed, parents continued the behavior of picking up their children late.

Be on the lookout for this crowding out phenomenon, especially when providing financial incentives. By shifting focus away from intrinsic motivations for engaging in environmental behaviors, financial incentives can impede *positive spillover* (where, after performing one behavior, your audience is more likely to perform future environmental behaviors). These incentives can also inhibit attitude shifts and the building of an environmental identity. To prevent this, pair financial rewards with other types of rewards, like social rewards or rewards that tap into identity.[5] See FOUNDATIONS: Process Chapter 1 for more about behavioral spillover.

It's important to note, however, that extrinsic motivation doesn't always crowd out intrinsic motivation. In fact, most incentives have both intrinsic and extrinsic features. Few Nobel Prize winners, for example, would say that extrinsic monetary and social rewards decreased their inherent scientific or artistic motivation to do their work. Many in your audience will respond to both types of motivation; the trick is to choose rewards that will motivate as many people as effectively (and affordably) as possible.

Offer a reward that is meaningful to your audience[19]

Because it's important to tailor your rewards to your audience, you will want to understand what is meaningful to them. A reward that might motivate one audience might not be meaningful to another. For example, a company's employees might prefer a group outing to a football game over a cash prize. Public recognition may be motivating to some but act as a disincentive to people who shy away from attention. An understanding of your audience's values and priorities (see ATTACHMENT: Building Block Chapter 4) will be helpful for tailoring your rewards and penalties.

REWARDS

Use your reward to address the barriers to the behavior

Rewards are especially impactful when they address the barriers of the desired behavior. For example, if you're trying to incentivize commuters to take the bus to work instead of driving, and you discover that affordability was a primary barrier to taking the bus to work, you could offer a discount if they take the bus more than a certain number of days in a month. However, if instead your research revealed that your audience avoids the bus because they think it's noisy, you may be better off handing out free noise-cancelling headphones. You wouldn't know your audience's barriers without conducting audience research; see UNCOVER: Process Chapter 3 for more on how to do this.

Make inherent yet invisible benefits more visible

We can sometimes fail to notice the positive consequences of performing a desirable behavior. Instead of creating an entirely new reward, check to see if your desired behavior has any inherent benefits that are "invisible" or that your audience just hasn't noticed yet. You can make invisible benefits more visible by vividly connecting action to impact and by providing feedback.

Vividly connect action to impact

Improving the environment can be its own reward. However, the environmental impacts of both negative or positive behaviors aren't always obvious. For example, when we use less paper, we are saving trees and helping reduce pollution related to ink production, and when we work from home, we reduce our carbon emissions, but these benefits can be invisible to us. As practitioners, we can make rewards like these more visible by vividly connecting behaviors to their impacts, such as through images, displays, and descriptive language. For example, we can design a water fountain that counts and displays how many plastic water bottles its use has prevented. See VIVID: Building Block Chapter 5 for many examples of how to make benefits like these stand out to our audience.

Provide feedback

Another way to make an unseen benefit seen is to provide your audience with feedback on their behaviors. For example, we can design walking apps to provide feedback on one's contribution to emission reduction in addition to steps completed. See HABITS: Building Block Chapter 3 for more on feedback.

Watch out for unintended consequences

As with penalties, rewards can also result in unintended consequences. Practitioners should seek to understand these potential consequences and to try to reduce their likelihood as much as possible.

Consider the magnitude of your reward

Offering a bigger reward may seem like it would result in an even stronger behavior change, but that isn't always the case. If a reward is too large, it can backfire if it sends a signal that the behavior is extremely difficult or onerous to complete.[29] For example, offering a $500 prize to a household who waters their lawn during acceptable hours might signal that the behavior is difficult or inconvenient, or that is has significant negative personal consequences; otherwise, why would such a large reward be offered? Larger rewards are of course also more expensive to implement, and sometimes a small reward is plenty sufficient. (In later sections about reward timing and how to "boost" rewards, we talk more about how to maximize the impact of your rewards, no matter what size they are.)

Keep an eye out for "creative misbehavior"

Just as they do to avoid penalties, people will sometimes "game the system" in order to get a reward. For example, if you reward people on the basis of how many miles they bike and give out pedometers to track their progress, they could shake the pedometer to make it look like they're biking when they aren't. Consider a bounty hunting program designed to eradicate the population of feral swine on a United States military base. Hunters were financially rewarded for each pig tail they collected. While many pig tails were brought in, the program failed to reduce the actual population of feral swine on the military base because many hunters picked tails up from meat processors to turn in for bounty.[2] Note that the larger the reward is, the more likely it becomes that people will try to game the system.

Be aware of inequitable impacts

While inequitable impacts are more commonly associated with penalties, even incentive systems can cause disproportionate negative effects. For example, emissions trading programs need to be designed to ensure that they don't unintentionally concentrate pollution in marginalized communities (e.g., industries located near those communities can emit at harmful levels if they purchase extra

REWARDS

emissions credits).[12,40] Make sure that your incentive achieves the purpose you want it to without harmful, disproportionate side effects.[20]

⚙️ Determine whether to reward behaviors or outcomes

Imagine you want to reduce energy usage in your community by rewarding people for saving energy. You can reward *specific behaviors* (e.g., replacing energy-inefficient appliances) to provide them with a predetermined roadmap to meet the outcome (in this case, "save energy by replacing the fridge"). Alternatively, you could reward *outcomes* (e.g., reducing energy use by 10%) to allow them to choose how to save energy. The option you choose depends on your audience and target outcome.

As discussed in INITIATE: Process Chapter 2, it's important to be specific about the behavior that you want your audience to complete. Rewarding specific behaviors has many advantages: explicitly describing a specific behavior is helpful if an audience isn't already familiar or experienced with the behavior, it can be easier to monitor whether people are doing a specific behavior than multiple behaviors, and repeating a single specific behavior can help your audience build habits (by pairing rewards and actions closely together,[38] like providing a discount when people use a reusable cup or bag; see HABITS: Building Block Chapter 3 for more on this topic).

However, there are cases where you might want to reward the outcome (instead of or in addition to rewarding a specific behavior). Rewarding outcomes can be advantageous when it's difficult to monitor specific behaviors, or when it's easy for your audience to "fake" specific behaviors to try to achieve the reward. Additionally, sometimes we as practitioners are not the experts on which behaviors can best achieve durable outcomes, but our audience is. In those cases, it can be more effective to allow the audience members to draw on their knowledge of the behaviors and choose how to achieve the desired outcome. (However, for non-expert audiences—those unfamiliar with the behaviors that they can complete to achieve the outcome—it's always best to provide suggestions of specific behaviors they can do.)

Providing certain audiences with options and autonomy can also increase ownership, buy-in, and motivation. For example, allowing households to decide how to save energy empowers them to take action by choosing the method that appeals to them most and that will result in the most energy reduction for their home. A household that cooks frequently might reduce energy by buying an energy-saving dishwasher or induction cooktop, whereas a household that doesn't cook frequently might instead focus on energy-efficient ways to heat their house.

⚙ Reward at the individual or group level

When rewarding behaviors, you'll have to decide whether to reward participants individually or as a group.

While we'll often be rewarding individuals or at the household level (e.g., rewarding each individual with a gift card if they adopt the desired behavior), sometimes you'll need to reward at the group level, such as when an individual behavior can't be measured (e.g., if you can't determine how much each university professor prints in a semester, but you can measure by department).

Additionally, if you want or need group collaboration toward a common goal, rewarding an entire group for achieving an outcome helps encourage them to reach the goal by working together and holding each other accountable. For example, you could reward an entire neighborhood by holding a block party when they reach an energy-saving goal. Even when you decide to reward at the group level, you might also provide individual rewards on top of that, as this example from Columbia University demonstrates.

Making Shift Happen: Rewarding Individuals and Groups for Reducing Paper Use

Columbia University's Mailman School of Public Health incentivized employees to reduce their paper consumption by offering them the ability to earn different levels of a sustainability certificate that could be publicly displayed to peers. The employees formed teams, signed a participation pledge, and completed actions from a checklist of behaviors. Teams must have completed all items from a specific level—gold, silver, and bronze—to receive that level of certificate. Examples of behaviors from each certificate level include:

- **Bronze:** Add a "think before printing" email tagline and host three paperless meetings.
- **Silver:** Adopt the Mailman School of Public Health paperless workflow guidelines for submitting items to the finance department.
- **Gold:** Create a paper allotment and individual incentives for those who comply.
- **Platinum:** Complete every listed action and create your own intervention.

By implementing these incentives, the school reported that overall paper use decreased by 23% in the first year of its ongoing program.[7,41]

Keep an Eye Out for Free Riders

One thing to keep in mind with group rewards, however, is the additional difficulties often posed by *free riders*: those in a group who benefit from rewards without significantly contributing to the collective goal.[24] It is important when designing group reward systems to discourage free riding, such as by assigning unique responsibilities, supporting individual accountability, and celebrating team spirit and success as much as possible. Don't be discouraged by the fact that it may be impossible to eliminate free riders and creative misbehavior. Well-designed reward systems will still succeed even with a certain amount of residual bad apples.

Consider the Timing of Rewards

Not only must you determine what type of reward to give, you must also decide when to administer it. Below are some ways to vary when and how often a reward is given, and some contexts in which each option can be beneficial.

Utilize the power of immediacy

People like to be rewarded immediately. For example, most of us know that eating seasonal foods is more environmentally friendly: when we choose to eat foods that are out of season, they have to be imported, increasing the number of "food miles" an item must travel to get to our plates. Yet, when we go to the grocery store, we're enticed by the immediate gratification of off-season fruits and vegetables and may not be willing to wait for those foods to be in-season locally. Why is that?

We are generally predisposed to prioritize immediate consequences over those that will occur in the future. Studies have shown that people routinely hold a *present bias:* living for today at the expense of tomorrow.[17,28] This means that we perceive the value of rewards that we get (and costs we incur) right now to be much higher than those that will be given in the future. Therefore, make your rewards as immediate as possible, even if that means they are small. Below are some examples of immediate rewards:

- Immediately provide a token of participation (e.g., sticker, button) when an audience member signs a pledge to reduce their energy use.

- Place incentives at or near the point where the target behavior takes place. For example, put a snack jar near the scrap paper bin.
- Offer discounts upon sign up, such as a 10% discount for signing up for email updates.

Lock in behavior with commitment devices

Present bias can make it hard to change our behavior. Behaviors like conserving energy or exercising can be hard to engage in because they cause us immediate inconvenience, and we won't always feel the benefits (such as cost savings or improved strength) until the future. To help ourselves complete behaviors like these, we can utilize *future lock-in*—making a commitment *right now* to do something inconvenient at a future point in time.[33]

One way to structure your rewards or penalties to utilize the future lock-in effect is to create a **commitment device**. Have your audience agree that if they do not engage in the desired environmental behavior in the future, they will automatically be subject to a penalty. For example, StickK.com is a commitment contract website where people commit to a goal (such as biking to work 3 days per week) and dedicate money (sometimes hundreds of dollars) that they will get back if they meet the goal, but that will be given to an organization they dislike (such as an opposing political party) if they don't.[15,39] For more on commitments, see IDENTITY: Building Block Chapter 6.

Reward one-time behaviors

Behaviors that can be easily audited, occur once or rarely, or have large up front costs can all benefit from a one-time reward. For example, you could provide a subsidy, tax break, or rebate for large one-time purchases of environmentally friendly appliances such as electric vehicles, low flush toilets, or solar panels.

Some one-time rewards can actually motivate people to keep doing the behavior even after the reward is removed.[14] For instance, if you subsidize compost bins for an entire neighborhood, you not only create a social norm, but you also give people tools to sustain a desired behavior.

Reward on a schedule for long-term change

If you need your audience to continue to do a behavior more than once, design a **schedule of reinforcement**[11] that promotes repetition and habit-formation. If well-designed, even temporary incentives can result in long-term behavior change.[14]

REWARDS

While your schedule of reinforcement might differ depending on your particular behavior and context, a good rule is to first establish the behavior by providing a reward *every time* the desired behavior is completed (a **continuous schedule**). Then, when your audience is reliably doing the behavior, you can start weaning them off the reward by only offering the reward *some of the time* (an **intermittent schedule**).[11,35] Intermittent schedules can be either fixed or variable. On a fixed ratio schedule, we would deliver the reward on a predictable schedule (e.g., every two times the person does the behavior, or for every second person that does the behavior), whereas with a variable ratio schedule, we would deliver the reward on an unpredictable or random schedule.

For example, if you are trying to get your audience to ride the bus, start with a continuous schedule that rewards every person who rides the bus, every time. Then, once enough people are consistently riding the bus, you can transition to an intermittent schedule that rewards every fifth person that rides the bus, or that rewards a random, unpredictable number of riders.[35] This way, the audience doesn't depend on receiving the reward every time they ride the bus, but they continue to build the habit because they anticipate that they might receive the reward.

Ideally, intermittent reward schedules (even fixed ones) aren't disclosed to the audience, so they never know when the next reward will be earned. As such, variable schedules are generally preferred to fixed schedules, because they are more unpredictable to the audience. (If you predictably reward every five times or every fifth rider, the audience might catch on to this fixed schedule.) The idea that the reward could happen any time can encourage the audience to keep engaging in the behavior. Over time, you can wean your audience off the reward by making the schedule more and more infrequent, but make sure to monitor the behavior for a while and have backup plans in place in case there is a regression away from the desired behavior.

See HABITS: Building Block Chapter 3 for more on using incentives to kickstart new habits and gradually ramp up to increasingly more challenging habits.

If you haven't been able to make the desired behavior a habit for your audience (either through rewards or other methods) but need them to continue engaging in the behavior for the long haul, you might need to provide a reward in perpetuity. If this is necessary, consider whether you can design a reward program that is self-sustaining (i.e., that pays for itself). Bottle collection programs, in which people receive money back for every bottle they recycle (a continuous schedule), are examples of self-sustaining incentive programs. The audience is motivated to get five cents back for returning the bottle, which is less than the value that the collecting agency can get for the bottle. At the very least, the rewards program is paying for itself, if not generating revenue. These programs have been successful in achieving positive environmental outcomes: many cities across the United States have seen vast reductions in litter and misplaced waste via these programs.[4]

Give Your Rewards a Boost

You can boost your incentives by appealing to behavioral principles, such as cognitive biases and our love of fun and games.

Use lotteries

Highly motivating for many people, lotteries are examples of variable schedules that many initiatives have used successfully to promote behavior change, such as Hydro-Québec's Energy Wise Home Diagnostic program, which offered households who participated in an energy audit the chance to win a car.[25]

One reason lotteries and raffle-style rewards work so well is that they increase a small reward's perceived value, so they are especially useful when you have limited resources to spend on rewards. We have a tendency to focus more on the size of the prize than the actual chance of winning, so a chance at winning $100 may be more powerful than a guaranteed $1. So, if you only have $100, splitting it among 100 participants (with each receiving $1) is unlikely to motivate action. However, if you offer a single reward of $100 and offer a 1 in 100 chance to win, the human tendency to overestimate the chance that we will win can increase motivation.[18]

In a real-world example of a small yet effective lottery reward in action, the city of Dayton, Ohio, began giving away $100 every two weeks to two randomly selected households that recycled. During the first month of the program, a city official reported that recycling participation was up by 40%.[21] Keep in mind that lottery prizes don't have to be financial—offering a free trip out in nature, such as a whale-watching excursion or guided nature hike, is a great way to foster a connection with nature.

⚙ Make it a game

A great way to engage with your audience is through fun and gamification. *Gamification*—turning your initiative into a game—can be effective because it can raise awareness, develop empathy for other stakeholders, and jumpstart habits by associating incentives with environmentally friendly behavior.[10,43] Rewards are an important part of games, but often just playing the game is the reward itself. People enjoy interactive challenges and many are highly motivated by competition. Points, levels, and badges that track and recognize progress,[32] or material rewards such as prizes, can be easily integrated into the game context, where appropriate. See HABITS: Building Block Chapter 3 more on providing feedback.

You can use a range of fun components to optimize your design:

Sustainability games

Computer or smartphone-based apps frequently use point systems and offer colorful and engaging animations to support individual or group progress. They often contain social comparison and progress markers over longer stretches of time. Sometimes, they involve competitions and lotteries for public recognition, supervisor appreciation, or tangible incentives. Many such applications and games have been developed and have concrete benefits, such as "Energy Chickens" discussed here.

Making Shift Happen: Using "Energy Chickens" to Decrease Energy Use

"Energy Chickens" is an example of gamification in which participants had to keep a virtual chicken alive by decreasing their energy use.[30] The game took information from plug-load sensors to measure energy consumption of the office worker participants. The less energy these participants used, the healthier their chicken was and the more eggs it laid. In the game, participants could then use these eggs to buy accessories for their chicken farms. This 20-week intervention proved effective, decreasing the workers' energy consumption by an average of 13%. Sixty-nine percent of participants reported that the experience helped them to be more energy-conscious, and some even reduced their energy behavior outside of the office.

Competitions and challenges

In competitions and challenges, individuals or groups compete against each other or their own baselines. For example, the electricity and natural gas utility Fortis BC offered a $15,000 energy makeover as a reward to the community with the highest number of participants committed to saving energy.[27] Tap into your audience's competitiveness using leaderboards or other ways of publicly acknowledging who has achieved the best results.

Simulations

Unlike the above types of games, simulations, which imitate the real-world, are more about exploring environmental issues than winning material rewards (although material rewards can still be used). Simulations can be very effective in helping audiences understand abstract new concepts and relate to other stakeholders. That being said, this type of experience can be very involved and is usually best when you have plenty of time with a captive audience, such as at a workshop or in the classroom. See ATTACHMENT: Building Block Chapter 4 for more on simulating environmental experiences.

Tap into loss aversion

You can leverage *loss aversion*, or the fact that, in general, we hate to lose more than we love to win,[23] when designing rewards or penalties. To do so, frame rewards as an avoidance of a potential loss. For example, instead of telling your audience that they will receive money for bringing their bottles and cans to be recycled at grocery stores (framing it as a gain), frame it as a loss by telling them that since they already paid for the bottle, they will lose that "deposit" if they don't recycle it.

Additional examples of using loss aversion include promising to give a reward when someone completes a desired behavior and emphasizing the potential for someone to "lose" the reward if they do not follow through, or highlighting lost opportunities for people who did not participate in an initiative. For example, on a college campus, perhaps only those who participate in the environmental ambassador training program are able to qualify for funding for their sustainability initiative; therefore, those who don't participate lose out on potential funding.

> Practitioners must be careful when tapping into loss aversion, as the threat of loss is often accompanied with negative emotions.[3] When using loss aversion, we strongly recommend testing your messages before implementing them. See ASSOCIATIONS: Building Block Chapter 9 for more on loss aversion.

⚙ Imply that the reward is scarce

We are more motivated to get things when there aren't many of them left, or when a lot of other people want them, too.[6,42] Online retailers take advantage of this all the time: how many times have you seen text saying, "only two left in stock—order soon!" or "this item is in three people's carts"? As a practitioner, you can imply that the reward you are offering is scarce (e.g., time-limited, diminishing) to increase its desirability.

To make a reward *time-limited*, restrict it to a certain time period or number of participants, such as by rewarding only the first 100 people who relinquish their desktop printer. To make a reward *diminishing*, offer each person who relinquishes their printer a smaller reward than the person who did it before them. This will create a race to relinquish printers first and can be especially powerful when a deadline to reach the goal is on the horizon.

Reducing the number of rewards increases the perceived value of each one. This can be especially useful when you have limited resources. You can place a cap or ceiling on rewards, like only supplying rewards to the first 25 people to claim them.

Making Shift Happen: Raising the "Sticker Price" of Hybrid Cars

How did the scarcity of California's Clean Air Vehicle stickers (which allow hybrid cars into carpool and High Occupancy Vehicle lanes even with only one occupant) lead to their increased resale price? These stickers were given to the first 85,000 purchasers of hybrid cars. After they ran out, hybrid cars with these stickers sold for $1,000 more than hybrids without the stickers![22, 36]

> Although implied scarcity is a powerful mechanism, beware that the word "scarcity" can have a negative connotation which could discourage participation. Instead, use words or phrases like "limited edition," "only a few left," "special issue," "deluxe version," "once-in-a-lifetime," "one of a kind," or "one time only."

Conclusion

Ultimately, every behavior has consequences of some kind. Therefore, every behavior involves a range of rewards and penalties, even when they are unintended, minor, or something that we may not have typically thought of as a reward (such as feedback). By recognizing this, we can begin to use incentives more intentionally and wisely.

An important part of using incentives more wisely is recognizing that people vary in the level and type of rewards that they may need to supplement their existing motivation. For some people, a bit of feedback can do the trick; for others, a financial incentive might be necessary. Additionally, remember that when people already have high levels of intrinsic motivation to take environmental action, we should be careful not to introduce incentives that aren't necessary, which can even backfire by reducing the intrinsic motivation that was already present. For example, if motivation is already present, someone might just need a reminder at the right time and place, or additional how-to information and skill building to increase their confidence that they can do the behavior.

Even if someone is not intrinsically motivated, rewards don't have to be financial; being part of the group—by adopting the behavior one's peers are doing—can be incentive enough. By remembering that incentives, especially financial ones, are not the answer to every environmental problem (just as the other shifters discussed in this book are also not panaceas), we can create more effective, and often more affordable, behavior change initiatives.

☷ Your Turn

How can you design incentives to increase motivation? Use the questions below to help you brainstorm.

Determine the incentive

❏ Is your audience facing a motivation problem? Should you provide an incentive to increase motivation (e.g., one that taps into intrinsic or extrinsic motivation, or both)?

❏ Are you able to positively reward a desired behavior? If not, consider penalizing the undesired behavior.

❏ What are some (tangible and intangible) rewards that you could give to your audience? Which rewards might they respond to best?

❑ Can you provide an incentive that will help address one or more of your audience's barriers?

❑ Before you add any new rewards, can you highlight any inherent yet invisible benefits that could be motivating to the audience?

❑ Do the circumstances align better with rewarding specific behaviors or rewarding outcomes? Do they align with rewarding individuals, or groups?

❑ Have you considered how your reward or penalty might create unintended consequences? How might you reduce the likelihood of those?

Consider the timing of rewards

❑ Can you deliver the reward as immediately as possible after the behavior is completed?

❑ Can you "lock in" your audience to commit to a behavior ahead of time?

❑ How can you structure a continuous or intermittent schedule to reward the audience for maximum behavior change?

❑ When will you start to wean your audience off the reward? How will you monitor when to start weaning? What plan do you have in case you wean too soon?

❑ If you need your audience to continue the behavior but they have not yet built the habit, can you develop a self-supporting incentive?

Give your rewards a boost

❑ Can you incorporate competitions, challenges, or games to make the desired behavior fun?

❑ Can you carefully tap into loss aversion, either with a penalty or by framing the lack of a reward as a loss?

❑ Can you utilize a lottery or raffle-style reward to maximize the effectiveness of limited resources?

❑ How can you make your reward more desirable by implying scarcity? Can you limit your reward by time or quantity in some way?

Building Block Chapter 9

....

Frame for the appropriate
ASSOCIATIONS

Key Takeaway: Framing information in a way that activates meaningful mental associations is essential for encouraging a shift in mindsets toward environmental engagement. As a community, we need to build deep frames to ensure that this engagement spreads and lasts.

What is framing?

WOULD YOU RATHER BUY MEAT that is 75% fat-free or meat that is 25% fat? When presented with these options, most people showed a strong preference for the 75% fat-free option,[20] even though both choices represented the same product, with only a difference in how the information was framed.

Frames, according to cognitive scientist George Lakoff, are the ways in which information is linked together in our brains. This can include the words, concepts, and relations to other frames that come to mind when you hear a word like "hospital" (e.g., doctor, patient, operating room, scalpel), or your ideas of what should happen in a hospital (e.g., the doctor operates on a patient). Since different frames are active at different times (you wouldn't necessarily think of a swimming pool when you are in a hospital), *framing* is the process of activating certain connections and associations with the experiences and information of the audience.[18] So, saying the word "hospital" is framing if it activates frames like doctor, operating rooms, etc. in someone's mind, whether or not they're activated purposefully.

Framing is the best way to communicate truth

Mental associations are activated—whether intentionally or not—every time we communicate.[18,27] The words or images we choose, the metaphors we employ, and the information we highlight all activate certain mental associations in the minds of our audience. These associations are often deeply rooted as beliefs, values, morals, narratives, and ideologies. They may also present as *cognitive biases*—mental shortcuts people use to process information. All information is processed in the context of the associations that are active in people's minds. Facts that do not resonate with these active associations will be misinterpreted or ignored.

Therefore, shaping your communications to activate specific mental associations is the most effective way to communicate truth to your audience. While some use framing to distort facts and spread misinformation, it is also the best tool that honest communicators have to help people understand the facts. Because all information (facts included) is interpreted according to the active mental associations of the audience, there is no truly "objective" way to convey facts. This belief that we can convey facts objectively is rooted in the idea that humans are "rational," meaning that we can consciously and unemotionally make decisions based on objective facts. This leads to the assumption that providing people with information (presented as "objectively" as possible) will be sufficient to get them to change their behavior or support a policy. This *information deficit model* is a flawed way of seeing the world; it is ineffective to present the facts about issues without framing them by appealing to deeply held mental associations that connect with our values and morals.[27]

Framing is both a short- and long-term strategy

It is common to mistake framing for "spinning" and assume that quickly rewording a message will be sufficient to change the minds of millions. However, while short-term framing can be highly successful in certain contexts, a long-term outlook on framing is required in many instances. This is because framing is effective when practitioners activate specific ***deep frames*** (our most deeply held mental associations) to affect how important issues are understood and acted upon.

Let's take the commonly used phrase "tax relief" as an example. The phrase creates and reinforces the idea that paying taxes is a painful burden from which we must be relieved. The phrase "tax relief" is a ***surface frame*** that is effective because it triggers deep frames—in this case, it taps into the American narrative about the need to be relieved of the burden of unjust government overreach. We might try to create our own catchy slogan (surface frame) to counter "tax relief," such as "national investment," to tap into values such as fairness and equality (deep frames). However, just creating this slogan would likely not be enough. Although the slogan would activate mental associations, it might not activate the ones intended; "national investment" may cause someone to remember that they haven't yet set up a retirement account, or may even activate a different deep frame that sees government services as commodities to be bought rather than as the rights of every citizen. For the slogan to become associated with values such as fairness and equality, we would have to repeatedly explain that taxes are like an investment in a country and that it is only fair that everyone pays for the benefits and services they receive. Connections between surface and deep frames can take years and a lot of repetition to form, which is why effective, deliberate framing isn't just "spinning" an issue. Where a connection between a surface frame and a deep frame doesn't already exist, a longer-term effort is required before we can start using catchy slogans to instantly convey our message.

In this Building Block, we discuss both short- and long-term aspects of framing. We provide guidance on how to deal with anti-environmental frames. We also provide advice on how you can intentionally frame for existing mental associations, such as by using existing environmental frames, appealing to values, framing uncertainty carefully, using well-chosen metaphors, and either triggering or avoiding cognitive biases. Finally, we make the case for a sustained, united effort to build and repeat frames that activate environmental values, beliefs, and actions. In this chapter we detail how framing works and how to leverage it in your communications, but it's important to note that framing is present in all of our Building Blocks. See the end of this chapter for an overview on how framing pairs with each Building Block.

Principles and Shifters for the ASSOCIATIONS Building Block

Avoid Mental Associations that Impede Environmental Action

Don't repeat the wrong message
Acknowledge skepticism, misinformation, uncertainty, and probability prudently

Connect with Existing Mental Associations

Use existing environmental frames
Frame for values, identities, and norms
Use metaphors for the big picture
Frame for cognitive biases

Change Mental Associations Over Time

Select the environmental frames that trigger deep frames
Test your frames
Repeat a unified message

 Avoid Mental Associations that Impede Environmental Action

For decades, groups that oppose environmental protection have developed frames that cast doubt on environmental threats such as climate change. These frames are widely used in public discourse, and unfortunately, they are rarely countered or challenged in an equally effective way. We must build our own equivalently ubiquitous frames, which takes time. In the meantime, we should stop using language that triggers the mental associations that impede environmental action.

⚙ Don't repeat the wrong message

Denying a frame activates the frame.
—George Lakoff, Distinguished Professor of
Cognitive Science and Linguistics

One easy way to combat deleterious frames right now? Stop using them.

Why? Our brains operate by connecting and categorizing information. When neurons (brain cells) are activated at the same time, their connection strengthens so that they may be more easily coactivated in the future.[17]

- If you see a dog on a leash, the cells associated with "dog" and "leash" will fire in your brain.

If the cells continue to fire together, the connection between them eventually becomes so strong that the activation of one set of cells will automatically activate the other set. Remember: "Neurons that fire together, wire together."[14]

- Now, if you see a leash, you may think of a dog even if you don't see a dog nearby.

Our brain cells will make these connections every time they fire together, even in the context of a denial or negation.

- Constantly repeating the phrase "a dog is not a cat" will cause the brain cells for "dog" and "cat" to form a connection, even though the phrase itself is designed to separate them.

This applies to environmental frames as well: repeating anti-environmental frames, even to negate them, only serves to strengthen those frames.

> Repeating anti-environmental frames, even to negate them, only serves to strengthen those frames.

ASSOCIATIONS

Climate Change or Global Warming?

"Global warming" was initially the most popular term to refer to the phenomenon of increased average temperature observed since the Industrial Revolution. This changed in 2002 when Republican strategist Frank Luntz advised the Bush administration to use the term "climate change" instead of "global warming." In his memo, Luntz said: "While global warming has catastrophic connotations attached to it, climate change suggests a more controllable and less emotional challenge." After that memo was sent, the term "climate change" became more and more frequently used, until it overtook "global warming," for progressives and conservatives alike.[17]

Should we try to go back to saying "global warming," then? Probably not. The term "global warming" is in itself problematic. By implying that the only consequence of greenhouse gas emissions is the planet getting hotter, it can cast uncertainty (how are longer winters caused by global warming?). In fact, research suggests that anti-environmentalists have returned to the use of "global warming" over "climate change" because it more easily supports the idea that the whole concept is a hoax.[12,19]

What about "climate crisis?" Some have suggested that we should instead use "climate crisis" to emphasize the urgency of the situation without resorting to oversimplified warming analogies. However, others have criticized emergency framing because it instills fear, rather than hope, which can capture short-term attention, but can be counterproductive to sustaining actions over the long term. See OPTIMISM: Building Block Chapter 7 for more on fear-based messaging and why we should avoid it.

So, what term should we use? Because the term "climate change" is widely used and now is the default way that many people understand and communicate about what is happening to our planet, we recommend using it. The fact that we must use an imperfect term is a learning opportunity: cases like this demonstrate the need for a coordinated effort on the part of environmental organizations to be proactive, rather than reactive, about framing environmental issues.

Examples for avoiding anti-environmental frames

Below are some suggestions for ways to avoid using anti-environmental frames. Although these suggestions are limited to climate change, the concepts can apply to many environmental issues.

Table 2.9.1: Evaluating the Language of Climate Change

Don't Use	Why
"Climate debate"	This suggests that there is a legitimate debate between two interpretations of data. Instead, state that "the vast majority of scientists and most Americans agree that climate change is human-caused, and it is happening now." This can also reinforce that it is the norm to be concerned about climate change, which we discuss further in BELONGING: Building Block Chapter 1.
"Climate change is not a hoax / fraud / lie."	Repeating this phrase just strengthens the association between "climate change" and "hoax."
"Climate change is real."	By repeating that climate change is real, you draw attention to outlying opinions. Consider the BBC's position on climate change coverage: "To achieve impartiality, you do not need to include outright deniers of climate change in BBC coverage, in the same way you would not have someone denying that Manchester United won 2–0 last Saturday."[10] Rather than spending time debating legitimacy, focus on consequences and mitigating actions.
"Alarmist / Alarmism"	The term "alarmist" has been used to discredit those who are concerned about climate change, painting them as people who are "crying wolf" unnecessarily. Other related terms include "warmist," "believer," and "catastrophist."[11] Don't repeat a negative frame—even to negate it.

⚙ Acknowledge skepticism, misinformation, uncertainty, and probability prudently

It is often impossible to avoid skepticism, misinformation, uncertainty, and probability altogether when dealing with environmental issues. Here we detail some ways that you can acknowledge complexities without creating unnecessary doubt.

Don't dwell on skepticism

If there is controversy around your issue and you fail to mention it, you can come off as manipulative and untrustworthy. Instead, acknowledge the controversy but stick to your frame, and don't repeat counter-productive frames.

Use a truth sandwich to counter misinformation or falsehoods

When countering falsehoods, a **truth sandwich** can be effective. Begin with a truth (the first piece of information in a communication establishes the frame), then paraphrase the falsehood (while repeating as little of its language as possible), and finish on another element of truth (always repeat truths more than lies).[24] For example, you could say: "The vast majority of scientists agree that climate change is already happening. Some people are trying to cast doubt about this even though there is strong consensus. The evidence is overwhelming that climate change is serious, human activity is responsible, there are solutions, and we are the ones that can fix it."

Avoid triggering uncertainty

Uncertainty is inevitable in scientific predictions of the future, such as the consequences of climate change. Precise communication requires us to state what *could* happen, or what is most *likely* to happen, rather than what *will* happen. This precision comes with a cost: "most likely" and "could" express uncertainty, and humans are averse to uncertainty.[25] Uncertainty can undermine our sense of control, which can, in turn, trigger avoidance and denial of the entire message.

Additionally, we may not feel that there's a need to act if the consequences of an environmental issue are uncertain—if sea levels *may* rise, then there is a chance they may not. If there is a climate "debate," we can proceed with our current behaviors until the scientists "figure it out." Groups invested in climate denial often capitalize on our discomfort with uncertainty, overstating disagreements among scientists and encouraging their audience to doubt the science altogether.[27]

Many environmental communicators simply sidestep uncertainty.[28] However, messages that oversimplify what people are seeing may engender skepticism, especially when forecasts that are presented as certain do not come to pass. Expressing uncertainty without triggering avoidance is challenging. Here are some basic rules of thumb:

- Don't use frames such as "debate" that trigger uncertainty.
- When communicating uncertainty, focus on specific, local consequences (see ATTACHMENT: Building Block Chapter 4, for more on why).
- When communicating uncertainty, focus on the solvability of the challenge (see OPTIMISM: Building Block Chapter 7, for more on efficacy messages).

• • •

Now that you have some ideas for how to avoid using deleterious frames, you will next learn how to craft frames that tap into existing mental associations that will encourage positive engagement with environmental action.

 Connect with Existing Mental Associations

While creating new deep environmental frames will take concerted effort over time, you can frame your communications to activate the existing mental associations in the minds of your audience.

Use existing environmental frames

There are many frames relating to environmental issues that have already been tested. Many are related to climate change and they are designed to engage a broad range of audiences. Below we present these frames, along with their strengths and weaknesses.

Table 2.9.2: Existing Environmental Frames

Economic cost of inaction	Inaction on climate change will cost the United States alone hundreds of billions of dollars by the end of the 21st century.[36] This frame is particularly effective with audiences interested in risk management, such as investors, money managers, and real estate firms.[6]
Economic development[27]	Environmental challenges can be reframed as opportunities for economic growth by using phrases like "innovative energy technology" and "sustainable economic prosperity." This frame can gain traction with labor advocates and conservatives who are driven by market opportunities, job growth, and tax benefits.
Environmental justice[5,9]	The environmental justice frame emphasizes that environmental issues disproportionately affect people depending on their race, gender, and class, among other social, cultural, and economic attributes. This frame has rallied a diverse group of supporters into what has become a robust social movement that revolves around a core value: equity. See ATTACHMENT: Building Block Chapter 4 for more on core values.

ASSOCIATIONS

Table 2.9.2: *Cont.*

Food security[37]	Framing climate change as imminently threatening to the world's food security can tap into a topic that's close to home for many—putting food on the table. Climate change already threatens agricultural production and fisheries. Strained natural resources such as land, water, and energy will also increase food prices. Some effects can already be felt (and were recently highlighted by the COVID-19 pandemic, which caused a rapid increase in food insecurity, partly due to the vulnerability of our food systems).
National security[37]	Framing climate change or loss of natural resources as a national security challenge can engage a wider audience, including conservatives, that may otherwise be uninterested in environmental issues. For example, more extreme weather caused by climate change increases migration from displaced populations, which can lead to border conflicts that strain government military operations.
Public health[27]	Appeals about climate change, pollution, or other environmental challenges may be more relatable if we connect them to familiar health problems. For example, this frame could emphasize the likelihood of climate change causing more frequent pandemics or an increase in allergies and asthma, especially among children and elderly populations.
Redemption[32]	This frame focuses on the idea that everyone makes mistakes, but we can all work to overcome them. For example, the work to repair the damage to the ozone layer can be expressed as a redemption effort on the part of a bipartisan group of people, from policymakers to everyday citizens, who are banding together to reverse the damage we created. We should be careful, however, as a redemption frame may trigger feelings of guilt, which can backfire, as we discuss in OPTIMISM: Building Block Chapter 7.
Resilience[23]	Building resilient ecological and social systems is critical to help ensure the safety and longevity of our society on a planet increasingly fraught with environmental challenges. Rising sea levels, for example, can be mitigated through restoration initiatives that reinforce natural infrastructure such as dunes and wetlands that help to protect coastal communities, increasing their resilience to environmental threats. This frame has been used by policymakers to shape progressive agendas on climate change adaptation.

As practitioners, you can select from these frames when communicating with your audience. Which frames you choose may depend on many factors: the issue you are trying to address, your audience's characteristics, or contextual factors like location or current events. For example, you can pair frames with current events to amplify their effects, like using the public health frame when the air is polluted to make the frame not only relatable but also available. No matter what, you should test how your selected frames perform with your audience before deploying them. We discuss a method for testing frames in more detail below.

⚙ Frame for values, identities, and norms

Tying your message to what your audience cares about is essential. Draw on the existing values of your audience to make your frames strong and persuasive. In fact, it has been argued that framing is only successful when the message appeals to deeply held values.[2,17] Additionally, you can frame your message to draw on the deeply held identities of your audience (see IDENTITY: Building Block Chapter 6) or on the norms of those people your audience cares about (see BELONGING: Building Block Chapter 1). For more on common values, morals, and ideologies and how they relate to the environment, see ATTACHMENT: Building Block Chapter 4.

⚙ Use metaphors for the big picture

Many environmental issues involve *systems*: interconnected networks of complex variables with often indirect links between causes and effects. It can be challenging to communicate about these systems to non-scientific audiences because systems thinking is something that humans struggle with in general.[17] But fortunately, *metaphors* are frames that make both systems and solutions easier to conceptualize by drawing on our knowledge of more familiar ideas. For example, saying that crime is a "beast" makes people want to fight it with force, and they are more likely to support measures like increasing the number of police officers. Characterizing crime as a "virus," however, is more likely to trigger systems thinking; viruses make communities "sick" just as crime does. When this metaphor was tested, people exposed to it were more likely to want to look for and address the root causes of crime, just as they would support programs like health and hygiene education and outbreak containment of a virus.[33]

Metaphors are pervasive in our language and culture, though we often do not notice them. We conceive of time as a valuable, finite resource: you can spend time or you can waste time.[16] We often conceive of the human mind as a machine: it can be operational or rusty, your wheels can be turning, or you can break down. Metaphors are essential to the way we comprehend our world, so they can be powerful vehicles (metaphor intended) to help audiences understand and connect to environmental concepts.

We have many metaphors for various environmental challenges at our disposal. For example, the "ecological footprint" is a popular way to convey the idea that each person has an impact on the environment, and that we can strive to leave as little impact as possible. Additionally, describing a national park as part of the "backbone" of the national park system encourages people to think of a park as an essential component of a larger system, while describing a park as a "pearl" merely emphasizes that it is beautiful.[35]

However, simply employing a metaphor is not a guarantee of effective communication. Consider the "Earth as spaceship" metaphor,[34] intended to signify that earth is all we have—a fragile life-support system afloat in the vast cosmos. When this metaphor was tested, more people had a negative response to this metaphor than a positive one, possibly because it made the earth seem man-made and artificial. They also thought scientists were more likely to use it than people like farmers, businesspeople, or religious leaders, which suggests that its potential to spread may be limited. Finally, the metaphor did not perform well in eliciting systems thinking. This is why it's important to always evaluate the effectiveness of our metaphors, whether these are metaphors that already exist, or are ones created anew to explain a particular issue.

So what makes a successful metaphor? Consider the following example by the FrameWorks Institute.[38]

"The oceans regulate the climate system the way your heart regulates the flow of blood throughout your body. The heart sustains the body by controlling the circulation of blood, making sure the right amount gets to all parts of the body—not too much and not too little. The oceans act as the climate's heart, sustaining the climate by controlling the circulation of things like heat and humidity.

"The oceans are the heart of a circulatory system that moves heat and moisture through all parts of the climate system, including oceans, land, and atmosphere. As the heart of this circulatory system, the oceans regulate the climate by helping to control the earth's temperature. By absorbing heat from the sun and emitting it back into the atmosphere, the oceans maintain a regular flow of heat and stabilize the earth's temperature. And ocean currents and winds move heat and moisture to different parts of the world, which keeps the climate stable."

This "Climate's Heart" metaphor has several characteristics that made it successful when tested.[38] These characteristics are detailed as best practices below.

Root it in a system that your audience understands well

Pick a subject for the metaphor that your audience is familiar with. We must be able to refer to what is familiar to understand what is unfamiliar. For example, if your audience is not familiar with how a car engine works, it wouldn't make sense to explain the concept of an ecosystem as a car engine with many working parts.

"Climate's Heart" brings to mind a system that is familiar to us (our own bodies), and it helps us conceptualize the ocean's crucial role in regulating things like temperature and humidity, just as the heart regulates blood flow within the body.

Provide enough detail to link cause and effect

Ensure that the metaphor provides an adequate amount of detail and provides the audience with the background necessary to quickly and easily understand all the links between causes and effects in a system. When people don't understand these links, they may fall back on their default beliefs or become unconsciously creative in inventing explanations.

When testing "Climate's Heart," researchers found that the explanation of how the ocean regulates heat and humidity increased people's ability to connect the ocean to the climate system as a whole. Without that piece, people would understand that the ocean was key to the climate system, but not how. This may limit discussions of solutions.

Facilitate solutions thinking

Another feature of successful metaphors is that they facilitate thinking about how the problem might be solved.

By relating the ocean to a part of our bodies for which health is extremely important, "Climate's Heart" equips its audience for discussions about preventative care.

Make the metaphor easy for your audience to communicate

Refine your metaphor until it is communicable: your audience should be able to remember it and explain it to others without misconstruing the meaning as it is spread.

When "Climate's Heart" was tested, participants were able to teach it to others, and the core concepts did not get lost in translation.

Shut down misinformation

Your metaphor should counter frames that allow for misinformation or confusion. It should help your audience understand why some default ways of thinking about the problem or even anti-environmental arguments don't actually work.

For example, "Climate's Heart" helped counter several unproductive frameworks, such as the idea that "nature is a self-correcting model." Just as the heart can't always repair itself and therefore needs to be taken care of, so too does the ocean.

• • •

Additionally, your metaphors should:

- Tell a story; metaphors that tell a story are more likely to be engaging than those that don't. See the "Tell a Story" principle in ATTACHMENT: Building Block Chapter 4 for more.
- Use vivid and attention-grabbing imagery by drawing on subjects that come to mind easily. See VIVID: Building Block Chapter 5 for more.

Strategic use of metaphors can activate helpful mental associations by relating new information to something the audience already understands and cares about. Metaphors can therefore frame complex ideas in a way that's easier to understand, ultimately helping people to engage with productive solutions to problems. Enduring, communicable metaphors engage deeply held mental associations and connect them in new ways, which, over time, can reshape the way society sees environmental issues.

> Enduring, communicable metaphors engage deeply held mental associations and connect them in new ways, which, over time, can reshape the way society sees environmental issues.

⚙ Frame for cognitive biases

We often use mental shortcuts to navigate our world. In the case of cognitive biases, these shortcuts result in predictable mistakes. Many cognitive biases can be triggered or avoided depending on how communications are framed. Below are some examples of how framing can take cognitive biases into account. We also discuss cognitive biases more thoroughly in FOUNDATIONS: Process Chapter 1.

Use anchoring

Anchoring can play a key role in how we perceive subsequent information.[31] On a daily basis, we make estimates by starting from an initial value, based on past experience, and then we adjust away from that value, like when we use the price we usually pay for a pair of jeans to determine if the current asking price is reasonable. When we don't have past experience as a guide, we tend to anchor on to the first piece of information that we receive, even when that information isn't relevant. We tend to rely too heavily on our anchors, and insufficiently adjust when we make decisions. As practitioners, we can incorporate anchors into our communications to promote the desired environmental action.

Making Shift Happen: Anchoring to Save Seabirds

When visitors to the San Francisco Exploratorium were asked if they were willing to donate money to save seabirds from offshore oil spills, they offered $64 on average.[8] However, when researchers introduced a low anchor by asking if they would be willing to donate $5, the average donations dropped to $20. And when they introduced a high anchor of $400, average donations rose to $143. This study illustrates that the design of a message can determine the anchors that people use, thereby influencing behavior.

Leverage loss aversion when appropriate

Generally speaking, we hate to lose more than we like to gain—a cognitive bias known as *loss aversion*.[13] In other words, we hate losing $100 more than we enjoy gaining $100. Environmental practitioners can frame issues to engage loss aversion. For example, when offering solutions that require an up front capital investment, emphasize what your audience would be losing if they did not make the investment. We created messaging like this for a local community energy services corporation: "We are offering a solar upgrade. Without this upgrade, you are losing $1500 per year."

Since people tend to be more motivated to prevent a loss than they are to achieve an equivalent gain, when people face a potential loss, they are much more willing to take risks, particularly if the risk gives them the chance to avoid the loss altogether.[13] Loss aversion can lead to pronounced behaviors such as risk-taking and cheating,[30] thus it is important to be aware of how loss aversion might motivate your audience.

While loss framing has been effective at swaying opinion and motivating action across environmental issues such as climate change and saving energy,[7] this is not

ASSOCIATIONS

always the case, and it is not necessarily always more effective than using gain frames. In recent years, some research has suggested that the effectiveness of loss aversion framing is nuanced and varies across audiences and contexts. Factors such as how much someone stands to lose or gain might make a difference in how they respond.[26] For example, loss frames may not be as effective when someone doesn't perceive much personal loss or risk from not taking action. On the other hand, gain frames can be effective when the actions you want to encourage have low risk and the rewards seem concrete and likely.[22] Finally, when it comes to climate change, a loss-framed climate message may be more persuasive at changing attitudes, but a gain-framed message can be more effective at actually mobilizing political action.[21] Given these nuances, gain vs. loss framing is an area where testing your messages is especially important.

Making Shift Happen: Loss Aversion as a Conservation Tool

Participants in a Southern California study were more likely to support a proposed program to manage an invasive pig species when it was framed as the prevention of further losses of native species and habitats, as opposed to equivalent gains like the potential benefits to those same native ecosystems and species.[4] By leveraging loss aversion, practitioners can increase support for their initiatives.

Loss frames can easily carry a "doom and gloom" message, potentially deterring your audience if the fear of loss is paralyzing or de-motivating them through a diminished sense of efficacy. Triggering loss aversion, like any fear-based or crisis messaging, may be better suited to one-time behaviors than it is to sustained change.[1] It is key to pair loss-framed messages with actions that suggest to the audience how they can prevent or mitigate the loss. See OPTIMISM: Building Block Chapter 7 for more on how to do this.

Pair loss aversion and anchoring

Whether we perceive something as a loss or a gain depends on our starting point, or reference point.[13] For example, if you started with $10 and paid $5 as a fine, you would consider it a loss, while another person who started with $0 and received $5 as a reward would consider it a gain, even though both of you ended up with $5. As environmental practitioners, one way we can invoke loss or gain frames is by using anchoring to influence our audience's reference points. For example, instead of saying "if we do nothing, there will only be 200 Sunda tigers left in five years," which anchors the audience to the low number, say "if we do nothing, the Sunda tiger population of 400 will be reduced to only 200 in five years" to set their baseline.

 ## Change Mental Associations Over Time

As this book was being finalized, the authors were all working from home to prevent the spread of COVID-19. Even though the world's response was certainly not free of mistakes, the massive, immediate behavior change on the part of both governments and individuals suggests an enormous potential for rapid change.[29] What if we had the frames in place to help policymakers and the public understand and respond to environmental issues as rapidly as they do to a pandemic? Developing these frames will require a long-term effort.

When framing for short-term behavior change, practitioners are constrained by the deep frames that are already the default ways that our audience sees the world. For example, if our audience is unaccustomed to thinking about taxation through the values of fairness and equality (as discussed in the introduction), it may be difficult in the short term to use or craft frames that both draw on these values and are still compatible with the audience's existing mental associations. This is where long-term effort is needed: by selecting and crafting strong frames that reinforce certain mental associations, and then repeating these frames over time, we can actually change the default mental associations that shape the way our audience interprets the world.

> By selecting and crafting strong frames that reinforce certain mental associations, and then repeating these frames over time, we can actually change the default mental associations that shape the way our audience interprets the world.

⚙ Select the environmental frames that trigger deep frames

The first step to building our own frames is to identify the deep frames that we are trying to connect with and strengthen in our audience. What are the systems that we are trying to help our audience understand? Strong environmental frames will contain metaphors or stories that capture the audience's attention and align with their deeply held values and morals. As discussed above, this process is more than just coming up with sayings or slogans. This effort will require collaboration, research, testing, and repetition before deep environmental frames become ubiquitous in public conversations.[17]

Fortunately, we don't have to start from scratch. In fact, we recommend using existing environmental frames when you can, because then you are repeating the same message as other organizations. However, in some cases, you may find that you need to modify existing environmental frames or create entirely new ones if the deep frames you wish to strengthen can't be effectively activated by existing environmental frames. If you do need to create a new environmental frame, you can find a discussion of values, morals, and ideologies and how they relate to the environment in ATTACHMENT: Building Block Chapter 4 that will help you brainstorm.

⚙ Test your frames

A strong frame must appeal to what motivates an audience, how they feel, and what they value. Surprises are inevitable; even if you understand your audience, you can't be certain how they will react to a message. To prevent disseminating a message that is doomed to fail, test it! We recommend the following method for testing frames.

Make it widely understandable

Using DESIGN: Process Chapter 4 as a guide, start with prototyping your potential frames. While evaluating your prototypes, consider the following questions, which are adapted from what the FrameWorks Institute uses to evaluate metaphors:[38]

- How well does your audience understand the frame?
- Does the frame help your audience perceive the challenge in a new way?
- Does the frame help your audience to process and discuss the challenge?
- Does the frame "fail" anywhere—does your audience fall back on undesired frames at any point in the process?

Experiment

Next, further refine your list of frames through a series of experiments by randomly assigning participants into control groups and treatment groups, and comparing the results. You can use experiments to test different frames or different variations of the same frame. Give all groups questions designed to measure their understanding of critical concepts and compare performance across groups. See METHODS: Process Chapter 6 for more on how to design and run experiments.

Alternatively, you can use focus groups and present multiple frames to the same group. This allows you to elicit direct feedback about how frames compare to each other. However, this approach is not as well-suited to testing whether frames help people understand issues because a person's knowledge will be affected by the first frame that they encounter. That means that for subsequent frames, you will not be able to tell how that person learned the information.

Ensure it's communicable

For a frame to be successful and scale, your audience needs to be able to share it faithfully—it must withstand the telephone game! The FrameWorks Institute recommends asking someone to whom you have taught the frame to teach it to another person.[38] Then, ask each participant questions designed to test their understanding. Continue through multiple "generations" to see if anything has been lost in translation.

• • •

Even if this full testing process is impractical for you or your organization, we encourage you to perform as many of these tests as possible before deploying any new frames.

> Have you tested any frames or metaphors? We'd love to publish your results on our website! To help us build a database of environmental frames, please send your results to hello@makingshifthappenbook.com.

Repeat a unified message

Once you have tested your frames, it's important to repeat them to your audience as much and as often as possible.

Connections between neurons only form if they fire together repeatedly; therefore, we can only build new frames if we repeat them often. Repetition can make messages easier to remember, and can even subconsciously lead people to have more positive regard for that message, in a phenomenon known as the *mere exposure effect*.[3,39] Establishing new frames will take a concerted effort. We need to present a united front by aligning our frames with those of other environmental communicators and by repeatedly exposing the audience to our message in as many contexts and locations as possible. At the very least, employing a unified set of well-designed frames now can be a solid insurance policy for the future. Doing this can supplement current change initiatives and lend the environmentalists of the future an upper hand as they work to improve society and the planet.

Conclusion

Emotion and unconscious thought play key roles in our ability to function, and we rely on our deeply held frames to help us process new information. The way information is framed affects the way messages are received, understood, and acted upon.

We believe that a sustained effort to change the way society thinks about the environment is essential to solving many of the world's large-scale environmental challenges. Framing is key to achieving this, but will not be effective until we can use surface frames to trigger deep frames and values that motivate action. This will in turn require coordinated work to create these frames and narratives, which must be repeated by as many people as possible in order to create the necessary mental associations. Once this is accomplished, environmental actions will seem like common sense because they will be ingrained in our deep frames and value systems.

Framing in other Building Blocks

All messages are framed in some way, intentionally or not. Because of this, framing plays a major role throughout our Building Blocks:

- **BELONGING:** We can frame desired behaviors as being the socially acceptable norm, and avoid drawing attention to instances when people aren't engaging in the desired behavior.

- **EASY:** Repeat frames that show how environmental behaviors are accessible and easy to adopt. Don't repeat frames that suggest that environmental behaviors are always inconvenient or difficult.

- **HABITS:** Even the way we set up a room (e.g., when we place cues to remind us to do a behavior) can evoke mental associations that then trigger habitual behaviors.

- **ATTACHMENT:** By framing your messages to engage your audience's emotions and align with their deeply held values, morals, and ideologies, you can engender understanding, support, and environmental behavior.

- **VIVID:** By framing environmental issues and solutions in more concrete, vivid, and less abstract terms, we can capture attention and motivate environmental behavior.

- **IDENTITY:** By carefully choosing our words to highlight different identities, we can inspire certain ways of thinking and behaving in our audience.

- **OPTIMISM:** Framing a message to emphasize solutions can foster efficacy and empower people to engage in environmental behaviors.
- **REWARDS:** We can amplify the existing intrinsic benefits of desired behaviors, and frame incentives so as to magnify their perceived value.
- **LONGEVITY:** By redefining our relationship to the planet, we can change the deep frames that inspire environmental action.

🗒 Your Turn

What are some ways that you can use framing to strengthen your communications? Use the questions below to brainstorm.

Avoid mental associations that impede environmental action

❑ Can you generate a list of words and frames that run counter to desirable environmental behaviors so you can avoid repeating them? What are alternative frames you can use instead?

❑ How can you create a "truth sandwich" around concepts of uncertainty or misinformation?

❑ What are some concrete solutions you can provide your audience in tandem with any messages that convey uncertainty?

Connect with existing mental associations

❑ Are there any existing environmental frames that are persuasive for your audience?

Frame for values, identities, and norms

❑ What are some of your audience's deeply held values and identities, and how can you connect your issue to them?

❑ How can you connect your issue to social norms that are particularly prominent among your audience members?

Use metaphors for the big picture

❑ Can you compare your environmental issue to a system that your audience already understands, like the human body or family/social structures?

❑ Does your metaphor explain the important causes and effects of your issue?

- ❑ How can your metaphor encourage your audience to think about solutions?
- ❑ Are there any metaphors already in use around your issue that align with your audience's values? What are their strengths and weaknesses? Can they be adapted to your specific target audience, or might you need to create new metaphors?

Frame for cognitive biases

- ❑ What information can you provide to your audience as an anchor that might shift their perspective on your issue or even change their behavior?
- ❑ What has your audience lost or what does it stand to lose if they don't take the desired action, and can you highlight that in your messaging?
- ❑ What are some of the potential gains or losses that your audience may realize as a result of the environmental issue, and how might you emphasize these in your communications?
- ❑ How can you test your messaging to see which type of frame is more effective?

Change mental associations over time

- ❑ What are the deep frames that you want to strengthen or build for your audience?
- ❑ Are there existing environmental frames that help strengthen or build your desired deep frames?
- ❑ How can you modify existing environmental frames to help build or strengthen your desired deep frames?
- ❑ Can you test your frames to see if they help your audience understand and discuss the issue?
- ❑ How can you work with other organizations or activists to create unified messaging and consistent frames?

Expanding the self to ensure nature's LONGEVITY

> *Key takeaway:* Through exposure to nature, other-focused emotions, and mindfulness, we can foster a change in our underlying relationship to the environment and its inhabitants and achieve permanent, society-wide environmental stewardship. As advocates, we must also use these tools to take care of ourselves, so that we have the endurance and empathy needed to continue our life's work.

Disconnection from other beings and the whole of nature separates us from our own humanity and impedes lasting change

LONG-TERM MOTIVATION isn't required for many behavioral changes. In fact, this is a key tenet of the *Making Shift Happen* approach—many of the shifters previously discussed are ways of working with people largely "as they are." Practitioners can use targeted shifters to protect the environment in specific ways for as long as the shifter can be sustained. That said, without an underlying change in humanity's relationship to nature that helps us see ourselves as part of—rather than separate from—nature, the behavior changes resulting from other shifters are, to varying degrees, temporary, or at least dependent on continued external application of some kind of shifter.

But what about the type of transformational change that can shift the mindset of an entire society? People need *intrinsic motivation*—motivation that arises from within—to continue to take action for the environment long after the shifter is gone. Unfortunately, our Western tendency toward dualism and separation can suppress our intrinsic motivation to protect the environment we are a part of and upon which we depend. In a society that values productivity and economic output above all else, it's hardly surprising that we find it difficult to slow down, to connect with nature, and even to know ourselves. In addition, we are continuously bombarded with bad news—and, as climate change accelerates, the news will get worse before it gets better. At worst, we may find ourselves isolated in a "bubble" that causes us to lose our empathy and compassion for others and nature. This loss of connection can lower our long-term motivation to care for others and protect our environment, making the barriers to behavior change even harder to overcome.

Transform mindsets via mindfulness, empathy, and compassion

This Building Block discusses how to change mindsets by building intrinsic motivation to protect the environment. Activating intrinsic motivation is essential to creating permanent, transformational changes in how we live on this planet. This is by no means a quick fix, but it is an enduring one. Researchers have consistently found that we can do this by reconnecting with nature, fostering an outward focus, and cultivating empathy, compassion, and mindfulness within ourselves and within our audiences.

By beginning to work the principles of the LONGEVITY Building Block into your initiatives, you may see some immediate increases in effectiveness in addition to long-term benefits. For example, bringing mindfulness practices into a workplace cafeteria initiative may lead to reduced food waste right away, even if it wouldn't result in a full mindset shift until much later. But shifting the mindset of society is a process that takes generations. This means that many of us may not see the full benefits of LONGEVITY shifters during our lifetimes, as the generational time scales are just not aligned with the resources available or with other practical constraints (for example, a political appointee who might want to launch a behavior change initiative may not be in office long enough to see the full effects of their program). However, even if you won't see the impacts right away, by utilizing the following principles, you are laying the foundation for long-lived transformational change in how people see their relationship with and responsibility to the earth.

Principles and Shifters for the LONGEVITY Building Block

Engage with Nature

Get into nature to restore directed attention
Get into nature to reduce psychological distance
View or remember scenes of nature

Foster an "Other-Focus"

Elicit other-directed emotions

Nurture empathy and compassion

Cultivate and Practice Mindfulness

Cultivate mindfulness

Use mindfulness to become aware of our own narratives and to mitigate cognitive biases

Use mindfulness to connect with your audience

Have Compassion for Yourself

 Engage with Nature

Simply put, being in nature makes us feel good. People seem to have an inherent love of nature—think of the delight that young children take in nature by playing in the mud, splashing in the sea, or watching animals. E.O. Wilson calls this inherent love of nature *biophilia*.[59] While outdoor experiences are particularly important for youth, they provide inspiration and deliver benefits to people of all ages.[47] Spending time in nature helps shape our cultural identities, provides us with a sense of place, has positive physiological effects, and promotes our physical well-being.[1,40,52] Nature can also provide us with psychological benefits. For example, taking a walk in a natural environment can reduce rumination on negative thoughts and emotions.[9,49]

Ultimately, being in nature makes most people happier and more willing to engage in prosocial behavior, which in turn makes us even happier: a positive feedback loop.[48] Experiencing nature can foster environmental behavior in two key ways: 1) it can help us replenish our capacity to pay attention, making us better environmental stewards, and 2) it can reduce our sense of being separate from nature, thereby making us more invested in protecting it. Though the systems and norms of our society can make us feel distant from nature, and the time we can spend outside may be constrained by geography and resources, there are many ways we can connect with nature, some of which we discuss here.

✿ Get into nature to restore directed attention

One of the most important benefits of being in nature stems from nature's ability to restore our *directed attention*. Directed attention—also called *voluntary attention*—requires effort, such as when focusing during meetings, or studying.[30] When our directed attention is fatigued, it reduces our capacity to make plans, try new things, make good decisions, and understand complex problems, which can lead to mistakes and poor performance.[30,58]

What does directed *attention fatigue* have to do with environmental stewardship? More than we might immediately think. When our directed attention is fatigued, we may make poor decisions related to the environment, such as forgetting to turn off the water when we brush our teeth, or buying things we don't really need. A policymaker experiencing directed attention fatigue might not conduct sufficient research on an issue, and as a result, could make a decision that ends up negatively affecting the environment. Even environmental practitioners who strive to act in the environment's best interest can't operate at their full potential if their directed attention is depleted. You may, therefore, find that you need to restore your own directed attention, or your audience's, if you need them to remember to take specific steps or think critically.

How can we restore directed attention in ourselves and our audiences? We can restore our capacity for directed attention by engaging in *involuntary attention*, which is attention that feels more like fascination—it requires little to no effort. When we do things like play a sport we love, listen to relaxing music, watch a sunset, or take a walk outside, our involuntary attentiveness to these pleasurable things reduces our mental fatigue by giving our brain a break.[5,26] This in turn regenerates our capacity for directed attention.[29]

Spending time in natural environments provides many opportunities for attention restoration. *Attention Restoration Theory*, originally developed by environmental psychologists Rachel and Stephen Kaplan, proposes that exposure to nature restores our directed attention, thus improving our focus and ability to concentrate.[28,29,30,31] Nature engages our sense of fascination and curiosity, making it easy to engage in involuntary attention.[29] For example, in nature, we engage in involuntary attention by noticing birds chirping and the plants and rocks around us. Even people seated near windows have been shown to exhibit improved executive functioning, which is related to enhanced capacity for attention and reduced mental fatigue.[28] This is especially important in urban environments, as exposure to natural environments is harder to come by and stress levels are generally higher.[34] Yet even within urban areas, residents who live in close proximity to parks and grassy areas have been found to demonstrate improved mental functioning and effectiveness compared to those who do not live near these natural areas.[33] In one study, researchers in Melbourne found that simply looking at a green roof (a roof with grass or other vegetation growing on it) for a short period of time (a 40-second "microbreak") can restore attention while a person is completing a task.[35]

There are endless ways to restore your own or your audience's attention in nature—be creative! For example, the next time you are out in nature, try imagining you are from another planet and that you are seeing nature for the first time. Walking through natural areas and noticing your surroundings or engaging in other pleasurable activities can help you and your audience regenerate the directed attention you need to plan and implement environmental protection initiatives. Taking breaks in nature can even mean stepping outside for just a few minutes. Try taking some of your favorite activities outside, like crafting, drawing, reading, or spending time with friends. Stop every now and then to notice what is around you—what do you see, hear, and smell? You don't need a national park nearby to do this; all you need is to get outdoors—whether that be in a courtyard, backyard, garden, or city park.

⚙️ Get into nature to reduce psychological distance

Separation and polarization are root causes of most conflicts, and conflicts between people and nature are no exception. To break down the barriers that make it seem like we are separate from nature, we can spend more time in nature and increase our awareness of it. Experiencing nature is one way to reduce our *psychological distance* from it, a concept we discuss in ATTACHMENT: Building Block Chapter 4.

Research and experience show us that when people feel connected to the natural world, they are more likely to engage in behaviors that have a positive effect on the environment.[4,39] Contact with nature also contributes to the ability to feel and express concern for other species.[10] Positive feelings, such as compassion, for other living creatures and for nature itself are powerful motivators for adopting long-lasting, positive environmental behaviors. One study showed that students who had many positive associations with nature were less likely to accept a free

> Positive feelings, such as compassion, for other living creatures and for nature itself are powerful motivators for adopting long-lasting, positive environmental behaviors.

plastic bag (representing an environmentally damaging behavior) offered as part of the study and reported taking part in positive environmental behaviors.[20]

To help rekindle our inherent connection to nature, try the following:

- Find a comfortable place to rest in nature, such as the crook of a tree, and enjoy the feeling of being held by the earth.
- Whether you are outside or indoors, reflect on nature (e.g., plants, pets, creatures) as being connected to you rather than as objects that are separate from you.
- While immersed in nature, note all of the ways that nature enriches your life—the air you breathe, the food you eat—and express gratitude.

⚙ View or remember scenes of nature

It's not always possible to get our audiences out in nature, so consider the use of photos to increase their sense of connection to nature. Though directly experiencing nature has been shown to have the most dramatic effects, research also shows that even just viewing scenes of nature is associated with self-reported feelings of connectedness.[39] Additionally, consider including photos that show (or imply) the presence of people in the natural world to demonstrate harmony with nature. Studies show that viewing humans in nature can emphasize our connection to nature and contribute to enhanced concern for the environment.[44] By using photos and stories to increase awareness of our connection to nature, we can begin to break down the illusion of separation that is so ingrained in mainstream culture, and that causes us to overlook the effects of our behavior toward the environment.

Prompting people to remember beloved experiences in nature can reconnect them to their love for it. Remembering these positive experiences can help stimulate compassion and empathy for the natural world. People can be prompted to recall a time they felt peace, awe, or joy in the natural world—focusing on the physical sensations, emotions, and positive thoughts they experienced—or to reflect on times they learned something or felt transformed by experiences in nature.

Foster an "Other-Focus"

Eliciting an "other-focus" through awe, gratitude, empathy, and compassion can expand our circle of care to all people affected by environmental problems and to nature itself. Other-focused motives and emotions (such as awe and gratitude) allow us to look outside ourselves, focus attention on the bigger picture, and take a long-term perspective.[11] When we feel empathy and

> Eliciting an "other-focus" through awe, gratitude, empathy, and compassion can expand our circle of care to all people affected by environmental problems and to nature itself.

compassion for other creatures and for nature itself, we are also more likely to care for and protect them. All of these shifts in perspective lead to increased positive environmental behaviors and help us build bridges to those with whom we may not see eye to eye.

Elicit other-directed emotions

Emotions can be self-directed—like the negative emotions of shame, fear, and guilt discussed in OPTIMISM: Building Block Chapter 7.[12] Intense self-focused emotions like these cause us to turn inward and focus on our current needs at the expense of attending to the big picture.

On the other hand, emotions can be positive and *other-directed*, such as gratitude and awe. These positive, other-directed emotions tend to broaden our focus to things that transcend the self—such as other people, other beings, and even the earth itself—and produce feelings of interconnectedness.[43] These emotions contribute to a long-term perspective that helps us to see the self as part of a larger, interconnected system.[11] For example, experimental evidence shows that feelings of awe can reduce people's focus on social hierarchies (thus making them feel more a part of, rather than separate from, other beings) which in turn is associated with more ecologically friendly behavior.[61]

Find ways to elicit these warm, positive, other-focused feelings: ask people to write about what they're grateful for in nature; guide them to remember experiences they have had in nature when they felt wonder, peace, or a sense of wisdom; elicit awe with images of Earth's beauty from outer space; or foster connectedness with experiential activities, like a gardening class or some of the mindfulness practices recommended in this Building Block.[43]

⚙ Nurture empathy and compassion

Our task must be to free ourselves by widening our circle of compassion to embrace all living creatures and the whole of nature and its beauty.

—Albert Einstein

While **empathy** refers to feeling with and taking the perspective of another, **compassion** refers to the desire to help and care for another.[55] Originally, as empathy became a subject of interest for scientists studying behavior change, research focused on understanding its role in motivating prosocial behavior toward other humans. Now, we know that feeling empathy for nature can generate a positive relationship with the environment. Studies have found notable correlations between self-reported feelings of empathy and favorable environmental attitudes, intentions, actions, and concerns.[7,46] In addition, researchers have found that participants who reported high levels of empathy after seeing negative human-caused consequences in nature also reported engaging in pro-environmental behaviors more often, consistent with other findings.[7,32,46]

In quantifying the relationship between empathy and environmentally beneficial behavior, a number of studies have measured the predictive power of empathy on participants' financial contributions to environmental causes. Using a widely accepted empathy metric called the Interpersonal Reactivity Index (IRI), one study found that participants who displayed empathetic tendencies donated larger amounts to environmental causes compared to those who did not display these tendencies.[15] In another study, those with the highest donations to environmental organizations demonstrated an ability to share the emotions of people less fortunate than themselves, to adopt others' point of view, and to experience distress in response to others' suffering.[32] These studies highlight the connection between having empathetic tendencies and engaging in environmentally beneficial behaviors.

Cultivate empathy and compassion through perspective taking

Empathy can be cultivated in a number of ways, most notably through the act of **perspective taking**, or seeing through the eyes of someone or something other than oneself.[53] Practitioners can elicit feelings of compassion and empathy through language, photos, and videos that encourage people to take the perspective of the subjects. For example, a study at the Autónoma University in Madrid, Spain, demonstrated that perspective taking can augment feelings of empathy toward nature. When shown images of trees felled by logging or a bird killed by oil pollutants, participants who were asked to imagine what it was like to be a tree in a logged forest or a bird covered in oil reported higher levels of empathy than those who were asked to remain objective.[7]

We can begin the process of building empathy and a desire to protect nature through perspective taking at an early age. A 2016 study found that preschoolers who were asked to role-play and take on the perspective of plants and animals, as well as to read nature-based books and go on nature excursions, showed a deeper caring for the emotional well-being of the natural world than kids who did not perform these actions.[36]

Cultivate empathy and compassion by personalizing nature

Personalizing nature, or associating human characteristics with the natural environment, is another method linked to increased connectedness to nature.[56] We talk about the planet having lungs and a circulatory system to help people understand the role forests and oceans play in maintaining life as we know it. John Muir wrote about the "childless sequoias" as he mourned for the forests.[42] Al Gore stated that "the planet has a fever."[23] As a practitioner, you can amplify the effectiveness of your communications by personalizing nature in your messages. See ASSOCIATIONS: Building Block Chapter 9 to learn more about framing and metaphors.

Making Shift Happen: Using Personalization of Nature to Inspire Positive Environmental Action

Would you act on behalf of Mr. Earth? A 2013 study examined the impact of personalization on feelings of connection with nature.[56] They did so by comparing newsletters discussing "Nature" and the "Current Condition of Nature" with one that referred to the Earth with personal pronouns (i.e., "Current Condition of Mr. Nature"). Using personal pronouns had an effect: participants who received the newsletter using personification demonstrated a significantly stronger connection to nature than those in the control groups, likely because assigning pronouns like "Mr." to nature led to an association between the environment and human beings. Practitioners can use personification to help their audience build a stronger connection to nature and the environment.

• • •

Include communications and practices that foster compassion and empathy as integral parts of new initiatives to positively affect underlying attitudes, concerns, and behaviors toward the natural environment. Environmental groups such as Amazon Watch and the Indigenous Environmental Network have put these principles into practice, basing their work in land and ecosystem preservation on underlying values of compassion and respect for the sacredness of the land. Activist authors, including Joanna Macy and Charles Eisenstein, advocate for a systematic, inclusive movement based on deep connection through compassion. As practitioners, you can help your audience increase their compassion and empathy for other people and for nature.

 ## Cultivate and Practice Mindfulness

Most of us use *fast thinking* methods to make many of our decisions—meaning that we make decisions automatically most of the time. Even if we intend to turn the lights off when we leave a room, turn the water off while we are brushing our teeth, or take even higher impact conservation actions, we often don't because we become distracted by other things or our actions are dictated by habit.

An antidote to this automatic behavior is mindfulness. The term mindfulness was coined by the scholar T. W. Rhys Davids in 1881 when he translated the Buddhist term "sati" into English.[14] The focus of sati, according to Rhys Davids, is to maintain awareness of reality—in other words, to be present. This awareness contrasts with our usual state of mind, where we dwell on the past, regret mistakes, or worry about the future. Paying attention to the present allows us to become more aware of our motivations and feelings, which in turn helps us to avoid engaging in behaviors driven by unsavory motivations like greed and hatred. The definition of mindfulness has since evolved to mean an awareness of your present surroundings and acceptance of each thought and feeling non-judgmentally.[21]

But how can mindfulness help us to become better environmentalists? Scientific evidence of the many benefits of mindfulness for cultivating positive environmental behavior is mounting.[2,16] By enhancing awareness of our surroundings, sensations, thoughts, and emotions, mindfulness can promote long-lasting positive environmental behavior in various, interrelated ways:[4,6,16,17,19,51,54]

- Mindfulness can help to restore directed attention.
- Mindfulness builds empathy and compassion and heightens our sense of commitment to the ethics of protecting nature.

- Mindfulness can help us bring our usually unconscious beliefs, motivations, and cognitive biases into awareness, helping us to better align our actions and habits with our environmental values and intentions.

- Mindfulness can foster happiness, which in turn is associated with more sustainable attitudes and behavior. Some studies have suggested that mindfulness helps us get off the "hedonic treadmill"—the quest to increase our happiness by consuming more. By consuming less, we can reduce a major driver of environmental degradation.

- In a world dominated by norms that reinforce consumption and separation from nature, mindfulness can increase our willingness to challenge these norms and act more in line with our values.

> Ultimately, to change our reactions and behaviors, we have to overcome our tendency toward fast thinking and achieve a certain level of mindfulness.

Together, this growing evidence supports the conclusion that mindfulness is associated with greater levels of positive environmental behavior.

Ultimately, to change our reactions and behaviors, we have to overcome our tendency toward fast thinking and achieve a certain level of mindfulness. We must first cultivate and then practice mindfulness within ourselves, so that we can design better behavioral initiatives and shifters. We can then begin to introduce and strengthen mindfulness practices in our audiences to promote environmental behavior.

✿ Cultivate mindfulness

Different methods of cultivating mindfulness work for different people. Seek out your favorite method—look for what suits you and promotes greater awareness of your surroundings, your thoughts, and emotions. This could be through sitting meditation, silent walks, yoga, breathing exercises, or myriad other techniques. When cultivating mindfulness with an audience, be sure to present them with multiple methods. Below are some exercises that illustrate the rich range of options available to you, from easy and fun to more serious and in-depth.

Meditation is a common method for cultivating mindfulness. In one study, researchers tested the effects of a short-term meditation program on 40 Chinese undergraduate students. The treatment group engaged in meditation for just 20 minutes each day over five days. This was followed by tests assessing attention levels and emotional management; students who meditated scored significantly higher than the control group in conflict resolution and reported significantly better moods, more energy, and fewer instances of depression and anger. Meditation training was also associated with reduced stress, as indicated by lower cortisol levels in the blood.[57] In another study, participants who underwent mindfulness training showed more capacity for directed attention.[27] People skilled in meditation—in any tradition—tend to experience unity with nature and the universe.[60]

Mindful breathing

A great way to begin cultivating mindfulness is by focusing on your breathing. Sit comfortably in an upright posture. Allow your gaze to rest softly on the floor in front of you. Close your eyes if that helps you focus on your breath. Bring awareness to the part of your body where you find it easiest to feel your breathing. Simply notice the sensations of your breath. When your mind begins to wander—which it will—gently bring your attention back to your breathing. Wandering is not failure; each return from wandering is another mindfulness training. Continue for a few minutes, and then gently bring your attention back to your surroundings. Notice the quality of your awareness after this exercise. How has it changed?

For a variation on this activity, with every breath in, notice that you are breathing in oxygen provided to you by phytoplankton in the ocean or trees in a forest. With every breath out, notice that you are exhaling carbon dioxide that provides for the plants and algae in return.

Loving-kindness meditation

Loving-kindness meditation is often used to cultivate compassion. It taps into our inherent capacity to care for a relatively small circle of people (e.g., our nuclear family), animals (e.g., our pets), and plants (e.g., flowers in the front yard), and expands this to broader and broader groups, until we are extending compassion to all of life. This meditation practice begins with participants taking calming breaths in silence. Then, participants visualize loved ones and consciously direct compassionate feelings toward them, and then gradually extend this visualization and compassion to others who are not as close to them, such as groups of people who are experiencing hardship on the other side of the globe. Participants can also extend this care to those whom they are upset with or feel in opposition to. Finally, participants visualize and extend compassion to all living beings.[55] Loving-kindness meditation has been shown to foster empathy: a study using brain imaging during loving-kindness meditations revealed that the more strongly developed meditation practice a person had, the more empathetic brain activity they exhibited when they were exposed to distressing sounds.[37] Using this and other tools, ecopsychologists and activists have begun to harness the power of human connectedness to nurture feelings of compassion.[38]

To generate increased compassion and empathy for nature, this meditation can focus on bringing loving-kindness to personally beloved places on the earth or places ravaged by environmental destruction.

Forest bathing (Shinrin-Yoku) to recharge and take action

People have reported increased feelings of tension and anger while in urban environments and a decrease in those feelings when exposed to forest environments.[45] Forest bathing is the practice of inducing a state of mental and physical relaxation by mindfully experiencing a forest through breathing exercises and by cultivating your sensory awareness. Research suggests that this practice can reduce cortisol levels, heart rate, and blood pressure, all of which indicate lower stress. Take the time to sit quietly in nature, taking in the sights, sounds, and smells surrounding you.

RAIN

The mindfulness practice RAIN is often used to connect to internal challenges but can also be broadened to all of humanity and nature.[8] RAIN stands for the four steps of the practice:

1. **Recognize** whatever is happening within yourself or in the world right now, instead of ignoring or suppressing it.
2. **Allow** it and any associated feelings to arise, including anger, rage, and other negative feelings.
3. **Investigate** it with interest and care (with a focus on bodily sensations you are feeling) so you can understand its true nature.
4. **Nurture** yourself with compassion.

RAIN is designed to counteract the tendency to engage in psychological distancing and othering that can lead us to hold such views as "poor people are inferior" or "plants and animals lack inherent rights to exist." Looking down upon others allows us to ignore, oppress, or exploit vulnerable people, creatures, and plants. For example, if we engage in RAIN when we see an insect, we may notice our initial inclination to react with disgust. However, if we allow ourselves to feel what we feel and investigate our feelings non-judgmentally, we may also notice that other thoughts and emotions are present when we look at the insect, like curiosity and fascination. We can nurture those thoughts and emotions, which could lead us to allow native insect species to thrive in our backyards instead of calling the exterminator.

You can also spend time engaging in mindfulness activities with your team or with core constituents whom you are cultivating to become environmental champions. Those who wish to deepen their mindfulness practice will benefit from the support of group participants, and from skillful teachers who can help them navigate challenges (such as boredom or antsiness) that sometimes arise when first attempting to meditate for longer periods of time. With guidance, practice, and compassion for ourselves, we can begin to look forward to the peace and increased awareness that comes with daily meditation.

⚙ Use mindfulness to become aware of our own narratives and to mitigate cognitive biases

Practicing mindfulness enables us to reevaluate some of our everyday decisions to better choose the actions we want to take. Mindfulness is particularly useful for helping us notice when our cognitive biases are unduly influencing our decisions. As we learned in FOUNDATIONS: Process Chapter 1, we all have cognitive biases and experience life through narratives, which affect our judgments, decisions, and behavior. *Cognitive biases* help us navigate everyday life with fast, automatic thinking. But they can also result in unhelpful or error-prone strategies.

Mindfulness helps us notice and overcome cognitive biases; we can't overcome a cognitive bias if we don't notice it when it arises. By creating space for slow thinking, mindfulness helps us distance ourselves from our thoughts, emotions, and automatic reactions so that we can observe them without immediately acting on them. Mindfulness also helps us to notice patterns in our narrative and biases; armed with this knowledge, we can do the work necessary to shift them to achieve long-term environmental behavior change.

For example, mindfulness can help us notice when we are making judgments based on the bias known as attribution error. If our audience is not turning off their outside lights at night, we might judge this to mean they don't care about saving energy or protecting the environment (i.e., attributing their behavior to certain characteristics). Approaching the audience without this bias, we may instead

Confirmation bias	Can result in selectively searching for evidence that supports our favorite hypotheses for why people engage in environmentally harmful behavior.
Attribution error	Can result in designing shifters aimed at changing beliefs or other personal characteristics related to behavior instead of addressing a structural driver that has a strong impact on that behavior.
Blind spot bias ***False consensus effect***	Our tendencies to believe that we have better judgment than others (blind spot bias), or that others agree with our views and opinions (false consensus effect) can lead us to misread our audiences and design ineffective shifters.
Moral licensing	Occurs when we give ourselves a "pass" (or license) to engage in a less desirable behavior after our self-image gets a boost from doing something virtuous.[22,41]

discover that they feel unsafe in their neighborhood and leave their lights on for protection, even though they do care about saving energy. Our attribution bias resulted in an incorrect belief about our audience. Designing shifters to convince the audience to care on the basis of that belief would have been ineffective.

Games, exercises, and activities, such as some of the mindfulness activities listed earlier in this Building Block, can be used to expose and increase our awareness of our biases. For example, participants can take the Implicit Association Test to see which stereotypes or other biases they unconsciously hold.[24] Similarly, the U.S. Defense Department's Sirius Program uses games to increase awareness of cognitive biases in intelligence analysts.[50] These types of exercises may allow some people to reduce the role of bias in their everyday lives.

When practitioners have significant decisions to make (such as making important organizational decisions or designing initiatives), we should consider convening intentionally structured spaces—like meetings or workshops—focused on understanding and overcoming biases that are likely to arise. In doing so, we are likely to design more effective and equitable initiatives.

When we are aware of our cognitive biases, we are less likely to mindlessly allow biases such as confirmation bias, attribution error, and moral licensing to determine our actions.[25] Mindfulness helps to bring such biases into conscious awareness and empowers us to decide not to allow biases to dictate our behavior.

✿ Use mindfulness to connect with your audience

We all notice and interpret information based on the frames and mental models stored in our brains. (See ASSOCIATIONS: Building Block Chapter 9 for more on this.) We can be blinded by our frames and mental models, which lead us to believe that our way of seeing and interpreting the information is the only "right" way. This can lead to judgment, which can shut down dialogue and collective action that protects the environment.

Fortunately, mindfulness can help us to uncover the assumptions and judgments we use to support our behavior and to deconstruct our thought processes, giving us more flexibility in our interactions with others. Mindfulness helps us to suspend our judgment and discern the bigger picture. When we are interacting with someone who we are disposed to view negatively, mindfulness can allow us to see that both of us are making assumptions and have different backgrounds and information sets. With this awareness, we can take the opportunity to examine the pool of data together (e.g., facts about an environmental issue) and proceed with open-mindedness to build consensus and move toward shared understanding.[3]

Mindfulness can help us detach from *positions* that can lead to polarization. Enhanced awareness of context can in turn help us facilitate discussions and negotiations based on interests, rather than on positions.[18] Generally, positions are what people say they want and *interests* reflect why they want the things they want. Many environmental problems persist because people with divergent, entrenched positions about how to address problems cannot agree on a course of action. For example, if one group of people wants to save water by regulating agricultural water use (a position), but another wants to focus on reducing household consumption (a competing position), the two groups may be in conflict even though their end goals are ultimately the same: they want to ensure ample drinking water for their stakeholders (their interests). If we can help people reduce their attachment to positions and consider their interests and those of other participants, common ground or win-win solutions can be found.[18] By taking a step back and suspending judgment, a group of people that can't agree on how to solve a problem may become better connected with why they want to solve it, facilitating a more productive discussion.[18] In advance of meetings with target audiences, do research such as interviews to discern and differentiate between positions and interests, and design the meetings to elicit the interests behind the positions.

Making Shift Happen: Using Mindfulness to Find Common Ground

Developers, environmentalists, landowners, fishers, and people in the tourist industry held strong positions for and against environmental regulations in the Florida Keys during the 1990s. Environmentalists were advocating for the creation of the Florida Keys National Marine Sanctuary along with a water quality improvement program to protect the coral reefs, mangroves, and seagrass meadows. Some fishers, developers, and landowners took very strong positions against these actions. During a workshop designed to resolve conflicts between these positions, each group of stakeholders was asked to discuss their interests—what they valued the most. When the stakeholders summarized these discussions in plenary, it became clear that everyone in the room valued high water quality and healthy marine ecosystems for a variety of reasons. The realization that they had common interests helped the participants set aside their positions and agree to form a coalition aimed at reducing the hydrological modifications and unsustainable farming practices that were degrading water quality and ecosystem health in the Keys. Help your audience identify their interests and find common ground when advocating for environmental initiatives.

• • •

When we cultivate and practice mindfulness, we create space for ourselves and our audiences to view ourselves and others in a way that suspends judgment and fosters dialogue. Mindfulness can increase our capacity to notice differences in context, and can help diverse groups of people find common ground.

 ## Have Compassion for Yourself

I have come to believe that caring for myself is not self-indulgent. Caring for myself is an act of survival.

—Audre Lorde

So far we have discussed how to cultivate compassion for other people and for nature. It is equally important to care for and have compassion for oneself. As environmental practitioners witnessing ecological loss, we might be experiencing grief, fear, a sense of urgency, or other thoughts and emotions that can be stressful, overwhelming, and heartbreaking.[13] We all need to care for ourselves, or risk hopelessness and depletion taking over. All of the mindfulness and compassion activities that we have discussed above can help you restore yourself through self-compassion. The Despair Ritual, detailed below, is also a good way to process negative emotions about the problems facing our world and to share compassion with our peers.

 ### Despair Ritual

The Despair Ritual is an interactive group practice designed to help people acknowledge their sorrows and other deep emotions they feel about the state of the world and to connect with their peers to share compassion for themselves and each other. This exercise was developed by Chellis Glendinning, following the nuclear accident at Three Mile Island in 1979, to help communities address feelings of fear and despair about the global environmental crisis that may inhibit them from taking positive environmental action. Studies suggest that many of us feel despair when we perceive a problem to be large and out of our control. As a result, we might not believe that our actions will result in significant change. (See OPTIMISM: Building Block Chapter 7 to learn more.) Skillful facilitation is essential for this practice—guidance can be found in Macy and Brown's book *Coming Back to Life*.[38]

The work of designing and implementing behavior change shifters requires a lot of information processing and directed attention. Sustaining our work to protect the environment over many years will therefore require us to have compassion for ourselves and to restore our capacity for directed attention regularly. By using practices like mindfulness and attention restoration for ourselves, we can reduce the influence of our cognitive biases, increase the accuracy of how we characterize our audiences and interpret data, and enhance our ability to focus and plan for the future. As they say on airplanes: "put on your own oxygen mask before assisting others." If we're not at our best and taking care of ourselves, we'll never have the endurance and empathy to continue our life's work.

Conclusion

As the authors of this book, and environmental practitioners ourselves, we know how easy it can be to get wrapped up in our everyday lives and lose touch with others and with nature. Yet, without that connection to others and the natural world, we won't be able to achieve long-lasting behavioral change. That's why it's important to connect with nature, elicit "other-focused" emotions, and foster empathy and compassion, both within ourselves and within our audiences. Our ultimate goal is to see ourselves as part of (rather than separate from) nature, thus making environmental action a greater priority. The practices described in this Building Block can help us reconnect with nature and act on our compassion for the earth. Mindfulness is equally important—through mindfulness, we can practice overcoming some of the many factors that pull us into mindless action, such as our hardwired tendency to use mental shortcuts. Ultimately, by engaging in these practices ourselves and with our audiences, we can increase the scale and longevity of environmental stewardship.

☑ Your Turn

What are some ways you can increase the longevity of your behavior change efforts? Use the questions below to brainstorm:

Engage with nature

❑ Does your initiative involve some outdoor time for participants, or engage them in nature in some way?

❑ What barriers make it difficult for your audience to experience nature? What measures have you included in your initiative to address these barriers?

❑ How can connection to nature be normalized socially? How can leaders within your audience promote connectedness to nature? Are there local cultural traditions or practices that can support connection to nature?

Foster an "other-focus"

❑ Which other-focused emotions can you draw out to cultivate behavior change? Which other-focused emotion is best suited for tackling your environmental problem?

❑ Are there activities that can elicit emotions that will connect people with your specific environmental problem?

❑ Does your initiative encourage the display of empathy and compassion? How could you use the strategies discussed in this chapter (such as perspective-taking exercises) to increase your audience's empathy and compassion?

Cultivate and practice mindfulness

❑ Does your initiative focus on common interests or on positions? What methods do you have in place to illuminate common interests and shared values across groups?

❑ What strategies have you developed to nurture a culture of open-mindedness? How can your initiative support a culture that values listening to and learning from others?

❑ Have you identified stereotyping, moral licensing, or other biases in yourself or your audience that could get in the way of creating lasting change?

❑ Does your initiative include practices that increase awareness of cognitive biases, such as mindfulness practices or exercises that illustrate the presence of implicit bias?

Have compassion for yourself

❑ Do you engage in mindfulness or compassion practices? If not, which practices can you start today?

❑ Do you give your brain a break by engaging in involuntary attention, especially by spending time in nature? If not, what kinds of attention restoration activities can you regularly include in your daily routine?

Conclusion

ENVIRONMENTAL ISSUES have grown increasingly complex and larger in scale. But take heart—efforts to protect the planet have also become more numerous and effective. The air is cleaner in many cities around the world. Many farmers are producing food sustainably. More people have access to clean water to drink and swim in. And more people than ever are concerned about climate change and environmental justice and are pressuring corporations and governments to take action.

Over the years, environmentalists have utilized many tools and approaches to protect nature and improve quality of life. At different points in time, the movement has focused on raising awareness and provoking fear or outrage, passing laws and regulations to regulate individual and institutional activities, and utilizing market-based approaches like cap and trade, among others. All of these approaches have yielded great environmental victories. There is much to celebrate.

But as environmental challenges accelerate, we need our solutions to scale with them, and for that to happen, solutions have to address the root causes of environmental problems. It may seem as if massive environmental problems like climate change or air pollution are caused by impersonal entities or forces like "industry" or "transportation." But at their root, environmental problems are caused by the beliefs and actions of people on all levels of the system—meaning that they're actually human behavior change problems. A policy may enable environmental degradation, but this policy is a result of a set of decisions by policymakers and their staff, who respond to their own values as well as to pressure from their constituents, each with their own values. A manufacturing plant may be spewing pollution, but this pollution is ultimately a result of the beliefs and actions of a group of people, like an executive board that is influenced by social norms or the incentive of making profit, or consumers that continue to demand certain products despite their harmful environmental impacts.

A fundamental challenge of our time is thus to change behavior at both individual and organizational levels. Designing solutions based directly on how humans think, make decisions, and act is critical for increasing the efficacy, durability,

471

and scale of conservation efforts—and requires adding evidence-driven behavior change tools and approaches to our conservation toolkit.

We created this book so that conservationists can use the tools of behavior change in their work with their audiences or even to improve their own individual behaviors. We hope this motivates the use of these techniques on a wider scale within the environmental movement and facilitates their application by activists across all environmental issues. We've used the *Making Shift Happen* process to address a variety of environmental problems, ranging from reducing the use of paper and plastic and decreasing single occupancy vehicle travel to preventing overfishing and eliminating marine debris. You now have the tools to *make shift happen.*

References

Introduction

1. Aramark Higher Education. (2008). *The business and cultural acceptance case for trayless dining* (PDF).

2. Cima, R. (2016, December 19). DARE: *The anti-drug program that never actually worked*. Priceonomics.

3. Ebeling, F., & Lotz, S. (2015). Domestic uptake of green energy promoted by opt-out tariffs. *Nature Climate Change, 5*(9), 868–871.

4. Farrelly, M. C., Davis, K. C., Duke, J., & Messeri, P. (2008). Sustaining "truth": Changes in youth tobacco attitudes and smoking intentions after 3 years of a national antismoking campaign. *Health Education Research, 24*(1), 42–48.

5. Ferro, S. (2013, April 15). The science of PSAs: Do anti-drug ads keep kids off drugs? *Popular Science.*

6. Gosnell, G. K., List, J. A., & Metcalfe, R. (2016). *A New Approach to an Age-Old Problem: Solving Externalities by Incenting Workers Directly* (Working Paper 22316). National Bureau of Economic Research. https://www.nber.org/system/files/working_papers/w22316/w22316.pdf.

7. Gulland, I. (2015, January 9). *Edinburgh "nudging" success in recycling.* Zero Waste Scotland.

8. Hicks, J. J. (2001). The strategy behind Florida's "truth" campaign. *Tobacco Control 10,* 3–5.

9. Hornik, R., Jacobsohn, L, Orwin, R., Piesse, A. & Kalton, G. (2008). Effects of the national youth anti-drug media campaign on youths. *American Journal of Public Health, 98*(12), 2229–2236.

10. Kallbekken, S., & Sælen, H. (2013). "Nudging" hotel guests to reduce food waste as a win-win environmental measure. *Economic Letters, 119*(3), 325–327.

11. Lambert, C., Harvey, E., Kistruck, D., Gosnell, G., List, J., Metcalfe, R. (2016). *The effects of giving captains feedback and targets on SOP fuel and carbon efficiency information: Results of the Virgin Atlantic University of Chicago and London School of Economics Captains' Study.*

12. Simis, M. J., Madden, H., Cacciatore, M. A., & Yeo, S. K. (2016). The lure of rationality: Why does the deficit model persist in science communication? *Public Understanding of Science, 25*(4), 400–414.

13. Sunstein, C. R. (2015). *Choosing not to choose: Understanding the value of choice.* Oxford.
14. The Behaviouralist. (2015). *Saving fuel by changing pilot behaviour.* https://the behaviouralist.com/portfolio-item/saving-fuel-by-changing-pilot-behaviour/.

Process Chapter 1: Foundations

1. Acumen Academy. (n.d.). *Environmental Sustainability: Module 2 Readings.* MAVA Fondation Pour la Nature.
2. Chan, K. M., Balvanera, P., Benessaiah, K., Chapman, M., Díaz, S., Gómez-Baggethun, E., Gould, R., Hannahs, N., Jax, K., Klain, S., Luck, G.W., Martín-López, B., Muraca, B., Norton, B., Ott, K., Pascual, U., Satterfield, T. Tadaki, M., Taggart, J. & Turner, N. (2016). Opinion: Why protect nature? Rethinking values and the environment. *PNAS, 113*(6), 1462–1465.
3. Cuncic, A. (2020). *Understanding internal and external validity.* Verywell Mind.
4. Damasio, A. (1994). *Descartes' error: Emotion, reason, and human brain.* Grosset/ Putnam.
5. Dolan, R.J. (2002). Emotion, Cognition, and Behavior. *Science, 298*(5596), 1191–1194.
6. Elf, P., Gatersleben, B., & Christie, I. (2019). Facilitating positive spillover effects: New insights from a mixed-methods approach exploring factors enabling people to live more sustainable lifestyles. *Frontiers in Psychology, 9,* 2699.
7. Fishbach, A. & Touré-Tillery, M. (2020). Motives and goals. In R. Biswas-Diener & E. Diener (Eds.), *Introduction to Psychology: The Full Noba Collection.* DEF publishers.
8. Gielen, A. C., & Green, L. W. (2015). The Impact of Policy, Environmental, and Educational Interventions: A Synthesis of the Evidence From Two Public Health Success Stories. *Health Education & Behavior, 42*(1_suppl), 20S–34S.
9. Gillingham, K., Kotchen, M. J., Rapson, D. S., & Wagner, G. (2013). The rebound effect is overplayed. *Nature, 493*(7433), 475–476.
10. Hansen, P. & Jespersen, A.M. (2013). Nudge and the manipulation of choice: Framework for the responsible use of the nudge approach to behaviour change in public policy. *European Journal of Risk Regulation, 2013*(1), 3–28.
11. Hwang, H. & Matsumoto, D. (2020). Functions of emotions. In R. Biswas-Diener & E. Diener (Eds.), *Noba textbook series: Psychology.* DEF publishers.
12. Kahn, M. E., & Kotchen, M. J. (2010). Environmental concern and the business cycle: The chilling effect of recession. National Bureau of Economic Research Working Paper 16241.
13. Kahneman, D. (2011). *Thinking, Fast and Slow.* Farrar, Straus, and Giroux.
14. Kemmis, S., McTaggart, R., & Nixon, R. (2013). *The action research planner: Doing critical participatory action research.* Springer.

15. Knight, A. T., Cook, C. N., Redford, K. H., Biggs, D., Romero, C., Ortega-Argueta, A., Norman, C. D., Parsons, B., Reynolds, M., Eoyang, G., & Keene, M. (2019). Improving conservation practice with principles and tools from systems thinking and evaluation. *Sustainability Science, 14*(6), 1531–1548.

16. Lades, L. K. & Delaney, L. (2020). Nudge FORGOOD. *Behavioural Public Policy,* 1–20.

17. Linville, P. W., & Fischer, G. W. (1991). Preferences for separating or combining events. *Journal of Personality and Social Psychology, 60*(1), 5–23.

18. Mann, T., De Ridder, D., & Fujita, K. (2013). Self-regulation of health behavior: Social psychological approaches to goal setting and goal striving. *Health Psychology, 32*(5), 487–498.

19. Meadows, D. H. (2008). *Thinking in Systems: A primer.* Chelsea Green Publishing.

20. Mullainathan, S. & Shafir, E. (2013). *Scarcity: Why having too little means so much.* Picador.

21. Nesterak, E. & Barnett, M. (2020). Research lead: Nudges work on Thaler too, psychology's racial blindspot, overestimating how much your political rivals hate you, and more. *Behavioral Scientist.*

22. Nilsson, A., Bergquist, M., & Schultz, W.P. (2017). Spillover effects in environmental behaviors, across time and context: A review and research agenda. *Environmental Education Research, 23*(4), 573–589.

23. Nisbet, M.C. (2011). *Climate shift: Clear vision for the next decade of public debate.* American University School of Communication.

24. *Our planet is drowning in plastic pollution* (2018). UN Environment.

25. Peters, E., Lipkus, I., & Diefenbach, M. (2006). The functions of affect in health communications and in the construction of health preferences. *Journal of Communication, 56*, S140–S162.

26. Proffitt. D.R. (2006). Embodied Perception and the Economy of Action. *Association for Psychological Science, 1*, 111–122.

27. Reijula, S. & Hertwig, R. (2020). Self-nudging and the citizen choice architect. *Behavioural Public Policy, First View,* 1–31.

28. Sen, A. (1992). Capability and well-being. In Nussbaum, M. & Sen, A. (Eds.) *The quality of life.* Clarendon Press.

29. Shome, D., & Marx, S. (2009). Section 4: Beware the overuse of emotional appeals. In Center for Research on Environmental Decisions. *The psychology of climate change communication: A guide for scientists, journalists, educators, political aides, and the interested public.*

30. Sintov, N., Geislar, S., & White, L. V. (2019). Cognitive accessibility as a new factor in proenvironmental spillover: Results from a field study of household food waste management. *Environment and Behavior, 51*(1), 50–80.

31. Smith, W.A. (2002). Social Marketing and its Potential Contribution to a Modern Synthesis of Social Change. *Social Marketing Quarterly, 8*(2), 46–48.

32. Sullivan, L. (2020). *How big oil misled the public into believing that plastic would be recycled.* NPR.

33. Sunstein, C. R. (2015). The ethics of nudging. *Yale Journal on Regulation, 32*, 413–450.

34. Sunstein C. R. & Reisch, L.A. (2019). *Trusting nudges: Toward a bill of rights for nudging.* Routledge.

35. Thaler, R. H., Sunstein, C. R., & Balz, J. P. (2010). *Choice architecture.* Available at SSRN.

36. Thøgersen, J. & Crompton, T. (2009). Simple and painless? The limitations of spillover in environmental campaigning. *Journal of Consumer Policy, 32*(2), 141–163.

37. Thomas, D. C. & Inkson, K. (2009). Making decisions across cultures. In *Cultural intelligence: Living and working globally* (2nd ed.). Berrett-Koehler.

38. Tiefenbeck, V., Staake, T., Roth, K., & Sachs, O. (2013). For better or for worse? Empirical evidence of moral licensing in a behavioral energy conservation campaign. *Energy Policy, 57,* 160–171.

39. Truelove, H. B., Carrico, A. R., Weber, E. U., Raimi, K. T., & Vandenbergh, M. P. (2014). Positive and negative spillover of pro-environmental behavior: An integrative review and theoretical framework. *Global Environmental Change, 29,* 127-138.

40. Weber, E. U. (1997). Perception and expectation of climate change: Precondition for economic and technological adaptation. In M. H. Bazerman, D. M. Messick, A. E. Tenbrunsel, & K. A. Wade-Benzoni (Eds.), *Environment, ethics, and behavior: The psychology of environmental valuation and degradation* (pp. 314–341). Lexington Books.

Notes Table 1.1.1:

a   Sherif, M., Taub, D., & Hovland C. I. (1958). Assimilation and contrast effects of anchoring stimuli on judgments. *Journal of Experimental Psychology, 55*(2), 150–155.

b   Gilovich, T., Griffin, D. W., & Kahneman, D. (2002). *Heuristics and Biases: The Psychology of Intuitive Judgement.* Cambridge.

c   Toffler, A. (1971). *Future Shock.* Bantam.

d   Gross, B. M. (1964). *The Managing of Organizations: The Administrative Struggle, Vols. I and II.* Free Press of Glencoe.

e   Festinger, L. (1957). *A Theory of Cognitive Dissonance.* Stanford.

f   Wason, P. C. (1960). On the failure to eliminate hypotheses in a conceptual task. *Quarterly Journal of Experimental Psychology, 12*(3), 129–140.

g   Nyhan, B., & Reifler, J. (2010). When corrections fail: The persistence of political misperceptions. *Political Behavior, 32*(2), 303–330.

h   Loomes, G., & Sugden, R. (1982). Regret theory: An alternative theory of rational choice under uncertainty. *The Economic Journal, 92*(368), 805–824; Bell, D. E. (1982). Regret in decision making under uncertainty. *Operations Research, 30*(5), 961–981; Fishburn, P. C. (1982). *The Foundations of Expected Utility.* Reidel.

i   Norton, M. I., Mochon, D., & Ariely, D. (2012). The IKEA effect: When labor leads to love. *Journal of Consumer Psychology, 22*(3), 453–460.

j   Loewenstein, G. (2005). Hot-cold empathy gaps and medical decision making. *Health Psychology, 24*(4S), S49–56.

k   Dai, H., Milkman, K. L., & Riis, J. (2014). The fresh start effect: Temporal landmarks motivate aspirational behavior. *Management Science, 10,* 2563–2582.

l   Ainslie, G., & Haendel, V. (1983). The motives of the will. In E. Gottheil, K. Druley, T. Skodola, & H. Waxman (Eds.), *Etiologic Aspects of Alcohol and Drug Abuse* (pp. 119–140). Charles C. Thomas.

m   Phelps, E. S., & Pollak, R. A. (1968). On second-best national saving and game-equilibrium growth. *The Review of Economic Studies, 35*(2), 185–199.

n   Schelling, T. C., Bailey, M. J., & Fromm, G. (1968). The life you save may be your own. In S.B. Chase (Ed.), *Problems in Public Expenditure Analysis* (pp.127–162). Brookings Institution.

o   Kahneman, D., & Tversky, A. (1979). Prospect theory: An analysis of decision under risk. *Econometrica, 47*(2), 263–291.

p   Fechner, G. T. (1876). *Vorschule der Aesthetik.* Breitkoff & Hartel.

q   Zajonc, R. B. (1968). Attitudinal effects of mere exposure. *Journal of Personality and Social Psychology, 9*(2), 1–27.

r   Monin, B., & Miller, D. T. (2001). Moral credentials and the expression of prejudice. *Journal of Personality and Social Psychology, 81*(1), 33–43.

s   Rozin, P., & Royzman, E. B. (2001). Negativity bias, negativity dominance, and contagion. *Personality and Social Psychology Review, 5*(4), 296–320.

t   Spranca, M., Minsk, E., & Baron, J. (1991). Omission and commission in judgement and choice. *Journal of Experimental Social Psychology, 27*(1), 76–105.

u   Sterns, S. C. (2000). Daniel Bernoulli (1738): Evolution and economics under risk. *Journal of Biosciences, 25,* 221–228; von Neumann, J., & Morgenstern, O. (1944). *Theory of games and economic behavior.* Princeton.

v   Desvousges, W. H., Johnson, F. R., Dunford, R. W., Boyle K. J., Hudson, S. P., & Wilson, K. N. (1992). *Measuring Nonuse Damages Using Contingent Valuation: An Experimental Evaluation of Accuracy.* RTI Press.

w   Weber, E. U. (1997). Perception and expectation of climate change: Precondition for economic and technological adaptation. In M. H. Bazerman, D. M. Messick, A. E. Tenbrunsel, & K. A. Wade-Benzoni (Eds.), *Environment, ethics, and behavior:*

The psychology of environmental valuation and degradation (pp. 314–341). Jason Aronson.

x   Kahneman, D., Knetsch, J. L., & Thaler, R. H. (1991). Anomalies: The endowment effect, loss aversion, and status quo bias. *Journal of Economic Perspectives, 5*(1), 193–206.

Process Chapter 2: Initiate

1. Acumen Academy. (n.d.). *Environmental Sustainability: Module 2 Readings.* MAVA Fondation Pour la Nature.
2. Doran, G. T. (1981). There's a S.M.A.R.T. way to write management's goals and objectives. *Management Review, 70*(11), 35–36.
3. Griffin, P., & Heede, C. R. (2017). *The carbon majors database.* CDP carbon majors report 2017, 14.
4. Hendrickson, M., Howard, P. H., & Constance, D. H. (2017). Power, food and agriculture: implications for farmers, consumers and communities. *Consumers and Communities.*
5. Holt-Giménez, E. (2019). Capitalism, food, and social movements: The political economy of food system transformation. *Journal of Agriculture, Food Systems, and Community Development.*
6. Locke, E. A., & Latham, G. P. (2002). Building a practically useful theory of goal setting and task motivation: A 35-year odyssey. *American Psychologist, 57*(9), 705.
7. Marsh, D. R., Schroeder, D. G., Dearden, K. A., Sternin, J., & Sternin, M. (2004). The power of positive deviance. *Bmj, 329*(7475), 1177–1179.
8. McKenzie-Mohr, D. (2011). *Fostering sustainable behavior: An introduction to community-based social marketing* (3rd ed). New Society Publishers.
9. Meadows, D. (1999). *Leverage points: Places to intervene in a system.* The Sustainability Institute.
10. Monast, M. (2020). *Financing Resilient Agriculture: How agricultural lenders can reduce climate risk and help farmers build resilience.* Environmental Defense Fund. https://www.edf.org/sites/default/files/content/Financing_Resilient_Agriculture_Report.pdf
11. Prochaska, J. O., Norcross, J. C., & DiClemente, C. C. (1995). *Changing for good: A revolutionary six-stage program for overcoming bad habits and moving your life positively forward.* Avon Books.
12. Rogers, Everett M. (2003) *The Diffusion of Innovations* (5th ed). Free Press.
13. Thøgersen, J. & Crompton, T. (2009). Simple and painless? The limitations of spillover in environmental campaigning. *Journal of Consumer Policy, 32,* 141–163.
14. Truelove, H. B., Carrico, A. R., Weber, E. U., Raimi, K. T., & Vandenbergh, M. P. (2014). Positive and negative spillover of pro-environmental behavior: An integrative review and theoretical framework. *Global Environmental Change, 29,* 127–138.

Process Chapter 3: Uncover

1. Armitage, C. J., & Conner, M. (2001). Efficacy of the theory of planned behaviour: A meta-analytic review. *British Journal of Social Psychology, 40*(4), 471–499.
2. Bandura, A. (1977). Self-efficacy: Toward a unifying theory of behavioral change. *Psychological Review, 84*(2), 191–215.
3. Booth-Kewley, S., & Vickers Jr, R. R. (1994). Associations between major domains of personality and health behavior. *Journal of personality, 62*(3), 281–298.
4. Bouman, T., Steg, L., & Kiers, H. A. L. (2018). Measuring values in environmental research: A test of an environmental portrait value questionnaire. *Frontiers in Psychology, 9,* 564.
5. Cialdini, R. B. (2008). *Influence: Science and practice* (4th ed.). Pearson Education.
6. Elf, P., Gatersleben, B., & Christie, I. (2019). Facilitating positive spillover effects: New insights from a mixed-methods approach exploring factors enabling people to live more sustainable lifestyles. *Frontiers in Psychology, 9,* 2699.
7. Fishbach, A. & Touré-Tillery, M. (2020). Motives and Goals. In R. Biswas-Diener & E. Diener (Eds), *Introduction to Psychology: The Full Noba Collection.* DEF publishers.
8. Gibbons, S. (2018). *Journey Mapping 101.* Nielsen Norman Group.
9. Gifford, R. (2011). The dragons of inaction: Psychological barriers that limit climate change mitigation and adaptation. *American Psychologist, 66*(4), 290–302.
10. Graham, S., Barnett, J., Fincher, R., Hurlimann, A., Mortreux, C., & Waters, E. (2013). The social values at risk from sea-level rise. *Environmental Impact Assessment Review, 41,* 45–52.
11. Gromet, D. M., Kunreuther, H., & Larrick, R. P. (2013). Political ideology affects energy-efficiency attitudes and choices. *Proceedings of the National Academy of Sciences, 110*(23), 9314–9319.
12. Haidt, J., & Joseph, C. (2004). Intuitive ethics: how innately prepared intuitions generate culturally variable virtues. *Daedalus, 133*(4), 55–66.
13. Kittle, B. (2017). *A practical guide to conducting a barrier analysis* (2nd ed.). Helen Keller International.
14. Lacroix, K., Gifford, R., & Chen, A. (2019). Developing and validating the Dragons of Inaction Psychological Barriers (DIPB) scale. *Journal of Environmental Psychology, 63,* 9–18.
15. Mullainathan, S. & Shafir, E. (2013). *Scarcity: Why having too little means so much.* Picador.
16. Pickering, J. (2018). *Nudges alone won't save Nemo: Conservation in the Great Barrier Reef.* Behavioral Scientist.
17. *Project Cane Changer.* (n.d.). Impact.

18. Skarin, F., Olsson, L. E., Roos, I., & Friman, M. (2017). The household as an instrumental and affective trigger in intervention programs for travel behavior change. *Travel Behaviour & Society, 6,* 83–89.

19. ecoAmerica. (2006). *The American Environmental Values Survey.* https://ecoamerica.org/wp-content/uploads/2013/02/AEVS_Report.pdf.

20. Staats, H., Harland, P., & Wilke, H. A. M. (2004). Effecting durable change: A team approach to improve environmental behavior in the household. *Environment and Behavior, 36*(3), 341–367.

21. The Community Guide (n.d.) *Physical activity: Social support interventions in community settings.*

22. Van der Werff, E., Steg, L., & Keizer, K. (2013). The value of environmental self-identity: The relationship between biospheric values, environmental self-identity and environmental preferences, intentions and behaviour. *Journal of Environmental Psychology, 34,* 55–63.

Process Chapter 4: Design

1. Chor, K. H. B., Wisdom, J. P., Olin, S-C. S., Hoagwood, K. E., & Horwitz, S. M. (2015). Measures for predictors of innovation adoption. *Administration and Policy in Mental Health and Mental Health Services Research, 42*(5), 545–573.

2. De Young, R. (1993). Changing behavior and making it stick: The conceptualization and management of conservation behavior. *Environment and Behavior, 25*(3), 485–505.

3. De Young, R. (2011). Slow wins: Patience, perseverance and behavior change. *Carbon Management, 2*(6), 607–611.

4. Fogg, B. J. (2009). A behavior model for persuasive design. In *Persuasive '09: Proceedings of the 4th international conference on persuasive technology* (pp. 1–7). Association for Computing Machinery.

5. Maguire, M. (2001). Methods to support human-centred design. *International Journal of Human-Computer Studies, 55*(4), 587–634.

6. Michie, S., Van Stralen, M. M., & West, R. (2011). The behaviour change wheel: a new method for characterising and designing behaviour change interventions. *Implementation science, 6*(1), 42.

7. Prochaska, J. O., Norcross, J. C., & DiClemente, C. C. (1995). *Changing for good: A revolutionary six-stage program for overcoming bad habits and moving your life positively forward.* Avon Books.

8. Rose, C. (2010). *How to win campaigns: Communications for change* (2nd ed.). Routledge.

9. Sussman, R., Tan, L. Q., & Kormos, C. E. (2020). Behavioral interventions for sustainable transportation: An overview of programs and guide for practitioners. In

J. Zhang (Ed.), *Transport and energy research: A behavioral perspective* (pp. 315–371). Elsevier.

10. West, R. & Michie, S. (2019). UBC Briefing 7: Evaluating behaviour change interventions using APEASE. Unlocking Behavior Change.

11. The World Bank. (2015). *World development report 2015: Mind, society, and behavior.*

Process Chapter 5: Implement

1. Battista, W., Tourgee, A., Wu, C., & Fujita, R. (2017). How to achieve conservation outcomes at scale: An evaluation of scaling principles. *Frontiers in Marine Science, 3,* 278.

2. Geiger, N., Swim, J. K., & Glenna, L. (2019). Spread the green word: A social community perspective into environmentally sustainable behavior. *Environment and Behavior, 51*(5), 561–589.

3. Green, D. P., Wilke, A., & Cooper, J. (2019). Countering violence against women at scale: A mass media experiment in rural Uganda [Unpublished Manuscript]. Columbia University.

4. Johanson, G. A., & Brooks, G. P. (2010). Initial scale development: Sample size for pilot studies. *Educational and Psychological Measurement, 70*(3), 394–400.

5. La Ferrara, E., Chong, A., & Duryea, S. (2012). Soap operas and fertility: Evidence from Brazil. *American Economic Journal: Applied Economics, 4*(4), 1–31.

6. Peace Corps. (2013). Peace Corps' Master Farmer Program Boosts Food Security and Economic Growth in Senegal.

7. Richards, D. A., & Hallberg, I. R. (Eds.). (2015). *Complex interventions in health: An overview of research methods.* Routledge.

Chapter 6: Methods

1. Bachman, R. D. & Schutt, R. K. (2020). Qualitative methods and data analysis. In R. D. Bachman, & R. K. Schutt (Eds.), *Fundamentals of research in criminology and criminal justice* (5th). Sage.

2. Namey, E. (2017) *Riddle me this: How many interviews (or focus groups) are enough?* R&E Search for Evidence.

3. Brookshire, B. (2013). *Psychology is WEIRD.* Slate.

4. Catalogue of Bias Collaboration, Spencer, E. A., Brassey J., & Mahtani K. (n.d.). *Recall bias.* In: Catalogue Of Bias 2017.

5. Cruz, S. M., & Manata, B. (2020). Measurement of environmental concern: A review and analysis. *Frontiers in Psychology, 11,* 363.

6. *Correlation vs. Causation* (n.d.). JMP.

7. Dewalt, K.M., Dewalt, B.R., & Wayland, C.B. (1998). Participant observation. In H. R. Bernard (Ed.), *Handbook of methods in cultural anthropology* (pp. 259–299). AltaMira Press.

8. Flisser, B. (2014, June 9). *How to find anything online with advanced search techniques.*

9. Jhangiani, R. (2020). Research methods in social psychology. In R. Biswas-Diener & E. Diener (Eds.), *Noba textbook series: Psychology*. DEF publishers.

10. Johnson, A., & Sackett, R. (1998). Direct systematic observation of behavior. In H. R. Bernard (Ed.), *Handbook of methods in cultural anthropology* (pp. 301–332). AltaMira Press.

11. Krosnick, J. A. and Presser, S. (2009). Question and questionnaire design. In J. D. Wright and P. V. Marsden (Eds.), *Handbook of survey research* (2nd ed.). Elsevier.

12. Morgan, D. L. (1997). *Focus groups as qualitative research; Vol. 16 Qualitative research methods series* (2nd ed). Sage.

13. Morgan, D. L. (2014). Research design and research methods. In *Integrating qualitative and quantitative methods: A pragmatic approach* (pp. 45–62). Sage.

14. OECD. (2012). Good Practices in Survey Design Step-by-Step. In *Measuring regulatory performance: A practitioner's guide to perception surveys*. OECD Publishing.

15. Almeida, F., Faria, D., & Queirós, A. (2017). Strengths and limitations of qualitative and quantitative research methods. *European Journal of Education Studies, 3*(9), 369–387.

16. Morgan, B. L., & Van Voorhis, C. R. W. (2007). Understanding power and rules of thumb for determining sample sizes. *Tutorials in Quantitative Methods for Psychology, 3*(2), 43–50.

17. Privitera, G. J. (2019). *Research methods for the behavioral sciences* (3rd ed.). Sage.

18. Yong, E. (2018). *Psychology's replication crisis is running out of excuses.* The Atlantic.

Section 2

Building Block Chapter 1: Highlight Norms to Leverage BELONGING

1. Abrahamse, W. (2019). *Encouraging pro-environmental behaviour: What works, what doesn't, and why.* Academic Press.

2. Baumeister, R. F., & Leary, M. R. (1995). The need to belong: Desire for interpersonal attachments as a fundamental human motivation. *Psychological Bulletin, 117*(3), 497–529.

3. Bicchieri, C. (2017). *Norms in the wild: How to diagnose, measure, and change social norms.* Oxford.

4. Cialdini, R. B. (2003). Crafting normative messages to protect the environment. Current *Directions in Psychological Science, 12*(4), 105–109.

5. Cialdini, R. B. (2009). *Influence: Science and practice* (5th ed.). Pearson.

6. Cialdini, R. B., Demaine, L. J., Sagarin, B. J., Barrett, D. W., Rhoads, K., & Winter, P. L. (2006). Managing social norms for persuasive impact. *Social Influence, 1*(1), 3–15.

7. Cialdini, R. B., Kallgren, C. A., & Reno, R. R. (1991). A focus theory of normative conduct: A theoretical refinement and reevaluation of the role of norms in human behavior. *Advances in Experimental Social Psychology, 24*, 201–234.

8. Cialdini, R. B., Reno, R. R., & Kallgren, C. A. (1990). A focus theory of normative conduct: Recycling the concept of norms to reduce littering in public places. *Journal of Personality and Social Psychology, 58*(6), 1015–1026.

9. Dwyer, P. C., Maki, A., & Rothman, A. J. (2015). Promoting energy conservation behavior in public settings: The influence of social norms and personal responsibility. *Journal of Environmental Psychology, 41,* 30–34.

10. Festinger, L. (1954). A theory of social comparison processes. *Human Relations, 7*(2), 117–140.

11. Gerber, A. S., & Green, D. P. (2000). The effects of canvassing, telephone calls, and direct mail on voter turnout: A field experiment. *American Political Science Review, 94*(3), 653–663.

12. Gershon, D. (2009). *Social change 2.0: A blueprint for reinventing our world.* High Point.

13. Goldstein, N. J., Cialdini, R. B., & Griskevicius, V. (2008). A room with a viewpoint: Using social norms to motivate environmental conservation in hotels. *Journal of Consumer Research, 35*(3), 472–482.

14. Kinzig, A. P., Ehrlich, P. R., Alston, L. J., Arrow, K., Barrett, S., Buchman, T. G., Daily, G. C., Levin, B., Levin, S., Oppenheimer, M., Ostrom, E., & Saari, D. (2013). Social norms and global environmental challenges: The complex interaction of behaviors, values, and policy. *BioScience, 63*(3), 164–75.

15. La Ferrara, E., Chong, A., & Duryea, S. (2012). Soap operas and fertility: Evidence from Brazil. *American Economic Journal: Applied Economics, 4*(4), 1–31.

16. Lawson, D. F., Stevenson, K. T., Peterson, M. N., Carrier, S. J., Strnad, R. L., & Seekamp, E. (2019). Children can foster climate change concern among their parents. *Nature Climate Change, 9*(6), 458–462.

17. Mildenberger, M., & Tingley, D. (2019). Beliefs about climate beliefs: The importance of second-order opinions for climate politics. *British Journal of Political Science, 49*(4), 1279–1307.

18. Noelle-Neumann, E. (1974). The spiral of silence: A theory of public opinion. *Journal of Communication, 24*(2), 43–51.

19. Nolan, J. M., Schultz, P. W., Cialdini, R. B., Goldstein, N. J., & Griskevicius, V. (2008). Normative social influence is underdetected. *Personality and Social Psychology Bulletin, 34*(7), 913–923.

20. Palm, A. (2017). Peer effects in residential solar photovoltaics adoption—A mixed methods study of Swedish users. *Energy Research & Social Science, 26,* 1–10.

21. Paluck, E. L., & Shepherd, H. (2012). The salience of social referents: A field experiment on collective norms and harassment behavior in a school social network. *Journal of Personality and Social Psychology, 103*(6), 899–915.

22. Rogers, E. M. (2003). *Diffusion of Innovations* (5th ed.). Free Press.

23. Shultz, P. W., Nolan, J. M., Cialdini, R. B., Goldstein, N. J., & Griskevicius, V. (2007). The constructive, destructive, and reconstructive power of social norms. *Psychological Science, 18*(5), 429–34.

24. Sparkman, G., & Walton, G.M. (2017). Dynamic norms promote sustainable behavior, even if it is counternormative. *Psychological Science, 28*(11), 1663–1674.

25. Sunstein, C.R. (2019). *How change happens.* MIT.

26. Sussman, R., & Gifford, R. (2013). Be the change you want to see: Modeling food composting in public places. *Environment and Behavior, 45*(3), 323–343.

27. Van Leuvan, N., Highleyman, L., Kibe, A., & Cole, E. (2019). *Turning the page: A behavior change toolkit for reducing paper use.* Root Solutions and Association for the Advancement of Sustainability in Higher Education.

28. Wellin, E. (1955). Water boiling in a Peruvian town. In B. D. Paul (Ed.), *Health, culture and community* (pp. 71–103). NY: Russell Sage.

29. The World Bank. (2015). *World development report 2015: Mind, society, and behavior.*

30. Yale Program on Climate Change Communication (2020). *Global warming's six Americas.*

Building Block Chapter 2: Make it EASY

1. Abrahamse, W., Steg, L., Vlek, C., & Rothengatter, T. (2005). A review of intervention studies aimed at household energy conservation. *Journal of Environmental Psychology, 25*(3), 273–291.

2. Abrams, K. M., Leong, K. M., Melena, S., & Teel, T. (2020) Encouraging safe wildlife viewing in national parks: Effects of a communication campaign on visitors' behavior. *Environmental Communication, 14*(2), 255–270.

3. Aramark Higher Education. (2008). *The business and cultural acceptance case for trayless dining.*

4. Austin, J., Hatfield, D. B., Grindle, A. C., & Bailey, J. S. (1993). Increasing recycling in office environments: The effects of specific, informative cues. *Journal of Applied Behavior Analysis 26*(2), 247–253

5. Bahr, S., Sparks, D., & Hoyer, K. M. (2018). *Why didn't students complete a Free Application for Federal Student Aid (FAFSA)? A detailed look.* Stats in brief (NCES 2018-061). National Center for Education Statistics.

6. Bandura, A. (1978). Self-efficacy: Toward a unifying theory of behavioral change. *Advances in Behaviour Research and Therapy, 1*(4), 139–161.

7. Banerjee, A. V., & Duflo, E. (2011). *Poor economics: A radical rethinking of the way to fight global poverty.* Public Affairs.

8. Bernstad, A. (2014). Household food waste separation behavior and the importance of convenience. *Waste Management, 34*(7), 1317–1323.

9. Black, J. (2020). How Google got its employees to eat their vegetables. *One Zero Medium*.

10. Brown, Z., Johnstone, N., Haščič, I., Vong, L., & Barascud, F. (2013). Testing the effect of defaults on the thermostat settings of OECD employees. *Energy Economics, 39,* 128–134.

11. Carroll, G. D., Choi, J. J., Laibson, D., Madrian, B. C., & Metrick, A. (2009). Optimal defaults and active decisions. *The quarterly journal of economics, 124*(4), 1639–1674.

12. City of Durham (North Carolina U.S.A.). (n.d.). Way to go Durham website.

13. DiGiacomo, A., Wu, D. W.-L., Lenkic, P., Fraser B., Zhao, J., & Kingstone, A. (2018). Convenience improves composting and recycling rates in high-density residential buildings. *Journal of Environmental Planning and Management, 61*(2), 1–23.

14. Duffy, S., & Verges, M. (2009). It matters a hole lot: Perceptual affordances of waste containers influence recycling compliance. *Environment and Behavior, 41*(5), 741–749.

15. Ebeling, F., & Lotz, S. (2015). Domestic uptake of green energy promoted by opt-out tariffs. *Nature Climate Change, 5*(9), 868–871.

16. Fishbein, M., & Ajzen, I. (2010). *Predicting and changing behavior: The reasoned action approach.* Psychology Press.

17. Gulland, I. (2015). *Edinburgh 'nudging' success in recycling.* Zero Waste Scotland.

18. Hart, P.S., & Feldman L. (2016). The impact of climate change-related imagery and text on public opinion and behavior change. *Science Communication, 38*(4), 415–441.

19. Hungerford, H. R., & Volk, T. L. (1990). Changing learner behavior through environmental education. *The Journal of Environmental Education, 21*(3), 8–21.

20. Iyengar, S. (2010). *The art of choosing.* Twelve.

21. Iyengar, S.S., & Lepper, M.R. (2000). When choice is demotivating: can one desire too much of a good thing? *Journal of Personality and Social Psychology, 79*(6), 995–1006.

22. Jilke, S., Van Ryzin, G. G., & Van de Walle, S. (2016). Responses to decline in marketized public services: An experimental evaluation of choice overload. *Journal of Public Administration Research and Theory, 26*(3), 421–432.

23. Kahneman, D., Knetsch, J. L., & Thaler, R. H. (1991). Anomalies: The endowment effect, loss aversion, and status quo bias. *Journal of Economic Perspectives. 5*(1), 193–206.

24. Kallbekken, S., & Sælen, H. (2013). 'Nudging' hotel guests to reduce food waste as a win-win environmental measure. *Economic Letters, 119*(3), 325–327.

25. Kassirer, J. and McKenzie-Mohr, D. (1998). *Tools of Change: Proven Methods for Promoting Environmental Citizenship.* National Round Table on the Environment and the Economy (Canada). Go Boulder.

26. Kassirer, J. & Meilleur, J. (2015). *Compost coaching: House-calls help reduce waste.*

27. Keep America Beautiful. (2010). *Litter in America. Key Findings: Cigarette Butt litter.* Resources.

28. Keller, P. A., Harlam, B., Loewenstein, G., & Volpp, K. G. (2011). Enhanced active choice: A new method to motivate behavior change. *Journal of Consumer Psychology, 21*(4), 376–383.

29. Knight C. (2013). *Novo Nordisk takes environmental responsibility to a higher level.* Green Fleet Operations.

30. Kollmuss, A., & Agyeman, J. (2002). Mind the gap: why do people act environmentally and what are the barriers to pro-environmental behavior? *Environmental Education Research, 8*(3), 239–260.

31. Levie, W.H., Lentz, R. (1982). Effects of text illustrations: A review of research. *ECTJ, 30*(4), 195–232.

32. Löfgren, Å., Martinsson, P., Hennlock, M., & Sterner, T. (2012). Are experienced people affected by a pre-set default option—Results from a field experiment. *Journal of Environmental Economics and Management, 63*(1), 66–72.

33. Macfayden, G., Huntington, T., & Cappell, T. (2009). *Abandoned, lost or otherwise discarded fishing gear.* United Nations Regional Seas Reports and Studies #185.

34. Madrian, B. C., & Shea, D. F. (2001). The power of suggestion: Inertia in 401(k) participation and savings behavior. *The Quarterly Journal of Economics, 116*(4), 1149–1187.

35. Maghy, S. J. (2015). Effectiveness of mnemonics on achievement of students in mathematics at highschool level. *International Journal of Modern Engineering Research (IJMER), 5*(4), 1–4.

36. Mind Tools. (n.d.). *Chunking: Grouping information so it's easier to understand.*

37. Monterey Bay Aquarium. Seafood Watch app. website.

38. National Fish and Wildlife Foundation. (2020). *Fishing for energy.*

39. The Newsroom. (2015, January 5). Edinburgh recycling rates soar 85 per cent. *Edinburgh Evening News.*

40. Patten, B. M. (1990). The history of memory arts. *Neurology, 40*(2), 346–352.

41. PaperKarma® website. (n.d.). *Stop paper junk mail with an app.*

42. Pichert, D., & Katsikopoulos, K. V. (2008). Green defaults: Information presentation and pro-environmental behaviour. *Journal of Environmental Psychology, 28*(1), 63–73.

43. Rozin, P., Scott, S. E., Dingley, M., Urbanek, J. K., Jiang, H., & Kaltenbach, M. (2011). Nudge to nobesity I: Minor changes in accessibility decrease food intake. *Judgment and Decision Making, 6*(4), 323–332.

44. Sarantis, H. (2002). *Business guide to paper reduction: A step-by-step plan to save money by saving paper* [PDF File]. ForestEthics.

45. Scheibehenne, B.Greifeneder, R. & Todd, P.(2010). Can there ever be too many options? A meta-analytic review of choice overload. *Journal of Consumer Research, 37*(3): 409–425.

46. Schultz, P. W. (2014). Strategies for promoting proenvironmental behavior: Lots of tools but few instructions. *European Psychologist, 19*(2), 107–117.

47. Shah, A. K., Mullainathan, S., & Shafir, E. (2012). Some consequences of having too little. *Science, 338*(6107), 682–685.

48. Sousa Lourenço, J., Ciriolo, E., Rafael Almeida, S., & Troussard, X. (2016). *Behavioural insights applied to policy: European report 2016.* European Union.

49. Stagg, B. C. & Donkin, M. E. (2015). Mnemonics are an effective tool for adult beginners learning plant identification. *Journal of Biological Education, 50*(1), 24–40.

50. Stern, P. C. (2000). New environmental theories: toward a coherent theory of environmentally significant behavior. *Journal of Social Issues, 56*(3), 407–424.

51. Suizo, G. L., & Dao, T. (2010). Fleets set out to cut GHG emissions. *Automotive Fleet* (September 2010), 20–25.

52. Sunstein, C. R. (2015). *Choosing not to choose: Understanding the value of choice.* Oxford.

53. Sunstein, C. R. (2016). Do people like nudges? *Admin Law Review, 68*(2), 177–232.

54. Sunstein, C. R., & Reisch, L. A. (2018). *Greener by default.* Harvard Public Law Working Paper No. 18–10.

55. Sunstein, C.R., & Thaler, R.H. (2003) Libertarian paternalism. *American Economic Review, 93*(2), 175–179.

56. U.S. Environmental Protection Agency website. (2020). *Reducing the impact of wasted food by feeding the soil and composting.*

57. Wagner, T. P., & Toews, P. (2018). Assessing the use of default choice modification to reduce consumption of plastic straws. *Detritus 4,* 113–121.

58. Wambuguh, O. (2011). Junk mail in residential homes in the United States: Insights from a sub-urban home in California. *Resources, Conservation and Recycling, 55*(8), 782–784.

59. Webb, T. L., & Sheeran, P. (2006). Does changing behavioral intentions engender behavior change? A meta-analysis of the experimental evidence. *Psychological Bulletin, 132*(2), 249–268.

60. Yale Office of Sustainability. (n.d.). *Printing—Think before you ink* (Squid vers.).

61. Yoeli, E., Budescu, D. V., Carrico, A. R., Delmas, M. A., DeShazo, J. R., Ferraro, P. J., Forster, H. A., Kunreuther, H. Larrick, R. P., Lubell, M., Markowitz, E. M., Tonn, B., Vandenberg, M.P. & Markowitz, E. M. (2017). Behavioral science tools to strengthen energy & environmental policy. *Behavioral Science & Policy, 3*(1), 69–79.

Building Block Chapter 3: Cultivate Powerful HABITS

1. Beshears, J., Lee, H. N., Milkman, K. L., & Mislavsky, R. (2020). Creating exercise habits using incentives: The trade-off between flexibility and routinization. *Management Science* Articles in Advance.

2. Brophy, J. (1981). Teacher praise: A functional analysis. *Review of Educational Research, 51*(1), 5–32.

3. Brown, B. B., Werner, C. M., & Kim, N. (2003). Personal and contextual factors supporting the switch to transit use: Evaluating a natural transit intervention. *Analyses of Social Issues and Public Policy, 3*(1), 139–160.

4. Buchanan, K. E., Russo, R., & Anderson, B. (2015). The question of energy reduction: The problem(s) with feedback. *Energy Policy, 77*, 89–96.

5. Cameron, J., & Pierce, W. D. (1994). Reinforcement, reward, and intrinsic motivation: A meta-analysis. *Review of Educational Research, 64*(3), 363–423.

6. Carrus, G., Passafaro, P., & Bonnes, M. (2008). Emotions, habits and rational choices in ecological behaviours: The case of recycling and use of public transportation. *Journal of Environmental Psychology, 28*(1), 51–62.

7. Clear, J. (2018). *Atomic habits: An easy & proven way to build good habits & break bad ones.* Penguin.

8. Dahl, M. (2015). Changing a habit can mess with your sense of self. *New York Magazine,* The Cut.

9. Dai, H., Milkman, K. L., & Riis, J. (2014). The fresh start effect: Temporal landmarks motivate aspirational behavior. *Management Science, 10*, 2563–2582.

10. Daniels, A. C. (2000). *Bringing out the best in people.* McGraw-Hill Audio.

11. Duhigg, C. (2012). *The Power of habit: Why we do what we do in life and business.* Random House.

12. Embry, D. D., & Biglan, A. (2008). Evidence-based kernels: Fundamental units of behavioral influence. *Clinical Child and Family Psychology Review, 11*, 75–113.

13. Finkelstein, S. R., & Fishbach, A. (2012). Tell me what I did wrong: Experts seek and respond to negative feedback. *Journal of Consumer Research, 39*(1), 22–38.

14. Fischer, C. (2008). Feedback on household electricity consumption: a tool for saving energy? *Energy Efficiency, 1*, 79–104.

15. Fogg, B. J. (2010). *3 Steps to new habits.* SlideShare.

16. Froehlich, J. (2009). *Sensing and feedback of everyday activities to promote environmentally sustainable behaviors.* Doctoral Colloquium in the Adjunct Proceedings of UbiComp, Orlando, Florida, USA.

17. Fujii, S., & Kitamura, R. (2003). What does a one-month free bus ticket do to habitual drivers? An experimental analysis of habit and attitude change. *Transportation, 30*(1), 81–95.

18. Fujii, S., & Taniguchi, A. (2005). Reducing family car-use by providing travel advice or requesting behavioral plans: An experimental analysis of travel feedback programs. *Transportation Research Part D: Transport and Environment, 10*(5), 385–393.

19. Gardner, B. (2012). Habit as automaticity, not frequency. *European Health Psychologist, 14*(2), 32–36.

20. Gollwitzer, P. M. (1993). Goal achievement: The role of intentions. *European Review of Social Psychology, 4*(1), 141–185.

21. Gollwitzer, P. M., & Sheeran, P. (2006). Implementation intentions and goal achievement: A meta-analysis of effects and processes. *Advances in Experimental Social Psychology, 38*(6), 69–119.

22. Harding, M., & Hsiaw, A. (2014). Goal setting and energy efficiency. *Journal of Economic Behavior and Organization 107*(A), 209–227.

23. Hunt, W. A., Matarazzo, J. D., Weiss, S. M., & Gentry, W. D. (1979). Associative learning, habit, and health behavior. *Journal of Behavioral Medicine, 2*(2), 111–124.

24. Kahneman, D., & Tversky, A. (1979). Intuitive prediction: Biases and corrective procedures. *TIMS Studies in Management Science, 12*, 313–32.

25. Karlin, B., Zinger, J. F., & Ford, R. (2015). The effects of feedback on energy conservation: A meta-analysis. *Psychological Bulletin, 141*(6), 1205–1227.

26. Karlsson, N., Loewenstein, G., & Seppi, D. (2009). The ostrich effect: Selective attention to information. *Journal of Risk and Uncertainty, 38*, 95–115.

27. Kassirer, J., & Boddy, S. (2016). *King County in motion.*

28. Kluger, A. N., & DeNisi, A. (1996). The effects of feedback interventions on performance: A historical review, a meta-analysis, and a preliminary feedback intervention theory. *Psychological Bulletin, 119*(2), 254–284.

29. Koo, M., & Fishbach, A. (2012). The small-area hypothesis: Effects of progress monitoring on goal adherence. *Journal of Consumer Research, 39*(3), 493–509.

30. Lally, P., van Jaarsveld, C. H. M., Potts, H. W. W., & Wardle, J. (2010). How are habits formed: Modelling habit formation in the real world. *European Journal of Social Psychology, 40*(6), 998–1009.

31. Langley Group. (n.d.). *The neuroscience of change: Why it's difficult and what makes it easier.*

32. Locke, E. A., & Latham, G. P. (2002). Building a practically useful theory of goal setting and task motivation: A 35-year odyssey. *American Psychologist, 57*(9), 705–717.

33. Martin, S. J., Goldstein, N., & Cialdini, R. (2014). *The small big: Small changes that spark big influence.* Hachette.

34. Martiros, N., Burgess, A. A., & Graybiel, A. M. (2018). Inversely active striatal projection neurons and interneurons selectively delimit useful behavioral sequences. *Current Biology, 28*(4), 560–573.

35. Milkman, K. L., Minson, J. A., & Volpp K. G. M. (2013). Holding the hunger games hostage at the gym: An evaluation of temptation bundling. *Management Science, 60*(2), 283–299.

36. Mowrer, O. H., & Jones, H. (1945). Habit strength as a function of the pattern of reinforcement. *Journal of Experimental Psychology, 35*(4), 293.

37. Neal, D. T., Wood, W., Labrecque, J. S., & Lally, P. (2012). How do habits guide behavior? Perceived and actual triggers of habits in daily life. *Journal of Experimental Social Psychology, 48*(2), 492–498.

38. Neal, D. T., Wood, W., & Quinn, J. M. (2006). Habits: A repeat performance. *Current Directions in Psychological Science, 15*(4), 198–202.

39. Neal, D., Vujcic, J., Hernandez, O., & Wood, W. (2015). *The science of habit: Creating disruptive and sticky behavior change in handwashing behavior.* USAID/WASHplus Project.

40. Poldrack, R. A., Clark, J., Paré-Blagoev, E. J., Shohamy, D., Moyano, J. C., Myers, C. E., & Gluck, M. A. (2001). Interactive memory systems in the human brain. *Nature, 414*(6863), 546-550.

41. Quinn, J. M., Pascoe, A. M., Wood, W., & Neal, D. T. (2010). Can't control yourself? Monitor those bad habits. *Personality and Social Psychology Bulletin, 36*(4), 499–511.

42. Rajbhandari-Thapa, J., Ingerson, K., & Lewis, K. H. (2018). Impact of trayless dining intervention on food choices of university students. *Archives of Public Health, 76*(1), 61.

43. Rogers, T., Milkman, K. L., John, L. K., & Norton, M. I. (2015). Beyond good intentions: Prompting people to make plans improves follow-through on important tasks. *Behavioral Science & Policy, 1*(2), 33–41.

44. Ross, J. (2014, July 7). *Information displays that change driver behavior.* UX Matters.

45. Sanguinetti, A., Dombrovski, K., & Sikand, S. (2018). Information, timing, and display: A design-behavior framework for improving the effectiveness of eco-feedback. *Energy Research & Social Science, 39*, 55–68.

46. Schneider, S. M. (2012). *The science of consequences: how they affect genes, change the brain, and impact our world.* Prometheus.

47. Sheeran, P., Webb, T. L., & Gollwitzer, P. M. (2005). The interplay between goal intentions and implementation intentions. *Personality and Social Psychology Bulletin. 31*(1), 87–98.

48. Sherwin, K. (2016). *Fresh start effect: How to motivate users with new beginnings.* Nielsen Norman Group.

49. Skinner, B. F. (1958). Reinforcement today. *American Psychologist, 13*(3), 94–99.

50. Swim, J., Clayton, S., Doherty, T., Gifford, R., Howard, G., Reser, J., Stern, P. & Weber, E. (2009). *Psychology and global climate change: Addressing a multi-faceted phenomenon and set of challenges* (pp. 66–67). American Psychological Association.

51. Thompson, S., Michaelson, J., Abdallah, S., Johnson, V., Morris, D., Riley, K., & Simms, A. (2011). *'Moments of change' as opportunities for influencing behaviour: A report to the Department for Environment, Food and Rural Affairs.*

52. Verplanken, B., Walker, I., Davis, A., & Jurasek, M. (2008). Context change and travel mode choice: Combining the habit discontinuity and self- activation hypotheses. *Journal of Environmental Psychology, 28*(2), 121–127.

53. Verplanken, B., & Roy, D. (2016). Empowering interventions to promote sustainable lifestyles: Testing the habit discontinuity hypothesis in a field experiment. *Journal of Environmental Psychology, 45,* 127–134.

54. Wood, W., & Neal, D. T. (2007). A new look at habits and the habit-goal interface. *Psychological Review, 114*(4), 843–863.

55. Wood, W., & Neal, D. T. (2016). Healthy through habit: Interventions for initiating & maintaining health behavior change. *Behavioral Science & Policy, 2*(1), 71–83.

56. Wood, W., Quinn, J. M., & Kashy, D. A. (2002). Habits in everyday life: Thought, emotion, and action. *Journal of Personality and Social Psychology, 83*(6), 1281–1297.

57. Wood, W., & Rünger, D. (2016). Psychology of habit. *Annual Review of Psychology, 67,* 289–314.

Building Block Chapter 4: Activate ATTACHMENT

1. Adams, K. (2013). *Back to the story spine.* Aerogramme Writers' Studio.

2. Ahn, S. J. (G.), Bailenson, J. N., & Park, D. (2014). Short- and long-term effects of embodied experiences in immersive virtual environments on environmental locus of control and behavior. *Computers in Human Behavior, 39,* 235–245.

3. Akerlof, K., Maibach, E. W., Fitzgerald, D., Cedeno, A. Y., & Neuman, A. (2013). Do people "personally experience" global warming, and if so how, and does it matter? *Global Environmental Change, 23*(1), 81–91.

4. Banse, L. (2013). *Seeing is believing: A guide to visual storytelling best practices.* Resource Media.

5. Bauer, M. A., Wilkie, J. E. B., Kim, J. K., & Bodenhausen, G. V. (2012). Cuing consumerism: Situational materialism undermines personal and social well-being. *Psychological Science, 23*(5), 517–523.

6. Bergquist, M., Nilsson, A., & Schultz, P. W. (2019). Experiencing a Severe Weather Event Increases Concern About Climate Change. *Frontiers in Psychology, 10,* 220.

7. Bicchieri, C. (2017). *Norms in the wild: how to diagnose, measure, and change social norms.* Oxford.

8. Bingham, S. (2009). Climate change: a moral issue. In S.C. Moser and L. Dilling (Eds.) *Creating a climate for change: Communicating climate change and facilitating social change* (pp. 153–166). Cambridge.

9. Blackmore, E., & Holmes, T. (2013). *Common cause for nature: Finding values and frames in the conservation sector.* Public Interest Research Centre.

10. Campbell, T. H., & Kay, A. C. (2014). Solution aversion: On the relation between ideology and motivated disbelief. *Journal of Personality and Social Psychology, 107*(5), 809–824.

11. Center for Research on Environmental Decisions. (2009). Beware the overuse of emotional appeals. In *The Psychology of Climate Change Communication.* Columbia University.

12. Clarke, C. E., Bugden, D., Hart, P. S., Stedman, R. C., Jacquet, J. B., Evensen, D. T. N., & Boudet, H. S. (2016). How geographic distance and political ideology interact to influence public perception of unconventional oil/natural gas development. *Energy Policy, 97,* 301–309.

13. Corner, A., Markowitz, E., & Pidgeon, N. (2014). Public engagement with climate change: the role of human values. *Wiley Interdisciplinary Reviews: Climate Change, 5*(3), 411–422.

14. Dahlstrom, M. F. (2014). Using narratives and storytelling to communicate science with nonexpert audiences. *Proceedings of the National Academy of Sciences, 111*(4), 13614–13620.

15. de Groot, J. I. M., & Steg, L. (2009). Mean or green: which values can promote stable pro-environmental behavior? *Conservation Letters, 2*(2), 61–66.

16. de Wit, J. B. F., Das, E., & Vet, R. (2008). What works best: Objective statistics or a personal testimonial? An assessment of the persuasive effects of different types of message evidence on risk perception. *Health Psychology, 27*(1), 110–115.

17. Desvousges, W. H., Johnson, F. R., Dunford, R. W., Boyle, K. J., Hudson, S. P. & Wilson, K. N. (2010). *Measuring nonuse damages using contingent valuation: An experimental evaluation of accuracy* (2nd ed., Monograph 92–1). Research Triangle Institute.

18. Dickinson, J. L., McLeod, P., Bloomfield, R., & Allred, S. (2016). Which moral foundations predict willingness to make lifestyle changes to avert climate change in the USA. *PLOS ONE, 11*(10).

19. Feinberg, M., & Willer, R. (2012). The moral roots of environmental attitudes. *Psychological Science, 24*(1), 56–62.

20. FrameWorks Institute. (2017). *Expanding our repertoire: Why and how to get collective climate solutions in the frame.*

21. Glick M. (2017). Believing is seeing: Confirmation bias. *Journal of the American Dental Association, 148*(3), 131–132.

22. Goodwin Simon Strategic Research & Wonder: Strategies for Good. (2019). *Heartwired to love the ocean: A messaging guide for advocates.*

23. Graham, S., Barnett, J., Fincher, R., Hurlimann, A., Mortreux, C., & Waters, E. (2013). The social values at risk from sea-level rise. *Environmental Impact Assessment Review, 41*, 45–52.

24. Haidt, J. (2012). *The righteous mind: Why good people are divided by politics and religion*. Pantheon.

25. Haidt, J., & Joseph, C. (2004). Intuitive ethics: how innately prepared intuitions generate culturally variable virtues. *Daedalus, 133*(4), 55–66.

26. Haluza-DeLay, R. (2014). Religion and climate change: varieties in viewpoints and practices. *Wiley Interdisciplinary Reviews: Climate Change, 5*(2), 261–279.

27. Hanel, P. H. P., Litzellachner, L. F., & Maio, G. R. (2018). An empirical comparison of human value models. *Frontiers in Psychology, 9*, 1643.

28. Hansla, A., Gamble, A., Juliusson, A., & Gärling, T. (2008). The relationships between awareness of consequences, environmental concern, and value orientations. *Journal of Environmental Psychology, 28*(1), 1–9.

29. Hardisty, D. J., Johnson, E. J., & Weber, E. U. (2009). A Dirty Word or a Dirty World?: Attribute Framing, Political Affiliation, and Query Theory. *Psychological Science, 21*(1), 86–92.

30. Isola, P., Xiao, J., Parikh, D., Torralba, A., & Oliva, A. (2013). What makes a photograph memorable? *IEEE Transactions on Pattern Analysis and Machine Intelligence, 36*(7), 1469–1482.

31. Kahneman, D., Knetsch, J. L., & Thaler, R. H. (1990). Experimental tests of the endowment effect and the coase theorem. *Journal of Political Economy, 98*(6), 1325–1348.

32. Kearney, A. R. (1994). Understanding global change: A cognitive perspective on communicating through stories. *Climatic Change, 27*(4), 419–441.

33. Kendall-Taylor, N. (2017). *Framing stories for change*. FrameWorks.

34. Lakoff, G. (2004). *Don't think of an elephant!: Know your values and frame the debate: The essential guide for progressives*. Chelsea Green.

35. Lakoff, G. (2007). *Whose freedom?: The battle over America's most important idea*. Picador.

36. Lakoff, G., & Wehling, E. (2012). *The little blue book: The essential guide to thinking and talking democratic*. Free Press.

37. Lee, S., & Feeley, T. H. (2016). The identifiable victim effect: a meta-analytic review. *Social Influence, 11*(3), 199–215.

38. Linville, P. W., & Fischer, G. W. (1991). Preferences for separating or combining events. *Journal of Personality and Social Psychology, 60*(1), 5–23.

39. Manzo, K. (2010). Beyond polar bears? Re-envisioning climate change. *Meteorological Applications, 17*(2), 196–208.

40. Markowitz, E., Hodge, C., & Harp, G. (2014). *Connecting on climate: A guide to effective climate change communication.* Center for Research on Environmental Decisions and ecoAmerica.

41. Markowitz, E. M., & Shariff, A. F. (2012). Climate change and moral judgment. Nature *Climate Change, 2*(4), 243–247.

42. Meisel, D. (2013). *Storytelling: Why it matters & how to get it right.* ClimateAccess.org.

43. Mercier, H. (2017). Confirmation bias—Myside bias. In R. F. Pohl (Ed.), *Cognitive illusions: Intriguing phenomena in judgement, thinking and memory* (pp. 99–114). Psychology Press.

44. Mirosa, M., Lawson, R., & Gnoth, D. (2011). Linking personal values to energy-efficient behaviors in the home. *Environment and Behavior, 45*(4), 455–475.

45. Moyer-Gusé, E., Tchernev, J. M., & Walther-Martin, W. (2019). The persuasiveness of a humorous environmental narrative combined with an explicit persuasive appeal. *Science Communication, 41*(4), 422–441.

46. Myers, T. A., Maibach, E. W., Roser-Renouf, C., Akerlof, K. & Leiserowitz, A. (2013). The relationship between personal experience and belief in the reality of global warming. *Nature Climate Change 3,* 343–347.

47. Nisbett, R. E., & Ross, L. (1980). *Human inference: Strategies and shortcomings of social judgement.* Prentice Hall.

48. Nyhan, B., & Reifler, J. (2010). When corrections fail: The persistence of political misperceptions. *Political Behavior, 32*(2), 303–330.

49. O'Brien, K. L., & Wolf, J. (2010). A values-based approach to vulnerability and adaptation to climate change. *Wiley Interdisciplinary Reviews: Climate Change, 1*(2), 232–242.

50. Olson, R. (2019). *Narrative is everything: The ABT framework and narrative evolution.* Prairie Starfish Productions.

51. Oreskes, N., & Conway, E. M. (2011). *Merchants of doubt: How a handful of scientists obscured the truth on issues from tobacco smoke to global warming.* Bloomsbury.

52. Paluck, E. L. (2009). Reducing intergroup prejudice and conflict using the media: a field experiment in Rwanda. *Journal of personality and social psychology, 96*(3), 574–587.

53. Sachdeva, S. (2016). Religious identity, beliefs, and views about climate change. In H. van Storch (Ed.), *Oxford Research Encyclopedia of Climate Science.* Oxford.

54. Scannell, L., & Gifford, R. (2011). Personally relevant climate change: The role of place attachment and local versus global message framing in engagement. *Environment and Behavior, 45*(1), 60–85.

55. Schwartz, S. H. (1992). Universals in the content and structure of values: Theoretical advances and empirical tests in 20 countries. *Advances in Experimental Social Psychology, 25,* 1–65.

56. Simon, A. F., Kendall-Taylor, N., & Lindland, E. (2013). *Using values to build public understanding and support for environmental health work.* FrameWorks Institute.

57. Slovic, P. (2000). *The perception of risk.* Routledge.

58. Small, D.A., Loewenstein, G. (2003). Helping a victim or helping the victim: Altruism and identifiability. *Journal of Risk and Uncertainty 26,* 5–16.

59. Spence, A., Poortinga, W., & Pidgeon, N. (2012). The psychological distance of climate change. *Risk Analysis: An International Journal, 32*(6), 957–972.

60. Steg, L., de Groot, J. I. M., Dreijerink, L., Abrahamse, W., & Siero, F. (2011). General antecedents of personal norms, policy acceptability, and intentions: The role of values, worldviews, and environmental concern. *Society & Natural Resources, 24*(4), 349–367.

61. Stern, P. C., & Dietz, T. (1994). The value basis of environmental concern. *Journal of Social Issues, 50*(3), 65–84.

62. Taquet, M., Quoidbach, J., de Montjoye, Y.-A., Desseilles, M., & Gross, J. J. (2016). Hedonism and the choice of everyday activities. *Proceedings of the National Academy of Sciences, 113*(35), 9769–9773.

63. Thomas, D. C. & Inkson, K. (2009). Making decisions across cultures. In *Cultural intelligence: Living and working globally* (2nd ed., pp. 85–112). Berrett-Koehler.

64. Trope, Y., & Liberman, N. (2010). Construal-level theory of psychological distance. *Psychological review, 117*(2), 440–463.

65. VanDeCarr, P. (2015). *3 tips for telling stories that move people to action.*

66. Vansen, D. (2013). *The Belizean radio soap opera: Puenta Fuego.* My Beautiful Belize.

67. Weaver, C. P., Moss, R. H., Ebi, K. L., Gleick, P. H., Stern, P. C., Tebaldi, C., Wilson, R. S., & Arvai, J. L. (2017). Reframing climate change assessments around risk: Recommendations for the US national climate assessment. *Environmental Research Letters, 12*(8).

68. Weber, E. U. (2010). What shapes perceptions of climate change? *Wiley Interdisciplinary Reviews: Climate Change, 1*(3), 332–342.

69. Whitmarsh, L. (2008). Are flood victims more concerned about climate change than other people? The role of direct experience in risk perception and behavioral response. *Journal of Risk Research, 11*(3), 351–374.

70. Whitmarsh, L. (2009). Behavioural responses to climate change: Asymmetry of intentions and impacts. *Journal of Environmental Psychology, 29*(1), 13–23.

Building Block Chapter 5: Design it to be VIVID

1. Aronson, E., & O'Leary, M. (1982). The relative effectiveness of models and prompts on energy conservation: A field experiment in a shower room. *Journal of Environmental Systems, 12*(3), 219–224.

2. Bailey, J. O., Bailenson, J. N., Flora, J., Armel, K. C., Voelker, D., & Reeves, B. (2015). The impact of vivid messages on reducing energy consumption related to hot water use. *Environment and Behavior, 47*(5), 570–592.

3.   Balkenius, C. (2000). Attention, habituation and conditioning: Toward a computational model. *Cognitive Science Quarterly, 1*(2), 171–204.

4.   The Behavioral Insights Team. (2020). *A menu for change.*

5.   The Behavioral Insights Team. (2013). *Applying behavioural insights to charitable giving.*

6.   Burn, S. M. (1991). Social psychology and the stimulation of recycling behaviors: The block leader approach. *Journal of Applied Social Psychology, 21*(8), 611–629.

7.   Cacioppo, J. T., & Petty, R. E. (1979). Effects of message repetition and position on cognitive response, recall, and persuasion. *Journal of Personality and Social Psychology, 37*(1), 97–109.

8.   Center for Research on Environmental Decisions and ecoAmerica. (2014). *Connecting on climate: A guide to effective climate change communication.*

9.   Centre for Social Innovation. (2015). *Case study: Green footprints.* www.keepbritaintidy. org/sites/default/files/resources/KBT_CFSI_Green_Footprints_Case_Study_ 2015.pdf.

10.   Chapman University. (n.d.). *Chapter 9: Waste management* (PDF). www.chapman. edu/campus-services/sustainability/_files/environmental-audit/pdfs/ch9-waste.pdf

11.   Corner, A., Webster, R., & Teriete, C. (2015). *Climate visuals: Seven principles for visual climate change communication* (based on international social research). Climate Outreach.

12.   Dayan, E., & Bar-Hillel, M. (2011). Nudge to nobesity II: Menu positions influence food orders. *Judgment and Decision Making, 6*(4), 333–342.

13.   Filkuková, P., & Klempe, S. H. (2013). Rhyme as reason in commercial and social advertising. *Scandinavian Journal of Psychology, 54*(5), 423–431.

14.   Food Recovery Network National Team. (2017). *Weigh the waste how-to guide.* www. foodrecoverynetwork.org/s/Weigh-the-Waste-How-to-Guide-v001.pdf.

15.   Frantz, C. M., Flynn, B., Atwood, S., Mostow, D., Xu, C., & Kahl, S. (2016). Changing energy behavior through community based social marketing. In W.L. Filho & M. Zint (Eds.), *The contribution of social sciences to sustainable development at universities* (pp. 259–272). Springer.

16.   Gonzales, M. H., Aronson, E., & Costanzo, M. A. (1988). Using social cognition and persuasion to promote energy conservation: A quasi-experiment. *Journal of Applied Social Psychology, 18*(12), 1049–1066.

17.   Goodhew, J., Pahl, S., Auburn, T., & Goodhew, S. (2015). Making heat visible: Promoting energy conservation behaviors through thermal imaging. *Environment and Behavior, 47*(10), 1059–1088.

18.   Guyader, H., Ottosson, M., & Witell, L. (2017). You can't buy what you can't see: Retailer practices to increase the green premium. *Journal of Retailing and Consumer Services, 34,* 319–325.

19. Hubbub & Common Works. (n.d.). *Ballot bin.* www.hubbub.org.uk/ballot-bin.

20. Hubbub. (n.d.). *Neat Streets impact report: Testing approaches to creating litter free streets.*

21. Hunt, E. (2017, September 1). Popsicles of pollution: Ice lollies highlight Taiwan's contaminated waterways. *The Guardian.*

22. iNudgeYou. (n.d.). *Green nudge: Nudging litter into the bin.*

23. Janiszewski, C., & Meyvis, T. (2001). Effects of brand logo complexity, repetition, and spacing on processing fluency and judgment. *Journal of Consumer Research, 28*(1), 18–32.

24. Jennings, R. (2017, July 16). Wastewater on a stick: The popsicles from Taiwan that you really, really don't want to eat. *Los Angeles Times.*

25. Johnson, K. (2006). *Cutting through advertising clutter.*

26. Kahn, M. E., & Kotchen, M. J. (2011). Business cycle effects on concern about climate change: The chilling effect of recession. *Climate Change Economics, 2*(3), 257–273.

27. Kahneman, D. (2011). Thinking, fast and slow. Farrar, Straus And Giroux.

28. Kaplan, S. & Kaplan, R. (1982). *Humanscape: Environments for people.* Ulrich's Books.

29. Kroese, F. M., Marchiori, D. R., & de Ridder, D. T. (2016). Nudging healthy food choices: A field experiment at the train station. *Journal of Public Health, 38*(2), e133–e137.

30. Lowry, W. R., & Joslyn, M. (2014). The determinants of salience of energy issues. *Review of Policy Research, 31*(3),153–172.

31. Meijers, M. H. C., Remmelswaal, P., & Wonneberger, A. (2019). Using visual impact metaphors to stimulate environmentally friendly behavior: The roles of response efficacy and evaluative persuasion knowledge. *Environmental Communication, 13*(8), 995–1008.

32. Meis-Harris, J., & Kashima, Y. (2017). Signage as a tool for behavioral change: Direct and indirect routes to understanding the meaning of a sign. *PLOS ONE, 12*(8), e0182975.

33. Miller, J. M., & Krosnick, J. A. (1998). The impact of candidate name order on election outcomes. *Public Opinion Quarterly 62*(3), 291-330.

34. Montazeri, S., Gonzalez, R., Yoon, C., & Papalambros, P. Y. (2012). *Color, cognition, and recycling: How the design of everyday objects prompt behavior change.* International Design Conference DESIGN 2012.

35. Nicholson-Cole, S. A. (2005). Representing climate change futures: A critique on the use of images for visual communication. *Computers, Environment and Urban Systems, 29*(3), 255–273.

36. Nisbett, R. E., & Ross, L. (1980). *Human inference: Strategies and shortcomings of social judgment.* Prentice Hall.

37. Nordman, E.C. (2017). *Flood risk and insurance.* CIPR Study Series 2017–1.

38. Goodwin Simon Strategic Research & Wonder: Strategies for Good. (2019). *Heartwired to love the ocean: A messaging guide for advocates.*

39. O'Neill, S. J., Boykoff, M., Niemeyer, S., & Day, S. A. (2013). On the use of imagery for climate change engagement. *Global Environmental Change, 23*(2), 413–421.

40. Petrolia, D. R., Landry, C. E., & Coble, K. H. (2013). Risk preferences, risk perceptions, and flood insurance. *Land Economics, 89*(2), 227–245.

41. Plotnikoff, R. C., McCargar, L. J., Wilson, P. M., & Loucaides, C. A. (2005). Efficacy of an e-mail intervention for the promotion of physical activity and nutrition behavior in the workplace context. *American Journal of Health Promotion, 19*(6), 422–429.

42. Rae, B., Eadie, D., & Stead, M. (2015). *NUDGE study implementation toolkit: Promoting the use of street litter bins.* Zero Waste Scotland.

43. Rao, T. (2017, September 20). San Francisco chefs serve up a message about climate change. *New York Times.*

44. Skov, L. R., Lourenco, S., Hansen, G. L., Mikkelsen, B. E., & Schofield, C. (2013). Choice architecture as a means to change eating behaviour in self-service settings: A systematic review. *Obesity Reviews, 14*(3), 187–196.

45. Stand for Trees. (2019). *Footprint calculator.* standfortrees.org/footprint-calculator/.

46. Stubbs, N. D., Sanders, S., Jones, D. B., Geraci, S. A., & Stephenson, P. L. (2012). Methods to reduce outpatient non-attendance. *The American Journal of the Medical Sciences, 344*(3), 211–219.

47. Sussman, R., & Gifford, R. (2012). Please turn off the lights: The effectiveness of visual prompts. *Applied Ergonomics, 43*(3), 596–603.

48. Takahashi, R., Todo, Y., & Funaki, Y. (2018). How can we motivate consumers to purchase certified forest coffee? Evidence from a laboratory randomized experiment using eye-trackers. *Ecological Economics, 150,* 107–121.

49. Thomas-Walters, L., & J Raihani, N. (2017). Supporting conservation: The roles of flagship species and identifiable victims. *Conservation Letters, 10*(5), 581–587.

50. United States Environmental Protection Agency. (2016). *Carbon footprint calculator.*

51. Urban Sustainability Directors Network. *The "Cool is Clean" slogan was created by the Urban Sustainability Directors Network (USDN) in conjunction with Action Research for a pilot program.*

52. Wallander, S., Ferraro, P., & Higgins, N. (2017). Addressing participant inattention in federal programs: A field experiment with the conservation reserve program. *American Journal of Agricultural Economics, 99*(4), 914–931.

53. Whitehouse, A. J. O., Maybery, M. T., & Durkin, K. (2006). The development of the picture-superiority effect. *British Journal of Developmental Psychology, 24*(4), 767–773.

Building Block Chapter 6: Leverage our need for consistent IDENTITY

1. Baca-Motes, K., Brown, A., Gneezy, A., Keenan, E. A., & Nelson, L. D. (2013). Commitment and behavior change: Evidence from the field. *Journal of Consumer Research, 39*(5), 1070–1084.

2. Bashir, N. Y., Lockwood, P., Chasteen, A. L., Nadolny, D., & Noyes, I. (2013). The ironic impact of activists: Negative stereotypes reduce social change influence. *European Journal of Social Psychology, 43*(7), 614–626.

3. Bauer, M. A., Wilkie, J. E. B., Kim, J. K., & Bodenhausen, G. V. (2012). Cuing consumerism: Situational materialism undermines personal and social well-being. *Psychological Science, 23*(5), 517–523.

4. Bryan, C. J., Walton, G. M., Rogers, T., & Dweck, C. S. (2011). Motivating voter turnout by invoking the self. *Proceedings of the National Academy of Sciences, 108*(31), 12653–12656.

5. Burger, J. M., & Caldwell, D. F. (2003). The effects of monetary incentives and labeling on the foot-in-the-door effect: Evidence for a self-perception process. *Basic and Applied Social Psychology, 25*(3), 235–241.

6. Center for Research on Environmental Decisions and ecoAmerica. (2014). *Connecting on climate: A guide to effective climate change communication.*

7. Cherry, E. (2019). "Not an environmentalist": Strategic centrism, cultural stereotypes, and disidentification. *Sociological Perspectives, 62*(5), 755–772.

8. Cialdini, R. B. (2009). *Influence: Science and practice* (5th ed.). Pearson.

9. Festinger, L. (1957). *A theory of cognitive dissonance.* Stanford University Press.

10. Freedman, J. L., & Fraser, S. C. (1966). Compliance without pressure: The foot-in-the-door technique. *Journal of Personality and Social Psychology, 4*(2), 195–202.

11. Gatersleben, B., Murtagh, N., Cherry, M., & Watkins, M. (2019). Moral, wasteful, frugal, or thrifty? Identifying consumer identities to understand and manage pro-environmental behavior. *Environment and Behavior, 51*(1), 24–49.

12. Gollwitzer, P. M. (1999). Implementation intentions: Strong effects of simple plans. *American Psychologist, 54*(7), 493-503.

13. Hart, P. S., & Nisbet, E. C. (2012). Boomerang effects in science communication: How motivated reasoning and identity cues amplify opinion polarization about climate mitigation policies. *Communication Research, 39*(6), 701–723.

14. Iyengar, S. & Lepper, M. M. (2000). When choice is demotivating: Can one desire too much of a good thing? *Journal of Personality & Social Psychology, 79*(6), 995–1006.

15. Knezevic, I. (2009). Hunting and environmentalism: Conflict or misperceptions. *Human Dimensions of Wildlife, 14*(1), 12–20.

16. Litwin, K. (2019, September 9). *McGill's sustainability programs awarded top prize for staff engagement.*

17. Lokhorst, A. M., van Dijk, J., Staats, H., van Dijk, E., & De Snoo, G. (2010). Using tailored information and public commitment to improve the environmental quality of farm lands: An example from the Netherlands. *Human ecology, 38*(1), 113–122.

18. Lokhorst, A. M., Werner, C., Staats, H., van Dijk, E., & Gale, J. L. (2013). Commitment and behavior change: A meta-analysis and critical review of commitment-making strategies in environmental research. *Environment and Behavior, 45*(1), 3–34.

19. Magno, F. & Dossena, G. (2020). Pride of being part of a host community? Medium-term effects of mega-events on citizen quality life: The case of the World Expo 2015 Milan. *Journal of Destination Marketing & Management, 15,* 100410.

20. Maki, A., Carrico, A. R., Raimi, K. T., Truelove, H. B., Araujo, B., & Yeung, K. L. (2019). Meta-analysis of pro-environmental behaviour spillover. *Nature Sustainability, 2*(4), 307–315.

21. Marsden, M., Bronner, L., Cunow, S., Rand, C., Searle, D., Hennelly, L. O., Rolfe-Redding, J., Zhou, J., Vidal, R. O., & Medina, E. O. (2019). *Climate action campaign action-taking test* (PDF).

22. McClure, T., & Spence, R. (2006). *Don't mess with Texas: the story behind the legend.* Idea City Press.

23. Nilsson, A., Bergquist, M., & Schultz, W. P. (2017). Spillover effects in environmental behaviors, across time and context: A review and research agenda. *Environmental Education Research, 23*(4), 573–589.

24. Nodjimbadem, K. (2017). The Trashy Beginnings of "Don't Mess With Texas." *Smithsonian Magazine.*

25. Norton, M. I., Mochon, D., & Ariely, D. (2011). The IKEA effect: When labor leads to love. *Journal of Consumer Psychology, 22*(3), 453–460.

26. Priolo, D., Milhabet, I., Codou, O., Fointiat, V., Lebarbenchon, E., & Gabarrot, F. (2016). Encouraging ecological behaviour through induced hypocrisy and inconsistency. *Journal of Environmental Psychology, 47,* 166–180.

27. Rare and The Behavioural Insights Team. (2019). *Behavior change for nature: A behavioral science toolkit for practitioners.* Rare Center for Behavior and the Environment.

28. Stone, J., & Fernandez, N. C. (2008). To practice what we preach: The use of hypocrisy and cognitive dissonance to motivate behavior change. *Social and Personality Psychology Compass, 2*(2), 1024–1051.

29. Stryker, S., & Burke, P. J. (2000). The past, present, and future of an identity theory. Social *Psychology Quarterly, 63*(4), 284–297.

30. Sumner, W. G. (1906). *Folkways: A study of the social importance of usages, manners, customs, mores, and morals.* Ginn & Co.

31. Theodore Roosevelt Conservation Partnership & Lori Weigel Public Opinion Strategies (2017). *TCRP's National Sportsmen Survey.* www.trcp.org/wp-content/uploads/2017/06/TRCP-Natl-Sportsmens-Poll_Complete.pdf.

32. Thøgersen, J. & Crompton, T. (2009). Simple and painless? The limitations of spillover in environmental campaigning. *Journal of Consumer Policy, 32*(2), 141–163.

33. Truelove, H. B., Carrico, A. R., Weber, E. U., Raimi, K. T., & Vandenbergh, M. P. (2014). Positive and negative spillover of pro-environmental behavior: An integrative review and theoretical framework. *Global Environmental Change, 29,* 127–138.

34. Unsworth, K. L., & Fielding, K. S. (2014). It's political: How the salience of one's political identity changes climate change beliefs and policy support. *Global Environmental Change, 27,* 131–137.

35. van der Werff, E., Steg, L., & Keizer, K. (2014). Follow the signal: When past environmental actions signal who you are. *Journal of Environmental Psychology, 40,* 273–282.

36. Vennard, D. (2017). *Don't put vegetables in the corner: A q&a with behavioral science researcher Linda Bacon.* Sustainable Brands.

37. Watt, S. (2019, May 17). *The McGill staff engagement ladder.* AASHE Sustainability Hub.

38. White, K., Habib, R., & Hardisty, D. J. (2019). How to SHIFT consumer behaviors to be more sustainable: A literature review and guiding framework. *Journal of Marketing, 83*(3), 22–49.

39. Whitmarsh, L., & O'Neill, S. (2010). Green identity, green living? The role of pro-environmental self-identity in determining consistency across diverse pro-environmental behaviours. *Journal of Environmental Psychology, 30*(3), 305–314.

40. Williams, L. A. & Desteno, D. (2008). Pride and Perseverance: The Motivational Role of Pride. *Journal of Personality and Social Psychology, 94*(6), 1007–1017.

Building Block Chapter 7: Empower Through Active OPTIMISM

1. Baker, A. (2016, May 16). *"A hard act to follow: After tackling a toilet, now what?"* Denver Water TAP.

2. Bandura, A. (1997). *Self-efficacy: The exercise of control.* W.H. Freeman and Company.

3. Bandura, A. (2000). Exercise of human agency through collective efficacy. *Current Directions in Psychological Science, 9*(3), 75–78.

4. Bandura, A. (2010). Self-efficacy. In I. B. Weiner & W. E. Craighead (Eds.), *The Corsini encyclopedia of psychology* (4th ed.). Wiley.

5. Bandura, A. (1977) *Social learning theory.* Prentice Hall.

6. Bissing-Olson, M. J., Fielding, K. S., & Iyer, A. (2016). Experiences of pride, not guilt, predict pro-environmental behavior when pro-environmental descriptive norms are more positive. *Journal of Environmental Psychology, 45,* 145–153.

7. Bonniface, L. & Henley, N. (2008). 'A drop in the bucket': Collective efficacy perceptions and environmental behaviour. *Australian Journal of Social Issues, 43*(3), 345–358.

8. Borg, K. & Goodwin, D. (2018, July 19) *Here's a funny thing: can comedy really change our environmental behaviors?* The Conversation.

9. Brown, B. (2006) Shame resilience: A grounded theory study on women and shame. *Families in Society: The Journal of Contemporary Social Services, 87*(1), 43–52.

10. Camilleri, A. R. & Larrick, R. P. (2019). The collective aggregation effect: Aggregating potential collective action increases prosocial behavior. *Journal of Experimental Psychology: General, 148*(3), 550–569.

11. Chang, C.-T. (2012). Are guilt appeals a panacea in green advertising? The right formula of issue proximity and environmental consciousness. *International Journal of Advertising, 31*(4), 741–771.

12. Chattoo, C. B. & Feldman, L. (2020). *A comedian and an activist walk into a bar: The serious role of comedy in social justice.* University of California.

13. Cohn, M. A., & Fredrickson, B. L. (2009). Positive emotions. In S. J. Lopez & C. R. Snyder (Eds.), *Oxford handbook of positive psychology* (2nd ed., p. 13–24). Oxford.

14. Corner, A., Webster, R., & Teriete, C. (2015). *Climate visuals: Seven principles for visual climate change communication (based on international social research).* Climate Outreach.

15. Courville, S. & Piper, N. (2004). Harnessing hope through NGO activism. *The Annals of the American Academy of Political and Social Science, 592*(1), 39–61.

16. Frantz, C. M. & Mayer, F. (2009). The emergency of climate change: Why are we failing to take action? *Analyses of Social Issues and Public Policy, 9*(1), 205–222.

17. Fredrickson, B. L. & Branigan, C. (2005). Positive emotions broaden the scope of attention and thought-action repertoires. *Cognition and Emotion, 19*(3), 313–332.

18. Galai, D. & Sade, O. (2006). The "ostrich effect" and the relationship between the liquidity and the yields of financial assets. *Journal of Business, 79*(5), 2741–2759.

19. Grazzini, L., Rodrigo, P. G.. K., Aiello, G., & Viglia, G. (2018). Loss or gain? The role of message framing in hotel guests' recycling behaviour. *Journal of Sustainable Tourism, 26*(1), 1–23.

20. Griese, K.-M., Alexandrov, A., Michaelis, C., & Lilly, B. (2018). Examining the effects of humor in environmentally-friendly advertising. *Marketing Management Journal, 28*(1), 30–47.

21. Health Communication Capacity Collaborative. (2014). *The extended parallel processing model.*

22. Heslin, P. A. (1999). Boosting empowerment by developing self-efficacy. Asia Pacific *Journal of Human Resources, 37*(1), 52–64.

23. Jaquet, J. (2015). *Is shame necessary? New uses for an old tool.* Vintage.

24. Kahneman, D., & Tversky, A. (1979). Prospect theory: An analysis of decision under risk. *Econometrica, 47*(2), 263–292.

25. Lewis, I. M., Watson, B., & White, K. M. (2010). Response efficacy: The key to minimizing rejection and maximizing acceptance of emotion-based anti-speeding messages. Accident *Analysis and Prevention, 42*(2), 459–467.

26. Manning, C. (2009). *The Psychology of Sustainable Behavior: Tips for empowering people to take environmentally positive action.* Minnesota Pollution Control Agency.

27. Markowitz, E., Hodge, C., & Harp, G. (2014). *Connecting on climate: A guide to effective climate change communication.* Center for Research on Environmental Decisions and ecoAmerica.

28. Marlon, J. R., Bloodhart, B., Ballew, M. T., Rolfe-Redding, J., Roser-Renouf, C., Leiserowitz, A., & Maibach, E. (2019). How hope and doubt affect climate change mobilization. *Frontiers in Communication, 4,* 20.

29. Martin, S. J., Goldstein, N., & Cialdini, R. (2014). *The small big: Small changes that spark big influence.* Hachette.

30. Moore, C. (2020). *What is the negativity bias and how can it be overcome?* Positive Psychology.com.

31. Moser, S. C. & Dilling, L. (2004). Making climate hot. Environment: *Science and Policy for Sustainable Development, 46*(10), 32–46.

32. Moussaoui, L. S. & Desrichard, O. (2016). Act local but don't think too global: The impact of ecological goal level on behavior. *The Journal of Social Psychology, 156*(5), 536–552.

33. Moyer-Gusé, E., Tchernev, J. M., & Walther-Martin, W. (2019). The Persuasiveness of Humorous Environmental Narrative Combined with an Explicit Persuasive Appeal. *Science Communication, 41*(4), 422–441.

34. Ojala, M. (2011). Hope and climate change: the importance of hope for environmental engagement among young people. *Environmental Education Research, 18*(5), 625–642.

35. O'Neill, S., & Nicholson-Cole, S. (2009). "Fear won't do it" Promoting positive engagement with climate change through visual and iconic representations. *Science Communication, 30*(3), 355–379.

36. O'Neill, S. J., Boykoff, M., Niemeyer, S., & Day, S. A. (2013). On the use of imagery for climate change engagement. *Global Environmental Change, 23*(2), 413–421.

37. Pike, C., Doppelt, B., Herr, M., & Climate Leadership Initiative. (2010). *Climate communications and behavior change: A guide for practitioners.*

38. Pink, D. H. (2009). *Drive: The surprising truth about what motivates us.* Riverhead.

39. Rare and The Behavioural Insights Team. (2019). *Behavior change for nature: A behavioral science toolkit for practitioners.* Rare Center for Behavior and the Environment.

40. Resource Media. (2014). *Beyond the CFL: Winning imagery for energy efficiency.*

41. Schneider, C. R., Zaval, L., Weber, E. U., & Markowitz, E. M. (2017). The influence of anticipated pride and guilt on pro-environmental decision making. *PLOS ONE, 12*(11), 1–14.

42. Sol Hart, P. & Feldman, L. (2016). The impact of climate change–related imagery and text on public opinion and behavior change. *Science Communication, 38*(4), 415–441.

43. Tannenbaum, M. B., Hepler, J., Zimmerman, R. S., Saul, L., Jacobs, S., Wilson, K., & Albarracín, D. (2015). Appealing to fear: A meta-analysis of fear appeal effectiveness and theories. *Psychological Bulletin, 141*(6), 1178–1204.

44. White, K., Habib, R., & Hardisty, D. J. (2019). How to SHIFT consumer behaviors to be more sustainable: A literature review and guiding framework. *Journal of Marketing, 83*(3), 22–49.

45. Williams, L. A. & DeSteno, D. (2008). Pride and perseverance: The motivational role of pride. *Journal of Personality and Social Psychology, 94*(6), 1007–1017.

46. Williams, S. J., Jones, J. P. G., Clubbe, C., & Gibbons, J. M. (2012). Training programmes can change behaviour and encourage the cultivation of over-harvested plant species. *PLOS ONE, 7*(3), e33012.

47. Witte, K. & Allen, M. (2000). A meta-analysis of fear appeals: Implications for effective public health campaigns. *Health Education & Behavior, 27*(5), 591–615.

Building Block Chapter 8: Judiciously use REWARDS

1. Adler, J. H. (2010). Perverse incentives and the endangered species act. In I. W.H. Parry & F. Day (Eds.), *Issues of the day: 100 commentaries on climate, energy, the environment, transportation, and public health policy* (1st ed., pp 128–129). Taylor & Francis.

2. Bevins, S. N., Pedersen, K., Lutman, M. W., Gidlewski, T., & Deliberto, T. J. (2014). Consequences associated with the recent range expansion of nonnative feral swine. *BioScience, 64*(4), 291–299.

3. Bilandzic, H., Kalch, A., & Soentgen, J. (2017). Effects of goal framing and emotions on perceived threat and willingness to sacrifice for climate change. *Science Communication, 39*(4), 466–491.

4. Bolderdijk, J. W., Lehman, P. K., & Geller, E. S. (2018). Encouraging pro-environmental behaviour with rewards and penalties. In L. Steg & J. I. M. de Groot (Eds.), *Environmental psychology: An introduction* (2nd ed., pp. 273–282). Wiley.

5. Bolderdijk, J. W., & Steg, L. (2015). Promoting sustainable consumption: The risks of using financial incentives. In *Handbook of research on sustainable consumption.* Cheltenham, UK: Edward Elgar Publishing. www.elgaronline.com/view/edc oll/9781783471263/9781783471263.00033.xml.

6. Cialdini, R. B. (2009). *Influence: Science and practice* (5th ed.). Pearson.

7. Columbia Mailman School of Public Health. (2014, August 13). *Paper reduction initiative.*

8. CTV News. (2018, February 18). *Model passenger: Driver busted using mannequin in HOV lane.*

9. Deci, E., & Ryan, R. M. (1985). *Intrinsic motivation and self-determination in human behavior.* Plenum.

10. de Suarez, J. M., Suarez, P., & Bachofen, C. (Eds.) (2012). *Games for a new climate: Experiencing the complexity of future risks.* Boston University.

11. Ferster, C. B., & Skinner, B. F. (1957). *Schedules of reinforcement.* Appleton-Century-Crofts.

12. Food and Water Watch. (2019, November). *Cap and trade: More pollution for the poor and people of color.*

13. Freemark, Y. (2014, December 10). Calgary's soaring transit use suggests high ridership is possible even in sprawling cities. *The Transport Politic.*

14. Fujii, S., & Kitamura, R. (2003). What does a one-month free bus ticket do to habitual drivers? An experimental analysis of habit and attitude change. *Transportation, 30*(1), 81–95.

15. Gino, F. (2018, August 21). Need more self-control? Try a simple ritual. *Scientific American.*

16. Gneezy, U., & Rustichini, A. (2000). A fine is a price. *The Journal of Legal Studies, 29*(1), 1–17.

17. Green, L., & Myerson, J. (2004). A discounting framework for choice with delayed and probabilistic rewards. *Psychological Bulletin, 130*(5), 769–792.

18. Griffiths, M. D., & Wood, R. (2001). The psychology of lottery gambling. *International Gambling Studies, 1*(1), 27–45.

19. Handgraaf, M. J. J., Van Lidth de Jeude, M. A., & Appelt, K. C. (2013). Public praise vs. private pay: Effects of rewards on energy conservation in the workplace. *Ecological Economics, 86,* 86–92.

20. Harvey, H., Orvis, R., & Rissman, J. (2018). *Designing climate solutions: A policy guide for low-carbon energy.* Island Press.

21. Heward, W. L., & Kimball, J. W. (2013, Spring/Summer). Sustaining sustainability with clueless contingencies. *Sustain Magazine, 28,* 4–15

22. Hsu, T. (2011, May 6). Yellow hybrid stickers for carpool lanes set to expire. *Los Angeles Times.*

23. Kahneman, D., & Tversky, A. (1979). Prospect theory: An analysis of decision under risk. *Econometrica, 47*(2), 263–292.

24. Karau, S. J., & Williams, K. D. (1993). Social loafing: A meta-analytic review and theoretical integration. *Journal of Personality and Social Psychology, 65*(4), 681–706.

25. LaLonde, M. (2008). *Save on energy, win a hybrid car. Hydro-Québec.* montrealgazette.com/news/local-news/save-on-energy-win-a-hybrid-car.

26. League of Conservation Voters. (2019). *National environmental scorecard.*

27. Mazur-Stommen, S., & Farley, K. (2013, December). *ACEEE field guide to utility-run behavior programs.* American Council for an Energy-Efficient Economy.

28. O'Donoghue, T., & Rabin, M. (1999). Doing it now or later. *American Economic Review, 89*(1), 103–124.

29. Oliver, R. L. (1974). Expectancy theory predictions of salesmen's performance. *Journal of Marketing Research, 11*(3), 243–253.

30. Orland, B., Ram, N., Lang, D., Houser, K. W., Kling, N., & Coccia, M. (2014). Saving energy in an office environment: A serious game intervention. *Energy and Buildings, 74,* 43–52.

31. Pink, D. H. (2006) *A whole new mind: Why right-brainers will rule the future.* Riverhead.

32. Ro, M., Brauer, M., Kuntz, K., Shukla, R., & Bensch, I. (2017). Making cool choices for sustainability: Testing the effectiveness of a game-based approach to promoting pro-environmental behaviors. *Journal of Environmental Psychology, 53,* 20-30.

33. Rogers, T., & Bazerman, M. H. (2008). Future lock-in: Future implementation increases selection of 'should' choices. *Organizational Behavior and Human Decision Processes, 106*(1), 1–20.

34. Ryan, R. M., & Deci, E. L. (2000). Intrinsic and extrinsic motivations: Classic definitions and new directions. *Contemporary Educational Psychology, 25*(1), 54–67.

35. Schneider, S. M. (2012). *The science of consequences: How they affect genes, change the brain, and impact our world.* Prometheus.

36. Shewmake, S., & Jarvis, L. (2014). Hybrid cars and HOV lanes. *Transportation Research Part A: Policy and Practice, 67,* 304–319.

37. Sirak-Schaeffer, L. & Kezios, S. (2020, July 21). *Turtle trash collectors goes virtual.* OR&R's Marine Debris Program.

38. Skinner, B. F. (1938). *The behavior of organisms.* Appleton-Century.

39. StickK. (2020). *Ready to finally stickK to your commitment?*

40. United States Environmental Protection Agency. (n.d.). *Economic incentives.*

41. Van Leuvan, N., Highleyman, L., Kibe, A., & Cole, E. (2019). Turning the Page: A Behavior *Change Toolkit for Reducing Paper Use.* Root Solutions and Association for the Advancement of Sustainability in Higher Education.

42. Verhallen, T. M. M. (1982). Scarcity and consumer choice behavior. *Journal of Economic Psychology, 2*(4), 299–322.

43. Wood, G., van der Horst, D., Day, R., Bakaoukas, A. G., Petridis, P., Liu, S., Smithson, E., Barnham, J., Harvey, D., Yang, B. & Pisithpunth, C. (2014). Serious games for energy social science research. *Technology Analysis & Strategic Management, 26*(10), 1212–1227.

Building Block Chapter 9: Frame for the appropriate ASSOCIATIONS

1. Bales, S. N., Sweetland, J., & Volmert, A. (2015, September 10). *How to talk about climate change and the ocean.* A FrameWorks MessageMemo.

2. Blackmore, E., & Holmes, T. (Eds.) (2013). *Common cause for nature: Finding values and frames in the conservation sector.* Public Interest Research Centre, UK.

3. Bornstein, R. F. (1989). Exposure and affect: Overview and meta-analysis of research, 1968–1987. *Psychological Bulletin, 106*(2), 265–289.

4. DeGolia, A. H., Hiroyasu, E. H. T., & Anderson, S. E. (2019). Economic losses or environmental gains? Framing effects on public support for environmental management. *PLOS ONE, 14*(7), e0220320.

5. Djoudi, H., Locatelli, B., Vaast, C., Asher, K., Brockhaus, M., & Sijapati, B. B. (2016). Beyond dichotomies: Gender and inequalities in climate change studies. *Ambio, 45,* 248–262.

6. Downeysmith, D. (2019, April 16). *Renewables and the cost of climate inaction.* Climate Solutions.

7. Frederiks, E. R., Stenner, K., & Hobman, E. V. (2015). Household energy use: Applying behavioural economics to understand consumer decision-making and behaviour. *Renewable and Sustainable Energy Reviews, 41,* 1385–1394.

8. Green, D., Jacowitz, K. E., Kahneman, D., & McFadden, D. (1998). Referendum contingent valuation, anchoring, and willingness to pay for public goods. *Resource and Energy Economics, 20*(2), 85–116.

9. Hadden, J. (2015, May 4). *From science to justice: What explains framing shifts in climate activism?* Mobilizing Ideas.

10. Hickman, L. (2018, September 7). *Exclusive: BBC issues internal guidance on how to report climate change.* ClimateChange.ie.

11. Howarth, C. C., & Sharman, A. G. (2015). Labeling opinions in the climate debate: A critical review. *Wiley Interdisciplinary Reviews: Climate Change, 6*(2), 239–254.

12. Jang, S. M., & Hart, P. S. (2015). Polarized frames on "climate change" and "global warming" across countries and states: Evidence from Twitter big data. *Global Environmental Change, 32,* 11–17.

13. Kahneman, D., & Tversky, A. (1979). Prospect theory: An analysis of decision under risk. *Econometrica, 47*(2), 263–292.

14. Keysers, C., & Gazzola, V. (2014). Hebbian learning and predictive mirror neurons for actions, sensations and emotions. *Philosophical Transactions of the Royal Society B: Biological Sciences, 369*(1644), 20130175.

15. Kolkman, M. J., van der Veen, A., & Geurts, P. A. T. M. (2007). Controversies in water management: Frames and mental models. *Environmental Impact Assessment Review, 27*(7), 685–706.

16. Lakoff, G., & Johnson, M. (2003). *Metaphors we live by.* University of Chicago.

17. Lakoff, G. (2004). *Don't think of an elephant!: Know your values and frame the debate: The essential guide for progressives.* Chelsea Green.

18. Lakoff, G. (2010). Why it matters how we frame the environment. *Environmental Communication, 4*(1), 70–81.

19. Leiserowitz, A., Feinberg, G., Rosenthal, S., Smith, N., Anderson, A., Roser-Renouf, C., & Maibach, E. (2014). *What's in a name? Global warming vs. climate change.* Yale University and George Mason University. New Haven, CT: Yale Project on Climate Change Communication. Retrieved from: environment.yale.edu/climate-communication-OFF/files/Global_Warming_vs_Climate_Change_Report.pdf.

20. Levin, I. P., & Gaeth, G. J. (1988). How consumers are affected by the framing of attribute information before and after consuming the product. *Journal of Consumer Research, 15*(3), 374–378.

21. Levine, A. S., & Kline, R. (2019). Loss-Framed Arguments Can Stifle Political Activism. *Journal of Experimental Political Science, 6*(3), 171–179.

22. Markowitz, E., Hodge, C., & Harp, G. (2014). *Connecting on climate: A guide to effective climate change communication.* Center for Research on Environmental Decisions and ecoAmerica.

23. McEvoy, D., Fünfgeld, H., & Bosomworth, K. (2013). Resilience and Climate Change Adaptation: The importance of framing. *Planning, Practice, & Research, 28*, 280–293.

24. Memmott, M. (2018, June 20). *Let's put "truth sandwiches" on our menu.* NPR.

25. Morton, T. A., Rabinovich, A., Marshall, D., & Bretschneider, P. (2011). The future that may (or may not) come: How framing changes responses to uncertainty in climate change communications. *Global Environmental Change, 21*(1), 103–109.

26. Mukherjee, S. (2019). Revise the belief in loss aversion. *Frontiers in Psychology, 10*, 2723.

27. Nisbet, M. C. (2009). Communicating climate change: Why frames matter for public engagement. *Environment: Science and Policy for Sustainable Development, 51*(2), 12–23.

28. Patt, A., & Dessai, S. (2005). Communicating uncertainty: Lessons learned and suggestions for climate change assessment. *Comptes Rendus Geoscience, 337*(4), 425–441.

29. Peters, A. (2020, March 11). *What would happen if the world reacted to climate change like it's reacting to the coronavirus?* Fast Company.

30. Schindler, S., & Pfattheicher, S. (2017). The frame of the game: Loss-framing increases dishonest behavior. *Journal of Experimental Social Psychology, 69*, 172–177.

31. Sherif, M., Taub, D., & Hovland CI. (1958). Assimilation and contrast effects of anchoring stimuli on judgments. *Journal of Experimental Psychology, 55*(2), 150–155.

32. Simon, A. and Pérez R. (2019). *Heartwired to love the ocean: A messaging guide for advocates. Goodwin Simon Strategic Research & Wonder: Strategies for Good.*

33. Thibodeau, P. H., & Boroditsky, L. (2011). Metaphors we think with: The role of metaphor in reasoning. *PLOS ONE, 6*(2): e16782.

34. Thibodeau, P. H., Frantz, C. M., & Berretta, M. (2017). The earth is our home: Systemic metaphors to redefine our relationship with nature. *Climatic Change, 142*(1–2), 287–300.

35. Thibodeau, P. H., Winneg, A., Frantz, C. M., & Flusberg, S. J. (2016). The mind is an ecosystem: Systemic metaphors promote systems thinking. *Metaphor & The Social World, 6*(2): 225–242.

36. United States Environmental Protection Agency. (2017, May). *Multi-Model Framework for Quantitative Sectoral Impacts Analysis.* A Technical Report for the Fourth National Climate Assessment.

37. U.S. National Intelligence Council. (2016, September 21). *Implications for US national security of anticipated climate change.* Office of the Director of National Intelligence.

38. Volmert, A. (2014, May 7). *Getting to the heart of the matter: Using metaphorical and causal explanation to increase public understanding of climate and ocean change.* A FrameWorks research report.

39. Zajonc, R. B. (1968). Attitudinal effects of mere exposure. *Journal of Personality and Social Psychology, 9*(2, Pt.2), 1–27.

Building Block Chapter 10: Expanding the self to ensure nature's LONGEVITY

1. Amberson, S., Biedenweg, K., James, J., & Christie, P. (2016). "The heartbeat of our people": identifying and measuring how salmon influences Quinault tribal well-being. *Society & Natural Resources, 29*(12), 1389–1404.

2. Amel, E. L., Manning, C. M., & Scott, B. A. (2009). Mindfulness and sustainable behavior: Pondering attention and awareness as means for increasing green behavior. *Ecopsychology, 1*(1), 14–25.

3. Argyris, C. (1982). *Reasoning, learning, and action: Individual and organizational.* Jossey-Bass.

4. Barrera-Hernández, L.F., Sotelo-Castillo, M.A., Echeverría-Castro, S.B., & Tapia-Fonllem, C.O. (2020). Connectedness to nature: Its impact on sustainable behaviors and happiness in children. *Frontiers in Psychology, 11*(276).

5. Basu, A., Duvall, J., & Kaplan, R. (2019). Attention restoration theory: Exploring the role of soft fascination and mental bandwidth. *Environment and Behavior, 51*(9–10), 1055–1081.

6. Bekoff, M. (Ed.). (2013). *Ignoring nature no more: The case for compassionate conservation.* University of Chicago.

7. Berenguer, J. (2007). The effect of empathy in proenvironmental attitudes and behaviors. *Environment and Behavior, 39*(2), 269–283.

8. Brach, T. (2019). *Radical compassion: Learning to love yourself and your world with the practice of RAIN.* Penguin.

9. Bratman, G. N., Hamilton, J. P., Hahn, K. S., Daily, G. C., & Gross, J. J. (2015). Nature experience reduces rumination and subgenual prefrontal cortex activation. *Proceedings of the National Academy of Sciences, 112*(28), 8567–8572.

10. Chawla, L. (2015). Benefits of nature contact for children. *Journal of Planning Literature, 30*(4), 433-452.

11. Crocker, J., & Canevello, A. (2016). Egosystem and ecosystem: Motivational o rientations of the self in relation to others. In K. W. Brown & M. R. Leary (Eds.) *The Oxford handbook of hypo-egoic phenomena,* (p. 271). Oxford University.

12. Crocker, J., Moeller, S., & Burson, A. (2010). The costly pursuit of self-esteem: Implications for self-regulation. In R. H. Hoyle (Ed.) *Handbook of personality and self-regulation.* Blackwell.

13. Cunsolo, A., & Ellis, N. R. (2018). Ecological grief as a mental health response to climate change-related loss. *Nature Climate Change, 8,* 275–281.

14. Davids, T. W. R. & Oldenberg, H. (1881). *Vinaya texts.* The Clarendon Press.

15. Davis, M. H. (1980). A multidimensional approach to individual differences in empathy. *JSAS Catalog of Selected Documents in Psychology, 10,* 85.

16. De Young, R. (2010). Restoring mental vitality in an endangered world: Reflections on the benefits of walking. *Ecopsychology, 2*(1), 13–22.

17. Ericson, T., Kjønstad, B. G., & Barstad, A. (2014). Mindfulness and sustainability. *Ecological Economics, 104,* 73–79.

18. Fisher, R., Ury, W., & Patton, B. (1992). *Getting to yes: Negotiating agreement without giving in* (2nd ed.). Houghton Mifflin Harcourt.

19. Fredrickson, B. L., Cohn, M. A., Coffey, K. A., Pek, J., & Finkel, S. M. (2008). Open hearts build lives: Positive emotions, induced through loving-kindness meditation, build consequential personal resources. *Journal of Personality and Social Psychology, 95*(5), 1045–1062.

20. Geng, L., Xu, J., Ye, L., Zhou, W., & Zhou, K. (2015). Connections with nature and environmental behaviors. *PLOS ONE, 10*(5), e0127247.

21. Gethin, R. (2011). On some definitions of mindfulness. *Contemporary Buddhism, 12*(1), 263–279.

22. Gneezy, A., Imas, A., Brown, A., Nelson, L. D., & Norton, M. I. (2012). Paying to be nice: Consistency and costly prosocial behavior. *Management Science, 58*(1), 179–187.

23. Gore, Al. (2007, March 21). *Planet has a fever, Gore warns.* Vail Daily / Associated Press.

24. Greenwald, A. G., McGhee, D. E., & Schwartz, J. L. (1998). Measuring individual differences in implicit cognition: the implicit association test. *Journal of Personality and Social Psychology, 74*(6), 1464–1480.

25. Hanley, A., Garland, E., Canto, A., Warner, A., Hanley, R., Dehili, V., & Proctor, A. (2015). Dispositional mindfulness and bias in self-theories. *Mindfulness, 6*, 202–207.

26. Herzog, T. R., Black, A. M., Fountaine, K. A. & Knotts, D. J. (1997). Reflection and attentional recovery as distinctive benefits of restorative environments. *Journal of Environmental Psychology, 17*(2), 165–170.

27. Jha, A. P., Krompinger, J., & Baime, M. J. (2007). Mindfulness training modifies subsystems of attention. *Cognitive, Affective, & Behavioral Neuroscience, 7*(2), 109–119.

28. Kaplan, R. (1993). The role of nature in the context of the workplace. *Landscape and Urban Planning, 26*(1–4), 193–201.

29. Kaplan, S. (1995). The restorative benefits of nature: Toward an integrative framework. *Journal of Environmental Psychology, 15*(3), 169–182.

30. Kaplan, S., & Berman, M. G. (2010). Directed attention as a common resource for executive functioning and self-regulation. *Perspectives on Psychological Science, 5*(1), 43–57.

31. Kaplan, R., & Kaplan, S. (1989). *The experience of nature: A psychological perspective.* Cambridge.

32. Kim, S.-J. & Kou, X. (2014). Not all empathy is equal: How dispositional empathy affects charitable giving. *Journal of Nonprofit & Public Sector Marketing, 26*(4), 312–334.

33. Kuo, F. E. (2001). Coping with poverty: Impacts of environment and attention in the inner city. *Environment and Behavior, 33*(1), 5–34.

34. Lederbogen, F., Kirsch, P., Haddad, L., Streit, F., Tost, H., Schuch, P., Wüst, S.S., Pruessner, J.C., Rietschel, M., Deuschle, M., & Meyer-Lindenberg, A. (2011). City living and urban upbringing affect neural social stress processing in humans. *Nature, 474*(7352), 498–501.

35. Lee, K. E., Williams, K. J. H., Sargent, L.D., Williams, N. S. G., & Johnson, K.A. (2015). 40 second green roof views sustain attention: The role of micro-breaks in attention restoration. *Journal of Environmental Psychology, 42,* 182–189.

36. Lithoxoidou, L. S., Georgopoulos, A. D., Dimitriou, A. T., & Xenitidou, S. C. (2017). "Trees have a soul too!" Developing empathy and environmental values in early childhood. *International Journal of Early Childhood Environmental Education, 5*(1), 68–88.

37. Lutz, A., Brefczynski-Lewis, J., Johnstone, T., & Davidson, R. J. (2008). Regulation of the neural circuitry of emotion by compassion meditation: effects of meditative expertise. *PLOS ONE, 3*(3), e1897.

38. Macy, J. & Brown, M. Y. (2014). *Coming back to life: The updated guide to the work that reconnects.* New Society.

39. Mayer, F. S. & Frantz, C. M. (2004). The connectedness to nature scale: A measure of individuals' feeling in community with nature. *Journal of Environmental Psychology, 24*(4), 503–515.

40. McCubbin, L. D., & Marsella, A. (2009). Native Hawaiians and psychology: The cultural and historical context of indigenous ways of knowing. *Cultural Diversity and Ethnic Minority Psychology, 15*(4), 374–387.

41. Merritt, A. C., Effron, D. A., & Monin, B. (2010). Moral self-licensing: When being good frees us to be bad. *Social and Personality Psychology Compass, 4*(5), 344-357.

42. Muir, J. (1876, February 9). God's first temples: How shall we preserve our forests? *Sacramento Daily Union,* 8.

43. Nelson-Coffey, S. K., Ruberton, P. M., Chancellor, J., Cornick, J. E., Blascovich, J., & Lyubomirsky, S. (2019). The proximal experience of awe. *PLOS ONE, 14*(5), e0216780.

44. Osbaldiston, R., & Schott, J. P. (2012). Environmental sustainability and behavioral science: Meta-analysis of proenvironmental behavior experiments. *Environment and Behavior, 44*(2), 257–299.

45. Park, B. J., Tsunetsugu, Y., Kasetani, T., Kagawa, T., & Miyazaki, Y. (2010). The physiological effects of Shinrin-yoku (taking in the forest atmosphere or forest bathing): Evidence from field experiments in 24 forests across Japan. *Environmental Health and Preventive Medicine, 15*(1), 18–26.

46. Pfattheicher, S., Sassenrath, C., & Schindler, S. (2016). Feelings for the suffering of others and the environment: Compassion fosters proenvironmental tendencies. *Environment and Behavior, 48*(7), 929–945.

47. Phenice, L. A. & Griffore, R. J. (2003). Young children and the natural world. *Contemporary Issues in Early Childhood, 4*(2), 167–171.

48. Piff, P. K., Dietze, P., Feinberg, M., Stancato, D. M., & Keltner, D. (2015). Awe, the small self, and prosocial behavior. *Journal of Personality and Social Psychology, 108*(6), 883–899.

49. Raanaas, R. K., Evensen, K. H., Rich, D., Sjøstrøm, G., & Patil, G. (2011). Benefits of indoor plants on attention capacity in an office setting. *Journal of Environmental Psychology, 31*(1), 99–105.

50. Richey, M. K. (2013). *A Games-Based Approach To Teaching Cognitive Biases.* [Doctoral Dissertation, Mercyhurst University].

51. Ruedy, N. E., & Schweitzer, M. E. (2010). In the moment: The effect of mindfulness on ethical decision making. *Journal of Business Ethics, 95*(1), 73–87.

52. Russell, R., Guerry, A. D., Balvanera, P., Gould, R. K., Basurto, X., Chan, K. M. A., Klain, S. K., Levine, J. & Tam, J. (2013). Humans and nature: how knowing and experiencing nature affect well-being. *Annual Review of Environment and Resources, 38*(1), 473–502.

53. Sevillano, V., Aragonés, J. I., & Schultz, P. W. (2007). Perspective taking, environmental concern, and the moderating role of dispositional empathy. *Environment and Behavior, 39*(5), 685–705.

54. Sheth, J. N., Sethia, N. K., & Srinivas, S. (2011). Mindful consumption: A customer-centric approach to sustainability. *Journal of the Academy of Marketing Science, 39*(1), 21–39.

55. Singer, T., & Klimecki, O. M. (2014). Empathy and compassion. *Current Biology, 24*(18), R875–R878.

56. Tam, K.-P., Lee, S.-L., & Chao, M. M. (2013). Saving Mr. Nature: Anthropomorphism enhances connectedness to and protectiveness toward nature. *Journal of Experimental Social Psychology, 49*(3), 514–521.

57. Tang, Y.-Y., Ma, Y., Wang, J., Fan, Y., Feng, S., Lu, Q., Yu, Q., Sui, D., Rothbart, M. K., Fan, M. & Posner, M. I. (2007). Short-term meditation training improves attention and self-regulation. *Proceedings of the National Academy of Sciences, 104*(43), 17152–17156.

58. van der Linden, D., Frese, M., & Meijman, T. (2003). Mental fatigue and the control of cognitive processes: Effects on perseveration and planning. *Acta Psychologica, 113*(1), 45–65.

59. Wilson, E. O. (1984). *Biophilia.* Harvard University.

60. Yaden, D. B., Haidt, J., Hood Jr., R. W., Vago, D. R., & Newberg, A. B. (2017). The varieties of self-transcendent experience. *Review of General Psychology, 21*(2), 143–160.

61. Zhao, H., Zhang, H., Xu, Y., Lu, J., & He, W. (2018). Relation between awe and environmentalism: The role of social dominance orientation. *Frontiers in Psychology, 9*, 2367.

Acknowledgments

Donors

W<small>E GRATEFULLY ACKNOWLEDGE</small> the Mary A. Crocker Trust, The Flora L. Thornton Foundation, William Crane, Yonatan Lerner, Elizabeth Culbertson, Mark Epstein, Kate Culbertson, Anne Thornton, Kirk Broaddus, John Culbertson, Annie Thornton, Jane Thornton, and Barbara Van Cleave Smith for their generous support of *Making Shift Happen*.

We would also like to thank Andrew Weisman, Anthony Filiberti, Brian Fan, Camille Herrera, Cat Toebe, Charlotte Rockwood, Cindy Linville, Claire Elise George, Cyril Azouley, Dona Williams, Dylan Leith, Elizabeth Bunnen, Erica Mack, Jacquie Broaddus, Jedd Parker, Jesse Bryant, Joe W. Graham, Katherine Siu, Katie Willis, Keith Pizzi, Kendra Karr, Kip Howard, Kristen Honey, Lily Wick, Lisa Moore, London Elise, Madeleine LePere, Madison Linville, Margaret Rockwood, Megan Rose Dickey, Michelle Lapinski, Millie Sutterman, Morgan Rogers, Nick Donahue, Paul Rich, Robert Gapasin, Ryan OMeara, Savannah Van Leuvan Smith, Yishai Lerner, and Wendy Weiden, whose early contributions laid the foundation for the writing of this book.

Contributors

Writing a book is harder than we anticipated and more rewarding than we could have ever imagined. We couldn't have done it without the substantial contributions of Pauline Miller, who helped formulate the Building Blocks, or Nicole Hilaire, Karina Mudd, and Susan Schneider, who coauthored multiple chapters and contributed to many others, or without Jess Beebe, Nicholas Janusch, Jessica Robbins, David Festa, Alex Michael Clark, Anjana Krishnan, Love Goyal, and Ted Toombs.

It really does take a team of superstars to write such a book as this. Thank you to everyone who helped research, develop content, fact-check, and edit: Lauren Balotin, Sonya Bengali, Shelby Bocks, Suzanne Burrows, Jennifer Chan, Phoebe Chiu, Kelly Chu, Madeline Chua, Emily J Clark, Sarah Ann Coffin, Alison Corn, Kirby Culbertson, Shruti Desai, Eli Fujita, Justine Zoe Gapayao, Robert Garcia, Lauren Genn, Fidel Gilchrist, Allie Goguen, Devin Grace Gill, Joe W Graham,

Julie Hassen, Amanda Hausman, Corinna Hong, Flannery Houston, Edwin Ip, Adrianna Nicole Jensen, Kevin Ji, Thomas Kelleher, Gavin Kellerman, Alison Kibe, Jackson Kuramoto, Sravya Lanka, Micaela Leonarte Paredes, Catherine Lopez, Cameron McKee, Kerry McKee, Cristina Morejón, Lucy Morrison, Elizabeth Muir, Aaron Pope, Ellen Robertson, Michael T Sheley, Alexandra May Smith, Haley Steinhauser, Mira Swaminathan, Gwyneth Teo, Elena Rose Thomas, Christine Tsai, Molly Watters, Nicola White, Jennifer Witherspoon, and Wendy Wu.

While this book wouldn't have been possible without the contributions of all of these people, any errors are our own.

•••

All authors and contributors worked on *Making Shift Happen* through Root Solutions to further our environmental mission. All royalties remain in the not-for-profit sector to be used on the dissemination of evidence-based tools to protect our planet. It is our deepest desire to get these tools right and as such, we welcome any feedback from those experienced in behavior design. Are there interventions you think should be included in future volumes? Are there case studies we should share? Or frames, metaphors, or stories that were particularly effective or ineffective in your work that others should know about? Please reach out to us through makingshifthappenbook.com.

Thank you to Multiplier, our fiscal sponsor, for providing the foundation upon which we could work, and to our colleagues Kate Wing, Rainer Romero-Canyas, Banny Banerjee, and Paul Brest, for providing invaluable guidance on how to best accelerate the use of behavior change to advance the public good. And thank you to New Society Publishers for believing in this book and working with us to spread world-changing solutions far and wide.

Personal Thanks

This book also would not have been possible without the support from many two- and four-legged family and friends. Nya is grateful for Kirby Culbertson, who helped us launch Root Solutions and this work, for Yonatan Lerner, David Festa, and Jasper Van Leuvan, who each supported this undertaking in critical ways, for Savannah Van Leuvan and Prisha Manwani who kept me motivated, and for those of you that still call me a friend after my disappearing act while writing *Making Shift Happen*. Lauren would like to thank her mother, Kathy Brenkle, and her late grandfather, Joe "Papa" Brenkle, for always encouraging her to explore and question, her husband Philip Castagnozzi Bush for his abounding love and support, and pets Penny, Pip, and Gryff for their great company! Ashleigh would like to thank Kathy and Gavin Kellerman for their support and encouragement, and Socks the cat for making sure she took some breaks. Rod is grateful for the loving support of Joyce Selkow and joins all the authors in drawing inspiration and hope from the work and passion of all the environmentalists that have worked alongside us over the decades.

Index

Page numbers in *italics* indicate tables.

availability heuristic, 347

B

backfire effect, *15*, 332
ballot order effect, 362
bandwagon effect, *14*
baseline data, 91, 94–98, 146, 200, 207–208
BEHAVIORAL Building Blocks
    principles, 5–6, *170*, 255
    structure of, 254
    See also individual Building Blocks
Behavioral Drivers Analysis (BDA) Survey
    analyze and interpret, 149–161
    behavioral sequence review, 131–133
    conducting survey, 148
    question types, 103
    questions for additional information, 145–147
    questions for demographic information, 144–145
    questions for eligibility, 133–134
    questions to identify Doers and Non-Doers, 134–141
    questions to identify drivers, 141–144
    research for, 93, 130–131
    structure of survey, 147–148
    value of, 128–129
behavioral economics, 21–22
behavioral sciences, 20–21, 24
behavioral sequences, 75–76, 131–133
behavioral spillover, 33–34, 77, 80, 371, 415
behaviors
    identification and evaluation, 69–73, 75–78
    inconveniencing undesirable, 296–298

measurements, 240–241
models, 102, 261
new to audience, 138–139
refining priority, 163
replacements for problematic, *74*
See also drivers
Belize Botanic Garden, 404
Belonging
    about, 5, 255
    brainstorming questions, 275–276
    as change motivator, 256–257
    changing norms, 271–273
    connection through social networks, 268–270
    developing positive norms, 262–267
    framing in, 448
    highlighting social proof, 258–262
    See also social networks; social norms
benefits. *See* Motivation drivers
benevolence, 324–325
biases
    availability, *14*
    blind spot, 465
    confirmation, 12, *15*, 332, 465
    in-group, 379
    negativity, *16*, 393–394
    observer, 223
    omission, *17*
    optimism, 12
    present, *16*, 127, 420
    in research, 215, 245
    response, 227–228
    self-selection, 206
    single action, *17*, 34
    status quo, *17*, 283
    in survey response, 227–228
    See also cognitive biases
biking to work example, 141–142, 145,

167, 235–237

Black, Indigenous, and People of Color (BIPOC), 28

blind spot bias, 465

block leaders, 269

brainstorming, 71

Brazilian novelas, 266

breathing, mindful, 462

C

Calgary, Alberta, 412

California Academy of Sciences, 354

carbon offset fees, *285*, 286

carbon sequestration example

  See farming carbon sequestration example

causality, 218

challenges, 424–425

Chapman University, 357

choice architecture, 22–23, 29–30

choice blindness, 12

choice overload, *14*, 288–290

choices

  arrangement of, 362–363

  influence with first choice, 305

  simplify, 282–291

chunking information, 294–295

cigarette butt disposal examples

  audience segmentation, 164

  ballot bins, 350–351

  drivers and shifters, *174*

  infrastructure access, 279

  normative messages, 263, *265*

climate change terminology, 434, *435*

"Climate's Heart metaphor," 440–442

closed-ended questions, 103, 225–226

cocktail party effect, 353

cognitive biases

  about, 12–13

  as driver, 128

  environmental change behavior and, *14–17*

  framing for, 442–445

  mindfulness and, 464–465

  in research, 215

cognitive burdens, 32

cognitive dissonance, *14*, 332, 385–386

cognitive neuroscience, 20

cognitive psychology, 21

cognitive systems, 11–12

collective action, 405–406

collectivist cultures, 29, 290

Columbia University, 419

commitment devices, 421

commitments, 379–383

community pioneers, 269–270

community pride, 378–379

compassion, 458–460, 467–468

competitions, 424–425

Compost Coaching initiative, 293

composting.

  See food composting campaigns

concentrated approach, for segmentation, 167, *168*

confidence intervals, 250

confirmation bias, 12, *15*, 332, 465

consequences, perceived, 112–114, 142, 151

conservation psychology, 21

consistency, 379–388

context

  awareness of, 279–281

  measurements, 242

  stable environment, 312

continuous reward schedules, 422

contrast in messaging, 351

convenience sampling, 244
core values, 323–329
correlation, 218
creative misbehavior, 417
cues
   design of, 311–314
   disruption of, 306–307
   in habit development, 303, *304*
   sources of, 125
   using feedback, 314–318
cultural context, 29, 218, 290
cultural values, 328
curiosity generation in messaging, 351
current events, 363–364

D
data cleaning, 248
decision regret, *17*
decisions, emotions and, 18–19
deep frames, 431, 445–446
default choice, 282–287
delayed feedback, 317–318
delivery mode, 178
demographics, 67, 144–145, 242
descriptive norms, 259–260, 263–264,
   265
Design
   about, 4–5
   audience segmentation, 164–168
   prototyping, 183–191
   research methods, *216*
   shifter design details, 178–179
   shifter evaluation, 174–177
   shifter generation, 168–174
   shifter suites, 179–183
design thinking, 26–27
Despair Ritual, 468
differences, testing for, 250

differentiated approach, for
   segmentation, 167, *168*
Diffusion of Innovation Theory,
   65, 166
diffusion of responsibility, 406
direct observation, 222–223
directed attention, 454
disruptions, temporary, 308–309
distribution and deviation, 250
Doers and Non-Doers
   analyzing BDA results for, 150–158
   designing BDA for, 129, 134–141,
      144, 146–147
   designing shifters for, 169
   motivations, 171
downstream audiences, 62
drivers
   categories of, 102–103, *104*
   characteristics of, 100–102
   determining influence of, 128–148
   determining significance, 150–152,
      158–161
   survey questions to identify, 141–144
   See also Means drivers; Memory
      drivers; Motivation drivers
drivers-to-shifters roadmap, 168–174
Drug Abuse Resistance Education
   (D.A.R.E.) program, 1
   anti-drug initiatives, 1–2
duration, 197, 207
dynamic norms, 264, *265*

E
Easy
   about, 5, 255
   brainstorming questions, 298–299
   contextual factors, 279–281
   framing in, 448

building intrinsic motivation, 451–452

engaging with nature, 453–456

framing in, 449

mindfulness practice, 460–467

other-focus, 457–460

self-compassion, 467–468

loss aversion, *16*, 284, 425, 443–445

lotteries, 423–424

loving-kindness meditation, 462–463

low-fidelity prototype, 188

M

Making Shift Happen process

characteristics of, 27

disciplines within, 20–27

principles, 28–36

mapping, 53–55

marginalized communities, 28

Master Farmer program, 203

materialism, 326

McGill University, 388

mean, 249

Means drivers

characteristics, 104–111

factors affecting, *104*

prioritizing, 159–161

shifters for, *170, 171*

survey questions to identify, 142

measurements

behaviors, 240–241

context and demographics, 242

evaluation of initiative, 198–202

of key variables, 239–240

psychological factors, 241–242

See also metrics

meat consumption, 109, 264, 311

media, 195

meditation, 461–463

memories, marked, 13

Memory drivers

factors affecting, *104*, 124–126

prioritizing, 159–161

shifters for, *170*, 171

survey questions to identify, 143

mental associations.

See Associations

mental models, 24, 25, 430

mere exposure effect, 12, *16*, 352–353, 447

messaging

abstract concepts, 353–361

competing values, 333–334

emotional responses and, 393–401

noticeable, 350–353

strategic timing, 362–368

messengers, 179

metaphors, 328, 439–442

Methods, about, 5, 215, *216*

See also research

metrics

to evaluate initiative, 198–202

for goals, 90–92

outcome metrics, 90, 200, 207–208, 209–210

process metrics, 201, 209

See also measurements

mindfulness practice, 460–467

mindsets, 452

misinformation, 436

mistaken norms, 115–116, 271

mnemonics, 295–296, 352

models, social, 259–262, 265–266, 269–270, 404

moral licensing, *16*, 34, 119–120, 465

morals, 122–124, 330–334

motivated reasoning, 12
Motivation drivers
   barriers vs., 101–102
   factors affecting, *104*, 111–124
   in habit development, 303, *304*, 306
   identification of significant drivers,
     150–154
   intrinsic and extrinsic, 412–415
   prioritizing, 159–161
   shifters for, *170*, 171–172
   survey questions to identify, 143
   See also Rewards

N

narratives, 19
national security, *438*
National Taiwan University of Arts, 350
nature, 453–456, 459
negativity bias, *16*, 393–394
nesting information, 294–295
neuroscience, 20
Non-Doers.
   See Doers and Non-Doers
norms.
   See social norms
novelty in messaging, 350–351
nudging, 22–23, 29, 362–368

O

Oberlin College, 367–368
observation, 94, 222–223, *238*
observer bias, 223
ocean health, *40*, 280
omission bias, *17*
online surveys, 95–96
open-ended questions, 103, 225–226
Optimism
   about, 6, 255

   brainstorming questions, 407
   emotional messaging, 393–401
   empowerment, 391–392
   framing in, 449
   through collective action, 405–406
   through efficacy, 401–404
optimism bias, 12
ostrich effect, 12, 395
other-focused emotions, 457
outcome metrics, 90, 200, 207–208,
   209–210
outcomes, rewarding, 418

P

paper reduction campaigns
   duration, 197
   misperceptions, 151
   multiple shifters in, 181–182
   process metrics, 201
   prototyping, 189–190
   rewards, 419
   using behavior change tools, 3
   using social networks, 268
paper towel dispensers, 356
participant bias, 245
participatory approach, 30
patterns of behavior, 24, *25*
peer educators, 269
penalties, 310, 409, 410–412
people in imagery, 358–359
perceived action efficacy, 117
perceived importance, 117
perceived negative consequences,
   113–114, 142, 151
perceived positive consequences,
   112–113, 142
perceived responsibility, 119–120
perceived severity, 118, 395

protection, 328
prototyping
    in design thinking process, 27
    piloting vs., 202
    shifters, 183–191
psychological distance, 334–339,
    455–456
psychological factors, measurements,
    241–242
psychological sciences, 20–21
public health, *438*

Q
qualitative data, 239–240, 247–248
quality of life, 335
quantitative data, 240, 248–250
quasi-experiments, 198–199, 222, 233,
    234, 235–237
question types, 103

R
racial diversity, 29
RAIN, 463–464
random sampling, 244
real-time feedback, 317
rebound effect, 34
receptivity questions, 146–147
recycling
    hotel campaign, 396
    increased convenience, 281
    penalties, 267
    using behavior change tools, 3
    visual aids, 293
redemption, *438*
reference groups, 261–262
reflective thinking, 11–12
reinforcers, 318–319
relationships, testing for, 250

religious ideology, 122, 331, 333
reminders, timing of, 364
renewable energy programs, 3, 282, *285*
replication, intentional, 193–194
representative samples, 243
research
    for audience selection, 60
    based on process stage, 215–216, *216*
    for BDA development, 130
    for behavior selection, 70
    biases, 215, 245
    in design thinking process, 26
    for Doer definition, 137–138
    of focus, 37–38, 46–56
    past initiatives, 172–173
    types of, 92, *93*
    See also primary research; secondary
        research
resilience, 44, 72, 73, 398, 399, 401, 405
    438
resource access, 107–109
resource gathering interviews, 217,
    220–221
respect, 31, 246–247
response, in habit development, 303,
    304, 306, 310–311
response bias, 227–228
responsibility
    diffusion of, 406
    perceived, 119–120
reusable serviceware example
    identify Doers and Non-Doers, 137,
        140
    participant eligibility questions,
        133–134
    survey bias, 228
    survey results analysis, 155–156, *156*,
        158

SMART goals, 88–89
smoking cessation initiatives, 3, 24
social acceptability. *See* social norms
social comparison, 257
social comparison feedback, 316
social diffusion, 268
social marketing, 23
social media, 272
social modeling, 259–262, 265–266,
  269–270, 404
social networks, 195, 257, 268–270
social norms
  as barrier, 101–102
  as change motivator, 256–257
  changing, 271–273
  defaults and, 284
  drawing attention to, 259–262
  emphasizing positive, 262–267
  perceived acceptability, 115–116, 151
  in prompts, 367
  spreading through networks, 195,
    268–270
social proof, 257, 258–262, 272
social psychology, 21
social sciences, 218
socioeconomic status, 31–32
sociology, 21
soil health example. *See* farming carbon
  sequestration example
spillover, 33–34, 77, 80, 371, 415
spiral of silence, 258–259, 271
spreadability of behavior, 58, 64, 77, 193
Stages of Change Model, 65, 166
stakeholders
  diversity of, 49–50
  interviews, 48
  system mapping and, 55
  training, 195–196, 198

standard deviation, 250
status quo bias, *17*, 283
Sternin, Jerry, 72
storyboards, 186
storytelling, 322, 328, 339–345, 361
stratified random sampling, 244
straws, 283, *285*, 287
student paper use reduction.
    See paper reduction campaigns
surface frames, 431
surveys, 95–98, 222, 224–229, *238*
    See also Behavioral Drivers Analysis
      Survey
susceptibility, perceived, 118–119, 395
sustainably fished seafood, 292
system structures, 24, 25
systems change, 193
systems thinking, 23–24, 25, 51–55

T
target population, 242
temporal distance, 336
temporary disruptions, 308–309
temptation bundling, 312–313
Texas anti-littering campaign, 378–379
thermal images, 355
threat appeals, 395–397
Tigana, Dembo, 203
timing, 179, 197, 207, 363–364
Toyota Prius, 317
tradition, 327
training, of stakeholders, 195–196, 198
transit, 50, 107, 126, 280, 289, 309, 313,
  318, 412
  public transit passes, *285*
transition moments, 273
transportation mode shift, *285*, 309,
  313–314, 318–319, 412